SOURCES OF JAPANESE TRADITION

VOLUME I

INTRODUCTION TO
ORIENTAL CIVILIZATIONS

WM. THEODORE DE BARY, EDITOR

Sources of
Japanese Tradition

VOLUME I

COMPILED BY

Ryusaku Tsunoda
Wm. Theodore de Bary
Donald Keene

COLUMBIA UNIVERSITY PRESS *New York and London*

The addition to the "Records of Civilization: Sources and Studies" of a group of translations of Oriental historical materials in a clothbound edition, from which this volume is taken, was made possible by funds granted by Carnegie Corporation of New York. That Corporation is not, however, the author, owner, publisher, or proprietor of this publication, and is not to be understood as approving by virtue of its grant any of the statements made or views expressed therein.

UNESCO Collection of Representative Works, JAPANESE SERIES

This work has been accepted in the Japanese Translation Series of the United Nations Educational, Scientific, and Cultural Organization (UNESCO).

SBN 231-08604-0

Text edition in two volumes published 1964

Printed in the United States of America

9 8 7 6

PREFACE

This book, representing part of a series dealing with the civilizations of Japan, China, India, and Pakistan, contains source readings that tell us what the Japanese have thought about themselves, the world they lived in, and the problems they faced living together. It is meant to provide the general reader with an understanding of the background of contemporary Japanese civilization, especially as this is reflected in intellectual traditions which remain alive today. Thus, much attention is given to religious and philosophical developments in early times that are still part of the national heritage and affect people's thinking today. On the other hand, equal attention is given to political and social questions which the ordinary history of philosophy or religion would not treat. Also, since the arts of Japan have such a unique importance in the modern world—indeed, are the embodiment of Japanese civilization to many—there must be a place for the discussion of Japanese aesthetics. Therefore we have not hesitated to make excursions into the fields of literature and dramatic art, just as readily as into politics or economics, even though we could not hope to take full stock of the riches in each of these domains.

Perhaps the greatest danger which besets the Western reader's attempt to understand Japanese civilization is the temptation to take one or another of its more striking aspects as representing the whole. There might be no great harm in this if, finding one gateway to Japanese culture especially inviting and congenial, through this he gained access to others in turn. But much that is popularly written about the Japanese (in particular, about "Japan Today") reflects the particular concerns of the moment, and these concerns shift so rapidly that the popular image of Japan is likely to become confused. A sense of bafflement or frustration may result, and the Westerner will then take what consolation he can find in the idea that Orientals are, after all, inscrutable. Just before and during the Second

World War, for instance, it was nationalism and militarism that served as the common theme of books about Japan, and one got the impression that the more engaging aspects of Japanese culture were no more than a mask for the underlying fanaticism and brutality which characterized these people. Not only did this one-sided view of the Japanese handicap Americans in their dealings with them after the war, by engendering suspicion or condescension, but also it produced in many persons a sense of having been duped when at last the finer aspects of Japanese character and culture were brought in upon them. Now, thirteen years after the surrender, there is danger in another kind of distortion, which sees nothing in Japan but its exoticism, aestheticism, and mysticism.

Obviously, then, the first requirement of a book such as this must be to achieve balance and perspective. It is unlikely that we have succeeded in this here, but, knowing our aim, the critical reader will at least understand why we have been tempted to spread ourselves so thin over the length and breadth of Japanese history and civilization, and have ventured to deal in a summary way with subjects that still call for much more intensive study and analysis. The fact is that we do not seek to identify causal factors in Japanese history, but merely to suggest the range and variety of Japanese thought, and some of the circumstances which called forth or conditioned these expressions of the Japanese mind. Considering the strangeness of the setting and the complexity of some subjects not readily presentable in translation, we have found it necessary to include far more historical and explanatory material than usual in a set of source readings. Nevertheless the reader unfamiliar with Japanese history who seeks a fuller knowledge of historical and institutional background will do well to supplement this text by reference to a general or cultural history. At the same time, given the limitations of an introductory text, we could not hope to deal with every thinker or movement of importance, but have had to select those examples which best illustrated the relation of divergent currents to the main stream of Japanese thought, and the relevance of intellectual attitudes to the most persistent problems of Japanese society. In the modern period the necessity for this is most apparent. We have ignored, for instance, some of the more striking examples of Western influence in favor of others which better demonstrate the adaptation or incorporation of Western attitudes in writers standing nearer the center of things. For much the same reason, in dealing with recent trends, we have focused attention on persons active in public life or organized political movements, close to the great events of their time, rather than upon intellectuals in the narrow sense, whose ultimate influence can only be conjectured with difficulty at such short range.

These readings were originally based on a series of essays and translations prepared by Ryusaku Tsunoda, for many years Curator of the Japanese Collection at Columbia University and lecturer on Japanese religion and thought. They have since been considerably supplemented, revised, and adapted for use in the general education program of Columbia College. Consequently, though Mr. Tsunoda's efforts contributed substantially to the work, the editor and not he must be held responsible for the contents and for any errors of fact or interpretation which they contain. Obviously, a project of this magnitude could not have been brought to completion without the collaboration of others possessing special qualifications. Donald Keene has helped especially with the chapters on Japanese aesthetics and poetry, the Shinto revival, the sub-section on Honda Toshiaki, and the final chapter, while also assisting in the editing of Chapters I–IX. It is also a pleasure to acknowledge our gratitude to colleagues in sister institutions from whose special knowledge of trends in modern Japanese history and thought we have greatly benefited in the preparation of Chapters XXIV–XXIX, in Volume II: Marius Jansen of the University of Washington at Seattle, who contributed the chapter on ultranationalism; Arthur Tiedemann of the College of the City of New York, for the chapter on modern liberalism; and Hyman Kublin of Brooklyn College, for the chapter on the Japanese social movement. Here again, since certain changes and additions have had to be made in adapting these contributions to the general plan of the work, final responsibility for them must rest with the editor. In the preparation of the entire manuscript for the press, and of several translations appearing in Chapters XV–XXI, and Chapters XXII–XXIX, in Volume II, Herschel Webb has been of great help in the final stages of this project. He has also prepared the chronological tables.

Among the more specific contributions made by individuals here and in Japan, that of Professor Abe Masao, a Rockefeller fellow at Columbia University and Union Theological Seminary, must be noted for the great care and time which he devoted to problems encountered in translations from *The Problem of Japanese Culture* by Nishida Kitarō. Dr.

Kōsaka Masaaki, Dean of the Faculty of Education, Kyoto University, and a leading authority on Nishida's philosophy, has also been most gracious with his advice. For help in selecting and obtaining key documents for Chapter XXVIII in Volume II we are indebted to Dr. Tsuru Shigeto, Visiting Professor at Harvard University; Dr. George O. Totten of the Fletcher School of Law and Diplomacy, Tufts University; and Mr. Oka Sumio. Dr. Totten, in particular, was most generous with his time, effort and special knowledge of the Japanese social movement, and contributed the translations from Abe Isoo and Kawai Eijirō. Mr. John F. Howes was responsible for the initial selection of readings from Uchimura Kanzō in the same chapter, and for background material used in the introduction. In the early phases of the project Dr. Minoru Shinoda, now of the University of Hawaii, was a valued assistant to Mr. Tsunoda in the work of translation. Dr. Jansen also wishes to acknowledge the help given him by William Naff and Noboru Hiraga in preparing Chapter XXVII in Volume II. Others to whom we are also indebted are Professor W. T. Chan of Dartmouth College; Professors Chi-chen Wang, Andrew Yarrow, and Royal Weiler of Columbia; Dr. Burton Watson, Cutting Traveling Fellow in Columbia University, 1956–57; Professor Roger Hackett of Northwestern University; Professor William G. Beasley of the University of London; Dr. Robert Scalapino of the University of California, Berkeley; Rev. J. J. Spae, C.I.C.M.; Mrs. Lien-che Tu Fang; Mr. Richard De Martino; Douglas Overton and Eugene Langston of the Japan Society of New York; and Mr. Howard Linton and the staff of the East Asiatic Library, Columbia University. In the early stages of compiling these readings, Nancy Sherman, Myrtle Hallam, and especially Miwa Kai rendered important services to the editor. To Eileen J. Boecklen thanks must go for her conscientious and capable work in preparing the manuscript for publication. Acknowledgment should also be made of her special contribution in the form of map making. Charles M. Saito handled with great skill the exacting assignment of preparing the chapter decorations. Lastly, Joan McQuary rendered the final editing process a far more pleasant experience than one would have thought possible.

This series of readings has been produced in connection with the Columbia College General Education Program in Oriental Studies, which has been encouraged and supported by the Carnegie Corporation of New York. For whatever value it may have to the general reader or college student seeking a liberal education that embraces both the East and West, a great debt is owed to Dean Emeritus Harry J. Carman, Professor James Gutmann, and Dean Lawrence H. Chamberlain of Columbia College. Their foresight and leadership are responsible for the progress that has been made toward reaching a goal long sought by members of the Columbia College faculty. Those who have joined in the preparation of this book know that it is only a beginning to the work that lies ahead, but it is offered nonetheless in tribute to the scholars and teachers who have set us on the road.

Columbia College
New York City
February, 1958

WM. THEODORE DE BARY

EXPLANATORY NOTE

In the pronunciation of Japanese words or names, the consonants are read as in English (with "g" always hard) and the vowels as in Italian. There are no silent letters. The name Abe, for instance, is pronounced "Ah-bay." The long vowels "ō" and "ū" are indicated except in the names of cities already well known in the West, such as Tokyo and Kyoto. All romanized terms have been standardized according to the Hepburn system for Japanese, the Wade-Giles for Chinese, and the McCune-Reischauer for Korean. Chinese philosophical terms used in Japanese texts are given in their Japanese readings (e.g., *ri* instead of *li* for "principle," "reason") except where attention is specifically drawn to the Chinese original. Sanskrit words appearing in italics, such as technical terms or titles, are rendered in accordance with the standard system of transliteration as found in Louis Renou's *Grammaire Sanskrite* (Paris, 1930), pp. xi–xiii. Other Sanskrit terms and names appearing in roman letters are rendered according to the usage of Webster's New International Dictionary, 2d edition Unabridged, except that here the macron is used to indicate long vowels and the Sanskrit symbols for ś (ç) and ṣ are uniformly transcribed "sh." Personal names have also been spelled in this manner except when they occur in the titles of works.

Japanese names are rendered here in their Japanese order, with the family name first and the personal name last. Dates given after personal names are those of birth and death except in the case of rulers whose reign dates are preceded by "r." Generally the name by which a person was most commonly known in Japanese tradition is the one used in the text. Since this book is intended for the general reader, rather than the specialist, we have not burdened the text with a list of the alternate names or titles which usually accompany biographical reference to a scholar in Chinese or Japanese historical works. For the same reason, the sources of translations, given at the beginning of each selection, are rendered as concisely as possible. In the reference at the head of each selection, unless otherwise indicated, the author of the book is the sources of translations, given at the beginning of each selection, are rendered as concisely as possible. Full bibliographical data can be obtained from the list of sources at the end of the book. In the reference at the head of each selection, unless otherwise indicated, the author of the book is the writer whose name precedes the selection. Where excerpts have been taken from existing translations, they have usually been adapted and edited to suit our purposes. In particular, unnecessary brackets and footnotes have been suppressed wherever possible, but if essential commentary could be inserted parenthetically in the text, we have preferred to do so rather than add a footnote. Those interested in the full text and annotations may, of course, refer to the original translation cited with each such excerpt. As sources for our own translations we have tried to use standard editions, if such exist, which would be available to other scholars.

W. T. DE B.

CONTENTS

[xvii]

CHRONOLOGICAL TABLE

A.D. 57 Envoy to the Han court from the Japanese kingdom of Nu. (Earliest date in Japanese history from a non-Japanese source.)

c. 260 Conjectural date for founding of the great shrine to the Sun Goddess at Ise.

552 Introduction of Buddhism to Japan.

562 Rising Korean kingdom of Silla destroys Japanese power in Korea.

592–628 Reign of Suiko Tennō. Shōtoku Taishi regent.

594 Buddhism proclaimed the state religion.

602 Kwallûk arrives in Japan, bringing with him books on geomancy and divination.

604 Seventeen-Article Constitution. First official use in Japan of the Chinese calendar.

607 First Japanese embassy to China.

645 Taika reform.

668 Silla becomes paramount in Korea.

672 Temmu Tennō usurps the throne.

702 Taihō code promulgated.

Nara Period

710 Establishment of the first permanent capital, Nara.

712 *Records of Ancient Matters (Kojiki)*.

720 *Chronicles of Japan (Nihongi)*.

741 Copies of *Golden Light Sūtra* distributed to all the provinces.

751 *Kaifūsō (Fond Recollections of Poetry)*. First collection of Chinese verse by Japanese poets.

752 Dedication of the Great Buddha at the Tōdai-ji in Nara.

754 The Chinese monk Ganjin establishes an ordination center at the Tōdai-ji in Nara.

764 Shōtoku Tennō resumes the throne and appoints a priest, Dōkyō, to be Prime Minister.

770 Dōkyō's rule brought to an end.

781 Kammu becomes emperor.

788 Saichō founds a temple (the Enryaku-ji) on Mt. Hiei.

Heian Period

794 Heian-kyō (Kyoto) becomes the capital.
805 Saichō (767–822) returns from study in China.
806 Kammu dies. Kūkai (774–835) returns from China.
812 Final subjugation of the Ainu (northern aborigines) by Japanese.
815 *New Compilation of the Register of Families (Shinsen Shōjiroku).*
816 Kōya-san monastery founded by Kūkai.
818 Saichō codifies regulations for monks at Mt. Hiei.
833 *Commentary on the Legal Code (Ryō no gige).*
838 Ennin goes to China as member of last official embassy to the T'ang, and returns (847) to found Tendai esotericism in Japan.
858 Establishment of hereditary civil dictatorship of the Fujiwara family. Enchin returns from China and founds a study center at Miidera.
905 *Kokin-shū.*
927 *Institutes of the Engi Period (Engi-shiki).*
933 Beginning of intermittent armed strife between Miidera and Hiei-zan factions of the Tendai sect.
972 Kūya (903–972), early popularizer of devotion to Amida.
c. 990– Classic age of Japanese prose. *Tale of Genji, Pillow Book,* works of
1020 Izumi Shikibu, *Honchō Monzui* (Chinese prose by Japanese).
1017 Genshin (942–1017), author of *Essentials of Salvation.*
1068 Go-Sanjō Tennō. Beginning of attempt to curb the power of the Fujiwara family.
1086 Establishment of "Cloistered Government" upon retirement into Buddhist orders of Shirakawa Tennō.
1095 First descent into the capital by marauding monks from Mt. Hiei.
1132 Ryōnin (1071–1132), forerunner of Pure Land sect.
1156 Taira Kiyomori, of the military and provincial aristocracy, controls the civil government in the capital.
1185 Defeat of the Taira clan. Minamoto Yoritomo supreme in Japan.
1191 Eisai (1141–1215) returns from China, bringing tea. Founds Rinzai branch of the Zen sect.

Kamakura Shogunate

1192 Yoritomo becomes first shogun.
1205 Beginning of hereditary regency to the shoguns of the Hōjō family.
1206 Hōnen (1133–1212) exiled because of his success in gaining converts to the Pure Land doctrine.
1222 Dōgen (1200–1253), founder of Sōtō branch of the Zen sect, goes to China.
1232 *Jōei shikimoku* (basic law code of the Kamakura Shogunate).

1260 Nichiren (1222–1282) first predicts a foreign invasion.
1262 Shinran (1173–1262), founder of the True Pure Land sect.
1268 Nichiren warns of the impending Mongol invasion.
1271 Nichiren sentenced to death, escapes, and is banished.
1274 First Mongol invasion.
1281 Second Mongol invasion.
1289 Ippen (1238–1289), popularizer of the Amida cult.
1325 Go-Daigo Tennō sends first official embassy to China since the T'ang, at suggestion of Zen master Musō Soseki (1275–1351).
c. 1331 *Essays in Idleness* (*Tsurezure gusa*).
1333 End of the Hōjō regency. Inauguration of direct imperial rule under Go-Daigo.
1336 Go-Daigo flees to Yoshino. Rival emperor reigns in Kyoto under the protection of Ashikaga Takauji.

Ashikaga Shogunate

WARRING STATES PERIOD

1338 Ashikaga Takauji becomes shogun.
1339 *Records of the Legitimate Succession of the Divine Sovereigns* (*Jinnō shōtō-ki*), by Kitabatake Chikafusa.
1368 Ashikaga Yoshimitsu succeeds to the shogunate. Fosters diplomatic and trade relations with China.
1384 Kan'ami (1333–1384), early master of Nō drama.
1392 Reunion of the Northern (Kyoto) and Southern (Yoshino) courts.
1443 Seami (1363–1443), master of Nō drama.
1467 Ōnin War. Commencement of endemic civil wars throughout Japan.
1488 Nisshin (1407–1488), evangelizer of Nichiren sect.
1499 Rennyo (1415–1499), priest of True Pure Land sect.
1511 Yoshida Kanetomo (1435–1511), of the "Primal Shinto" movement.
1542 First Europeans to visit Japan, Portuguese merchants, land on Kyushu.
1549 St. Francis Xavier reaches Japan.
1568 Nobunaga controls the capital.

Tokugawa Shogunate

1571 Nobunaga destroys the Enryaku-ji on Mt. Hiei.
1582 Nobunaga murdered. Hideyoshi succeeds to power.
1587 First persecution of Christians.
1592 First Korean expedition.
1593 Ieyasu meets Fujiwara Seika. Subsequently, Chu Hsi Confucianism adopted as official cult of Tokugawa Japan.
1597 Second Korean expedition.
1598 Death of Hideyoshi.

1600 Victory of Ieyasu at Sekigahara.

1603 Establishment of Tokugawa Shogunate.

1608 Hayashi Razan becomes Confucian tutor to the shogun.

1615 *Laws Governing the Military Households* promulgated. Osaka Castle destroyed; final defeat of Hideyoshi's heirs.

1616 Death of Ieyasu.

1617 Christians again persecuted.

1624 Spaniards expelled.

1637–1638 Shimabara revolt. Japanese forbidden to leave Japan.

1639 Portuguese expelled.

1640 Other Europeans excluded.

1647 Kumazawa Banzan, having studied Ōyōmei philosophy under Nakae Tōju, enters the service of Lord Ikeda of Okayama.

1648 Nakae Tōju (1608–1648).

1657 Great Fire in Edo. *Dai-Nihon-shi* started.

1665 The Chinese émigré Chu Shun-Shui settles in Mito as adviser to Mito school.

1670 *General History of Our State* (*Honchō Tsugan*) completed by Hayashi school.

1682 Yamazaki Ansai (1618–1682).

1685 Yamaga Sokō (1622–1685), early proponent of the "Way of the Warrior" (*Bushidō*).

1687 Reform program of Kumazawa Banzan (1619–1691) arouses the shogunate's wrath.

1688–1704 Genroku period, featuring novels of Saikaku, plays of Chikamatsu, poems of Bashō, and Ukiyo prints.

1691 Hayashi Hōkō named hereditary Head of the State University.

1703 Incident of the 47 *rōnin*.

1705 Itō Jinsai (1627–1705), proponent of "Ancient Studies."

1709 Arai Hakuseki (1657–1725) becomes Confucian consultant to the shogunate.

1714 Kaibara Ekken (1630–1714).

1715 Yoshimune becomes shogun. Arai Hakuseki dismissed as Confucian adviser; Muro Kyūsō (1688–1734) employed.

1716 Relaxation of edicts against foreign learning gives impetus to Dutch studies.

1728 Ogyū Sorai (1666–1728). High tide of Chinese studies. Kada Azumamaro (1669–1736) petitions shogunate to establish school of national (Shinto) learning.

1732 Great famine.

1746 Tominaga Nakamoto (1715–1746), rationalist philosopher.

1783–1786   Serious famines and epidemics.
1787   Matsudaira Sadanobu institutes various fiscal and social reforms in Shogun's administration.
1789   Miura Baien (1723–1789), rationalist philosopher.
1790   Shogunate issues edict suppressing heterodox learning.
1817   Kaiho Seiryō (1755–1817), rationalist thinker.

CHAPTER I

THE EARLIEST RECORDS OF JAPAN

The oldest extant annals in Japanese are the *Records of Ancient Matters* (A.D. 712) and the *Chronicles of Japan* (720).[1] Both open with chapters on the mythological Age of the Gods, but little of the material from the ancient Japanese past can be taken seriously as history. It is not until we reach the reign of the Empress Suiko (592–628) that consciously written history became a reality; indeed, the name Suiko itself may be translated "conjecture of the past," and suggests that this posthumous title was bestowed on the empress because the writing of history was considered to be an outstanding event of her reign.

For information about the earlier periods of Japanese history it is usually safer to rely on accounts found in the Chinese dynastic histories than on the native literature. By the time that Japan first came into the ken of the Chinese, the writing of history had left far behind the rather primitive level of the *Book of History* and was approaching a science. In contrast to the highly tendentious and even fictional Japanese descriptions of their early history, the Chinese accounts of Japan, brief as they are, possess comparative reliability, if for no other reason than that the Chinese had no axe to grind with respect to a semicivilized people living at what was for them the end of the world.

According to the *Chronicles of Japan* the foundation of the Japanese empire took place at a date corresponding to 660 B.C., but the first mention of Japan in the Chinese histories occurs only in A.D. 57. At this latter date, Japan, far from being a unified country with a heritage of 700 years of civilization, consisted of more than a hundred scattered tribal communities. Even as late as the Chinese Three Kingdoms Period (220–265) Japan was still divided into some forty communities.

The Chinese histories do not inform us how the people now known as

[1] The *Kojiki* and the *Nihongi*.

[1]

the Japanese first found their way to the islands. In the absence of positive information on this subject, modern scholars have attempted to expound various theories based on linguistics, archeology, architecture, and a great many criteria, some contending that the Japanese originally came from Southeast Asia, others insisting that they were a northern people. It is probable, however, that the Japanese had diverse origins, with various elements entering from different directions. The main stream of cultural influence came from the continent by way of Korea. It seems likely that when the first Ch'in emperor (247–210 B.C.) unified China and built the Great Wall to prevent the northern barbarians from making incursions on the fertile plains of the Yellow River, it helped to set a definite direction to the migrations of different peoples, eastwards or westwards along the wall. Disturbances resulting from the movement of tribes were at times so severe as to compel the Emperor Wu (r. 140–87 B.C.) of the Han dynasty to send expeditionary forces to restore order. An outpost of the Han empire was established in northern Korea which served as a model of organized government to the surrounding tribes including, possibly, the Japanese.

It may seem surprising that there were Japanese in Korea in the first century A.D., but no fixed boundary appears in fact to have existed at the time between the territories of the Koreans and of the Japanese. A constant eastward migration from northern China to the Korean peninsula and thence to the Japanese archipelago made for a fluidity in the composition of the population. Despite Korean references of the fourth century A.D. to "Japanese invaders," there continued to be Japanese holdings on the continent until A.D. 562 when the Japanese political center in the peninsula was destroyed by the rising power of the Korean kingdom of Silla. As late as A.D. 478 the Japanese emperor was recognized by the Chinese court as being ruler of Korea, although the Japanese emperor in turn proclaimed his fealty to the Chinese sovereign. During the course of the seventh century Silla, with Chinese aid, subjugated the rival kingdoms of Koguryŏ and Paekche, and unified the peninsula. These successes of the combined forces of Silla and T'ang China drove the Japanese from the continent into the relative isolation of their islands, an event which may have helped to bring about the birth of historical Japan. The rise of powerful dynasties in China and Korea impelled Japan to achieve a unified government if it were not to be overwhelmed.

For an understanding of some important influences upon Japanese thought since the earliest periods of their history, we may turn to the geographical features of the islands. The first Chinese account of Japan opens with the words, "The people of Wa live on mountainous islands in the ocean," and the two elements of water and mountains, together with a kind of sun worship have always been very close to the Japanese. Of course we are likely to find in the religious beliefs of any country worship of the striking or beneficial aspects of nature, but the combination of these three elements is especially characteristic of Japan. The numerous clear streams and the ever present ocean have always delighted the Japanese, as we may tell from their earliest poetry. To their love of water the Japanese have joined a passion for lustration and cleanliness, and in our own day for swimming. The Japanese love of mountains is not surprising in a country renowned for its numerous peaks, especially the incomparable Mt. Fuji, and the worship of the sun is not unnatural in a country blessed with a temperate climate. Today we can still appreciate what an awe-inspiring experience it must have been for the Japanese of any age to stand on the summit of Mt. Fuji and greet the glowing sun as it rose from the waters of the Pacific. Other characteristics of the Japanese found in the early Chinese accounts and which still seem true today include honesty, politeness, gentleness in peace and bravery in war, and a love of liquor.

The Japanese accounts of the birth of the gods and of the foundation of Japan belong of course to the realm of mythology rather than history, but they afford us a glimpse of Japanese attitudes toward life and the universe when civilization was just beginning to glimmer. Also since great importance was attached to these legends by later Japanese, some knowledge of them is indispensable to the study of Japanese thought.

JAPAN IN THE CHINESE DYNASTIC HISTORIES

The following extracts are from the official histories of successive Chinese dynasties beginning with the Latter Han (A.D. 25–220). However, the first of these accounts to be written was that for the Kingdom of Wei (220–265), compiled about A.D. 297. The *History of the Latter Han* was compiled about 445 and incorporates much from the earlier description of the Japanese.

These accounts are contained in a section devoted to the barbarian neighbors of China at the end of each history. Thus they do not occupy a prominent place in these works, being more in the nature of an afterthought or footnote. Particularly in the earlier accounts the information is apt to be scattered and disconnected, and of course is presented by official chroniclers who view Japanese affairs with an eye to Chinese interests and prestige.

Nevertheless, some of the main outlines of Japan's development in these early centuries may be discerned. In the first accounts Japan appears to be a heterogeneous group of communities in contact with China, with one ruling house bidding for Chinese recognition of its supremacy over the others. In one case the influence of the Chinese ambassador is said to have been the decisive factor in settling a dispute over succession to the Yamato throne. The kings of Wa, as the Yamato rulers were known, also made strong claims to military supremacy in Korea which were at times acknowledged by the Chinese court. In the later accounts unification of Japan has progressed noticeably. The sovereignty of the Yamato house has been asserted over hitherto autonomous regions, and its government displays many of the trappings of the Chinese imperial structure. On occasion the Japanese court is rebuked for its pretensions to equality with the Chinese, and even for its hinted superiority, as when the Japanese ruler addressed the Chinese, "The Son of Heaven in the land where the sun rises addresses a letter to the Son of Heaven in the land where the sun sets."

ACCOUNTS OF THE EASTERN BARBARIANS

History of the Kingdom of Wei (Wei Chih) c. A.D. 297
[Adapted from Tsunoda and Goodrich, *Japan in the Chinese Dynastic Histories*, pp. 8–16]

The people of Wa [Japan] dwell in the middle of the ocean on the mountainous islands southeast of [the prefecture of] Tai-fang. They formerly comprised more than one hundred communities. During the Han dynasty, [Wa] envoys appeared at the court; today, thirty of their communities maintain intercourse with us through envoys and scribes. . . .

The land of Wa is warm and mild. In winter as in summer the people live on raw vegetables and go about barefooted. They have [or live in] houses; father and mother, elder and younger, sleep separately. They smear their bodies with pink and scarlet, just as the Chinese use powder. They serve food on bamboo and wooden trays, helping themselves with their fingers. When a person dies, they prepare a single coffin, without an outer one. They cover the graves with earth to make a mound. When death occurs, mourning is observed for more than ten days, during which

[4]

period they do not eat meat. The head mourners wail and lament, while friends sing, dance, and drink liquor. When the funeral is over, all members of the family go into the water to cleanse themselves in a bath of purification.

When they go on voyages across the sea to visit China, they always select a man who does not comb his hair, does not rid himself of fleas, lets his clothing get as dirty as it will, does not eat meat, and does not lie with women. This man behaves like a mourner and is known as the "mourning keeper." When the voyage meets with good fortune, they all lavish on him slaves and other valuables. In case there is disease or mishap, they kill him, saying that he was not scrupulous in observing the taboos. . . .

Whenever they undertake an enterprise or a journey and discussion arises, they bake bones and divine in order to tell whether fortune will be good or bad. First they announce the object of divination, using the same manner of speech as in tortoise shell divination; then they examine the cracks made by the fire and tell what is to come to pass.

In their meetings and in their deportment, there is no distinction between father and son or between men and women. They are fond of liquor. In their worship, men of importance simply clap their hands instead of kneeling or bowing. The people live long, some to one hundred and others to eighty or ninety years. Ordinarily, men of importance have four or five wives; the lesser ones, two or three. Women are not loose in morals or jealous. There is no theft, and litigation is infrequent. In case of violation of law, the light offender loses his wife and children by confiscation; as for the grave offender, the members of his household and also his kinsmen are exterminated. There are class distinctions among the people, and some men are vassals of others. Taxes are collected. There are granaries as well as markets in each province, where necessaries are exchanged under the supervision of the Wa officials. . . .

When the lowly meet men of importance on the road, they stop and withdraw to the roadside. In conveying messages to them or.addressing them, they either squat or kneel, with both hands on the ground. This is the way they show respect. When responding, they say "ah," which corresponds to the affirmative "yes."

The country formerly had a man as ruler. For some seventy or eighty years after that there were disturbances and warfare. Thereupon the people agreed upon a woman for their ruler. Her name was Pimiko. She occupied herself with magic and sorcery, bewitching the people. Though mature in age, she remained unmarried. She had a younger brother who assisted her in ruling the country. After she became the ruler, there were few who saw her. She had one thousand women as attendants, but only one man. He served her food and drink and acted as a medium of communication. She resided in a palace surrounded by towers and stockades, with armed guards in a state of constant vigilance. . . .

In the sixth month of the second year of Ching-ch'u [A.D. 238], the Queen of Wa sent the grandee Nashonmi and others to visit the prefecture [of Tai-fang], where they requested permission to proceed to the Emperor's court with tribute. The Governor, Liu Hsia, dispatched an officer to accompany the party to the capital. In answer to the Queen of Wa, an edict of the Emperor, issued in the twelfth month of the same year, said as follows: "Herein we address Pimiko, Queen of Wa, whom we now officially call a friend of Wei. The Governor of Tai-fang, Liu Hsia, has sent a messenger to accompany your vassal, Nashonmi, and his lieutenant, Tsushi Gori. They have arrived here with your tribute, consisting of four male slaves and six female slaves, together with two pieces of cloth with designs, each twenty feet in length. You live very far away across the sea; yet you have sent an embassy with tribute. Your loyalty and filial piety we appreciate exceedingly. We confer upon you, therefore, the title 'Queen of Wa Friendly to Wei,' together with the decoration of the gold seal with purple ribbon. The latter, properly encased, is to be sent to you through the Governor. We expect you, O Queen, to rule your people in peace and to endeavor to be devoted and obedient." . . .

When Pimiko passed away, a great mound was raised, more than a hundred paces in diameter. Over a hundred male and female attendants followed her to the grave. Then a king was placed on the throne, but the people would not obey him. Assassination and murder followed; more than one thousand were thus slain.

A relative of Pimiko named Iyo, a girl of thirteen, was [then] made queen and order was restored. Cheng [the Chinese ambassador] issued a proclamation to the effect that Iyo was the ruler. Then Iyo sent a delegation of twenty under the grandee Yazaku, General of the Imperial Guard, to accompany Cheng home [to China]. The delegation visited the capital and presented thirty male and female slaves. It also offered to the court five thousand white gems and two pieces of carved jade, as well as twenty pieces of brocade with variegated designs.

History of the Latter Han Dynasty (*Hou Han Shu*) c. A.D. 445
[Adapted from Tsunoda and Goodrich, *Japan in the Chinese Dynastic Histories*, pp. 1–3]

The Wa dwell on mountainous islands southeast of Han [Korea] in the middle of the ocean, forming more than one hundred communities. From the time of the overthrow of Chao-hsien [northern Korea] by Emperor Wu [r. 140–87 B.C.], nearly thirty of these communities have held intercourse with the Han (Chinese) court by envoys or scribes. Each community has its king, whose office is hereditary. The King of Great Wa resides in the country of Yamadai. . . .

In the second year of the Chien-wu Chung-yüan era [A.D. 57], the Wa country Nu sent an envoy with tribute who called himself *ta-fu*. This country is located in the southern extremity of the Wa country. Emperor Kuang-wu bestowed on him a seal. . . .

During the reigns of Huan-ti [147–168] and Ling-ti [168–189] the country of Wa was in a state of great confusion, war and conflict raging on all sides. For a number of years, there was no ruler. Then a woman named Pimiko appeared. Remaining unmarried, she occupied herself with magic and sorcery and bewitched the populace. Thereupon they placed her on the throne. She kept one thousand female attendants, but few people saw her. There was only one man who was in charge of her wardrobe and meals and acted as the medium of communication. She resided in a palace surrounded by towers and stockade, with the protection of armed guards. The laws and customs were strict and stern.

History of the Liu Sung Dynasty (*Sung Shu*) c. A.D. 513
[Adapted from Tsunoda and Goodrich, *Japan in the Chinese Dynastic Histories*, pp. 23–24]

The following extract is preceded by an account of four successive Japanese rulers who asked to be confirmed in their titles by the Chinese court. One of these titles was "Generalissimo Who Maintains Peace in the East Commanding with Battle-Ax All Military Affairs in the Six Countries of Wa, Paekche, Silla, Imna, Chin-han and Mok-han." Wa refers to Japan, and the other five names

[7]

to states comprising most of the Korean peninsula. On at least two occasions in the fifth century the Chinese court, while accepting the fealty of the Japanese "king," confirmed his claim to military supremacy in Korea. . . .

Kō died and his brother, Bu,[1] came to the throne. Bu, signing himself King of Wa, Generalissimo Who Maintains Peace in the East Command-ing with Battle-Ax All Military Affairs in the Seven Countries of Wa, Paekche, Silla, Imna, Kala, Chin-han, and Mok-han, in the second year of Sheng-ming, Shun-ti's reign [478], sent an envoy bearing a memorial which read as follows: "Our land is remote and distant; its domains lie far out in the ocean. From of old our forebears have clad themselves in armor and helmet and gone across the hills and waters, sparing no time for rest. In the east, they conquered fifty-five countries of hairy men; and in the west, they brought to their knees sixty-six countries of various barbarians. Crossing the sea to the north, they subjugated ninety-five countries. The way of government is to keep harmony and peace; thus order is established in the land. Generation after generation, without fail, our forebears have paid homage to the court. Your sub-ject, ignorant though he is, is succeeding to the throne of his predecessors and is fervently devoted to your Sovereign Majesty. Everything he com-mands is at your imperial disposal. In order to go by way of Paekche, far distant though it is, we prepared ships and boats. Koguryŏ,[2] however, in defiance of law, schemed to capture them. Borders were raided, and murder was committed repeatedly. Consequently we were delayed every time and missed favorable winds. We attempted to push on, but when the way was clear, Koguryŏ was rebellious. My deceased father became indignant at the marauding foe who blocked our way to the sovereign court. Urged on by a sense of justice, he gathered together a million archers and was about to launch a great campaign. But because of the death of my father and brother, the plan that had been matured could not be carried out at the last moment. Mourning required the laying down of arms. Inaction does not bring victory. Now, however, we again set our armor in array and carry out the wish of our elders. The fighting men are in high mettle; civil and military officials are ready; none have fear of sword or fire.

"Your Sovereign virtue extends over heaven and earth. If through it we can crush this foe and put an end to our troubles, we shall ever

---

[1] Emperor Yūryaku, 456–479.　　　　[2] State in North Korea.

continue loyally to serve [Your Majesty]. I therefore beg you to appoint me as supreme commander of the campaign, with the status of minister, and to grant to others [among my followers] ranks and titles, so that loyalty may be encouraged."

By imperial edict, Bu was made King of Wa and Generalissimo Who Maintains Peace in the East Commanding with Battle-Ax all Military Affairs in the Six Countries of Wa, Silla, Imna, Kala, Chin-han, and Mok-han.

History of the Sui Dynasty (Sui Shu) c. A.D. 630

[Adapted from Tsunoda and Goodrich, *Japan in the Chinese Dynastic Histories*, pp. 29-32]

During the twenty years of the K'ai-huang era (581-600), the King of Wa, whose family name was Ame and personal name Tarishihoko, and who bore the title of Ahakomi, sent an envoy to visit the court. The Emperor ordered the appropriate official to make inquiries about the manners and customs [of the Wa people]. The envoy reported thus: "The King of Wa deems heaven to be his elder brother and the sun, his younger. Before break of dawn he attends the court, and, sitting cross-legged, listens to appeals. Just as soon as the sun rises, he ceases these duties, saying that he hands them over to his brother." Our just Emperor said that such things were extremely senseless,[1] and he admonished [the King of Wa] to alter [his ways].

[According to the envoy's report], the King's spouse is called Kemi. Several hundred women are kept in the inner chambers of the court. The heir apparent is known as Rikamitahori. There is no special palace. There are twelve grades of court officials. . . .

There are about 100,000 households. It is customary to punish murder, arson, and adultery with death. Thieves are made to make restitution in accordance with the value of the goods stolen. If the thief has no property with which to make payment, he is taken to be a slave. Other offenses are punished according to their nature—sometimes by banishment and sometimes by flogging. In the prosecution of offenses by the court, the knees of those who plead not guilty are pressed together by placing them

---

[1] According to Chinese tradition a virtuous ruler showed his conscientiousness by attending to matters of state the first thing in the morning. Apparently the Japanese emperor was carrying this to a ridiculous extreme by disposing of state business before dawn.

[9]

between pieces of wood, or their heads are sawed with the stretched string of a strong bow. Sometimes pebbles are put in boiling water and both parties to a dispute made to pick them out. The hand of the guilty one is said to become inflamed. Sometimes a snake is kept in a jar, and the accused ordered to catch it. If he is guilty, his hand will be bitten. The people are gentle and peaceful. Litigation is infrequent and theft seldom occurs.

As for musical instruments, they have five-stringed lyres and flutes. Both men and women paint marks on their arms and spots on their faces and have their bodies tattooed. They catch fish by diving into the water. They have no written characters and understand only the use of notched sticks and knotted ropes. They revere Buddha and obtained Buddhist scriptures from Paekche. This was the first time that they came into possession of written characters. They are familiar with divination and have profound faith in shamans, both male and female. . . .

Both Silla and Paekche consider Wa to be a great country, replete with precious things, and they pay her homage. Envoys go back and forth from time to time.

In the third year of Ta-yeh [607], King Tarishihoko sent an envoy to the court with tribute. The envoy said: "The King has heard that to the west of the ocean a Bodhisattva of the Sovereign reveres and promotes Buddhism. For that reason he has sent an embassy to pay his respects. Accompanying the embassy are several tens of monks who have come to study Buddhism." [The envoy brought] an official message which read: "The Son of Heaven in the land where the sun rises addresses a letter to the Son of Heaven in the land where the sun sets. We hope you are in good health." When the Emperor saw this letter, he was displeased and told the official in charge of foreign affairs that this letter from the barbarians was discourteous, and that such a letter should not again be brought to his attention.

New History of the T'ang Dynasty (Hsin T'ang Shu) [1]
[Adapted from Tsunoda and Goodrich, *Japan in the Chinese Dynastic Histories*, pp. 38–40]

Japan in former times was called Wa-nu. It is 24,000 *li* distant from our capital, situated to the southeast of Silla in the middle of the ocean.

[1] Compiled in the eleventh century on the basis of earlier materials relating to the T'ang dynasty, 618–906.

It is five months' journey to cross Japan from east to west, and a three months' journey from south to north. There are no castles or stockades in that country, only high walls built by placing timbers together. The roofs are thatched with grass. There are over fifty islets there, each with a name of its own, but all under the sovereignty of Japan. A high official is stationed to have surveillance over these communities.

As for the inhabitants the women outnumber the men. The people are literate and revere the teachings of Buddha. In the government there are twelve official ranks. The family name of the King is Ame. The Japanese say that from their first ruler, known as Ame-no-minaka-nushi, to Hiko-nagi, there were altogether thirty-two generations of rulers, all bearing the title of *mikoto* and residing in the palace of Tsukushi. Upon the enthronement of Jimmu, son of Hikonagi, the title was changed to *tennō* and the palace was moved to the province of Yamato. . . .

In the fifth year of Chen-kuan [631], the Japanese sent an embassy to pay a visit to the court. In appreciation of this visit from such a distance, the sovereign gave orders to the official concerned not to insist on yearly tribute. . . .

At this time, Silla was being harassed by Koguryo and Paekche. Emperor Kao Tsung sent a sealed rescript to Japan ordering the King to send reinforcements to succor Silla. But after a short time, King Kōtoku died [654] and his son Ame-no-toyo-takara was enthroned. Then he also died, and his son Tenchi was enthroned. In the following year [663] an envoy came to the court accompanied by some Ainus. The Ainus also dwell on those islands. The beards of the Ainus were four feet long. They carried arrows at their necks, and without ever missing would shoot a gourd held on the head of a person standing several tens of steps away.

Then Tenchi died [671] and his son, Temmu, came to the throne. He died, and his son Sōji was enthroned.

In the first year of Hsien-heng [670] an embassy came to the court from Japan to offer congratulations upon the conquest of Koguryŏ. About this time, the Japanese who had studied Chinese came to dislike the name Wa and changed it to Nippon. According to the words of the Japanese envoy himself, that name was chosen because the country was so close to where the sun rises. Some say [on the other hand], that Nippon was a small country which had been subjugated by the Wa, and that the latter took over its name. As this envoy was not truthful, doubt still remains. Besides the envoy was boastful, and he said that the domains of his country were many thousands of square *li* and extended to the ocean on the south and on the west. In the northeast, he said, the country was bordered by mountain ranges beyond which lay the land of the hairy men.

THE EARLIEST JAPANESE CHRONICLES

The great native chronicles of early Japan, the *Records of Ancient Matters* (*Kojiki*) and *Chronicles of Japan* (*Nihongi*), were compiled as late as the first decades of the eighth century A.D., when Japanese writers were already strongly influenced by Chinese traditions.[1] It is therefore difficult to distinguish any pure native traditions in these works or any reliable account of Japan's early history. Many of the events described are anachronistic, and many of the legends are selected with a view to confirming the religious or political claims of the ruling dynasty. The emphasis on ancestry is already quite apparent, though other evidence indicates that family genealogies were in a very confused state before the introduction of writing and the Chinese practice of compiling genealogical records (see Chapter IV).

Passages betraying significant Chinese influence are included elsewhere. The following excerpts from the translations of Chamberlain and Aston are selected to show what seem to be the most unsystematic and unsophisticated of legends dealing with the Age of the Gods and the founding of the dynasty. Especially evident are the great number of gods, their close association with natural phenomena, and the near-chaos of the supernatural world. It should be noted that in the creation of the imperial line gods representing the Sun, Mountains and the Sea each made an important contribution.

From the Preface to *Records of Ancient Matters* (*Kojiki*)
[Adapted from Chamberlain, *Ko-ji-ki*, pp. 11–13]

Hereupon, regretting the errors in the old words, and wishing to correct the misstatements in the former chronicles, [the Empress Gemmyō], on the eighteenth day of the ninth moon of the fourth year of Wadō [November 3, 711], commanded me Yasumaro to select and record the old words, learned by heart by Hieda no Are according to the imperial decree, and dutifully to lift them up to Her.

In reverent obedience to the contents of the decree, I have made a

[1] Footnotes to translations from the *Kojiki* and *Nihongi*, unless otherwise identified, are those of Chamberlain and Aston respectively, in some cases abbreviated or adapted to the usage in this text. [Ed.]

careful choice. But in high antiquity both speech and thought were so simple, that it would be difficult to arrange phrases and compose periods in the characters.[2] To relate everything in an ideographic transcription would entail an inadequate expression of the meaning; to write altogether according to the phonetic method would make the story of events unduly lengthy.[3] For this reason have I sometimes in the same sentence used the phonetic and ideographic systems conjointly, and have sometimes in one matter used the ideographic record exclusively. Moreover where the drift of the words was obscure, I have by comments elucidated their signification; but need it be said that I have nowhere commented on what was easy? . . . Altogether the things recorded commence with the separation of Heaven and Earth, and conclude with the august reign at Oharida.[4] So from the Deity Master-of-the-August-Centre-of-Heaven down to His Augustness Prince-Wave-Limit-Brave-Cormorant-Thatch-Meeting-Incompletely makes the First Volume; from the Heavenly Sovereign Kamu-Yamato-Ihare-Biko down to the august reign of Homuda makes the Second Volume; from the Emperor Ō-Sazaki down to the great palace of Oharida makes the Third Volume.[5] Altogether I have written Three Volumes, which I reverently and respectfully present. I, Yasumaro, with true trembling and true fear, bow my head, bow my head.

Reverently presented by the Court Noble Futo no Yasumaro, an Officer of the Upper Division of the First Class of the Fifth Rank and of the Fifth Order of Merit, on the 28th day of the first moon of the fifth year of Wadō [March 10, 712].

[2] That is, the simplicity of speech and thought in early Japan renders it too hard a task to rearrange the old documents committed to memory by Are in such a manner as to make them conform to the rules of Chinese style.

[3] That is, if I adopted in its entirety the Chinese ideographic method of writing, I should often fail of giving a true impression of the nature of the original documents. If, on the other hand, I consistently used the Chinese characters, syllable by syllable, as phonetic symbols for Japanese sounds, this work would attain to inordinate proportions, on account of the great length of the polysyllabic Japanese as compared with the monosyllabic Chinese.

[4] That is, commence with the creation, and end with the death of the Empress Suiko (A.D. 628), who resided at Oharida.

[5] Kamu-Yamato-Ihare-Biko is the proper native Japanese name of the emperor commonly known by the Chinese "canonical name" of Jimmu. Homuda is part of the native Japanese name of the Emperor Ōjin. Ō-Sazaki is the native Japanese name of the Emperor Nintoku.

Birth of the Sun Goddess

Note that in this account from the *Nihongi* the Sun Goddess, Amaterasu, is identified not as the first of the gods or as the creator of the world, but simply as one among many offspring of the primal pair, Izanagi and Izanami.

[Adapted from Aston, *Nihongi*, I, 18–20]

Izanagi no Mikoto and Izanami no Mikoto consulted together, saying: "We have now produced the Great-eight-island country, with the mountains, rivers, herbs, and trees. Why should we not produce someone who shall be lord of the universe?" They then together produced the Sun Goddess, who was called Ō-hiru-me no muchi.[1]

(Called in one writing Amaterasu no Ō kami.[2])

(In one writing she is called Amaterasu-ō-hiru-me no Mikoto.[3])

The resplendent luster of this child shone throughout all the six quarters.[4] Therefore the two Deities rejoiced, saying: "We have had many children, but none of them have been equal to this wondrous infant. She ought not to be kept long in this land, but we ought of our own accord to send her at once to Heaven, and entrust to her the affairs of Heaven."

At this time Heaven and Earth were still not far separated, and therefore they sent her up to Heaven by the ladder of Heaven.

They next produced the Moon-god.

(Called in one writing Tsuki-yumi[5] no Mikoto, or Tsuki-yomi no Mikoto.)

His radiance was next to that of the Sun in splendor. This God was to be the consort of the Sun-Goddess, and to share in her government. They therefore sent him also to Heaven.

Next they produced the leech-child, which even at the age of three years could not stand upright. They therefore placed it in the rock-camphor-wood boat of Heaven, and abandoned it to the winds.

Their next child was Sosa no o no Mikoto.[6]

(Called in one writing Kami Sosa-no-o no Mikoto or Haya Sosa-no-o no Mikoto.[7])

---

[1] Great-noon-female-of-possessor.   [2] Heaven-illumine-of-great-deity.

[3] Heaven-illumine-great-noon-female-of-augustness.

[4] North, South, East, West, Above, Below.

[5] *Yumi* means bow; *yomi*, darkness. Neither is inappropriate as applied to the moon.

[6] Better known as Susa no o, a god particularly associated with the Izumo people, who was probably relegated to a subordinate role when these people were displaced or eclipsed in power by the Yamato group. [Ed.]

[7] *Kami*, deity; *haya*, quick.

This God had a fierce temper and was given to cruel acts. Moreover he made a practice of continually weeping and wailing. So he brought many of the people of the land to an untimely end. Again he caused green mountains to become withered. Therefore the two Gods, his parents, addressed Sosa no o no Mikoto, saying: "Thou art exceedingly wicked, and it is not meet that thou shouldst reign over the world. Certainly thou must depart far away to the Nether-land." So they at length expelled him.

The Divine Creation of the Imperial Ancestors

In the following excerpt from the *Kojiki* it should be observed that the divine offspring from which the imperial line is traced were the joint creation of Amaterasu, the Sun Goddess, and Susa-no-o, the unruly storm god. They were actually produced from the mouth of Susa-no-o after he had chewed up the ornaments of Amaterasu, but she claimed them as her own on the ground that the seed or stuff of which they were made came from her. Thus the ordinary male and female functions are reversed in establishing the genetic relationship, which gives priority to the Sun Goddess but suggests the absorption of Susa-no-o's power into the imperial line.

[Adapted from Chamberlain, *Ko-ji-ki,* pp. 45–49]

So thereupon His-Swift-Impetuous-Male-Augustness (Susa-no-o) said: "If that be so, I will take leave of the Heaven-Shining-Great-August-Deity (Amaterasu),[1] and depart." [With these words] he forthwith went up to Heaven, whereupon all the mountains and rivers shook, and every land and country quaked. So the Heaven-Shining-Deity, alarmed at the noise, said: "The reason of the ascent hither of His Augustness my elder brother is surely no good intent. It is only that he wishes to wrest my land from me." And she forthwith, unbinding her august hair, twisted it into august bunches; and both into the left and into the right august bunch, as likewise into her august head-dress and likewise on to her left and her right august arm, she twisted an augustly complete [string] of curved jewels eight feet [long] of five hundred jewels; and, slinging on her back a quiver holding a thousand [arrows], and adding [thereto] a quiver holding five hundred [arrows], she likewise took and slung at her side a mighty and high [-sounding] elbow-pad, and brandished and stuck her bow upright so that the top shook; and she stamped her feet into the hard ground up to her opposing thighs, kicking away [the earth] like

[1] In what follows, the names of deities appearing frequently in these accounts are standardized and given an abbreviated translation or transliteration in place of the full title. [Ed.]

rotten snow, and stood valiantly like unto a mighty man, and waiting, asked: "Wherefore ascendest thou hither?" Then Susa-no-o replied, saying: "I have no evil intent. It is only that when the Great-August-Deity [our father] spoke, deigning to enquire the cause of my wailing and weeping, I said: 'I wail because I wish to go to my deceased mother's land'; whereupon the Great-August-Deity said: 'Thou shalt not dwell in this land,' and deigned to expel me with a divine expulsion. It is therefore, solely with the thought of taking leave of thee and departing, that I have ascended hither. I have no strange intentions." Then the Heaven-Shining-Deity said: "If that be so, whereby shall I know the sincerity of thine intentions?" Thereupon Susa-no-o replied, saying: "Let each of us swear, and produce children." So as they then swore to each other from the opposite banks of the Tranquil River of Heaven, the august names of the Deities that were born from the mist [of her breath] when, having first begged Susa-no-o to hand her the ten-grasp saber which was girded on him and broken it into three fragments, and with the jewels making a jingling sound having brandished and washed them in the True-Pool-Well of Heaven, and having crunchingly crunched them, the Heaven-Shining-Deity blew them away, were Her Augustness Torrent-Mist-Princess, another august name for whom is Her Augustness Princess-of-the-Island-of-the-Offing; next Her Augustness Lovely-Island-Princess, another august name for whom is Her Augustness Good-Princess; next Her Augustness Princess-of-the-Torrent. The august name of the Deity that was born from the mist [of his breath] when, having begged the Heaven-Shining-Deity to hand him the augustly complete [string] of curved jewels eight feet [long] of five hundred jewels that was twisted in the left august bunch [of her hair], and with the jewels making a jingling sound having brandished and washed them in the True-Pool-Well of Heaven, and having crunchingly crunched them, Susa-no-o blew them away, was His Augustness Truly-Conqueror-I-Conquer-Conquering-Swift-Heavenly-Great-Great-Ears. The august name of the Deity that was born from the mist [of his breath] when again, having begged her to hand him the jewels that were twisted in the right august bunch [of her hair], and having crunchingly crunched them, he blew them away, was His Augustness Ame-no-hohi. The august name of the Deity that was born from the mist [of his breath] when again, having begged her to hand him the jewels that were twisted in her august head-dress, and

having crunchingly crunched them, he blew them away, was His Augustness Prince-Lord-of-Heaven. The august name of the Deity that was
born from the mist [of his breath] when again, having begged her to
hand him the jewels that were twisted on her left august arm, and having
crunchingly crunched them, he blew them away, was His Augustness
Prince-Lord-of-Life. The august name of the Deity that was born from
the jewels that were twisted on her right august arm, and having crunchingly crunched them, he blew them away, was His-Wondrous-August-
ness-of-Kumanu. [Five Deities in all.]

The August Declaration of the Division of the August Male
Children and the August Female Children
[Adapted from Chamberlain, *Ko-ji-ki,* pp. 49–50]

Hereupon the Heaven-Shining-Deity said to Susa-no-o: "As for the seed
of the five male Deities born last, their birth was from things of mine;
so undoubtedly they are my children. As for the seed of the three female
Deities born first, their birth was from a thing of thine; so doubtless they
are thy children." Thus did she declare the division.

Descent of the Divine Grandson with the
Three Imperial Regalia
[Adapted from Aston, *Nihongi,* I, 76–77]

"All the Central Land of Reed-Plains is now completely tranquilized."
Now the Heaven-Shining-Deity gave command, saying: "If that be so, I
will send down my child." She was about to do so, when in the meantime, an August Grandchild was born, whose name was called Ama-tsu-
hiko-hiko-ho-no-ninigi no Mikoto. Her son represented to her that he
wished the August Grandchild to be sent down in his stead. Therefore the
Heaven-Shining-Deity gave to Ama-tsu-hiko-hiko-ho-no-ninigi no Mikoto
the Three Treasures, viz. the curved jewel of Yasaka gem, the eight-hand
mirror, and the sword Kusanagi, and joined to him as his attendants Ame
no Koyane no Mikoto, the first ancestor of the Naka-tomi; Futo-dama no
Mikoto, the first ancestor of the Imbe; Ame no Uzume no Mikoto, the first
ancestor of the Sarume; Ishi-kori-dome no Mikoto, the first ancestor of the
mirror-makers; and Tamaya no Mikoto, the first ancestor of the jewel-

makers; in all Gods of five *be*.[1] Then she commanded her August Grand-child, saying: "This Reed-plain-1500-autumns-fair-rice-ear Land is the re-gion which my descendants shall be lords of. Do thou, my August Grand-child, proceed thither and govern it. Go! and may prosperity attend thy dynasty, and may it, like Heaven and Earth, endure for ever."

His Marriage with the Daughter of the Great Mountain Deity
[Adapted from Aston, *Nihongi*, I, 70–71]

Then Taka-mi-musubi no Mikoto took the coverlet which was on his true couch, and casting it over his August Grandchild, Ama-tsu-hiko-hiko-ho-ninigi no Mikoto, made him to descend. So the August Grand-child left his Heavenly Rock-seat, and with an awful path-cleaving, clove his way through the eight-fold clouds of Heaven, and descended on the Peak of Takachiho of So[2] in Hyūga.

After this the manner of the progress of the August Grandchild was as follows: From the Floating Bridge of Heaven on the twin summits of Kushibi, he took his stand on a level part of the floating sand-bank. Then he traversed the desert land of Sojishi from the Hill of Hitao in his search for a country, until he came to Cape Kasasa, in Ata-no-nagaya. A certain man of that land appeared and gave his name as Koto-katsu-kuni-katsu Nagasa. The August Grandchild inquired of him, saying: "Is there a country, or not?" He answered, and said: "There is here a coun-try, I pray thee roam through it at thy pleasure." The August Grand-child therefore went there and took up his abode. Now there was a fair maid in that land whose name was Ka-ashi-tsu-hime.

(Also called Kami Ata-tsu-hime or Ko no hana no saku-ya-hime.)

The August Grandchild inquired of this fair maid, saying: "Whose daughter art thou?" She answered and said: "Thy handmaiden is the child of a Heavenly Deity by his marriage with the Great Mountain Deity."[3]

The August Grandchild accordingly favored her, whereupon in one night she became pregnant.

---

[1] *Be*—hereditary guilds or corporations of craftsmen. [Ed.]

[2] It is this word which forms the second part of Kumaso, the general name of the tribes which inhabited the south of Kyushu.

[3] Ō-yama-tsu-mi Kami.

The Heavenly Grandchild and the Sea-God's Daughter
[Adapted from Aston, *Nihongi*, I, 92–95]

The elder brother Ho-no-susori no Mikoto had by nature a sea-gift; the younger brother Hiko-hoho-demi no Mikoto had by nature a mountain-gift.[4] In the beginning the two brothers, the elder and the younger, conversed together, saying: "Let us for a trial exchange gifts." They eventually exchanged them, but neither of them gained aught by doing so. The elder brother repented his bargain, and returned to the younger brother his bow and arrows, asking for his fish-hook to be given back to him. But the younger brother had already lost the elder brother's fish-hook, and there was no means of finding it. He accordingly made another new hook which he offered to his elder brother. But his elder brother refused to accept it, and demanded the old hook. The younger brother, grieved at this, forthwith took his cross-sword and forged from it new fish-hooks, which he heaped up in a winnowing tray, and offered to his brother. But his elder brother was wroth, and said: "These are not my old fish-hook: though they are many, I will not take them." And he continued repeatedly to demand it vehemently. Therefore Hiko-hoho-demi's grief was exceedingly profound, and he went and made moan by the shore of the sea. There he met Shiho-tsutsu[5] no Oji. The old man inquired of him saying: "Why dost thou grieve here?" He answered and told him the matter from first to last. The old man said: "Grieve no more. I will arrange this matter for thee." So he made a basket without interstices, and placing in it Hoho-demi no Mikoto, sank it in the sea. Forthwith he found himself at a pleasant strand, where he abandoned the basket, and, proceeding on his way, suddenly arrived at the palace of the Sea-God. This palace was provided with battlements and turrets, and had stately towers. Before the gate there was a well, and over the well there grew a many-branched cassia-tree, with wide-spreading boughs and leaves. Now Hiko-hoho-demi went up to the foot of this tree and loitered about. After some time a beautiful woman appeared, and, pushing open the door, came forth. She at length took a jewel-vessel and approached. She was about to draw water, when, raising her eyes, she saw

[4] A talent for fishing and a talent for hunting. The two brothers were the twin offspring of the August Grandchild and the daughter of the Great Mountain Deity. [Ed.]
[5] Salt-sea-elder.

him, and was alarmed. Returning within, she spoke to her father and mother, saying: "There is a rare stranger at the foot of the tree before the gate." The God of the Sea thereupon prepared an eight-fold cushion and led him in. When they had taken their seats, he inquired of him the object of his coming. Then Hiko-hoho-demi explained to him in reply all the circumstances. The Sea-God accordingly assembled the fishes, both great and small, and required of them an answer. They all said: "We know not. Only the Red-woman [6] has had a sore mouth for some time past and has not come." She was therefore peremptorily summoned to appear, and on her mouth being examined the lost hook was actually found.

After this, Hiko-hoho-demi took to wife the Sea-God's daughter, Toyo-tama [7]-hime, and dwelt in the sea-palace. . . . When the Heavenly Grandchild was about to set out on his return journey, Toyo-tama-hime addressed him, saying: "Thy handmaiden is already pregnant, and the time of her delivery is not far off. On a day when the winds and waves are raging, I will surely come forth to the sea-shore, and I pray thee that thou wilt make for me a parturition house, and await me there." . . .

After this Toyo-tama-hime fulfilled her promise, and, bringing with her her younger sister, Tama-yori-hime, bravely confronted the winds and waves, and came to the sea-shore. When the time of her delivery was at hand, she besought Hiko-hoho-demi, saying: "When thy hand-maiden is in travail, I pray thee do not look upon her." However, the Heavenly Grandchild could not restrain himself, but went secretly and peeped in. Now Toyo-tama-hime was just in childbirth, and had changed into a dragon. She was greatly ashamed, and said: "Hadst thou not disgraced me, I would have made the sea and land communicate with each other, and forever prevented them from being sundered. But now that thou hast disgraced me, wherewithal shall friendly feelings be knit together?" So she wrapped the infant in rushes, and abandoned it on the sea-shore. Then she barred the sea-path, and passed away. Accordingly the child was called Hiko-nagisa-take-u-gaya-fuki-aezu [8] no Mikoto.

A long time after, Hiko-hoho-demi no Mikoto died, and was buried in the imperial mound on the summit of Mount Takaya in Hyūga.

[6] Aka-me, a name of the Tai (pagrus).   [7] Rich-jewel.
[8] Prince-beach-brave-cormorant-rush-thatch-unfinished.

CHAPTER II

EARLY SHINTO

Western scholars, intrigued by what they imagined to be the indigenous nature of Shinto, from the early days of the opening of Japan devoted considerable attention to this religion. By the turn of the century there were scholars from the important Western nations studying what has been termed the "National Faith of Japan," in the hope of discovering in it an explanation of Japanese characteristics long obscured to foreigners by the self-imposed isolation of the country. Strictly speaking, however, Shinto was not an indigenous religion, for the Japanese were not the first inhabitants of the islands, and their religion apparently came with them from elsewhere. Shamanistic and animistic practices similar to those of Shinto have also been found throughout Northeast Asia, especially in Korea, and we thus cannot say of Shinto that it is a purely Japanese faith.

Shinto was diverse in its origins and remained an aggregate of heterogeneous cults well into historical times. Its failure to develop into a unified religion resulted largely from the natural features of Japan and a strong sense of regionalism among the people. The numerous tribal communities living in the river basins held to their own beliefs even after the unified control of the central government began to assert its authority early in the seventh century.

The objects of worship in all Shinto cults were known as *kami,* a term for which it is difficult to find any translation. A famous student of Shinto, Motoori Norinaga (1730–1801), wrote:

I do not yet understand the meaning of the term *kami.* Speaking in general, however, it may be said that *kami* signifies, in the first place, the deities of heaven and earth that appear in the ancient records and also the spirits of the shrines where they are worshipped.

It is hardly necessary to say that it includes human beings. It also includes such objects as birds, beasts, trees, plants, seas, mountains, and so forth. In ancient usage, anything whatsoever which was outside the ordinary, which possessed superior power, or which was awe-inspiring was called *kami.* Eminence here does not refer merely to the superiority of nobility, goodness, or meritorious deeds. Evil and mysterious things, if they are extraordinary and dreadful, are called *kami*. It is needless to say that among human beings who are called *kami* the successive generations of sacred emperors are all included. The fact that emperors are also called "distant kami" is because, from the standpoint of common people, they are far-separated, majestic, and worthy of reverence. In a lesser degree we find, in the present as well as in ancient times, human beings who are *kami*. Although they may not be accepted throughout the whole country, yet in each province, each village, and each family there are human beings who are *kami,* each one according to his own proper position. The *kami* of the divine age were for the most part human beings of that time and, because the people of that time were all *kami*, it is called the Age of the Gods (*kami*).[1]

Primitive Shinto embraced cults of exceedingly diverse origins, including animism, shamanism, fertility cults, and the worship of nature, ancestors, and heroes. In the course of time the distinctions between these various cults tended to disappear. The Sun Goddess, for instance, became the chief deity not only of nature worshipers, but also of ancestor worshipers as well. She was also considered to be the dispenser of fertility and of the fortunes of the nation. Similarly, an object of animistic worship could assume the role of a fertility god or a shamanistic deity, or even pose as the ancestor of the land on which a community lived. Before Shinto could become the "national faith" of Japan, however, it had to be bolstered successively by the philosophical and religious concepts of Han Confucianism, Esoteric Buddhism, Neo-Confucianism, and, finally, Christianity. The forms which these influences took will be discussed in later chapters; in the early period with which we are here concerned, Shinto was still a primitive and almost inarticulate group of cults.

The oldest center of Shinto worship was that of the Izumo Shrine on the Japan Sea coast, and thus close to the Korean peninsula, by way of which continental civilization had reached Japan. The Kashima and Katori shrines in the Tone River basin to the north for a long time marked the frontier between the lands of the Japanese and those of the less civilized aborigines. The shrine at Ise, that of the Sun Goddess, came to be the most important, and it was there that various symbols of the imperial power were displayed.

[1] Holtom, *The National Faith of Japan*, pp. 23–24.

The buildings of the shrines were architecturally very simple. They consisted generally of a single room (although it was sometimes partitioned), raised from the ground and entered by steps at the side or front. It was invariably of wood, with whole tree-trunks used for beams. A mirror or a sword might be enshrined within, but often the building served merely as a place where the *kami,* visible or invisible, might be worshiped.

Outside the main building of the shrine two other architectural features usually may be found, a gateway called a *torii,* and a water basin where the mouth and hands of worshipers may be washed. The characteristic Japanese insistence on cleanliness finds its expression in many forms. Two important acts of worship at Shinto shrines, the *harai* and the *misogi,* both reflect this tendency. The former apparently originated in the airing of the cave or pit dwellings of prehistoric times, and came to refer to both the sweeping out of a house and the special rites of chasing out evil spirits; the latter refers to the washing of the body, an act of increasingly spiritual significance. In addition to these formal acts of religion, there were formulas, prayers, and ritual practices associated with almost all human activities (but especially in the arts and crafts), whereby divine power was invoked to assure success.

Worship at a Shinto shrine consisted of "attendance" and "offering." "Attendance" meant not only being present and giving one's attention to the object of worship, but often also performing ceremonial dances or joining in processions, which have always been an important part of Shinto ritual. The offerings usually consisted of the first-born of a household, the first fruits of the season or the first catch from the water, but might also include booty of war, such as the heads of enemies. The shrine was in the charge of a medium who transmitted messages both from the *kami* and from the political rulers. The mediums were assisted by supplicators, the general term for officers of the shrine, and by ablutioners. Some of the texts of the prayers and rituals of this early time have been preserved. The following is part of a prayer for the harvest festival:

More especially do I humbly declare in the mighty presence of the Great-Heaven-Shining Deity who dwells in Isé. Because the Great Deity has bestowed on him [the sovereign] the lands of the four quarters over which her glance extends as far as where the walls of Heaven rise, as far as where the bounds of Earth stand up, as far as the blue sky extends, as far as where the white clouds settle down; by the blue sea-plain, as far as the prows of ships can reach without letting dry their poles and oars; by land, as far as the hoofs of horses can go, with tightened baggage-cords, treading their way among rock-beds and tree-roots where the long roads extend, continuously widening the narrow regions and making the steep regions level, in drawing together, as it were, the distant regions by throwing over them [a net of] many ropes—therefore let the first-fruits for the Sovran Deity be piled up in her mighty presence like a range of hills, leaving the remainder for him [the sovereign] tranquilly to partake of.

Moreover, whereas you bless the Sovran Grandchild's reign as a long reign, firm and enduring, and render it a happy and prosperous reign, I plunge down my neck cormorant-wise in reverence to you as our Sovran's dear, divine ancestress, and fulfill your praise by making these plenteous offerings on his behalf.[2]

The texts of these ancient prayers are often beautiful, with a simplicity that is characteristic of Shinto. The above example indicates moreover that at the time of its composition the cult of the Sun Goddess of Ise was closely associated with the imperial house and had already come to dominate the various other beliefs. It was, in fact, just when Shinto was first assuming the features of a more homogeneous and developed religion that the arrival of Buddhism caused it to be relegated to a position of minor importance for many centuries.

LEGENDS CONCERNING SHINTO DEITIES

There is virtually no documentary evidence to indicate the original character of Shinto belief. Before the introduction of Chinese writing and Chinese ideas, the Japanese were unable to record their religious beliefs and there is little reason to believe that they had produced an articulate body of doctrine or dogma. The legends in the *Kojiki* and *Nihongi,* often cited as containing the original deposit of Shinto folklore, are late compilations in which political considerations and specifically Chinese conceptions intrude themselves almost everywhere. This fact was recognized by the great Neo-Shinto scholars of the eighteenth and nineteenth centuries who tried almost in vain to find in these texts any evidence of pure Japanese beliefs. Elements of Chinese cosmology are most apparent in rationalistic passages explaining the origin of the world in terms of the yin and yang principles, which seem to come directly from

[2] Anesaki, *History of Japanese Religion,* pp. 32–33.

Chinese works such as the *Huai-nan tzu*. The prevalence of paired male and female deities, such as Izanagi and Izanami, may also be a result of conscious selection with the yin and yang principles in mind. Also the frequency of numerical sets of deities, such as the Five Heavenly Deities of the *Kojiki* and Seven Generations of Heavenly Deities of the *Nihongi,* may represent an attempt at selection and organization in terms of Chinese cosmological series, in this case the Five Elements and Seven Heavenly Luminaries.

With these major reservations in mind, we may still discern in these legends some features of early Japanese belief in regard to questions which might arise in almost any country or culture. But since Shinto cults were so closely associated with nature worship and the topographical aspects of Japan, one obvious question was "How was the Japanese archipelago created?" This led to another, "Who has a rightful claim to occupy and rule over this land?", a question answered in favor of the Yamato people and their rulers by the passages cited in the previous section. Still other passages, attempting to assert Yamato supremacy, betray the existence of diverse and competing cults, such as that associated with Susa-no-o and the Izumo people. It should be noted in the following excerpts how the names of deities and semi-divine beings are composed of vivid images from nature, and how often their activities suggest a concern with fertility, ritual purification, ancestor or hero worship, and animism.

Birth of the Land

[Adapted from Aston, *Nihongi,* I, 10–14]

Izanagi and Izanami stood on the floating bridge of Heaven, and held counsel together, saying:

"Is there not a country beneath?"

Thereupon they thrust down the jewel-spear of Heaven,[1] and groping about therewith found the ocean. The brine which dripped from the point of the spear coagulated and became an island which received the name of Ono-goro-jima.

The two Deities thereupon descended and dwelt in this island. Accordingly they wished to become husband and wife together, and to produce countries.

So they made Ono-goro-jima the pillar of the center of the land.

Now the male deity turning by the left, and the female deity by the right, they went round the pillar of the land separately. When they met together on one side, the female deity spoke first and said: "How de-

[1] Considered by some commentators to resemble the phallus. Cf. Aston, *Nihongi,* I, 10. [Ed.]

lightful! I have met with a lovely youth." The male deity was displeased, and said: "I am a man, and by right should have spoken first. How is it that on the contrary thou, a woman, shouldst have been the first to speak? This was unlucky. Let us go round again." Upon this the two deities went back, and having met anew, this time the male deity spoke first, and said: "How delightful! I have met a lovely maiden."

Then he inquired of the female deity, saying: "In thy body is there aught formed?" She answered, and said: "In my body there is a place which is the source of femininity." The male deity said: "In my body again there is a place which is the source of masculinity. I wish to unite this source-place of my body to the source-place of thy body." Hereupon the male and female first became united as husband and wife.

Now when the time of birth arrived, first of all the island of Ahaji was reckoned as the placenta, and their minds took no pleasure in it. Therefore it received the name of Ahaji no Shima.[2]

Next there was produced the island of Ō-yamato no Toyo-aki-tsu-shima.[3]

(Here and elsewhere [the characters for Nippon] are to be read Yamato.[4])

Next they produced the island of Iyo no futa-na,[5] and next the island of Tsukushi.[6] Next the islands of Oki and Sado were born as twins. This is the prototype of the twin-births which sometimes take place among mankind.

Next was born the island of Koshi,[7] then the island of Ō-shima, then the island of Kibi no Ko.[8]

Hence first arose the designation of the Great Eight-island Country.

Then the islands of Tsushima and Iki, with the small islands in various parts, were produced by the coagulation of the foam of the salt-water.

---

[2] "The island which will not meet," i.e., is unsatisfactory. Ahaji may also be interpreted as "my shame." The characters with which this name is written in the text mean "foam-road." Perhaps the true derivation is "millet-land."

[3] Rich-harvest (or autumn)-island of Yamato.

[4] Yamato means probably mountain-gate. It is the genuine ancient name for the province which contained Nara and many of the other capitals of Japan for centuries, and it was also used for the whole country. Several emperors called themselves Yamato-neko. It is mentioned by the historian of the Later Han dynasty of China (A.D. 25–220) as the seat of rule in Japan at that time.

[5] Now called Shikoku.   [6] Now called Kyushu.

[7] Koshi is not an island. It comprises the present provinces of Etchū, Echigo, and Echizen.

[8] These two are not clear. Kibi is now Bingo, Bizen, and Bitchū. Ko, "child" or "small," perhaps refers to the small islands of the Inland Sea.

Legends Concerning Susa-no-o

The part of Amaterasu's unruly brother, Susa-no-o, in the creation of the imperial line has already been described in Chapter I. His other activities are of interest because they reflect the importance of regional cults incorporated into the Yamato system of Shinto. After his banishment from Heaven, Susa-no-o is reported in one account to have gone to Korea, an indication that the activities of the Gods were no more limited to Japan alone than were those of the people themselves. In any case this black sheep of the gods settled in Izumo, where he married the local princess and rid the land of a dreaded serpent, in whose body was found the Great Sword which became one of the Three Imperial Regalia (another of the Regalia is a curved stone or jewel produced in both Izumo and Korea).

THE SUN GODDESS AND SUSA-NO-O

[Adapted from Aston, *Nihongi*, I, 40–45]

After this Susa-no-o no Mikoto's behavior was exceedingly rude. In what way? Amaterasu [the Heaven-Shining-Deity] had made august rice fields of Heavenly narrow rice fields and Heavenly long rice fields. Then Susa-no-o, when the seed was sown in spring, broke down the divisions between the plots of rice, and in autumn let loose the Heavenly piebald colts, and made them lie down in the midst of the rice fields. Again, when he saw that Amaterasu was about to celebrate the feast of first-fruits, he secretly voided excrement in the New[9] Palace. Moreover, when he saw that Amaterasu was in her sacred[10] weaving hall, engaged in weaving garments of the Gods, he flayed a piebald colt of Heaven, and breaking a hole in the roof-tiles of the hall, flung it in. Then Amaterasu started with alarm, and wounded herself with the shuttle. Indignant of this, she straightway entered the Rock-cave of Heaven, and having fastened the Rock-door, dwelt there in seclusion. Therefore constant darkness prevailed on all sides, and the alternation of night and day was unknown.

Then the eighty myriads of Gods met on the bank of the Tranquil River of Heaven, and considered in what manner they should supplicate her. Accordingly Omoi-kane[11] no Kami, with profound device

[9] For the sake of greater purity in celebrating the festival.
[10] The Chinese character here translated sacred has the primary meaning of abstinence, fasting. In the *Nihongi*, however, it represents avoidance, especially religious avoidance of impurity.
[11] Thought-combining or thought-including.

and far-reaching thought, at length gathered long-singing birds [12] of the Eternal Land and made them utter their prolonged cry to one another. Moreover he made Ta-jikara-o [13] to stand beside the Rock-door. Then Ame no Koyane no Mikoto, ancestor of the Nakatomi Deity Chieftains,[14] and Futo-dama no Mikoto,[15] ancestor of the Imibe [16] Chieftains, dug up a five-hundred branched True Sakaki [17] tree of the Heavenly Mt. Kagu.[18] On its upper branches they hung an august five-hundred string of Yasaka jewels. On the middle branches they hung an eight-hand mirror.[19]

(One writing says Ma-futsu no Kagami.)

On its lower branches they hung blue soft offerings and white soft offerings. Then they recited their liturgy together.

Moreover Ama no Uzume [20] no Mikoto, ancestress of the Sarume [21] Chieftain, took in her hand a spear wreathed with Eulalia grass, and standing before the door of the Rock-cave of Heaven, skillfully performed a mimic dance.[22] She took, moreover, the true Sakaki tree of the Heavenly Mount Kagu, and made of it a head-dress, she took club-moss and made of it braces, she kindled fires, she placed a tub bottom upwards,[23] and gave forth a divinely-inspired utterance.

Now Amaterasu heard this, and said: "Since I have shut myself up in the Rock-cave, there ought surely to be continual night in the Central Land of fertile reed-plains. How then can Ama no Uzume no Mikoto be so jolly?" So with her august hand, she opened for a narrow space the Rock-door and peeped out. Then Ta-jikara-o no Kami forthwith

[12] The cock is meant.   [13] Hand-strength-male.

[14] Nakatomi probably means ministers of the middle, mediating between the Gods and the Emperor, and the Emperor and the people. In historical times their duties were of a priestly character. Worship and government were closely associated in ancient times in more countries than Japan. *Matsurigoto*, government, is derived from *matsuri*, worship. It was they who recited the Harai or purification rituals.

[15] *Futo-dama*, big-jewel.

[16] Imi-be or imbe is derived from *imi*, root of *imu*, to avoid, to shun, to practise religious abstinence, and *be*, a hereditary corporation.

[17] The Sakaki, or Cleyera Japonica, is the sacred tree of the Shinto religion. It is still used in Shinto religious ceremonies.

[18] Mt. Kagu is the name of a mountain in Yamato. It is here supposed to have a counterpart in Heaven.

[19] It is said to be this mirror which is worshiped at Ise as an emblem of the Sun Goddess.

[20] Terrible female of Heaven.   [21] Monkey-female.

[22] This is said to be the origin of the Kagura or pantomimic dance now performed at Shinto festivals.

[23] The *Nihongi* strangely omits to say that, as we learn from the *Kojiki*, she danced on this and made it give out a sound.

took Amaterasu by the hand, and led her out. Upon this the Gods Naka-tomi no Kami and Imibe no Kami [24] at once drew a limit by means of a bottom-tied rope [25] (also called a left-hand rope) and begged her not to return again [into the cave].

After this all the Gods put the blame on Susa-no-o, and imposed on him a fine of one thousand tables,[26] and so at length chastised him. They also had his hair plucked out, and made him therewith expiate his guilt.

SUSA-NO-O IN IZUMO

[Adapted from Chamberlain, *Ko-ji-ki,* pp. 60–64]

So, having been expelled, Susa-no-o descended to a place [called] Tori-kami at the head-waters of the River Hi in the land of Izumo. At this time some chopsticks came floating down the stream. So Susa-no-o, think-ing that there must be people at the head-waters of the river, went up it in quest of them, when he came upon an old man and an old woman—two of them—who had a young girl between them, and were weeping. Then he deigned to ask: "Who are ye?" So the old man replied, saying: "I am an Earthly Deity,[1] child of the Deity Great-Mountain-Possessor.[2] I am called by the name of Foot-Stroking-Elder, my wife is called by the name of Hand-Stroking-Elder, and my daughter is called by the name of Wondrous-Inada-Princess." Again he asked: "What is the cause of your crying?" [The old man] answered, saying: "I had originally eight young girls as daughters. But the eight-forked serpent of Koshi has come every year and devoured [one], and it is now its time to come, wherefore we weep." Then he asked him: "What is its form like?" [The old man] answered, saying: "Its eyes are like *akakagachi,* it has one body with eight heads and eight tails. Moreover on its body grows moss, and also chamaecyparis [3] and cryptomerias. Its length extends over eight valleys and eight hills, and if one look at its belly, it is all constantly bloody and inflamed." (What is here called *akakagachi* is the modern *hohozuki.*) [4]

---

[24] These Gods' names were properly Koyane no Mikoto and Futo-dama no Mikoto (see above), but here the names of their human descendants are substituted.
[25] A rope made of straw of rice which has been pulled up by the roots.
[26] By tables are meant tables of offerings.
[1] Or "Country Deity," "Deity of the Land."   [2] O-yama-tsu-mi-no-kami.
[3] A coniferous tree, the *Chamaecyparis obtusa,* in Japanese *hi-no-ki.* The cryptomeria is *Cryptomeria japonica.*
[4] The winter-cherry, *Physalis Alkekengi.*

Then Susa-no-o said to the old man: "If this be thy daughter, wilt thou offer her to me?" He replied, saying: "With reverence, but I know not thine august name." Then he replied, saying: "I am elder brother to the Heaven-Shining-Deity. So I have now descended from Heaven." Then the Deities Foot-Stroking-Elder and Hand-Stroking-Elder said: "If that be so, with reverence will we offer [her to thee]." So Susa-no-o, at once taking and changing the young girl into a multitudinous and close-toothed comb which he stuck into his august hair-bunch, said to the Deities Foot-Stroking-Elder and Hand-Stroking-Elder: "Do you distill some eight-fold refined liquor.[5] Also make a fence round about, in that fence make eight gates, at each gate tie [together] eight platforms, on each platform put a liquor-vat, and into each vat pour the eight-fold refined liquor, and wait." So as they waited after having thus prepared everything in accordance with his bidding, the eight-forked serpent came truly as [the old man] had said, and immediately dipped a head into each vat, and drank the liquor. Thereupon it was intoxicated with drinking, and all [the heads] lay down and slept. Then Susa-no-o drew the ten-grasp sabre, that was augustly girded on him, and cut the serpent in pieces, so that the River Hi flowed on changed into a river of blood. So when he cut the middle tail, the edge of his august sword broke. Then, thinking it strange, he thrust into and split [the flesh] with the point of his august sword and looked, and there was a sharp great sword [within]. So he took this great sword, and, thinking it a strange thing, he respectfully informed [6] Amaterasu. This is the Herb-Quelling Great Sword.[7]

So thereupon Susa-no-o sought in the land of Izumo for a place where he might build a palace. Then he arrived at a place [called] Suga, and said: "On coming to this place my august heart is pure," [8] and in that place he built a palace to dwell in. So that place is now called Suga. When this Great Deity first built the palace of Suga, clouds rose up thence. Then he made an august song. That song said:

Eight Clouds arise. The eight-fold fence
of Izumo makes an eight-fold fence
for the spouses to retire [within]. Oh!
that eight-fold fence.

[5] In Japanese, sake.   [6] According to some sources: "sent it with a message to."
[7] Reputedly one of the Three Imperial Regalia. [Ed.]
[8] That is, "I feel refreshed." The Japanese term used is suga-sugashi, whence the origin ascribed to the name of the place Suga. But more probably the name gave rise to this detail of the legend.

Princess Yamato and Prince Plenty

The Shinto shrine in Izumo, Kitsuki-no-miya, dedicated to the son of Susa-no-o, is the most ancient shrine in Japan and therefore is called "the shrine ahead of those to all other gods" (*Kami-mae no Yashiro*). Perhaps because it was here that Susa-no-o, from the Yamato line, married the Izumo princess, and their son Prince Plenty or the Great Landlord God (Ōnamochi or Ō-mono-nushi) married a Yamato princess, this shrine is particularly thought of as symbolizing union and compromise. A visit to the Izumo shrine has been regarded as especially beneficial to those with hopes of marriage or those desirous of promoting greater harmony and understanding in their own families.

[Adapted from Aston, *Nihongi*, I, 158–59]

After this Yamato-toto-hi-momo-so-bime no Mikoto [Princess Yamato] became the wife of Ō-mono-nushi no Kami [Prince Plenty].[1] This God, however, was never seen in the day-time, but came at night. Princess Yamato said to her husband: "As my Lord is never seen in the day-time, I am unable to view his august countenance distinctly; I beseech him therefore to delay a while, that in the morning I may look upon the majesty of his beauty." The Great God answered and said: "What thou sayest is clearly right. Tomorrow morning I will enter thy toilet-case and stay there. I pray thee be not alarmed at my form." Princess Yamato wondered secretly in her heart at this. Waiting until daybreak, she looked into her toilet-case. There was there a beautiful little snake,[2] of the length and thickness of the cord of a garment. Thereupon she was frightened, and uttered an exclamation. The Great God was ashamed, and changing suddenly into human form, spake to his wife, and said: "Thou didst not contain thyself, but hast caused me shame: I will in my turn put thee to shame." So treading the Great Void, he ascended to Mount Mimoro. Hereupon Princess Yamato looked up and had remorse. She flopped down on a seat and with a chopstick stabbed herself in the pudenda so that she died. She was buried at O-chi. Therefore the men of that time called her tomb the Chopstick Tomb. This tomb was made by men in the daytime, and by Gods at night. It was built of stones carried from Mount O-saka. Now the people standing close to each other passed the stones from hand to hand, and thus transported them from the mountain to the tomb. The men of that time made a song about this, saying:

[1] Or "The Great Landlord God." [Ed.]
[2] This is one of numerous evidences of serpent-worship in ancient Japan.

If one passed from hand to hand
The rocks
Built up
On Ō-saka,[3]
How hard 'twould be to send them! [4]

Enshrinement of Amaterasu

The following entries in the *Nihongi,* for the twenty-fifth year of the Emperor Suinin's reign (5 B.C. according to traditional dating, but more probably around A.D. 260), describe the founding of the great shrine to Amaterasu at Ise. The moving of the Sun Goddess no doubt refers to the transporting of the mirror thought to be her embodiment.

[Adapted from Aston, *Nihongi,* I, 175–76]

25th year, Spring, 2nd month, 8th day. The Emperor commanded the five officers, Takenu Kaha-wake, ancestor of the Abe no Omi; Hiko-kuni-fuku,[5] ancestor of the Imperial Chieftains; O-kashima, ancestor of the Nakatomi Deity Chieftains; Tochine, ancestor of the Mononobe Deity Chieftains; and Take-hi, ancestor of the Ōtomo Deity Chieftains, saying: "The sagacity of Our predecessor on the throne, the Emperor Mimaki-iri-hiko-inie, was displayed in wisdom: he was reverential, intelligent, and capable. He was profoundly unassuming, and his disposition was to cherish self-abnegation. He adjusted the machinery of government, and did solemn worship to the Gods of Heaven and Earth. He practiced self-restraint and was watchful as to his personal conduct. Every day he was heedful for that day. Thus the weal of the people was sufficient, and the Empire was at peace. And now, under Our reign, shall there be any remissness in the worship of the Gods of Heaven and Earth?" [6]

3rd month, 10th day. The Great Goddess Amaterasu was taken from

[3] The great acclivity.

[4] The tombs of men of rank at this period of Japanese history consisted of a round mound of earth varying in size according to the station of the person interred, and containing a vault of megalithic stones, with an entrance gallery similar to those of the Imperial Mausoleum, but of much smaller size. Many of these are still to be seen in Japan, especially in the provinces near Yamato. Of course it is utterly impossible to pass from hand to hand stones of the size used in constructing these tombs.

[5] Both these men are named in Sūjin Tennō's reign, 10th year, eighty-five years before according to the traditional reckoning. [Ed.]

[6] This speech is thoroughly Chinese. It contains numerous phrases borrowed from the Chinese classics.

[the princess] Toyo-suki-iri-hime,[7] and entrusted to [the princess] Yamato-hime no Mikoto. Now Yamato-hime sought for a place where she might enshrine the Great Goddess. So she proceeded to Sasahata in Uda. Then turning back from thence, she entered the land of Omi, and went round eastwards to Mino, whence she arrived in the province of Ise.

Now the Great Goddess Amaterasu instructed Yamato-hime, saying: "The province of Ise, of the divine wind,[8] is the land whither repair the waves from the eternal world, the successive waves. It is a secluded and pleasant land. In this land I wish to dwell." In compliance, therefore, with the instruction of the Great Goddess, a shrine was erected to her in the province of Ise. Accordingly an Abstinence Palace [9] was built at Kawakami in Isuzu. This was called the palace of Iso. It was there that the Great Goddess Amaterasu first descended from Heaven.

[7] To whom she had been entrusted in 92 B.C., eighty-seven years before.

[8] This is a stock epithet (*makura kotoba*) of this province.

[9] Abstinence Palace or Worship Palace. "On the accession of an Emperor, an unmarried Princess of the Imperial House was selected for the service of the Shrine of Ise, or if there was no such unmarried Princess, then another Princess was fixed upon by divination and appointed worship-princess. The Worship-Palace was for her residence." Cf. Aston, I, 176. [Ed.]

CHAPTER III

PRINCE SHŌTOKU AND HIS CONSTITUTION

The reign of the Empress Suiko (592–628) was one of the most remarkable periods in Japanese history. A crisis had developed in Japan
toward the end of the sixth century as a result of the loss of the ancient
Japanese domains on the Korean peninsula and the defeat of her ally,
the kingdom of Paekche. Within the country there was also serious dis-
sension among the powerful clans, partly on account of developments in
Korea. The large numbers of Korean refugees who fled to Japan from
the turmoil of the peninsula added to the difficulties of the authorities. Not
only were there problems of a political and economic nature, but the
arrival of Buddhism some fifty years before had caused bitter controversies. Some of the important clans, representing the traditional
Shinto views, were violent in their opposition to what they considered a
foreign and harmful religion. Above all these difficulties was the fact that
a unified and expanding China under the Sui and a unifying Korea
under Silla were now facing a weak and decentralized Japan. Apart
from whatever threat to their security the Japanese felt to lie in the
changing conditions on the continent, there was also of course the desire
to emulate the superior achievements of the rising Chinese and Korean
dynasties.

In this situation the Yamato court attempted to enhance its power and
prestige in the eyes of foreigners and domestic rivals alike by adopting
many features of the superior Chinese civilization and especially its political institutions. The first measures included a reorganization of court
ranks and etiquette in accordance with Chinese models, the adoption of
the Chinese calendar, the opening of formal diplomatic relations with
China, the creation of a system of highways, the erection of many Buddhist temples, and the compilation of the chronicles of the government.
Most important, perhaps, was the proclamation of a "constitution"—a

set of principles of government in seventeen articles, this number probably having been derived from the combination of eight, the largest yin number, and nine, the largest yang number.

The chief architect of these great changes was the Prince Shōtoku (573–621), who served as "regent" during much of the reign of his aunt, the Empress Suiko. The veneration in which he was held after his death may be inferred from his name itself, which might be translated "sovereign moral power." Shōtoku was a member of the powerful Soga family, which had been the main support of Buddhism during its early days in Japan, and always showed a deep interest in the religion. He also appears to have been widely read in Confucian literature. His military achievements were less conspicuous than his civil ones, but at one time he had under his control in Kyushu a considerable army whose function was to have been the reassertion of Japanese influence in Korea.

Although Shōtoku was a devout Buddhist, it was to Confucian models that he turned for guidance when faced with the enormous task of reorganizing the government. His most crucial problem, the establishment of the court as the central authority, was well met by the teachings of Confucianism as it had developed under the great Han empire. According to these teachings, the universe consisted of three realms, Heaven, Earth, and Man, with Man occupying a place between the other two. The basis of all authority and order lay in Heaven, and was demonstrated to Earth by the ·stately progress of the sun, moon, and planets across the firmament. A sovereign was a sovereign only because of Heaven's will, and the good or ill fortune that might befall a nation or individual was likewise determined entirely by Heaven. It may be seen, then, why it was considered that no more important duty existed for a ruler than to make sure that his country was governed ·in accordance with the pattern established by Heaven. This is the reason for the great importance of the calendar in countries dominated by Confucian thought; unless the "time" were correct, the government on Earth would be out of step with the movements of Heaven.

A regular, determined system of government was exactly what was needed in Japan during Shōtoku's time. The Seventeen Article Constitution (A.D. 604) on first reading may seem to be little more than a set of ethical platitudes, but more careful study will give us clear indications of the chaotic conditions prevailing at the time. The insistence on harmony

(Article I) reflects the disharmony and factionalism of the court; similarly, the condemnation of bribery (Article II) or of the exaction of forced labor from the peasants at improper times (Article XVI) must have been expressions of views on existing problems rather than mere Confucian generalizations. The statement of the Han Confucian ideal of government itself is found in Article III: "The lord is Heaven; the vassal, Earth. Heaven overspreads; Earth upbears. When this is so, the four seasons follow their due course, and the powers of Nature develop their efficiency."

Buddhism is specifically mentioned in Article II, and the dictum that decisions should be discussed by many people may also have a Buddhist origin. Hints of Legalist and other non-Confucian ideas may be detected elsewhere. By and large, however, it is Han Confucianism which dominates the writing of the Constitution. The Confucian ideology of government adopted by Shōtoku was actually quite contradictory to Buddhist teachings on the subject, particularly the Buddhism of Nāgārjuna brought from India to China by Kumārajīva. These doctrines stressed the necessity for the individual to obey the guidance of his own inner light (*prajñā*) rather than any external guide. Buddhism recognized no unvarying universal order except the law of constant change. Thus, while the good Confucian sovereign was obliged to follow the unvarying motions of the celestial spheres in governing the country, the good Buddhist ruler needed to pay no attention to the stars or anything else but his inner light. This opposition of ideas does not appear to have disturbed Shōtoku very much. Where the two ideologies did not conflict he adopted both; in cases of conflict Confucianism was considered supreme in secular matters and Buddhism in spiritual ones. Buddhism and Confucianism were able thus to exist side by side in Japan for a thousand years without any serious quarrels.

Shōtoku's policy of internal reforms was complemented by his attitude toward China. He realized how much Japan had to learn from China and desired to cultivate good relations with her. Japanese students (though possibly of Chinese or Korean ancestry) were sent to Sui China to study both Confucianism and Buddhism. Shōtoku's own respect for Chinese learning is obvious from his Constitution, where no mention is made of traditional Japanese religious practices or of the Japanese principle of the hereditary line of emperors. However, many Japanese historians have professed to discover an assertion of equality with China in the letters which Shōtoku sent to the Sui court. One of them, as we have seen in the excerpts from the Chinese dynastic histories, bore the superscription "The Son of Heaven of the Land of the Rising Sun to the Son of Heaven of the Land of the Setting Sun," and another "The Eastern Emperor Greets the Western Emperor." Whether these letters represented real attempts on Shōtoku's part to show that Japan did not join with the other "barbarian" nations in groveling before mighty China, or were merely a case of ignorance of the correct procedure, is difficult to determine. In any case it is recorded that the Sui emperor was highly displeased.

CIVIL STRIFE IN THE LATE SIXTH CENTURY

In these excerpts we get a glimpse of the struggle for power at court between the Mononobe and Soga clans just before Empress Suiko and Prince Shōtoku came to power. Against this background it becomes more apparent what relevance the seeming platitudes of Shōtoku's Constitution had to the political situation in his time. These passages also testify to a growing interest in Buddhism, which will be dealt with more fully in the next chapter. Many of the portions deleted from the account here pertain to this subject or to intercourse with the Korean kingdoms.

The episode involving Yorozu, an adherent of the defeated Mononobe, has been retained as an early example of the indomitable spirit and resourcefulness long admired in the Japanese warrior, even before these traits became systematized in the cult of the warrior, *Bushidō*, in recent centuries. Yorozu, though a rebel, is pictured as a loyalist at heart. The story of his tragic end is told with a sympathy for the underdog and the martyr which has continued to find expression in the literature and political life of Japan until the present day.

As in passages cited earlier from the *Nihongi*, these accounts are interspersed with comments on questionable points or alternative accounts from different sources, indicating at least a rudimentary sense of critical historiography.

[Adapted from Aston, *Nihongi*, II, 112–20] [1]

[1] Important personal titles left untranslated by Aston are rendered here according to the usage of R. K. Reischauer in *Early Japanese History*. [Ed.]

The Emperor Tachibana no Toyohi[2] died in the second year of his reign [c. A.D. 587], Summer, the 4th month. In the 5th month the army of the Great Deity Chieftain[3] Mononobe made a disturbance thrice. The Great Deity Chieftain from the first wished to set aside the other Imperial Princes and to establish the Imperial Prince Anahobe[4] as Emperor. He now hoped to make use of a hunting party to devise a plan for raising him to the throne instead. So he secretly sent a messenger to the Imperial Prince Anahobe, to say: "I should like to hunt with the Imperial Prince in Awaji." The plot leaked out.

6th month, 7th day. Soga no Mumako no Sukune and other Ministers, on behalf of Kashikiya hime no Mikoto, commissioned Nifute, the Deity Chieftain of Saheki; Iwamura, the Deity Chieftain of Hashi; and Makuhi, the Imperial Chieftain of Ikuba; saying: "Do ye with rigorous discipline of arms proceed at once to execute the Imperial Prince Anahobe and the Imperial Prince Yakabe." On this day, at midnight, Nifute, the Deity Chieftain of Saheki, and his colleagues surrounded the Palace of the Imperial Prince Anahobe. Upon this the guardsmen, having first climbed up into the upper story, smote the Imperial Prince Anahobe on the shoulder. The Imperial Prince fell down from the upper story, and ran away into an outhouse. Then the guardsmen, holding up lights, executed him.

8th day. The Imperial Prince Yakabe was executed.

(The Imperial Prince Yakabe was the son of the Emperor Hinokuma[5] and father of Princess Kamutsu hime. This is not clear.)

He was put to death because he approved the Imperial Prince Anahobe.

9th day. The nun Zen-shin and the others addressed the Great Imperial Chieftain, saying: "Discipline is the basis of the method of those who renounce the world; we pray thee to let us go to Paekche to receive instruction in the Law of Discipline."[6] This month tribute Envoys from Paekche arrived at court. The Great Imperial Chieftain addressed the Envoys, saying: "Take these nuns with you, and when you are about to cross over to your country, make them learn the Law of Discipline.

[2] Yōmei Tennō.

[3] Hereditary title of clan chieftains (other than imperial clan) tracing their ancestry to deities of heaven and earth.

[4] Half-brother of the reigning emperor.   [5] Senka Tennō.

[6] That is, the monastic discipline of Buddhism. Paekche was the state in Southwest Korea which first sent Buddhist missionaries to Japan. [Ed.]

When they have done, send them off." The Envoys answered and said: "When we return to our frontier State, we shall first of all inform the King of our country, and it will afterwards be not too late to send them off."

Autumn, 7th month. The Great Imperial Chieftain, Soga no Mumako no Sukune, incited the Imperial Princes and the Ministers to plot the destruction of the Great Deity Chieftain, Mononobe no Moriya. . . . [Soga, the Imperial Prince Mumayado (Shōtoku), and others advanced to attack.] The Great Deity Chieftain, in personal command of the young men of his family and of a slave-army, built a rice-fort and gave battle. Then the Great Deity Chieftain climbed up into the fork of an elm at Kisuri, from which he shot down arrows like rain. His troops were full of might. They filled the house and overflowed into the plain. The army of the Imperial Princes and the troops of the Ministers were timid and afraid, and fell back three times. At this time the Imperial Prince Mumayado (Shōtoku), his hair being tied up on the temples [the ancient custom was for boys at the age of fifteen or sixteen to tie up their hair on the temples; at the age of seventeen or eighteen it was divided, and made into tufts, as is the case even now], followed in the rear of the army. He pondered in his own mind, saying to himself: "Are we not going to be beaten? Without prayer we cannot succeed." So he cut down a *nuride* tree, and swiftly fashioned images of the four Heavenly Kings.[7] Placing them on his top-knot, he uttered a vow: "If we are now made to gain the victory over the enemy, I promise faithfully to honor the four Heavenly Kings, guardians of the world, by erecting to them a temple with a pagoda." The Great Imperial Chieftain Soga no Mumako also uttered a vow: "Oh! all ye Heavenly Kings and great Spirit King, aid and protect us, and make us to gain the advantage. If this prayer is granted, I will erect a temple with a pagoda in honor of the Heavenly Kings and the great Spirit King, and will propagate everywhere the three precious things."[8] When they had made this vow, they urged their troops of all arms sternly forward to the attack. Now there was a man named Ichihi, Tomi no Obito, who shot down the Great Deity Chieftain from his branch and killed him and his children. His troops accordingly gave way

[7] Buddhist guardian gods.
[8] The three treasures of Buddhism: Buddha, the law, the monastic orders. [Ed.]

suddenly. Joining their forces, they every one put on black clothes,[9] and going hunting on the plain of Magari in Hirose, so dispersed. . . .

A dependent of the Great Deity Chieftain Mononobe no Moriya, named Yorozu [the personal name], of the Tottori-be, in command of one hundred men, guarded the house at Naniwa, but hearing of the Chieftain's downfall, he urged his horse into a gallop, and made his escape by night in the direction of the village of Arimaka in the district of Chinu, where, having passed his wife's house, he at length concealed himself among the hills. The court took counsel together, saying: "Yorozu cherishes traitorous feelings, and therefore has concealed himself among these hills. Let his kindred be extirpated promptly, and no remissness shown." Yorozu, in tattered and filthy raiment, and with a wretched countenance, came forth alone, of his own accord, bow in hand and girt with a sword. The officials sent several hundred guardsmen to surround him. Yorozu, accordingly, was afraid, and hid himself in a bamboo thicket, where he tied cords to the bamboos and pulled them so as to shake the bamboos, and thus make the people to doubt where he had gone in. The guardsmen were deceived, and pointing to the quivering bamboos, ran forward, saying: "Yorozu is here!" Yorozu forthwith shot his arrows, not one of which missed its mark, so that the guardsmen were afraid, and did not dare to approach. Yorozu then unstrung his bow, and taking it under his arm, ran off toward the hills. The guardsmen accordingly pursued him, shooting their arrows at him from both sides of a river, but none of them were able to hit him. Hereupon one of the guardsmen ran on swiftly, and got before Yorozu. Lying down by the river's side, he aimed at him, and hit him on the knee. Yorozu forthwith pulled out the arrow, and stringing his bow, let fly his arrows. Then prostrating himself on the earth, he exclaimed aloud: "A shield of the Emperor, Yorozu would have devoted his valor to his service, but no examination was made, and, on the contrary, he has been hard pressed, and is now at an extremity. Let some one come forward and speak with me, for it is my desire to learn whether I am to be slain or to be made a prisoner." The guardsmen raced up and shot at Yorozu, but he warded off the flying shafts, and slew more than thirty men. Then he took the sword, flung it into the midst of the water of the river. With a dagger

---

[9] It is explained here that "black" was the color of underlings' clothes, and that the chiefs put on this color for disguise. The "hunting" was only a pretense.

which he had besides, he stabbed himself in the throat, and died. The Governor of Kawachi reported the circumstances of Yorozu's death to the court, which gave an order by a stamp[10] that his body should be cut into eight pieces and disposed for exposure among the eight provinces. The Governor of Kawachi accordingly, in obedience to the purport of the stamped order, was about to dismember him for exposure, when thunder pealed, and a great rain fell. Now, there was a white dog which had been kept by Yorozu. Looking up, and looking down, he went round, howling beside the corpse, and at last, taking up the head in his mouth, placed it on an ancient mound. He then lay down close by, and starved to death in front of it. The Governor of Kawachi, thinking that dog's conduct very strange, reported it to the court. The court could not bear to hear of it for pity, and issued a stamped order to this effect: "The case of this dog is one that is rarely heard of in the world, and should be shown to after ages. Let Yorozu's kindred be made to construct a tomb and bury their remains." The kindred of Yorozu accordingly assembled together, and raised a tomb in the village of Arimaka, where they buried Yorozu and his dog. . . .

8th month, 2nd day. The Emperor,[11] upon the advice of Kashikiya hime no Mikoto and the Ministers, assumed the Imperial Dignity. Soga no Mumako no Sukune was made Great Imperial Chieftain as before. The Ministers and high officials were also confirmed in their previous ranks. . . .

4th year, Autumn, 8th month, 1st day. The Emperor addressed his Ministers, saying: "It is our desire to establish Imna.[12] What do ye think?" The Ministers said to him: "The Miyake of Imna should be established. We are all of the same opinion as Your Majesty."

Winter, 11th month, 4th day. Ki no Omaro no Sukune [and others] were appointed as Generals. Taking with them the Imperial Chieftains and Deity Chieftains of the various Houses as Adjutant-Generals of the divisions of the army, they marched out in command of over 20,000 men and stationed themselves in Tsukushi.[13] Kishi no Kana was sent to Silla and Kishi no Itahiko to Imna to make inquiry respecting Imna.

5th year, Winter, 10th month, 4th day. A wild boar was presented to

[10] *Oshide.* A stamp of red or black ink on the palm of the hand as token of authority.
[11] Sujun.
[12] A Japanese outpost in South Korea from which they had previously been driven. [Ed.]
[13] Northern Kyushu.

the Emperor. Pointing to it, he said: "When shall those to whom We have an aversion be cut off as this wild boar's throat has been cut?" An abundance of weapons was provided beyond what was customary.

10th day. Soga no Mumako no Sukune, having been told of the pronouncement of the Emperor, and alarmed at his detestation of himself, called together his people and conspired with them to assassinate the Emperor.

In this month, the Hall of Worship and the covered gallery of the great Hōkōji Temple were built.

11th month, 3rd day. Mumako no Sukune lied to the Ministers, saying: "Today I present the taxes of the Eastern provinces," and sent Koma, Yamato no Aya no Atae, who killed the Emperor.

One book says: "Koma, Yamato no Aya no Atae, was the son of Ihai, Yamato no Aya no Atae."

On this day the Emperor was buried in the Misasagi [14] on the hill of Kurahashi.

(One book says: The Imperial concubine Ōtomo no Koteko, incensed at her declining favor, sent a man to Soga no Mumako no Sukune with a message, saying: "Recently a wild boar was presented to the Emperor. He pointed to it and said: 'When shall the man We think of be cut off as this wild boar's throat has been cut?' Besides weapons are being made in abundance in the Palace." Now Mumako no Sukune, hearing this, was alarmed.)

5th day. Mounted messengers were sent to the General's quarters in Tsukushi, saying: "Do not let foreign matters be neglected in consequence of the internal troubles."

THE REIGN OF SUIKO AND RULE OF SHŌTOKU

From the many entries in the *Chronicles of Japan* for Suiko's reign a few have been selected to show how greatly this Empress and Prince Shōtoku came to be revered for the accomplishments of their joint rule. Particularly noteworthy is Shōtoku's reputation as a profound student of Buddhism, such that he could expound some of the great sūtras at a time when few Japanese could read any Chinese. In addition to the legendary feats of this Prince are recorded the building of many temples, the adoption of Chinese court cere-

[14] Imperial mound or mausoleum.

monial in the form of cap ranks, the sending of embassies (including students) to China, and the first project to write an official history of Japan comparable to the great Chinese histories.

[Adapted from Aston, *Nihongi*, II, 121–50]

The Empress Suiko, A.D. 592–628

The Empress Toyo-mike Kashiki-ya-hime[1] was the second daughter of the Emperor Ame-kuni oshi-hiraki hiro-niha[2] and a younger sister by the same mother of the Emperor Tachibana no toyo-hi.[3] In her childhood she was called the Princess Nukada-be. Her appearance was beautiful, and her conduct was marked by propriety. At the age of eighteen, she was appointed Empress-consort of the Emperor Nunakura futo-dama-shiki.[4] When she was thirty-four years of age, in the 5th year and the 11th month of the reign of the Emperor Hatsuse-be,[5] the Emperor was murdered by the Great Imperial Chieftain Mumako no Sukune, and the succession to the Dignity being vacant, the Ministers besought the Empress-consort of the Emperor Nunakura futo-dama-shiki, viz. the Princess Nukada-be, to ascend the throne. The Empress refused, but the public functionaries urged her in memorials three times until she consented,[6] and they accordingly delivered to her the Imperial Seal. . . .

1st year [A.D. 593], Summer, 4th month, 10th day. The Imperial Prince Mumayado no Toyotomimi [Shōtoku] was appointed Prince Imperial. He had general control of the Government, and was entrusted with all the details of administration. He was the second child of the Emperor Tachibana no Toyo-hi. The Empress-consort his mother's name was the Imperial Princess Anahobe no Hashibito. The Empress-consort, on the day of the dissolution of her pregnancy, went round the forbidden precinct, inspecting the different offices. When she came to the Horse Department, and had just reached the door of the stables,[7] she was suddenly delivered of him without effort. He was able to speak as soon as he was born, and was so wise when he grew up that he could attend to the suits of ten men at once and decide them all without error. He knew beforehand what was going to happen. Moreover he learnt the Inner

[1] *Toyo*, abundant; *mi*, august; *ke*, food; *Kashikiya*, cook-house; *hime*, princess.
[2] Kimmei.　　　　　[3] Yōmei.　　　　　[4] Bidatsu.　　　　　[5] Sujun.
[6] It was the Chinese custom to decline such an honor twice and accept only when offered a third time.
[7] Hence his name, Muma-ya-do, which means stable door.

Doctrine [8] from a Koryo Priest named Hye-cha, and studied the Outer Classics [9] with a doctor called Kak-ka. In both of these branches of study he became thoroughly proficient. The Emperor his father loved him, and made him occupy the Upper Hall South of the Palace. Therefore he was styled the Senior Prince Kamu-tsu-miya,[10] Muma-ya-do Toyotomimi. [pp. 121–23]

. . . .

11th year [604], 12th month, 5th day. Cap-ranks [11] were first instituted in all twelve grades:

Dai-toku . .	greater virtue
Shō-toku . .	lesser virtue
Dai-nin . .	greater humanity
Shō-nin . .	lesser humanity
Dai-rei . .	greater decorum
Shō-rei . .	lesser decorum
Dai-shin . .	greater faith
Shō-shin . .	lesser faith
Dai-gi . .	greater righteousness
Shō-gi . .	lesser righteousness
Dai-chi . .	greater knowledge
Shō-chi . .	lesser knowledge

Each was made of sarcenet of a special color.[12] They were gathered up on the crown in the shape of a bag, and had a border attached. Only on the first day of the year were hair-flowers [13] worn.

[In this year also a Chinese-style calendar was officially adopted for the first time.[14]] [pp. 127–28]

. . . .

[8] That is, Buddhism.

[9] That is, the Chinese Classics. Inner and Outer have here something of the force of our words sacred and secular.

[10] Kamu-tsu-miya means upper palace.

[11] The Chinese custom of distinguishing rank by the form and materials of the official cap. In modern times a button on the top of the cap serves this purpose.

[12] In imitation of the contemporary Sui dynasty of China, purple was for officials of the fifth rank and upwards. *Nin* was green, *rei* red, *shin* yellow, *gi* white, and *chi* black. Princes and chief ministers wore the cap of the highest rank, viz. *toku.*

[13] Hair ornaments of gold or silver in the shape of flowers. Specimens are preserved in the Nara Museum.

[14] Cf. R. K. Reischauer, *Early Japanese History,* A, 140. [Ed.]

14th year [606], 5th month, 5th day. The imperial commands were given to Kuratsukuri no Tori, saying: "It being My desire to encourage the Inner doctrines, I was about to erect a Buddhist Temple, and for this purpose sought for relics. Then thy grandfather, Shiba Tattō, offered Me relics. Moreover, there were no monks or nuns in the land. Thereupon thy father, Tasuna, for the sake of the Emperor Tachibana no Toyohi, took priestly orders and reverenced the Buddhist law. Also thine aunt Shimame was the first to leave her home and, becoming the forerunner of all nuns, to practice the religion of Shākya. Now, We desired to make a sixteen-foot Buddha, and to that end sought for a good image of Buddha. Thou didst provide a model which met Our wishes. Moreover, when the image of Buddha was completed, it could not be brought into the Hall, and none of the workmen could suggest a plan of doing so. They were, therefore, on the point of breaking down the doorway, when thou didst manage to admit it without breaking down the doorway. For all these services of thine, We grant thee the rank of Dainin, and We also bestow on thee twenty *chō* of water-fields [15] in the district of Sakata in the province of Afumi." With the revenue derived from this land, Tori built for the Empress the Temple of Kongō-ji, [16] now known as the nunnery of Sakata in Minabuchi.

Autumn, 7th month. The Empress requested the Prince Imperial to lecture on the *Sūtra of Queen Śrīmālā*. [17] He completed his explanation of it in three days.

In this year the Prince Imperial also lectured on the *Lotus Sūtra* [18] in the Palace of Okamoto. The Empress was greatly pleased, and bestowed on the Prince Imperial one hundred *chō* of water-fields in the Province of Harima. They were therefore added to the Temple of Ikaruga. [pp. 134–35]

. . . .

16th year [608], "Autumn, 9th month. At this time there were sent to the land of T'ang [19] the students Fukuin [and others], together with student priests Nichibun [and others], in all eight persons.

[15] That is, rice-land.   [16] Diamond-temple.
[17] Skt. *Srīmālādevisiṃhanāda;* Jap. *Shōmangyō.* [Ed.]
[18] The *Saddharmapuṇḍarīka- Sūtra;* Jap. *Hokke-kyō.* [Ed.]
[19] China, ruled when this occurred by the Sui dynasty, but at the time of writing by the T'ang dynasty. [Ed.]

In this year many persons from Silla came to settle in Japan. [p. 139]

· · · ·

22nd year [614], 6th month, 13th day. Mitasuki, Lord of Inugami, and Yatabe no Miyakko were sent to the Land of Great T'ang. [p. 145]

· · · ·

30th year [622], Autumn, 7th month. . . . At this time the Buddhist priests E-sai and E-kō, with the physicians E-jitsu and Fuku-in, students of the learning of the Great T'ang, arrived in company with . . . others. Now E-jitsu and the rest together made representation to the Empress, saying: "Those who have resided in T'ang to study have all completed their courses and ought to be sent for. Moreover, the Land of Great T'ang is an admirable country, whose laws are complete and fixed. Constant communication should be kept up with it." [p. 150]

· · · ·

28th year [620]. This year, the Prince Imperial, in concert with the Great Imperial Chieftain Soga, drew up a history of the emperors, a history of the country, and the original record of the Imperial Chieftains, Deity Chieftains, Court Chieftains, Local Chieftains, the 180 hereditary Corporations and the common people.[20] [p. 148]

· · · ·

29th year [621], Spring, 2nd month, 5th day. In the middle of the night the Imperial Prince Mumayado no Toyotomimi no Mikoto died in the Palace of Ikaruga. At this time all the Princes and Imperial Chieftains, as well as the people of the empire, the old, as if they had lost a dear child, had no taste for salt and vinegar[21] in their mouths; the young, as if they had lost a beloved parent, filled the ways with the sound of their lamenting. The farmer ceased from his plough, and the pounding woman laid down her pestle. They all said: "The sun and moon have lost their brightness; heaven and earth have crumbled to ruin: henceforward, in whom shall we put our trust?"

In this month the Prince Imperial Kamitsumiya[22] was buried in the Shinaga Misasagi.

At this time Hye-cha, the Buddhist priest of Koryo, heard of the death of the Prince Imperial Kamitsumiya, and was greatly grieved thereat. He

[20] Almost all of this work was burned during disturbances in 645 and the remainder is no longer extant. [Ed.]
[21] To be understood generally of well-flavored food.   [22] Prince Shōtoku.

invited the priests, and in honor of the Prince Imperial gave them a meal, and explained the sacred books in person. On this day he prayed, saying: "In the Land of Nippon there is a sage, by name the Imperial Prince Kamitsumiya Toyotomimi. Certainly Heaven has freely endowed him with the virtues of a sage.[23] Born in the Land of Nippon, he thoroughly possessed the three fundamental principles,[24] he continued the great plans of the former sages. He reverenced the Three Treasures,[25] and assisted the people in their distress. He was truly a great sage. And now the Prince Imperial is dead. I, although a foreigner, was in heart closely united to him. Now what avails it that I alone should survive? I have determined to die on the 5th day of the 2nd month of next year.[26] So shall I meet the Prince Imperial Kamitsumiya in the Pure Land, and together with him pass through the metempsychosis of all living creatures." Now when the appointed day came, Hye-cha died, and all the people of that day said one to another: "Prince Kamitsumiya is not the only sage, Hye-cha is also a sage." [pp. 148–49]

The Seventeen-Article Constitution of Prince Shōtoku

The influence of Confucian ethical and political doctrines is almost everywhere apparent in this set of basic principles of government. In Article II, however, Buddhism is specifically subscribed to as contributing to the ideal of social harmony. The fact that most of these principles are stated in very general terms reflects the characteristic outlook of Confucianism: the ruler should offer his people moral guidance and instruction, not burden them with detailed laws which involve compulsion rather than elicit cooperation. Therefore this Constitution exhorts the people to lay aside partisan differences and accept imperial rule in order to achieve social harmony. Ministers and officials are urged to be diligent and considerate, prompt and just in the settlement of complaints or charges, careful in the selection of assistants and wary of flatterers, conscientious in the performance of their duties while not overreaching their authority, and ever mindful of the desires of the people so that public good is put above private interest. Articles XII and XV alone refer to specific functions or prerogatives of the imperial government: the power to raise taxes, which is essential to any government, and the seasons in which forced labor is to be exacted, likewise an aspect of the power to tax. Both of these represent practical measures indispensable to establishment of the imperial

[23] According to the Confucian conception. [Ed.]
[24] Viz. Heaven, Earth, and Man. The meaning is that he was a philosopher.
[25] Of Buddhism.   [26] The anniversary of the Prince's death.

authority over a hitherto uncentralized society, no doubt with a view to achieving the uniformity and centralization which the Chinese empire exemplified.

[Adapted from Aston, *Nihongi*, II, 128–33]

12th year [604], Summer, 4th month, 3rd day. The Prince Imperial in person prepared for the first time laws. There were seventeen clauses, as follows:

I. Harmony is to be valued,[27] and an avoidance of wanton opposition to be honored. All men are influenced by partisanship, and there are few who are intelligent. Hence there are some who disobey their lords and fathers, or who maintain feuds with the neighboring villages. But when those above are harmonious and those below are friendly, and there is concord in the discussion of business, right views of things spontaneously gain acceptance. Then what is there which cannot be accomplished?

II. Sincerely reverence the three treasures. The three treasures, viz. Buddha, the Law, and the Monastic orders, are the final refuge of the four generated beings,[28] and are the supreme objects of faith in all countries. Few men are utterly bad. They may be taught to follow it. But if they do not betake them to the three treasures, wherewithal shall their crookedness be made straight?

III. When you receive the imperial commands, fail not scrupulously to obey them. The lord is Heaven, the vassal is Earth. Heaven overspreads, and Earth upbears. When this is so, the four seasons follow their due course, and the powers of Nature obtain their efficacy. If the Earth attempted to overspread, Heaven would simply fall in ruin. Therefore is it that when the lord speaks, the vassal listens; when the superior acts, the inferior yields compliance. Consequently when you receive the imperial commands, fail not to carry them out scrupulously. Let there be a want of care in this matter, and ruin is the natural consequence.

IV. The ministers and functionaries should make decorous behavior their leading principle, for the leading principle of the government of the people consists in decorous behavior.[29] If the superiors do not behave with decorum, the inferiors are disorderly: if inferiors are wanting in proper behavior, there must necessarily be offenses. Therefore it is that when

[27] From the *Analects* of Confucius, I, 12.

[28] That is, the beings produced in transmigration by the four processes of being born from eggs, from a womb, moisture-bred, or formed by metamorphosis (as butterflies from caterpillars).

[29] The Chinese *li*, decorum or ceremony (rites).

lord and vassal behave with decorum, the distinctions of rank are not confused: when the people behave with decorum, the government of the commonwealth proceeds of itself.

V. Ceasing from gluttony and abandoning covetous desires, deal impartially with the suits which are submitted to you. Of complaints brought by the people there are a thousand in one day. If in one day there are so many, how many will there be in a series of years? If the man who is to decide suits at law makes gain his ordinary motive, and hears cases with a view to receiving bribes, then will the suits of the rich man be like a stone flung into water,[30] while the plaints of the poor will resemble water cast upon a stone. Under these circumstances the poor man will not know whither to betake himself. Here too there is a deficiency in the duty of the minister.

VI. Chastise that which is evil and encourage that which is good. This was the excellent rule of antiquity. Conceal not, therefore, the good qualities of others, and fail not to correct that which is wrong when you see it. Flatterers and deceivers are a sharp weapon for the overthrow of the State, and a pointed sword for the destruction of the people. Sycophants are also fond, when they meet, of dilating to their superiors on the errors of their inferiors; to their inferiors, they censure the faults of their superiors. Men of this kind are all wanting in fidelity to their lord, and in benevolence towards the people. From such an origin great civil disturbances arise.

VII. Let every man have his own charge, and let not the spheres of duty be confused. When wise men are entrusted with office, the sound of praise arises. If unprincipled men hold office, disasters and tumults are multiplied. In this world, few are born with knowledge: wisdom is the product of earnest meditation. In all things, whether great or small, find the right man, and they will surely be well managed: on all occasions, be they urgent or the reverse, meet but with a wise man, and they will of themselves be amenable. In this way will the State be lasting and the Temples of the Earth and of Grain will be free from danger. Therefore did the wise sovereigns of antiquity seek the man to fill the office, and not the office for the sake of the man.

VIII. Let the ministers and functionaries attend the court early in the morning, and retire late. The business of the State does not admit of

[30] That is, they meet with no resistance.

remissness, and the whole day is hardly enough for its accomplishment. If, therefore, the attendance at court is late, emergencies cannot be met: if officials retire soon, the work cannot be completed.

IX. Good faith is the foundation of right. In everything let there be good faith, for in it there surely consists the good and the bad, success and failure. If the lord and the vassal observe good faith one with another, what is there which cannot be accomplished? If the lord and the vassal do not observe good faith towards one another, everything without exception ends in failure.

X. Let us cease from wrath, and refrain from angry looks. Nor let us be resentful when others differ from us. For all men have hearts, and each heart has its own leanings. Their right is our wrong, and our right is their wrong. We are not unquestionably sages, nor are they unquestionably fools. Both of us are simply ordinary men. How can any one lay down a rule by which to distinguish right from wrong? For we are all, one with another, wise and foolish, like a ring which has no end. Therefore, although others give way to anger, let us on the contrary dread our own faults, and though we alone may be in the right, let us follow the multitude and act like them.

XI. Give clear appreciation to merit and demerit, and deal out to each its sure reward or punishment. In these days, reward does not attend upon merit, nor punishment upon crime. Ye high functionaries who have charge of public affairs, let it be your task to make clear rewards and punishments.

XII. Let not the provincial authorities or the Kuni no Miyakko [31] levy exaction on the people. In a country there are not two lords; the people have not two masters. The sovereign is the master of the people of the whole country. The officials to whom he gives charge are all his vassals. How can they, as well as the Government, presume to levy taxes on the people?

XIII. Let all persons entrusted with office attend equally to their functions. Owing to their illness or to their being sent on missions, their work may sometimes be neglected. But whenever they become able to attend to business, let them be as accommodating as if they had had cognizance

[31] The Kuni no Miyakko were the old local nobles, whose power was at this time giving way to that of the central government, represented in the provinces by the *kokushi*, or local governors.

of it from before, and not hinder public affairs on the score of their not having had to do with them.

XIV. Ye ministers and functionaries! Be not envious. For if we envy others, they in turn will envy us. The evils of envy know no limit. If others excel us in intelligence, it gives us no pleasure; if they surpass us in ability, we are envious. Therefore it is not until after a lapse of five hundred years that we at last meet with a wise man, and even in a thousand years we hardly obtain one sage. But if we do not find wise men and sages, wherewithal shall the country be governed?

XV. To turn away from that which is private, and to set our faces towards that which is public—this is the path of a minister. Now if a man is influenced by private motives, he will assuredly feel resentments, and if he is influenced by resentful feelings, he will assuredly fail to act harmoniously with others. If he fails to act harmoniously with others, he will assuredly sacrifice the public interests to his private feelings. When resentment arises, it interferes with order, and is subversive of law. Therefore in the first clause it was said, that superiors and inferiors should agree together. The purport is the same as this.

XVI. Let the people be employed [in forced labor] at seasonable times. This is an ancient and excellent rule. Let them be employed, therefore, in the winter months, when they are at leisure. But from Spring to Autumn, when they are engaged in agriculture or with the mulberry trees, the people should not be so employed. For if they do not attend to agriculture, what will they have to eat? if they do not attend to the mulberry trees, what will they do for clothing?

XVII. Decisions on important matters should not be made by one person alone. They should be discussed with many. But small matters are of less consequence. It is unnecessary to consult a number of people. It is only in the case of the discussion of weighty affairs, when there is a suspicion that they may miscarry, that one should arrange matters in concert with others, so as to arrive at the right conclusion.

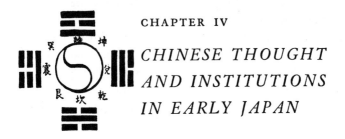

CHAPTER IV

CHINESE THOUGHT
AND INSTITUTIONS
IN EARLY JAPAN

At this point a chapter devoted especially to Chinese influences in early Japan may seem needless, for under every topic discussed so far this influence has been quite conspicuous. As the Yamato people consolidated their position in central Japan, and as their rulers attempted to win undisputed supremacy over other clans of the confederacy, it was to the Chinese example that they turned more and more for political guidance and cultural direction. In Prince Shōtoku we have already seen the embodiment of this tendency to adopt and adapt all that China might contribute to the unification and pacification of a restless, turbulent people.

But the most striking examples of this trend are to be found in the series of imperial edicts issued during the period of Great Reform (Taika), which began in 645. Proceeding from the theory enunciated in Shōtoku's Constitution that "In a country there are not two lords; the people have not two masters," these reforms asserted the doctrine that "Under the heavens there is no land which is not the king's land. Among holders of land there is none who is not the king's vassal." On this ground an ambitious program was launched to curb the powers of the clan leaders, who had frequently jeopardized the Throne itself in their struggles for power. In place of the old political organization based on clan units was set up the systematic territorial administration of the Chinese, with local governors sent out by the court, centrally directed and executing a uniform law which represented the paramount authority of the emperor. In keeping with this the central administration itself was overhauled so as to provide a close replica of the vast, symmetrical bureaucracy of the great T'ang empire. A new aristocracy was thereby created of those who held office and court rank conferred by the Throne. Thus the old and complex class structure, along with the clan hierarchy based on birth and blood, was to be replaced by a simpler division of society into two main classes, the rulers and the common people, characteristic of imperial China.

The reformers did not, however, limit their actions to the political sphere. Indeed, implicit in the erection of this state machinery was the need for economic changes which would channel the wealth of the country toward the center of political power. Thus it was recognized from the first that the T'ang tax system was indispensable to the functioning of the T'ang-type administration. The T'ang tax system, moreover, presupposed a system of land nationalization and redistribution such as that instituted during the early years of that dynasty by the famous monarch, T'ai-tsung. Accordingly the Japanese reformers attempted to abolish "private" property, nationalize the land, redistribute it on the basis of family size, and adopt the Chinese system of triple taxation on land, labor, and produce. In fact, so meticulously was the Chinese example followed that land and tax registers for this period, preserved in the imperial repository at Nara, are almost identical in form and terminology to contemporary Chinese registers discovered recently at the western outpost of the Chinese empire, Tun-huang. Furthermore, by their assertion of the imperial right to universal labor and military service, the reformers went far toward achieving for the ruling house that absolute control over all the elements of power characteristic of the greatest Chinese dynasties. But with this wholesale imitation of China came likewise the chronic difficulties experienced by these dynasties, which were to undermine the new state almost from the start.

There was, however, a more profound and lasting influence exerted by China in these early years than the political changes inaugurated in the seventh century. This was the vast system of coordinated knowledge and belief of which the Chinese imperial structure was indeed the most imposing terrestrial symbol, but which stretched out into realms of thought and action both transcending and penetrating beneath the immediate political order. Like the imperial pattern itself this far-reaching syncretism was a product of the Han dynasties (202 B.C.–A.D. 220), in which parallel tendencies worked to unify and organize both the political and intellectual life of China. In the realm of thought this development was most apparent in the adoption of Confucianism as the state creed

[53]

and cult, expounded in the imperial university, incorporated into the civil service examinations, and systematized by scholars working for the Throne who tried to arrive at a definite version of the Confucian classics.

However, the Confucianism of the Han dynasties, introduced to Japan at the latest by the sixth and seventh centuries A.D., represented more than the essential ethical teachings of Confucius and his early followers. These teachings were there, at the base of the new intellectual edifice, but they had become overlaid and to some extent obscured by the great weight of correlative learning and doctrine which had taken shelter under its copious roof. This was not necessarily due to the fact that many popular beliefs sought to gain respectability by association with doctrines having the sanction of tradition and the state. Rather Confucianism itself had to battle with other potent philosophies for official favor, and in the process the fundamental rationalism of this school penetrated into realms of thought which it had previously not fully explored. By so doing it absorbed much from other traditions, such as the Taoist and Five Elements (or yin-yang) schools, to fill out its own lean frame.

Modern minds may find a great deal here that seems to have been poorly digested. Yet it must be recognized that in terms of the knowledge then available this synthesis is remarkable for its order and coherence, and in the hands of an articulate spokesman such as Tung Chung-shu, it served well to reinforce some of the fundamental political doctrines of the Confucian school, persuading absolute monarchs to use their power wisely and with restraint. It must also be remembered that, if much of its cosmology and the "sciences" derived from it were put to superstitious use, people in all times and places have been forced to act on the basis of incomplete knowledge, and therefore we must be careful to judge the activities of these people by their standards as well as our own.

At the heart of all such Confucian speculation is the doctrine, which it shared in common with other influential schools of thought, that the universe is a harmonious whole in which man and nature constantly interact on each other in all aspects of life. From this doctrine it was concluded that the actions of men, particularly as represented by their rulers, affect the natural order, which is sensitive above all to the ethical quality of their acts. If man fails to fulfill his proper function, nature acts or operates to restore the total balance or harmony. For this reason it was believed that natural occurrences, especially spectacular aberrations from the normal course of nature, would reveal when properly interpreted the extent to which a man or ruler had lapsed from his duty or the proper course of conduct for him to follow.

The importance in China of divination and other primitive arts or sciences is evident when we consider that the earliest Chinese writing now preserved is found on oracle bones, recording the questions and responses that the diviners obtained by scrutinizing cracks made when the bones were heated. In later times we find that the astrologers were called "historians" (*shih*), and combined the functions of both diviners and compilers of records. Their influence is apparent in the Chinese view of history as the expression of the Will of Heaven. For the early Chinese historians a noteworthy event was not merely a fact to be recorded—it was to be interpreted either as an ill-omen or as a sign of Heaven's approval. Eclipses and comets were evident attempts of Heaven to express its desires, but the sight of an unusually shaped cloud was also sometimes considered important enough to warrant changing the name by which a part of an emperor's reign was known. The close connection persisting between the diviner and the historian is attested by the statement in the preface to the *True Records of Three Japanese Reigns* (A.D. 901) where the compilers declare their intent of fully recording the "auspicious signs with which Heaven favors the Lord of Men and the portents with which Heaven admonishes the Lord of Men." The application of this method is already fully evident in such an early history as the *Nihongi*.

Behind such a statement lay the belief in the necessary correspondences between the worlds of Heaven and earth. When the astronomers reported that the heavenly bodies had reached their spring positions, the rites suitable to spring had to be performed on earth. Or, if a lucky cloud indicated that some favorable change had been decreed by Heaven, a corresponding change, such as one of the reign name, had to be made on earth. Even Confucius was reported to have changed his countenance on hearing a clap of thunder. A failure to observe the changes in Heaven might lead to disasters on earth. If, for example, a rite suitable to winter were performed in the spring because of a faulty calendar, the crops would be blasted in the bud by wintry weather. The proper rites, on the other hand, could insure such blessings as seasonal rainfall. Tung Chung-shu, the Han philosopher, described various ways to insure that rain fell when it was needed: one of them was to have the government employees and other subjects cohabit with their wives on a day chosen by yin-yang methods.

Different sciences were evolved to deal with events in the Three Realms —Heaven, Earth, and Man. These were astrology, geomancy, and the art of "avoiding calamities" respectively. Astrology enabled man to discover what was to be the fate of a kingdom or of an individual. The twelve divisions of the heavens (based on the twelve-year period of the planet Jupiter) had corresponding divisions on earth and when, for example, Jupiter was in the division of the heavens "controlling" a particular country, that country was safe from invasion. By learning the Will of Heaven from the stars one could predict events on earth. By geomancy and the art of "avoiding calamities," on the other hand, the Will of Heaven could be cooperated with in the interests of man. Thus, when the site of Kyoto was chosen because it possessed the "proper" number of rivers and mountains, it represented an attempt to secure by geomancy the most auspicious surroundings for the new capital. Heaven had designed such a place for a capital and man could benefit by it. An even more important method of obtaining benefits from Heaven, particularly in Japan, was the art of "avoiding calamities."

It was in A.D. 602 that the Korean monk Kwallŭk brought some books on geomancy and "avoiding calamities" to Japan. Several members of the court were selected to study with Kwallŭk, and some of the extraordinary changes which took place in the next few years may be attributed to the success of the new learning. In 604, a year whose astrological signs marked it for the adepts of "avoiding calamities" as a "revolutionary year," Prince Shōtoku's Constitution in seventeen articles was proclaimed. (The number of articles, it will be remembered, was derived from the combination of eight, the largest yin number, and nine, the largest yang number.) In the same year also appeared the first Japanese calendar, an event of immense importance both in the writing of history and in the development of the rites of state.

It may be, of course, that these events did not actually occur in 604, but were credited to that year by later historians anxious to impart additional significance to them by the association with a "revolutionary year." It seems clear now, for example, that the events attributed to the reign of the legendary Emperor Jimmu were assigned to "revolutionary years" by the compilers of the *Chronicles of Japan* for a similar reason.

There is in any case ample evidence of the prevalence of yin-yang (by which the whole Han Confucian ideology is meant) thinking in both the *Records of Ancient Matters* (712) and the *Chronicles of Japan* (720). The preface to the former work begins:

Now when chaos had begun to condense, but force and form were not yet manifest, and there was nought named, nought done, who could know its shape? Nevertheless Heaven and Earth first parted, and the Three Deities performed the commencement of creation; the yin and the yang then developed, and the Two Spirits became the ancestors of all things.[1]

The *Chronicles of Japan* begins:

Of old, Heaven and Earth were not yet separated, and the yin and the yang not yet divided. They formed a chaotic mass like an egg which was of obscurely defined limits and contained germs. The purer and clearer part was thinly drawn out, and formed Heaven, while the heavier and grosser element settled down and became Earth.[2]

Perhaps the chief purpose of the compilation of the *Records of Ancient Matters* was to establish the legitimacy of the claim of the Emperor Temmu and his descendants to the throne. This was done in terms of both genealogy and virtue or accomplishment. It was declared of Temmu, among other things, that "he held the mean between the Two Essences [yin and yang], and regulated the order of the Five Elements." We can see, then, how intimately yin-yang thinking was connected with early Japanese historiography.

Mention of the five elements brings us to the center of the art of "avoiding calamities." An elaborate system of correspondences was evolved between the planets, the elements, the directions, the seasons, the signs of the zodiac, and various other categories, as follows:

Planet	Element	Direction	Season	Signs of the Zodiac
Jupiter	wood	east	spring	tiger, hare
Mars	fire	south	summer	serpent, horse
Saturn	earth	center	solstices[3]	dog, ox, dragon, sheep
Venus	metal	west	autumn	monkey, cock
Mercury	water	north	winter	boar, rat

According to the theory of the five elements, the two elements bordering any particular element were beneficial to it, while the two separated elements were harmful. Thus, both wood and earth were beneficial to

[1] Chamberlain, *Ko-ji-ki*, p. 4.   [2] Aston, *Nihongi*, I, 1–2.
[3] Summer and winter intervals between the seasons.

fire, but metal and water were harmful. Thus too, a person born under the sign of Mars would make a suitable spouse for one born under Jupiter and Saturn, but not for one born under Venus or Mercury. It was possible to "avoid calamity" by preventing a marriage or partnership between people born under conflicting elements.

In Japan life came to be ruled very largely by such beliefs. When we read novels of the Heian Period (794–1186) we cannot but be struck by the frequent mentions of "unlucky directions" or "unlucky days." For each person, depending on the planet which governed him, different directions were auspicious or inauspicious on a certain day. Diaries giving the astrological conditions of each day of the year were popular with the great men of the state, who regulated their plans according to the heavenly influences present. To advise the government on all matters of yin-yang lore, there was a department of yin-yang (*Onyôryô*) as early as A.D. 675, and detailed provisions for its organization were given in the Taihō Code of 701–2.

The yin-yang teaching was not confined to members of the court, however. It spread to all levels of Japanese society and affected almost every phase of daily living, though unlike Buddhism or Shinto, it had no organized clergy to promote or perpetuate it. The layout of a house and even the position of articles of furniture were determined by yin-yang. Thus, it was not advisable to place a chest containing valuables in the southern part of the house, for the south was the direction governed by the element fire, and anything left there was likely to be burned. To avoid such calamities care had to be given to the yin-yang directives on all matters.

The yin-yang attempt to explain the phenomena of the universe, both physical and spiritual, in terms of the five elements was increasingly successful and met little serious opposition. Some Buddhists appear to have been hostile at first to fortune-telling on the basis of the five elements, but later attempted to do much the same with five elements of their own choosing. By and large, however, the yin-yang teachings were widely accepted and remained unchallenged until modern times. Up to 1861, for example, the reign names continued to change regularly when one of the "revolutionary years" turned up in the cycle. The yin-yang system was resorted to on many occasions even in recent decades; lucky days were still chosen by yin-yang methods, and the zodiacal sign under which a person was born was rarely ignored in making marriages.

Yin-yang was not the only variety of Chinese thought familiar to the Japanese court of the Nara and Heian periods. The classics of Confucianism and Taoism were relatively well known, as is evinced by the poetry of the *Manyōshū,* an anthology completed in the eighth century. Here we find frequent echoes of Chinese thought in a form which indicates their familiarity even at that early date. Outright imitations of Chinese thought and literature may be found in the *Kaifūsō,* a collection of poetry in Chinese dating from A.D. 751. However, it was not only in literary works that Japanese writers showed their indebtedness to Chinese style and sentiments. When, for example, the commentary on the legal code of A.D. 833 was submitted to the Throne, it was accompanied by a memorial which is a tissue of allusions to Chinese literature. Thus, not only did Japan borrow the legal institutions of the T'ang dynasty for her own purposes, but she borrowed the flowery phraseology in which the Chinese were accustomed to give their reasons for the existence of laws. The use of such language undoubtedly had a profound influence on the development of thought in Japan, and specimens of it may be found in innumerable prefaces and memorials.

The lasting remains of the introduction of Chinese thought to early Japan are apparent in every field, but especially in the concept of imperial rule, sometimes called Tennōism. It is often thought that this concept is based mainly on the Japanese rulers' claim to unbroken succession from the Sun Goddess, but the only authority for this notion in the early period comes from writers anxious to emulate or outdo Chinese dynastic traditions. As for the assumption of absolute powers, which made of the Japanese king a divine emperor (Tennō), it plainly derives from the already fully developed autocracy of China, justified by the Mandate of Heaven. The successive steps taken toward the establishment of a strong central government reflect Japanese adherence to the Chinese concept of the sovereign as the possessor of the Mandate of Heaven. Prince Shōtoku's Constitution, the Taika Reforms, the adoption of Chinese legal and bureaucratic institutions, were all intended to strengthen the claims of the emperor to being a true Son of Heaven, a polar star about whom the lesser celestial luminaries turned. Symbolic of this trend is the choice of posthumous titles for the two great rulers of the late seventh century, Tenchi (Heavenly Wisdom) and Temmu (Heavenly Might).

The establishment of a permanent capital at Nara in 708 was also necessary for the prestige of the emperor in the eyes of his people as well as in those of such Chinese dignitaries as might visit the country. The capital at Kyoto was built in imitation of Ch'ang-an, closely following yin-yang theories. The city was divided by eight streets and nine avenues. The palace, situated in the north in accordance with yin-yang, was surrounded by nine-fold walls. The emperor was served by a bureaucracy organized into nine departments of state, with eight ranks of officials. And, as if to protect the capital from baleful influences coming from the northeast, the unlucky quarter, a Buddhist monastery was built on Mt. Hiei, which lay in that direction. But prior to this event Buddhism itself had become a force to be reckoned with by the government, and to this development we shall turn in the next chapter.

CHINESE-STYLE HISTORY AND THE IMPERIAL CONCEPT

The following excerpts should be read in conjunction with those from the *Records of Ancient Matters* (*Kojiki*) and *Chronicles of Japan* (*Nihongi*), contained in the first chapter, which were used to illustrate the legendary beginnings of the Japanese people and ruling house. The selections here, while related to the same subject, are intended to show especially how in the writing of history on Chinese models the imperial line is clothed with all the attributes of the ideal Chinese ruler, and how the Chinese concept of sovereignty is arbitrarily applied to the Japanese situation so as to strengthen the claims of the Yamato kings. This is the beginning of Tennōism.

Most of the Preface to the *Kojiki* is given here (the part preceding the excerpt in Chapter I) to show the compiler's aim and the general view of early Japanese history which is elaborated in the text itself. The *Kojiki* (712) has been thought to show less Chinese influence than the later *Nihongi* (720), but, as the notes amply demonstrate, Chinese conceptions are almost everywhere apparent.

Preface to *Records of Ancient Matters* (*Kojiki*)
[Adapted from Chamberlain, *Ko-ji-ki,* pp. 4–10]

Now when chaos had begun to condense, but force and form were not yet manifest, and there was nought named, nought done, who could know its shape? Nevertheless Heaven and Earth first parted, and the Three Deities performed the commencement of creation; the Passive and Active

Essences then developed, and the Two Spirits became the ancestors of all things. Therefore did he enter obscurity and emerge into light, and the Sun and Moon were revealed by the washing of his eyes; he floated on and plunged into the sea-water, and Heavenly and Earthly Deities appeared through the ablutions of his person. So in the dimness of the great commencement, we, by relying on the original teaching, learn the time of the conception of the earth and of the birth of islands; in the remoteness of the original beginning, we by trusting the former sages, perceive the era of the genesis of Deities and of the establishment of men. Truly we do know that a mirror was hung up, that jewels were spat out, and that then an Hundred Kings succeeded each other; that a blade was bitten, and a serpent cut in pieces, so that a Myriad Deities did flourish. By deliberations in the Tranquil River the Empire was pacified; by discussions on the Little Shore the land was purified. Wherefore His Augustness Ho-no-ni-ni-gi[1] first descended to the Peak of Takachi, and the Heavenly Sovereign Kamu-Yamato[2] did traverse the Island of the Dragon-Fly.[3] A weird bear put forth its claws, and a heavenly saber was obtained at Takakura. They with tails obstructed the path, and a great crow guided him to Eshinu. Dancing in rows they destroyed the brigands, and listening to a song they vanquished the foemen. Being instructed in a dream he was reverent to the Heavenly and Earthly Deities, and was therefore styled the Wise Monarch;[4] having gazed on the smoke, he was benevolent to the black-haired people,[5] and is therefore remembered as the Emperor-Sage.[6] Determining the frontiers and civilizing the country, he issued laws from the Nearer Afumi;[7] reforming the surnames and selecting the gentile names, he held sway at the Further Asuka.[8] Though each differed in caution and in ardor, though all were unlike in accomplishments and in intrinsic worth, yet was there none who did not by contemplating antiquity correct manners that had fallen to ruin, and by illumining modern times repair laws that were approaching dissolution.[9]

In the august reign of the Heavenly Sovereign who governed the Eight

---

[1] The abbreviated form of the name of the Sun Goddess' grandson.
[2] That is, the first "human emperor" Jimmu.   [3] That is, Japan.
[4] "The Emperor Sūjin" must be mentally supplied as the logical subject of this clause.
[5] Chinese term for the people of China which is applied here to the Japanese.
[6] "The Emperor Nintoku" is referred to.
[7] "The Emperor Seimu" is referred to.   [8] "The Emperor Ingyō" is referred to.
[9] Characteristics of the Chinese sage-kings which are hardly appropriate here.

Great Islands from the Great Palace of Kiyomihara at Asuka,[10] the Hidden Dragon put on perfection, the Reiterated Thunder came at the appointed moment.[11] Having heard a song in a dream, he felt that he should continue the succession; having reached the water at night, he knew that he should receive the inheritance. Nevertheless Heaven's time was not yet,[12] and he escaped like the cicada to the Southern Mountains; both men and matters were favorable, and he marched like the tiger to the Eastern Land. Suddenly riding in the imperial Palanquin, he forced his way across mountains and rivers: the Six Divisions rolled like thunder, the Three Hosts sped like lightning. The erect spears lifted up their might, and the bold warriors arose like smoke: the crimson flags glistened among the weapons, and the ill-omened crew were shattered like tiles. Or ere a day had elapsed, the evil influences were purified: forthwith were the cattle let loose and the horses given repose, as with shouts of victory they returned to the Flowery Summer; the flags were rolled up and the javelins put away, as with dances and chants they came to rest in the capital city. The year was that of the Cock, and it was in the Second Moon.[13] At the Great Palace of Kiyomihara did he ascend to the Heavenly seat: in morality he outstripped the Yellow Emperor, in virtue he surpassed the kings of Chou. Having grasped the celestial seals, he was paramount over the Six Cardinal Points; having obtained the heavenly supremacy, he annexed the Eight Wildernesses. He held the mean between the Two Essences,[14] and regulated the order of the Five Elements. He established divine reason wherewith to advance good customs; he disseminated brilliant usages wherewith to make the land great. Moreover the ocean of his wisdom, in its vastness, profoundly investigated the highest antiquity; the mirror of his heart, in its fervor, clearly observed former ages.[15]

Hereupon the Heavenly Sovereign commanded, saying: "I hear that the chronicles of the emperors and likewise the original words in the

[10] Viz., the Emperor Temmu, who struggled for the crown in the latter part of the seventh century of our era against the contending claims of Prince Ōtomo.

[11] Chinese metaphors referring to the heir-apparent.

[12] According to the Han Confucian view of sovereignty, hereditary right alone did not guarantee succession. One had to await the Mandate of Heaven. [Ed.]

[13] That is, March, A.D. 673 as represented by the Chinese calendar.

[14] Yang and yin. In this case the meaning is probably that Temmu was neither excessively strict nor excessively lax. [Ed.]

[15] Sentiments typical of Han Confucianism. [Ed.]

possession of the various families deviate from exact truth, and are mostly amplified by empty falsehoods. If at the present time these imperfections be not amended, ere many years shall have elapsed, the purport of this, the great basis[16] of the country, the grand foundation of the monarchy, will be destroyed. So now I desire to have the chronicles of the emperors selected and recorded, and the old words examined and ascertained, falsehoods being erased and the truth determined, in order to transmit [the latter] to after ages."[17] At that time there was a retainer whose surname was Hieda, and his personal name Are. He was twenty-eight years old, and of so intelligent a disposition that he could repeat with his mouth whatever met his eyes, and record in his heart whatever struck his ears. Forthwith Are was commanded to learn by heart the genealogies of the emperors, and likewise the words of former ages. Nevertheless time elapsed and the age changed, and the thing was not yet carried out.[18]

Prostrate I consider how Her Majesty the Empress, having obtained Unity, illumines the empire, being versed in the Triad, nourishes the people.[19] Ruling from the Purple Palace,[20] Her virtue reaches to the utmost limits of the horses' hoof-marks: dwelling amid the Somber Retinue, Her influence illumines the furthest distance attained to by vessels' prows. The sun rises, and the brightness is increased; the clouds disperse, neither is there smoke. Never cease the historiographers from recording the good omens of connected stalks and double rice-ears; never for a single moon is the treasury without the tribute of continuous beacon-fires and repeated interpretations.[21] In fame She must be pronounced superior to Wen-ming, in virtue more eminent than T'ien-i.[22]

[16] Literally "warp and woof," typical Confucian terminology.

[17] This is the imperial decree ordering the compilation of the *Records of Ancient Matters*.

[18] That is, the Emperor Temmu died before the plan of the compilation of these "Records" had been carried into execution.

[19] The phrase "obtained Unity" is borrowed from Lao Tzu. The "Triad" is the threefold intelligence of Heaven, Earth, and Man. The general meaning of the sentence is that the Empress' perfect virtue, which is in complete accord with the heavenly ordinances, is spread abroad throughout the empire, and that with her all-penetrating insight she nourishes and sustains her people.

[20] In the following four sentences the compiler expresses his respectful admiration of the Empress Gemmyō, who was on the throne at the time when he wrote, and tells us how wide was her rule and how prosperous her reign. The "Purple Palace" is one of the ornamental names borrowed from the Chinese to denote the imperial residence.

[21] The whole sentence is borrowed scarcely without alteration from the Chinese work *Wen Hsüan*, ch. 46, preface to "Ch'ü-shui-shih," by Yen Yen-nien. [Ed.]

[22] The Great Yü and T'ang the Completer, legendary Chinese rulers.

The First Emperor, Jimmu

The following extracts from the *Chronicles of Japan* deal with the reign of the Emperor Jimmu, who reputedly founded the earthly domain of the imperial line. It is clear that the concept of sovereignty and pretensions to universal rule advanced here (and made much of in the emperor-centered nationalism of modern times) are based on Han Chinese models. Hence the incongruities which appear when the historian, obviously with one eye on the claims of imperial China to being the Central Kingdom of the world, makes similar claims for this remote island kingdom.

[Adapted from Aston, *Nihongi*, I, 109–32]

The Emperor Kami Yamato Ihare-biko's personal name was Hiko-hoho-demi. He was the fourth child of Hiko-nagisa-take-u-gaya-fuki-aezu no Mikoto. His mother's name was Tama-yori-hime, daughter of the Sea God. From his birth, this Emperor was of clear intelligence and resolute will. At the age of fifteen he was heir to the throne. When he grew up, he married Ahira-tsu-hime, of the district of Ata in the province of Hyūga, and made her his consort. By her he had Tagishi-mimi no Mikoto and Kisu-mimi no Mikoto.

When he reached the age of forty-five, he addressed his elder brothers and his children, saying: "Of old, Our Heavenly Deities Taka-mi-musubi no Mikoto, and Ō-hiru-me no Mikoto, pointing to this land of fair rice-ears of the fertile reed-plain, gave it to Our Heavenly ancestor, Hiko-ho no ninigi no Mikoto. Thereupon Hiko-ho no ninigi no Mikoto, throwing open the barrier of Heaven and clearing a cloud-path, urged on his superhuman course until he came to rest. At this time the world was given over to widespread desolation. It was an age of darkness and disorder. In this gloom, therefore, he fostered justice, and so governed this western border.[1] Our imperial ancestors and imperial parent, like gods, like sages, accumulated happiness and amassed glory. Many years elapsed. From the date when Our Heavenly ancestor descended until now it is over 1,792,470 years.[2] But the remote regions do not yet enjoy the blessings of imperial rule. Every town has always been allowed to have its lord, and every village its chief, who, each one for himself,

---

[1] That is, Kyushu.

[2] This is in imitation of the great number of years ascribed to the reigns of the early Chinese monarchs.

makes division of territory and practices mutual aggression and conflict.

"Now I have heard from the Ancient of the Sea³ that in the East there is a fair land encircled on all sides by blue mountains. Moreover, there is there one who flew down riding in a Heavenly Rock-boat. I think that this land will undoubtedly be suitable for the extension of the Heavenly task,⁴ so that its glory should fill the universe. It is, doubtless, the center of the world.⁵ The person who flew down was, I believe, Nigi-haya-hi.⁶ Why should we not proceed thither, and make it the capital?"

All the Imperial Princes answered, and said: "The truth of this is manifest. This thought is constantly present to our minds also. Let us go thither quickly." This was the year Kinoe Tora [51st] of the Great Year.⁷ [pp. 109–11]

. . . .

The year Tsuchinoto Hitsuji, Spring, 3rd month, 7th day. The Emperor made an order⁸ saying: "During the six years that Our expedition against the East has lasted, owing to My reliance on the Majesty of Imperial Heaven, the wicked bands have met death. It is true that the frontier lands are still unpurified, and that a remnant of evil is still refractory. But in the region of the Central Land⁹ there is no more wind and dust. Truly we should make a vast and spacious capital, and plan it great and strong.

"At present things are in a crude and obscure condition, and the people's minds are unsophisticated. They roost in nests or dwell in caves.¹⁰ Their manners are simply what is customary. Now if a great man were to establish laws, justice could not fail to flourish. And even if some gain should accrue to the people, in what way would this interfere with the

---

³ Shiho tsutsu no oji.   ⁴ That is, for the further development of the imperial power.

⁵ The world is here the six quarters, North, South, East, West, Zenith, Nadir. This is, of course, Chinese, as indeed is this whole speech.

⁶ Nigi-haya-hi means soft-swift-sun.

⁷ The great year is the Chinese cycle of sixty years. It is needless to add that such dates are, in this part of the *Nihongi,* purely fictitious.

⁸ This whole speech is thoroughly Chinese in every respect, and it is preposterous to put it in the mouth of an Emperor who is supposed to have lived more than a thousand years before the introduction of Chinese learning into Japan.

⁹ Claiming for Japan the name always used for China: "Central Kingdom." [Ed.]

¹⁰ The reader must not take this as any evidence of the manners and customs of the ancient Japanese. It is simply a phrase suggested by the author's Chinese studies.

Sage's [11] action? Moreover, it will be well to open up and clear the mountains and forests, and to construct a palace. Then I may reverently assume the Precious Dignity, and so give peace to My good subjects. Above, I should then respond to the kindness of the Heavenly Powers in granting Me the Kingdom, and below, I should extend the line of the imperial descendants and foster rightmindedness. Thereafter the capital may be extended so as to embrace all the six cardinal points, and the eight cords may be covered so as to form a roof.[12] Will this not be well?

"When I observe the Kashiwa-bara plain, which lies SW of Mount Unebi, it seems the Center of the Land. I must set it in order."

Accordingly he in this month commanded officers to set about the construction of an imperial residence. [pp. 131–32]

Nintoku: Rule of Benevolence

Here is a striking example of the legendary Japanese emperor who is clothed in all the attributes of the Chinese sage-king, as the virtuous father of his people. The benevolent paternalism ascribed to Nintoku, a much later successor to Jimmu, became an important element in the glorification of the emperor as an embodiment, not simply of awesome power, but of divine virtue and love.

[Adapted from Aston, Nihongi, I, 278–79]

4th year, Spring, 2nd month, 6th day. The Emperor addressed his ministers, saying: "We ascended a lofty tower and looked far and wide, but no smoke arose in the land. From this We gather that the people are poor, and that in the houses there are none cooking their rice. We have heard that in the reigns of the wise sovereigns of antiquity,[13] from everyone was heard the sound of songs hymning their virtue, in every house there was the ditty, 'How happy are we.' But now when We observe the people, for three years past, no voice of eulogy is heard; the smoke of cooking has become rarer and rarer. By this We know that the five grains [14] do not come up, and that the people are in extreme want. Even

[11] Meaning the Emperor's action, because in Chinese tradition the early rulers were "sage-kings." [Ed.]

[12] The character for roof also means the universe. The eight cords, or measuring tapes, simply means "everywhere."

[13] Actually Chinese antiquity. [Ed.]

[14] Hemp, millet, rice, wheat and barley, pulse—the Five Grains of ancient China.

in the Home provinces [15] there are some who are not supplied; what must it be in the provinces outside of Our domain?"

3rd month, 21st day. The following decree was issued: "From this time forward, for the space of three years, let forced labor be entirely abolished, and let the people have rest from toil." From this day forth his robes of state and shoes did not wear out, and none were made. The warm food and hot broths did not become sour or putrid, and were not renewed. He disciplined his heart and restrained his impulses so that he discharged his functions without effort.

Therefore the Palace enclosure fell to ruin and was not rebuilt; the thatch decayed, and was not repaired; the wind and rain entered by the chinks and soaked the coverlets; the starlight filtered through the decayed places and exposed the bed-mats. After this the wind and rain came in due season,[16] the five grains produced in abundance. For the space of three autumns the people had plenty, the praises of his virtue filled the land, and the smoke of cooking was also thick.

7th year, Summer, 4th month, 1st day. The Emperor was on his tower, and looking far and wide, saw smoke arising plentifully. On this day he addressed the Empress, saying: "We are now prosperous. What can there be to grieve for?" The Empress answered and said: "What dost thou mean by prosperity?" The Emperor said: "It is doubtless when the smoke fills the lands, and the people freely attain to wealth." The Empress went on to say: "The Palace enclosure is crumbling down, and there are no means of repairing it; the buildings are dilapidated so that the coverlets are exposed. Can this be called prosperity?" The Emperor said: "When Heaven establishes a Prince, it is for the sake of the people. The Prince must therefore make the people the foundation. For this reason the wise sovereigns of antiquity, if a single one of their subjects was cold and starving, cast the responsibility on themselves. Now the people's poverty is no other than Our poverty; the people's prosperity is none other than Our prosperity. There is no such thing as the people's being prosperous and yet the Prince in poverty." [17]

[15] The territory round the capital ruled immediately by the emperor. This is a Chinese phrase, not properly applicable to Japan at this period.

[16] The notion that the virtues of the emperor have a direct influence on the weather is, of course, Chinese.

[17] This whole episode is the composition of someone well acquainted with Chinese literature. The sentiments are throughout characteristically Chinese, and in several cases whole sentences are copied verbatim from Chinese works.

THE REFORM ERA

The way was cleared for the inauguration of the Taika reforms in 645 by the overthrow of the powerful Soga clan. Prior to this the *Nihongi* records many strange occurrences and calamities, as if Heaven were showing its displeasure over the Soga usurpation of imperial power. Then Fujiwara Kamatari and the future Emperor Tenchi appear on the scene as leaders of a "restoration." Kamatari, from the Nakatomi clan traditionally charged with Shinto priestly functions, is said to have declined several times the post of Superintendent of the Shinto religion. After his successful coup the Emperor he installed on the throne is likewise identified in the *Nihongi* as one who "despised the Way of the Gods (Shinto)." Kamatari devoted himself to Chinese learning and is cast by the historian in the role of the Duke of Chou, the statesman instrumental in founding the Chou dynasty in China and in establishing what was regarded by Confucianists as the ideal social order.

[Adapted from Aston, *Nihongi*, II, 184–239]

Fujiwara Kamatari and the Future Emperor Tenchi
[Adapted from Aston, *Nihongi*, II, 184–85]

The Deity Chieftain Nakatomi no Kamako [Fujiwara Kamatari] was a man of an upright and loyal character and of a reforming disposition. He was indignant with Soga no Iruka for breaking down the order of Prince and Vassal, of Senior and Junior, and cherishing veiled designs upon the State. One after another he associated with the Princes of the imperial line, trying them in order to discover a wise ruler who might establish a great reputation. He had accordingly fixed his mind on Naka no Ōe, but for want of intimate relations with him he had been so far unable to unfold his inner sentiments. Happening to be one of a football [1] party in which Naka no Ōe [the future Tenchi] played at the foot of the keyaki tree of the Temple of Hōkōji, he observed the [Prince's] leathern shoe fall off with the ball. Placing it on the palm of his hand, he knelt before the Prince and humbly offered it to him. Naka no Ōe in his turn knelt down and respectfully received it. From this time they became mutual friends, and told each other all their thoughts. There was no longer any concealment between them. They feared, however, that jealous suspicions might be caused by their frequent meetings

[1] What kind of football—like ours, or in Chinese fashion, knocking the ball from one to another like a shuttle-cock—does not appear.

and they both took in their hands yellow rolls,[2] and studied personally the doctrines of Chou [3] and Confucius with the learned Minabuchi. Thus they at length while on their way there and back, walking shoulder to shoulder, secretly prepared their plans. On all points they were agreed.

Inauguration of the Great Reform Era

After the assassination of the Soga leaders, the reigning empress abdicated and a new government was formed with the future Tenchi as Crown Prince and Kamatari as Chief Minister actually directing affairs. A new reign and era title was therefore announced, Taika, meaning "Great Transformation."

[Adapted from Aston, *Nihongi,* II, 197–98]

4th year of Kōkyoku (645), 6th month, 19th day. The Emperor, the Empress Dowager, and the Prince Imperial summoned together the Ministers under the great tsuki tree, and made an oath appealing to the Gods of Heaven and Earth, and saying:

"Heaven covers Us: Earth upbears Us: the imperial way is but one. But in this last degenerate age, the order of Lord and Vassal was destroyed, until Supreme Heaven by Our hands put to death the traitors. Now, from this time forward, both parties shedding their heart's blood, the Lord will eschew double methods of government, and the Vassal will avoid duplicity in his service of the sovereign! On him who breaks this oath, Heaven will send a curse and earth a plague, demons will slay them, and men will smite them. This is as manifest as the sun and moon." [4]

The style 4th year of the Empress Ame-toyo-takara ikashi-hi tarashi-hime was altered to Taika, 1st year.

Reform Edicts

Only a few of the most important edicts are included here, outlining the major steps taken by the court to extend its political and fiscal control over the country. These aimed at establishing centralized administration of the Chinese type over areas which previously had enjoyed considerable autonomy under hereditary clan chieftains.

[Adapted from Aston, *Nihongi,* II, 200–226]

[2] Chinese books.
[3] The Duke of Chou, statesman and sage instrumental in founding the Chou dynasty in China. [Ed.]
[4] It may be noted that there is nothing Buddhist or Shinto in this vow. It is pure Chinese. It is not exactly an oath according to our ideas, but an imprecation on rebellion.

1st year of Taika [645], 8th month, 5th day. Governors of the Eastern provinces were appointed. Then the Governors were addressed as follows: "In accordance with the charge entrusted to Us by the Gods of Heaven, We propose at this present for the first time to regulate the myriad provinces.

"When you proceed to your posts, prepare registers of all the free subjects of the State and of the people under the control of others, whether great or small. Take account also of the acreage of cultivated land. As to the profits arising from the gardens and ponds, the water and land, deal with them in common with the people. Moreover it is not competent for the provincial Governors, while in their provinces, to decide criminal cases, nor are they permitted by accepting bribes to bring the people to poverty and misery. When they come up to the capital they must not bring large numbers of the people in their train. They are only allowed to bring with them the Local Chieftains and the district officials. But when they travel on public business they may ride the horses of their department, and eat the food of their department. From the rank of Suke [5] upwards those who obey this law will surely be rewarded, while those who disobey it shall be liable to be reduced in cap-rank. On all, from the rank of Hangan [6] downwards, who accept bribes a fine shall be imposed of double the amount, and they shall eventually be punished criminally according to the greater or less heinousness of the case. Nine men are allowed as attendants on a Chief Governor, seven on an assistant, and five on a secretary. If this limit is exceeded, and they are accompanied by a greater number, both chief and followers shall be punished criminally.

"If there be any persons who lay claim to a title [7] but who, not being Local Chieftains, Imperial Chieftains, or Custodians [8] of districts by descent, unscrupulously draw up lying memorials, saying: 'From the time of our forefathers we have had charge of this Miyake or have ruled this district,' in such cases, ye, the Governors, must not readily make application to the court in acquiescence in such fictions, but must ascertain particularly the true facts before making your report.

"Moreover on waste pieces of ground let arsenals be erected, and let the swords and armor, with the bows and arrows of the provinces and

[5] Assistant to a governor.
[7] Literally, name.
[6] Assistant district chief.
[8] Collectors and guardians of tax grain.

districts, be deposited together in them. In the case of the frontier provinces which border close on the Emishi,[9] let all the weapons be mustered together, and let them remain in the hands of their original owners. In regard to the six districts of the province of Yamato, let the officials who are sent there prepare registers of the population, and also take into account the acreage of cultivated land.

"This means to examine the acreage of the cultivated ground, and the numbers, houses, and ages of the people." [pp. 200–201]

. . . .

9th month, 19th day. Commissioners were sent to all the provinces to take a record of the total numbers of the people. The Emperor on this occasion made an edict, as follows:

"In the times of all the Emperors, from antiquity downwards, subjects have been set apart for the purpose of making notable their reigns and handing down their names to posterity. Now the Imperial Chieftains and Deity Chieftains, the Court Chieftains and Local Chieftains, have each one set apart their own vassals, whom they compel to labor at their arbitrary pleasure. Moreover they cut off the hills and seas, the woods and plains, the ponds and rice-fields belonging to the provinces and districts, and appropriate them to themselves. Their contests are never-ceasing. Some engross to themselves many tens of thousand of *shiro*[10] of rice-land, while others possess in all patches of ground too small to stick a needle into. When the time comes for the payment of taxes, the Imperial Chieftains, the Deity Chieftains and the Court Chieftains, first collect them for themselves and then hand over a share. In the case of repairs to palaces or the construction of misasagi, they each bring their own vassals, and do the work according to circumstances. The Book of Changes says: 'Diminish that which is above: increase that which is below: if measures are framed according to the regulations, the resources [of the State] suffer no injury, and the people receive no hurt.'

"At the present time, the people are still few. And yet the powerful cut off portions of land and water,[11] and converting them into private ground, sell it to the people, demanding the price yearly. From this time forward the sale of land is not allowed. Let no man without due authority make

---

[9] Ainu.   [10] A land measure of 15.13 acres.
[11] That is, rice ground and other cultivated land.

himself a landlord, engrossing to himself that which belongs to the helpless."

The people were greatly rejoiced. [pp. 204–5]

. . . .

2nd year [646], Spring, 1st month, 1st day. As soon as the ceremonies of the new year's congratulations were over, the Emperor promulgated an edict of reform, as follows:

"I. Let the people established by the ancient Emperors, etc., as representatives of children be abolished, also the Miyake of various places and the people owned as serfs by the Wake, the Imperial Chieftains, the Deity Chieftains, Court Chieftains, Local Chieftains and the Village Headmen. Let the farmsteads [12] in various places be abolished." Consequently fiefs [13] were granted for their sustenance to those of the rank of Daibu and upwards on a descending scale. Presents of cloth and silk stuffs were given to the officials and people, varying in value.

"Further We say. It is the business of the Daibu to govern the people. If they discharge this duty thoroughly, the people have trust in them, and an increase of their revenue is therefore for the good of the people.

"II. The capital is for the first time to be regulated, and Governors appointed for the Home provinces and districts. Let barriers, outposts, guards, and post-horses, both special and ordinary, be provided, bell-tokens [14] made, and mountains and rivers regulated.[15]

"For each ward in the capital let there be appointed one alderman, and for four wards one chief alderman, who shall be charged with the superintendence of the population, and the examination of criminal matters. For appointment as chief alderman of wards let men be taken belonging to the wards, of unblemished character, firm and upright, so that they may fitly sustain the duties of the time. For appointment as aldermen, whether of rural townships or of city wards, let ordinary subjects be taken belonging to the township or ward, of good character and solid capacity. If such men are not to be found in the township or ward in

[12] Of serfs.

[13] Not a true feudal domain, but lands from which these officials could draw the tax proceeds as a form of salary. [Ed.]

[14] Signs of rank indicating the number of horses an official was entitled to—a Chinese practice.

[15] By the regulation of mountains and rivers is meant the provision of guards at ferries and mountain passes which serve as boundaries between different provinces.

question, it is permitted to select and employ men of the adjoining township or ward.

"The Home provinces shall include the region from the River Yokogawa at Nabari on the east, from Mount Senoyama in Kii on the south, from Kushibuchi in Akashi on the west, and from Mount Afusakayama in Sasanami in Afumi on the north. Districts of forty townships[16] are constituted Greater Districts, of from thirty to four townships are constituted Middle Districts, and of three or fewer townships are constituted Lesser Districts. For the district authorities, of whatever class, let there be taken Local Chieftains of unblemished character, such as may fitly sustain the duties of the time, and made Tairei and Shōrei.[17] Let men of solid capacity and intelligence who are skilled in writing and arithmetic be appointed assistants and clerks.

"The number of special or ordinary post-horses given shall in all cases follow the number of marks on the posting bell-tokens. When bell-tokens are given to [officials of] the provinces and barriers, let them be held in both cases by the chief official, or in his absence by the assistant official.

"III. Let there now be provided for the first time registers of population, books of account and a system of the receipt and regranting of distribution-land.[18]

"Let every fifty houses be reckoned a township, and in every township let there be one alderman who shall be charged with the superintendence of the population,[19] the direction of the sowing of crops and the cultivation of mulberry trees, the prevention and examination of offenses, and the enforcement of the payment of taxes and of forced labor.

"For rice-land, thirty paces in length by twelve paces in breadth shall be reckoned a tan.[20] Ten tan make one chō. For each tan the tax is two sheaves and two bundles [such as can be grasped in the hand] of rice; for each chō the tax is twenty-two sheaves of rice. On mountains or in valleys where the land is precipitous, or in remote places where the population is scanty, such arrangements are to be made as may be convenient.

[16] A township consisted of 50 houses.   [17] Greater and Lesser Governors.
[18] The Denryō (Land Regulations) says, "In granting Kō-bun-den (land shared in proportion to population) men shall have two tan, women a third less, and children under five years of age none. Lands are granted for a term of six years."
[19] That is, of the registers of population.
[20] Allowing five feet to the pace, this would make the tan 9,000 square feet.

"IV. The old taxes and forced labor are abolished, and a system of commuted taxes instituted. These shall consist of fine silks, coarse silks, raw silk, and floss silk, all in accordance with what is produced in the locality. For each *chō* of rice-land the rate is one rod [21] of fine silk, or for four *chō* one piece forty feet in length by two and a half feet in width. For coarse silk the rate is two rods [per *chō*], or one piece for every two *chō* of the same length and width as the fine silk. For cloth the rate is four rods of the same dimensions as the fine and coarse silk, i.e., one *tan* [22] for each *chō*. [No rates of weight are anywhere given for silk or floss silk.] Let there be levied separately a commuted house tax. All houses shall pay each one rod and two feet of cloth. The extra articles of this tax, as well as salt and offerings, will depend on what is produced in the locality. For horses for the public service, let every hundred houses contribute one horse of medium quality. Or if the horse is of superior quality, let one be contributed by every two hundred houses. If the horses have to be purchased, the price shall be made up by a payment from each house of one rod and two feet of cloth. As to weapons, each person shall contribute a sword, armor, bow and arrows, a flag, and a drum. For coolies, the old system, by which one coolie was provided by every thirty houses, is altered, and one coolie is to be furnished from every fifty houses (one is for employment as a menial servant) for allotment to the various functionaries. Fifty houses shall be allotted to provide rations for one coolie, and five *masu* [23] of rice in lieu of service.

"For waiting women in the Palace, let there be furnished the sisters or daughters of district officials of the rank of Shōrei or upwards—good-looking women (with one male and two female servants to attend on them) and let one hundred houses be allotted to provide rations for one waiting-woman. The cloth and rice supplied in lieu of service shall, in every case, follow the same rule as for coolies." [pp. 206–9]

. . . .

Autumn, 8th month, 14th day. An edict was issued saying:
"Going back to the origin of things, We find that it is Heaven and Earth with the male and female principles of nature,[24] which guard the four seasons from mutual confusion. We find, moreover, that it is this

---

[21] Ten feet.

[22] There are two *tan* to the *hiki* or piece, which now measures about 21½ yards.

[23] Or *shō* = 109 cubic inches.   [24] The yin and yang of Chinese philosophy.

Heaven and Earth [25] which produces the ten thousand things. Amongst these ten thousand things Man is the most miraculously gifted. Among the most miraculously gifted beings, the sage takes the position of ruler. Therefore the sage-rulers, viz. the Emperors, take Heaven as their exemplar in ruling the World, and never for a moment dismiss from their breasts the thought of how men shall gain their fit place.

"Now as to the names of the early Princes, the Imperial Chieftains, Deity Chieftains, Court Chieftains and Local Chieftains have divided their various hereditary corporations [26] and allotted them severally to their various titles (or surnames). They afterwards took the various hereditary corporations of the people, and made them reside in the provinces and districts, one mixed up with another. The consequence has been to make father and child to bear different surnames, and brothers to be reckoned of distinct families, while husbands and wives have names different from one another. One family is divided into five or split up into six, and both court and country are therefore filled with contentious suits. No settlement has been come to, and the mutual confusion grows worse and worse. Let the various hereditary corporations, therefore, beginning with those of the reigning Emperor and including those in the possession of the Imperial and Deity Chieftains, etc., be, without exception, abolished, and let them become subjects of the State. Those who have become Court Chieftains by borrowing the names of princes, and those who have become Imperial or Deity Chieftains on the strength of the names of ancestors, may not fully apprehend Our purport, and might think, if they heard this announcement without warning, that the names borrowed by their ancestors would become extinct. We therefore make this announcement beforehand, so that they may understand what are Our intentions." [pp. 223-24]

. . . .

"Let the local Governors who are now being dispatched, and also the Local Chieftains of the same provinces, give ear to what We say. In regard to the method of administration notified last year to the Court Assembly, let the previous arrangement be followed, and let the rice lands which are received and measured be granted equally to the people, with-

---

[25] That is, Nature.
[26] Instituted in commemoration of princes and bearing their names, or names intended to recall their memory.

out distinction of persons. In granting rice lands the peasants' houses should adjoin the land. Those whose houses lie near the lands must therefore have the preference. In this sense receive Our injunctions.

"In regard to commuted taxes,[27] they should be collected from males [only].

"Laborers should be supplied at the rate of one for every fifty houses. The boundaries of the provinces should be examined and a description or map prepared, which should be brought here and produced for Our inspection. The names of the provinces and districts will be settled when you come.

"With respect to the places where embankments are to be constructed, or canals dug, and the extent of rice land to be brought under cultivation, in the various provinces, uniform provision will be made for causing such work to be executed.

"Give ear to and understand these injunctions." [pp. 225–26]

The White Pheasant

Just as in the years preceding the Great Reform many calamities and bad omens are recorded in the *Nihongi* to justify a change of rule, so in after years auspicious events are recorded to show how Heaven favored the new regime. The greatest stir at court was over the discovery of a white pheasant, a sign interpreted with reference to Chinese legendry as if this were the authentic heritage of Japan itself. The episode is thus an apt illustration of the Han Confucian view in politics and the writing of history.

[Adapted from Aston, *Nihongi,* II, 236–39]

Hakuchi era, 1st year [650], 2nd month, 9th day. Shikofu, Deity Chieftain of Kusakabe, Governor of the Province of Anato, presented to the Emperor a white pheasant, saying: "Nihe, a relation of Obito, the Local Chieftain, caught it on the 9th day of the first month on Mount Onoyama." Upon this inquiry was made of the Lords of Paekche, who said: "In the eleventh year of Yung-p'ing [A.D. 68], in the reign of Ming Ti of the Later Han dynasty, white pheasants were seen in a certain place." Further, inquiry was made of the Buddhist priests, who answered and said: "With our ears we have not heard, nor with our eyes have we seen such. May it please Your Majesty to order a general amnesty; and so give joy to the hearts of the people."

. . . .

[27] Of other things than rice.

[76]

The Priest Bin said: "This is to be deemed a lucky omen, and it may reasonably be accounted a rare object. I have respectfully heard that when a Ruler extends his influence to all four quarters, then will white pheasants be seen. They appear, moreover, when a Ruler's sacrifices are not in mutual disaccord, and when his banquets and costumes are in due measure. Again, when a Ruler is of frugal habits, white pheasants are made to come forth on the hills. Again, they appear when the Ruler is sage and humane. In the time of the Emperor Ch'ēng Wang of the Chou Dynasty, the Yüeh-shang[28] family brought and presented to the Emperor a white pheasant, saying: 'We were told by the old men of our country: "What a long time it has been since there have been any exceptional storms or long-continued rains, and that the great rivers and the sea have not surged up over the land! Three years have now elapsed. We think that in the Central Land there is a Sage. Would it not be well to go and pay your respects at his court?" We have therefore come, having tripled our interpreters.' Again, in the first year of Hsien-ning[29] in the reign of Wu-ti of the Tsin Dynasty, one was seen in Sung-tzu. This is accordingly a favorable omen. A general amnesty ought to be granted."

Upon this the white pheasant was let loose in the garden.

15th day. The array of guards at court was like that on the occasion of a New Year's reception. The Great Ministers of the Right and Left and all the functionaries formed four lines outside of the purple gate. Ihimushi, Imperial Chieftain of Ahata, and three others were made to take the pheasant's litter and move off ahead. . . . These four men . . . taking up the pheasant's litter in turn, advanced in front of the Hall. Then the Great Ministers of the Right and Left approached and held the litter by the forward end. The Prince of Ise, Maro, Lord of Mikuni, and Oguso, Imperial Chieftain of Kura, took hold of the hinder end of the litter and placed it before the imperial throne. The Emperor straightway called the Prince Imperial, and they took it and examined it together. The Prince Imperial having retired, made repeated obeisances, and caused the Great Minister Kose to offer a congratulatory address, saying: "The Ministers and functionaries offer their congratulations. Inasmuch as Your Majesty governs the Empire with serene virtue, there is here a white pheasant, produced in the western region. This is a sign that Your Majesty will continue for a thousand autumns and ten thousand years peacefully to govern the Great eight-islands of the four quarters. It is

[28] The name of a region lying to the south of China.   [29] A.D. 275.

the prayer of the Ministers, functionaries, and people that they may serve Your Majesty with the utmost zeal and fidelity."

Having finished this congratulatory speech, he made repeated obeisances. The Emperor said:

"When a sage Ruler appears in the world and rules the Empire, Heaven is responsive to him, and manifests favorable omens. In ancient times, during the reign of Ch'ēng-wang of the Chou Dynasty, a ruler of the Western land,[30] and again in the time of Ming Ti of the Han Dynasty, white pheasants were seen. In this Our Land of Japan, during the reign of the Emperor Homuda,[31] a white crow made its nest in the Palace. In the time of the Emperor Ō-sazaki,[32] a Dragon-horse appeared in the West.[33] This shows that from ancient times until now, there have been many cases of auspicious omens appearing in response to virtuous rulers. What we call phoenixes, unicorns, white pheasants, white crows, and such like birds and beasts, even including herbs and trees, in short all things having the property of significant response, are favorable omens and auspicious signs produced by Heaven and Earth. Now that wise and enlightened sovereigns should obtain such auspicious omens is meet and proper. But why should We, who are so empty and shallow, have this good fortune? It is no doubt wholly due to Our Assistants, the Ministers, Imperial Chieftains, Deity Chieftains, Court Chieftains and Local Chieftains, each of whom, with the utmost loyalty, conforms to the regulations that are made. For this reason, let all, from the Ministers down to the functionaries, with pure hearts reverence the Gods of Heaven and Earth, and one and all accepting the glad omen, make the Empire to flourish."

Again he commanded, saying:

"The provinces and districts in the four quarters having been placed in Our charge by Heaven, We exercise supreme rule over the Empire. Now in the province of Anato, ruled over by Our divine ancestors, this auspicious omen has appeared. For this reason We proclaim a general amnesty throughout the Empire, and begin a new year-period, to be called White Pheasant. Moreover We prohibit the flying of falcons within the limits of the province of Anato."

[30] China. [31] Ōjin Tennō. [32] Nintoku Tennō.
[33] The dragon-horse has wings on its head. It crosses water without sinking. It appears when an illustrious sovereign is on the throne.

THE COMMENTARY ON THE LEGAL CODE
(RYŌ NO GIGE)

One of the principal Chinese influences on the thought of early Japan was exerted by the legal codes of T'ang China. As early as the reign of the Emperor Tenchi (662–71) there appears to have been compiled a Japanese code, but almost nothing of it remains. The Taihō Code of 701–2, on the other hand, continued to be the basic law of Japan until after the Meiji Restoration of 1868. In this code many Chinese institutions were taken over directly in spite of their unsuitability for the far less developed society of Japan. An elaborate bureaucracy was organized based on the merit system. The Taihō Code was not, however, a mere copy of T'ang precedents. New provisions were also made for the Shinto priesthood and other peculiarly Japanese institutions.

The laws themselves came to assume an even greater importance for the Japanese than they did for the Chinese, and occupied a central place in Japanese thinking for many centuries. The commentary on the legal code of 834 was an extremely successful attempt to interpret the laws and show their significance for Japanese society.

Memorial on the Submission of the Commentary on the Legal Code
[From the Kokushi Taikei, XXII, 348–50]

Your subjects, Natsuno [1] and others, report: the study of the successive rulers of old and the perusal of early writings show that whenever a sovereign assuming the succession mounted the throne, took his position facing South,[2] and declared himself Emperor, decrees were invariably announced and the law proclaimed as the warp and woof of the government of the country. Rites and punishments were also established to serve as a bulwark in the protection of the dynasty. Although, just as dragons and phoenixes differ in their appearance, some rulers favored literary pursuits and others the simple virtues, they all arrived by different roads at the same end of instructing the common people and protecting them.

Your subjects prostrate themselves and state as their considered opinion: Your Majesty, whose Way shines to the four quarters and whose Virtue surpasses that of all kings, sits impassively in marble halls, a model to the world. Wherever in your domains human society exists, rites and music

[1] Kiyohara no Natsuno (782–837).
[2] In the yin-yang cosmology the ruler's place was in the north, facing south. He was likened to the North Star, to which all the other stars "bow."

are in honor; and as far as your powerful influence extends, all men, civilized and barbarian alike, show joyful appreciation. Now Your Majesty, who rises so early he dresses in darkness, lest the conduct of government go amiss; and who neglects eating until it is late because of his concern for the people's happiness, has issued an edict decreeing that experts in law be found. It was your consideration that the interpretations of earlier scholars were at times contradictory; the shallow observations tended to get mixed with the profound; and their merits were difficult to judge.

Your subjects cannot approach Chang Ts'ang in scholarship, nor Ch'en Ch'ung in achievements.[3] Mediocre of talent as we are, how great was our honor in accepting your appointment! We have attempted to revise and correct the legal writings, now adding and now deleting. Whenever there were problems which we could not solve, or ambiguities which could not be cleared up, we always looked up to Your Majesty's august rulings for our authority. New times require new laws, which are in the spirit of those of ancient times, but suited to the present. Indeed, these laws will change the ways of thought of the people, and will also serve as a guide for all rulers. The compilation is in ten volumes and is entitled the *Commentary on the Legal Code.* Five years elapsed before the fair copy could be completed and respectfully submitted.

Your subjects, Natsuno and others, bow their heads and, with awe and trepidation, offer these words. [28th January 834.]

Regulations for Fitness Reports

A merit system of recruitment and promotion was the heart of the imperial bureaucracy in China. Here the Japanese attempt to duplicate it. Eventually inability to overcome by these means the strong native tradition of hereditary rank and office-holding completely vitiated the civil service system and with it the whole bureaucratic structure.

[From *Kokushi Taikei,* XXII, 149–56]

Fitness reports must be submitted annually by the chief of every department for all civil and military officers under his command in the court or in the provinces. The merits, demerits, conduct, and abilities of all persons for whom reports are made should be recorded in detail, so

---

[3] Chang Ts'ang (d. 161 B.C.) and Ch'en Ch'ung (d. A.D. 107) were noted statesmen and lawgivers of the Han dynasty.

that they may be consulted in classifying the officers into nine grades of merit. The reports must be completed by the thirtieth day of the eighth moon. Reports on officers stationed in the capital or the provinces of the Inner Circuit should be submitted to the Great Council of State by the first day of the tenth moon; reports for officers in other provinces should be submitted not later than the first day of the eleventh moon through the Imperial Inspectors. Acts of merit or demerit performed after the submission of reports should be entered in the records of the following year. In case a department is without a chief, the fitness reports should be made by a vice-chief.

Reports on the acts and merits of all officers should be in the form of a day-to-day account. In cases where a private offense committed during a previous term of office is uncovered and judgment is to be passed on it, it should be treated as though it had been committed during the present term. If it is then decided to remove the officer from his position, the length of his previous service and his record should be taken into consideration.

Chiefs of department submitting fitness reports must state only the facts with no interpolations of either favorable or unfavorable material. If a false report results in an unwarranted promotion or demotion, or if an officer's actual fitness is concealed so that his rank will be raised or lowered, the reporting officer responsible shall be demoted in accordance with the seriousness of his error. An imperial inspector who promotes or demotes an officer in disregard of his record shall similarly be held responsible.

Merits:
1. When an officer has a reputation for virtue and a sense of duty, it is to be counted as a merit.
2. When an officer's honesty and conscientiousness are evident, it is to be counted as a merit.
3. When an officer's devotion to public good and justice arouses praise, it is to be counted as a merit.
4. When an officer performs faithful and diligent service, it is to be counted as a merit.

Articles of Excellence:
To carry out the festivals and ceremonies of the Deities of Heaven and

Earth in exact compliance with established procedure is to be counted the excellence of a Shinto official.

To address memorials in favor of that which is advantageous to the state and against that which is harmful; and to discuss government business in accordance with reason are to be counted the excellence of a Major Counsellor.

To act in strict accord with instructions received; and to be clear and fluent of speech are to be counted the excellence of a Minor Counsellor.

To handle general state business; and to dispose of it without delay are to be counted the excellence of a Controller.

To wait in attendance on the Emperor and transmit memorials to him; and to be prompt in the execution of his duties are to be counted the excellence of an officer of the Ministry of Central Affairs.

To evaluate men; and to select all those of ability and talent are to be counted the excellence of an officer of the Ministry of Ceremony.

To hold monks and nuns to the teachings of Buddha; and to keep registered subjects under control are to be counted the excellence of an officer of the Ministry of Civil Administration.

To maintain order among the population; and to ensure abundant supplies in the storehouses are to be counted the excellence of an officer of the Ministry of the Interior.

To select military officers; and to prepare munitions of war are to be counted the excellence of an officer of the Ministry of Military Affairs.

To pass judgments without delay; and to give rewards or exact punishments justly are to be counted the excellence of an officer of the Ministry of Justice.

To be scrupulous in the care of deposits; and to be well-informed of expenditures and receipts are to be counted the excellence of an officer of the Ministry of the Treasury.

To be competent in furnishing provisions; and to expedite the management of the various departments of the Palace are to be counted the excellence of an officer of the Ministry of the Imperial Household.

To be energetic in investigations and competent in the arraignment of suspects is to be counted the excellence of a Censor.

To promote good manners and morals; and to suppress robbery and banditry are to be counted the excellence of an Officer of the Capital.

To prepare the imperial meals; and to observe faultless cleanliness are to be counted the excellence of a Commissioner of Food.

To maintain rigid discipline and constant vigilance is to be counted the excellence of a Guards officer.

To ensure that music is well harmonized and does not fall into discord is to be counted the excellence of an officer of the Bureau of Music.

To keep order among monks and nuns; and to see to it that aliens are lodged in suitable quarters are to be counted the excellence of an officer of the Bureau of Buddhism and Aliens.

To budget court expenditures; and to be accurate in accounting are to be counted the excellence of an officer of the Bureau of Statistics.

To be scrupulous in the care of storehouses; and to be well-informed about incoming and outgoing shipments are to be counted the excellence of an officer of the Bureau of Tax Collection.

To feed, train, and stable horses; and to have grooms available are to be counted the excellence of an officer of the Bureau of Horses.

To dry in the sun or air stores with care; and to be well-informed about incoming and outgoing shipments are to be counted the excellence of an officer of the Bureau of Military Storehouses.

To serve in constant attendance at court; and to repair omissions and supplement deficiencies are to be counted the excellence of a Chamberlain.

To engage in unremitting supervision; and to be accurately informed about all incoming and outgoing property are to be counted the excellence of an Inspector-Official.

To perform night watch in the Palace; and to behave in perfect conformity to etiquette are to be counted the excellence of a Lord in Waiting.

To regulate official business; and to see to it that office hours are properly observed are to be counted the excellence of all officers of the secondary rank and above.

To promote the pure and to remove evil-doers; and to ensure that praise or censure is properly given are to be counted the excellence of a Commissioner of Personnel.

To carry out examinations in a thorough and detailed manner; and to be familiar with all types of affairs are to be counted the excellence of a judge.

To engage unremittingly in public service; and to perform one's work without oversights are to be counted the excellence of all officers.

To be assiduous in keeping records; and to examine into failings without glossing over them are to be counted the excellence of a clerk.

To keep detailed records in model order; and to excel both in language and in reasoning are to be counted the excellence of an historian.

To be clear in the recording of facts; and to communicate successfully imperial orders are to be counted the excellence of a palace scribe.

To be methodical in instruction; and to fit students for their work are to be counted the excellence of a Learned Scholar.

To be effective in yin-yang divination, astronomy, medicine, and fortunetelling is to be counted the excellence of a diviner.

To observe the motions of the celestial bodies; and to be accurate in the calculation of their movements are accounted the excellence of a Scholar of the Calendar.

To supervise markets and shops; and to prevent cheating and other forms of deception are accounted the excellence of a Markets Officer.

To investigate the facts of a case; and to reveal their circumstances are accounted the excellence of a Constable.

To perform state ceremonies; and to maintain suitable military preparations are accounted the excellence of the Governor General of Kyūshū.

To be strict in the administration of all business; and to insist on the honesty of his subordinates are accounted the excellence of a provincial governor.

To be impartial in his dealings with local people; and accomplished in his official duties are accounted the excellence of an assistant governor.

To keep the coast guard in fighting trim; and to have munitions ready for an emergency are accounted the excellence of the Coast Guards Officer.

To be brief in his questions and not to delay travelers unnecessarily is accounted the excellence of a barrier-keeper.

An officer who possesses four merits in addition to the excellence suited to his post is to be classified Superior, First Class.

An officer who possesses three merits in addition to his excellence, or who possesses four merits without his excellence, is to be classified Superior, Second Class.

An officer who possesses two merits in addition to his excellence, or who possesses three merits without his excellence, is to be classified Superior, Third Class.

An officer who possesses one merit in addition to his excellence, or who possesses two merits without his excellence, is to be classified Medium, First Class.

An officer who possesses his excellence but no merits, or who possesses one merit without his excellence, is to be classified Medium, Second Class.

An officer who has a crude competence in his position, but possesses neither a merit nor his excellence, is to be classified Medium, Third Class.

An officer who indulges in his own likes and dislikes and who is unreasonable in his judgments is to be classified Inferior, First Class.

An officer who acts against the public interest for personal reasons and fails in his official duties is to be classified Inferior, Second Class.

An officer who flatters and lies, or who appears avaricious and dishonest, is to be classified Inferior, Third Class.

Special consideration should be given when an officer's record is being reviewed whether he possesses praiseworthy characteristics not covered under the list of merits or excellences; or whether, if he is guilty of some offense, there are not extenuating circumstances; or whether, if he is technically guiltless, he should nevertheless be condemned.

NEW COMPILATION OF THE REGISTER OF FAMILIES

The importance of genealogy in determining claims to sovereignty was demonstrated by the *Records of Ancient Matters* (A.D. 712). The Japanese, who thus stressed the divine descent of the imperial family, were confirmed in this by the Han view of the Mandate of Heaven as conferred, not on individuals, but on dynasties which themselves had been provided with genealogies going back to the sage-kings. However, in the following preface, in that to the *Kojiki,* and in several Taika edicts, there is evidence that Japanese family genealogies were in a great state of confusion until the seventh century, when Chinese histories were brought over containing well-ordered genealogies of important families. This no doubt inspired the Japanese to draw up similar records, not only of the imperial house, but of all important families. The *New Compilation of the Register of Families (Shinsen shōji-roku,* A.D. 815) is one result of this development.

The influx of Korean and Chinese immigrants during the Nara Period and earlier had in some respects presented a challenge to the Japanese, for the immigrants were clearly superior to the Japanese in their knowledge of the techniques of civilization. The advantage that the Japanese claimed was their descent from the gods, and to this heritage they jealously clung.

In the *Register of Families,* the names given are divided into three classes: "All descendants of heavenly and earthly deities are designated as the Divine Group; all branches of the families of Emperors and royal princes are called the Imperial Group; and families from China and Korea are called the Alien Group." It perhaps seems surprising that the "descendants of heavenly and earthly deities" (who must have included a good part of the Japanese population) should have been mentioned before the imperial family. However, since these deities ruled over the land of Japan before the arrival of the imperial family from Heaven, they deserved their pride of place.

Preface in the Form of a Memorial to Emperor Saga
[From the *Kōgaku Sōsho,* IV, 123–24]

They say that the Divine Dynasty had its inception when the Grandson of Heaven descended to the land of So [1] and extended his influence in the West,[2] but no written records are preserved of these events. In the years when Jimmu assumed command of the state and undertook his campaign to the East, conditions grew steadily more confused, and some tribal leaders rose in revolt. When, however, the Heaven-sent sword appeared and the Golden Kite flew to earth,[3] the chieftains surrendered in great numbers and the rebels vanished like mist. Jimmu, accepting the Mandate of Heaven, erected a palace in the central province and administered justice. Peace reigned throughout the country. Land was allotted to men who were deemed virtuous in accordance with their merits. Heads of clans were granted such titles as Local Chieftain [*Kuni-no-miyatsuko*] and District Chieftain [*Agata-nushi*] for the first time.

Suinin [4] cultivated good fortune by his ever-renewed benevolent favors. Through such acts the Golden Mean was attained. [At this time] clans and families were gradually distinguished one from the other. More-

[1] An ancient name for the southern part of the island of Kyūshū. Location of Mount Takachiho where Ninigi, the Grandson of Heaven, made his descent. (See p. 18.)

[2] Kyūshū is in the west of Japan.

[3] Signs confirming Jimmu's divine right to imperial dominion. (See Aston, *Nihongi,* I, 115, 126.)

[4] The name Suinin means "to be benevolent" (of an emperor), and may have that meaning here rather than that of a proper name.

over, Imna came under our influence and Silla brought tribute. Later, barbarians from other countries, in due reverence for his virtue, all wished to come to Japan. Out of solicitude for these aliens, he bestowed family names on them. This was an outstanding feature of the time.

During the reign of Inkyō,[5] however, family relationships were in great confusion. An edict was accordingly issued, ordering that oaths be tested by the trial of boiling water. Those whose oaths were true remained unscathed, while the perjurers were harmed. From this time onwards the clans and families were established and there were no impostors. Rivers ran in their proper courses.

While Kōgyoku held the Regalia,[6] however, the provincial records were all burnt, and the young and defenseless had no means of proving their antecedents. The designing and the strong redoubled their false claims. Then, when the Emperor Tenchi was Heir Apparent, Eseki, an archivist of the Funa family, presented to the court the charred remains of the records. In the year of metal and the horse (A.D. 670) the family registers were re-compiled and the relationships of clans and families were all clarified. From this time on revisions were always made by succeeding sovereigns from time to time.

During the Tempyō Shōro era (749–57), by special favor of the court, all aliens who had made application were granted family names. Since the same surnames were given to the immigrants as Japanese families possessed, uncertainty arose as to which families were of alien and which of native origin. There were commoners everywhere who pretended to be the scions of the high and the mighty, and immigrant aliens from the Korean kingdoms claimed to be the descendants of the Japanese deities. As time passed and people changed scarcely anyone was left who knew the facts.

During the latter part of the Tempyō Hōji era (757–65) controversies about these matters grew all the more numerous. A number of eminent scholars were therefore summoned to compile a register of families. Before their work was half completed, however, the government became involved in certain difficulties. The scholars were disbanded and the compilation was not resumed. . . .

Our present Sovereign,[7] of glorious fame, desired that the work be resumed at the point where it was abandoned. . . . We, his loyal sub-

[5] Traditional dates: A.D. 411–53.   [6] A.D. 642–45.   [7] Saga (809–23).

jects, in obedience to his edicts, have performed our task with reverence and assiduity. We have collected all the information so as to be able to sift the gold from the pebbles We have cleared the old records of confusion and have condensed into this new work the essential facts contained in them. New genealogies have been purged of fictitious matter and checked with the old records. The concision and simplicity of this work are such that its meaning will be apparent as the palm of one's hand. We have searched out the old and new, from the time of the Emperor Jimmu to the Kōnin era (811–24) to the best of our abilities. The names of 1,182 families are included in this work, which is in thirty volumes. It is entitled the "New Compilation of the Register of Families." It is not intended for pleasure-reading, and the style is far from polished. Since, however, it is concerned with the key to human relationships, it is an essential instrument in the hands of the nation.

Preface to the *Kaifūsō*

The *Kaifūsō*—"Fond Recollections of Poetry"—is the first anthology of poetry in Chinese written by Japanese. It was compiled in A.D. 751 but includes verses dating back some seventy-five years previous, to the reign of the Emperor Tenchi. The *Kaifūsō* is today chiefly of historical interest. It contains some of the earliest attempts by Japanese writers (including emperors and princes) to compose in literary Chinese, and therefore often gives more the effect of copybook exercises than true poetry. Even when the subject of a poem is Japanese—such as a visit to the Yoshino River—the main effort of the writer appears to be directed towards including as many allusions to Chinese literature and history as possible.

The preface to the *Kaifūsō* is an example of Chinese parallel prose. The style is rather clumsily handled by the unknown compiler, who is sometimes driven to desperate measures to maintain a parallel. Almost every sentence is jammed with allusions, some of them now extremely difficult to understand fully.

However imperfect the style and technique of this preface, it is important because it clearly shows how great the prestige of Chinese literature (and thought) was even during this early period.

[From (*Shinsen*) *Meika Shishū*, pp. 499–500]

From what I have heard of ancient practices and seen of the records of long ago, in the age of the divine descent from Heaven on the mountain of So and in the time when the country was founded at Kashiwabara,

Heaven's work was at its bare inception, and human culture was yet to flourish. When the Empress Jingū led the expedition over the water and the Emperor Ōjin mounted the throne, Paekche brought homage to the court and revealed the dragon-writing. Koguryo presented memorials inscribed with crow-writing and bird-writing. It was Wani who first brought learning to Karushima; Shinji later spread his teachings in the field of translation. He caused the people to become imbued with the breeze from the riversides dear to Confucius and Mencius, and made them direct their steps towards the doctrines of Ch'i and Lu.[1] With Prince Shōtoku the ranks of honor were established; the offices of government were demarcated; and court rites and ceremonies were for the first time regulated. However, because of the exclusive devotion shown to Buddhism, there was no time for literature. But when the former Emperor Ōmi received Heaven's mandate he vastly expanded the imperial achievements and widely extended the sovereign's counsels. His virtue reached to heaven and earth; his merit shone through the universe like sunlight. Thus did he long meditate: "To regulate customs and bring culture to the people, nothing is more valuable than literature; to cultivate virtues and make oneself resplendent in them, what could come before learning?" Therefore he founded schools and sought persons of flourishing talent. He determined the Five Rites and fixed the Hundred Regulations. The principles of government, the laws, and the rules of state were promulgated far and wide, as never before in history. Then the Three Classes enjoyed peace and glory; within the Four Seas reigned prosperity and wealth. The great dignitaries had surcease from their labors; the palace galleries knew much leisure. At times the emperor summoned men of letters; often great banquets were held. On these occasions the imperial brush let fall prose; the courtiers offered their eulogies in verse. Many more than a hundred were the pieces of chiseled prose and exquisite calligraphy. But with the passage of time, disorders reduced all these writings to ashes. How heart-rending it is to think of the destruction!

In later times men of letters occasionally appeared. A prince, a dragon apparent, made cranes soar in the clouds with his brush; a phoenix-like emperor floated his moonlit boat on misty waters. Ōkami, the Councillor of State, lamented his greying hair, and demonstrated the flourishing

[1] Native states of Mencius and Confucius.

fruits of his art during the last emperor's reign; Fujiwara, the Grand Minister, celebrated the imperial rule and caused his glorious voice to echo through later times.

My minor position at the court has permitted me the leisure to let my fancy wander in the garden of letters and to read the works left by the men of former days. When I recall now those sports with the moon and poetry, how blurred are my remembrances—yet, the words left by old brushes remain. As I go over the titles of the poems my thoughts are carried far away, and the tears flow without my realizing it. As I lift the lovely compositions, my mind searches the distant past, and I long for those voices which are now stilled.

Thus it has come about that I have collected the scraps left in the wall at Lu, and assembled the fragments remaining in the ashes left by Ch'in,[2] beginning with the long-ago reign at Ōmi and coming down to the court of Nara. Altogether I have included 120 pieces, enough to make a volume. I have listed in detail the names, court ranks, and origins of the sixty-four authors. Since my reason for making this anthology was to keep from oblivion the poetry of the great men of former days, I think it is proper to call the collection *Kaifū*—Fond Reminiscences.

It is the eleventh moon of the third year of Tempyō Shōhō [751], and the stars are at the juncture of metal and hare.

[2] Likening himself to the Han dynasty scholars who rediscovered and preserved the Confucian texts.

CHAPTER V

NARA BUDDHISM

In the tenth moon of A.D. 552 the King of Paekche sent to Japan an envoy with presents of an image of Buddha and sacred writings, apparently hoping thereby so to ingratiate himself with the Japanese court as to win their military support. Together with his presents he submitted a memorial lauding Buddhism in these terms:

This doctrine is amongst all doctrines the most excellent, but it is hard to explain and hard to comprehend. Even the Duke of Chou and Confucius could not attain a knowledge of it. This doctrine can create religious merit and retribution without measure and without bounds, and so lead on to a full appreciation of the highest wisdom. Imagine a man in possession of treasures to his heart's content, so that he might satisfy all his wishes in proportion as he used them. Thus it is with the treasure of this wonderful doctrine. Every prayer is fulfilled and naught is wanting. Moreover, from distant India it has extended hither to Korea, where there are none who do not receive it with reverence as it is preached to them.[1]

We are told that the Emperor Kimmei was so delighted with these tidings that he leapt for joy. The head of the Soga clan, no less affected, urged that Japan follow the lead of all other civilized nations in adopting the new religion. More conservative elements at the court objected, however, saying that the worship of foreign deities could not but incense the national gods. Soga was presented with the image and allowed to worship it, but when, shortly afterwards, a pestilence broke out, the Shinto adherents persuaded the emperor that it was a manifestation of the wrath of the gods. The image of Buddha was thrown into a moat, and the temple built by the Soga family was razed.

Nothing much more was heard of Buddhism until 584, when another member of the Soga clan was given two Buddhist images that had come from Korea. He erected a temple to enshrine them, and had three girls ordained as nuns by a Korean priest who happened to be living in Japan.

[1] Aston, *Nihongi*, II, 66.

This, we are informed by the *Chronicles of Japan,* marked the real beginning of Buddhism in the country. However, it was not long before another plague caused the Shinto factions to throw the holy images into the moat and to defrock the nuns. When these rigorous measures failed to halt the spread of the disease, the emperor finally agreed to allow the Soga family to worship Buddhism as it chose, and the nuns were given back their robes.

Within a few years of the second start of Buddhism in Japan, a number of learned Korean priests began to arrive. Among their most eager disciples was Prince Shōtoku, who is credited with having delivered lectures on three important sūtras to the Empress Suiko. Most of the emperors and empresses in the century following were devout Buddhists; indeed, the Nara Period (709–84) in some ways marks the high point of Buddhism in Japan.

It is not difficult to understand the success of the new religion. At the time of its introduction to Japan Buddhism was nearly a thousand years old and, as the first world religion, had marched triumphantly to the east and west, raising temples and monasteries, and filling grottoes and caves with an amazing profusion of art. It had become a well organized and tested faith constituted under its Three Treasures—Buddha, the Law (Dharma), and the Monastic orders (Sangha). It possessed a highly developed and decorated pantheon as its objects of worship, a tremendous accumulation of literature called the *Tripitaka,* and a priesthood dedicated to the propagation of the teachings by oaths of celibacy, sobriety, and poverty.

In this connection it should be stressed that the importance of Buddhist missionary activity in Japan went far beyond the propagation of the faith alone. Chinese and Korean monks, carried across stormy seas by religious zeal, at the same time served as the carriers of superior Chinese culture. They were no doubt well aware that identification or association with this high culture lent them great prestige in the eyes of admiring Japanese, but whether they chose to capitalize on this or not, it would in any case have been impossible to disengage this new religion from its cultural embodiment in China, the land of its adoption. To establish the new faith in Japan required the transplanting of essential articles— images, vestments, books, ritual devices—as well as of ideas. The Japanese apprenticeship in the study of Chinese writing was undoubtedly served in the copying by hand of large numbers of Buddhist sūtras, distributed by imperial order to the various temples and monasteries. Furthermore, to erect temples and monasteries carpenters and artisans had to be brought over along with missionary priests. This is illustrated by an entry in the *Nihongi* for the reign of Sujun (c. 588):

This year the land of Paekche sent envoys, and along with them the Buddhist priests, Hyejong [and others] with a present of Buddhist relics. The land of Paekche sent the Buddhist ecclesiastics Susin [and others] with tribute and also with a present of Buddhist relics, the Buddhist priest Yongjo, the ascetics Yongwi [and others], the temple carpenters Taeryangmidae and Mungagoja, a man learned in the art of making braziers and chargers, . . . men learned in pottery . . . and a painter named Poega.[2]

But it is apparent, too, that Buddhist priests were vessels for the transmission of branches of learning having no direct connection with religious doctrine or institutions, yet which they evidently regarded as being in no way incompatible with the former. Thus during the tenth year of Suiko (602) it is recorded:

A Paekche priest named Kwallŭk arrived and presented by way of tribute books of calendar-making, of astronomy and of geomancy, and also books on the art of invisibility and magic. At this time three or four pupils were selected and made to study under Kwallŭk. Ōchin, the ancestor of the scribes of Yako, studied the art of calendar-making. Kōsō, Otomo no Suguri, studied astronomy and the art of invisibility. Hinamitatsu, the Imperial Chieftain of Yamashiro, studied magic. They all studied so far as to perfect themselves in these arts.[3]

In the forms it took, Nara Buddhism was an extension of that of T'ang China. For example, it is in the Nara Period that we first hear of Buddhist sects in Japan, and it is usual to speak of the "Six Sects" then introduced from China. Some of them, particularly the two Hīnayāna sects, appear never to have been independent, having served primarily as forms of academic discipline for the priesthood. The three main philosophical features of Nara Buddhism were the dialectics of negation (Sanron or "Three-Treatises" sect, associated with the great Indian scholar Nāgārjuna and transmitted by Kumārajīva), the doctrine of the attainment of enlightenment through the powers of the mind (Hossō or

[2] Aston, *Nihongi*, II, 117.   [3] Aston, *Nihongi*, II, 126.

"Dharma-Character" sect, associated with Vasubandhu and Hsüan-tsang), and the metaphysics of the harmonious whole (taught by the Kegon or "Flower-Wreath" sect).

Common to these seemingly disparate ideas was the basic Buddhist doctrine of change, the antithesis of the rigidity of the Han Confucian picture of the world. Heaven was not considered as the unvarying model for life on earth, but as an outward manifestation of universal evolution. Buddhism insisted on the need to free ourselves from a reliance on external things in our attempt to reach ultimate reality. Externals are so changeable that they can only deceive. They must therefore be negated exhaustively, until all the usual distinctions of becoming, which arise from incomplete knowledge, are denied and perfect knowledge can be attained. Such was the teaching of Nāgārjuna. For the followers of the Hossō sect, the school of the great Chinese pilgrim Hsüan-tsang, the outer world did not exist at all, but was a creation of our own minds. How could man turn to the motions of the stars for guidance when they were illusory and without permanent reality? Even in the Kegon school, which preached a cosmological harmony governed by Lochana Buddha, who sits on a lotus throne of a thousand petals, each of which is a universe containing millions of worlds like ours, it is the mutable nature of this system and not its permanence (like the Confucian Heaven) which is emphasized. Within the great harmony of the Kegon (or Flower Wreath) all beings are related, and capable of mutual penetration until they attain a fundamental communion with Buddha and through him with all other beings.

It is highly problematical how much of these abstruse doctrines was understood by Japanese Buddhists of the Nara Period. Expressions of religious fervor generally assumed a tangible form. The patronage of Buddhism by the court led to the building of the magnificent temples and monasteries of Nara, some of which still survive. Certain court ceremonies such as the open confession of sins (*keka*) show how the strong desire to lead a religious life permeated ruling circles. Buddhist influence led also to the making of highways and bridges, to the use of irrigation, and to exploration of distant parts of the country by itinerant monks (who drew the earliest Japanese maps). Such features of Japanese life as the public bath and cremation also date from Buddhist inspiration of this time.

For the small number of priests and scholars of the Nara Period who were well-versed in Buddhist literature, three sūtras were of especial importance: the *Sūtra of Past and Present, Cause and Effect;* the *Sūtra of the Golden Light;* and the *Kegon,* or *Flower Wreath Sūtra.* The first-mentioned of these sūtras is a biography of Buddha which declares his extraordinary attainments to have been the cumulative merit of his meritorious deeds from the infinitely distant past to the present. This concept offers a marked contrast to the Han Confucian doctrine of kingly attainment being based on conformity with the Way of Heaven, or the theory of the *Kojiki,* where we find genealogy to be the essential factor governing kingship.

The responsibilities of a ruler, and indeed the entire question of the relationship between the state and Buddhism, were most completely discussed in the *Sūtra of the Golden Light.* This masterpiece of Buddhist literature is a synthesis of the creative doctrines of Mahāyāna Buddhism, presented in a form as satisfying aesthetically as it is ethically. The *Sūtra of the Golden Light* played a more important role than any other in establishing Buddhism as the religion of Japan, and its influence continued undiminished for centuries. It opens with an eloquent proclamation of the eternity of Buddha's life, and declares that he exists not only as a historical figure with a human form, but in the cosmos as the ultimate Law or Truth, and in the life hereafter as the savior possessed of an all-embracing love. Since Buddha is omnipresent, everything that exists is subject to his eternal vigilance of boundless compassion. The sūtra declares further that the gates of the Paradise of the Lotus where Buddha dwells are always open to all of humanity, for anyone can become a Buddha. The methods the sūtra especially recommends for bringing about this change for the better are expiation and self-sacrifice; the climax of the entire narration is the parable of Buddha giving himself up to a hungry lion.

The central theme of the entire sūtra, however, is the life of reason— *prajñā,* which distinguishes good from evil and right from wrong. Everyone, from the king to his lowliest subject, must obey the dictates of the inner light of reason. The religious life starts with an awareness of one's sins and the desire to atone for them. It is reason which enables us to surmount these failings, and the highest expression of the triumph of reason is in an act of self-sacrifice. Reason is associated also with healing;

Buddha is not only supremely possessed of reason but is the great healer. It was this aspect of Buddha which appealed most to Japanese of the Nara Period as is witnessed by the predominant role of Yakushi, or the Healing Bodhisattva, not only in temples specifically dedicated to him, but in all centers of worship. The *Sūtra of the Golden Light* contains a chapter entirely devoted to medicine and healing, illustrating the close connection between religious belief and medicine. (It should be noted also that Buddhist priests introduced many medicines from China during the Nara Period.)

The political aspects of the sūtra are most clearly stated in the chapter on laws (*Ōbōshō-ron*). It is declared that government and religion are united by the Buddhist Law (or Dharma). The law of men must be universal but not final, always subject to change, with peace as its ultimate end. Any king who violates the Law will be punished; but as long as he is faithful to it, Buddha will see to it that he enjoys immeasurable blessings. Japanese monarchs during the Nara Period held this sūtra in such reverence that they attempted to make of it an instrument of state policy. Copies of the sūtra were distributed in all the provinces in A.D. 741 by order of the Emperor Shōmu, one of the most devout rulers. At about the same time Shōmu ordered each province to build a seven-storied pagoda, and to establish a Guardian Temple of the Province and an Atonement Nunnery of the Province.

It was Shōmu also who was responsible for the building of the Great Image of Lochana Buddha, the most famous monument of the Nara Period. Just as Lochana Buddha is the central figure of the cosmogony of the *Kegon* sūtra, the Great Image and its temple were intended as the center of the provincial temples and nunneries. The *Kegon* sūtra is said to have been the teaching delivered by Buddha immediately after attaining enlightenment, when he made no attempt to simplify the complexities of his doctrines for the benefit of the less capable. Its difficulty kept it from attaining the popularity of the *Sūtra of the Golden Light,* but its importance is evident from the efforts devoted to the completion of the Great Image (over fifty feet high). When in 749 gold was discovered in Japan for the first time, it was regarded as an auspicious sign for the completion of the monument. The Emperor Shōmu declared:

This is the Word of the Sovereign who is the Servant of the Three Treasures, that he humbly speaks before the Image of Lochana.

In this land of Yamato since the beginning of Heaven and Earth, Gold, though it has been brought as an offering from other countries, was thought not to exist. But in the East of the land which We rule . . . Gold has been found.

Hearing this We were astonished and rejoiced, and feeling that this is a Gift bestowed upon Us by the love and blessing of Lochana Buddha, We have received it with reverence and humbly accepted it, and have brought with Us all Our officials to worship and give thanks.

This We say reverently, reverently, in the Great Presence of the Three Treasures whose name is to be spoken with awe.[4]

We cannot but be struck by the humility of the terms employed by Shōmu. For him to have claimed to be a "servant" of the Three Treasures marks an astonishing departure from the previously held ideas of kingship in Japan. There seemingly remained only one further step to be taken to make Japan into a true Buddha-land: to have a sovereign who was a priest of Buddha's Law so that the country could be governed in perfect consonance with these teachings. During the reign of Shōmu's daughter, the Empress Shōtoku, the transference of rule to a Buddhist priest all but happened.

In A.D. 764 the Empress Shōtoku, who had previously abdicated, suddenly decided to reassume the throne in spite of the Buddhist vows she had taken. In the same proclamation she declared that she was appointing Dōkyō, a Master of the Hossō sect, to be her chief minister. Dōkyō steadily rose in power. In 766 he was appointed "king of the law" (*hōō*), and several years later the Empress, acting on a false oracle, was on the point of abdicating the throne in his favor. However, the powerful conservative forces at the court blocked this move, and Japan never again came so close to becoming a Buddha-land. The Empress Shōtoku died in 770, Dōkyō was disgraced, and the new rulers turned away from Nara to Kyoto, where new forms of Buddhism were to dominate the scene.

THE SŪTRA OF THE GOLDEN LIGHT

The full title of this work, *Sūtra of the Sovereign Kings of the Golden Light Ray* (*Konkō myō saishō ō gyō*), refers to the Deva Kings who came to pay homage to the Buddha. To its inspiration is due the first temple built by

[4] Sansom, "The Imperial Edicts in the Shoku-Nihongi," *TASJ*, 2d series, I, 26.

the court, the Shitennō (or Four Deva Kings). When Temmu seized the throne in 672, this sūtra appears to have influenced his decision to promote Buddhism in the interest of the new regime. His predecessor, Tenchi, had been clearly associated with the Confucian political order, and, as we have seen, Tenchi's assumption of power was justified by numerous portents indicating that he had received the Mandate of Heaven. Temmu found a similar justification in the *Golden Light Sutra,* which set forth a doctrine of kingship based on merit—merit achieved in former existences and through wholehearted support of Buddhism. It is thus strongly implied that kings rule by a kind of "divine right," which is not based on any hereditary claim but rather on the ruler's proper performance of his duties. In the latter case, not only will his realm enjoy the peace and harmony from the beneficial influence of Buddhist teachings on public morality, but even the cosmic order will respond to the ruler's virtue and bestow blessings upon him and his people. Here, then, is a Buddhist parallel to the Han Confucian view of sovereignty, without the concessions made by Han theorists to dynastic inheritance. It is no wonder that Temmu held this sūtra in particular honor, and fostered the growth of Buddhism by ordering every family to have a Buddhist shrine in its house.

The Protection of the Country by the Four Deva Kings
[From Tsuji, *Nihon Bukkyō Shi,* Jōsei-hen, 194–95]

Then the Four Deva Kings, their right shoulders bared from their robes in respect, arose from their seats and, with their right knees touching the ground and their palms joined in humility, thus addressed Buddha:

"Most Revered One! When, in some future time, this *Sūtra of the Golden Light* is transmitted to every part of a kingdom—to its cities, towns and villages, its mountains, forests and fields—if the king of the land listens with his whole heart to these writings, praises them, and makes offerings on their behalf, and if moreover he supplies this sūtra to the four classes of believers, protects them and keeps all harm from them, we Deva Kings, in recognition of his deeds, will protect that king and his people, give them peace and freedom from suffering, prolong their lives and fill them with glory. Most Revered One! If when the king sees that the four classes of believers receive the sūtra, he respects and protects them as he would his own parents, we Four Kings will so protect him always that whatever he wishes will come about, and all sentient beings will respect him." . . .

Then Buddha declared to the Four Deva Kings:

"Fitting is it indeed that you Four Kings should thus defend the holy

[98]

writings. In the past I practiced bitter austerities of every kind for 100,-000 kalpas [eons]. Then, when I attained supreme enlightenment and realized in myself universal wisdom, I taught this law. If any king upholds this sūtra and makes offerings in its behalf, I will purify him of suffering and illness, and bring him peace of mind. I will protect his cities, towns and villages, and scatter his enemies. I will make all strife among the rulers of men to cease forever.

"Know ye, Deva Kings, that the 84,000 rulers of the 84,000 cities, towns and villages of the world shall each enjoy happiness of every sort in his own land; that they shall all possess freedom of action, and obtain all manner of precious things in abundance; that they shall never again invade each other's territories; that they shall receive recompense in accordance with their deeds of previous existences; that they shall no longer yield to the evil desire of taking the lands of others; that they shall learn that the smaller their desires the greater the blessing; and that they shall emancipate themselves from the suffering of warfare and bondage. The people of their lands shall be joyous, and upper and lower classes will blend as smoothly as milk and water. They shall appreciate each other's feelings, join happily in diversions together, and with all compassion and modesty increase the sources of goodness.

"In this way the nations of the world shall live in peace and prosperity, the peoples shall flourish, the earth shall be fertile, the climate temperate, and the seasons shall follow in the proper order. The sun, moon, and the constellations of stars shall continue their regular progress unhindered. The wind and rain shall come in good season. All treasures shall be abundant. No meanness shall be found in human hearts, but all shall practice almsgiving and cultivate the ten good works. When the end of life comes, many shall be born in Heaven and increase the celestial multitudes."

THE VIMALAKĪRTI SŪTRA (YUIMA-KYŌ)

This sūtra eulogizes Buddha's lay disciple, Vimalakīrti, who lives as a householder and yet achieves a saintliness unmatched even by those following monastic discipline. At the Japanese court this ideal of the Buddhist layman found favor among men taking an active part in state affairs, and under Fujiwara auspices a date was reserved on the court calendar for the reading and expounding of this sūtra. An extant commentary on the *Vimalakīrti* text has been traditionally ascribed to Prince Shōtoku, but it is more likely that Shōtoku only sponsored or joined in its preparation by Korean monks.

The second chapter, given here, describes the virtues of Vimalakīrti and presents his discourse on the nature of the human body as contrasted to the body of the Buddha.

[Adapted from Hokei Idumi, "Vimalakīrti's Discourse," *The Eastern Buddhist*, III, No. 2, 138–41]

At that time, there dwelt in the great city of Vaishālī a wealthy house-holder named Vimalakīrti. Having done homage to the countless Buddhas of the past, doing many good works, attaining to acquiescence in the Eternal Law, he was a man of wonderful eloquence,

Exercising supernatural powers, obtaining all the magic formulas [dhāranīs], arriving at the state of fearlessness,

Repressing all evil enmities, reaching the gate of profound truth, walk-ing in the way of wisdom,

Acquainted with the necessary means, fulfilling the Great Vows, com-prehending the past and the future of the intentions of all beings, under-standing also both their strength and weakness of mind,

Ever pure and excellent in the way of the Buddha, remaining loyal to the Mahāyāna,

Deliberating before action, following the conduct of Buddha, great in mind as the ocean,

Praised by all the Buddhas, revered by all the disciples and all the gods such as a Shakra and the Brahmā Sahāpati ["lord of the world"],

Residing in Vaishālī only for the sake of the necessary means for saving creatures, abundantly rich, ever careful of the poor, pure in self-discipline, obedient to all precepts,

Removing all anger by the practice of patience, removing all sloth by the practice of diligence, removing all distraction of mind by intent meditation, removing all ignorance by fullness of wisdom;

Though he is but a simple layman, yet observing the pure monastic discipline;

Though living at home, yet never desirous of anything;

Though possessing a wife and children, always exercising pure virtues;

Though surrounded by his family, holding aloof from worldly pleas-ures;

Though using the jeweled ornaments of the world, yet adorned with spiritual splendor;

Though eating and drinking, yet enjoying the flavor of the rapture of meditation;

Though frequenting the gambling house, yet leading the gamblers into the right path;

Though coming in contact with heresy, yet never letting his true faith be impaired;

Though having a profound knowledge of worldly learning, yet ever finding pleasure in things of the spirit as taught by Buddha;

Revered by all as the first among those who were worthy of reverence;

Governing both the old and young as a righteous judge;

Though profiting by all the professions, yet far above being absorbed by them;

Benefiting all beings, going wheresoever he pleases, protecting all beings as a judge with righteousness;

Leading all with the Doctrine of the Mahāyāna when in the seat of discussion;

Ever teaching the young and ignorant when entering the hall of learning;

Manifesting to all the error of passion when in the house of debauchery; persuading all to seek the higher things when at the shop of the wine dealer;

Preaching the Law when among wealthy people as the most honorable of their kind;

Dissuading the rich householders from covetousness when among them as the most honorable of their kind;

Teaching kshatriyas [i.e., nobles] patience when among them as the most honorable of their kind;

Removing arrogance when among brahmans as the most honorable of their kind;

Teaching justice to the great ministers when among them as the most honorable of their kind;

Teaching loyalty and filial piety to the princes when among them as the most honorable of their kind;

Teaching honesty to the ladies of the court when among them as the most honorable of their kind;

Persuading the masses to cherish the virtue of merits when among them as the most honorable of their kind;

Instructing in highest wisdom the Brahmā gods when among them as the most honorable of their kind;

Showing the transient nature of the world to the Shakra gods when among them as the most honorable of their kind;

Protecting all beings when among the guardians as the most honorable of their kind;

—Thus by such countless means Vimalakīrti, the wealthy householder, rendered benefit to all beings.

Now through those means he brought on himself sickness. And there came to inquire after him countless visitors headed by kings, great ministers, wealthy householders, lay-disciples, brahman princes and other high officials. Then Vimalakīrti, taking the opportunity of his sickness, preached to any one who came to him, and said:

"Come, ye gentlemen, the human body is transient, weak, impotent, frail, and mortal; never trustworthy, because it suffers when attacked by disease;

Ye gentlemen, an intelligent man never places his trust in such a thing; it is like a bubble that soon bursts.

It is like a mirage which appears because of a thirsty desire.

It is like a plantain tree which is hollow inside.

It is like a phantom caused by a conjurer.

It is like a dream giving false ideas.

It is like a shadow which is produced by karma.

It is like an echo which is produced by various relations.

It is like a floating cloud which changes and vanishes.

It is like the lightning which instantly comes and goes.

It has no power as the earth has none.

It has no individuality as the fire has none.

It has no durability as the wind has none.

It has no personality as the water has none.

It is not real and the four elements are its house.

It is empty when freed from the false idea of me and mine.

It has no consciousness as there is none in grasses, trees, bricks or stones.

It is impotent as it is revolved by the power of the wind.

It is impure and full of filthiness.

It is false and will be reduced to nothingness, in spite of bathing, clothing, or nourishment.

It is a calamity and subject to a hundred and one diseases.

It is like a dry well threatened by decay.

It is transient and sure to die.

It is like a poisonous snake or a hateful enemy or a deserted village as it is composed of the (five) *skandhas,* the (twelve) *āyatanas* and the (eighteen) *dhātus.*[1]

O ye gentlemen, this body of ours is to be abhorred, and the body of Buddha is to be desired. And why?

The body of Buddha is the body of the law.

It is born of immeasurable virtues and wisdom.

It is born of discipline, meditation, wisdom, emancipation, wisdom of emancipation.

It is born of mercy, compassion, joy, and impartiality.

It is born of charity, discipline, patience, diligence, meditation, emancipation, samādhi, learning, meekness, strength, wisdom, and all the Pāramitās.

It is born of the necessary means.

It is born of the six supernatural powers.

It is born of the threefold intelligence.

It is born of the thirty-seven requisites of enlightenment.

It is born of the concentration and contemplation of mind.

It is born of the ten powers, threefold fearlessness, and the eighteen special faculties.

It is born by uprooting all wicked deeds and by accumulating all good deeds.

It is born of truth.

It is born of temperance.

Of these immeasurable pure virtues is born the body of Tathāgata.[2] Ye

---

[1] Components of the human being, the five *skandhas* are form (body), sensation, perception, psychic construction, and consciousness. The twelve *āyatanas* are the six senses and six sense organs. The eighteen *dhātus* are the six sense organs, six sense objects, and six senses.

[2] A title of the Buddha—the Truth-revealer, literally, "He who comes thus."

gentlemen, if one wishes to obtain the body of Buddha and exterminate the diseases of all beings he should cherish the thought of supreme enlightenment."

Thus Vimalakīrti, the wealthy householder, rightly preached for the profit of those who came to visit him on his bed of sickness and made all these countless thousand people cherish the thought of supreme enlightenment.

STATE SPONSORSHIP AND CONTROL OF BUDDHISM

Proclamation of the Emperor Shōmu on the Erection of the Great Buddha Image
[From *Shoku Nihongi*, in *Rikkokushi*, III, 320–21]

Having respectfully succeeded to the throne through no virtue of Our own, out of a constant solicitude for all men We have been ever intent on aiding them to reach the shore of the Buddha-land. Already even the distant sea-coasts of this land have been made to feel the influence of Our benevolence,and regard for others,[1] and yet not everywhere in this land do men enjoy the grace of Buddha's Law. Our fervent desire is that, under the aegis of the Three Treasures, the benefits of peace may be brought to all in heaven and on earth, even animals and plants sharing in its fruits, for all time to come.

Therefore on the fifteenth day of the tenth month of the fifteenth year of the Tempyō reign [743], which is the year of the Goat and Water Junior,[2] We take this occasion to proclaim Our great vow of erecting an image of Lochana Buddha in gold and copper. We wish to make the utmost use of the nation's resources of metal in the casting of this image, and also to level off the high hill on which the great edifice is to be raised, so that the entire land may be joined with Us in the fellowship of Buddhism and enjoy in common the advantages which this undertaking affords to the attainment of Buddhahood.

It is We who possess the wealth of the land; it is We who possess all

---

[1] Cardinal Confucian virtues which here signify the spread of Confucian ethics as exemplified by the Imperial rule.

[2] Year designation according to the Chinese sexagenary cycle (see Chapter IV).

power in the land. With this wealth and power at Our command, We have resolved to create this venerable object of worship. The task would appear to be an easy one, and yet a lack of sufficient forethought on Our part might result in the people's being put to great trouble in vain, for the Buddha's heart would never be touched if, in the process, calumny, and bitterness were provoked which led unwittingly to crime and sin.

Therefore all who join in the fellowship of this undertaking must be sincerely pious in order to obtain its great blessings, and they must daily pay homage to Lochana Buddha, so that with constant devotion each may proceed to the creation of Lochana Buddha.[3] If there are some desirous of helping in the construction of this image, though they have no more to offer than a twig or handful of dirt, they should be permitted to do so. The provincial and county authorities are not to disturb and harass the people by making arbitrary demands on them in the name of this project. This is to be proclaimed far and wide so that all may understand Our intentions in the matter.

Two Edicts of the Empress Shōtoku Concerning Dōkyō

These edicts, one making the priest Dōkyō chief minister of the court and the other naming him King of the Law, preceded the Empress Shōtoku's attempt to abdicate the imperial throne in his favor.
[From *Shoku Nihongi*, in *Rikkokushi*, IV, 93–141]

EDICT OF OCTOBER 19, 764

It has been represented to Us, in view of the Master's constant attendance on Us, that he has ambitions of rising to high office like his ancestors before him, and We have been petitioned to dismiss him from Our Court. However, We have observed his conduct and found it to be immaculate. Out of a desire to transmit and promote Buddha's Law, he has extended to Us his guidance and protection. How could We lightly dismiss such a teacher?

Although Our head has been shaven and We wear Buddhist robes, We feel obliged to conduct the government of the nation. As Buddha declared in the [*Bommō, Brahmajāla*] Sūtra, "Kings, ye who take up

---

[3] Though to Western minds it might seem impious that the Cosmic Buddha himself could be so created, in the Kegon philosophy the particular and the universal are one and inseparable, so that an image properly conceived with a devout realization of the Buddha's true nature might stand for the Buddha himself.

thrones, receive the ordination of the bodhisattvas!" These words prove that there can be no objection even for one who has taken holy orders in administering the government. We deem it proper therefore, since the reigning monarch is ordained, that the Chief Minister should also be an ordained priest. Hearken, all ye people, to Our words: We confer on the Master Dōkyō the title of Chief Minister and Master, though the title is not of his seeking. [pp. 93-94]

EDICT OF NOVEMBER 26, 766

We do affirm in this edict Our belief that when the Law of Buddha, the Supreme One, is worshiped and revered with perfect sincerity of heart, he is certain to vouchsafe some unusual Sign. The sacred bone of the Tathāgata which has now been manifested, of perfect shape and unusually large, is brighter and more beautiful of color than ever We have seen; the mind cannot encompass its splendor. Thus it is that night and day alike We pay it humble reverence with Our unwavering attention. Indeed, it appears to Us that when the Transformation Body of the Buddha extends its guidance to salvation in accordance with circumstances, his compassionate aid is manifested with no delay. Nevertheless, the Law depends on men for the continuation and spread of its prosperity. Thus, it has been due to acts of leadership and guidance in consonance with the Law performed by Our Chief Minister and Master, who stands at the head of all priests, that this rare and holy Sign has been vouchsafed Us. How could so holy and joyous a thing delight Us alone? Hearken, all ye people, to your sovereign's will: We bestow on Our teacher, the Chief Minister, the title of King of the Law.[4] We declare again that such worldly titles have never been of his seeking; his mind is set, with no other aspiration, on performing the acts of a bodhisattva and leading all men to salvation. Hearken, all ye people, to your sovereign's will: We confer this position on him as an act of reverence and gratitude. [pp. 140-41]

Regulation of Buddhist Orders by the Court

Not all of those who embraced Buddhism, "left the world," and joined monastic orders, did so with a full realization of what would be required of them in the religious life. Consequently it was not long after the first estab-

[4] Sometimes translated as "pope."

lishment of monasteries and nunneries in Japan that charges were made of flagrant violations of Buddhist vows in regard to the taking of life, sexual incontinence, and drunkenness. Since the Throne had taken a prominent part in the establishment of Buddhist institutions, it was to be expected that the court would likewise assert its control over them, as indicated by the measures taken by Suiko as early as A.D. 623. However, such external controls proved largely ineffective, for serious violations were frequent throughout the seventh and eighth centuries, and it remained for reformers in the priesthood itself, such as Ganjin and Saichō (see Chapter VI), to attempt the tightening of discipline from within.

[Adapted from Aston, *Nihongi*, II, 152–54]

31st year [623], Spring, 4th month, 3rd day. There was a Buddhist priest who took an axe and smote therewith his paternal grandfather. Now the Empress, hearing of this, sent for the Great Imperial Chieftain Soga, and gave command, saying: "The man who has entered religion should be devoted to the Three Treasures, and should cherish devoutly the prohibitions of the Buddhist law. How can he without compunction be readily guilty of crime? We now hear that there is a priest who has struck his grandfather. Therefore, let all the priests and nuns of the various temples be assembled, and investigation made. Let severe punishment be inflicted on any who are convicted of offenses." Hereupon the priests and nuns were all assembled, and an examination held. The wicked priests and nuns were all about to be punished, when Kwallŭk, a Buddhist priest of Paekche, presented a memorial, as follows: "The law of Buddha came from the Western Country to Han.[1] Three hundred years later it was handed on to Paekche, since which time barely one hundred years had elapsed, when Our King, hearing that the Emperor of Nippon was a wise man, sent him tribute of an image of Buddha and of Buddhist sūtras. Since that time, less than one hundred years have passed, and consequently the priests and nuns have not yet learned the Buddhist laws, and readily commit wickedness. On this account all the priests and nuns are afraid, and do not know what to do. I humbly pray that with the exception of the wicked [priest who struck his grandfather] all the other priests and nuns be pardoned and not punished. That would be a work of great merit."

Accordingly the Empress granted [his petition].

13th day. A decree was made as follows: "If even the priests continue

[1] The Chinese dynasty of that name.

to offend against the law, wherewithal shall the laymen be admonished? Therefore from this time forward we appoint a Sōjō and a Sōzu for the superintendence of the priests and nuns."

Autumn, 9th month, 3rd day. There was an inspection of the temples, and of the priests and nuns, and an accurate record made of the circumstances of the building of the temples, and also of the circumstances under which the priests and nuns embraced religion, with the year, month and day of their taking orders. There were at this time 46 temples, 816 priests, and 569 nuns—in all, 1,385 persons.

32nd year [624], Spring, 1st month, 7th day. The King of Koryo sent tribute of a Buddhist priest, named Hyegwan. He was appointed Sōjō [superintendent of priests and nuns].[2]

[2] The Japanese were still such novices in Buddhism that Korean priests were generally selected as religious authorities. [Ed.]

MAHĀYĀNA UNIVERSALISM AND THE SENSE OF HIERARCHY

The name Heian means "peace and tranquillity," and was originally given to the imperial capital, Kyoto, which remained the actual seat of ruling power throughout this period (eighth to twelfth centuries A.D). During its earlier years, at least, the period lived up to its name. After removal of the court to Kyoto in 795 the struggles for power around the throne, which had marked the Nara Period, diminished in intensity, and there was no recrudescence of the drastic reforms attempted earlier to remake Japan on the Chinese model. Not that complete success had been achieved in unifying Japan and centralizing its administration—on the contrary, control of the so-called "provinces," tenuous even at the start, was in the ninth and tenth centuries almost entirely lost to great families who made a mockery of the land and tax system imported from T'ang China. And if there was a greater stability and continuity of power at the court itself, this too was gained, not through a strengthening of the bureaucratic structure or civil service, but through the complete triumph of the hereditary principle and the concentration of power in a single family, the Fujiwara. Such peace as the Heian Period enjoyed, then, was due to the skill of the Fujiwara in managing their own interests and those of the imperial house so as to preserve their dominance even in the new circumustances. That the diffusion of power from the court was a long and gradual process, during which the imperial capital remained the unrivaled center of national life, is due also to the great weight of tradition and to the enormous prestige of the capital in cultural affairs. Indeed, Kyoto's position as the cynosure of civilization was even further enhanced during this period by the relative decline of T'ang China, to which the Japanese looked less and less as a final authority in all matters. In religion, it is true, the two great movements inaugurated in the early ninth century, the Tendai Buddhism introduced by Saichō and the Esoteric Buddhism ably propagated by Kūkai, were direct imports from China. Nevertheless, their progress was furthered by close association with the court and their characteristic forms of expression increasingly reflected the attitudes and manner of life which predominated at court. Thus, although both these forms of Buddhism were egalitarian in theory —that is, as outgrowths of the Mahāyāna teaching they stressed that all men had the potentialities for Buddhahood—in the Japanese setting their activities were strongly conditioned by the aristocratic nature of court society. Again, despite the universalistic claims of the Mahāyāna as revealed in Tendai and Shingon eclecticism—that is, their readiness to find a place for all religious teachings and all forms of the religious life in a comprehensive view of Truth—there was a noticeable tendency to stress the hierarchic order of these forms of religious consciousness in the ascent to Truth (a retrospective view of this contradiction in Heian Buddhism is afforded by the fifteenth century Nō play, *Sotoba Komachi*). Thus, even though Tendai and Shingon Buddhism contained within them the seeds later sown abroad by the popular religious movements of the medieval period, in the Heian Period itself the germination process was long delayed.

Meanwhile, however, the Heian court attained great heights of cultural achievement. Increasingly the Japanese asserted their independence of the Chinese forms in literature and art, and developed a native script better suited to the expression of their own language. The great monuments of this period of cultural efflorescence are the famous *Tale of Genji* by Lady Murasaki and the *Pillow Book* of Sei Shonagon, which mirror the court life of the time and the aesthetic preoccupations of the Heian aristocrats, as well as the great imperial collections of native poetry and the magnificent scroll paintings of this period. In them we find elegant expressions of the Heian passion for aesthetic refinement and the first clear intimations of the classic canons of Japanese taste, which inspired and guided the later development of a distinctive and highly distinguished artistic tradition.

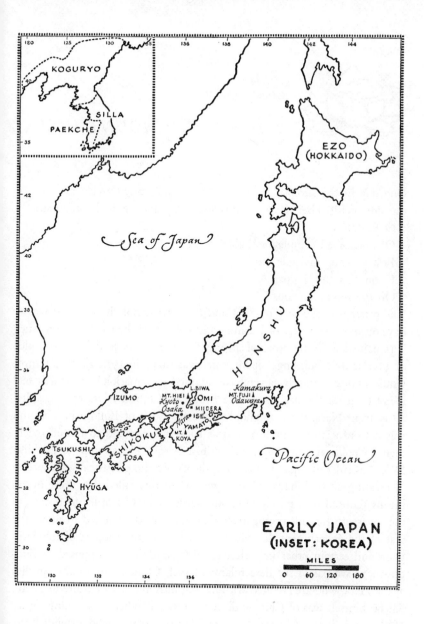

EARLY JAPAN
(INSET: KOREA)

KOGURYO

SILLA

PAEKCHE

Sea of Japan

EZO
(HOKKAIDO)

HONSHU

IZUMO

L. BIWA

MT. HIEI OMI

Kamakura

Kyoto MT. FUJI
Osaka MIIDERA *Odawara*

Nara ISE

YAMATO

MT.
KOYA

TSUKUSHI

SHIKOKU

TOSA

Pacific Ocean

KYUSHU HYUGA

MILES

0   60 120 180

One day in the seventh moon of 788 a young priest made his way up
the side of Mt. Hiei repeating this song of prayer he had composed:
  O Buddhas
  Of unexcelled complete enlightenment
  Bestow your invisible aid
  Upon this hut I open
  On the mountain top.[1]
The priest was Saichō (767–822) and the little temple he founded was to
develop into the center of learning and culture of the entire nation; such
it remained until, by order of an impetuous military leader, the complex
of 3,000 temple buildings on Mt. Hiei was razed in 1571. Saichō's temple
would almost certainly never have attained so remarkable a growth had
it not been for the decision of the Emperor Kammu to move the capital
away from Nara, the stronghold of the Six Sects of Buddhism. Kammu
was a Confucian by training and as such was opposed to the encroach-
ment of political power by the Buddhist clergy. The attempt to establish
Dōkyō as ruler of Japan represented the closest the priests came to success
in creating a "Buddha-land," but even when this failed they were by no
means reduced to a purely religious status. It was in order to restore to
the sovereign his full prerogatives that Kammu determined to move the
seat of the government. In this decision he had the support of the Fujiwara and certain other important families traditionally opposed to Buddhism, as well as of the descendants of such Chinese immigrant families
as the Hata, who are credited with having introduced sericulture to Japan.
Saichō himself was of Chinese descent, as was another outstanding figure
of the period, the General Sakanoue Tamuramaro, who extended the
imperial domains to the northern end of the main island of Japan.
  Although Kammu's dislike of the secular ambitions of the priests and

[1] *Dengyō Daishi zenshū*, IV, 756.

[112]

his impatience at their interminable wrangling had made him generally anti-Buddhist, he realized that he needed Buddhist support for the reforms he intended to effect. Saichō met ideally Kammu's needs. He had originally left Nara because of his dissatisfaction with the worldliness and, as he considered, the decadence of the priesthood there. He became convinced that only in an entirely different environment could a true moral purge and ethical awakening take place. When he first established his little temple, the area around Mt. Hiei was mainly uncultivated marshland, but six years later, in 794, it was chosen as the site of the capital. Saichō may have been instrumental in the adoption of this site; in any case, once the removal there had been effected he enjoyed the patronage of the Emperor Kammu. Saichō was sent to China in 804, chiefly to gain spiritual sanction for the new Buddhist foundation on Mt. Hiei. China was considered to be the "fatherland" of Japanese Buddhism, and without Chinese approval Saichō's monastery had no standing alongside those of the powerful sects in Nara.

Saichō does not appear originally to have desired to found a new sect. When his first temple was opened, the Healing Buddha was enshrined there, just as in so many of the Nara temples. While he was in China, however, he studied the Tendai (T'ien-t'ai) teachings, and he brought back this doctrine to Japan after a year abroad. The Tendai sect, as founded by Saichō, was essentially the same as its parent sect in China, and was based like it on the teachings of the *Lotus Sūtra*. The Nara sects, with the exception of the Kegon, had derived authority for their doctrines from secondary sources—the commentaries—instead of from the sūtras. Saichō denounced this feature of Nara Buddhism in pointing out the superiority of the Tendai teachings based on Buddha's own words.

Saichō referred often to the "Two Vehicles" of Nara Buddhism. By this he meant Hīnayāna and what may be called Quasi-Mahāyāna, the latter referring to such schools as the Hossō and Sanron. Against these doctrines Saichō upheld the "One Vehicle" of the true Mahāyāna. The emphasis on "oneness" took various forms. It meant, most importantly, universality, in contrast, say, to the Hossō sect, which had evolved as an aristocratic and hierarchic religion, with certain persons excluded by their inborn shortcomings from Buddhist perfection; Tendai Buddhism preached enlightenment for all. Saichō declared that all men had innate in them the possibility of gaining enlightenment:

In the lotus-flower is implicit its emergence from the water. If it does not emerge, its blossoms will not open; in the emergence is implicit the blossoming. If the water is three feet deep, the stalk of the flower will be four or five feet; if the water is seven or eight feet deep, the stalk will be over ten feet tall. That is what is implied by the emergence from the water. The greater the amount of water, the taller the stalk will grow; the potential growth is limitless. Now, all human beings have the lotus of Buddhahood within them. It will rise above the mire and foul water of the Hīnayāna and Quasi-Mahāyāna, and then through the stage of the bodhisattvas to open, leaves and blossoms together, in full glory.[2]

Another aspect of oneness as found in Tendai Buddhism was the insistence on the basic unity of Buddha and all other beings. In every person is the Buddha-nature which must be realized. No matter how wicked a man may be, he is potentially a Buddha. The way that one may attain Buddhist perfection is to follow the way of Buddha by leading a life of moral purity and contemplation. Indeed, it was his emphasis on moral perfection rather than any more metaphysical aspect of the Tendai philosophy which most conspicuously appeared in Saichō's teachings.

In contrast, again, with the Nara Buddhists who lived in the old capital, Saichō required Tendai monks to remain in the seclusion of the monastery on Mt. Hiei for twelve years. There they received the "training of a bodhisattva," including a study of the Mahāyāna sūtras (especially the *Lotus*), and a kind of mystic contemplation known as "Concentration and Insight" (*shikan*). The discipline on Mt. Hiei was severe, necessarily so if, as Saichō hoped, the monastery was to supply the nation with its teachers and leaders.

There was a close connection between Mt. Hiei and the court, but it was a relationship quite unlike that which existed between the sovereigns and the great temples when the court was in Nara. The Emperor Shōmu had proclaimed himself to be the slave of the Three Treasures, and his daughter was willing to yield the throne to a priest, but the new Buddhism was in the service of the court and not its master. Saichō's monastery was declared to be the "Center for the Protection of the Nation," and Saichō constantly reiterated his belief that Mahāyāna Buddhism was the great benefactor and protector of Japan. He distinguished three classes of monks among those who would "graduate" from Mt. Hiei. The first class was those gifted both in their actions and words; they were the "treasure of

[2] *Dengyō Daishi zenshū*, I, 436.

the nation" and more precious than the richest jewels. Such monks were to remain on Mt. Hiei and serve their country by their religious practices. Monks who were not so gifted either in actions or in words would leave the mountain and become servants of the state. Some would teach; others would engage in agricultural and engineering projects for the nation's benefit.

Saichō's writings sometimes appear to be tinged with nationalism, probably because of his strong feelings for the prestige of the court. Many of the important Buddhist monks of the Nara Period had been Chinese or Koreans and showed little specific attachment for the Japanese court or Japan itself. Saichō, on the other hand, in spite of his Chinese ancestry was thoroughly Japanese in his love of what he called "the country of Great Japan" (*Dai-Nippon-Koku*) and in his reverence for the sovereign. In the oath which the Tendai monks were required to swear, Saichō included a moving acknowledgment of the sect's debt to the Emperor Kammu. The fortunes of Tendai Buddhism were in fact so closely linked at first to Kammu that when he died in 806 Tendai's supremacy was immediately threatened. The Nara priests were bitterly opposed to Saichō because of his part in the removal of the capital, and because of their jealousy over the honors that Kammu had later bestowed on the Tendai monk. One of the charges against Saichō was that he was not properly qualified to pose as a "monk who sought the Buddhist Law in China" (the title Saichō often used) because he had failed to visit Ch'ang-an, the Chinese capital. The accusations exchanged between Nara and Mt. Hiei became increasingly acrimonious.

Another threat to the prosperity of Tendai came in the same year as Kammu's death—the return to Japan of Kūkai, who was to become the great religious leader of the period. Kūkai quickly ingratiated himself with Kammu's successor by presenting him with many treasures from China. Before long Kūkai's Shingon Buddhism, with its emphasis on aestheticism, was in higher favor with the court than the severely moral Tendai school.

The relations between Saichō and Kūkai were at first very friendly. Saichō eagerly sought to learn the teachings which Kūkai brought back from China. This was one of the most appealing sides of Saichō's character—his genuine desire to improve his knowledge and understanding of Buddha's Law regardless of whether or not the material he studied formed part of the Tendai teachings. He stated as his principle:

A devout believer in Buddha's Law who is also a wise man is truly obliged to point out to his students any false doctrines, even though they are principles of his own sect. He must not lead the students astray. If, on the other hand, he finds a correct doctrine, even though it is a principle of another sect he should adopt and transmit it. This is the duty of a wise person. If a man maintains his partisan spirit even when his teachings are false; conceals his own errors and seeks to expose those of other people; persists in his own false views and destroys the right views of others—what could be more stupid than that? From this time forward, priests in charge of instruction in the Law must desist from such practices.[3]

Saichō was much impressed by the esoteric teachings. He was baptized by Kūkai at the latter's first initiation rites, and frequently borrowed works on esotericism from him. Saichō even sent Taihan, one of his favorite disciples, to study with Kūkai. The happy relations between Saichō and Kūkai came to an abrupt end, however, when Kūkai, writing on Taihan's behalf, refused Saichō's request that he return to Mt. Hiei. When Saichō asked to borrow a certain esoteric sūtra, Kūkai this time replied that if he wished to study the Truth it was everywhere apparent in the cosmos, but if he wished to learn about Esoteric Buddhism he would have to become a regular student. The tone of Kūkai's letter was extremely unpleasant, and we cannot be surprised that Saichō was embittered by it. Saichō's last years were unhappily spent. His most ardent wish, that a Mahāyāna ordination center be established on Mt. Hiei, so that Tendai Buddhists might be completely free from the Nara ordination hall with its Hīnayāna practices, was successfully opposed by the Nara Buddhists. Only after Saichō's death in 822 was permission finally granted.

Saichō's lasting contributions to Buddhism were probably more in the field of organization than of doctrine. His writings are in an undistinguished and even tedious style, often repetitious, seldom engrossing. They possess, however, an earnestness and sincerity which tell us much about the man. Saichō may not dazzle us by the brilliance of his achievements the way Kūkai does, but the student of Buddhism may well turn to him for an example of the highest ideals of the Buddhist priesthood.

THE LOTUS SŪTRA

The *Lotus Sūtra,* which was the chief text of Saichō's Tendai sect in Japan, was also one of the most influential and popular sūtras among Mahāyāna

[3] *Dengyō Daishi zenshū,* I, 447.

Buddhists in the Far East. Its authorship and date are obscure, but the *Lotus* was first translated from Sanskrit into Chinese during the third century A.D. In vivid language overpowering the imagination, it relates the final discourse on Vulture Peak of Shākyamuni, before his entry into Nirvāna. Here he offers to his assembled disciples a vision of infinite Buddha-worlds, illuminated by Buddhas revealing the Truth to innumerable disciples, just as Shākyamuni does in this world. This is a foreshadowing of the later revelation that Shākyamuni is just one manifestation of the Eternal Buddha, who appears in these infinite realms whenever men threaten to be engulfed by evil. The saving Truth which he reveals, called the Mahāyāna (Great Vehicle or Career), is so profound that only beings possessed of the highest intelligence can comprehend it. These are the bodhisattvas, destined for Buddhahood, to whom Shākyamuni entrusts the truth of this Wonderful Law and who, by the display of their transcendent virtues, provide the example which men are to follow in seeking release from this world. Through the inspiration and compassionate care of these bodhisattvas, all men may ultimately achieve salvation.

The Lotus, as vital a symbol of Buddhism as the Cross is of Christianity, represents purity and truth rising above evil just as the lotus flower rises above turbid waters. In its wider aspect it represents the Universe, one and infinite, flowering in innumerable Buddha-realms.

The passages which follow tell of Shākyamuni's revelation of the Mahāyāna doctrine. He is aware that many who have followed his earlier teachings, including the practice of severe disciplines, will feel cheated rather than be rejoiced by the news that Buddhahood is open to all, even the humblest of the faithful, rather than only to the few who have prepared themselves for the attainment of Nirvāna. These are identified as followers of the Hīnayāna (Lesser Vehicle or Career). Shākyamuni proceeds to explain why it has been necessary for him first to preach the Hīnayāna doctrine, intended for the self-improvement of individuals, as a preparation for the final revelation of Universal Salvation. One of the outstanding features of Tendai Buddhism as developed in China and carried to Japan, was its elaboration of this doctrine to show that the principal divisions and sects of later Buddhism all represented valid expressions of Buddha's teaching, adapted so as to accommodate people in varying stages of spiritual development.

[From the abridged translation of W. E. Soothill, *The Lotus of the Wonderful Law*, pp. 71–153]

The Revelation of the Mahāyāna

The dull, who delight in petty rules,
Who are greedily attached to mortality,
Who have not, under countless Buddhas,
Walked the profound and mystic Way,

Who are harassed by all the sufferings—
To these I [at first] preach Nirvāna.
Such is the expedient I employ
To lead them to Buddha-wisdom.
Not yet could I say to them,
"You all shall attain to Buddhahood,"
For the time had not yet arrived.
But now the very time has come
And I must preach the Great Vehicle.

. . . .

The Buddha appears in the world
Only for this One Reality,
The other two not being real;
For never by a smaller Vehicle (Hīnayāna)
[Could a Buddha] save any creature.
The Buddha himself is in the Great Vehicle (Mahāyāna)
And accordant with the Truth he has attained,
Enriched by meditation and wisdom,
By it he saves all creatures.
I, having proved the Supreme Way,
The universality of the Great Vehicle,
If, by a Small Vehicle, I converted
Were it but one human being,
I should fall into grudging selfishness,
A thing that cannot be.
If men turn in faith to the Buddha,
The Tathāgata will not deceive them,
Having no selfish, envious desires,
Being free from all sins of the Law.
Hence, the Buddha, in the universe,
Is the One being perfectly fearless.

. . . .

Know, O Shāriputra!
Of yore I made a vow,
In desire to cause all creatures
To rank equally with me.

. . . .

[118]

Whene'er I meet any of the living
I teach them the Buddha-Way;
The unwise remain confused
And, deluded, accept not my teaching.

. . . .

I know that all these creatures
Have failed in previous lives,
Are firmly attached to base desires
And, infatuated, are in trouble.

. . . .

They suffer the utmost misery.
Received into the womb in embryo,
They pass from generation to generation,
Poor in virtue and of little happiness,
Oppressed by all the sorrows
And dwelling in the thickets of debate,
Such as, Existence? or Non-existence?
Relying on their propositions,
Sixty-two in number,
They became rooted in false philosophy,
Tenacious and unyielding,
Self-sufficient and self-inflated,
Suspicious, warped, without faith.
During thousands and milliards of kalpas
Such hear not the name of Buddha,
Nor ever learn of the Truth;
These men are hard to save.
For this reason, Shāriputra,
I set up an expedient for them,
Proclaiming a Way to end suffering,
Revealing it as Nirvāna.
Yet, though I proclaim Nirvāna,
It is not real extinction;
All things from the beginning
Are ever of Nirvāna nature.
When a Buddha-son fulfils [his] course,
In the world to come he becomes Buddha.

It is because of my adaptability
That I tell of a Three-Vehicle Law,
[But truly] the World-honored Ones
Preach the One-Vehicle Way.

. . . .

If there are any beings
Who have met the former Buddhas,
If, after hearing the Truth,
They have given kindly alms,
Or kept the commands, enduring,
Been zealous, meditative, wise,
Cultivating blessedness and virtue,
Such men and beings as these
Have all attained to Buddhahood.
If, after the Nirvāna of Buddhas,
Men have become gentle of heart,
All such creatures as these
Have all attained to Buddhahood.
After the Nirvāna of Buddhas,
Those who worshiped their relics,
And built myriads, koṭis [millions] of stūpas,
With gold, silver, and crystal,
With moonstone and with agate,
With jasper and lapis lazuli,
Purely and abundantly displayed,
Superbly shown on every stūpa;
Or those who built shrines of stone,
Of sandal-wood or aloes,
Of eagle-wood or other woods,
Of brick and tiles, or clay;
Or those who, in the wilds,
Built Buddha-shrines of earth;
Even children who, in play,
Gathered sand for a Buddha's stūpa;
Such men and beings as these,
Have all attained to Buddhahood.
If men, for the sake of Buddhas,

Have erected images of them,
Carved with the [sacred] signs,
They have all attained to Buddhahood.

        . . . .

Even boys, in their play,
Who with reed, wood, or pen,
Or, even with finger-nail,
Have drawn Buddha's images;
Such men and beings as these
Gradually accumulating merit,
And becoming pitiful in heart,
Have all attained to Buddhahood,
And converted many bodhisattvas,
Saving countless creatures.

        . . . .

If men, to the stūpas and shrines,
To a precious image or painting,
With flowers, incense, flags and umbrellas,
Have paid homage with respectful hearts;
Or employed others to perform music,
Beat drums, blow horns and conches,
Pan-pipes and flutes, play lutes and harps,
Gongs, guitars and cymbals,
Such mystic sounds as these,
Played by way of homage;
Or with joyful hearts have sung
Praise to the merits of Buddhas,
Though with but one small sound,
[These, too,] have attained to Buddhahood.
Even one who, distracted of mind,
With but a single flower,
Has paid homage to a painted image,
Shall gradually see countless Buddhas.
Or, those who have offered worship,
Were it merely by folding the hands,
Or even by raising a hand,
Or by slightly bending the head,

By thus paying homage to the images,
Will gradually see countless Buddhas,
Attain the Supreme Way,
Widely save numberless creatures
And enter the perfect Nirvāna.

. . . .

[For] all Buddhas take the one vow:
"The Buddha-way which I walk,
I will universally cause all the living
To attain this same Way with me."
Though Buddhas in future ages
Proclaim hundreds, thousands, *koṭis,*
Countless ways into the doctrine,
In reality there is but the One-Vehicle.

. . . .

In the perilous round of mortality,
In continuous, unending misery,
Firmly tied to the passions
As a yak is to its tail;
Smothered by greed and infatuation,
Blinded and seeing nothing;
Seeking not the Buddha, the Mighty,
And the Truth that ends suffering,
But deeply sunk in heresy,
By suffering seeking riddance of suffering;
For the sake of all these creatures
My heart is stirred with great pity.

. . . .

Know, Shāriputra!
The stupid and those of little wit,
Those tied to externals and the proud,
Cannot believe this Truth.
But now I gladly and with boldness
In the midst of [you] bodhisattvas,
Straightway put aside expediency
And only proclaim the Supreme Way.

. . . .

In the same fashion that the Buddhas,
Past, present, and future, preach the Law,
So also will I now proclaim
The one and undivided Law.

. . . .

Even in infinite, countless kalpas,
Rarely may this Law be heard,
And those able to hearken to it,
Such men as these are rare.

. . . .

Who hears and joyfully extols it,
Though but by a single word,
Has thus paid homage to
All Buddhas in the three realms.

. . . .

Know, all of you, Shāriputra,
That this Wonderful Law
Is the secret of all the Buddhas.

. . . .

Rejoice greatly in your hearts,
Knowing that you will become Buddhas.

The Efficacy of the Lotus Sūtra

The *Lotus Sūtra* directs the veneration and faith of the Mahāyāna believer
not only to the compassionate bodhisattvas, custodians of Buddha's saving
Truth, but also to the sūtra itself. In the following passage Shākyamuni explains to the Bodhisattva King of Healing what merits and rewards will accrue
to those who honor this sūtra.

[From the abridged translation of W. E. Soothill, *The Lotus of the
Wonderful Law*, pp. 151–53]

Should one wish to dwell in Buddhahood
And attain to intuitive Wisdom,
He must always earnestly honor
The keepers of the Flower of the Law.
Should one wish quickly to attain
To complete omniscience,

He must receive and keep this sūtra
And honor those who keep it.
Should one be able to receive and keep
The Wonderful Law-Flower Sūtra,
Let him know he is the Buddha's messenger,
Who compassionates all living beings.
He who is able to receive and keep
The Wonderful Law-Flower Sūtra,
Casting aside his Paradise, and,
From pity for the living, being re-born,
Know, such a man as this,
Free to be born where he will,
Is able, in this evil world,
Widely to preach the Supreme Law.
You should, with celestial flowers and perfumes,
Robes of heavenly jewels, and heaps
Of wonderful celestial jewels,
Pay homage to such a preacher of the Law.
In evil ages after my extinction
Those who are able to keep this sūtra
Must be worshiped with folded hands,
As if paying homage to the World-honored One.
With the best of dainties and sweets,
And every kind of garment,
This son of Buddha should be worshiped
In hope of hearing him if but for a moment.
In future ages, if one is able
To receive and keep this sūtra,
I will send him to be amongst men,
To perform the task of the Tathāgata.

SAICHŌ

Vow of Uninterrupted Study of the Lotus Sūtra
(Taken by Monks of Mt. Hiei)
[From *Dengyō Daishi zenshū*, IV, 749]

The disciple of Buddha and student of the One Vehicle [name and court rank to be filled in] this day respectfully affirms before the Three

Treasures that the saintly Emperor Kammu, on behalf of Japan and as a manifestation of his unconditional compassion, established the Lotus Sect and had the *Lotus Sutra,* its commentary, and the essays on "Concentration and Insight," copied and bound, together with hundreds of other volumes, and installed them in the seven great temples. Constantly did he promote the Single and Only Vehicle, and he united all the people so that they might ride together in the ox-cart of Mahāyāna[1] to the ultimate destination, enlightenment. Every year festivals[2] of the *Golden Light Sutra* were held to protect the state. He selected twelve students, and established a seminary on top of Mt. Hiei, where the *Tripiṭaka,* the ritual implements, and the sacred images were enshrined. These treasures he considered the guardian of the Law and its champion during the great night of ignorance.

It was for this reason that on the fifteenth day of the second moon of 809 Saichō with a few members of the same faith, established the uninterrupted study of the *Sutra of the Lotus of the Wonderful Law.*

I vow that, as long as heaven endures and earth lasts, to the most distant term of the future, this study will continue without the intermission of a single day, at the rate of one volume every two days. Thus the doctrine of universal enlightenment will be preserved forever, and spread throughout Japan, to the farthest confines. May all attain to Buddhahood!

A Manifestation of the Discipline

The rather long essay of this title, of which an excerpt is given here, was written and presented to the Emperor Saga in 819. It was intended as an answer to the attacks on Saichō and the Tendai teachings which were being made by the Nara monks.

The first paragraph of the translation is in verse in the original.
[From *Dengyō Daishi zenshū,* I, 16–17]

I now initiate the discipline of the One Vehicle in order to profit and delight all sentient beings; this essay has been written to initiate the discipline of universality. I offer my prayers to the everlasting Three Treasures to extend their invisible and visible protection, so that the

[1] Three vehicles are described in the *Lotus Sutra;* of them the ox-cart stands for Mahāyāna.
[2] These festivals, often called *gosaie* ("imperial vegetarian entertainments" of priests), were held during the first moon in the Imperial Palace from 802, when Kammu founded them, until 1467. (See De Visser, *Ancient Buddhism in Japan,* pp. 471–79.) The text studied was that of the *Golden Light Sutra.*

discipline will be transmitted unhampered and unharmed, protecting the nation for all time to come. May all sentient beings who lead worldly or spiritual lives ward off what is wrong, put an end to all evil, and protect the seed of Buddhahood; may they awaken to the universal nature of things and partake of spiritual joy in the land of tranquil light.

I have heard that a gentleman of the laity should not pride himself on his superiority—how much less should I, a monk, discuss the failings of others? If, however, I followed such a philosophy and kept silent, the discipline of universality might perish. If, on the other hand, I were to speak out boldly, as is the fashion nowadays, there would be a never-ending controversy. I have therefore compiled this essay elucidating the discipline. I submit it to the Emperor.[3]

His Majesty the Emperor is equal to the sun and the moon in enlightenment, and his virtue does not differ from that of heaven and earth. His administration is in accord with the five human relationships,[4] and his religious faith is based on the teachings of Buddha. Nothing falls outside the scope of his great benevolence; there is no wise statesman but serves the court. The Buddha-sun shines brightly again, and the Way of inner realization flourishes. Now is the moment for the Mahāyāna discipline of the Perfect Doctrine to be proclaimed and promoted; it is the day when the temple should be erected. I have therefore cited the texts which describe the three kinds of temples[5] in making my request for a Mahāyāna Hall where Manjushrī may be installed and bodhisattva-monks be trained. When a white ox-cart is granted, the three other vehicles are unnecessary.[6] When a positive teaching has been found, why should we use the negativism of others?[7] The *Lotus Sūtra* says, "Choose the straight way and cast aside expediencies; preach the peerless doctrine." It also says, "What we should practice now is Buddha's wisdom alone."

At present the six supervisors[8] wield so much power as to suppress the Buddha's discipline. The hordes of monks have vociferously been demanding that I debate with them: in three hundred ways have they

---

[3] The Emperior Saga, reigned 809–23. [4] Of Confucianism.

[5] Mahāyāna, Hīnayāna, and combined Mahāyāna-Hīnayāna.

[6] The white ox was frequently used as a symbol for Mahāyāna. The other three vehicles were the means of enlightenment expounded by Hīnayāna and Quasi-Mahāyāna sects.

[7] Saichō considered that the Hīnayāna desire to achieve Nirvāna, extinction of the self, was as negative as "getting rid of excrement," the image he uses here.

[8] Each of the Six Sects of the Nara Period had its "supervisor" or nominal head.

slashed my heart. How then can I remain silent? Instead of speech, however, I have used my brush to express the barest fraction of my thoughts.

Regulations for Students of the Mountain School I

Saichō's importance as a religious organizer is apparent in these regulations for the students who were annually appointed by the government to study Tendai Buddhism. The ideal he held up for the monks was a lofty and demanding one: that they should combine the religious dedication of the bodhisattva with the Confucian virtues of service to the State and society.

The stylistic failings of Saichō's writings are also apparent in this work, but his repetition of such words as "treasure of the nation" has a certain cumulative power.

The original version of these regulations is in three sections of which the first two are translated here.

[From *Dengyō Daishi zenshū*, I, 5–10]

What is the treasure of the nation? The religious nature is a treasure, and he who possesses this nature is the treasure of the nation. That is why it was said of old that ten pearls big as pigeon's eggs do not constitute the treasure of a nation, but only when a person casts his light over a part of the country can one speak of a treasure of the nation. A philosopher of old [9] once said that he who is capable in speech but not in action should be a teacher of the nation; he who is capable in action but not in speech should be a functionary of the nation; but he who is capable both in action and speech is the treasure of the nation. Apart from these three groups, there are those who are capable neither of speech nor action: these are the betrayers [10] of the nation.

Buddhists who possess the religious nature are called in the west bodhisattvas; in the east they are known as superior men.[11] They hold themselves responsible for all bad things, while they credit others with all good things. Forgetful of themselves, they benefit others: this represents the summit of compassion.

Among Buddha's followers there are two kinds of monks, Hīnayāna

[9] Mou Tzu, a late Han philosopher, who attempted to make a synthesis of Buddhism, Confucianism, and Taoism, according to Buddhism the highest position. (Saichō quotes from *Mou Tzu*, p. 13b, *Ping-chin-kuan ts'ung-shu* edition.)

[10] This word seems far too strong for the offense. There may be a corruption in the text: Mou Tzu calls these people "mean" (or "lowly").

[11] Or "gentlemen"—the name given by Confucius to the people who followed his code.

and Mahāyāna; Buddhists possessing a religious nature belong to the latter persuasion. However, in our eastern land only Hīnayāna images are worshiped,[12] and not the Mahāyāna ones. The Great Teaching is not yet spread; the great men have not been able to rise. I fervently pray that, in accordance with the wishes of the late Emperor,[13] all Tendai students annually appointed will be trained in the Mahāyāna doctrines and become bodhisattva monks.[14]

REGULATIONS FOR THE TWO STUDENTS ANNUALLY APPOINTED BY THE COURT

1. All annually appointed Tendai Lotus students, from this year 818 to all eternity, shall be of the Mahāyāna persuasion. They shall be granted Buddhist names, without however losing their own family names. They shall be initiated into the Ten Precepts of Tendai before they become novices, and when they are ordained government seals will be requested for their papers.

2. All Mahāyāna students, immediately after their ordination, shall be administered the oaths of Sons of Buddha, and then become bodhisattva monks. A government seal will be requested for the certificates of oaths. Those who take the Vow will be required to remain on Mt. Hiei for twelve years without ever leaving the monastery. They shall study both disciplines.

3. All monks who study the Concentration and Insight (*shikan*) discipline shall be required every day of the year to engage in constant study and discussion of the *Lotus, Golden Light, Benevolent Kings, Protector* and other Mahāyāna sūtras for safeguarding the nation.[15]

4. All monks who study the Vairochana discipline shall be required every day of the year to recite the True Words (*mantra*) of the Vairochana, the Peacock, the Eternal, the Crown and other sūtras for safeguarding the nation.[16]

5. Students of both disciplines shall be appointed to positions in keeping with their achievements after twelve years' training and study. Those

---

[12] Even though Nara Buddhism was predominantly Mahāyāna, for the most part the images worshiped were Hīnayāna.

[13] Emperor Kammu (reigned 781–806) shortly before his death issued this order.

[14] That is, Mahāyāna monks, for the bodhisattva was held up by Mahāyāna Buddhism as the ideal to be followed.

[15] Japanese names for the sūtras: Hokke-kyō, Konkō-kyō, Ninnō-kyō, and Shugo-kyō.

[16] Japanese names for the sūtras: Dainichi-kyō, Kujaku-kyō, Fukū Kensaku Kannon-gyō, Ichiji Chōrinnō-gyō. These represent the esoteric discipline.

who are capable in both action and speech shall remain permanently on the mountain as leaders of the order: these are the treasure of the nation. Those who are capable in speech but not in action shall be teachers of the nation, and those capable in action but not in speech shall be the functionaries of the nation.

6. Teachers and functionaries of the nation shall be appointed with official licenses as Transmitters of Doctrine and National Lecturers. The national lecturers shall be paid during their tenure of office the expenses of the annual summer retreat and provided with their robes. Funds for these expenses shall be deposited in the provincial offices, where they will be supervised jointly by provincial and district governors.

They shall also serve in such undertakings which benefit the nation and the people as the repair of ponds and canals, the reclamation of uncultivated land, the reparation of landslides, the construction of bridges and ships, the planting of trees and ramie [17] bushes, the sowing of hemp and grasses, and the digging of wells and irrigation ditches. They shall also study the sūtras and cultivate their minds, but shall not engage in private agriculture or trading.

If these provisions are followed, men possessing the religious nature will spring up one after another throughout the country, and the Way of the Superior Man shall never die.

The above six articles are based on the teachings of mercy and will lead all sentient beings to the Great Teaching. The Law of Buddha is eternal; because the nation will always remain strong, the seeds of Buddhism will not die.

Overcome by profound awe, I offer these articles of Tendai and respectfully request the imperial assent.

Saichō, the Monk who Formerly Sought the Law in China. [19 June 818]

Regulations for Students of the Mountain School II

1. Twelve regular students of the Tendai Sect will be appointed for terms of six years each. If during the course of a year two places fall vacant, they will be filled by two other men.

The method of examining students will be as follows. All Tendai

---

[17] A plant whose fibers are similar to those of hemp in their properties and uses.

teachers will assemble in the Seminary Hall and there examine candidates on their recitations of the *Lotus* and *Golden Light* sūtras. When a student passes the examinations his family name and the date of the examination will be reported to the government.

Students who have completed six years of study will be examined in the above manner. Students who fail to complete the course will not be examined. If any students withdraw, their names, together with those of candidates for their places, should be reported to the government.

2. Regular students must provide their own clothing and board. Students who possess the proper mental ability and whose conduct is excellent, but who cannot provide their own clothing and board, shall be furnished by the monastery with a document authorizing them to seek alms throughout the country for their expenses.

3. If a regular student's nature does not accord with the monastic discipline and he does not obey the regulations, a report will be made to the government requesting his replacement in accordance with the regulations.

4. Regular students are required to receive the Mahāyāna initiation during the year of their ordination. After the ceremony they shall remain for twelve years within the gates of the monastery engaged in study. During the first six years the study of the sūtras under a master will be their major occupation, with meditation and the observance of discipline their secondary pursuits. Two-thirds of their time will be devoted to Buddhism, and the remaining third to the Chinese classics. An extensive study of the sūtras will be their duty, and teaching others about Buddhism their work. During the second six years in residence, meditation and the observance of discipline will be their chief occupation, and the study of the sūtras their secondary pursuit. In their practice of Concentration and Insight (*shikan*) students will be required to observe the four forms of concentration, and in their esoteric practices will be required to recite the three sūtras.[18]

5. The names of Tendai students registered at the Ichijō Shikan Monastery[19] on Mt. Hiei, whether students with annual grants or privately enrolled, should not be removed from the rolls of temples to

[18] The three basic sūtras of esoteric Buddhism: the Dainichi-kyō, the Kongōchō-gyō, and the Soshichi-kyō.
[19] The temple's name may be translated literally "the Vehicle of One-ness; Concentration and Insight."

which they were originally affiliated. For the purposes of receiving provisions, they should nevertheless be assigned to one of the wealthy temples in Ōmi.[20] In keeping with Mahāyāna practices, alms will be sought throughout the country to provide them with summer and winter robes. With the material needs of their bodies thus taken care of, they will be able to continue their studies without interruption. Once admitted to the monastery it will be a fast rule for these students that a thatched hut will serve as their quarters and bamboo leaves as their seats.[21] They will value but slightly their own lives, reverencing the Law. They will strive to perpetuate the Law eternally and to safeguard the nation.

6. If ordained priests belonging to other sects and not recipients of annual appointments wish of their own free will to spend twelve years on the mountain in order to study the two disciplines, their original temple affiliation and the name of their master, together with documents from this monastery, must be deposited in the government office. When they have completed twelve years of study they will be granted the title of Master of the Law as in the case of the annual appointees of the Tendai sect. If they should fail to live up to the regulations they are to be returned to the temple with which they were originally affiliated.

7. The request will be made that the court bestow the title of Great Master of the Law on students who have remained twelve years on the mountain, and have studied and observed the disciplines in strict adherence to the regulations. The request will be made that the court bestow the title of Master of the Law on students who, although they may not be accomplished in their studies, have spent twelve years on the mountain without ever having left it.

If any members of the sect fail to observe the regulations and do not remain on the mountain, or if, in spite of their having remained on the mountain, they have been guilty of numerous infractions of the Law or have failed to remain the full period, they will be removed permanently from the official register of the Tendai sect and returned to the temple with which they were originally affiliated.

8. Two lay intendants will be appointed to this Tendai monastery to supervise it alternately, and to keep out robbers, liquor, and women. Thus the Buddhist Law will be upheld and the nation safeguarded.

[20] The region near Lake Biwa where many rich immigrants were domiciled.
[21] That is, they will lead a life of poverty.

The above eight articles are for the maintenance of the Buddhist Law and the benefit of the nation. They should serve to guide all men and to encourage future generations in the way of goodness.

The imperial assent is respectfully requested.

Saichō, the Monk who Formerly Sought the Law in China. [30 September 818.]

CHAPTER VII

KŪKAI AND ESOTERIC
BUDDHISM

Outstanding among the Buddhist leaders of the Heian Period was Kūkai (774–835), a man whose genius has well been described, "His memory lives all over the country, his name is a household word in the remotest places, not only as a saint, but as a preacher, a scholar, a poet, a sculptor, a painter, an inventor, an explorer, and—sure passport to fame—a great calligrapher." [1]

Kūkai came from one of the great aristocratic families. At the time of the decision to move the capital from Nara, Kūkai's family was closely associated with the group opposed to the move, and was even implicated in the murder of the leader of the opposing faction. The subsequent disgrace of his family may have been a factor in Kūkai's eventual decision to become a Buddhist monk rather than to win the high place in the government that his talents and birth should have guaranteed him. Even as a small boy he showed exceptional ability in his studies, and was taken under the protection of his maternal uncle, a Confucian scholar. In 791 Kūkai entered the Confucian college in the capital. According to some sources, it was in the same year that he completed the first version of his *Indications to the Teachings of the Three Religions,* a work which treats the doctrines of Confucianism, Taoism, and Buddhism more or less novelistically. In its early form the book may actually have been intended more as a literary exercise than as an interpretation of the three religions. If it was in fact composed in 791, it was an amazing achievement for a youth of seventeen, but, as often in the case of the great men of former ages, it may be that Kūkai's admirers have sought to make him appear even more of a prodigy than he was.

The 797 version of the *Indications* was Kūkai's first major work. In it he proclaimed the superiority of Buddhism over the other two religions

[1] G. B. Sansom, *Japan, a Short Cultural History* (London, 1946), p. 230.

[133]

discussed because it went beyond them in its concern for man's future existence. Kūkai did not deny the validity of Confucian and Taoist beliefs as such, but pointed out how inadequate they were. For Kūkai Buddhism was not only superior, but actually contained all that was worthwhile in the other two beliefs. We can thus find even in this early work signs of the syncretism which marked his mature philosophy. Although Kūkai clearly reveals himself as Buddhist in the *Indications,* we know that he was not satisfied with the forms of the religion known to him in Japan. In later years he recalled that period of his life: "Three vehicles, five vehicles, a dozen sūtras—there were so many ways for me to seek the essence of Buddhism, but still my mind had doubts which could not be resolved. I beseeched all the Buddhas of the three worlds and the ten directions to show me not the disparity but the unity of the teachings." [2]

In the hope of finding the unifying Buddhism he sought, Kūkai sailed to China in 804 with the same embassy that Saichō also accompanied, although on a different ship. At this early date a voyage to China was extremely hazardous; ships which arrived safely were the exception and not the rule. When Kūkai's ship was about to sail, apprehension of the dangers was so great that the ambassadors' "tears fell like rain and everybody present also wept." [3] The crossing took thirty-four days, and instead of arriving at the mouth of the Yangtze, the probable goal, the ship reached the coast of Fukien, where the authorities were at first unwilling to let the Japanese ashore. Kūkai's mastery of written Chinese here served the embassy in good stead; the governor was so impressed that he created no further obstacles.

Kūkai proceeded with the embassy to the capital at Ch'ang-an. There he met his great master Hui-kuo (746–805) who was immediately struck by the young Japanese and treated him as his chosen disciple. After Hui-kuo's death in the following year Kūkai was selected to write the funeral inscription, a signal honor for a foreigner. He returned to Japan late in 806. The Emperor Kammu, who had strongly favored the removal of the capital from Nara, and who was thus presumably not so well disposed towards Kūkai, had died in the spring of that year, and his successor showed Kūkai every kindness. After Kūkai had been granted many

[2] From Kūkai's so-called *Testament,* written by another hand. Quoted in Moriyama (ed.), *Kōbō Daishi Den,* p. 85.

[3] Kuwabara Jitsuzo, "Daishi no Nyūtō" in *Kōbō Daishi to Nihon Bunka,* p. 479.

honors, he asked in 816 for permission to build a monastery on Mt. Kōya, which later became the center of the Shingon Sect. In 822 Saichō, Kūkai's rival, died, and in the following year Kūkai was appointed Abbot of the Tōji, the great Buddhist temple which commanded the main entrance to the capital. He died in 835 on Mt. Kōya.

The Buddhism which Kūkai learned in China and brought back to Japan was known as the True Words (*Mantrayāna* in Sanskrit, *Shingon* in Japanese). The name itself indicates the importance accorded to speech as one of the Three Mysteries—body, speech, and mind. These three faculties are possessed by every human being, but in them resides all secrets, and through them one can attain to Buddhahood. The mysteries of the body include the various ways of holding the hands (known as mudrā) in accordance with the Buddha or bodhisattva invoked, the postures of meditation, and the handling of such ritual instruments as the symbolic thunderbolt (*vajra*) and lotus flowers. The mysteries of speech included the "true words" and other secret formulas. The mysteries of the mind referred mainly to the "five wisdoms," methods of perceiving truth. In Shingon Buddhism these mysteries are transmitted orally from master to disciple and not written in books where anyone might read of them. This constitutes one of the main differences between esoteric (for the initiated) and exoteric (for the public) Buddhism. The reason given for keeping these teachings secret is that, unlike the doctrines of Shākya-muni, the historical Buddha, which were expounded with the limitations of his audience in mind, the esoteric teachings were voiced for his own enjoyment by Vairochana, the cosmic Buddha. The truths of the esoteric teachings were considered to be absolute, independent of place or time, and uniting in them the truths of all schools of thought. Only the initiated could hope to understand fully doctrines of such magnitude.

In the Esoteric school of Buddhism the relation between a master and his disciples was extremely close. Often the master would divulge all of his knowledge of the secret teachings only to one pupil of outstanding ability. Kūkai related how his master, Hui-kuo, waited almost until his death before he found in the Japanese an adequate receptacle for his knowledge. The personal nature of the transmission of the teachings was such that no independent Shingon sect was formed in China. It was left to Kūkai to present the Shingon teachings as a systematized doctrine and thus establish a sect. The immediate occasion for Kūkai's *Ten Stages of the Religious Consciousness,* in which Shingon is treated as a separate philosophy, was a decree issued in 830 by the Emperor Junna ordering the six existing Buddhist sects to submit in written form the essentials of their beliefs. Of the works submitted at this time, Kūkai's *Ten Stages* was by far the most important, both in quality and magnitude. It consisted of ten chapters, each one presenting a successive stage upward of religious consciousness. The work was written entirely in Chinese, not merely good Chinese for a Japanese writer, but with an ornate poetical style which may remind one somewhat of Pope's attempt in the *Essay on Man* to present philosophical ideas in rhymed couplets. Kūkai's use of this cumbersome medium of expression was dictated largely by the fashion of his time. We may regret this today, for in spite of Kūkai's remarkable mastery of the techniques of Chinese composition, his statement of the doctrines of Shingon Buddhism was inevitably hampered by the necessity of casting his words into a rigid and unsuitable mold. His writings are today difficult to understand, and his attempts at parallel constructions made him at times prolix, but in spite of such handicaps Kūkai remains the towering intellectual figure of Japanese Buddhism.

The *Ten Stages* was the first attempt made by a Japanese to appraise existing Buddhist literature of every variety preliminary to his elucidation of the doctrines of a new sect. Kūkai even went beyond the field of Buddhism in his discussion of the stages of the religious life: Confucianism and Taoism were considered as two stages of the ten. At the bottom of the ten stages Kūkai placed the animal life of uncontrolled passions, the life without religious guidance. Only one step upwards was Confucianism, where the mind is as yet ignorant of the true religion, but is led by teaching to the practice of secular virtues. The third stage was Taoism (and, according to some authorities, Brāhmanism), where the believers hope for heaven but ignore its nature. Two Hīnayāna stages follow; here there is a partial understanding only, and the highest aspiration is that of personal extinction in Nirvāna. This is in contrast to the Mahāyāna belief that even those who have attained Heaven must descend to the lower stages of existence to help save others. The sixth stage is the first of Mahāyāna belief sometimes identified as Quasi- or Pseudo-Mahāyāna. It is that of Hossō Buddhism which "aims at discovering the ultimate entity of cosmic existence in contemplation, through investigation into the specific characteristics of all existence, and through the realization of the fundamental nature of the soul in mystic illumination." [4] Because it is Mahāyāna, it is also characterized by its compassion for those who still wallow in ignorance. The seventh stage is the Sanron, which follows Nāgārjuna in the "Eightfold Negations" as a means of eliminating all false conceptions which hinder the mind in its search for the truth. The eighth stage is that of the universality of Tendai, where one moment contains eternity and a sesame seed may hold a mountain. The Kegon teachings, with its insistence on interdependence and convertibility, form the ninth stage. At the summit are the esoteric teachings of Shingon.

Although Kūkai insisted on the difference between the exoteric teachings of other schools of Buddhism and the esoteric Shingon teachings, an examination of doctrine would seem to show that the concept of Vairochana, the cosmic Buddha, had been anticipated by the Tendai concept of the eternal Buddha or the Kegon interpretation of Lochana Buddha. The essential difference was that the latter two concepts of Buddhahood were purported to have been visions revealed to the historical Buddha, while the Vairochana Buddha discussed by Kūkai was not merely an ideal, but the cosmos itself, limitless, without beginning or end. The cosmos was held to consist of six elements: earth, water, fire, air, space, and consciousness. Unlike certain other Buddhist schools, Shingon did not consider the world to be consciousness only; matter and mind are inseparable, "two but not two." In the Shingon insistence on consciousness as an element it differed from the Chinese Five Elements which were physical forces. Esoteric Buddhism was able to synthesize both the previous Buddhist concepts of the universe and the yin-yang theory of five elements. It was later also to absorb Shinto.

The great appeal of Esoteric Buddhism for Heian Japan lay in its aesthetic qualities. Kūkai himself excelled in the arts, and this fact may partially explain the important role which art played in his teachings. Kūkai's master, Hui-kuo, had told him that only through art could the profound meaning of the esoteric scriptures be conveyed, and when Kūkai returned to Japan he elaborated this theory:

The law [dharma] has no speech, but without speech it cannot be expressed. Eternal truth [*tathatā*] transcends color, but only by means of color can it be understood. Mistakes will be made in the effort to point at the truth, for there is no clearly defined method of teaching, but even

---

[4] M. Anesaki, *History of Japanese Religion*, p. 95.

when art does not excite admiration by its unusual quality, it is a treasure which protects the country and benefits the people.

In truth, the esoteric doctrines are so profound as to defy their enunciation in writing. With the help of painting, however, their obscurities may be understood. The various attitudes and mudrās of the holy images all have their source in Buddha's love, and one may attain Buddhahood at sight of them. Thus the secrets of the sūtras and commentaries can be depicted in art, and the essential truths of the esoteric teaching are all set forth therein. Neither teachers nor students can dispense with it. Art is what reveals to us the state of perfection.[5]

The arts were generally considered by Kūkai's school under four aspects: 1) painting and sculpture, 2) music and literature, 3) gestures and acts, and 4) the implements of civilization and religion. Ability in any or all of the arts may be achieved by a mastery of the Three Mysteries, and can result in the creation of flowers of civilization which are Buddhas in their own right. For Kūkai whatever was beautiful partook of the nature of Buddha. Nature, art and religion were one. It is not difficult, then, to see why so aesthetic a religion found favor at a time when Japanese civilization was at the height of its flowering.

Probably the most important use of painting made by the Shingon school was in the two Mandalas, representations of the cosmos under the two aspects of potential entity and dynamic manifestations. The indestructible potential aspect of the cosmos is depicted in the Diamond (*Vajra*) Mandala. In the center Vairochana Buddha is shown in contemplation, seated on a white lotus and encircled by a white halo. Around him are various Buddhas and the sacred implements. The dynamic aspect of the cosmos is depicted in the Womb (*Garbha*) Mandala, "wherein the manifold groups of deities and other beings are arrayed according to the kinds of the powers and intentions they embody. In the center there is a red lotus flower, with its seed-pod and eight petals, which symbolizes the heart of the universe. . . ."[6] Vairochana Buddha is seated on the seed-pod of the lotus and the petals are occupied by other Buddhas.

The Mandalas were used to represent the life and being of Vairochana Buddha, and also served to evoke mysterious powers, much in the way that the mudrās were performed. One important ceremony where the Mandalas figured was that in which an acolyte was required to throw

[5] From Kūkai's *Memorial on the Presentation of the List of Newly Imported Sūtras,* quoted in Moriyama (ed.), *Kōbō Daishi Den,* p. 249.

[6] Anesaki, *History of Japanese Religion,* pp. 126–27.

a flower on the Mandalas. The Buddha on which his flower alighted was the one he was particularly to worship and emulate. It is recorded that Kūkai's flower fell on Vairochana Buddha both in the Diamond and Womb Mandalas. His master was amazed at this divine indication of the great destiny in store for the young Japanese.

An unusual feature of Kūkai's teachings was the emphasis placed on a knowledge of Sanskrit. It is not certain what degree of proficiency Kūkai himself was able to attain in Sanskrit after his relatively brief study of the language in China, but with his unusual gifts he may well have gained a considerable command. He described the importance of Sanskrit:

Buddhism had its inception in India. The lands of the West and those of the East are culturally and geographically far removed, and both in language and writing India differs from China. Thus we have had to rely on translations in order to study the Buddhist texts. However, the True Words in the original language are exceedingly abstruse, each word possessing a profound meaning. This meaning is changed when its sound is altered, and can easily be falsified by different punctuation. One may get a rough impression of the meaning, but no clear understanding. Unless one reads the Sanskrit original it is impossible to distinguish the qualities of the vowels. That is why we must go back to the source.[7]

According to traditional accounts at least, Kūkai put his Sanskrit to excellent use in the invention of the Japanese syllabary (*kana*), a contribution which made possible the glorious literature of the Heian Period. Regardless of Kūkai's part, it is certain that the syllabary was evolved in imitation of Sanskrit use.

Esoteric Buddhism became the most important religion of Heian Japan. Although its profound secrets could be transmitted only from masters to their disciples, the main features of the doctrines could be grasped quite easily. Life was conceived of in terms of constant change, upwards to Buddhahood, or downwards to hell, when Mahāyāna compassion led the enlightened ones to seek the salvation of those still living as "butting goats." However, the esoteric teachings did not deny the importance of this world and of happiness in this life. By correct performance of the mysteries, material benefits could immediately be obtained. This belief led at first towards a spirit of intellectual curiosity in the things of this world which distinguishes Shingon from most other forms of Buddhism. Later, however, the hope of securing practical advantages through the

[7] Moriyama, *Kōbō Daishi Den*, p. 246.

intermediary of an adept in magical formulae led to many superstitious excesses. It was largely in protest against this latter development of Shingon Buddhism that the Jōdo and other dissident sects first arose.

KŪKAI

Kūkai and His Master

This passage and the one following are taken from the *Memorial Presenting a List of Newly Imported Sūtras* which Kūkai wrote to the emperor upon his return from studying in China. In addition to listing the many religious articles which he brought back with him, Kūkai reported on the results of his studies and extols the doctrines into which he was initiated. Among the points which he especially emphasizes are 1) his personal success in gaining acceptance by the greatest Buddhist teacher of the day in China; 2) the authenticity of this teaching in direct line of succession from the Buddha; 3) the great favor in which this teaching was held by the recent emperors of the T'ang dynasty, to the extent that it represented the best and most influential doctrine current in the Chinese capital; and 4) the fact that this teaching offers the easiest and quickest means of obtaining Buddhahood, probably an important recommendation for it in the eyes of a busy monarch.

[From *Kōbō Daishi zenshū*, I, 98–101]

During the sixth moon of 804, I, Kūkai, sailed for China aboard the Number One Ship, in the party of Lord Fujiwara, ambassador to the T'ang court. We reached the coast of Fukien by the eighth moon, and four months later arrived at Ch'ang-an, the capital, where we were lodged at the official guest residence. The ambassadorial delegation started home for Japan on March 15, 805, but in obedience to an imperial edict, I alone remained behind in the Hsi-ming Temple where the abbot Yung-chung had formerly resided.

One day, in the course of my calls on eminent Buddhist teachers of the capital, I happened by chance to meet the abbot of the East Pagoda Hall of the Green Dragon Temple. This great priest, whose Buddhist name was Hui-kuo, was the chosen disciple of the Indian master Amoghavajra. His virtue aroused the reverence of his age; his teachings were lofty enough to guide emperors. Three sovereigns revered him as their master and were ordained by him. The four classes of believers looked up to him for instruction in the esoteric teachings.

I called on the abbot in the company of five or six monks from the

Hsi-ming Temple. As soon as he saw me he smiled with pleasure, and he joyfully said, "I knew that you would come! I have been waiting for such a long time. What pleasure it gives me to look on you today at last! My life is drawing to an end, and until you came there was no one to whom I could transmit the teachings. Go without delay to the ordination altar with incense and a flower." I returned to the temple where I had been staying and got the things which were necessary for the ceremony. It was early in the sixth moon, then, that I entered the ordination chamber. I stood in front of the Womb Mandala and cast my flower in the prescribed manner. By chance it fell on the body of the Buddha Vairochana in the center. The master exclaimed in delight, "How amazing! How perfectly amazing!" He repeated this three or four times in joy and wonder. I was then given the fivefold baptism and received the instruction in the Three Mysteries that bring divine intercession. Next I was taught the Sanskrit formulas for the Womb Mandala, and learned the yoga contemplation on all the Honored Ones.

Early in the seventh moon I entered the ordination chamber of the Diamond Mandala for a second baptism. When I cast my flower it fell on Vairochana again, and the abbot marveled as he had before. I also received ordination as an āchārya early in the following month. On the day of my ordination I provided a feast for five hundred of the monks. The dignitaries of the Green Dragon Temple all attended the feast, and everyone enjoyed himself.

I later studied the Diamond Crown Yoga and the five divisions of the True Words teachings, and spent some time learning Sanskrit and the Sanskrit hymns. The abbot informed me that the Esoteric scriptures are so abstruse that their meaning cannot be conveyed except through art. For this reason he ordered the court artist Li Chen and about a dozen other painters to execute ten scrolls of the Womb and Diamond Mandalas, and assembled more than twenty scribes to make copies of the Diamond and other important esoteric scriptures. He also ordered the bronzesmith Chao Wu to cast fifteen ritual implements. These orders for the painting of religious images and the copying of the sūtras were issued at various times.

One day the abbot told me, "Long ago, when I was still young, I met the great master Amoghavajra. From the first moment he saw me he treated me like a son, and on his visit to the court and his return to the temple I was as inseparable from him as his shadow. He confided to me, 'You will be the receptacle of the esoteric teachings. Do your best! Do your best!' I was then initiated into the teachings of both the Womb and Diamond, and into the secret mudrās as well. The rest of his disciples, monks and laity alike, studied just one of the mandalas or one Honored One or one ritual, but not all of them as I did. How deeply I am indebted to him I shall never be able to express.

"Now my existence on earth approaches its term, and I cannot long remain. I urge you, therefore, to take the two mandalas and the hundred volumes of the Esoteric teachings, together with the ritual implements and these gifts which were left to me by my master. Return to your country and propagate the teachings there.

"When you first arrived I feared I did not have time enough left to teach you everything, but now my teaching is completed, and the work of copying the sūtras and making the images is also finished. Hasten back to your country, offer these things to the court, and spread the teachings throughout your country to increase the happiness of the people. Then the land will know peace and everyone will be content. In that way you will return thanks to Buddha and to your teacher. That is also the way to show your devotion to your country and to your family. My disciple I-ming will carry on the teachings here. Your task is to transmit them to the Eastern Land. Do your best! Do your best!" These were his final instructions to me, kindly and patient as always. On the night of the last full moon of the year he purified himself with a ritual bath and, lying on his right side and making the mudrā of Vairochana, he breathed his last.

That night, while I sat in meditation in the Hall, the abbot appeared to me in his usual form and said, "You and I have long been pledged to propagate the esoteric teachings. If I am reborn in Japan, this time I will be your disciple."

I have not gone into the details of all he said, but the general import of the Master's instructions I have given. [Dated 5th December 806.]

The Transmission of the Law
[From *Kōbō Daishi zenshū*, I, 83–84]

The ocean of the Law is one, but sometimes it is shallow and sometimes deep, according to the capacity of the believer. Five vehicles have been distinguished, sudden or gradual according to the vessel. Even among the teachings of sudden enlightenment, some are exoteric and some esoteric. In Esotericism itself, some doctrines represent the source while others are tributary. The masters of the Law of former times swam in the tributary waters and plucked at leaves, but the teachings I now bring back reach down to the sources and pull at the roots.

You may wonder why this is so. In ancient times Vajrasattva personally received the teachings from Vairochana. After many centuries it was transmitted to the Bodhisattva Nāgārjuna, who later transmitted it to the Āchārya Nāgabodhi. He in turn transmitted it to the Āchārya Vajrabodhi, the master of Indian and Chinese learning, who first taught the esoteric doctrines in China during the K'ai-yüan era [713-42]. Although the emperor himself reverenced his teachings, Vajrabodhi could not spread them very widely. Only with our spiritual grandfather Amoghavajra, the great master of broad wisdom, did the teachings thrive. After he had been initiated by Vajrabodhi, Amoghavajra visited the place in southern India where Nāgabodhi had taught, and silently mastered the eighteen forms of yoga. After attaining a complete understanding of the Womb Mandala and other parts of the esoteric canon, he returned to China during the T'ien-pao Era [742-65]. At this time the Emperor Hsüan-tsung was baptized; he revered Amoghavajra as his teacher.

In later years both the Emperors Su-tsung and Tai-tsung in turn received the Law. Within the imperial palace the Monastery of the Divine Dragon [1] was established, and in the capital ordination platforms were erected everywhere. The Emperor and the government officials went to these platforms to be formally baptized. This was the period when the Esoteric sect began to flourish as never before; its methods of baptism were widely adopted from this time on.

According to exoteric doctrines, enlightenment occurs only after three existences; the esoteric doctrines declare that there are sixteen chances of enlightenment within this life. In speed and in excellence the two doctrines differ as much as Buddha with his supernatural powers and a lame donkey. You who reverence the good, let this fact be clear in your minds! The superiority of the doctrines and the origins of the Law are explained at length in the five esoteric formulas of Vajrasattva and in the memorials and answers written by Benshō.

---

[1] "Divine dragon" was an era (705-6) during the reign of the Emperor Chung-tsung.

THE DIFFERENCE BETWEEN EXOTERIC
AND ESOTERIC BUDDHISM
(BEN KEMMITSU NIKYŌ-RON)

This work of Kūkai was probably an outgrowth of disputations among the sects established in or near the capital, and is intended to show the superiority of the Shingon doctrine to all others. Kūkai puts Shingon in a class by itself as the Esoteric (private) teaching of the Buddha, while other sects, whether identified as Mahāyāna or Hīnayāna, are classed together as exoteric (public) teachings. The superiority of the former is based on its claim to represent the inner experience of the Buddha in his absolute, spiritual aspect, as revealed in secret formulas to his closest disciples. Although shrouded in mystery, this Truth is attainable by all because each individual has the potentiality for Buddhahood as the very Law of his being. Properly understood and practiced this teaching offers the quickest and surest means of attaining Buddhahood in this life.

Kūkai's argument is carefully and systematically presented, taking up one by one the positions of the other schools and commenting upon them. Often he makes effective use of the impersonal dialogue form. After examining passages from the sūtras upon which the other teachings are based, he cites his own scriptural passages to show that the supreme knowledge of the Cosmic Buddha, Vairochana, was not totally incommunicable, as other sects maintained, and that certain of Buddha's followers possessed the secret keys to the storehouse of Truth. Kūkai's introduction to this work summarizes the arguments elaborated in the body of the text.

Introduction
[From *Kōbō Daishi zenshū*, pp. 474–75]

Buddha has three bodies;[2] his doctrines are in two forms. The doctrine expounded by Nirmāna Buddha is called exoteric, since the words are open and brief, and adapted to those taught. The doctrine taught by Dharma Buddha is called the esoteric treasury; the words are secret and of absolute truth. The sūtras used in exotericism number in the millions. The collection is divided by some into fifteen and by others into eleven parts. They speak of single, double, triple, quadruple, and quintuple

[2] The three bodies are called in Sanskrit Dharmakāya, Sambhogakāya, and Nirmānakāya, respectively the Buddha-body in its essential nature; Buddha's body of bliss, which he "receives" for his own "use"; and his body of transformation, by which he can appear in any form. In the Esoteric sect, the Dharma-body is associated with Vairochana, the Sambhoga-body with Amitābha, and the Nirmāna-body with the historical Buddha, Shākyamuni.

[144]

Vehicles. In discussing actions, the six ways of obtaining salvation are one of their main tenets; in explanations of the absolute, three great characteristics are delimited. The reasons why these complicated doctrines arose was clearly explained by the Great Sage. According to the esoteric *Diamond Crown Sūtra,* Buddha manifested himhelf in human form and taught the doctrine of the Three Vehicles of gradual enlightenment for the sake of bodhisattvas-to-be and the believers in Hīnayāna and Quasi-Mahāyāna.[3] Buddha also manifested himself in his Sambhoga-body and taught the exoteric doctrine of the One Vehicle of universal enlightenment for the benefit of bodhisattvas on earth. Both of these teachings were exoteric. The Dharma Buddha who manifested himself for his own sake, for his own enjoyment, expounded the doctrine of the Three Mysteries, with only his own retinue[4] present. These were the esoteric teachings. The doctrine of the Three Mysteries lies in the realm of the inner wisdom of the Buddha, and even bodhisattvas who have attained ten steps of enlightenment cannot penetrate it, much less the ordinary believers of the Hīnayāna and Quasi-Mahāyāna. Therefore, though the *Jiron* and *Shakuron*[5] declare that the Truth does not depend on the faculties, and the *Yuishiki* and *Chūkan*[6] praise the Truth as a thing beyond words or thought, the absolute truth of which they speak was known to the compilers of these commentaries (shāstras) only in theory; they were not the work of men who had attained Buddhahood.

How can we know the Truth? Within the Buddhist canon itself is clear evidence, and in the following pages I shall indicate it in detail. It is hoped that all who seek Buddha will understand their import. Some may become entangled in the net of exotericism, and thereby get into inextricable difficulties. Or, blocked by the barrier of the Quasi-Mahāyāna, they may waste their days. They will be lotus-eaters in the false Nirvāna of the Hīnayāna, children prizing yellow willow-leaves like gold. How can they hope to preserve the glorious treasures which lie within themselves, numberless as the sands of Ganges? They will be casting away the rich liquor skimmed from butter[7] to look for milk; or

---

[3] Hossō, Sanron and various other Mahāyāna schools were so termed.

[4] That is, the bodhisattvas, dragon kings, etc.

[5] Shāstras—commentaries—written not by Buddha but by bodhisattvas and other holy men, in this case Vasubandhu and Nāgārjuna respectively.

[6] Commentaries by Dharmapāla and Kumārajīva respectively.

[7] Used for the perfect Buddha-truth as found, according to Tendai, in the *Nirvāna* and *Lotus* sūtras.

discarding pearls[8] to pick up fish-eyes. Such believers are victims of a mortal disease before which even the King of Medicine would fold his hands in despair, a disease for which even the most precious medicine would be of no avail.

If men and women once catch the fragrance of these teachings, they will behold the source of knowledge reflected as in a flawless mirror, and the differences between the temporal and the real doctrines will melt away.

THE PRECIOUS KEY TO THE SECRET TREASURY

In his master work, *The Ten Stages of Religious Consciousness,* Kūkai presented a systematic evaluation of the principal schools of Buddhist teaching, as well as of Confucianism, Taoism and Brāhmanism. When it was shown to the reigning Emperor, the latter praised it highly but requested that Kūkai compose a simplified and condensed version which would make less formidable reading. His *Precious Key to the Secret Treasury* was written in response to this request.

In the opening lines of his Introduction, Kūkai acknowledges how difficult it is to make a comprehensive study of the numerous scriptures and texts representing the development of Buddhist doctrine, yet he insists that only by referring to them (as he does in the body of this work) can the manifold aspects of religious truth be made known. As a result the condensation itself is an imposing monument of scriptural scholarship. In the Introduction, however, Kūkai gives a concise résumé of his views, presented in verse, prose, and tabular form. His language is highly rhetorical and at times so obscure or allusive that a variety of interpretations or translations may be derived from a few words of text.

Introduction
[From *Kōbō Daishi zenshū,* I, 417–19]

From the deep, dim, most distant past,
A thousand thousand tomes we hold
Of sacred texts and learned lore.
Profound, abstruse, obscure and dark,
Teachings diverse and manifold—
Who can encompass such a store?

[8] A symbol of Buddha and his doctrines (in Sanskrit, *mani*).

Yet, had no one ever written such,
And if no one read what they have told,
What should we know, what should we know?
However hard they strove in thought,
The saint today, the sage of old
Would still be lost, have naught to show.

The ancient god with herb and balm [9]
Took pity on the stricken host
Of suffering, sore humanity.
And he who made the compass-cart [10]
Showed them the way whose way was lost,
A guide in their perplexity.

Yet senseless dawdlers in this world,
The three-fold realm of fantasy,
Mad, their madness do not perceive;
And all the four-fold living things
Are blinded so they cannot see
How blind they are, the self-deceived.

Born, reborn, reborn and reborn
Whence they have come they do not know.
Dying, dying, ever dying
They see not where it is they go.

. . . .

How could the Great Enlightened One, feeling a fatherly compassion
for all sentient beings and seeing the misery of their existence, silently
let it pass? It was for this reason indeed that He provided many sorts of
remedies to guide them in their perplexities. To this end he established
the following teachings:

1. [The first stage of religious consciousness is the brutish existence
described above.]

2. That which, through personal cultivation of the Five Cardinal
Virtues and Three Human Relationships, promotes social order by

---

[9] Shen-nung, the early Chinese God of Agriculture.
[10] The Duke of Chou, statesman instrumental in founding the Chou dynasty of Ancient
China, was said to have provided a "south-pointing chariot" for some foreign emissaries
who could not find their way back home.

enabling prince and minister, father and son each to fulfill his proper mission in life. [Confucianism.]

3. That which, through practice of the six disciplines and the four methods of mental concentration, produces contempt for the world below and desire for that above, from which one may proceed to the attainment of happiness in heaven. [Brāhmanism and popular Taoism.]

4. That which, recognizing that the self is unreal and represents only a temporary combination of the Five Components[11] strives to achieve the eight forms of disentanglement and six supernatural powers that come from concentrated meditation. [The Shrāvaka vehicle of Hīnayāna Buddhism practiced by the direct disciples of the Buddha.]

5. That which, through personal practice of the meditation on the Twelve Links of Causation,[12] makes one aware of the impermanence and ego-lessness of all things, and thus uproots the seeds of karma. [The Pratyeka-Buddha vehicle of Hīnayāna Buddhism, practiced by those seeking enlightenment for themselves.]

6. That which, from a sense of unlimited compassion for others, and following the highest inner knowledge which transcends all external circumstances, overcomes all impediments within the mind to transform the eight consciousnesses into the Fourfold Wisdom of the Buddha.[13] [Hossō school of Quasi-Mahāyāna.]

7. That which, by understanding one's nature through the method of eightfold negation[14] and by transcending ordinary forms of argument through realization that Truth is void of name or character, brings the mind to a state of tranquility, absolute and indescribable. [Sanron school of Quasi-Mahāyāna.]

8. That which, by realizing the absolute and universal way in one's primal nature, causes the Bodhisattva of Mercy, Kannon,[15] to smile with delight. [Tendai school of Mahāyāna.]

[11] Form (body), sensation, perception, psychic construction, and consciousness.

[12] Blindness, will to live, subconsciousness, name and form, sense organs, contact, perception, desire, cleaving, formation of being, birth and death—together making up the Wheel of Life or Cycle of Causations and Becomings.

[13] According to the psychological doctrines of the Hossō school there are eight consciousnesses: five sense consciousnesses, the sense-center, thought-center, and ideation center. These are transformed into the wisdom of accomplishing works, awareness of diversity, awareness of equality, and the wisdom of mirror-like objectivity.

[14] Negation of all specific features: no production, no extinction; no annihilation, no permanence; no unity, no diversity; no coming, no going.

[15] Avalokiteshvara—here a symbol of the Tendai doctrine of the One in the Many, the identity of noumenon and phenomenon.

9. That which, by embracing cosmic existence in the first awakening of religious consciousness, causes the Bodhisattva Fugen [16] to beam with satisfaction. [Kegon school of Mahāyāna.]

10. By these teachings the dust and stains of the world are cleansed away, revealing the splendor and solemnity of the world of the Mandalas. As the performer of the Mantra meditates on the syllables *Ma* and *Ta,* the Buddha's nature shines forth and dispels the darkness of ignorance. In the lasting light of sun and moon appear the Bodhisattvas of Wisdom, while the Five Buddhas [17] reign supreme, each making his characteristic sign of the hand. The universe is filled with the radiance of the Four Mandala Circles [18] representing the Buddha-world.

Achala, the God of Fire, with his left eye closed and right wide open, glares out over the realm of sentient beings and stills the stormy winds of worldly desire. The King of Triumph, Trailokyavijaya, three times roars forth his mighty *"Hūṃ,"* evaporating the unruly waves of lust. The Eight Angelic Maidens [19] [at the corners of the Diamond Mandala] float through the clouds and over the seas to make their exquisite offerings, while the Four Queens of Wisdom [20] are enraptured by the bliss of the Law.

Such is this state that even those most advanced in the various stages of ordinary Buddhism are unable even to glimpse it, and those who have diligently cultivated the Three Divisions of the Eight-fold Path [21] cannot approach it. It is the secret of all secrets, the enlightenment of all enlightenments. [Esoteric Buddhism.]

Alas, men are ignorant of the treasures they possess, and in their confusion consider themselves enlightened. What is it but utter foolishness! The Buddha's compassion is indeed profound, but without his teaching

[16] Samantabhadra—here a symbol of the Kegon doctrine of the interdependence of all things, all-embracing love.

[17] The Cosmic Buddha, the Buddhas of the four quarters and the Bodhisattvas of the four corners make up the central figures of the Mandalas.

[18] The Great Circle, consisting of graphic Buddha-figures; the Symbol Circle, consisting of the articles carried by each; the Law Circle, consisting of letters representing saintly beings; and the Circle of Works, represented by sculptured figures.

[19] Those of the first division, serving inside, representing the smile, hair tresses, song and dance; those of the second division, serving outside, representing incense, flowers, lanterns and ointment.

[20] Representing the Diamond (*Vajra*), Jewel (*Cintāmaṇi*), Law (Dharma) and Action (Karma).

[21] Right Views, Thought, Speech and Action are the elements of human character or self-control; Right Mindfulness, Endeavor and Livelihood are the elements of human life or self-purification; Right Concentration is the element of self-development.

how can they be saved? The remedies have been provided, yet if men refuse to take them, how can they be cured? If we do naught but spend our time in vain discussion and vain recitation, the King of Healing will surely scold us for it.

Now there are nine kinds of medicine [22] for the diseases of the mind, but the most they can do is sweep away the surface dust and dispel the mind's confusion. Only in the Diamond Palace [23] do we find the secret treasury opened wide to dispense its precious truths. To enjoy them or reject them—this is for everyone to decide in his own mind. No one else can do it for you; you must realize it for yourself.

Those who seek Buddha's wisdom must know the difference between a true jewel and an ordinary stone, between cow's milk and the milk of an ass. They must not fail to distinguish them; they must not fail to distinguish them.

The ten stages of religious experience, as revealed in the scriptures and their commentaries, are clearly and systematically presented in what follows.

Recapitulation of the Ten Stages of Religious Consciousness
[From *Kōbō Daishi zenshū*, I, 420]

1. The mind animal-like and goatish in its desires.
   The mass-man in his madness realizes not his faults.
   He thinks but of his lusts and hungers; he is like a butting goat.
2. The mind ignorant and infantile yet abstemious.
   Influenced by external causes, the mind awakens to temperance in eating.
   The will to do kindnesses sprouts, like a seed in good soil. [Confucianism.]
3. The mind infantile and without fears.
   The pagan hopes for birth in heaven, there for a while to know peace.
   He is like an infant, like a calf that follows its mother. [Brāhmanism or popular Taoism.]
4. The mind recognizing only the objects perceived, not the ego.
   The mind understands only that there are Elements, the ego it completely denies.

[22] The first nine teachings or stages of religious consciousness.   [23] Esoteric Buddhism.

The *Tripiṭaka* of the Goat-Cart is summed up by this verse. [Shrāvaka vehicle of Hīnayāna Buddhism.]

5. The mind freed from the causes and seeds of karma.

Having mastered the 12-divisioned cycle of causations and beginning, the mind extirpates the seeds of blindness.

When karma birth has been ended, the ineffable fruits of Nirvāna are won. [Pratyeka-Buddha vehicle of Hīnayāna Buddhism.]

6. The Mahāyāna mind bringing about the salvation of others.

When compassion is aroused without condition, the Great Compassion first appears.

It views distinctions between "you" and "me" as imaginary; recognizing only consciousness it denies the external world. [The Hossō sect.]

7. The mind aware of the negation of birth.

Through eightfold negations, foolishness is ended; with one thought the truth of absolute Voidness becomes apparent.

The mind becomes empty and still; it knows peace and happiness that cannot be defined. [The Sanron sect.]

8. The mind which follows the one way of Truth.

The universe is by nature pure; in it knowledge and its objects fuse together.

He who knows this state of reality has a cosmic mind. [The Tendai sect.]

9. The mind completely lacking characteristics of its own.

Water lacks a nature of its own; when met by winds it becomes waves.

The universe has no determined form, but at the slightest stimulus immediately moves forward. [The Kegon sect.]

10. The mind filled with the mystic splendor of the cosmic Buddha.

When the medicine of exoteric teachings has cleared away the dust, the True Words open the Treasury.

When the secret treasures are suddenly displayed, all virtues are apparent. [The Shingon sect.]

CHAPTER VIII

THE SPREAD OF ESOTERIC BUDDHISM

A student of the history of Japanese Buddhism is likely to get the impression that the various sects represented successive stages in the development of the religion. He may thus imagine that the sects of the Nara Period gave way to Tendai and Shingon Buddhism, which in turn were replaced by one after another of the popular sects of the medieval period. More careful examination will show, however, that instead of following a regular pattern of rise, flourishing, decline and extinction, most of the sects continued to exist long after their period of glory, oblivious to the signs of decline which the historian might observe, and capable always of unexpected revivals. This was certainly true of the Nara sects, some of which not only preserved their identity throughout the Heian and medieval periods but still exist today. Similarly Esoteric Buddhism, by which is meant here both Tendai and Shingon, continued to make its influence felt long after Kūkai's time. Esoteric Buddhism set the predominant tone of religious life in the Heian Period, and its influence extended to all the other schools. Even the popular sects that turned away from its excessive emphasis on ritual drew much of their inspiration from doctrines contained in the vast storehouse of Esoteric Buddhism. Its syncretism lent itself readily to combination with other beliefs, whether the Buddhism of other sects, Shinto, or even alien teachings like yin-yang. And a place for some new god could always be found in its spacious pantheon.

When, however, the hundreds of deities who populated the maṇḍalas proved too much even for the polytheistic Japanese, their number was gradually reduced to thirteen selected objects of worship: Fudō, Shaka, Monju, Fugen, Jizō, Miroku, Yakushi, Kannon, Seishi, Amida, Ashiku, Dainichi, and Kokūzō. Of these thirteen the most exalted were considered to be Dainichi (Vairochana), Ashiku (Akshobhya), Amida (Amitābha), Miroku (Maitreya) and Shaka (Shākyamuni). Dainichi occupied the center of the pantheon of Esoteric Buddhism. To the east of him sat Ashiku, the source of life, and to the west Amida, the dispenser of infinite love. Miroku, the Buddha of the future, and Shaka, the historical Buddha, completed this group of Tathāgatas.

Each of the thirteen deities had claims to the worshipers' attention, but by the late Heian Period two of them came to occupy a special place in the religious life of Japan: Kannon (Avalokiteshvara), one of the Bodhisattva attendants of Amida, who came to be worshiped as a Goddess of Mercy (although a male deity in India), and Fudō (Achala), a fierce god apparently of Indian origin although neither a Buddha nor a Bodhisattva. Statues of Kannon were erected at thirty-three sites of remarkable beauty in Japan, and pilgrimages to the different shrines were popular with all classes, from the imperial family downwards. The famous temple of the "33,333 Kannons," each with a "thousands hands" for dispensing mercy, was built in the twelfth century, and serves as an indication of the extreme popularity of this deity during the late Heian Period. In contrast to the merciful Kannon, Fudō was represented as "a terrible figure, livid blue in color and of a ferocious expression. He is surrounded by flames and carries a sword and a rope to smite and bind evil. He is generally explained as typifying the fierce aspect assumed by Vairochana when resenting wrong doing."[1] If Kannon represented the female (or *Garbha* mandala), Fudō stood for the male (or *vajra*), and as such was popular with the rising warrior class, who may have likened themselves, the guardians of the state in the face of disorder, to the powerful Fudō. The cult of Fudō spread not to the charming scenic spots chosen for Kannon but to regions where nature presented her severest face—rocky crags and the shores of the sea.

Probably the most important event in the history of Esoteric Buddhism in the years following the death of Kūkai (who had established the teachings in Japan) was its triumph on Mt. Hiei, the stronghold of Tendai. Saichō himself had studied Esoteric learning with Kūkai, but it remained for his disciple and successor Ennin (794–864) to found Tendai esotericism (*Taimitsu*). Ennin had led a rather colorless life as a priest and teacher and was already in his forties when he was sent to China for study in 838. At first unable to obtain the necessary authoriza-

[1] Eliot, *Japanese Buddhism*, pp. 348–49.

tion to visit either Wu-t'ai shan or T'ien-t'ai shan, the two most important Buddhist centers, he managed with great difficulty to be set ashore on the Chinese coast, and was later fortunate enough to meet a general who secured permission for him to visit Wu-t'ai shan and other holy sites. Ennin finally returned to Japan in 847 after extensive study with the masters of each of the Tendai disciplines. Upon his return to Mt. Hiei he organized study of the two maṇḍala, initiated Esoteric baptism and promoted other branches of Esoteric learning. Ennin also introduced to Japan the invocation of Buddha's name (*nembutsu*) which he had heard at Wu-t'ai shan, and had a special hall built for this purpose. *Nembutsu* was to become in some of the popular sects an all-sufficient means of gaining salvation, but for Ennin it appeared to be of less importance than Esoteric learning.

The establishment of Tendai esotericism marked a new phase in the relations between Tendai and Shingon. The Tendai monks had never forgiven Kūkai for having placed Tendai below Kegon in his *Ten Stages,* and for a long time they had sought some way of emerging from under the domination of Shingon. With the development of Tendai esotericism it was believed on Mt. Hiei that Shingon's claim to stand at the head of the Ten Stages in unique splendor had been at last rendered untenable. The two schools of esoteric teaching had many points in common, but at least one basic difference: Shingon had originated in China as the esoteric teachings of the Kegon school, and held as its central tenet the incompatibility of Exoteric and Esoteric Buddhism; Tendai esotericism, on the other hand, originated in China as the esoteric discipline of Tendai itself, which taught that the exoteric and esoteric teachings were one.

The contest between Tendai and Shingon for recognition as the center of esotericism resulted in victory for the Hiei monks. Their success was due partially to the failure of Shingon to produce great leaders in the generations after Kūkai, and partially to the advantage which geographical proximity to the capital gave to Hiei over the more distant Kōya. However, the split in the ranks of Tendai esotericism caused by the founding of the Miidera school prevented the Mt. Hiei monks from taking full advantage of the supremacy they gained over Shingon, and led to some of the least attractive episodes in the history of Japanese Buddhism.

Miidera was a temple founded originally in 674 by the shores of Lake

Biwa. It was associated with the Ōtomo family, and with the decline in the fortunes of the Ōtomo the temple had fallen into ruins. Enchin (814–891), a nephew of Kūkai, founded a center of study at the Miidera shortly after his return to Japan in 858 from six years' study in China of the Tendai and esoteric teachings. In 864 the temple was attached to the Enryaku-ji on Mt. Hiei. Enchin's appointment in 868 as abbot of the Enryaku-ji made him the most important figure in Tendai Buddhism, and his strong personality earned for him devoted followers and bitter enemies. The immediate successors of Enchin to the abbacy of the Enryaku-ji were of his school, but they were followed by a line of men who were identified with Ennin. When in 933 a supporter of Enchin's was unexpectedly appointed as abbot by the emperor, the Ennin faction rebelled against him, and as a result the followers of Enchin marched from Mt. Hiei to the Miidera, where they formed an almost entirely in- dependent school. Violent disputes frequently broke out between the two branches of Tendai esotericism. In 1039, for example, the appoint- ment of a Miidera man resulted in a demonstration by 3,000 Hiei monks before the house of the regent in Kyoto, thereby compelling the deposi- tion of the unwanted abbot. Violence reached its height in 1081 when Hiei monks burst into the confines of the Miidera and set it afire, destroying most of the buildings. They returned three months later to finish off the job. In the course of the next three centuries the Miidera was burned seven times, usually by Hiei monks, and reconstructed each time by the determined followers of Enchin.

The rise of the "warrior-monks" was a prominent feature of medieval Buddhism. Their lawlessness was at its peak during the reigns of the Emperor Shirakawa (1072–1086) and his immediate successors. When- ever the monks had some demand to make, they would march in force on the capital, bearing with them the palanquins of the Shinto god Sannō, the guardian deity of Mt. Hiei. The first such descent took place in 1095, and almost every one of the thirty or forty following years saw at least one visitation either of the Tendai "warrior-monks" or those of the Hossō sect from the Kōfuku-ji in Nara, who periodically stormed into the capi- tal with the sacred tree of the Kasuga (Shinto) Shrine. Frequent battles between the Tendai and the Hossō monks disturbed the peace of the capital for about a century from Shirakawa's reign onwards. In 1165 the Hiei monks burned the Kiyomizu-dera, the stronghold of the Hossō sect in Kyoto, and the Hossō monks attempted unsuccessfully to burn the Enryaku-ji.

Beset by such internecine warfare, Esoteric Buddhism also had to struggle against a tendency for the impressive rituals associated with the Three Mysteries to degenerate into mere superstition. The spells recited to prolong life were typical of this trend in the late Heian Period. Texts of these spells had been brought to Japan from China by Kūkai, Ennin, and Enchin, but the earliest mention of the performance of the secret rituals accompanying them dates from 1075, during the reign of Shirakawa, when the abbot of the Enryaku-ji executed the ceremony. It was performed again in 1080 in the imperial palace. This ritual was carried out in exact conformity to the texts. It was prescribed that before the presiding priest could perform the spell he had to bathe with perfumed water, don newly purified clothes, receive the Eight Commandments, and eat a meal of plain rice, honey, and milk. The actual ceremony required twenty-one small platforms built on top of a large platform, and different types of rare incense and flowers to accompany each part of the prayers. Such a ceremony was open to serious criticism not only because of its costliness, but because the prolongation of life on earth by means of spells seemed clearly contrary to the teachings of the Buddha.

As time went on, moreover, various heresies gained currency which tended to bring discredit on all of Esoteric Buddhism. The most notorious of them was the so-called Tachikawa school, founded in the early twelfth century by a Shingon believer with the aid of a yin-yang teacher whom he met while in exile. They evolved a doctrine teaching that "the Way of man and woman, yin and yang, is the secret art of becoming a Buddha in this life. No other way exists but this one to attain Buddhahood and gain the Way." [2] As authority for this statement, the *Vajra* and *Garbha Mandalas* were declared to be symbols of the male and female principles, and other elaborate yin-yang correspondences were drawn. The immoral rites practiced by the somewhat similar Shāktist sects of Tibet appear also to have been indulged in by the Tachikawa school. In 1335 as the result of a memorial submitted by the Mt. Kōya monks against the Tachikawa school, its leader was exiled and books which expounded its principles were ordered to be burned. Traces of its doctrines still survive in existing Buddhist sects.

[2] Statement in the *Hōkyōshō*, an anti-Tachikawa work which is one of our chief sources of information on the school.

Prayer of the Retired Emperor Shirakawa on Offering the Tripiṭaka to Hachiman

In November of 1128 the retired Emperor Shirakawa, father, grandfather, and great-grandfather of emperors reigning in his own lifetime, offered his prayer to the god Hachiman for ten years more of life. On this occasion he presented a copy of the *Tripiṭaka,* to be read uninterruptedly by six priests, and in his prayer he enumerated other acts of piety already performed. These reflect the Esoteric Buddhism then prevalent at court, especially in its iconographic forms. The syncretic tendencies of Esoteric Buddhism are also apparent in its association with notions concerning immortality and longevity which are typical of popular Taoism. These same tendencies account for the making of such an offering to Hachiman. It may seem curious that the Shinto God Hachiman was favored with a copy of the Buddhist scriptures, but·in the ages of the Combined Faith Hachiman was worshiped as a great bodhisattva, and such a gift seemed wholly appropriate. In spite of the fervent prayers made to him, however, Shirakawa died the following year.

The practice of a sovereign abdicating and becoming a Buddhist priest, while continuing to rule in the name of a boy emperor, was inaugurated by the Emperor Uda (r. 889–97) and became an established institution with Shirakawa. Not only a devout Buddhist but an astute politician, the latter saw the advantages of governing from behind the scenes with the title "Emperor of the [Buddhist] Law (*hōō*)." This represents a fusion of the *Tennō* concept deriving from Chinese absolutism with the title *hōō* (King of the Law) once accorded the priest Dōkyō, who was thwarted in his attempt to become emperor in the Nara period. Now when emperors themselves became priests, the parallel development of Chinese political institutions and Buddhist religious ideals became merged in a single symbol of sovereignty.

Shirakawa's prayer was actually written by a courtier, Fujiwara no Atsumitsu (1062–1144). It is in balanced-prose, the ornate Chinese style which Kūkai had popularized in Japan.

[From Tsuji, *Nihon Bukkyō Shi,* Jōsei Hen, pp. 728–33]

This copy of the *Tripiṭaka,* transcribed by imperial order, is composed as follows:

Mahāyāna sūtras	2,395 volumes
Hīnayāna sūtras	618 volumes
Mahāyāna vinayas	55 volumes
Hīnayāna vinayas	441 volumes
Mahāyāna shāstras	515 volumes
Hīnayāna shāstras	695 volumes
Biographies of the Bodhisattvas and Arhats	593 volumes
Total	5,312 volumes

The above enumerated sūtras, vinayas, shāstras and biographies are respectfully offered to the Hachiman Temple at Iwashimizu, to be used for lectures and sermons.

I recall that when I was still young and inexperienced, the former sovereign transmitted to me the imperial rank. Grave though the responsibility was, I remained ignorant of the ways of administration. When I received the documents and records of the domains within the four seas, I felt as though I stood before a profound abyss, and when I tried to control the multifarious activities of government, it was like driving a team of horses with rotting reins. How, I wondered, could I devise a good plan, so that I might rule my land in peace? I placed my faith in the spirits of my ancestors, and relied on the powers of the gods of Heaven and Earth.

Soon after my assumption of the imperial rank, in the year 1074, I paid homage at the palace of the Bodhisattva Hachiman. Since that time I have arranged an imperial visit every year in the third moon. In the morning, when the petals of the palace cherry-blossoms are wet with dew, I leave the purple gate in my palanquin; in the evening, when the mountain nightingales are singing in the mist, I stand in worship by the fence of the shrine while voices and flutes harmoniously blend. This has become an established practice, although unknown in former times.

More than forty years have passed since my abdication. Often have I urged my carriage forward through stormy winds in the pine-clad hills; many times have I offered my devotion on the steps of the shrine in the woods. I have made this pilgrimage twenty-five times. During this period I have built a pagoda at the Usa Shrine to help establish the prestige of the sacred precincts. I have had the *Great Sūtra of Wisdom* copied in gold to extol the bliss of the temporal and real Law. It would be hard to recall all the treasures that have been offered, the lectures on the holy writings that have been sponsored, and the devotion expressed by my pilgrimages of thanks. During all this time, whenever I have stood in thought by the window, my mind has been drawn to the moon [1] of clear insight, and whenever I have sat in meditation, my graying brows have been knitted in concentration.

My descendants, always increasing in numbers, have succeeded one after another to the imperial rank,[2] and each one has enjoyed a long

_____
[1] In Buddhist writings the moon is often used as a symbol of wisdom.
[2] Shirakawa reigned from 1072–86. He abdicated in favor of his seven-year-old son

reign devoted to solicitude for the people. That now, despite my advanced age, I am able to help my lord, the boy sovereign, is indeed a sign that I have obtained the grace of Heaven and the favor of the gods. For me to have witnessed my great-grandson receive the prognostications for his reign [3] shows that I have attained an age approaching a rarity.

"It is not the millet which has a piercing fragrance; it is bright virtue." [4] Buddha's teachings and not bright gems are precious. All the true teachings we possess are those preached by the peerless Shākyamuni during his lifetime. At his birth he stood on the lotus, and the air of the Lumbinī Grove first was replete with his fragrance. [5] In his wanderings he saw the Tree, and the moon of enlightenment attained its fullness. On high mountains and level fields alike the sun of mercy shone everywhere. In the Deer Park and on Vulture Peak the fructifying rain of the Law fell in abundance. The Greater and the Lesser Vehicles ran abreast and the Basic and the Complete Schools [6] both opened their gates. The teachings traveled 10,000 leagues over the boundless seas, above the high-tossing billows, to be transmitted at last from those distant lands to our imperial realm. Here sovereigns and subjects have all offered devout reverence; the high and the mighty have vied with each other in acts of piety. The prosperity of the land has no other source but this.

Therefore, I have had several copies of the sūtras, vinayas and shāstras made on behalf of the Three Bodies of the Buddha, in order to promote the Surpassing Cause of enlightenment and to bring about the perfect and ultimate Enlightenment of the Buddha. Now, in early winter, the seventeenth of November, the maigre repast [7] has been spread out on the sacrificial altar. To the shrine among the elms and oaks have come the gorgeous carriages of the court, and the illustrious officials follow behind;

Horikawa, who reigned from 1086–1107. On his death his four-year-old son Toba succeeded (Shirakawa's grandson). He reigned from 1107–23, abdicating in favor of his four-year-old son Sutoku (Shirakawa's great-grandson). In 1128, the year of this document, Shirakawa was seventy-five years old, his son was dead, his grandson Toba was twenty-five years old, and his great-grandson Sutoku was nine years old.

[3] Prepared at the beginning of an emperor's reign by specialists in the Chinese art of prognostication.

[4] A quotation from the Book of History. See Legge, The Chinese Classics, Shoo-King, Part V, Book XXI, p. 2.

[5] Important episodes in the life of the historical Buddha are given here: his birth in the Lumbinī Grove, his attainment of enlightenment under the Bodhi Tree, his first sermon at the deer park in Benares, and his teaching to the ascetics of Vulture Peak.

[6] The two vehicles and two schools refer to Mahāyāna and Hīnayāna.

[7] A vegetarian feast for monks.

to the mountain of paulownia and cedar have repaired the splendidly robed priests, and the numberless monks are gathered like clouds. Present also is my dutiful grandson, who inclines his dark cap in profound piety; it was the reigning Emperor, my great-grandson, who gave instructions to the officials for this maigre feast. The rhythmic flutes alternately play, transmitting their lovely melodies to the Cloud Gates; [8] dancing sleeves frequently twist, capturing a wonderful charm on the dewy ground. This day of the year has been established as a day of ceremony, known as the Feast of the *Tripitaka,* a precedent for all ages to follow. In order to continue what has been begun today throughout future years, six priests will permanently reside here, to read aloud the whole of the scriptures. The recitation is to continue without a break; when once finished, it is to be started again. In one year, one complete reading may be accomplished; in ten years ten readings may be performed. Through the merit that accrues from ten readings my life will be prolonged ten years. I do not venture to describe what may happen in this life when once I have attained that age. Let the readings then continue perpetually, to the glory of the Law, so that all living creatures may rely on the divine aid. May this unending reading lead to a true awakening.

It is my conviction that Buddhism renders help to the gods; it also protects the imperial rule. Therefore, early in my reign, I solemnly vowed to have a beautiful site selected east of the capital for the erection of a great monastery. This was the Hōshō Temple. In the Golden Pavilion were installed a gilt image 32 feet tall of the Buddha Vairochana, images 20 feet tall of four Buddhas of the Womb Mandala, two 9-feet-tall polychrome images of the Two Guardian Kings, and 8-feet-tall images of the Four Deva Kings. In the Lecture Hall were installed a 20-feet-tall gilt image of Shākyamuni and 16-feet-tall images of Samantabhadra and Manjushrī. Every year in the tenth moon I had priests and monks of the different sects lecture on the five parts of the Mahāyāna Sūtras. In the Amida Hall were installed nine gilt images of the Buddha Amitābha, each 16 feet tall, together with 10-feet-tall images of the Bodhisattvas Avalokiteshvara and Mahāsthāmaprāpta, attended by polychrome images of the Four Deva Kings, each 6 feet tall. In the Yakushi Hall were installed seven gilt images of the Healing Buddha, with his two attendant Bodhisattvas, Sunlight and Moonlight. In the Hall of the Five Illustrious

[8] Meaning the heavens and also suggesting a kind of classical Chinese music.

Deities [9] were installed a polychrome image 26 feet tall of Achala, together with 16-feet-tall images of the Four Deva Kings. In the Lotus Hall was installed a pagoda of the Seven Treasures, and six priests remain there to perform the samādhi discipline. An octangular, nine-storied pagoda enshrined within it gilt images 8 feet tall of the Five Tathāgatas who embody the five wisdoms of Buddha.

[At this point are omitted the details of other donations by the Emperor Shirakawa, including temples, statues, and the copying of the *Tripiṭaka*.]

Of the six fundamental disciplines, the observance of the commandments is considered the most important; of the ten commandments, the prohibition on the taking of life is the prime one. All living creatures are our dear friends; successive generations are of one flesh and blood. There is no end to the turning of the Wheel, and no escape from the torments of hell. There is no one source of life, but fish, insects, birds, and beasts are variously born from transformation, moisture, eggs, and the womb.[10] However tiny a creature may be, it clings to its life as though more important than Mt. T'ai. However fierce an animal may be, its love for its young surpasses that found among human beings. And yet the practice has been transmitted of making a living by the slaughter of animals. Some urge forward their horses in sanguinary pursuit of hart and hind. Some carry blue falcons on their wrists for flying at pheasants and hares. In the desolate fields, some shoot captive arrows [11] above the evening clouds; on the vast expanse of the sea, some delight to catch the fish of the icy waves. The pangs of sympathy were not to be borne; the desire for penitence rose within me. When word reached me that various provinces offered a tribute of fish, in accordance with regulations, I forbade this practice completely. Eleven provinces halted their offerings of regional maritime produce; the people left off their tribute. As time went on, fish could dart about without fear.[12] In addition, 8,823 fine-meshed

[9] These were gods of wrath especially worshipped in Shingon Buddhism. The most important was Fudō (Achala).

[10] The four modes of birth: 1) birth from the womb as animals; 2) birth from the egg as birds; 3) from moisture as fish and insects; 4) sudden birth without any apparent cause, as bodhisattvas.

[11] Arrows having a cord attached, used in shooting birds.

[12] An allusion to Chuang Tzu 17, "See how the minnows are darting about! That is the pleasure of fishes" (tr. Giles, *Chuang Tzu,* 218). Here it simply means that the fish were now protected from fishermen and could dart about happily.

fishing-nets were burnt, and in more than 45,300 places hunter's trails were covered. Those who violated the edicts were severely punished.

The virtue of sparing life comes from the fact that it arouses divine retribution. Brahmā, sitting in his lofty palace in Heaven, scrutinizes the minds of men and clearly knows their thoughts. Shakra, dallying in his pleasure garden, turns his compassionate glance and illuminates all actions. He who accomplishes an act of mercy will have a prayer accomplished; he who increases the happiness of others will have his span of life increased. When the Yellow Emperor asked Heaven about old age, he learned that 120 years was considered a very long life. The Emperor Wu of Han by praying to Mt. T'ai lived until his eightieth year. When I consider my own life and attempt to calculate how long it will last, I realize that if I pray to live 120 years, there are but rare precedents for such a great age. If I hope for eighty years, not much remains of my old age. The most I desire is to prolong my life ten years more. Then, as progenitor of three successive sovereigns, I shall be without peer in the world, and as the senior by six years of Shākyamuni,[13] I shall have all I desire in this mortal world. If the Great Bodhisattva Hachiman extends his divine protection, the gods will answer my great prayer; if the Tathāgatas of the ten directions [14] vouchsafe their aid, my life will be strong as the Diamond. I shall then be able to attain enlightenment, and I shall certainly be born in the paradise of peace and purity. The moral force of good actions brings neighbors; [15] their merit has no bounds. This one good action will reach alike the reigning Emperor, the retired Emperor, the Empress Dowager, the Empress, the princes and the princesses, and they will enjoy great longevity. The nation will boast a reign of peace and harmony; all people will be at liberty to enjoy their pleasures. Thus may all, from the pillars of Heaven above, to the circle of the wind below,[16] taste the savor of the Law and sojourn in the garden of enlightenment. [17th November 1128.]

[13] Shirakawa, by Japanese reckoning, was seventy-six years old. Since Shākyamuni is said to have died at the age of eighty, if Shirakawa lived ten more years he would be six years older than Shākyamuni was.

[14] The eight points of the compass plus up and down.

[15] A quotation from the *Analects*. "The Master said: Moral force never dwells in solitude; it will always bring neighbors." (IV, 25. tr. Waley).

[16] The lowest circle of the world in the Buddhist cosmogony was that of the wind.

Sex and Buddhahood—A Shingon Heresy
(Selections from *The Precious Mirror* [*Hōkyōshō*])

This short work written by the Shingon priest Yūkai (1345–1416) is of interest in tracing certain developments in the later history of Esoteric Buddhism. In its emphasis on the pedigree of the Shingon teachings, it was no more than echoing Kūkai's words of six hundred years before, but in the meantime the orthodox tradition had suffered much from the numerous heresies which developed out of the Tantric aspects of the religion. In the excerpts here given Yūkai attacks one of the most notorious heresies, the so-called Tachikawa School; in other parts of his essay he mentions how Shingon's name had been lent to magical arts which bore little relation to the doctrines taught by Kūkai, including the art of discovering buried treasure and the art of flying about at will. Even the most outlandish heresy was capable of producing scriptural evidence for the validity of its view, for the Buddhist canon as transmitted to Japan contained an incredible variety of texts, some of them little more than thinly disguised formulae for magical rites. The Tachikawa School was almost extinct by Yūkai's day, as he himself states, but other bizarre heresies continued to dominate Esoteric Buddhism.

[From *Taishō daizōkyō*, Vol. 77, pp. 847–49]

Shingon Esotericism is the secret doctrine taught by Vairochana, the King of Enlightenment, and transmitted by the Eight Founders. It is called the Supreme Highest Vehicle of the Buddha, and bears the title of the Realm Surpassing all Sects. Indeed, only through this teaching can one exterminate the extremely heavy burdens of karma, or save the living creatures difficult of conversion, or quickly realize the Buddhist knowledge. That is why in ancient times eight wise philosophers who went to China to seek the Law received instruction in Shingon. The Eastern temple [Shingon] had five transmitters of the teachings: Kūkai, Shūei, Eun, Engyō and Jōgyō.[1] The other school [Tendai] had three transmitters: Saichō, Ennin and Enchin. . . . Among the teachings received from China, those obtained by Kūkai are the senior ones, because they were passed down from one heir to the traditions to the next, from the Great Founder Vairochana to Hui-kuo, the abbot of The Green Dragon Temple in China. I cannot enter into details here, but although Hui-kuo transmitted the Law to many people . . . only Kūkai and I-ming were in-

---

[1] Shūei (808–84), Eun (798–869), Engyō (799–852) and Jōgyō (d. 866), together with the more famous Kūkai, Saichō, Ennin and Enchin are often spoken of as the eight priests who sought the Law in China.

structed in the two maṇḍalas, and I-ming was not fully instructed. He died without transmitting the Law to anyone. Only Kūkai was the true heir of Hui-kuo. . . . Kūkai in turn transmitted the teachings to many disciples. [Genealogical tables omitted.]

Someone asked, "It is indeed true that the Shingon teachings are the highest of all the sects, and are the direct road for attaining Buddhahood. However, in late years the false and the true have become confused. To enter a false path and to violate the true way of becoming a Buddha is like saying East is West, and the point of view becomes topsy-turvy. How then can one attain the goal of becoming a Buddha? I crave your instruction on this matter."

I replied, "It is difficult to distinguish jade and stone; it is easy to be misled by worthless things, and difficult to establish the difference between the false and the true. For example, among the disciples of the Daigo Sambō-in there was a man called the *ajari* Ninkan. On account of some crime of which he was found guilty, he was exiled to the province of Izu, and there he earned his living by teaching Shingon to married laity and to meat-eating, defiled people, whom he made his disciples. A yin-yang teacher from a place called Tachikawa in the province of Musashi studied Shingon with Ninkan and combined it with his yin-yang doctrines. The false and the true were thus confounded; the inner and the outer learning were indiscriminately mixed. He called it the Tachikawa School, and expounded it as a branch of Shingon. This was the origin of the heresy. . . .

The principle of this sect was to consider the way of men and women, yin and yang, to be the secret art of obtaining Buddhahood in this flesh, and the only means of obtaining Buddhahood and gaining the Way. They made outrageous assertions that the Buddha had previously taught their doctrines, a diabolic invention deserving of eternal punishment in hell. Ignorant people, not realizing this, upheld it as the most profound and secret Law. How can one say that they possessed true views and genuine knowledge? The *Śūraṅgama Sūtra* declares, "Those who secretly desire to perform acts of greed and lust are fond of saying that the eyes, ears, nose, and tongue are all 'pure land' and that the male and female organs are the true places of perfect knowledge [bodhi] and Nirvāna. The ignorant people believe these foul words. They are to be called poisoners, hinderers, and demons. When they die they become devils who afflict and unsettle people in this world, causing them to become confused and unwittingly to fall into the hell of eternal punishment." How can people belonging to that hell be called Shingon believers? . . .

This Tachikawa School later spread to the province of Etchū. In successive generations two teachers, Kakumei and Kakuin, lived on Mount Kōya [and taught Tachikawa doctrine there]. At this time many secret manuals and texts of this heretical school were in circulation, often called "oral transmission of the secrets of esoteric doctrine." To this day there are ignorant people who study such works and believe them to possess the loftiest thoughts. In truth they are neither exoteric nor esoteric, but merely so many stones wrapped in jade. . . . Many people studied these teachings, but they did not meet with divine favor, and for the most part both the teachings and the men have perished. A few are left, but I do not know how many.

Prayers for the Shogun

This letter was written to the Shogun Yoriie by the Shingon monk, Mongaku, who had been a close adviser of Yoriie's father, Minamoto Yoritomo. In refusing to offer prayers for the shogun, Mongaku does not hesitate to scold him for his failings as a ruler. The forthrightness and independence of mind displayed by even this priest of the formalistic Shingon sect show that these were not qualities characteristic of Zen alone but of Kamakura Buddhism in general. Nothing could better illustrate than this letter both the abuse of esoteric practices by those with little understanding of them, and the reaffirmation of true men of religion like Mongaku that the performance of these rituals must go hand in hand with genuine piety and exemplary moral conduct.
[From *Kokushi Taikei*, XXXII, *Azuma Kagami*, 579–84]

LETTER OF THE PRIEST MONGAKU TO SHOGUN YORIIE A.D. 1200
I respectfully acknowledge your second letter. I sent you an answer before, but since you have written me again, I am replying again in the same tenor. While reading your letter, I repeatedly felt that I was listening to a message from the late Generalissimo and I was deeply moved.

[You ask me] to offer prayers—and I remember with gratitude beyond expression that the Generalissimo rebuilt the East Temple [1] and made possible through his generosity the re-establishment of the Takao mon-

---

[1] Tōji in the original text, but it must refer to the Tōdaiji in Nara, which Yoriie's father, Yoritomo, helped to rebuild in 1190.

astery. Through these merits, he will be saved in the life hereafter. It is also due only to his generosity that I, Mongaku, have been able to do something for Buddhism and accomplish something for the good of man. I therefore have remained ever grateful for his generosity and happy beyond words. Even before you asked me to offer prayers, it was always my fervent desire that you should enjoy peace and security.

[May I say], however, that prayer takes effect only for those who practice virtue and who love the good. In the dwellings of those who offend, prayer is of no avail. By offenders, I mean those who destroy life without proper cause, and those who live a life of pleasure and indulge themselves with liquor, women, and wealth, ignoring the grief of others and disregarding the well-being of the nation. When men are virtuous and good, on the other hand, it means that they reverence both the law of Buddha and the law of the state and are ever concerned with the welfare of the people. In short, it means that they must have character such as is expected of a parent by all people, even the lowliest man or woman—peasants and those in all walks of life.

When a man who has no concern for these things, or who is ruthless and offensive, or who has only selfish motives, orders a monk or other spiritual intermediary to offer prayers, there may be those who will reply with favorable words because the order comes from a lofty source. But if the petitioner is not a good man, he must not only expect that there will be no answer to his prayers, but he must expect that he may be worse off than before.

Therefore, if you must have prayers offered, Your Highness should command only those monks or astrologers who are not dishonest or subservient, but are straightforward. Your Highness should tell them your misdemeanors and try at all times to make amends. This Your Highness should by all means do. If your actions are not good and you tell others to pray for you, you are really putting yourself in a precarious situation.

Your Highness is the Generalissimo of Japan. He who is asked to pray for you should be a man of great mind and great integrity. A person of steadfast virtue and lofty disdain of flattery, but yet of compassionate heart, must be selected to be the master of your prayers.

When it is a question of offering prayer as a sovereign as well as an individual, the first object of prayer should be the whole country and the whole people. How one may pray depends upon one's position in life. He whose influence does not affect the nation may offer prayers for his own benefit. But in these days the rulers as well as the ruled offer up prayers on their own account. Such prayers have no effect, for they are not in accord with the invisible mind of Buddha and are in discord with the transparent light of Heaven. I beg Your Highness, and must repeat it again and again, that you deem it your duty to merit the confidence of all, so that with you as Generalissimo in Kamakura, complaints of injustice will nowhere be heard and unreason will nowhere prevail.

If Your Highness acts in that way, you have no need for prayers for yourself. [The Goddess of] the Great Shrine of Ise, the Bodhisattva Hachiman, [the deities of] Kamo and Kasuga will all be pleased; and all Buddhas, sages, gods, and goddesses, without exception, will extend their hands to safeguard you.

Even before Buddhism came into existence, there were in India and in China, as well as in Japan, wise kings and sage rulers under whom all the land was prosperous and all the people lived a happy life. The sovereigns, long of life, were like father and mother to the people. The Five Emperors and the Three Sovereigns, among whom were Yao and Shun, were rulers who came before the time of Buddha. Your Highness is more fortunate [than they] in that you are acquainted with the Three Treasures of Buddhism [2] which those others could not know. Your Highness, therefore, should put your mind on the life hereafter. You should endeavor to get away from this "house of fire" of the three existences and, rising above the troubles of repeated transmigration, attain to Buddhahood. Such should be the first prayer of the ruler as well as of the ruled.

Needless to say, Buddhism, like other religions, helps to extirpate evil and to bring good fortune. Throughout its history in three countries, there are records of answers to prayer and of benefits received. If Your Highness will first pay strict attention to your own conduct and then proceed to put your administration in order, then when you offer prayer, an answer will come just as surely as sound follows when a word is spoken. There will be no failure.

In these days, however, all religious works and rituals sponsored by the great are merely for the eye and are only an expense to the country and a burden to the people. Buddha and the deities do not accept them at all.

---

[2] The Three Treasures: The Buddha, the Dharma (Law, or Scriptures containing the Law), and Saṅgha (Monastic Orders).

Those who pray should know that Buddha and the deities accept only virtue and faith; material treasures have no appeal for them.

It is with this in mind that Your Highness, at the head of your warriors, should guard the Emperor and become the mainstay of the whole nation. If you go astray in any way or have evil in your heart, you will prove to be only an enemy of the country. Its downfall will be the logical result.

It would be possible for me, without going into detailed reasons and unmindful of Buddha and the deities, to reply favorably to Your Highness and offer up prayers. But that would mean wasting the land's substance without benefiting anyone and only harming Your Highness. I myself would have to pay the penalty also. How can I permit Your Highness to carry out a project so injurious to yourself? I say again that the Goddess of Ise and Hachiman and the other deities will never consent to be indulgent because of material offerings; they extend their hands only to those whose heart is pure and whose conduct is proper. The Bodhisattva Hachiman said, according to the oracle: "Even if I should have to drink molten copper, I would not accept offerings from those whose hearts are tainted." He said again, according to another oracle: "Day and night I stand guard over the land. If the ruler is evil, he will be unpleasing to the Three Treasures and to all the Devas.[3] Such a thing would be most lamentable, most deplorable." Also, according to the oracle of the temple of Jingo in Takao, self-reliance only can be depended upon; in that lies the strength of Buddha. One should rely first upon the efficacy of one's own power, not upon the gods, who themselves depend upon the Three Treasures to protect the Throne and nurture the people. Your Highness should bear in mind that through your prestige you can make all temples and monasteries prosper.

Just as water runs together into the ocean because the land lies lower there, so good fortune and happiness will accumulate for him whose heart is undefiled. When Hachiman said that he would extend his hand to the pure in heart, he meant that the Emperor, the ministers and the shogun, if their hearts were pure, would have no thought for their own pleasures, but would have extreme solicitude that the labor of the people be not wasted, that unreasonable taxes be not exacted, that the land be kept in peace and prosperity, with winter and summer following each

[3] Guardian powers who protect the Three Treasures.

other, with all in good order, and with post-horses and river-ferries going regularly without war or disturbance—in short, with peace reigning supreme throughout the land. Your Highness should endeavor to live up to each and every one of these requirements.

Your Highness should refrain from destroying men who are not traitors, or who do not treat Your Highness as an enemy, or who do not wickedly harass others and seek means to ruin them. A good shogun, also, is one who does not devote himself to hunting and fishing; who does not destroy life for pleasure but preserves life.

If Your Highness does not conduct yourself well, all men throughout the land will come to believe that you are not a good man. Then mountain bandits, sea marauders, highwaymen, and thieves will abound and in the end will bring ruin to your regime. You may issue prohibitory edicts one after the other but your orders will more and more be treated lightly. Put one man to death and ten other criminals will come back at you. The situation will go from bad to worse. Then Your Highness, not realizing that all this is your own fault, but believing it to be the work of criminals, will merely go on arresting men, punishing them, imprisoning them and cutting off their heads or their limbs to the detriment of the country. It is necessary to think of the retribution waiting in the life to come.

When Your Highness once realizes that these crimes are not always the offenses of others but are due to your own recklessness, and when you are sincerely convinced of it, if you ask any learned man how best to govern, the answer will be simple—as simple as shooting at a target, as the saying goes. As long as Your Highness knows how to rule yourself, there is no need for regulations about this or that, no need for prohibitions, orders or proclamations, because the people will be submissive and obedient. Then the land will naturally be at peace and well ordered.

Even under such a good administration, however, evil-minded men will not disappear, as history shows. But if Your Highness would first exercise self-control and safeguard the people, proceeding then to get rid of evil men, your acts would be like the special acts of a bodhisattva. The people would remain tranquil, your proclamations would carry weight, and Your Highness would not have to fear retribution. I am here repeating [what I wrote you before].

The late shogun always thought Mongaku to be a man of tough fiber and straightforward speech. I have never been in the personal service of Your Highness; it must have been offensive to Your Highness for me to write to you in the way I did. For this I beg your forgiveness. However, it has seemed to me that Your Highness is too much addicted to pleasures and has no regard for the complaints or the sufferings of the people. I thought this so deplorable that I told the late shogun confidentially that you should be sent away somewhere into exile—that such a course would be a real act of love toward you.

It is whispered in the capital that Your Highness is addicted to hunting and that you pay no attention to grievances. As you only go from bad to worse, people do not speak out but say only that you are a great shogun. Your Highness is unaware of what they are whispering in denunciation of you.

Under these circumstances, how can you be a worthy successor to your father—watching over the Sovereign on the one hand, and on the other safeguarding the country? Until Your Highness changes your ways, pray as one may, there will be no answer at all. As for myself, I cannot offer prayers for you.

Because I am frank and outspoken, I am certain that Your Highness hates me. That I do not mind. I have written you thus only because I desire you to be good, and more than that, to grow in virtue.

A learned scholar quotes a text to the effect that a good word spoken for the sake of the ruler and the people is more valuable than hundreds and thousands of gold offerings. To this the ancient Sage Kings bore testimony. To one like Your Highness, gold is of no account. The important thing is to keep the land at peace and to have food produced in abundance and the people prosperous. That is the greatest act of loyalty. Therefore do not fail to listen to those who tell you your shortcomings. If Your Highness tries to keep the nation in order without being mindful of your own faults, you will be like a man who expects to get rid of illness without taking medicine.

There are men of loyalty and faithfulness from whom you can learn your shortcomings, who do not change their colors in the service of Her Highness your mother. Let them speak to you in secret, not in public. Listen to them directly; do not heed the lip-service of monks. If they speak ill of you, you will be apt to become angry; but you must practice patience. Cure by fire is painful but it is only through endurance that illness can be cured.

There are none more despicable than those who change their colors. There are none more loyal than those who tell you your faults. I pray Your Highness to remember this. Even if a man is agreeable and likable, beware of him if he is a cheat. But if there be one whom you dislike and do not wish to see, give him his due if he be of sterling character. The art of government, it seems to me, lies in nothing more nor less than in this awareness of true character.

I cannot thank Your Highness enough for the two letters with which you have honored me. This is my answer, written with all reverence and respect.

Tenth day of the first month of the second year of Shōji.

CHAPTER IX

THE VOCABULARY OF
JAPANESE AESTHETICS I

It is surprising how often we find the same few terms used to express the preferences or ideals of Japanese creative artists throughout the ages, so often indeed that we can identify them as a special "vocabulary of Japanese aesthetics." Such terms varied in meaning with the times and with the individual critics, as was only to be expected of words employed for well over a thousand years in some cases. Nevertheless, some knowledge of this vocabulary may serve as a key to Japanese canons of taste in literature and the other arts.

The most famous of these words, and one which has had whole volumes of serious research devoted to it, is *aware*. In old texts we find it first used as an exclamation of surprise or delight, man's natural reaction to what an early Western critic of Japanese literature called the "ahness" of things, but gradually it came to be used adjectivally, usually to mean "pleasant" or "interesting." One scholar who analyzed the uses of *aware* in the *Manyōshū*, the great eighth-century collection of poetry, discovered that an *aware* emotion was most often evoked in the poets by hearing the melancholy calls of birds and beasts. An inscription from the year 763 contains the word *aware* used to describe the writer's emotions on seeing the spring rain. Gradually, therefore, *aware* came to be tinged with sadness. By the time of *The Tale of Genji* only the lower classes (or the upper classes in moments of great stress) used the word *aware* as a simple exclamation: elsewhere it expressed a gentle sorrow, adding not so much a meaning as a color or a perfume to a sentence. It bespoke the sensitive poet's awareness of a sight or a sound, of its beauty and its perishability. It was probably inevitable that with the steady heightening of the sensitivity of poets to the world around them the tone of sadness deepened.

The famous eighteenth-century critic of Japanese literature Motoori

Norinaga (1730–1801) once characterized the whole of *The Tale of Genji* as a novel of *mono no aware,* a phrase which has sometimes been translated as "the sadness of things." Motoori, however, seems to have meant by it something closer to a "sensitivity to things"—sensitivity to the fall of a flower or to an unwept tear.

Some of the early works of criticism use the word *aware* so often as to make it almost the exclusive criterion of merit. In a work written about the year 1200, for example, there occurs this discussion of *The Tale of Genji.*

"Someone asked, 'Which chapter is the best and creates the most profound impression?'

" 'No chapter is superior to *Kiritsubo.* From the opening words, "At the Court of an Emperor (he lived it matters not when)" to the final description of Genji's initiation to manhood, the whole chapter is filled with a moving (*aware*) pathos which colors the language, the circumstances portrayed, and everything else. In *The Broom-Tree* the discussion on a rainy night of the categories of women contains many praiseworthy things. The chapter *Yugao* is permeated with a moving (*aware*) sadness. *The Festival of Red Leaves* and *The Flower-Feast* are unforgettable chapters, each possessed of its own charm (*en*) and interest. *Aoi* is an extremely moving (*aware*) and absorbing chapter. The chapter *Kashiwagi* contains the scene of the departure for Ise, which is at once charming (*en*) and magnificent. The scene when, after the death of the Emperor, Fujitsubo takes vows as a nun is moving (*aware*). *Exile at Suma* is a moving (*aware*) and powerful chapter. The descriptions of Genji leaving the capital for Suma and of his life in distant exile are extremely moving (*aware*).' " [1]

As this excerpt shows, the word *aware* was used to describe almost every chapter considered to be of unusual beauty, and in each case the meaning, though vague, was associated with deep emotions, and not a mere exclamation as in early times. But *aware* had not yet darkened to its modern meaning of "wretched," which represents perhaps the final evolution in its long history.

In the same excerpt one other word appears several times—*en,* which may be translated as "charming." Its use as a term of praise indicates that not only the melancholy but the colorful surface of the *Genji* was

[1] *Mumyō sōshi,* pp. 17–18.

appreciated. Indeed, if we look at the superb horizontal scroll illustrating the *Genji,* which is roughly contemporary with this piece of criticism, we are struck far more by its exquisite charm than by the sadness of the scenes (although, of course, the two conceptions are not mutually exclusive). *En* evokes the visual beauty in which much of the literature of the time was clothed.

Another term of aesthetic criticism of a cheerful nature was *okashi,* a word we find in many Heian works, in particular the celebrated *Pillow Book.* It seems originally to have meant something which brought a smile to the face, either of delight or amusement. It was not applied to the serious or sad things of life except ironically and thus, as one Japanese critic has pointed out, in its making light of the tragic was just the opposite of the attitude of *aware* which sought to impart to the otherwise meaningless cries of a bird or the fall of a flower a profound and moving meaning.

Both *aware* and *okashi*—the former best represented by Murasaki Shikibu, who saw the *aware* nature of a leaf caught in the wind, the latter by Sei Shōnagon, whose witty essays are dotted with the word *okashi* —are standards which are typical of an aristocratic society of great refinement. That aristocrats of the Heian Period were aware of the special nature of their society is attested by one other word of their aesthetic vocabulary—*miyabi,* literally "courtliness" but in general "refinement." The court was a small island of refinement and sophistication in a country otherwise marked by ignorance and uncourtliness; it is therefore not surprising that people at court tended to think with horror of the world outside the capital. By "courtliness" was meant not only the appropriate decorum for lords and ladies at the palace, but also the Japanese reflection of the culture which had originally come from China. One can imagine in our own day a somewhat similar situation existing somewhere in Africa, where the Oxford-educated prince of a still largely uncivilized tribe listens to records of the music of Debussy or tries his hand at composing avant-garde verse.

Miyabi was perhaps the most inclusive term for describing the aesthetics of the Heian Period. It was applied in particular to the quiet pleasures which, supposedly at least, could only be savored by the aristocrat whose tastes had been educated to them—a spray of plum blossoms, the elusive perfume of a rare wood, the delicate blending of colors in a robe. In

[174]

lovemaking too, the "refined" tastes of the court revealed themselves. A man might first be attracted to a woman by catching a glimpse of her sleeve, carelessly but elegantly draped from a carriage window, or by seeing a note in her calligraphy, or by hearing her play a lute one night in the dark. Later, the lovers would exchange letters and poems, often attached to a spray of the flower suitable for the season. Such love affairs are most perfectly portrayed in *The Tale of Genji*, and even if somewhat idealized in that novel, suggest to what lengths a feeling for "refinement" could govern the lives of those at court. Perhaps nowhere is this insistence upon the refinement of taste more clearly revealed than in the passage known as the Gradations of Beauty,[2] in which Prince Genji and his sophisticated companions discuss the relative virtues of the women they have known. In love, no less than in art, the same aristocratic hierarchy of values, the same subtlety of discrimination prevailed as in social relations. Indeed, it was in just such a society as this that so much importance was attached, even in religious matters and contrary to the equalitarian trend of Mahāyāna Buddhism, to the ascending hierarchy or gradations of religious consciousness.

The influence of *miyabi* was not wholly beneficial, it must be admitted. In refining and polishing down the cruder emotions such as may be found in the *Manyōshū*, it severely limited the range of Japanese poetry and art. *Miyabi* led poets to shun the crude, the rustic, and the unseemly, but in so doing it tended to remove or dilute real feeling. In reading today much of the later Japanese poetry we cannot help wishing at times that the poet would venture forth from the oft-sung themes of the moon, the cries of birds, and the fall of cherry blossoms, and treat instead harsher and more compelling subjects.

Miyabi was in a sense a negation of the simple virtues, the plain sincerity (*makoto*) which *Manyōshū* poets had possessed and which poets many centuries later were to rediscover. "Refinement" gave to the courtiers a justification for their own way of living and at the same time a contempt for the non-courtly similar to the attitude which has given the English words "peasant-like," "boorish," and "countrified" their uncomplimentary meanings. But in a curious way this specifically aristocratic standard was transmitted to the military classes when the latter rose to power, and later to the common people and even the peasantry, so that

[2] Shina no sadame—literally, "the determination of rank or value."

today much of what it represented is part of the common heritage of all Japanese. The hackneyed imagery of Heian poetry—the falling of the cherry blossoms, the reddening of the autumn leaves, and the rest—has become very much a part of even the least aesthetic of Japanese. Steel mills dismiss their employees for the day to enable them to admire the cherry-blossoms (and to drink *sake* under them), and the hardest-headed businessman will not begrudge an afternoon off that is spent at Takao when the maples are their most brilliantly colored. Even the shoeshine boy in front of the railway station may in summer talk of the flickering beauty of the fireflies. Nothing in the West can compare with the role which aesthetics has played in Japanese life and history since the Heian Period. If *aware* and *okashi* are no longer used in the present-day vocabulary of aesthetic criticism, the *miyabi* spirit of refined sensibility is still very much in evidence.

MURASAKI SHIKIBU

On the Art of the Novel
(From *The Tale of Genji*)

The Tale of Genji has been read and commentated on ever since it was first written, almost a thousand years ago, and many theories have been advanced as to what the author Murasaki Shikibu was attempting to express in her novel. In this excerpt from *The Tale of Genji* we find what is perhaps the best answer to this question. It seems likely that Murasaki was here, in one of the earliest and most famous examples of Japanese criticism, stating her own views on the function of the novel.
[From Waley (tr.), *A Wreath of Cloud*, pp. 253–57]

One day Genji, going the round with a number of romances which he had promised to lend, came to Tamakatsura's room and found her, as usual, hardly able to lift her eyes from the book in front of her. "Really, you are incurable," he said, laughing. "I sometimes think that young ladies exist for no other purpose than to provide purveyors of the absurd and improbable with a market for their wares. I am sure that the book you are now so intent upon is full of the wildest nonsense. Yet knowing this all the time, you are completely captivated by its extravagances and follow them with the utmost excitement: why, here you are on this hot day, so hard at work that, though I am sure you have not the least idea

[176]

of it, your hair is in the most extraordinary tangle. . . . But there; I know quite well that these old tales are indispensable during such weather as this. How else would you all manage to get through the day? Now for a confession. I too have lately been studying these books and have, I must tell you, been amazed by the delight which they have given me. There is, it seems, an art of so fitting each part of the narrative into the next that, though all is mere invention, the reader is persuaded that such things might easily have happened and is as deeply moved as though they were actually going on around him. We may know with one part of our minds that every incident has been invented for the express purpose of impressing us; but (if the plot is constructed with the requisite skill) we may all the while in another part of our minds be burning with indignation at the wrongs endured by some wholly imaginary princess. Or again we may be persuaded by a writer's elo-quence into accepting the crudest absurdities, our judgment being as it were dazzled by sheer splendor of language.

"I have lately sometimes stopped and listened to one of our young peo-ple reading out loud to her companions and have been amazed at the advances which this art of fiction is now making. How do you suppose that our new writers come by this talent? It used to be thought that the authors of successful romances were merely particularly untruthful peo-ple whose imaginations had been stimulated by constantly inventing plausible lies. But that is clearly unfair. . . ." "Perhaps," she said, "only people who are themselves much occupied in practicing deception have the habit of thus dipping below the surface. I can assure you that for my part, when I read a story, I always accept it as an account of something that has really and actually happened."

So saying she pushed away from her the book which she had been copy-ing. Genji continued: "So you see as a matter of fact I think far better of this art than I have led you to suppose. Even its practical value is immense. Without it what should we know of how people lived in the past, from the Age of the Gods down to the present day? For history-books such as the *Chronicles of Japan* show us only one small corner of life; whereas these diaries and romances which I see piled around you contain, I am sure, the most minute information about all sorts of people's private affairs. . . ." He smiled, and went on: "But I have a theory of my own about what this art of the novel is, and how it came into being. To begin with, it does not simply consist in the author's telling a story about the adventures of some other person. On the contrary, it happens because the storyteller's own experience of men and things, whether for good or ill— not only what he has passed through himself, but even events which he has only witnessed or been told of—has moved him to an emotion so passionate that he can no longer keep it shut up in his heart. Again and again something in his own life or in that around him will seem to the writer so important that he cannot bear to let it pass into oblivion. There must never come a time, he feels, when men do not know about it. That is my view of how this art arose.

"Clearly then, it is no part of the storyteller's craft to describe only what is good or beautiful. Sometimes, of course, virtue will be his theme, and he may then make such play with it as he will. But he is just as likely to have been struck by numerous examples of vice and folly in the world around him, and about them he has exactly the same feelings as about the pre-eminently good deeds which he encounters: they are more important and must all be garnered in. Thus anything whatsoever may become the subject of a novel, provided only that it happens in this mundane life and not in some fairyland beyond our human ken.

"The outward forms of this art will not of course be everywhere the same. At the court of China and in other foreign lands both the genius of the writers and their actual methods of composition are necessarily very different from ours; and even here in Japan the art of storytelling has in course of time undergone great changes. There will, too, always be a distinction between the lighter and the more serious forms of fiction. . . . Well, I have said enough to show that when at the beginning of our conversation I spoke of romances as though they were mere frivolous fabrications, I was only teasing you. Some people have taken exception on moral grounds to an art in which the perfect and imperfect are set side by side. But even in the discourses which Buddha in his bounty allowed to be recorded, certain passages contain what the learned call *Upāya* or 'Adapted Truth'[1]—a fact that has led some superficial persons to doubt whether a doctrine so inconsistent with itself could possibly command our credence. Even in the scriptures of the Greater Vehicle there are, I confess, many such instances. We may indeed go so far as to say that there is an actual mixture of Truth and Error. But

---

[1] Sutras presenting divergent doctrines were said to represent different formulations of the same teaching, adjusted by the Buddha to his hearers' level of comprehension. [Ed.]

the purpose of these holy writings, namely the compassing of our Salvation, remains always the same. So too, I think, may it be said that the art of fiction must not lose our allegiance because, in the pursuit of the main purpose to which I have alluded above, it sets virtue by the side of vice, or mingles wisdom with folly. Viewed in this light the novel is seen to be not, as is usually supposed, a mixture of useful truth with idle invention, but something which at every stage and in every part has a definite and serious purpose."

FUJIWARA NO TEIKA
Introduction to the Guide to the Composition of Poetry

Fujiwara no Teika (1162–1241), more than any other individual, was responsible for the formation of Japanese literary taste. Attempting in the early medieval period to preserve the best of the classical tradition, he defined for all time the classic canons of Japanese verse. His judgments influenced not only writers who consulted his books of poetry and criticism, but, indirectly, the entire nation: the *Hundred Poets, a Poem Each* (*Hyakunin Isshū*), which Teika is generally believed to have compiled, is the most popular anthology of Japanese verse, and almost every Japanese knows its contents by heart, largely through a game based on them. Teika also helped give direction to later trends in Japanese poetry by his selection of the works to be included in the *New Collection* (1205), the last of the great anthologies and the most influential. Finally, it may be noted that the principal works of Heian literature which are extant today were all edited by Teika, and our picture of that glorious period of Japanese literature has thus been conditioned by his taste.

In the field of literary criticism, Teika's *Guide to the Composition of Poetry* has long been considered an authoritative statement of the ideals of Japanese poetry. It is brief to the point of being cryptic at times; later men have expanded it to seventy times its original length in the attempt to elucidate Teika's meanings. Perhaps the most striking feature of this little essay is its insistence on the use of the language of former poets. To the degree that this counsel was followed—the *Guide* became in fact a set of golden rules for later court poets—the result tended to be sterility in poetry. Any new conceit or turn of phrase was considered to be a sufficiently original contribution, even though a poem differed very little from earlier ones, and the use of outmoded clichés robbed the poetry of even the vitality that fresh language can impart.

[From *Eika taigai* in Hisamatsu, *Chūsei karon shū*, pp. 188–89]

In the expression of the emotions originality merits the first consideration. (That is, one should look for sentiments unsung by others and sing them.) The words used, however, should be old ones. (The vocabulary should be restricted to words used by the masters of the Three Anthologies:[1] the same words are proper for all poets, whether ancient or modern.)

The style should imitate the great poems of the masters of former times. One must discard every last phrase of the sentiments and expressions written by men of recent times. (Expressions which appear in the poetry of the last seventy or eighty years must be avoided at all cost.)

It has become a popular practice to borrow many of the same expressions that appear in the poetry of former masters for use in making new poems. It is, however, rather excessive to borrow as many as three of the five lines,[2] and betrays a lack of originality. Three or four words over two lines are permissible, but it is simply too exasperating if in the remaining lines the same imagery as in the original poem is used. . . .[3]

One should impregnate one's mind with a constant study of the forms of expression of ancient poetry. The *Kokinshū,* the *Tales of Ise,*[4] the *Gosen,* and the *Shūi* are truly deserving of study. One should especially concentrate on the outstanding poems in the collections of the Thirty-Six Poets (e.g., those of Hitomaro, Tsurayuki, Tadamine, Ise, and Komachi). The first and second books of Po Chü-i's *Collected Works*[5] should be gone over constantly; although he was not a master of Japanese poetry, his works are remarkable for their descriptions of the time, and for their portrayal of the splendors and decline of his age.

There are no teachers of Japanese poetry. But they who take the old poems as their teachers, steep their minds in the old style, and learn their words from the masters of former time—who of them will fail to write poetry?

[1] The *Kokinshū* (905), the *Gosenshū* (951), and the *Shūi Wakashū* (c. 1005–8)—three anthologies of poetry compiled by imperial order.

[2] The *waka* is written in five lines of 5, 7, 5, 7, and 7 syllables respectively. This is the standard Japanese verse-form.

[3] Some examples of phrases which often occur in poetry have been omitted in this translation.

[4] A tenth-century work consisting of 125 episodes, most of them relating to the great lover Ariwara no Narihira. Each of these episodes contains one or more poems. For the other works mentioned in this sentence see footnote 1 above.

[5] Po Chü-i (772–846) was the most widely read Chinese poet in Japan, partially at least because the simplest to understand. During the Heian Period his writings were so popular that the word *Works* itself, with no other qualification, meant Po's collected poetry and prose.

DESPAIR, DELIVERANCE,
AND DESTINY

The term "medieval Japan" represents only a general phase in a continuing process of historical evolution. For convenience' sake, we may
consider it to embrace the twelfth through sixteenth centuries, including
those periods identified politically with the Kamakura and Ashikaga
shogunates. Actually, the characteristic feudal institutions of medieval
Japan had their roots far back in the Heian Period, but it was only in
the twelfth century that the power of these feudal forces became fully
manifest in the bloody struggles for military ascendancy between the
Taira and Minamoto clans, climaxed by the establishment of a military
government in Kamakura which effectively terminated rule by the old
Kyoto court. Thereafter, in one form or another, under one family or
another, military government endured into the nineteenth century. What
marks off the medieval period, especially, is the prevailing disorder and
instability as compared to the "peace and tranquillity" with which the
earlier Heian Period had been identified, and the stable rule of the
Tokugawa, who brought unity and lasting peace to Japan at the end of
the sixteenth century. Medieval Japan began and ended in protracted
feudal warfare and enjoyed only the loosest, most precarious kind of
political organization. Thus, despite our natural tendency to think of
historical periods in terms of political unities or continuities like the
Kamakura and Ashikaga regimes, it is rather disunity and violent change
that give this period its distinctive character.

Medieval literature sharply reflects the sudden transition Japan underwent in the eleventh and twelfth centuries. In contrast to the still atmosphere, the gentle sophistication and refinement of life expressed in
earlier writing, there is a turbulence, a wild, ebullient tenor of life, and
a background of danger and stark brutality which inspires in some a new
sense of realism and bold adventure, while in others, especially those

identified with the old regime or imbued with the old culture, it produces a sense of shock and impending doom, often coupled with nostalgic yearning for the past. Whether in the first romantic tales of the epic wars that loosed this fury over the land, or in the more contemplative and still highly refined art of the Nō which flourished during the fourteenth century, there is an intense awareness of the tragedy of life. In religion, too, there is a deepening of that pessimism toward the world that had always pervaded Buddhism. "The end of the Law," an expression for the final stage in the devolution of Buddha's teaching, when it would become almost totally obscured in an age of ignorance and corruption, was more and more frequently heard.

Yet in religion, as in Japanese society as a whole, on the threshold of death appeared new life. If the collapse of the old order brought new blood and more vigorous leaders on the scene, and if the eclipse of the aristocratic Kyoto court signified a greater participation by the provinces in the national life, so too in these circumstances the older forms of religion gave way to new ones, responding to the needs of the country as a whole. Thus, for example, the sense of despair, of inability to rise above the evils of the times, was met by a powerful movement offering salvation through faith alone, which brought the hope of new life and light to thousands of Japanese untouched by the older forms of Buddhism. The cult of Amida, who shared the bliss of his Pure Land with those who put their trust in him, is the most striking example of this tendency. In the teaching of Nichiren, also, there is great emphasis upon faith in the *Lotus Sūtra* as the key to salvation, and it was a notable trait of both these movements that their leaders sought converts among the humblest folk in the farthest reaches of Japan, especially in the near-wilderness of the north. Even in Zen Buddhism, which insisted upon individual effort rather than a reliance upon faith in something external, we find evidences of the same tendency. Aristocratic though it was in spirit, and intimately associated with the most sophisticated arts of the Ashikaga period, Zen not only embodied the vigorous simplicity of this age, but, in the most concrete and practical manner, raised to a new artistic dignity the humblest activities of the Japanese household: the preparing of tea, the arranging of flowers, the designing of house and garden, and many other everyday pursuits of the medieval Japanese. In this way religion, while making a place for itself in the new society, contributed to the development of a new and more broadly based culture. To call this trend "democratic" would be going too far, since it was unattended by any significant increase in political freedom or activity on the part of the people as a whole. Nevertheless, there can be no doubt that the spread of popular religions contributed to the general uplift of the people and to a sense of unity transcending class distinctions. At the same time, we have already in the medieval period, from such men as Nichiren and Kitabatake Chikafusa, the exponent of a nationalism linked to Shinto traditions, intimations of a special destiny reserved for the Japanese people, an idea which gained potency in the age that followed.

CHAPTER X

AMIDA AND THE PURE LAND

"There is only one Way," the *Lotus Sūtra* says again and again, "not two or three." All human beings are to achieve Buddhahood through the same Great Vehicle, Mahāyāna. No class or group is to be disqualified; there are to be no separate categories, such as the Hīnayāna and pseudo-Mahāyāna sects distinguish, for those of different social status or individual capability. No matter what means men avail themselves of, all find their ultimate fulfillment in the single, universal Way of Mahāyāna.

This was the central truth of the Buddhist faith which reigned supreme in the Heian Period. The two leading sects, Tendai and Shingon, both acknowledged such an idealistic and egalitarian view of man's potentialities for enlightenment. But, as we have seen, in the practice of this Mahāyāna faith compromises were made which reflected the more aristocratic character of Japanese society in this period, especially the strong consciousness of rank and status which pervaded the life of the Heian court. There was an established hierarchy in almost every sphere of activity: there were three grades of royal princes, called *hon,* and there were eight ranks for government officials, each subdivided into Senior and Junior. Even court gossip gave voice to the passion for making distinctions of grade and quality, as evidenced by the sharp judgments of a Lady Shōnagon, in her *Pillow Book,* or by the second chapter of *The Tale of Genji,* in which young men of the court assess the beauty and talents of women they have known in terms of *shina,* "grade."

In a sense, too, Kūkai's *Ten Stages of Religious Consciousness* exemplifies the same tendency, for in assigning each type of belief its proper place in the total scheme of salvation, Kūkai also assigned it a certain relative value and made clear its peculiar limitations. This quality perhaps in Kūkai's Esoteric Buddhism, as well as its emphasis on art and ritual, accounts for the high favor which his new faith won in the citadels of

Heian culture. For the Esoteric doctrine, which entrenched itself not only at court but at Nara, the old center of Buddhism, and at Mt. Hiei, the Tendai center, put far less stress in practice on the universal hope of attaining Buddhahood than it did on the special means to be employed by each individual. The Buddha and all creatures were made of the same stuff, the same six elements. But in the diverse manifestations of the Mandala might be seen the different aspects and functions of the Three Mysteries: Body, Speech, and Mind. Through their proper functioning alone could Buddhahood be attained, and the secret knowledge of these functions was possessed by the Shingon priesthood alone. Inasmuch as Shingon Buddhism was esoteric, it also tended to be exclusive.

In the twelfth century, with the sudden collapse of the Kyoto court and the onset of the feudal era, among the swift and bewildering changes that ensued was a sweeping redirection of the religious life of Japan. It is not surprising that the established sects of Buddhism should have declined with the waning fortunes of their aristocratic patrons, but in an age often seen as dominated by hardened warriors and held in the tight grip of military government, it may seem paradoxical that Japanese Buddhism should for the first time have become a mass movement, a democracy of faith, offering to everyone tangible hope for salvation in this life. Yet this is the most evident and significant feature of medieval Buddhism: that it was not preserved as a mere heirloom of the *ancien régime,* but elbowed its way out among the people and made itself at home in the households of humble folk.

In this popularization of Buddhism no doctrine or sect was more influential than that associated with the Buddha Amida, whose Western Paradise or "Pure Land" offered a haven to weary souls in that strife-torn age. It was Amida,[1] the Buddha of Boundless Light, who eons ago vowed that all should be saved who called on his name, a pledge which became known as the "Original Vow." It was to the Pure Land, a special place prepared by Amida, that the Buddha welcomed those who had won eternal bliss by calling on his name, *Namu Amida Butsu,* with single-minded and wholehearted devotion. This was the invocation which became known as the *Nembutsu,* a term which originally signified meditation on the name of Amida, but later meant simply the fervent repetition of his name. The scriptural authority for this teaching came from a sūtra

[1] Skt: Amitābha.

in which Shākyamuni describes his former existence as a Buddha-to-be (bodhisattva), who accepts Buddhahood only on condition that he can establish a land of bliss for all who invoke his name (as Amida) in perfect trust. In another sūtra Shākyamuni offers a devout queen her choice of many Buddha-lands and, after she has chosen that of Amida, he instructs her in the meditation which will lead to her admission there.

This faith was not by any means the creation of medieval Japan. It derived from the Mahāyāna Buddhism of Northern India and Central Asia, and for centuries the worship of Amida had been tremendously popular in China. Nevertheless the spread of Pure Land doctrines in medieval times represented a striking change in outlook for the Japanese, and in the process of establishing itself, the doctrine too underwent profound changes. For one thing, the earlier forms of Japanese Buddhism had all stressed the attainment of Buddhahood, the achieving of enlightenment, whereas this faith aimed at rebirth in a land of bliss. At the same time there was a shift in emphasis away from the individual's efforts to achieve enlightenment toward an exclusive reliance on the saving power of the Buddha. This meant a strong monotheistic tendency —all honor and devotion to Amida alone—in contrast to the strong polytheistic tendency of Esoteric Buddhism, with its .multitude of icons directing worship to a vast pantheon of Buddhas and bodhisattvas.

From the social as well as the religious standpoint two far-reaching changes wrought by the spread of Amidism were the transformation of the Buddhist clergy and the recognizing of women's right to equal opportunities for salvation along with men. The champions of Amida-worship started a trend away from the traditional concept of the Buddhist clergy, who had left the world as celibate followers of a monastic discipline, toward a new role as religious leaders living in society a life which differed little from the layman's. One of the reasons which led them out of the isolation of the monasteries was a desire to bring religion directly to those outside, including women. When the great monastic centers of Hiei and Kōya were established, their founders ordained that these sacred precincts should never be visited by women. An incidental advantage of this ban was no doubt to insure against violations of the vows of celibacy, but what primarily dictated it was the view that women were a source of defilement (probably because they were subject to menstruation, long regarded as a form of pollution). Women were thus effectively excluded from participation in some of the more important religious observances. But the new religious leaders were determined that women should enjoy every opportunity for salvation open to men.

PIONEERS OF PURE LAND BUDDHISM

The rise of Pure Land Buddhism was not merely an outgrowth of the new feudal society, translating into religious terms the profound social changes which then took place. Already in the late Heian period we find individual monks who sensed the need for bringing Buddhist faith within the reach of the ordinary man, and thus anticipated the mass religious movements of medieval times. Kūya (903–972), a monk on Mt. Hiei, was one of these. The meditation on the Buddha Amida, which had long been accepted as an aid to the religious life, he promoted as a pedestrian devotion. Dancing through the city streets with a tinkling bell hanging from around his neck, Kūya called out the name of Amida and sang simple ditties of his own composition, such as:

Hito ·tabi mo	He never fails
Namu Amida bu to	To reach the Lotus Land of Bliss
Yū hito no	Who calls,
Hasu utena ni	If only once,
Noboranu wa nashi.	The name of Amida.

And—

Gokuraku wa	A far, far distant land
Harukeki hodo to	Is Paradise,
Kikishi kado	I've heard them say;
Tsutomete itaru	But those who want to go
Tokoro narikeri.	Can reach there in a day.

In the market places all kinds of people joined him in his dance and sang out the invocation to Amida, "Namu Amida Butsu." When a great epidemic struck the capital, he proposed that these same people join him in building an image of Amida in a public square, saying that common folk could equal the achievement of their rulers, who had built the Great Buddha of Nara, if they cared to try. In country districts he built bridges and dug wells for the people where these were needed, and to show that no one was to be excluded from the blessings of Paradise, he traveled into regions inhabited by the Ainu and for the first time brought to many of them the evangel of Buddhism.

As Kūya became known as "the saint of the streets" for his dancing, so another Tendai monk, Ryōnin (1072–1132), later became known especially for his propagation of the *Nembutsu* through popular songs. Ryōnin's great success in this medium reflected his own vocal talents and his mastery of traditional liturgical music. At the same time his advocacy of the *Nembutsu* chant reflected the influence upon him of Tendai and Kegon doctrine. From the former philosophy he drew the idea that "one act is all acts, and all acts are one act." From the *Flower Wreath (Kegon) Sūtra* he took the doctrine of the interrelation and interdependence of all things: "one man is all men and all men are one man." Joining these to faith in Amida, he produced the "circulating *Nembutsu*" or "Nembutsu in communion" (*Yūzū nembutsu*). If one man calls the name of Amida, it will benefit all men; one man may share in the invocations of all others. Spreading this simple but all-embracing idea in a musical form, Ryōnin became an evangelist on a vast scale. Among his early converts were court ladies, and the Emperor Toba was so deeply impressed that he gave Ryōnin a bell made from one of his own mirrors. With this he traveled the length and breadth of the land, inviting everyone to join him in the "circulating *Nembutsu*" and asking them to sign their names in a roster of participants. According to tradition the entries accumulated during a lifetime of evangelizing added up to the modest figure of 3,282.

In the thirteenth century these same methods were employed by the evangelist Ippen (1239–1289), who believed that the grace of Amida was present everywhere, in Shinto shrines as well as Buddhist temples of all denominations. For him the important thing was not to build new places of worship, but for the faithful to dance and sing together in praise of Amida, anywhere, any time. In the roster he kept of persons joining in his movement the names were said to have reached the incredible total of 2,300,001,724.

A man who did as much as Kūya and Ryōnin to popularize faith in Amida, without ever leaving the monastic life, was Genshin (942–1017). He too was from Mt. Hiei, to which the great Ennin had first brought the practice of meditation on the name of Amida. From his early study of the *Lotus Sūtra* and his great devotion to his aged mother, Genshin became convinced that there must be some means of obtaining salvation which was open to all, laymen as well as monks, women as well as men. And the method he espoused after years of pious study—loving trust in the saving power of Amida—he wished to bring to all in a vivid and forceful manner. This he did in his *Essentials of Salvation,* which brought together in one book passages from the great body of Buddhist scriptures describing various aspects of the religious life. For Genshin, as for all Tendai schoolmen, there are ten realms of existence with the world of the Buddha at one end and Hell at the other, human existence standing in between. Man's religious life starts with an aversion for Hell, the perpetual battleground of human greed, lust, and desire for power. As he shrinks from those actions which result in the miseries of Hell, man is drawn to the land made blissful by the light, life, and love of Amida. This is the essence of religion: disgust for Hell and desire for the Pure Land. Genshin's work was to inspire all men with these sentiments by depicting in lucid and graphic terms the horrors of Hell and attractions of the Western Paradise. So effectively did he convey in popular form the fruits of his scriptural studies that his book, *The Essentials of Salvation,* not only won the acclaim of Chinese authorities to whom he sent a copy, but it became a sort of "best-seller" in medieval times, going through several printed editions. With so learned a monk as its champion, the popularization of Amidism gained added impetus.

But Genshin was not content to express himself in literary form alone and turned to painting and sculpture as well. The written word could only be appreciated by those able to read, and since Genshin wrote in a modified form of Chinese, his work was not accessible to many. Painting and sculpture, on the other hand, had the advantage of direct and in-stantaneous appeal to all. Unfortunately we do not possess much reliable evidence of Genshin's work in these media, but there can be no doubt that he was the originator of a new religious art. Liberating Buddhist painting from the stiff and stereotyped forms of Shingon iconography, he introduced new subjects such as the torments of Hell, the glories of Paradise, and the compassionate Amida with his attendant bodhisattvas welcoming the blessed to the Pure Land. These scenes he represented with a freshness of imagination and devotional atmosphere reflecting his own deep piety. The diary of a court lady of that time testifies to the effectiveness of his painting, for when one of his screens was brought

[189]

into the palace the ladies-in-waiting had nightmares over the realistic treatment of hell-fire and its screaming victims. There is an enormous painting attributed to him, now in the Mt. Kōya Museum, which shows Amida and his retinue coming out to receive the souls of the redeemed. It is recognized as probably the greatest of Japanese religious paintings. Another famous painting believed to be his is called "Amida Beyond the Hill." It shows Buddha rising like the moon over Genshin's mountain-home and bathing Lake Biwa in the resplendent light of his benign countenance.

Thus the pioneers of Pure Land Buddhism developed new means of communication—dancing, music, painting, sculpture, and popular religious tracts—in order to bring the Buddhaland within sight of all. With these available Buddhism was ready to take a wider and deeper hold on the life of the people than ever before.

IPPEN

Precepts for Followers of the Timely Teaching (Jishū Seikai)

The evangelist Ippen, who popularized devotion to Amida by means of song and dance, did not organize his followers into a separate sect, since he believed that any temple or shrine, any place or time, was suitable for the invocation of Amida's name. When he identified his disciples as "Followers of the Timely Teaching (Jishū)," he meant that the practice of the Nembutsu was the most appropriate to that degenerate age. Therefore the precepts given below are simple rules which anyone could practice without special training or discipline. Later his followers organized a sect of their own and called it the Ji (Time) School. The "time" referred to here, however, was not the "present degenerate age," but the "six-hour invocation of the Nembutsu" each day. Moreover, the "six hours" indicated the time divisions of one day according to the usual Japanese reckoning, and consequently does not mean "at six appointed hours" but rather the equivalent of our "twenty-four hours a day." The real sense of this name is therefore "School of the Perpetual Invocation of the Name of Amida," and in actual practice this invocation might be chanted any number of times a day depending on the circumstances at each temple.[1]

[From *Ippen Shōnin Goroku*, pp. 28–29]

Devoutly adore the glory of God;
Do not ignore the original one's virtue.

[1] Not six specific times of the day as indicated by Takakusu, *Essentials of Buddhist Philosophy*, p. 174.

Devoutly revere the Buddha, the Law, and the Priesthood;
Do not forget the power of communion.

Devoutly practice the invocation;
Do not engage in superfluous disciplines.

Devoutly trust the law of love;
Do not denounce the creeds of others.

Devoutly promote the sense of equality;
Do not arouse discriminatory feelings.

Devoutly awaken the sense of compassion;
Do not forget the sufferings of others.

Devoutly cultivate an amicable disposition;
Do not display an angry countenance.

Devoutly preserve a humble manner;
Do not arouse the spirit of arrogance.

Devoutly visualize the sources of defilement;
Do not develop a sense of attachment.

Devoutly study the law of evanescence;
Do not arouse the sense of greed.

Devoutly examine your own faults;
Do not make comment on the faults of others.

Devoutly go on trying to influence others;
Do not forget your own proper business.

Devoutly beware of the three evil ways: [lust, greed, and anger];
Do not indulge in wanton acts.

Devoutly yearn for the bliss of the happy land;
Do not forget the tortures of Hell.

Devoutly persevere in the aim of rebirth;
Do not neglect the practice of the invocation.

Devoutly concentrate on the vision of the West;
Do not let your attention stray to the nine regions.

Devoutly follow the path of enlightenment;
Do not mix with pleasure seekers.

Devoutly follow the teacher's guidance;
Do not indulge your own desires.

To all my followers:

Abide by these precepts to the end of the world. Exert yourself and do not be negligent. The activities of body, speech and mind have as their ultimate end a single devotion to Amida. [Signed:] Ippen

Psalm of the Six Hundred Thousand People

The following is an example of the type of hymn used by Ippen to popularize his teaching. The original is extremely simple and suggestive, consisting merely of four lines of seven syllables each. Each of the first three lines contains his religious name, Ippen, meaning "one and all" or "all in one."

[From *Ippen Shōnin Goroku*, p. 42]

The six-letter invocation is the Law, one and all.
The beings of the ten realms of existence are the Buddha, one and all.
Freedom from self-interest and partiality brings Realization for one and all. He who achieves this is supreme among men, an exquisite Lotus.

GENSHIN

The Essentials of Salvation

This famous work, describing the torments of Hell, the Pure Land, and the advantages of the Nembutsu, is in ten divisions as listed below by the author. The following excerpts are the initial chapters in the first two divisions, dealing with Hell and the Pure Land. Scriptural authorities cited by Genshin are deleted from the text.

[From Yampolsky, *The Essentials of Salvation*, pp. 10–16, 90–94]

The teaching and practice which leads to birth in Paradise is the most important thing in this impure world during these degenerate times.[1] Monks and laymen, men of high or low station, who will not turn to it? But the literature of the exoteric and the esoteric teachings of Buddha are not one in text, and the practices of one's work in this life in its ritualistic and philosophical aspects are many. These are not difficult for men of keen wisdom and great diligence, but how can a stupid person such as I

[1] Reference is to *mappō*, the last of the three periods of Buddhist law, that of degeneration and destruction of the law which extends for countless years. The first period, *shōbō*, the period of the true law, lasted 500 years. The second period, *zōbō*, the period of the simulated doctrine, endured 1,000 years.

achieve this knowledge? Because of this I have chosen the one gate to salvation of *nembutsu*.[2] I have made selections from the important sūtras and shāstras and have set them forth so that they may be readily understood and their disciplines easily practiced. In all there are ten divisions, divided into three volumes. The first is the corrupt life which one must shun, the second is the pure land for which one should seek, the third is the proof of the existence of the pure land, the fourth is the correct practice of *nembutsu*, the fifth is the helpful means of practicing the *nembutsu*, the sixth is the practice of *nembutsu* on special occasions, the seventh is the benefit resulting from *nembutsu*, the eighth is the proof of the benefit accruing from *nembutsu* alone, the ninth is the conduct leading to birth in Paradise, and the tenth comprises questions and answers to selected problems. These I place to the right of where I sit lest I forget them.

The first division, the corrupt land which one must shun, comprises the three realms[3] in which there is no peace. Now, in order to make clear the external appearances of this land, it is divided into seven parts: 1) hell; 2) hungry demons; 3) beasts; 4) fighting demons; 5) man; 6) Deva; and 7) a conclusion.

The first of these, hell, is furthermore divided into eight parts: 1) The hell of repeated misery; 2) The hell of the black chains; 3) The hell of mass suffering; 4) The hell of wailing; 5) The hell of great wailing; 6) The hell of searing heat; 7) The hell of great searing heat, and 8) The hell of incessant suffering.

The hell of repeated misery is one thousand yojanas[4] beneath the Southern Continent[5] and is ten thousand yojanas in length and breadth. Sinners here are always possessed of the desire to do each other harm. Should they by chance see each other, they behave as does the hunter when he encounters a deer. With iron claws they slash each other's bodies until blood and flesh are dissipated and the bones alone remain. Or else the hell-wardens, taking in their hands iron sticks and poles, beat the sinners' bodies from head to foot until they are pulverized like grains of sand. Or else, with a sword of awful sharpness, they cut their victims' bodies in regular pieces as the kitchen worker slices the flesh of fish. And then a cool wind arises, and blowing, returns the sinners to the

---

[2] Meditation on or repetition of the name of Amida Buddha.
[3] Past, present, and future.
[4] The distance an army can march in one day.   [5] India and adjoining regions.

same state in which they were at the outset. Thereupon they immediately arise and undergo torment identical to that which they had previously suffered. Elsewhere it is said that a voice from the sky above calls to the sentient beings to revive and return to their original state. And again, it is said that the hell-wardens beat upon the ground with iron pitchforks calling upon the sinners to revive. I cannot tell in detail of the other sufferings similar to those already told. . . .

Fifty years of human life is equivalent to one day and night in the realm of the Four Deva Kings,[6] and there life lasts five hundred years. The life in the realm of the Four Deva Kings is the equivalent of one day and night in this hell, and here life lasts five hundred years. People who have taken the life of a living creature fall into this hell. . . .

Outside the four gates of this hell are sixteen separate places which are associated with this hell. The first is called the place of excrement. Here, it is said, there is intensely hot dung of the bitterest of taste, filled with maggots with snouts of indestructible hardness. The sinner here eats of the dung and all the assembled maggots swarm at once for food. They destroy the sinner's skin, devour his flesh and suck the marrow from his bones. People who at one time in the past killed birds or deer fall into this hell. Second is the place of the turning sword. It is said that iron walls ten yojanas in height surround it and that a terrible and intense fire constantly burns within. The fire possessed by man is like snow when compared to this. With the least of physical contact, the body is broken into pieces the size of mustard-seeds. Hot iron pours from above like a heavy rainfall, and in addition, there is a forest of swords, with blades of exceptional keenness, and these swords, too, fall like rain. The multitude of agonies is in such variety that it cannot be borne. Into this place fall those who have killed a living being with concupiscence. Third is the place of the burning vat. It is said that the sinner is seized and placed in an iron vat, and boiled as one would cook beans. Those who in the past have taken the life of a living creature, cooked it, and eaten of it, fall into this hell. Fourth is the place of many agonies. In this hell there are a trillion different numberless tortures which cannot be explained in detail. Those who at some time in the past bound men with rope, beat men with sticks, drove men and forced them to make long journeys, threw men down steep places, tortured men with smoke,

[6] The lowest of the six heavens in the world of desire.

frightened small children, and in many other ways brought suffering to their fellow man, fall into this hell. Fifth is the place of darkness. It is said that here is pitch blackness that burns constantly with a dark flame. A powerful and intense wind blows against the adamantine mountains causing them to grind against each other and to destroy each other, so that the bodies of the sinners in between are broken into fragments like grains of sand. Then a hot wind arises which cuts like a sharply honed sword. To this place fall those who have covered the mouths and noses of sheep or who have placed turtles between two tiles and crushed them to death. Sixth is the place of joylessness. Here, it is said, is a great fire which burns intensely night and day. Birds, dogs, and foxes with flaming beaks whose intensely evil cries cause the sinner to feel the greatest of fear, come constantly to eat of the sinner, whose bones and flesh lie in great confusion. Hard-snouted maggots course about inside the bone and eat of the marrow. Those who once blew on shells, beat drums, made frightening sounds, or killed birds and animals fall to this hell. Seventh is the place of extreme agony. It is located beneath a precipitous cliff where a fire of iron burns continuously. People who once killed living creatures in a fit of debauchery descend to this hell. . . .

The second division is the Pure Land towards which one must aspire. The rewards of Paradise are of endless merit. Should one speak of them for a hundred kalpas or even for a thousand kalpas, one would not finish describing them; should one count them or give examples of them, there would still be no way to know of them. At present, ten pleasures in praise of the Pure Land will be explained, and they are as but a single hair floating upon the great sea.

First is the pleasure of being welcomed by many saints. Second is the pleasure of the first opening of the lotus.[7] Third is the pleasure of obtaining in one's own body the ubiquitous supernatural powers of a Buddha. Fourth is the pleasure of the realm of the five wonders. Fifth is the pleasure of everlasting enjoyment. Sixth is the pleasure of influencing others and introducing them to Buddhism. Seventh is the pleasure of assembling with the holy family. Eighth is the pleasure of beholding the Buddha and hearing the Law. Ninth is the pleasure of serving the Buddha according to the dictates of one's own heart. Tenth is the pleasure of progressing in the way of Buddhahood. . . .

[7] The pleasure of being first born into this land.

First is the pleasure of being welcomed by many saints. Generally when an evil man's life comes to an end, the elements of wind and fire leave first, and as they control movement and heat, great suffering is felt. When a good man dies, earth and water depart first, and as they leave gently, they cause no pain. How much less painful then must be the death of a man who has accumulated merit through *nembutsu!* The man who carries this teaching firmly in his mind for a long time feels a great rejoicing arise within him at the approach of death. Because of his great vow, Amida Nyorai,[8] accompanied by many bodhisattvas and hundreds of thousands of monks, appears before the dying man's eyes, exuding a great light of radiant brilliance. And at this time the great compassionate Kanzeon[9] extending hands adorned with the hundred blessings and offering a jeweled lotus throne, appears before the faithful. The Bodhisattva Seishi[10] and his retinue of numberless saints chant hymns and at the same time extend their hands and accept him among them. At this time the faithful one, seeing these wonders before his eyes, feels rejoicing within his heart and feels at peace as though he were entering upon meditation. Let us know then, that at the moment that death comes, though it be in a hut of grass, the faithful one finds himself seated upon a lotus throne. Following behind Amida Buddha amid the throng of bodhisattvas, in a moment's time he achieves birth in the Western Paradise. . . .

The pleasures in the Thirty-three-fold heaven[11] which last a billion years, the pleasures of deep meditation in the palace of the Great Brahma heaven,[12] are not pleasures at all, for the cycle of transmigration is not at an end, and one cannot escape the evils of the three worlds. But once one is in the embrace of Kannon and is seated upon the treasure lotus throne, one has crossed the sea of suffering and is born for the first time in the Pure Land. The pleasure felt in the heart at this time cannot be put into words.

A *gāthā* by Nāgārjuna says, "If upon death a man attains birth in this land, the virtue he attains is endless. That is why I devote my life to Amida." . . .

Second is the pleasure of the first opening of the Lotus. After the believer is born into this land and when he experiences the pleasures

---

[8] Amitābha Tathāgata.
[9] More commonly Kannon.
[10] Mahāsthāmaprāpta.
[11] Tōri-ten.
[12] Daibon.

of the first opening of the lotus, his joy becomes a hundred times greater than before. It is comparable to a blind man gaining sight for the first time, or to entering a royal palace directly after leaving some rural region. Looking at his own body, it becomes purplish gold in color. He is gowned naturally in jeweled garments. Rings, bracelets, a crown of jewels, and other ornaments in countless profusion adorn his body. And when he looks upon the light radiating from the Buddha, he obtains pure vision, and because of his experiences in former lives, he hears the sounds of all things. And no matter what color he may see or what sound he may hear, it is a thing of marvel. Such is the ornamentation of space above that the eye becomes lost in the traces of clouds. The melody of the wheel of the wonderful Law as its turns, flows throughout this land of jeweled sound. Palaces, halls, forests, and ponds shine and glitter everywhere. Flocks of wild ducks, geese, and mandarin ducks fly about in the distance and near at hand. One may see multitudes from all the worlds being born into this land like sudden showers of rain. And one may see a throng of saints, numerous as the grains of sand in the Ganges, arriving from the many Buddhalands. There are some who climb within the palaces and look about in all directions. There are those who, mounted upon temples, dwell in space. Then again there are some who, living in the sky, recite the sūtra and explain the Law. And again there are some who, dwelling in space, sit in meditation. Upon the ground and amid the forests there are others engaged in the same activities. And all about there are those who cross and bathe in the streams and those who walk among the palaces singing and scattering flowers and chanting the praises of the Tathāgata. In this way the numberless celestial beings and saints pursue their own pleasures as they themselves desire. How indeed can one tell in detail of the throng of incarnate Buddhas and bodhisattvas which fills this land like clouds of incense and flowers!

HŌNEN

What we have so far referred to as Pure Land Buddhism or Amidism was not a separate sect or school. Images of Amida and his two attendant bodhisattvas, Seishi and Kannon (known to the West as the Goddess of Mercy), were to be found in the temples of every sect, and recitation of the Nembutsu was a common adjunct to meditative practices that aimed at a state of enlightenment or ecstasy. The popularization of this formula did not, therefore, break down the walls of sectarian allegiance or seriously undercut existing religious observances. It was only with the appearance of Hōnen (1133–1212) that such a sharp break with other forms of Buddhism occurred.

In his epoch-making work *Senchakushū,* which translated in full means "Collection of Passages on the Original Vow of Amida, in which the Nembutsu is Chosen Above All Other Ways of Achieving Rebirth," Hōnen made it unmistakably clear that the Invocation to Amida was superior to all other religious practices. Traditional methods he characterized as the Path of Personal Sanctity, which involved the practice of severe disciplines leading to enlightenment, and which relied for their efficacy upon the personal merits and effort of the aspirant. The other Path was that of the Pure Land, involving only the recitation of the Nembutsu and complete reliance on the grace of Amida, not upon oneself. Since it was widely accepted that the world was passing through a stage of utter religious degeneration, as foretold by the Buddha, Hōnen believed that the Path of Personal Sanctity was beyond the capability of most men to pursue successfully. Their only sure hope of salvation in such times was to follow the second Path, since its success was dependent only on the unfailing mercy and power of Amida. In Hōnen's terms the former way was the "difficult path," relying on "one's own power," whereas the Nembutsu offered an "easy path," relying on the "power of another." The Nembutsu was therefore the greatest and most excellent of all disciplines, and enjoyed the protection of all other Buddhas as well as of Amida.

When this book, originally written for the edification of the premier, Fujiwara Kanezane, was eventually published, monks from Mt. Hiei seized all available copies, together with the blocks from which they were printed, and consigned them to the flames. Hōnen had already exposed himself to attack on personal grounds. Being a man of deep charity and believing that all men were equally immersed in sin, on one occasion he gave shelter in his mountain hermitage to a young court lady, about to deliver a child by a secret union. Some people insinuated that Hōnen was the real father of the expected baby, but in spite of such calumny Hōnen continued to treat the lady with the deepest solicitude

[198]

and tender care. Later the father was proven to be a young Taira warrior who had died in battle.

At the age of seventy-four Hōnen's success in winning converts to the new Pure Land Sect, which he had founded, resulted in his condemnation and exile. His biography tells us that in "the first year of Ken-ei (1206), . . . on the ninth day of the twelfth month, the retired Emperor Go-Toba happened to make a visit to the shrines at Kumano. It so happened that at this time Jūren and Anraku and some other disciples of Hōnen were holding a special service for the practice of the *Nembutsu* at Shishigatani in Kyoto, in which they were chanting the hymns appointed for each of the six hours of the day and night. The chanting was so impressive and awe-inspiring, with its peculiar irregular intonation, that those who heard it were strangely swayed by mingled feelings of sorrow and joy, so that many were led into the life of faith. Among them there were two maids of honor to the ex-emperor, who in his absence had gone to the service. On the emperor's return from Kumano, it would appear as if someone told him about these ladies having become nuns, suggesting that there was something wrong about their relations with these priests, so that the emperor was very angry with them, and on the ninth of the second month in the second year of Ken-ei (1207), he summoned them to the court and imposed on them quite a severe penalty."[1]

On his way into exile in a remote region of Shikoku, from which he returned by Imperial pardon only a year before his death, Hōnen fashioned a papier-mâché image of himself while passing away the hours aboard ship. It shows him with an enormous head having two unusual protuberances. One of these is said by his followers to represent his great scriptural erudition, which gained him the soubriquet *Chie Daiichi* (Foremost in Wisdom). The other, even more prominent, is considered a sign of his compassionate nature.

HONEN

Letter to Tsukinowa's Wife

Written in answer to questions raised by the wife of the ex-Regent, Kanezane Tsukinowa, who had already been converted to Hōnen's faith, this letter de-

[1] Coates and Ishizuka, *Honen*, p. 598.

fends the exclusive practice of the Nembutsu, which the lady was thereby persuaded to take up.

[From Coates and Ishizuka, *Honen,* pp. 371–73]

I have the honor of addressing you regarding your inquiry about the *Nembutsu.* I am delighted to know that you are invoking the sacred name. Indeed the practice of the *Nembutsu* is the best of all for bringing us to Ōjō,[1] because it is the discipline prescribed in Amida's Original Vow. The discipline required in the Shingon, and the meditation of the Tendai, are indeed excellent, but they are not in the Vow. This *Nembutsu* is the very thing that Shākya himself entrusted to his disciple Ānanda. As to all other forms of religious practice belonging to either the meditative or non-meditative classes, however excellent they may be in themselves, the great Master did not specially entrust them to Ānanda to be handed down to posterity. Moreover the *Nembutsu* has the endorsation of all the Buddhas of the six quarters; and, while the discipline of the exoteric and esoteric schools, whether in relation to the phenomenal or noumenal worlds, are indeed most excellent, the Buddhas do not give them their final approval. And so, although there are many kinds of religious exercise, the *Nembutsu* far excels them all in its way of attaining Ōjō. Now there are some people who are unacquainted with the way of birth into the Pure Land, who say, that because the *Nembutsu* is so easy, it is all right for those who are incapable of keeping up the practices required in the Shingon, and the meditation of the Tendai sects, but such a cavil is absurd. What I mean is, that I throw aside those practices not included in Amida's Vow, nor prescribed by Shākyamuni, nor having the endorsement of the Buddhas of all quarters of the universe, and now only throw myself upon the Original Vow of Amida, according to the authoritative teaching of Shākyamuni, and in harmony with what the many Buddhas of the six quarters have definitely approved. I give up my own foolish plans of salvation, and devote myself exclusively to the practice of that mightily effective discipline of the *Nembutsu,* with earnest prayer for birth into the Pure Land. This is the reason why the abbot of the Eshin-in Temple in his work *Essentials of Salvation* makes the *Nembutsu* the most fundamental of all. And so you should now cease from all other religious practices, apply yourself to the *Nembutsu* alone, and in this it is all-important to do it with undivided attention. Zendō,[2]

[1] Rebirth in the Pure Land.　　　　　[2] Chinese patriarch of Pure Land Sect.

who himself attained to that perfect insight (samādhi) which apprehends the truth, clearly expounds the full meaning of this in his Commentary on the *Meditation Sūtra,* and in the *Two-volumed Sūtra* the Buddha (Shākya) says, "Give yourself with undivided mind to the repetition of the name of the Buddha who is in Himself endless life." And by "undivided mind" he means to present a contrast to a mind which is broken up into two or three sections, each pursuing its own separate object, and to exhort to the laying aside of everything but this one thing only. In the prayers which you offer for your loved ones, you will find that the *Nembutsu* is the one most conducive to happiness. In the *Essentials of Salvation,* it says that the *Nembutsu* is superior to all other works. Also Dengyō Daishi,[3] when telling how to put an end to the misfortunes which result from the seven evils, exhorts to the practice of the *Nembutsu.* Is there indeed anything anywhere that is superior to it for bringing happiness in the present or the future life? You ought by all means to give yourself up to it alone.

Declaration on Going into Exile

After Hōnen was sentenced to exile in Tosa, many of his disciples tried to persuade the aged and decrepit monk that he should give up open propagation of the Nembutsu and thereby seek to stay execution of the sentence. But Hōnen in comforting them welcomed banishment as an opportunity to spread his faith in remote regions.

[From Coates and Ishizuka, *Honen,* pp. 601–2]

We must not resent this penalty of exile that has come upon me at all, for I am now an old man in my eighth decade. Mountains and seas may divide us, but we are sure of meeting again in that Pure Land. Man is a being who goes on living when he grows weary of life, and is most likely to die when life is most dear. What difference does it make as to where we happen to be? But not only this, the fact is, I have labored here in the capital these many years for the spread of the *Nembutsu,* and so I have long wished to get away into the country to preach to those on field and plain, but the time never came for the fulfillment of my wish. Now, however, by the august favor of His Majesty, circumstances have combined to enable me to do so. Man may try to put a stop to the spread of this Law of the Buddhas, but it cannot be done. The

---

[3] Saichō.

vows which the many Buddhas have made to save men have come forth from their hearts' depths, and the unseen divine powers have conspired together to protect the Law against all opposition. Why, then, should we have any anxiety over incurring the world's displeasure, and make that a ground for concealing from the public the real import of the sūtras and the commentaries which explain them? The only thing I am concerned about, is lest the gods who extend their constant protection over that Law of the Jōdo of which I, Genkū (Hōnen), am an exponent, should mete out punishment to those who of evil purpose thrust obstacles in the way of its propagation. For of all other ways of salvation known, this of the Jōdo is the most important, because it makes salvation certain, in these latter degenerate times, for all sentient beings. Let all those who outlive me take note that a fitting penalty will surely not fail to come upon all such offenders. If that law of affinity (karma) which operates in our mutual fellowship has not run its course, we may yet meet once more here in this present world.

The One-Page Testament

Written by Hōnen two days before he died for a disciple who asked that he "write me something with your own hand that you think will be good for me, so that I may keep it as a memento." After Hōnen's death this note was honored as his final testament and as a complete credo for the faithful.

[From Coates and Ishizuka, Honen, pp. 728–29]

The method of final salvation that I have propounded is neither a sort of meditation, such as has been practiced by many scholars in China and Japan, nor is it a repetition of the Buddha's name by those who have studied and understood the deep meaning of it. It is nothing but the mere repetition of the "Namu Amida Butsu," without a doubt of His mercy, whereby one may be born into the Land of Perfect Bliss. The mere repetition with firm faith includes all the practical details, such as the three-fold preparation of mind and the four practical rules. If I as an individual had any doctrine more profound than this, I should miss the mercy of the two Honorable Ones, Amida and Shāka, and be left out of the Vow of the Amida Buddha. Those who believe this, though they clearly understand all the teachings Shāka taught throughout his whole life, should behave themselves like simple-minded folk, who know not a single letter, or like ignorant nuns or monks whose faith is implicitly simple. Thus without pedantic airs, they should fervently practice the repetition of the name of Amida, and that alone. [pp. 728–29]

SHINRAN AND THE TRUE PURE LAND SECT

Among those banished from Kyoto at the same time as Hōnen was Shinran (1173–1262), who later claimed to be Hōnen's true disciple and is regarded as the founder of the most important of all Pure Land sects. Shinran's crime, for which he was exiled to the northern province of Echigo, was that he had taken a wife in violation of the clerical vow of celibacy. His followers later alleged that Shinran had married this woman, identified by them as a daughter of the Fujiwara regent, Kanezane, at the express request of Hōnen in order to demonstrate that monastic discipline was not essential to salvation and that the family rather than the monastery should be the center of the religious life.

Letters (recently found in Echigo) written by Shinran's wife cast doubt on her Fujiwara origin, but there can be no doubt that these traditions accurately reflect Shinran's own view of his relationship to Hōnen. He saw himself as merely following out in practice the full implications of his master's teaching. The more conservative of Hōnen's followers, who made their headquarters at the former site of his hermitage, held to the traditional monastic discipline of Buddhism, including the vows of celibacy and sobriety. But Shinran believed that if salvation truly depended on nothing but the grace of Amida, it was needless and perhaps dangerous to act as if one's conduct, or one's state in life, could have any bearing on ultimate redemption.

Shinran's experience in exile convinced him that propagation of the faith among all classes of people required its apostles to identify themselves as closely as possible with the ordinary man. During the remaining years of his life he was in fact compelled to live among the people, not as an outspoken preacher boldly proclaiming his mission, but as one condemned, a social outcast, whose faith had been proscribed and was allowed, like him, only a fugitive existence. Yet Shinran never sought to justify himself before the world, to make virtues of the vices for which others condemned him. He was, he admitted, a lost soul, unsure of himself and of all else in this life except the abiding grace of Amida. His only aim was to bring this faith in Amida to those like himself who needed it most, to those ignorant and illiterate souls who could not distinguish good from bad, to "bad people" rather than "good people." Shinran even went so far as to say that wicked men might be more acceptable to Amida than good men, since the former threw themselves entirely on the mercy of the Buddha, while the latter might be tempted to think that their chances of salvation were improved by their own meritorious conduct. "If even good people can be reborn in the Pure Land, how much more the wicked man!"

Shinran's utter reliance on the power of Amida is also emphasized by his attitude toward the recitation of the Nembutsu. The conservative followers of Hōnen believed that one's devotion to Amida was deepened by continual invocation of his name, a practice Hōnen is said to have encouraged and exemplified throughout his life. But to Shinran this too seemed to imply that there was something the individual could do to win salvation; it was another manifestation of the tendency to rely on "one's own power." A single, sincere invocation is enough, said Shinran, and any additional recitation of the Name should merely be an expression of thanksgiving to Amida. Indeed on certain occasions Shinran indicated that even one audible invocation was unnecessary, providing one had inward faith in Amida's saving grace.

Another way in which Shinran stressed exclusive reliance on Amida was by discouraging the worship of any other Buddhas. The historical Buddha himself, Shākyamuni, was merely an agent for the transmission of the true faith, a teacher and messenger but not someone to be worshiped. As might be expected, Shinran was also ready to dispense with all the sūtras except that which revealed Amida's Original Vow, even setting aside two other texts relating to Amida and the Pure Land which Hōnen had prized. Finally, of three vows attributed to Amida in this sūtra and recognized by Hōnen, Shinran discarded two. These promised a welcome to the Pure Land for all who performed meritorious deeds or repeated Amida's name. Shinran did not actually revoke them, but asserted that anyone who relied on the performance of meritorious deeds or the recitation of Buddha's name would have to endure a sort of purgatory before achieving rebirth in the Pure Land. The eighteenth or

Original Vow of Amida, which placed sole trust in the Buddha, alone assured direct rebirth in the Land of Bliss.

Though Shinran reduced Buddhism to the simplest of faiths, it must not be thought that this resulted from any ignorance on his part of the depth or complexity of Buddhist doctrine. On the contrary he, like Hōnen and Genshin, had made a thorough study of traditional teachings, as his writings on doctrinal questions testify. Nevertheless it is plain that Shinran grounded himself in tradition only to overturn it. The Buddhism he so unobtrusively but persistently propagated bore little resemblance to the original creed. The Three Treasures had been transformed into one: Amida's Original (or Fundamental) Vow. Virtually nothing remained of the Buddha as manifested by Shākyamuni, of the Law as embodied in scripture, or of the Priesthood as represented by a celibate clergy following monastic discipline. Gone too was the traditional emphasis on ethical and intellectual excellence, on the search for enlightenment through strenuous personal effort. All of these were now but particles of dust dancing in the radiant light of Amida.

In his own lifetime Shinran made no attempt to organize a new sect around his own creed, but he did leave numerous religious communities, consisting mostly of townspeople, bound together by loyalty to him and his teachings. Eventually they were organized into the True Pure Land Sect by Shinran's lineal descendants. The most famous of these was Rennyo (1415–1499), an able organizer as well as religious leader. In an age torn by conflicting feudal loyalties, Rennyo welded his adherents together into a disciplined band, ready to fight for their faith and their independence of other feudal powers. The bond of devotion between teacher and disciple became a personal bond of militant loyalty. Shinran had urged his followers to make every act an act of thanksgiving to Amida. Now this sense of obligation was redirected to Shinran's heir, identified as the official representative of Amida in this life. "The mercy of Buddha should be recompensed even by pounding flesh to pieces. One's obligation to the Teacher should be recompensed even by smashing bones to bits!" This was the battle cry of those who defended the Temple of the Original Vow in Osaka, withstanding for ten years the attacks of Nobunaga in the late sixteenth century. By such fanatic devotion they had won for themselves the name "Single-Minded" (*Ikkō*), and had maintained their independence in defensive strongholds throughout the country, taking a leading part in the century of warfare which ended with Nobunaga's rise to power.

Though the True Pure Land Sect ceased to be a feudal power after the unification of Japan, it has retained one important vestige of feudalism. This is the hereditary succession of its leadership, to which Shinran's abandonment of celibacy had opened the way. Generation after generation the abbots of both the Western and Eastern branches of the Temple of the Original Vow in Kyoto, primates of what is now one of the most numerous and affluent sects in Japan, have been descendants of Shinran. For those who recognize only the supreme value of Amida's love and never the claims of individual merit, such an arrangement no doubt involves the least danger of self-assertion. Moreover the discarding of the vow of celibacy has had its effect on other sects as well, which have belatedly followed Shinran's lead. Today, although a few monasteries and individuals elect to follow this rule, in none of the important sects is its observance a strict requirement.

SHINRAN

Hymn to the True Faith in the Nembutsu
(Shōshin Nembutsu Ge)

In this hymn, part of the daily devotions of Shinran's followers, he sums up the basic tenets of the Pure Land faith and its transmission from India through China to Japan.
[Adapted from Lloyd, *Shinran and His Works*, pp. 46–56]

I put my trust in the great Tathāgata of Infinite Life and Boundless Light!

Hōzō[1] the Bodhisattva, in the days of his humiliation, being in the presence of the Tathāgata Lord of the World, examining the degree of excellence of the Paradises of all the Buddhas, the causes of their formation, and the angels and men in them, made his great Vow and proclaimed his mighty Oath, which he meditated and selected for the space of five long kalpas; and he repeated the Vow of announcing his Holy Name "Amida" in all the Ten Quarters.

[1] Japanese form of the name given to Amida during his earthly existence. [Ed.]

Universally doth he send forth his endless, boundless, all-pervading unrivaled, supreme Light, his Light of Purity, of Joy, of Wisdom, His changeless, unconceivable, unexplainable Light, brighter than the brightness of Sun or Moon. His Light illuminates worlds more numerous than dust, and all sentient creatures enjoy it and are illuminated thereby.

His Holy Name which was revealed by his Vow of Salvation, is the fundamental Power that justly determines us to enter into his Pure Land. His Vow to make us put our sincere trust in it is the effective cause which produces perfect Enlightenment. His Vow to lead us without fail into Nirvāna has been fulfilled; in consequence of it, we can acquire the same rank as the bodhisattva in this life, and Nirvāna [2] in the next.

The reason why the Tathāgata Shākyamuni was revealed to the world was solely that he might proclaim the Boundless Ocean of Amida's Fundamental Vow. Men, numerous as the Ocean Waves, who are subject to the Five Obstacles and entangled in Evil, should certainly listen to the Tathāgata's true words.

If once there be aroused in us but one thought of joy and love [in consequence of the Vow], we turn just as we are with our sins and lusts upon us, towards Nirvāna. Laymen and saints alike, even those who have committed the five deadly sins, and slandered the Holy Laws of Buddha, will yet, by faith in the power of the Tathāgata, enter into the enjoyment and taste of his mercy, as surely as the water in the mountain stream ultimately reaches the Ocean and becomes salt.

The Light of the Buddha's Heart which has taken hold of us, illuminates and protects us continually, and dispels the darkness of Ignorance. It is true that the dark mist of covetousness and passion constantly overhangs the sky that is above the believing heart. Yet, though the sky above may be constantly overcast, beneath the cloud it is light, there is no darkness.

When we have made Faith our own, and have received a sight of the great mercy and a thought of pious joy, we pass away sideways [3] from the five evil spheres of life. If any layman, whether good or bad, hears and believes the all-embracing Vow of Amida-Buddha, him will the Tathāgata Shākyamuni praise for his wisdom, and will call him a lotus-flower among men.

[2] Which is to be obtained in the Pure Land. [Ed.]
[3] Not by a steep ascent, but passing directly over to the Pure Land. [Ed.]

For sentient creatures, who are heretical, evil, and proud, to believe and accept the practice of Amida's Fundamental Vow, is indeed a hard matter, there is nothing harder than this.

Abhidharma Doctors of Western India, noble priests of China and Japan, have declared to us that the true meaning of the Great Saint's (Shākyamuni's) appearance was to point to the true Vow of Amida, and the Vow is just the way for us.

Shākyamuni the Tathāgata, on the mountain peak in Lankā [Ceylon], prophesied for the people assembled to hear him that there should appear in South India, a great teacher, Nāgārjuna by name, who should destroy the conflicting views of Entity and Non-Entity, who should clearly teach the excellent law of the Mahāyāna, who should reach the Class of Joy and be born in Paradise.

He (Nāgārjuna) taught that the way of Salvation by one's own efforts is like a toilsome journey by land, that the Way of Faith in the Merits of Another is as an easy voyage in a fair ship over smooth waters, that if a man put his trust in the Fundamental Vow of Amida, he will enter at once, by Buddha's power, into the class of those destined to be born in the Pure Land. Only let him ever call upon the Name of the Tathāgata, and gratefully commemorate the great all-embracing Vow.

Vasubandhu, also, the Bodhisattva, composed his praise of the Pure Land, put his whole trust and confidence in the Tathāgata of Boundless Light, established the truth by the sūtras, and made clear the way of 'crosswise going-out' through the merits of the great Fundamental Vow.

[Vasubandhu taught], with a view to the Salvation of Men through the Faith in Another's merits which Amida bestows upon us, the mystery of the One Heart. If a man enter into this Faith, he will acquire the merit of the Great Ocean of Divine Treasures, and will certainly be admitted to the Great Company of the Saints, in the present life. In the future life, he will go to the Pure Land which shines with the Light of Wisdom like the lotus, and having acquired the Holy Existence with divine power he will return to the forest of human passions, and there, in the garden of life and death, [for the salvation of his fellow creatures], will manifest himself in various transformations.

Take Donran [4] our teacher, whom the king [Wu-ti] of the Liang Dynasty reverenced as a Bodhisattva. From Bodhiruchi, the Master of the

[4] Tan-luan, regarded in Japan as first Chinese patriarch of the Pure Land Sect. [Ed.]

Tripitaka, he received the teaching of the Pure Land, and burning the ascetic books [in which he had hitherto put his trust], put his faith in the Paradise of Bliss. He followed the teachings of Vasubandhu [which he learned from Bodhiruchi] and clearly taught that Amida's Great Vow was the effective cause of Birth in Paradise.

[Donran taught] that the Grace of new birth into Paradise, as well as that whereby we can return to Earth to aid our fellow-beings, is a gift which we receive through the Buddha's power, and that the effective cause whereby we are justly determined to be born in the Pure Land, is only the believing heart. Wherefore, if we, blind and sinful persons, arouse this believing heart, we can perceive Nirvāna in this life. Afterwards, without fail, we reach the Pure Land of Boundless Light, and teaching all sentient creatures that are involved in misery of Earth, lead them to salvation.

Dōshaku[5] taught that the innumerable practices for perfecting righteousness by one's own efforts are of no value, and the invocation of the Name which comprises all virtues, he praised as beneficial. He spoke much of the three marks of Non-Faith and Faith, and showed that in all three Ages it is the principle of Mercy that alone rules and draws men. Though a man had done evil all his life, yet, if he were once brought near to the Great Vow, he would reach the Land of Bliss and enjoy the fruits of Salvation.

Zendō[6] was the first that understood the true will of Buddha Shākyamuni in his age, and that had pity, alike for those who practiced meditation or moral good, as for those who lived in wickedness.

Zendō taught that the Effect of Salvation is given by the Holy Light and the Sacred Name of Amida, and expounded the Great Ocean of Wisdom contained in the Fundamental Vow. The believer, having rightly received the adamantine heart of firm faith, and having answered to the calling of the Tathāgata with a joyful heart, like Vaidehī[7] receives the threefold assurance and immediately enters into the happiness of the Eternal Life.

Genshin studied all the teachings of Shākyamuni, and earnestly aspired to go to the Buddha's Land. He exhorted all men to go there too.

[5] Tao-ch'o, Chinese patriarch of the seventh century. [Ed.]
[6] Shan-tao, d. 681. [Ed.]
[7] Queen to whom Shākyamuni was said to have taught the meditation on Amida and the Pure Land. [Ed.]

Genshin established a difference between a pure and an impure Faith, the one deep and the other shallow. Also, he taught that there are two forms of Paradise, as places of rest for those of deep and shallow faith respectively. O deadly sinner! Invoke but once Amida-Buddha! He is taking hold of us. Though our eyes of flesh can not clearly see him owing to our sins, yet is his mercy constantly present to illuminate our minds.

My teacher Genkū [Hōnen] threw light on Buddhism, and had deep compassion for the laity, good or bad. It was he who originated the True Sect's teachings in this country, and propagated in this wicked world the doctrine of Amida's Selected Vow.

Genkū taught that the reason why men keep constantly returning to the Home of Error [bodily life], is entirely due to our being fast bound with doubt. In order that we may enter straight into the peaceful and eternal abode of Nirvāṇa, it is necessary for us to receive the believing heart.

Thus prophets and teachers, propagating the teachings of the sūtras, have saved countless men from countless evils. Monks and laymen in the present age! We must put our hearts together; and believe the words that these exalted monks have spoken.

Selections from the *Tannishō*

This collection of Shinran's sayings is said to have been made by his disciple Yuiembō, who was concerned over heresies and schisms developing among Shinran's followers and wished to compile a definitive statement of his master's beliefs. The title *Tannishō* means "Collection Inspired by Concern over Heresy." These words attributed to Shinran reveal above all his utter self-abasement and glorification of Amida.

[From *Shinshū seiten*, pp. 1203–5, 1207, 1224–25]

Your aim in coming here, traveling at the risk of your lives through more than ten provinces, was simply to learn the way of rebirth in the Pure Land. Yet you would be mistaken if you thought I knew of some way to obtain rebirth other than by saying the Nembutsu, or if you thought I had some special knowledge of religious texts not open to others. Should this be your belief, it is better for you to go to Nara or Mt. Hiei, for there you will find many scholars learned in Buddhism and from them you can get detailed instruction in the essential means of obtaining rebirth in the Pure Land. As far as I, Shinran, am concerned, it is only because the worthy Hōnen taught me so that I believe salvation comes from Amida by saying the Nembutsu. Whether the Nembutsu brings rebirth in the Pure Land or leads one to Hell, I myself have no way of knowing. But even if I had been misled by Hōnen and went to Hell for saying the Nembutsu, I would have no regrets. If I were capable of attaining Buddhahood on my own through the practice of some other discipline, and yet went down to Hell for saying the Nembutsu, then I might regret having been misled. But since I am incapable of practicing such disciplines, there can be no doubt that I would be doomed to Hell anyway.

If the Original Vow of Amida is true, the teaching of Shākyamuni cannot be false. If the teaching of the Buddha is true, Zendō's commentary on the *Meditation Sūtra* cannot be wrong. And if Zendō is right, what Hōnen says cannot be wrong. So if Hōnen is right, what I, Shinran, have to say may not be empty talk.

Such, in short, is my humble faith. Beyond this I can only say that, whether you are to accept this faith in the Nembutsu or reject it, the choice is for each of you to make. . . .

"If even a good man can be reborn in the Pure Land, how much more so a wicked man!"

People generally think, however, that if even a wicked man can be reborn in the Pure Land, how much more so a good man! This latter view may at first sight seem reasonable, but it is not in accord with the purpose of the Original Vow, with faith in the Power of Another. The reason for this is that he who, relying on his own power, undertakes to perform meritorious deeds, has no intention of relying on the Power of Another and is not the object of the Original Vow of Amida. Should he, however, abandon his reliance on his own power and put his trust in the Power of Another, he can be born in the True Land of Recompense. We who are caught in the net of our own passions cannot free ourselves from bondage to birth and death, no matter what kind of austerities or good deeds we try to perform. Seeing this and pitying our condition, Amida made his Vow with the intention of bringing wicked men to Buddhahood. Therefore the wicked man who depends on the Power of Another is the prime object of salvation. This is the reason why Shinran said, "If even a good man can be reborn in the Pure Land, how much more so a wicked man!" . . .

It is regrettable that among the followers of the Nembutsu there are some who quarrel, saying "These are my disciples, those are not." There is no one whom I, Shinran, can call my own disciple. The reason is that, if a man by his own efforts persuaded others to say the Nembutsu, he might call them his disciples, but it is most presumptuous to call those "my disciples" who say the Nembutsu because they have been moved by the grace of Amida. If it is his karma to follow a teacher, a man will follow him; if it is his karma to forsake a teacher, a man will forsake him. It is quite wrong to say that the man who leaves one teacher to join another will not be saved by saying the Nembutsu. To claim as one's own and attempt to take back that faith which is truly the gift of Amida—such a view is wholly mistaken. In the normal course of things a person will spontaneously recognize both what he owes to the grace of Amida and what he owes to his teacher [without the latter having to assert any claims]. . . .

The Master was wont to say, "When I ponder over the Vow which Amida made after meditating for five kalpas, it seems as if the Vow were made for my salvation alone. How grateful I am to Amida, who thought to provide for the salvation of one so helplessly lost in sin!"

When I now reflect upon this saying of the Master, I find that it is fully in accordance with the golden words of Zendō. "We must realize that each of us is an ordinary mortal, immersed in sin and crime, subject to birth and death, ceaselessly migrating from all eternity and ever sinking deeper into Hell, without any means of delivering ourselves from it."

It was on this account that Shinran most graciously used himself as an example, in order to make us realize how lost every single one of us is and how we fail to appreciate our personal indebtedness to the grace of Amida. In truth, none of us mentions the great love of Amida, but we continually talk about what is good and what is bad. Shinran said, however, "Of good and evil I am totally ignorant. If I understood good as Buddha understands it, then I could say I knew what was good. If I understood evil as Buddha understands it, then I could say I knew what was bad. But I am an ordinary mortal, full of passion and desire, living in this transient world like the dweller in a house on fire. Every judgment of mine, whatever I say, is nonsense and gibberish. The Nembutsu alone is true."

CHAPTER XI

NICHIREN: THE SUN AND THE LOTUS

The story of Nichiren (1222–1282) is one, to use his own words, of "a son of the shūdras (lowest caste)" on the seacoast of Japan, who was destined to become "the pillar of Japan, the eye of the nation and the vessel of the country." Like most of the great religious leaders of that age, this son of a humble fisherman spent years in study and training at the great monastic center of Mt. Hiei. Unlike many others, however, he found new faith, not by turning away from the teachings of its Tendai founder, Saichō, but by turning back to them. In doing so he was forced to depart from Mt. Hiei itself, which had long since become a stronghold of Esoteric Buddhism, and to embark upon a preaching career of unceasing hardship, conflict, and persecution. But through it all he became ever more convinced of his mission to save his country and Buddhism.

For Nichiren the *Lotus Sūtra,* upon which the Tendai teaching had been based, is the key to everything. It is the final and supreme teaching of the Buddha Shākyamuni, revealing the one and only way of salvation. In this sūtra the three forms of the Buddha—his Universal or Law Body (Dharmakāya), Eternal Body or Body of Bliss (Sambhogakāya), and Transformation Body (Nirmānakāya)—are seen as one and inseparable. What the prevailing schools of Buddhism had done was to emphasize one form at the expense of the others. Esoteric Buddhism stressed the Universal Buddha, Vairochana or Dainichi; Amidism worshipped the Body of Bliss or Eternal Buddha, Amitābha. By thus dispensing with the historical Buddha, Shākyamuni (the Transformation Body), they committed the inexcusable crime of mutilating Buddha's perfect body. On the other hand Zen Buddhism and the Vinaya school, which was undergoing something of a revival at that time, ignored the universal and eternal aspect of the Buddha in favor of the historical or actual Buddha. The *Lotus*

Sūtra alone upholds the truth of the triune Buddha. And only in this trinity is the salvation of all assured.

So it is the name of the *Lotus Sūtra,* not the name of Amida Buddha, which should be on the lips of every Buddhist. "Namu myōhō renge-kyō" is the Buddha's pledge of salvation, which Nichiren often called out to the beat of a drum—"dondon dondoko dondon." Like Shinran, Nichiren was a man of no slight intelligence, and in his years of exile or enforced seclusion he devoted himself to an intensive study of scripture and doctrine; but this erudition only served to adorn a simple conviction, arrived at early in life and held to with single-minded devotion throughout his stormy career, that faith in the *Lotus of the Wonderful Law* was all one needed for salvation.

Unlike Shinran, Nichiren stressed the importance of one's own efforts and became ever more deeply convinced that he himself was destined to fulfill a unique mission in the world. A man of active temperament, who commanded attention because of his forceful and magnetic personality, Nichiren thought the *Lotus Sūtra* should be "read by the body" and not just with the eyes. To him among its most significant passages were those describing the saints destined to uphold and spread abroad the truths of the Lotus. One of these was the Bodhisattva of Superb Action,[1] who was to be a stalwart pioneer in propagating the Perfect Truth. Another was the Bodhisattva Ever-abused,[2] who suffered continual insults from others because he insisted on saluting everyone as a Buddha-to-be, convinced that every man was ultimately destined to be such. The Lotus' account of these two saints he regarded as prefiguring his own mission, and often he referred to himself as a reincarnation of them, especially of the Bodhisattva Superb Action. Nichiren also found special meaning in the vows taken by Buddha's disciples when His eternal aspect was revealed to them at the climax of the *Lotus Sūtra.* In these vows they took upon themselves to proclaim the Supreme Scripture in evil times, and promised to endure all the injury and abuse which was certain to descend on them. In this too Nichiren saw a prophecy of his own sufferings.

The immediate cause of his sufferings was Nichiren's unrelenting attack on the established sects and his outspoken criticism of Japan's rulers for patronizing these heretics. The repeated calamities suffered by the country at large and the threat of foreign invasion, which he hinted at ten years before the Mongol fleet appeared in Japanese waters, he regarded

[1] Vishishtachāritra (Viśiṣṭacāritra).   [2] Sadāparibhūta.

as the inevitable retribution for the false faith of the nation's leaders, ecclesiastical and political. Contrasted to this sad state of affairs was Nichiren's vision of Japan as the land in which the true teaching of the Buddha was to be revived and from which it was to spread throughout the world. The name Nichiren, which he adopted, symbolizes this exalted mission and his own key role in its fulfillment, for *nichi,* "the sun," represents both the Light of Truth and the Land of the Rising Sun, while *ren* stands for the Lotus.

To accomplish this aim Nichiren urged all his followers to imitate the bodhisattva ideal of perseverance and self-sacrifice. In an age of utter decadence, everyone must be a man of Superb Action, ready to give his life if necessary for the cause. Nichiren himself was sentenced to death for his bold censure of the Hōjō regency in Kamakura, and was saved only by miraculous intervention, according to his followers, when lightning struck the executioner's blade. Banished then to a lonely island in the Sea of Japan, Nichiren wrote, "Birds cry but shed no tears. Nichiren does not cry, but his tears are never dry." Ever after his narrow escape at the execution ground, Nichiren regarded himself as one who had risen from the dead, who had been reborn in the faith. "Tatsunokuchi is the place where Nichiren renounced his life. The place is therefore comparable to a paradise; because all has taken place for the sake of the Lotus of Truth. . . . Indeed every place where Nichiren encounters perils is Buddha's land." [3] In this way Nichiren made of suffering a glorious thing, and set an example for his disciples which did more to confirm their faith in the Lotus than volumes of scripture.

At least three of Nichiren's adherents followed in his footsteps as Bodhisattvas of Superb Action. One was Nichiji (1250-?), who undertook foreign missionary work at the age of forty-six, going first to Ainuland in Hokkaido and thence it is said to Siberia, from which he never returned. A stone monument he erected in northern Japan testifies to his indefatigable zeal for spreading faith in the Lotus among the heathen of unknown lands. In his youth he had accompanied his master into exile off the Sea of Japan coast, opposite Siberia. Known as a master of prose and poetry, who wrote for Nichiren in the latter's old age, Nichiji might have settled down to a quiet life of study and writing, but chose instead a strenuous life exploring the unknown, with only his faith to sustain him.

[3] M. Anesaki, *Nichiren, the Buddhist Prophet,* pp. 58–59.

A later follower of Nichiren, named Nisshin (1407–1488), went to Kyushu at the other end of Japan and was made superintendent of the mission there. But he too was a Bodhisattva of Superb Action, and, dissatisfied with the easy life of a successful missionary, returned alone to Kyoto. In this stronghold of tradition and conservatism, Nisshin started out as a street-corner evangelist, calling out the name of the *Lotus Sūtra* to the beat of a drum, "dondon dondoko dondon." Openly he challenged the ruling shogun to suppress all other Buddhist sects and recognize the Lotus alone. When the shogun, who had quit the priesthood to become military dictator, was persuaded by his former clerical associates to command Nisshin to keep silent, the evangelist only beat his drum louder. Thrown into jail and tortured, he still would not yield to the shogun's order. Finally a brass pot was jammed down over his head so as to keep him from talking, and thus he became known as the "pot-wearer (*nabe-kaburi*)." Among the converts which he made through his almost superhuman endurance under such suffering were the Prime Minister Konoe, the master craftsman Hon-ami, and also the head of the eminent Kano school of painting.

Lastly there is Nichiō (1565–1630), who led a group of the Nichiren sect known as the *Fuju-fuse*—from their slogan: "Accept nothing [from nonbelievers] and give nothing." So uncompromising was he in regard to all other schools of Buddhism that when Hideyoshi, upon unifying the country, invited all sects to send delegates for a festival of celebration, Nichiō refused on the ground that the conqueror was not a follower of Nichiren. A repetition of this incident occurred when the next shogun, Ieyasu, had unified the country, but this time Nichiō's refusal of such an invitation led to his banishment for more than ten years. Thereafter the *Fuju-fuse* school was subjected to repeated persecutions by the Tokugawa Shogunate, and yet somehow it has managed to survive into the present, though limited in numbers.

NICHIREN

Dedication to the Lotus
[From Anesaki, *Nichiren*, pp. 46–47]

If you desire to attain Buddhahood immediately, lay down the banner of pride, cast away the club of resentment, and trust yourselves to the unique Truth. Fame and profit are nothing more than vanity of this life; pride and obstinacy are simply fetters to the coming life. . . . When you fall into an abyss and some one has lowered a rope to pull you out, should you hesitate to grasp the rope because you doubt the power of the helper? Has not Buddha declared, "I alone am the protector and savior"? There is the power! Is it not taught that faith is the only entrance [to salvation]? There is the rope! One who hesitates to seize it, and will not utter the Sacred Truth, will never be able to climb the precipice of Bodhi (Enlightenment). . . . Our hearts ache and our sleeves are wet [with tears], until we see face to face the tender figure of the One, who says to us, "I am thy Father." At this thought our hearts beat, even as when we behold the brilliant clouds in the evening sky or the pale moonlight of the fast-falling night. . . . Should any season be passed without thinking of the compassionate promise, "Constantly I am thinking of you"? Should any month or day be spent without revering the teaching that there is none who cannot attain Buddhahood? . . . Devote yourself wholeheartedly to the "Adoration to the Lotus of the Perfect Truth," and utter it yourself as well as admonish others to do the same. Such is your task in this human life.

Condemnation of Hōnen

Nichiren's famous tract, "The Establishment of the Legitimate Teaching for the Security of the Country (*Risshō ankoku ron*)" brought his banishment from Kamakura after he had boldly presented it to the authorities. Writing in dialogue form, Nichiren denounced Japan's rulers for countenancing false teachings and prophesied grievous calamities for the nation, including foreign invasion, unless all other Buddhist sects were suppressed in favor of the Lotus. His sharpest attacks were directed at the worshipers of Amida, among whose number was a high official of the regime.

[From Lloyd, *The Creed of Half Japan*, pp. 315–18]

In the reign of Go-Toba (1183–1198) there was a monk of the name of Hōnen, who wrote a book called the *Senchakushū*, in which he abused the holy teachings of the age, and misled men by the thousands. Now this man, basing his arguments on a mistaken interpretation of Nāgārjuna's writings, in which he follows Dōshaku, Donran, and Zendō, his predecessors in heresy, divides Buddhism into two gates, the gate of Holy Practices, and the gate of Faith in the Pure Land, and advises all men, in this age of decay, to embrace the latter. As to the other forms of Buddhism, and as to the other sūtras, including even the *Lotus* and the sūtras of the Shingon tradition, he uses four words to describe what should be our attitude towards them. "Give them up," he says, "close the books, lay them aside, fling them away." By means of this doctrine he has misled thousands of his followers, both lay and clerical.

Now, this teaching is in direct contradiction to one of Amida's Vows, as contained in the three *Pure Land Sūtras* in which alone he puts his trust. I mean the Vow that Amida takes to "clear away the five obstacles to the truth, and to remove the abuses of true Buddhism." It is in contradiction, likewise, to the teachings of the "whole life according to the five periods."[1] It can lead its author nowhere but to the lowest hell. We live in an age when saints are few; there are not many that can discern the dangerous nature of these teachings. Woe unto them! They do not smite the offender. Woe, woe! they acquiesce in the propagation of a false faith. From the princes and barons down to the common people, every one is now saying, that there are no Scriptures but the Three of the Pure Land, and no Buddha but the Triune Amida. . . .

As a consequence of his preaching, men refused to make contributions to temples that were not dedicated to Amida, and forgot to pay their tithes to priests who were not of the Nembutsu. Thus temples and halls have fallen into ruin, so that for a long time they have been uninhabitable, and many cloisters have fallen into disrepair, and are covered with rank vegetation on which the dew lies thick and undisturbed. But none heeded the ruin of the temples, none would repair or give support; and therefore the priests who lived there, and the deities who protected the people, have left the temples and refuse to return. For all this who is to blame but Hōnen and his *Senchaku?*

Woe, woe! During the last thirty or forty years, thousands of people have been enchanted and led astray, so that they wander in Buddhism as men without a guide. Is it not to be expected that the good deities should be angry when men depart from the truth? Is it not natural that evil spirits should make the most of their opportunities, when they see men forsake justice and love unrighteous deeds? It is better far to exert ourselves to stay an impending calamity than to repeat the vain Nembutsu.

[1] According to the Tendai school Shākyamuni's teaching career was divided into five periods, in terms of which the whole body of Buddhist scripture might be classified. [Ed.]

Warning of Foreign Invasion

Nichiren first predicted a foreign invasion in 1260. In 1268, upon the arrival of an envoy from the Mongols demanding tribute, Nichiren reiterated his warning to the authorities and wrote his followers:
[From Anesaki, *Nichiren*, p. 53]

In consequence of the arrival of the Mongol envoy, I have sent eleven letters to various officials and prelates. Prosecution will surely overtake Nichiren and his followers, and either exile or death will be the sentence. You must not be at all surprised. Strong remonstrances have intentionally been made, simply for the purpose of awakening the people. All is awaited by Nichiren with composure. Do not think of your wives and children and households; do not be fearful before the authorities! Make this your opportunity to sever the fetters of births and deaths, and to attain the fruit of Buddhahood!

Nichiren as a Prophet
[From Anesaki, *Nichiren*, p. 115]

The Lord Shākya proclaimed to all celestial beings that when, in the fifth five hundred years after his death, all the truths of Buddhism should be shrouded in darkness, the Bodhisattva of Superb Action (Vishishṭa-chāritra) should be commissioned to save the most wicked of men who were degrading the truth, curing the hopeless lepers by the mysterious medicine of the Adoration of the Lotus of the Perfect Truth. Can this proclamation be a falsehood? If this promise be not vain, how can the rulers of the people of Japan remain in safety, who, being plunged in the whirlpool of strife and malice, have rebuked, reviled, struck, and banished the messenger of the Tathāgata and his followers commissioned by Buddha to propagate the Lotus of Truth?

When they hear me say this, people will say that it is a curse; yet, those who propagate the Lotus of Truth are indeed the parents of all men living in Japan. . . . I, Nichiren, am the master and lord of the sovereign, as well as of all the Buddhists of other schools. Notwithstanding this, the rulers and the people treat us thus maliciously. How should the sun and the moon bless them by giving them light? Why should the earth not refuse to let them abide upon it? . . . Therefore, also, the Mongols are

[219]

coming to chastise them. Even if all the soldiers from the five parts of India were called together, and the mountain of the Iron Wheel (Chakravāla) were fortified, how could they succeed in repelling the invasion? It is decreed that all the inhabitants of Japan shall suffer from the invaders. Whether this comes to pass or not will prove whether or not Nichiren is the real propagator of the Lotus of Truth.

A Challenge to Hachiman

After he was condemned at Kamakura a second time, Nichiren was forced to ride through the streets bareback to his appointed place of execution. When the procession passed the shrine of Hachiman, Shinto deity regarded as the protector of the nation and also as a Bodhisattva, Nichiren stopped and called upon the god to save him.

[Adapted from Satomi, *Japanese Civilization*, pp. 150–51]

Oh, Hachiman! Art Thou in truth a Divine Being? . . . When the Great Master Dengyō preached on the *Lotus Sūtra*, didst Thou not do homage to him by laying at his feet a gown of purple color? I now say unto Thee that I am the Only One whose life is the *Lotus Sūtra*. There is no fault in me whatsoever; I am proclaiming the Truth, for the sole purpose of saving the people who dwell in the land from sinking into the deepest of Hells on account of degrading the Lotus. If it came to pass that this land were subjugated by the Mongols, wouldst Thou, O Hachiman, alone with the Sun Goddess be in safety? Let me now say unto Thee that when our Lord Shākyamuni preached the Lotus, all the Buddhas gathered together from ten quarters, like unto a sun and a sun, a moon and a moon, stars and stars, mirrors and mirrors, and were ranged face to face with one another; and with hosts of heaven within their midst, deities and saints of India, China, Japan, etc., present in the congregation, all of them vowed to watch over those who should labor to perpetuate the *Lotus Sūtra*.

Now shouldst Thou come hither and fulfill what Thou hast sworn. Why then comest Thou not to fulfill Thy Promise! When, I, Nichiren, this night shall have been beheaded and shall have passed away to the Paradise of Vulture Peak, I shall declare unto Our Lord Shākyamuni that Thou, Hachiman, and the Sun Goddess have not fulfilled the vows. Therefore, if Thou fearest, tarry not, but do Thy duty!

[220]

The Value of Suffering
[From Anesaki, *Nichiren*, p. 74]

That Nichiren suffers so much is not without remote causes. As is explained in the chapter on the Bodhisattva Ever-abused (Sadāparibhūta), all abuses and persecutions heaped upon the bodhisattva were the results of his previous karma. How much more, then, should this be the case with Nichiren, a man born in the family of an outcast fisherman, so lowly and degraded and poor! Although in his soul he cherishes something of the faith in the Lotus of Truth, the body is nothing but a common human body, sharing beastlike life, nothing but a combination of the two fluids, pink and white, the products of flesh and fish. Therein the soul finds its abode, something like the moon reflected in a muddy pool, like gold wrapped up in a dirty bag. Since the soul cherishes faith in the Lotus of Truth, there is no fear even before [the highest deities, such as] Brahmā and Indra; yet the body is an animal body. Not without reason others show contempt for this man, because there is a great contrast between the soul and the body. And even this soul is full of stains, being the pure moonlight only in contrast to the muddy water; gold, in contrast to the dirty bag.

Who, indeed, fully knows the sins accumulated in his previous lives? . . . The accumulated karma is unfathomable. Is it not by forging and refining that the rough iron bar is tempered into a sharp sword? Are not rebukes and persecutions really the process of refining and tempering? I am now in exile, without any assignable fault; yet this may mean the process of refining, in this life, the accumulated sins [of former lives], and being thus delivered from the three woeful resorts. . . .

The world is full of men who degrade the Lotus of Truth, and such rule this country now. But have I, Nichiren, not also been one of them? Is that not due to the sins accumulated by deserting the Truth? Now, when the intoxication is over, I stand here something like a drunken man who having, while intoxicated, struck his parents, after coming to himself, repents of the offense. The sin is hardly to be expiated at once. . . . Had not the rulers and the people persecuted men, how could I have expiated the sins accumulated by degrading the Truth?

Nichiren as the Bodhisattva of Superb Action
[From Anesaki, *Nichiren*, pp. 83–85]

I, Nichiren, a man born in the ages of the Latter Law, have nearly achieved the task of pioneership in propagating the Perfect Truth, the task assigned to the Bodhisattva of Superb Action (Vishishṭachāritra). The eternal Buddhahood of Shākyamuni, as he revealed himself in the chapter on Life-duration, in accordance with his primeval entity; the Buddha Prabhūtaratna, who appeared in the Heavenly Shrine, in the chapter on its appearance, and who represents Buddhahood in the manifestation of its efficacy; the Saints [bodhisattvas] who sprang out of the earth, as made known in the chapter on the Issuing out of Earth—in revealing all these three, I have done the work of the pioneer [among those who perpetuate the Truth]; too high an honor, indeed, for me, a common mortal! . . .

I, Nichiren, am the one who takes the lead of the Saints-out-of-Earth. Then may I not be one of them? If I, Nichiren, am one of them, why may not all my disciples and followers be their kinsmen? The Scripture says, "If one preaches to anybody the Lotus of Truth, even just one clause of it, he is, know ye, the messenger of the Tathāgata, the one commissioned by the Tathāgata, and the one who does the work of the Tathāgata." How, then, can I be anybody else than this one? . . .

By all means, awaken faith by seizing this opportunity! Live your life through as the one who embodies the Truth, and go on without hesitation as a kinsman of Nichiren! If you are one in faith with Nichiren, you are one of the Saints-out-of-Earth; if you are destined to be such, how can you doubt that you are the disciple of the Lord Shākyamuni from all eternity? There is assurance of this in a word of Buddha, which says: "I have always, from eternity, been instructing and quickening all these beings." No attention should be paid to the difference between men and women among those who would propagate the Lotus of the Perfect Truth in the days of the Latter Law. To utter the Sacred Title is, indeed, the privilege of the Saints-out-of-Earth. . . .

When the Buddha Prabhūtaratna sat in the Heavenly Shrine side by side with the Tathāgata Shākyamuni, the two Buddhas lifted up the banner of the Lotus of the Perfect Truth, and declared themselves to be the Commanders [in the coming fight against vice and illusion]. How can this be a deception? Indeed, they have thereby agreed to raise us mortal beings to the rank of Buddha. I, Nichiren, was not present there in the congregation, and yet there is no reason to doubt the statements of the Scripture. Or, is it possible that I was there? Common mortal that I am, I am not well aware of the past, yet in the present I am unmistakably the one who is realizing the Lotus of Truth. Then in the future I am surely destined to participate in the communion of the Holy Place. Inferring the past from the present and the future, I should think that I must have been present at the Communion in the Sky. [The present assures the future destiny, and the future destiny is inconceivable without its cause in the past.] The present, future, and past cannot be isolated from one another. . . .

In this document, the truths most precious to me are written down. Read, and read again; read into the letters and fix them into your mind! Thus put faith in the Supreme Being, represented in a way unique in the whole world! Ever more strongly I advise you to be firm in faith, and to be under the protection of the threefold Buddhahood. March strenuously on in the ways of practice and learning! Without practice and learning the Buddhist religion is nullified. Train yourself, and also instruct others! Be convinced that practice and learning are fruits of faith! So long as, and so far as, there is power in you, preach, if it be only a phrase or a word [of the Scripture]! *Namu Myōhō-renge-kyō! Namu Myōhō-renge-kyō!* [Adoration to the Lotus of Perfect Truth].

His Destiny to Convert Japan
[From Anesaki, *Nichiren,* p. 119–20]

So far as, and so much as, my—Nichiren's—compassion is vast and comprehensive, the Adoration of the Lotus of the Perfect Truth shall prevail beyond the coming ages of ten thousand years, nay, eternally in the future. This is the merit I have achieved, which is destined to open the blind eyes of all beings in Japan [the world], and to shut off the ways to the nethermost avīchi hell. These merits surpass those of Dengyō and Tendai, and are far beyond those of Nāgārjuna and Kāshyapa. Is it not true that one hundred years' training in a heavenly paradise does not compare with one day's work in the earthly world, and that all service done to the Truth during the two thousand years of the ages of the Perfect Law and the Copied Law is inferior to that done in one span of time in the age of the Latter Law?[1] All these differences are due, not to Nichiren's own wisdom, but to the virtues inherent in the times. Flowers bloom in spring, and fruits are ripe in autumn; it is hot in summer, and cold in winter. Is it not time that makes these differences? Buddha announced, "This Truth shall be proclaimed and perpetuated in the whole Jambudvīpa [world], in the fifth five hundred years after my death; and it will avail to save all kinds of devils and demons, celestial beings, and serpent tribes," etc. If this prediction should not be fulfilled, all other prophecies and assurances will prove false, the Lord Shākyamuni will fall to the avīchi hell, the Buddha Prabhūtaratna will be burned in the infernal fires, while all other Buddhas in the ten quarters will transfer their abodes to the eight great hells, and all bodhisattvas will suffer from pains, one hundred and thirty-six in kind. How should all this be possible? If it is not, the whole of Japan [the world] will surely be converted to the Adoration of the Lotus of the Perfect Truth.

Japan as the Center of Buddhism's Regeneration
[From Anesaki, *Nichiren*, p. 110]

When, at a certain future time, the union of the state law and the Buddhist Truth shall be established, and the harmony between the two completed, both sovereign and subjects will faithfully adhere to the Great Mysteries. Then the golden age, such as were the ages under the reign of the sage kings of old, will be realized in these days of degeneration and corruption, in the time of the Latter Law. Then the establishment of the Holy See will be completed, by imperial grant and the edict of the Dictator, at a spot comparable in its excellence with the Paradise of Vulture Peak. We have only to wait for the coming of the time. Then the moral law (*kaihō*) will be achieved in the actual life of mankind. The Holy See will then be the seat where all men of the three countries [India, China, and Japan] and the whole Jambudvīpa [world] will be initiated into the mysteries of confession and expiation; and even the great deities, Brahmā and Indra, will come down into the sanctuary and participate in the initiation.

[1] That is, the present degenerate times, in which Buddha's teaching has almost been lost.

Nichiren's Transfiguration (*While Living in Retirement*)
[From Anesaki, *Nichiren,* p. 129]

This spot among the mountains is secluded from the worldly life, and there is no human habitation in the neighborhood—east, west, north, or south. I am now living in such a lonely hermitage; but in my bosom, in Nichiren's fleshly body, is secretly deposited the great mystery which the Lord Shākyamuni revealed on Vulture Peak, and has entrusted to me. Therefore I know that my breast is the place where all Buddhas are immersed in contemplation; that they turn the Wheel of Truth upon my tongue; that my throat is giving birth to them; and that they are attaining the Supreme Enlightenment in my mouth. This place is the abode of such a man, who is mysteriously realizing the Lotus of Truth in his life; surely such a place is no less dignified than the Paradise of Vulture Peak. As the Truth is noble, so is the man who embodies it; as the man is noble, so is the place where he resides. We read in the chapter on the "Mysterious Power of the Tathāgata" as follows:

"Be it a forest, or at the foot of a tree, or in a monastery . . . on that spot erect a stūpa dedicated to the Tathāgata. For such a spot is to be regarded as the place where all Tathāgatas have arrived at the Supreme Perfect Enlightenment; on that spot all Tathāgatas have turned the Wheel of Truth, on that spot all Tathāgatas have entered the Great Decease." Lo, whoever comes to this place will be purged of all sins and depravities which he has accumulated from eternity, and all his evil deeds will at once be transformed into merits and virtues.

CHAPTER XII

ZEN BUDDHISM

To bring salvation within the reach of ordinary men—this was the common aim of the Buddhist sects which spread abroad in medieval Japan. Yet to achieve this same end, and to guide men through the uncertainties, turmoil and suffering of that difficult age, these new movements sometimes employed quite different means. The Pure Land and Nichiren sects, as we know, stressed the need for complete faith in something beyond oneself: the saving power of Amida or of the *Lotus Sūtra*. To find rest and security, they said, man had to turn from himself and this world to the Other World. By contrast Zen Buddhism, which first rose to prominence in these same times, firmly opposed the idea that Buddhahood is something to be sought outside oneself or in another world. Every man has a Buddha-nature, and to realize it he need only look within. Self-understanding and self-reliance are the keynote of Zen.

The means by which this inner realization may be achieved is indicated by the term Zen, meaning "meditation" or "concentration." To speak of it as a "means," however, is appropriate only with reference to the specific procedure involved in the practice of meditation: sitting erect, cross-legged and motionless, with the mind concentrated so as to achieve, first, tranquility, and then active insight. But in the light of this insight the method and realization are seen to be one; no "means" is employed, no "end" is attained.

Meditative practices of this sort were an essential feature of Buddhism from the earliest times and are related to the yogic practices of ancient India. The founder of Buddhism himself retired into the solitude of nature where, sitting silently in restful but intent contemplation, he realized the Truth which was later to be taught throughout East Asia. In both the Hīnayāna and Mahāyāna the specific type of meditation known as dhyāna was an integral part of Buddhist discipline, and, while more fully developed in some schools such as the idealistic Yogāchāra, remained the common property of all. It was in China that the practice of dhyāna became the basis of a separate school of Buddhism for the first time. There, as a protest against the prevailing scholasticism of North China, with its attention to scripture and philosophical discussion, a movement developed which became especially strong in the South, stressing intuitive enlightenment and the rejection of all scriptural or ecclesiastical authority. At its inception this movement was associated, significantly enough, with the monastic centers of the Vinaya school devoted to the precise performance of religious disciplines, of which the dhyāna meditation was one. While the emphasis upon strict discipline remained characteristic of those who attached the highest value to this particular form of meditation, their independence of mind and rejection of all external authority led eventually to the establishment of a separate school of Buddhism known as Ch'an, the Chinese equivalent of dhyāna. That such a distinctive school should have sprung up on Chinese soil, characterized by the same quietistic, individualistic and iconoclastic tendencies as early Taoism, is suggestive of the manner in which this alien religion underwent a striking transformation in the Chinese environment. But how much this is to be understood as an adaptation to Chinese tastes of something already implicit in Indian Buddhism, or how much it represents a dressing up of essentially Taoist attitudes in Buddhist guise, is a question which it is difficult to settle on the basis of historical evidence.

While we have spoken of Ch'an Buddhism as a separate school or teaching, organizationally it was not one school but many, each assembled around the person of an individual master and claiming an authoritative patriarchal transmission of vital truth from the first teacher, Buddha. According to a widespread tradition this transmission was inaugurated by the Buddha at Vulture Peak when Brahmā offered him a flower and requested him to preach the Law. Buddha took the flower and turned it in his fingers, but said nothing. Everyone in the assemblage was mystified except the wise Kāshyapa who smiled in acknowledgment of the Buddha's sign-teaching and was thereupon entrusted with the handing down of this truth to posterity. Thus the transmission went on from generation to generation without verbal preaching or written scripture, but with cryptic signs as the only overt form of communication from one patriarch to another. According to tradition, the twenty-eighth patriarch in this succession, Bodhidharma, carried this teaching to China.

The supposed meeting between Bodhidharma and Emperor Wu of the

Liang dynasty in A.D. 520 is one of the most celebrated stories in Zen tradition. The Emperor said to the monk, "Since my enthronement I have built many monasteries, had many scriptures copied and had many monks and nuns invested. How great is the merit thus achieved?" "No merit at all," was Bodhidharma's answer. The Emperor then asked, "What is the Noble Truth in its highest sense?" "It is empty, no nobility whatever." "Who is it then that is facing me?" "I do not know, Sire." [1] The Emperor, as might be expected, could make nothing of this. Bodhidharma went away and later spent nine years sitting in meditation, facing a cliff in silence. In this pose, Daruma, as he is known to the Japanese, has been a favorite subject of Buddhist painting and sculpture. The patriarchal succession eventually passed to a resolute man in search of truth named Hui-k'o, who got no reply when he first asked Bodhidharma for instruction. To show his determination to win the Truth at any cost, Hui-k'o, standing in the snow, cut off his left arm. Thereupon Bodhidharma accepted him as a disciple and later gave him a robe and bowl as a sign of the patriarchal transmission.

The historicity of such accounts is a question of little importance; their value lies in the striking way these episodes suggest the character of Ch'an (Zen) Buddhism: its rejection of all temporal or scriptural authority, its refusal to commit itself to words, its independence of the world, and its emphasis upon moral character rather than intellectual attainments. Perhaps most significant of all is the focusing of attention upon the individual Ch'an master as the living embodiment of Truth. This characteristic of Ch'an Buddhism proved to be a great source of strength through the years. Since it depended less on the maintenance of any physical establishment or ecclesiastical organization, such as monasteries and temples, than it did on the commanding personality of its masters, Ch'an was in a better position to withstand the great religious persecutions of A.D. 841–846 than most other sects in China. Its propagation required only teachers and students, and these were not lacking even after the closing up of monasteries and dissolution of religious communities. Thus, by the Sung dynasty (960–1279), Ch'an was virtually all that remained of Buddhism in China and it had a very deep influence on many aspects of the brilliant Sung culture, especially in art, poetry, and philosophy.

[1] Adapted from Takakusu, *Essentials of Buddhist Philosophy*, p. 159.

The Sung is also known as a period of remarkable activity in overseas trade, which at least for a time was conducted largely under private auspices, rather than as a government monopoly. Here too Ch'an played an important role, for its resourceful and adventurous adherents took part in commercial enterprises, and their temples along the southeast coast of China served as hostels for merchants and distribution centers for foreign goods. Ch'an missionaries often accompanied trading missions to Japan. It is understandable, then, why Ch'an Buddhism should have deeply implanted itself on Japanese soil at this time, during the twelfth and thirteenth centuries.

Actually Ch'an, or Zen, had been introduced to Japan several times in earlier centuries with court sponsorship, both as a special meditative discipline adopted by men of other sects (Saichō was one of these) and as a separate, exclusive teaching. None of these earlier attempts was lasting, however, and it remained for two great Japanese pioneers of Zen to establish this teaching firmly on native ground. These pioneers were Eisai (1141–1215) and Dōgen (1200–1253). We have already seen that the history of Zen centers upon the personality of its great masters, and that anecdotes from the lives of these masters were a favorite means of conveying the essential teachings of Zen. In the case of Chinese Zen the anecdotes preserved to us deal mostly with the experience of achieving enlightenment and the act of transmission from one patriarch to another. But Zen is much more than a single "enlightenment-experience"; it is a whole way of life. And we are fortunate that in the biographies of these two Zen pioneers we have a much fuller account of their activities, providing us with the important links between Zen as they saw it, Zen as they lived it, and Zen as it had an impact on many aspects of Japanese life and culture.

ZEN PIONEERS IN JAPAN

The first pioneer, Eisai, started his religious life in the center of Esoteric Buddhism, Mt. Hiei, but became determined that he should pursue his studies further in China and if possible make the long journey to India, homeland of Buddhism. He never achieved the latter ambition, but did visit China twice at a time when regular communication with the mainland had long since ceased and when only the most enterprising embarked on such a venture. In twelfth-century China Eisai found Zen to be the only form of Buddhism still flourishing, and after studying at the Zen center of T'ien-t'ung shan, returned to Japan in 1191 as a full-fledged Zen master of the Rinzai (in Chinese, *Lin-ch'i*) School. On his return Eisai brought with him something else which had newly won favor among the Chinese: tea. Back in Kyoto he set about urging the adoption of both Zen and tea by the Japanese, but soon encountered opposition to his new teaching from the traditional strongholds of Esoteric Buddhism in and around the capital. Resourceful and adaptable, in keeping with the spirit of Zen itself, Eisai escaped from the hostile atmosphere of Kyoto and moved on to the new center of political power in the northeast, Kamakura. Here in the seat of military government Eisai's teachings won great favor among the hardy and adventurous warriors who found Zen particularly congenial to their way of life. With support from the Hōjō regents, and with the patronage of the third ruling shogun as well as of the widow of the first, Eisai established a new center for the study of Zen and inaugurated what was to become a historic *rapprochement* between this sect and the military warlords of Japan. Nevertheless when Eisai returned to preach in Kyoto during his last years, he was forced to compromise with the established order. He was free to propagate Zen only on condition that other Buddhist disciplines, as represented by Tendai and Shingon practices, be accorded a place in his teaching. Thus it is characteristic of Eisai's pioneer work that, by allying himself with the new political order and compromising with the established religions, he did much to legitimize Zen in Japan.

If Eisai was in this way a personification of the virtue of adaptability, which is a notable feature of Zen, his successor Dōgen equally personified the opposite virtue in Zen: rugged determination and uncompromising independence. High born, with an emperor as an ancestor on his father's side and a Fujiwara prime minister on his mother's, Dōgen had the advantage of an excellent education in Chinese studies and showed such promise as a youth that the Fujiwara regents wished to adopt him into their own family and groom him for the prime ministership. Dōgen, however, rejected this opportunity for worldly advancement in order to take up a religious life, which was to prove for him far more difficult. At the historic centers of Buddhist monasticism, Mt. Hiei and Miidera near

Lake Biwa, Dōgen was disappointed to find no true refuge from worldly life and only an academic or ritualistic interest in the Buddhist ideal. "It is taught that 'we are all born Buddhas,' but I have been unable to find among the inmates [of Mt. Hiei] a single person who looks like a Buddha," he complained. "It seems that a collection of Scriptures is worth nothing unless someone puts it to real use."

From Mt. Hiei Dōgen went to see Eisai, who died soon thereafter. Even when he undertook to follow in Eisai's footsteps to China, his quest seemed doomed to failure. At T'ien-t'ung monastery, where Eisai had studied, Dōgen's hunger for the truth was still unsatisfied after a stay of two years. He went on from one monastery to another, not drifting aimlessly but pursuing a relentless search for a true Master, a living Buddha. His disappointment was only heightened by the ease with which he himself won acceptance from some so-called "masters" who indicated their readiness to confer master's papers upon him in return for a gift of money. Worldliness and commercialism had infiltrated even the sanctuaries of the Buddha.

At last, when Dōgen was about to return home in despair, a new master, Ju-ching, came to preside over the T'ien-t'ung monastery. One night Ju-ching was explaining to the monks that the practice of Zen meant "dropping off both body and mind [transcending the dualism of matter and spirit]," and Dōgen was suddenly enlightened. Afterward he went to the master's room and started to burn incense, a sign that one has achieved enlightenment and acknowledges the Buddhahood of his master. "What has happened," Ju-ching asked, "that you should be burning incense?" Dōgen replied, "Both body and mind are dropped." "Both body and mind are dropped," Ju-ching repeated. "You have really dropped both body and mind!" Dōgen was not exactly pleased that his own claim should be accepted so readily, however. "That is rather a little thing to achieve," he countered. "Please don't set your seal on me so easily." "No, I am not setting my seal on you so easily," his teacher assured him. But Dōgen pressed on, almost as if he were the examiner and Ju-ching the disciple. "What do you mean by not setting your seal so easily?" "I mean that you really have dropped both body and mind," reaffirmed Ju-ching. At this Dōgen finally bowed in homage, acknowledging Ju-ching's acceptance of him. "That's dropping off the dropping," said Ju-ching.

Dōgen continued to show his independence after returning to Japan. In Kyoto and nearby Uji he refused to teach anything but Zen, and when put under pressure to change his ways, preferred to move on to the remote province of Echizen rather than give in to the established order. There is a legend, without historical basis but suggestive of Dōgen's reputation for independence, which tells of his visiting Kamakura to urge the Hōjō regent, Tokiyori, to restore ruling power to the emperor in Kyoto. Obtaining no satisfaction from Tokiyori, Dōgen quit Kamakura in disgust rather than serve in Eisai's role as adviser to an illegitimate ruler. Nevertheless, Tokiyori was much impressed by Dōgen's strength of character, and sent one of the latter's pupils to him bearing a grant of land for his temple. At this Dōgen was so incensed that he not only sent his pupil away, but, in a manner reminiscent of Taoist sages in China who refused the throne, ordered that the chair the monk had sat in be destroyed, the ground under the chair dug three feet deep and the earth thrown away.

Still, for all of his independence and intransigeance, Dōgen's attitude toward traditional Buddhism was notably softer than most of his Zen predecessors in China. The danger of intellectualism and of reliance upon the written word had stirred up controversy among Zen schools on the continent, with some taking the extreme view that the patriarchal man-to-man transmission alone was authentic and that the scriptural transmission was not true Buddhism. Dōgen sided with those who upheld the essential unity of the two forms of teaching. The study of scripture was not to be condemned, except where it lead to the sūtras gaining mastery over the student rather than the student gaining mastery over the sūtras. "Stay on top of the Lotus; don't let it get on top of you." Far from being a passive receptacle for the written word, Dōgen himself devoted much of his life to writing and achieved a remarkable literary output. Believing in the fundamental unity of the various schools, in his writings he sought less to establish the correctness of Zen than to assert the fundamental truths of Buddhism. The "Zen" label he had little use for; it was the teaching of the Buddha, "Buddhism," with which he identified himself. Accordingly he was drawn more and more to the Indian, especially the Hīnayāna sources, of this teaching than to the Chinese. In the personal example of the Founder he found the simplest and best method of achieving enlightenment. Shākyamuni's way of sitting in meditation under the Tree of Enlightenment was the "proven" or "tested" method of realizing the Truth. Yet sitting in meditation with the object of achieving enlightenment is too selfish an approach; Buddhahood cannot be sought after or obtained for oneself, but only for its own sake. Dōgen quoted an earlier master of his school who said, "If you want to obtain a certain thing, you must first be a certain man. Once you have become a certain man, obtaining that certain thing won't be a concern of yours any more."

In this respect Dōgen took issue with the Rinzai school of Zen, which Eisai had introduced to Japan. Rinzai had developed a special technique and discipline, the *kōan,* leading to the sudden attainment of enlightenment. The *kōan* was a theme upon which the student might focus his mind, consisting of a problem or dilemma together with the resolution of it worked out by some earlier master. Since the solution was beyond the reach of ordinary logical processes, few students could comprehend it without spending days and weeks in intent absorption with the *kōan.* Then all at once realization took place, induced perhaps by some accidental occurrence—a sound or sight—impinging upon the consciousness of the individual, or else by some deliberate act of the master—a shout or blow on the head—intended to startle and awaken the mind of the disciple. This sudden intuition or realization is what D. T. Suzuki, the best-known interpreter of Zen to the West in recent times, has called "Enlightenment-experience."

From the point of view of Dōgen, and of the Sōtō (Chinese *Ts'ao-tung*) school of Zen which he introduced to Japan,[2] this preoccupation with the momentary experience of enlightenment and the deliberate use of the *kōan* formula to achieve it, was directed too much toward "obtaining a certain thing" and might be too self-assertive. It also placed too great stress on mental perception, realization through the mind alone rather than through all of the faculties and activities of the "whole man." Therefore Dōgen minimized the value of the *kōan* and stressed instead the importance of "sitting in meditation" (*zazen*) without any thought of acquisition or attainment, without any specific problem in mind. Through such a discipline, bodily as well as mental, moral as well as intellectual,

---

[2] Dōgen himself emphatically repudiated any sectarian allegiance, but his later followers identified him with this school because he was most sympathetic to and influenced by the teachings of Sōtō masters. As a school Sōtō became far more influential in Japan than it ever was in China.

a gradual and life-long realization took place rather than a sudden awakening.

From the Rinzai point of view the defect of this method was its emphasis upon stillness in meditation, which led to empty passivity on the part of the individual rather than to the active, dynamic self-introspection stimulated by the *kōan*. Yet on Dōgen's part, at least, there was no lack of dynamism, the difference being that for him it was applied to the conduct of life rather than to the achievement of a particular experience. In this again he reflected the strongly ethical character of the Sōtō school in China. Just as the practice of sitting is not just a means to an end, but the realization of Buddhahood itself, so Buddhahood is realized constantly in life by selfless action and strenuous effort, with no thought of achieving an end apart from the means. Man's only possession is time, and this is his only insofar as he uses it creatively, because Buddhahood is not a static thing to be achieved once but something that grows with each effort. Thus life is a work of art and Zen is the flowering of life—the discipline of creative labor.

In another section we shall discuss the ways in which the creative powers of Zen were brought to bear upon some of the humblest activities of men and the lowliest objects of nature to raise them to the level of great art, and thereby to permeate the Japanese way of life to its core. Among the Zen masters responsible for this, however, was one who also had such outstanding success in the political sphere as to be worthy of mention here. He is Musō Soseki (1275–1351), who came to be known as Musō Kokushi, or "Musō the National Master." In his time there were already several full-fledged Zen masters in Japan, both native and Chinese domiciled in Japan. Yet, like Dōgen, Musō found his way to Zen with difficulty. Leaving his teachers, he wandered all over Japan to seek a revelation of Truth in its mountain fastnesses and forests, by its lakesides and seashores. Finally, spending the night deep in a lonely wood, he found his answer in the sight of embers catching fire again. Thereafter Musō served as an adviser to several rulers in succession at a time when political power was changing hands with startling rapidity. First the Hōjō regents invited him to preside over a monastery in Kamakura. Then Go-Daigo, attempting to reassert imperial rule in Kyoto, enlisted Musō's services and at his suggestion in 1325 sent the first official mission to China in almost five centuries, opening a new era in foreign commerce and diplomacy. Finally the new shogun, Ashikaga Takauji, after disposing of Go-Daigo, asked Musō to serve as his spiritual mentor and seems to have experienced a deep religious conversion under Musō's influence. Takauji built for him the famous monastery of Tenryū-ji, and when in 1339 the shogun also sent a mission to China, almost certainly at Musō's urging, it sailed in a ship bearing the name of this temple. Musō also inspired Takauji to erect a temple and pagoda in each province, reviving the idea of a state-established Buddhist church first instituted by the Emperor Shōmu in the seventh century, as a means both of propagating Buddhist teaching and of creating good will among the people toward the Ashikaga regime.

Thus, as the recognized "National Master of Seven Reigns," a title awarded him three times during his life and four after death, Musō did much to gain for Zen a favored position at court and to solidify the alliance initiated by Eisai between it and Japan's military rulers. With such advantages, even though it failed to win converts in such great numbers as the Pure Land and Nichiren sects did among the more humble folk, Zen was nevertheless able to make its influence felt among the political, intellectual, and artistic leaders of medieval times and thus to shape to a remarkable extent the cultural traditions deriving from this period.

EISAI

PROPAGATION OF ZEN FOR THE PROTECTION OF THE COUNTRY

(Preface to *Kōzen gokoku ron*)

In this tract Eisai attempted to win for Zen a legitimate place in the religious life of the nation, arguing that this teaching was conducive to the general welfare and national security, and defending it against the charge of the established sects that it was negativistic and obscurantist. The title indicates that political and nationalistic considerations loomed large in Eisai's mind, just as they had with Saichō centuries before when winning for Tendai the patronage of the imperial house against opposition from the older Nara sects. Ironically Eisai's chief adversaries at the Kyoto court were the monks of Mt. Hiei monastery, which Saichō had founded. For this reason Eisai stresses Saichō's reputed part in the introduction of Zen meditative practices earlier, as well as the legitimate succession of Zen patriarchs from Shākyamuni Buddha, scriptural authorities for the teaching, the endorsement of it by leading Buddhists of the past—in short, all the necessary points for rendering it socially acceptable in the orthodox world. Eisai's preface gives a brief summary of his position.

[From *Taishō daizōkyō,* Vol. 80, Zoku shoshūbu, p. 2]

Great is Mind. Heaven's height is immeasurable, but Mind goes beyond heaven; the earth's depth is also unfathomable, but Mind reaches below the earth. The light of the sun and moon cannot be outdistanced, yet Mind passes beyond the light of sun and moon. The macrocosm is limitless, yet Mind travels outside the macrocosm. How great is Space! How great the Primal Energy! Still Mind encompasses Space and generates the Primal Energy. Because of it heaven covers and earth upbears. Because of it the sun and moon move on, the four seasons pass in succession, and all things are generated. Great indeed is Mind! Of necessity we give such a name to it, yet there are many others: the Highest Vehicle, the First Principle, the Truth of Inner Wisdom, the One Reality, the Peerless Bodhi, the Way to Enlightenment as taught in the *Laṅkāvatāra Sūtra,* the Treasury of the Vision of Truth, and Insight of Nirvāna. All texts in the Three Vehicles of Buddhism[1] and in the eight treasuries of Scripture, as well as all the doctrines of the four schools and five denominations of Zen are contained in it. Shākya, the greatest of all teachers, transmitted this truth of the Mind to the golden-haired monk [Kāshyapa], calling it a special transmission not contained in the scriptures. From the Vulture Peak it moved to Cockleg Cave, where it was greeted with a smile.[2] Thus with the mere twist of a flower a thousand trees were made to bloom; from one fountainhead sprang ten thousand streams of Truth.

As in India, so in China this teaching has attracted followers and disciples in great numbers. It propagates the Truth as the ancient Buddha did, with the robe of authentic transmission passing from one man to the next. In the matter of religious discipline, it practices the genuine method of the sages of old. Thus the Truth it teaches, both in substance and appearance, perfects the relationship of master and disciple. In its rules of action and discipline, there is no confusion of right and wrong.

[1] Hīnayāna, Quasi-Mahāyāna, and True Mahāyāna.

[2] When the Hindu god Brahmā came to Shākyamuni Buddha at the Vulture Peak offering him a flower and requesting him to teach the Law, Buddha took the flower and turned it in his fingers without saying a word. Everyone in the assemblage was mystified, but at the nearby Cockleg Cave the disciple Kāshyapa smiled in joyful recognition. Buddha thereupon entrusted to Kāshyapa the secret transmission of the Law, which was later passed on to others by similar "mind-signs."

After the Great Master [Bodhidharma] sailed by way of the South Seas and planted his staff of Truth on the banks of East River in China, the vision of the Law soon made its appearance in Korea and the Ox-head School of Zen from North China made its way to Japan. Studying it, one discovers the key to all forms of Buddhism; practicing it, one's life is brought to fulfillment in the attainment of enlightenment. Outwardly it favors discipline over doctrine, inwardly it brings the Highest Inner Wisdom. This is what the Zen sect stands for.

In our country the Divine Sovereign shines in splendor and the influence of his virtuous wisdom spreads far and wide. Emissaries from the distant lands of South and Central Asia pay their respects to his court. Lay ministers conduct the affairs of government; priests and monks spread abroad religious truth. Even the truths of the Four Hindu Vedas are not neglected. Why then reject the five schools of Zen Buddhism?

There are, however, some persons who malign this teaching, calling it "the Zen of dark enlightenment." There are also those who question it on the ground that it is "utter Nihilism." Still others consider it ill-suited to these degenerate times, or say that it is not what our country needs. Or else they may express contempt for our mendicant ways and our alleged lack of documentary support for our views. Finally there are some who have such a low opinion of their own capabilities that they look upon Zen as far beyond their power to promote. Out of their zeal for upholding the Law, these people are actually suppressing the treasures of the Law. They denounce us without knowing what we have in mind. Not only are they thus blocking the way to the gate of Zen, but they are also ruining the work of our great forebear at Mt. Hiei [Saichō]. Alas, alas, how sad, how distressing!

It is for this reason that I venture to make a general survey of the Three Vehicles for consideration of philosophers today, and to record the essential teachings of our sect for the benefit of posterity. The work is in three chapters consisting of ten sections, and is entitled *The Propagation of Zen for the Protection of the Country*.

DRINK TEA AND PROLONG LIFE

(From the *Kissa yōjō ki*)

Though Zen is a meditative school of Buddhism, far from encouraging passivity it attaches the highest value to action. There is nothing incongruous,

[237]

therefore, in the fact that its leading exponents led a very active life and devoted themselves to practical enterprises such as commerce and diplomacy. One of the most enduring of Eisai's contributions to Japanese life was his advocacy of tea-drinking, which did much to make it the national beverage. Typically too, Zen monks in later years went on to make the preparation and imbibing of this common drink one of the most highly refined of household arts: the Tea Ceremony.

[From *Gunsho ruijū*, XV, 899–901]

Tea is the most wonderful medicine for nourishing one's health; it is the secret of long life. On the hillsides it grows up as the spirit of the soil. Those who pick and use it are certain to attain a great age. India and China both value it highly, and in the past our country too once showed a great liking for tea. Now as then it possesses the same rare qualities, and we should make wider use of it.

In the past, it is said, man was coeval with Heaven, but in recent times man has gradually declined and grown weaker, so that his four bodily components and five organs have degenerated. For this reason even when acupuncture and moxa cautery are resorted to the results are often fatal, and treatment at hot springs fails to have any effect. So those who are given to these methods of treatment will become steadily weaker until death overtakes them, a prospect which can only be dreaded. If these traditional methods of healing are employed without any modification on patients today, scarcely any relief can be expected.

Of all the things which Heaven has created, man is the most noble. To preserve one's life so as to make the most of one's allotted span is prudent and proper [considering the high value of human life]. The basis of preserving life is the cultivation of health, and the secret of health lies in the well-being of the five organs. Among these five the heart is sovereign, and to build up the heart the drinking of tea is the finest method. When the heart is weak, the other organs all suffer. It is more than two thousand years since the illustrious healer, Jīva, passed away in India, and in these latter degenerate days there is none who can accurately diagnose the circulation of the blood. It is more than three thousand years since the Chinese healer, Shen-nung, disappeared from the earth, and there is no one today who can prescribe medicines properly. With no one to consult in such matters, illness, disease, trouble, and danger follow one another in endless succession. If a mistake is made in the method of healing, such as moxa cautery, great harm may be done. Someone has

[238]

told me that as medicine is practiced today, damage is often done to the heart because the drugs used are not appropriate to the disease. Moxa cautery often brings untimely death because the pulse is in conflict with the moxa. I consider it advisable, therefore, to reveal the latest methods of healing as I have become acquainted with them in China. Accordingly I present two general approaches to the understanding of diseases prevalent in these degenerate times, hoping that they may be of benefit to others in the future.

I. Harmonious Functioning of the Five Organs

According to the esoteric scripture known as the Conquest of Hell the liver likes acid foods, the lungs pungent foods, the heart bitter ones, the spleen sweet, and the kidney salty. It also correlates them with the Five Elements and five directions as follows:

Organ	Direction	Season	Element	Color	Spirits	Sensory Organs
Liver	East	Spring	Wood	Blue	Soul	Eyes
Lungs	West	Autumn	Metal	White	Soul	Nose
Heart	South	Summer	Fire	Red	Spirit (*shin*)	Tongue
Spleen	Center	Between seasons	Earth	Yellow	Will	Mouth
Kidney	North	Winter	Water	Black	Imagination	Ears

Thus the five organs have their own taste preferences. If one of these preferences is favored too much, the corresponding organ will get too strong and oppress the others, resulting in illness. Now acid, pungent, sweet, and salty foods are eaten in great quantity, but not bitter foods. Yet when the heart becomes sick, all organs and tastes are affected. Then, eat as one may, one will have to vomit and stop eating. But if one drinks tea, the heart will be strengthened and freed from illness. It is well to know that when the heart is ailing, the skin has a poor color, a sign that life is ebbing away. I wonder why the Japanese do not care for bitter things. In the great country of China they drink tea, as a result of which there is no heart trouble and people live long lives. Our country is full of sickly-looking, skinny persons, and this is simply because we do not drink tea. Whenever one is in poor spirits, one should drink tea. This will put the heart in order and dispel all illness. When the heart is vigorous, then even if the other organs are ailing, no great pain will be felt.

[Then follows a section explaining the five organs in correlation with the various Buddhas, symbols, gestures, and regions of the esoteric Mandalas (see Chapters VII and VIII) together with the esoteric secrets of healing disorders in each.]

[239]

In regard to the Five Tastes: acid foods include oranges, lemons, and other citrus fruits; pungent foods include onions, garlic, and peppers; sweets include sugar, etc. (all foods are sweet by nature); bitter foods include tea, herb teas, etc.; salty foods include salt, etc.

The heart is the sovereign of the five organs, tea is the chief of the bitter foods, and bitter is the chief of the tastes. For this reason the heart loves bitter things, and when it is doing well all the other organs are properly regulated. If one has eye trouble, something is wrong with the liver and acid medicine will cure it. If one has ear trouble, something is wrong with the kidney and salty medicine will cure it. [And so forth through the table of correspondences above.] When, however, the whole body feels weak, devitalized, and depressed, it is a sign that the heart is ailing. Drink lots of tea, and one's energy and spirits will be restored to full strength.

DŌGEN

CONVERSATIONS

The following excerpts from the conversations of Dōgen as recorded by his disciple Ejō have an air of intimacy and a simple directness not usually found in the formal writings of the master. The first selections reveal the radical faith of this Zen pioneer, and incidentally provide a valuable commentary on the life and character of Dōgen's predecessor, Eisai.

[From the *Shōbō genzō zuimonki*, pp. 35-36]

Spoken during an evening conversation:

The late Abbot [Eisai] once said: "The food and clothing which each of you monks uses should not be thought of as something I have given you. They are all gifts from Heaven, and I am nothing but an intermediary. Everyone receives what is needed to sustain his allotted life and there is no sense in making a fuss over it. Don't think you are under any obligation to me for these things," he always used to tell us. In my opinion no finer words could be spoken.

When the T'ien-t'ung monastery [in China] was presided over by the Zen Master Hung-chih, provision was made for one thousand students, seven hundred of them inmates and three hundred transients. With such a fine master presiding, however, monks flocked there from all over the country. The number of inmates mounted to one thousand, while the transients increased to five hundred. So the steward appealed to Hung-chih: "We have provisions for only one thousand. With this great crowd there will never be enough to go round. Please send some away." Hung-chih replied, "Every man has a mouth to feed, but that is not your fault, so stop complaining!"

When I think about this now, it seems to me that everyone is born with his share of clothing and food. Seeking for food does not make it appear; abandoning the search does not make it disappear. Remember that even laymen leave such matters in the hands of Providence, while they strive for the virtues of loyalty and piety. How much less should monks who have left the world be concerned over such external matters! The Buddha prescribes their fortunes and the heavens provide their food and clothing. Moreover, everyone has his own share of life; without seeking for it or thinking about it, this allotted share comes from the natural course of things. Suppose you run after more and pile up great treasures—what will you do with them when Evanescence pays you a visit? Therefore the student should drive all thought of such external matters from his mind, and devote himself single-mindedly to the pursuit of Truth.

Yet some say that the propagation of Buddhism in these latter degenerate days, on this remote island, would be facilitated if a secure and peaceful abode were prepared where monks could practice the teachings of Buddha without any worries over food, clothing, and the like. To me this seems wrong. Such a place would only attract men who are selfish and worldly, and among them could be found no one at all with a sincere religious intention. If we give ourselves over to the comforts of life and the enjoyment of material pleasures, then even though hundreds of thousands were induced to come here, it would be worse than having no one here at all. We would acquire only a propensity for evil, not a disposition for the practice of Buddha's Law.

If on the contrary you live in spotless poverty and destitution, or go begging for your food, or live on the fruits of the field, pursuing your study of the Truth while suffering real deprivation, then if even one man hears of your example and comes to study with you out of genuine devotion to the Truth, it will be a real gain for Buddhism. If, however, you feel that spotless poverty and destitution will discourage people, and consequently provide an abundance of food and clothing, a great many may come but they will have no real interest in Buddhism. In the former case you will obtain eight ounces of gold, and in the latter a half-pound of tinsel.

Sacrifice
[From the *Shōbō genzō zuimonki*, pp. 31–32]

When the late Abbot [Eisai] was still at Kenninji monastery, a poor man once came and said "My family is so destitute that they have had nothing to cook for several days. Myself, my wife, and our three children are on the verge of starvation. For pity's sake, please help us!" At the time there was in the Abbot's quarters nothing whatever—no food, no clothing, no money—for him to give away, and he was almost at the end of his wits. There was, however, some beaten copper which was to be used in making a halo for the statue of the Lord of Healing. He took it and broke it up in his hands. Then, tying it in a little package, he gave the copper to the poor man. "Exchange this for food and save your family from starvation." The man went away overjoyed.

But some of the Abbot's disciples criticised his action, saying, "This was no less than the halo of the Buddha statue. Giving it to a layman constitutes the crime of using what belongs to the Buddha for one's own private purposes. Isn't that wrong?"

"You are right," the Abbot replied, "but just consider the will of the Buddha. He sacrificed his very flesh and limbs for the sake of all mankind. If some men are about to die of starvation, would he not want us to give the whole Buddha figure to save them? Even if I should go to Hell for this crime, I would want to save people from starvation." Such loftiness of purpose is well worth reflecting upon. You students should keep this in mind.

There was another time when his disciples observed to the Abbot that the site of the Kenninji monastery buildings was too close to the river, so close, in fact, that in years to come the monastery would be likely to suffer flood damage. The Abbot told them, "Do not worry about the damage our monastery may suffer in years to come. The first temple of the Buddha, in the Jetavana Park of India, has now disappeared and only stone ruins remain. Nevertheless the merit of building a temple or monastery should not be lost sight of. To practice the way of the Buddha in such a place, if only for six months or a year, is a work of enormous merit."

Thinking back on this, the building of a temple or monastery seems indeed to be the greatest undertaking of a man's life. It is only natural that one should want it to endure for all time. And yet this did not keep him from realizing in the depths of his soul a very profound truth, which is well worth remembering.

True Dedication
[From the *Shōbō genzō zuimonki*, pp. 110–11]

The concerns of the disciple of Buddhism are different from those of the ordinary man. During the lifetime of the Abbot of Kenninji, it once happened that there was no food for those in the monastery. At that time, however, a patron of the monastery invited the Abbot to visit him, and then presented him with a roll of silk as an offering. Overjoyed, the Abbot took it with him back to the monastery and turned it over to the steward, saying, "Use it to buy food for the morrow."

Just at that time, however, there was a layman who, seeing this, went up to the Abbot and begged, "I have a desperate need for two or three rolls of silk. If you have anything at all, I would deeply appreciate it." The Abbot thereupon took back from the steward what he had just turned over to him, and gave the silk to the layman while the steward and all the other monks watched in amazement. Later the Abbot said to them, "You all probably think that it was a rash thing for me to do. But it occurred to me that the inmates of this monastery have all dedicated themselves to the way of the Buddha, and even if they should have to go without food for a day, or perhaps even starve to death, they would still have no cause for complaint. So if by this means the distress of some layman should be relieved in a time of dire need, each of you should regard it as a work of personal gratification and merit." Truly this is the sort of thing that reflects an enlightened mind.

Exertion
[From *Zenshū seiten, zokuhen, Shōbō genzō gyōji*, pp. 676–78]

The great Way of the Buddha and the Patriarchs involves the highest form of exertion, which goes on unceasingly in cycles from the first dawn-

[243]

ing of religious truth, through the test of discipline and practice, to enlightenment and Nirvāna. It is sustained exertion, proceeding without
lapse from cycle to cycle. Accordingly it is exertion which is neither self-
imposed nor imposed by others, but free and uncoerced. The merit of this
exertion upholds me and upholds others. The truth is that the benefits of
one's own sustained exertion are shared by all beings in the ten quarters
of the world. Others may not be aware of this, and we may not realize it,
but it is so. It is through the sustained exertions of the Buddhas and
Patriarchs that our own exertions are made possible, that we are able to
reach the high road of Truth. In exactly the same way it is through our
own exertions that the exertions of the Buddhas are made possible, that
the Buddhas attain the high road of Truth. Thus it is through our exertions that these benefits circulate in cycles to others, and it is due only to
this that the Buddhas and Patriarchs come and go, affirming Buddha and
negating Buddha, attaining the Buddha-mind and achieving Buddhahood,
ceaselessly and without end. This exertion too sustains the sun, the moon,
and the stars; it sustains the earth and sky, body and mind, object and
subject, the four elements, and five compounds.

This sustained exertion is not something which men of the world naturally love or desire, yet it is the last refuge of all. Only through the exertions of all Buddhas in the past, present, and future do the Buddhas of
past, present, and future become a reality. The merits of these exertions
are sometimes disclosed, and thus arises the dawn of religious consciousness which is then tested in practice. Sometimes, however, these merits lie
hidden and are neither seen, nor heard, nor realized. Yet hidden though
they may be, they are still available because they suffer no diminution or
restriction whether they are visible or invisible, tangible or intangible. . . .

The exertion that brings the exertion of others into realization is our
exertion right at this moment. This exertion of the moment is not innate
or inherent in us, nor does it come and go, visiting or departing. What we
call the "moment" does not precede exertion. The "moment" is when
exertion is actually being performed. That is to say, the exertion of a day
is the seed of all Buddhas, it is the exertion of all Buddhas.[1] By this exertion

---

[1] The sense of this passage seems to be: "Exertion is not inherent in our nature in the sense
that it operates automatically and can be taken for granted; nor on the other hand is it
extraneous to our nature in the sense that it must be acquired. Our nature is only realized
insofar as we exert our efforts. Similarly time does not exist apart from exertion, and all
exertion is one in time, the reality of the moment. Thus our exertions today contribute to the

Buddhahood is realized, and those who do not make an exertion when exertion is possible are those who hate Buddha, hate serving the Buddha, and hate exertion; they do not want to live and die with Buddha, they do not want him as their teacher and companion.

At this moment a flower blossoms, a leaf falls—it is a manifestation of sustained exertion. A mirror is brightened, a mirror is broken—it is a manifestation of sustained exertion. Everything is exertion. To attempt to avoid exertion is an impossible evasion, for the attempt itself is exertion. And to belabor oneself, because it is impossible to be otherwise than one is, is to be like the rich man's son who left home to seek his fortune, only to endure poverty in a foreign land.[2] Though in his wanderings the son may be fortunate enough not to lose his life altogether, it would still have been better had he not abandoned his father's treasures in the first place. Nor should we risk losing the treasures of the Law, which never allows of any abandonment of exertion. Our benevolent father and great master, Shākyamuni Buddha, began his exertions deep in the mountains at the age of nineteen. At the age of thirty he labored to achieve the Enlightenment which embraced all sentient beings. Until the age of eighty he labored in the forests and in monasteries, without any thought of returning to his royal palace or of sharing in the wealth of his kingdom. Not once did he put on a new robe; not once did he exchange his bowl for another. Not for one day, not for an hour, did he seek to take care of himself, but lived on the offerings of others and endured the ridicule of heretics. His whole life was one long exertion of begging food and clothing, a life that knew nothing but sustained exertion.

Realizing the Solution (Genjō Kōan)
[From Hashida, Shōbō genzō shakui, I, 142–69]

[Against the notion that enlightenment is a single, momentary experience]
To study the way of the Buddha is to study your own self. To study your own self is to forget yourself. To forget yourself is to have the objective world prevail in you. To have the objective world prevail in you, is to let go of your "own" body and mind as well as the body and mind of "others." The enlightenment thus attained may seem to come to an

realization of Buddhahood in the past, and the Buddha's exertions contribute to our realization."
[2] The parable of a prodigal son in the Lotus Sūtra.

end, but though it appears to have stopped this momentary enlightenment should be prolonged and prolonged. [p. 142]

[Against the notion that the objective world is merely a projection of one's own mind]

When you go out on a boat and look around, you feel as if the shore were moving. But if you fix your eyes on the rim of the boat, you become aware that the boat is moving. It is exactly the same when you try to know the objective world while still in a state of confusion in regard to your own body and mind; you are under the misapprehension that your own mind, your own nature, is something real and enduring [while the external world is transitory]. Only when you sit straight and look into yourself, does it become clear that [you yourself are changing and] the objective world has a reality apart from you. [p. 149]

[The fullness of enlightenment]

Our attainment of enlightenment is something like the reflection of the moon in water. The moon does not get wet, nor is the water cleft apart. Though the light of the moon is vast and immense, it finds a home in water only a foot long and an inch wide. The whole moon and the whole sky find room enough in a single dewdrop, a single drop of water. And just as the moon does not cleave the water apart, so enlightenment does not tear man apart. Just as a dewdrop or drop of water offers no resistance to the moon in heaven, so man offers no obstacle to the full penetration of enlightenment. Height is always the measure of depth. [The higher the object, the deeper will seem its reflection in the water.] [p. 164]

When your body and mind are not yet filled with enlightenment, you may feel that you are enlightened enough. But when enlightenment fills your whole body and mind, then you may be aware that something is still lacking. It is like taking a boat out into a vast expanse of water. When you look in all directions, that expanse looks round all around and nothing more. But the ocean is not merely round or square; its virtues are truly inexhaustible, like the Dragon's palace with its innumerable reflecting jewels. Only as far as our eyesight can reach does the ocean appear to be round. It is the same with the real world; inside and out it has numerous features, but we can see only as far as our spiritual eyesight reaches. Once we learn the true features of the real world, it is more than round, more than square. Its virtues are illimitable, as is the vastness of the ocean and the immensity of the mountain. There are worlds on all four sides of us, and not on all sides only, but underneath as well and even in the little dewdrop. [pp. 168–69]

Sitting and the Kōan
[From the Shōbō genzō zuimonki, pp. 98–99]

In the pursuit of the Way [Buddhism] the prime essential is sitting (zazen). . . . By reflecting upon various "public-cases" (kōan) and dialogues of the patriarchs, one may perhaps get the sense of them but it will only result in one's being led astray from the way of the Buddha, our founder. Just to pass the time in sitting straight, without any thought of acquisition, without any sense of achieving enlightenment—this is the way of the Founder. It is true that our predecessors recommended both the kōan and sitting, but it was the sitting that they particularly insisted upon. There have been some who attained enlightenment through the test of the kōan, but the true cause of their enlightenment was the merit and effectiveness of sitting. Truly the merit lies in the sitting.

The Importance of Sitting
[From the Shōbō genzō zuimonki, pp. 50–52]

When I stayed at the Zen lodge in T'ien-t'ung [China], the venerable Ching used to stay up sitting until the small hours of the morning and then after only a little rest would rise early to start sitting again. In the meditation hall he went on sitting with the other elders, without letting up for even a single night. Meanwhile many of the monks went off to sleep. The elder would go around among them and hit the sleepers with his fist or a slipper, yelling at them to wake up. If their sleepiness persisted, he would go out to the hallway and ring the bell to summon the monks to a room apart, where he would lecture to them by the light of a candle.

"What use is there in your assembling together in the hall only to go to sleep? Is this all that you left the world and joined holy orders for? Even among laymen, whether they be emperors, princes, or officials, are there any who live a life of ease? The ruler must fulfill the duties of the sovereign, his ministers must serve with loyalty and devotion, and commoners must work to reclaim land and till the soil—no one lives a life of ease. To escape from such burdens and idly while away the time in a monastery—what does this accomplish? Great is the problem of life and death; fleeting indeed is our transitory existence. Upon these truths both the scriptural and meditation schools agree. What sort of illness awaits us tonight, what sort of death tomorrow? While we have life, not to practice Buddha's Law but to spend the time in sleep is the height of foolishness. Because of such foolishness Buddhism today is in a state of decline. When it was at its zenith monks devoted themselves to the practice of sitting in meditation (*zazen*), but nowadays sitting is not generally insisted upon and consequently Buddhism is losing ground." . . .

Upon another occasion his attendants said to him, "The monks are getting overtired or falling ill, and some are thinking of leaving the monastery, all because they are required to sit too long in meditation. Shouldn't the length of the sitting period be shortened?" The master became highly indignant. "That would be quite wrong. A monk who is not really devoted to the religious life may very well fall asleep in a half hour or an hour. But one truly devoted to it who has resolved to persevere in his religious discipline will eventually come to enjoy the practice of sitting, no matter how long it lasts. When I was young I used to visit the heads of various monasteries, and one of them explained to me, 'Formerly I used to hit sleeping monks so hard that my fist just about broke. Now I am old and weak, so I can't hit them hard enough. Therefore it is difficult to produce good monks. In many monasteries today the superiors do not emphasize sitting strongly enough, and so Buddhism is declining. The more you hit them the better,' he advised me."

Body and Mind
[From the *Shōbō genzō zuimonki*, p. 52]

Is the Way [of liberation] achieved through the mind or through the body? The doctrinal schools speak of the identity of mind and body, and so when they speak of attaining the Way through the body,[1] they explain

---

[1] A famous example is the doctrine of Kūkai, who asserted the identity of mind and body and the possibility of achieving liberation "in the body" (i.e., in this life). See Chapter VII.

it in terms of this identity. Nevertheless this leaves one uncertain as to what "attainment by the body" truly means. From the point of view of our school, attainment of the Way is indeed achieved through the body as well the mind. So long as one hopes to grasp the Truth only through the mind, one will not attain it even in a thousand existences or in eons of time. Only when one lets go of the mind and ceases to seek an intellectual apprehension of the Truth is liberation attainable. Enlightenment of the mind through the sense of sight and comprehension of the Truth through the sense of hearing are truly bodily attainments. To do away with mental deliberation and cognition, and simply to go on sitting, is the method by which the Way is made an intimate part of our lives. Thus attainment of the Way becomes truly attainment through the body. That is why I put exclusive emphasis upon sitting.

Contempt for the Scriptures
[From Etō, *Shūso to shite no Dōgen Zenji*, p. 246]

There are Zen masters of a certain type who join in a chorus to deny that the sūtras contain the true teaching of the Buddha. "Only in the personal transmission from one patriarch to another is the essential truth conveyed; only in the transmission of the patriarchs can the exquisite and profound secrets of Buddha be found." Such statements represent the height of folly, they are the words of madmen. In the genuine tradition of the patriarchs there is nothing secret or special, not even a single word or phrase, at variance with the Buddhist sūtras. Both the sūtras and the transmission of the patriarchs alike represent the genuine tradition deriving from Shākyamuni Buddha. The only difference between them is that the patriarchs' transmission is a direct one from person to person. Who dares, then, to ignore the Buddha's sūtras? Who can refuse to study them, who can refuse to recite them? Wisely has it been said of old, "It is you who get lost in the sūtras, not the sūtras that lead you astray." Among our worthy predecessors there were many who studied the Scriptures. Therefore these loose-tongued individuals should be told, "To discard the sūtras of the Buddha, as you say, is to reject the mind of the Buddha, to reject the body of the Buddha. To reject the mind and body of the Buddha is to reject the children [followers] of the Buddha. To reject the children of the Buddha is to reject the teaching of the

Buddha. And if the teaching of the Buddha itself is to be rejected, why should not the teaching of the patriarchs be rejected? And when you have abandoned the teaching of the Buddha and the patriarchs, what will be left except a lot of bald-headed monks? Then you will certainly deserve to be chastized by the rod. Not only would you deserve to be enslaved by the rulers of this world, but to be cast into Hell for punishment."

MUSŌ KOKUSHI

Reflections upon the Enmity between Emperor Go-Daigo and the Shogun, Ashikaga Takauji
(From *Musō Kokushi goroku*)

This extract is from a sermon delivered by Musō Kokushi upon resumption of his presidency over the Tenryū monastery in 1351, in which he reflects upon the reasons for dedicating this temple to the memory of Go-Daigo and analyzes the causes of the rupture between the latter and Ashikaga Takauji, his erstwhile supporter. In Buddhist terms he attributes the break to one of the Three Evil Impulses: anger arising from jealousy of another's power, which blinded Go-Daigo and estranged him from his obedient servant. The writer's frank censure of the deceased emperor shows both how low the imperial house had fallen and how little awed by it was this Zen master, who considered it a purely human institution and not divine.
[From the *Taishō daizōkyō*, Vol. 80, pp. 463–64]

In the realm of True Purity there is no such thing as "I" or "He," nor can "friend" and "foe" be found there. But the slightest confusion of mind brings innumerable differences and complications. Peace and disorder in the world, the distinction between friend and foe in human relationships, follow upon one another as illusion begets delusion. A man of spiritual insight will immediately recognize what is wrong and before long rid himself of such an illusion, but the shallow-minded man will be ensnared by his own blindness so that he cannot put an end to it. In such a case one's true friend may seem a foe and one's implacable foe may appear a friend. Enmity and friendship have no permanent character; both of them are illusions.

During the disorders of the Genkō era [1331–34] the shogun, acting promptly on the imperial command, swiftly subdued the foes of the state [the Hōjō regents], as a result of which he rose higher in the ranks of government day by day and his growing prestige brought a change in the attitude of others toward him. Ere long slander and defamation sprang up with the violence of a tiger, and this unavoidably drew upon him the imperial displeasure. Consider now why this should have happened. It was because he performed a meritorious task with such despatch and to the entire satisfaction of his sovereign. There is an old saying that intimacy invites enmity. That is what it was. Thereupon amity and good will were scattered to the winds and the imperial authority was endangered. The emperor had to take refuge in the mountains to the South, where the music of the court was no longer heard and whence the imperial palanquin could never again return to the capital.

With a great sigh the Military Governor [Takauji] lamented, "Alas, due to slander and flattery by those close to the Throne, I am consigned to the fate of an ignominious rebel without any chance to explain my innocence." Indeed his grief was no perfunctory display, but without nurturing any bitterness in his heart he devoutly gave himself over to spiritual reflection and pious works, fervently praying for the enlightenment of the Emperor and eventually constructing [in the name of the Emperor] this great monastery for the practice of Buddhism. . . .

The virtuous rule of Emperor Go-Daigo was in accord with Heaven's will and His wisdom was equal to that of the ancient sage-kings. Therefore the imperial fortunes rose high and the whole country was brought under His sway. A new calendar was proclaimed and a new era of magnificence and splendor was inaugurated. The barbarian peoples showed themselves submissive and His subjects were well-disposed. This reign, men thought, would be like that of the Sage-Emperor Yao [in ancient China]; it would endure and never come to an end. Who would have thought that this Sage-like Sun would soon set and disappear into the shadows? And what are we to make of it—was it a mere trick of fate? No, I surmise that His late Majesty paid off all the debt of karma incurred in the world of defilement and straightway joined the happy assemblage of the Pure Land. It is not so much that His august reign was brought to an untimely end, but that the great mass of the people were caused so much suffering and distress. As a result from the time of His passing right up to the present there has been no peace, clergy and laity alike have become displaced, and there is no end to the complaints of the people.

What I have stated above is all a dream within a dream. Even if it were true, there is no use finding fault with what is past and done—how much less with what has happened in a dream! We must realize that the Throne, the highest position among men, is itself but something cherished in a dream. Even the kings of highest Heaven know nothing but the pleasure of a dream. That is why Shākyamuni, the Tathāgata, gave up his royal rank and took up a solitary life of religious discipline. Why did he do this? To teach all men that the Sovereign of Enlightenment is far superior to the highest position among men. The four castes [1] differ from one another, but they are all alike in being disciples of the Buddha and should behave accordingly.

I pray therefore that our late Emperor will turn away from his past confusions and free himself from bondage to illusion, bid farewell to karma-consciousness and prove himself the master of enlightened knowledge. Thus he may pass safely beyond the dark crossroad of differences between friend and foe, and attain that spiritual region wherein the identity of confusion and clear insight may be seen. Yet may he not forget the request of the Buddha at Vulture Peak, and extend an invisible hand to protect his teaching, so that with his spirit ever-present in this monastery of Kameyama his blessings may extend to all mankind.

This is indeed the wish of the Military Governor [Takauji], and so we have reason to believe that the imperial wrath will be appeased. Such a worthy intention [on the part of Takauji] is no trifling thing, and the Buddhas in their profound compassion are certain to bestow their unseen favor and protection upon us. Then may warfare come to an end, the whole country enjoy true peace, and all the people rest secure from disturbances and calamities. May the rule of the Military Governor pass on to his heirs, generation after generation. Our earnest desire is that all mankind should share in its blessings.

Sermon at the Opening of Tenryū Monastery
(From *Musō Kokushi goroku*)

The following sermon was delivered at the original opening of the Tenryū monastery, dedicated to the memory of Go-Daigo, when Musō Kokushi became its founding abbot. In it he reminds his audience that even among the

---

[1] Speaking the language of Indian Buddhism.

patriarchs of Zen the transmission of the Buddhist Law involved some form of preaching to proclaim its Truth to the world, and accordingly he proceeds to explain or suggest the fundamentals of Zen teaching.

[From the *Taishō daizōkyō*, Vol. 80, pp. 460c–61a]

In the tenth month of the second year of the Rekiō period [1339] an imperial decree ordered the conversion of the detached palace of the ex-Emperor Kameyama into a monastery dedicated to the memory of the ex-Emperor Go-daigo, and also nominated the Master to be its founding prior. In the fourth year of Kōei [1345], 4th month, 8th day, the Meditation Hall was opened for the first time (with their lordships General Takauji and Vice-general Tadayoshi in attendance). At the Hall the Master first performed the ceremony in commemoration of the Buddha's birth and then proceeded to say:

"The appearance in this world of all Buddhas, past, present, and future, is solely for the purpose of preaching the Law and helping all creatures to cross over to the shore of Liberation. The arts of oratory and types of intonation employed by Shākya were all meant to serve as a guide to the preaching of the Law, while the Deer Park and Vulture Peak served as places of spiritual instruction. The school of the Patriarch Bodhidharma stressed the method of individual instruction directed toward the essential nature, thus setting themselves off from the schools which stressed the teaching of doctrine. But closer examination of their aims reveals that Bodhidharma's followers likewise sought to transmit the Law and rescue men from the confusions of this world. Thus all of the patriarchs, forty-seven in India and twenty-three in China, each signalized his succession to the patriarchate by making a statement on the transmission of the Law. The Great Master Bodhidharma said, 'I came here primarily to transmit the Law and save men from their blinding passions.' So it is clear that Hui-k'o's cutting off his arm in the snow [2] and the conferring of the robe at midnight upon Hui-neng [3] were both meant to signify transmission of the true Law from one patriarch to another. In all circumstances, whether under a tree, upon

[2] Hui-k'o, the second Chinese patriarch, cut off his arm to show that he would stop at nothing in his determination to pursue Zen, and thereupon was confirmed by Bodhidharma as his successor.

[3] The ceremony of transmission was performed secretly at night to shield Hui-neng, the sixth Chinese patriarch, from the recriminations of a disappointed contender for that honor.

a rock, in the darkness of a cave or deep in a glen, the Law has been set forth and transmitted by such signs to whoever possessed the right qualifications. . . .

"What is that which we call the 'Law'? It is the Truth inherent in all its perfection in every living creature. The sage possesses it in no greater measure than does the ordinary man. Enlarge it and it will fill the universe; restrict it and it can be contained in a fraction of an inch. Yesterday or today, it undergoes no change or variation. All that the Buddhas have taught, whether as the Mahāyāna, the Hīnayāna, the pseudo or the authentic, the partial or the complete—all are embraced in it. This is the meaning of the 'Law.'

"Everything the world contains—grass and trees, bricks and tile, all creatures, all actions and activities—are nothing but manifestations of this Law. Therefore is it said that all phenomena in the universe bear the mark of this Law. If the significance of this were only grasped, then even without the appearance in this world of a Tathāgata [Buddha], the enlightenment of man would be complete, and even without the construction of this Hall the propagation of the Law would have achieved realization.

"As for myself, appearing before you today on this platform, I have nothing special to offer as my own interpretation of the Law. I merely join myself with all others—from the founder Shākya Tathāgata, the other Buddhas, bodhisattvas, saints and arhats, to all those here present, including patrons and officials, the very eaves and columns of this hall, lanterns and posts, as well as all the men, animals, plants and seeds in the boundless ocean of existence—to keep the wheel of the Law in motion.

"On such an occasion as this, you may say, 'What can we do?'" Holding out his cane, he exclaimed, "Look here, Look here! Don't you see Shākyamuni here right now walking around on the top of my cane? He points to heaven and then to earth, announcing to the entire audience, 'Today I am born again here with the completion of this new hall. All saints and sages are assembling here to bring man and heaven together. Every single person here is precious in himself, and everything here— plaques, paintings, square eaves and round pillars—every single thing is preaching the Law. Wonderful, wonderful it is, that the true Law lives

on and never dies. At Vulture Peak, indeed, this Law was passed on to
the right man!'

"It is thus that Shākya, the most venerable, instructs us here. It is the
teaching which comes down to men in response to the needs of their
situation. But perhaps, gentlemen, you wish to know the state of things
before Shākya ever appeared in his mother's womb?" [He tapped his
cane on the floor.] "Listen, Listen!"

The Vigorous Treatment of Zen
  [From *Muchū mondō* in *Kōso meicho zenshū*, XVI, Musō Kokushi hen,
  p. 145]

Clear-sighted masters of the Zen sect do not have a fixed doctrine which
is to be held to at any and all times. They offer whatever teaching occasion demands and preach as the spirit moves them, with no fixed course
to guide them. If asked what Zen is, they may answer in the words of
Confucius, Mencius, Lao Tzu or Chuang Tzu, or else in terms of the
doctrines of the various sects and denominations, and also by using
popular proverbs. Sometimes they draw attention to the immediate
situation confronting us, or they swing their mace and shout out *"katsu,"*
or perhaps they just raise their fists or fingers. All of these are methods
used by the Zen master and known as the "vigorous treatment of the
Zen Buddhist." They are incomprehensible to those who have not yet
ventured into this realm.

ZEN AND THE ARTS

At the time Eisai and Dōgen ventured forth to China, the Japanese
government had long since abandoned official relations with that country
and took little interest in the course of events on the mainland. But the
Mongol conquest of China and Korea in the thirteenth century suddenly
posed a threat for the Japanese themselves, and when the Hōjō regency
had to make momentous decisions Zen monks were chosen as its advisers
because they were considered to have a firsthand knowledge of China.
This was the beginning of a long history of secular service by Zen monks,
especially in the realm of foreign affairs, which lasted almost until the

seventeenth century. Later when the third Ashikaga Shogun Yoshimitsu (1358–1408) had successfully entered into foreign trade with the Chinese Ming dynasty in the hope of restoring the finances of the shogunate, he celebrated his new prosperity by building a great Zen monastery. Yoshimitsu in effect instituted a department of foreign affairs with a Zen monk as its head, and from his time onwards every delegation sent overseas by the government was led by a Zen monk. In the sixteenth century and later, local maritime potentates who engaged in foreign trade followed the example of the central government in appointing a Zen monk as commissioner or chief delegate. The influence of Zen in medieval Japan was thus not confined to religious activities but was also highly utilitarian.

Because of the strategic position the Zen monks occupied in the government, it was not difficult for them to extend the influence of Zen teachings to much of medieval culture. Virtually the only institutions of popular education during the period were the *tera-koya* (temple schools) run by Zen monks. All literature came under the spell of Zen, although the influence of Zen is perhaps most striking in the Nō theatre, which had got its start under the tutelage of Esoteric Buddhism. The bare simplicity of the Nō stage and scenery is a reflection of Zen aesthetic principles, and the movements of the actors themselves are based largely on those of swordsmanship, with which Zen had many intimate connections. Sometimes we find Zen teachings voiced by characters in a Nō play, but it is more in the underlying aesthetic concepts that we may detect Zen's great influence on the Nō.

In painting, no less than in literature, Zen aesthetics played a role of considerable magnitude. Shingon Buddhism had emphasized the artistic aspects of religion and had been responsible for many works of lasting beauty, most characteristic of which were the elaborate maṇḍala and the polychromed images of the different bodhisattvas. With Zen, however, simplicity and suggestion came to assume a dominant role in Japanese painting. In place of the brightly colored images of raging Fudō or of the thousand-armed Kannon, we find monochrome sketches of Zen masters, of sweeping landscapes, or of a single bird on a withered bough.

The great influence on literature and art of Zen Buddhism did not originate in Japan. Already in Sung China Zen had been considered to be one in essence with both poetry and painting, but although Zen reached the height of its influence at that time in China, its overall effect on secular culture appears of strictly limited magnitude when compared with that of Taoism and Confucianism. In Japan, however, Zen had no serious rivals at court or in the intellectual and artistic circles of the Ashikaga Period. And Zen monks occupied a favorable position for asserting their leadership in cultural matters, particularly in poetry and painting, because their special contacts (as trade commissioners) with China enabled them to introduce into their poetry and paintings the latest continental developments, which greatly enhanced their prestige.

The influence of Zen on Japanese culture was not limited to literature and art. As has been mentioned, there was a close connection between Zen and the Japanese warrior. Many samurai found Zen's stern masculinity and emphasis on intuitive action particularly congenial. For the believer in Zen swordsmanship might even be considered "an art of protecting life" rather than a means of killing others, and during the Tokugawa Period under Zen influence swordsmanship tended to become a peaceful art rather than a brutal contest.

Perhaps, however, Zen's influence was nowhere more marked than in the evolution of the Japanese tea ceremony. The cult of tea was not exclusively affiliated with Zen Buddhism; during the Tokugawa shogunate when Neo-Confucianism was the state philosophy, the tea ceremony came to be considered an effective means of training young women in the concept of *li*, here interpreted as the etiquette of the hearth. The tea cult also had its commercial aspects from the outset. Zen priests not only introduced the new beverage to Japan but also the pottery in which it was served, and the tea ceremony thus came to be not only a social attraction but the source of mercantile enterprise. These features of the background of the tea ceremony should not be ignored; nevertheless it remains true that it was the expression of many of the ideals of Buddhism, in particular of Zen Buddhism.

Three Zen masters were largely responsible for the growth of the tea cult in Japan. First was the founder of Japanese Zen, Eisai, who brought tea seeds home with him on his return from a second visit to China in 1191, and had them planted on a hillside near Kyoto. In 1214, as we have seen, he wrote the *Kissa yōjō-ki,* "Drink Tea To Improve Health and Prolong Life" in the hope of saving the Shogun Sanetomo from alcoholism by extolling the virtues of "the cup that cheers but does not inebriate."

[257]

In order to popularize the use of tea it was considered desirable to improve the quality of the cups in which it was served. Accordingly, when Dōgen visited China in 1222 to study Zen, he was accompanied by an artisan who later established a thriving center of pottery production in Japan.

The next step was to create a setting for the demonstration of the methods of enjoying the new drink. It thus happened that when another Zen master, Musō Kokushi (1275–1351), had built a simple cottage in a secluded garden for the purpose of solitary meditation, it was found agreeable to have a nonintoxicating beverage as a mild stimulant. The three elements of the tea ceremony—the actual beverage, the pottery, and the setting—having thus been supplied, a cult before long developed with the active participation of Zen masters.

The tea hut was considered to consist of three elements—the exterior of the hut, the garden, and the interior. These were equated with three prime characteristics of Buddhist teaching: the evanescence of all things, the selflessness of all elements (dharmas), and the bliss of Nirvāna.

Outside the cottage three things call one's attention to the first lesson in Buddhism, that life is everlasting change. The first is a little roof by the fence which, protecting the visitor from the weather, reminds him that nature is always changeable. This part is known as the *machiai*, or waiting house (a name which later acquired quite another meaning as a rendezvous for lovers). The second thing lies to the right in a thicket or under the shade of trees—a simple privy. Some may think that a privy hardly fits in with the exquisite refinement of the tea ceremony, but in fact it symbolizes better than anything else the incessant changes through which the human body passes. The third thing is the gate of the cottage, through which visitors constantly pass in and out, bending their heads and drawing up their legs as they do so, for the gate does not permit one to enter while standing upright.

The first lesson, the incessant changes of nature, is succeeded by the second one, in which three stone objects in the garden teach us the selflessness of the elements. These are the stepping stones, the stone water-basin, and the stone lantern, each silently teaching its lesson in selflessness. The flag-stones are willing to remain below and to be stepped on. The water-basin, where every visitor washes himself before entering the hut, may awaken the thought that the cleansing of the hands is made possible only by the willingness of the water to take away the dirt, the second example of selflessness. Lastly, there is a stone lantern which sheds a pale light. A little thought may lead to the realization of the selflessness of the wick, which is willing to be consumed in flame in order to illumine, however faintly, a dark corner of the garden.

The visitor is next led inside, into the room where the tea is to be served. After virtually doubling his body in order to pass through the low door, he suddenly finds himself in a realm of the most absolute peace. The room is small—only nine feet square and high—but everything in it is a marvel of purity and simplicity.

The first thing that greets the visitor is the scent of incense, which magically and indefinably transforms the atmosphere. Not only by its fragrance but by the faint wisp of its smoke does the incense catch the imagination. The ever-rising smoke symbolizes the constant aspiration of the terrestrial towards the celestial.

While the visitor sits motionlessly, watching in silence the course of the smoke, he is certain to hear the cries of a solitary bird flying by the hut, or the dripping of water in the fountain outside, or the rustle of the wind in the pines above the roof. Like the pealing of a distant temple bell, such sounds come from nowhere and lose themselves in timelessness, to awaken the enveloping silence from which all music comes and into which all music returns. Because these sounds are so fleeting, so transitory, the presence of silence is felt all the more profoundly. A moment has communion with eternity when sound meets silence to create music: this is the Buddhist philosophy of music expressed in the Avatamsaka doctrines.

At the far end of the room, in the center, is an alcove in which hangs a scroll painting. Before it flowers are arranged. These two finite examples of form and color help to make visible the infinite, just as a single note can make us more aware of the eternal silence. Without forms or color the immense space surrounding us would remain forever a stupendous blank, an unnamable vacuum. When lines or colors cut through infinite space, painting, which is the meeting of the finite with the infinite, comes into being. The *Lotus Sutra* says, "Everything finite tells of infinity."

The appeal of the infinite having thus been made to the senses of smell, hearing, and sight, the visitor is now ready for the enjoyment of the tea. He will be mistaken, however, if he expects to witness anything extraordinary in the preparation. The host is seated by a small open fire with the paraphernalia required, including bamboo implements, lacquerware, pots, kettles, and silk napkins. There is not a single thing which the average Japanese family does not possess, for, as the Zen masters were accustomed to say, "Religion is a most ordinary thing." The teacups are somewhat larger than the usual ones and may be works of art, but they are made of nothing more extraordinary than clay; to the Zen believer the transformation of clay into a lovely teacup is religion itself.

In the actual preparation of the tea, the host must pay special attention to four things—the fire, the water, the spoon, and the bamboo whisk. The first two are powerful elements which in other circumstances require all of man's efforts to control; the second two, the spoon to measure the powdered tea and the whisk to stir it, require delicacy and care in order to ensure a perfect balance. When the host has placed the proper measure of tea in the cup, he pours in boiled water and stirs the mixture with the whisk until it is exactly right. Then it is placed before the visitor, who must lift the cup in both hands, feeling its texture and warmth. He drinks the tea, not in one gulp but three sips, savoring the liquid as refreshing as some precious elixir though made of a most common, ordinary leaf. Thus also is sometimes transformed the common clay of humanity into an arhat, a bodhisattva, or a Buddha.

CHAPTER XIII

SHINTO IN MEDIEVAL JAPAN

The introduction of Buddhism and its subsequent acceptance by the Japanese court resulted in the submergence of Shinto, the native religion, for many years. It was said of the Emperor Kōtoku (who reigned at the time of the Great Reform of 646) that he "honored the religion of Buddha and despised the Way of the Gods." [1] Other sovereigns generally had more respect for Shinto, although the brilliant Buddhist ceremonies that marked the Nara and Heian periods occupied the court far more than the simple observances of the native religion. The ethical teachings of Shinto, later the subject of so much attention by scholars of the native learning, had little importance in early Japan. Except for a few prayers (*norito*) Shinto did not produce religious writings; it was thus natural that the constitution attributed to Prince Shōtoku should have been formulated entirely in terms of Confucian and Buddhist teachings.

It should not be thought, however, that Shinto was entirely absent from the scene of early Japan. The gods had their functions, chiefly concerned with natural phenomena—rain, drought, earthquakes, etc. This meant that among the peasants (and, in general, most people living away from the capital in the provinces), the local cults of Shinto continued to be the prevailing religion even when Buddhism was triumphant at the court. But even the court recognized the importance of the gods. Over and over in the *Chronicles of Japan* we find such entries as the following (for A.D. 599): "There was an earthquake which destroyed all the houses. So orders were given to all quarters to sacrifice to the God of Earthquakes." [2] An entry for 689 contains the first mention of a state "department of Shinto," and in the eleventh month of 691 we are told that: "The festival of first-fruits was held. Ōshima, Nakatomi no Ason, Minister of the De-

---

[1] Aston, *Nihongi*, II, 195. [2] *Ibid.*, II, 124.

partment of the Shinto religion, recited the prayers invoking the blessing of the Heavenly Deities."[3]

By the early tenth century, when the Institutes of the Engi Era were completed, more than 6,000 Shinto shrines were enumerated where annual offerings were to be made by the court or the provincial governments. This official recognition of Shinto represented a great landmark in the systematization of the native cults, which until then had tended to remain loosely connected aggregates of local shrines. We may detect the influence of Buddhist practices in this attempt to systematize Shinto. Already in the late Nara Period (in 765) Buddhist priests and nuns had participated in the Great Thanksgiving Festival, one of the most sacred Shinto celebrations, and the Empress Shōtoku declared on that occasion that she considered her duty (having returned to the throne as a nun), "first to serve the Three Treasures, then to worship the Gods, and next to cherish the people."[4] The union of the two religions was further promoted in 768 when a Buddhist temple was erected by the Ise Shrine, the holiest Shinto sanctuary, and from this time on many Shinto shrines had their temples and Buddhist priests who served both religions.

The fusion of Buddhism with another religion did not originate in Japan. In India, Buddha himself had recognized the popular gods, the devas, as deities possessing powers far less considerable than his own, but superior to those of ordinary men. There are frequent references in early texts to the conversion of the Indian gods [devas] to Buddhism after they had heard Buddha preach. In later Buddhist writings Brahmā and the lesser deities were explained as avatārs of Buddha and the bodhisattvas who had appeared on earth to save mankind. This concept was later adopted by the Mahāyāna sects. It is found in such works as the *Saddharma Puṇḍarīka*, the *Vimalakīrti*, and *Vairocana* sūtras, and in the Shingon mandalas.

In China, the Buddhists at times claimed that Confucius, Lao Tzu, and other famous philosophers were sent by Buddha to help mankind. By the middle of the T'ang dynasty we find the first mention of the phrase "original substance manifests traces" (*honji suijaku*) which was to figure so importantly in Japan; in an explanation of the *Vairochana* sūtra a com-

---

[3] Aston, *Nihongi*, II, 404. The Nakatomi family was one of the chief supporters of Shinto. It was later renamed Fujiwara.

[4] Sansom, *Japan*, p. 135.

mentator stated that the spirits and gods were avatārs of Vairochana—
traces on earth of the original substance of divinity.

Although the fusion of Buddhism and native religions may thus be
discovered in both India and China, it was in Japan that it assumed its
most significant form. Kūkai is often mentioned as the originator of
honji suijaku, but in spite of the numerous forged works on the subject
which are attributed to him, there is nothing to indicate that the *honji
suijaku* formula was known in his time. It was natural enough for later
supporters to bring in Kūkai's name in order to lend greater authority to
honji suijaku, and this fact may also explain the tales of how Kūkai taught
the Emperor Saga about the mysteries of Shinto, or such supposed quotations as, "Unless one studies Shinto one will not understand the pro-
fundities of my school of Buddhism." Whether we believe such stories or
not, it is certain that Kūkai did pay considerable attention to the gods.
When he built his temple on Mt. Kōya, which had been known as
the seat of various gods, he called out to them: "All evil spirits and gods,
who may be to the east, south, north, west, above, or below this monastery: you hinderers and destroyers of the True Law, hie you seven
leagues hence from my altar! If however there be any good spirits and
gods who are beneficial to the Buddhist Law and protect it, you may
dwell as you choose in this monastery and protect the Buddhist Law." [5]

The first clear evidence of *honji suijaku* thought in Japan seems to date
from 937, when two gods were declared to be avatārs of bodhisattvas. In
time every god was established as an avatār of one or another Buddha or
Bodhisattva. Most of the "original substances" of the different gods proved
to be the thirteen Buddhas of Shingon, a fact indicative of the special ties
between this sect and Shinto. Shinto adopted the incantations, ritual fire
ceremonies, charms, signs, and methods of instruction of Shingon, and
these alien features soon became so much a part of Shinto that even pur-
ists later considered them to be part of the religion in its pristine form. The
most important form of union between Buddhism and Shinto was called
"Dual Shinto" (*Ryōbu Shintō*), a term derived from the equation made
between the two mandalas of Shingon Buddhism and the Inner and
Outer Shrines at Ise. The Tendai monasteries of Mt. Hiei and Miidera,
which had become strongholds of Esoteric Buddhism, consummated their
union with Shinto by adopting local tutelary deities as had the Shingon

[5] *Kōbō Daishi Zenshū, III, Shōryōshū,* 530–31.

center of Mt. Kōya.[6] But Shingon was considered by most Shinto scholars to be closest to the native religion. Kitabatake Chikafusa declared that the "traditions from the Age of the Gods tally most closely with the teachings of this sect [Shingon]. That is probably why, though it enjoyed only brief popularity in China, it has persisted in Japan."

In medieval Japan the fusion of Buddhist and Shinto ceremonies became almost invariable. Most of the shrines of the nation were controlled by Buddhists. Within the shrines themselves Buddhist images were worshiped as representations of the gods, and Buddhist implements (principally Shingon) were used alongside the traditional paper streamers and ropes. The pantheism of Tendai and the cosmotheism of Shingon led easily to an incorporation of Shinto beliefs and legends, and even in the remote regions of Japan, where the Way of the Gods remained strongest, a *rapprochement* of the two religions regularly took place. Although it is true that monks were not allowed to penetrate the Inner Shrine at Ise, and certain Buddhist sects failed to show much interest in Shinto, by and large the union of Buddhism and Shinto, usually stated in *honji suijaku* terms, became a general feature of Japanese religious life and remained such at least until the Meiji Restoration of 1868.

At first Shinto's part in the combined religion was relatively minor, but with the downfall of the court aristocracy at the end of the Heian Period, men from the outlying provinces were brought to power, and they still retained a strong attachment to Shinto. Thus, the Taira clan proclaimed its loyalty to the goddess Itsukushima, and the Minamoto clan worshiped Hachiman, the god of war. As early as the year 750 Hachiman is reported to have paid his respects to the Great Statue of the Buddha in Nara, and it was not many years afterwards that he acquired the title of "great Bodhisattva." Later the Minamoto shoguns adopted Hachiman as their clan deity and enshrined him in their capital at Kamakura, just as the imperial house had established his worship in Nara and Kyoto. He was considered as a manifestation of Amida Buddha, while Itsukushima was the "manifested trace" of Kannon (Avalokiteshvara), further examples of *honji suijaku*.

The Mongol invasions of 1274 and 1281 created a strong sentiment of

[6] At Mt. Kōya it was the female deity Tanjō who allegedly turned the mountain over to Kūkai; at Hiei, the mountain god Sannō; and at Miidera the Korean goddess, Shiragi Myōjin (Korean influence was well-established in this region).

national consciousness among the Japanese. The "divine winds" (*kami-kaze*) which had driven off the invaders were interpreted as signs of the protection afforded to Japan by the native gods (the Sun Goddess and Hachiman), and it was less than fifty years afterwards that Kitabatake wrote his *Records of the Legitimate Succession of the Divine Sovereigns*, in which he proclaimed the supremacy of Japan over China and India because of Japan's single line of emperors descended from the gods. Kitabatake's work was primarily political, but from about the same time (or somewhat earlier) date the Five Classics of Shinto, forgeries purporting to have been composed in remote antiquity. The Five Classics are concerned mainly with the history of the Ise Shrine, and attempt to set forth a Shinto philosophy and ethics. Whatever philosophical or ethical significance these books possess was borrowed from Buddhism, but the adherents of the "Primal Shinto" (*Yuiitsu Shintō*) school of the fifteenth century and later, referred to the Five Classics as a treasury of pure Shinto teachings.

The chief figure in the "Primal Shinto" school was Yoshida Kanetomo (1435–1511). Yoshida did not attempt, like certain later Shinto scholars, to discredit Buddhism; he sought instead to shift the emphasis in the combined religion from Buddhism to Shinto although maintaining the union. He interpreted *honji suijaku* as meaning that the Japanese gods were the original substance, and Buddha and the bodhisattvas the manifested traces. (This may be compared to a similar switch-about in India, where brāhmans came to consider Buddha as the ninth avatār of Vishnu, or in China, where Buddha was said by Taoists to be an avatār of Lao Tzu.) Yoshida relied heavily on the forged Five Classics, and where they were insufficient to meet his needs, he appears not to have been above forgery of his own. In one of Yoshida's works we find his most famous statement of the relations of Shinto, Buddhism, and Confucianism:

During the reign of the Empress Suiko, the thirty-fourth sovereign, Prince Shōtoku stated in a memorial that Japan was the roots and trunk [of civilization], China its branches and leaves, and India its flowers and fruit. Similarly, Buddhism is the flowers and fruit of all laws, Confucianism their branches and leaves, and Shinto their roots and trunk. Thus all foreign doctrines are offshoots of Shinto.[7]

[7] Yoshida, *Yuiitsu Shintō Myōhō Yōshū*, quoted in Kiyowara, *Shintō-shi*, p. 237. The reversal of the order in the parallels between Japan and Shinto, China and Confucianism, and India and Buddhism was a common literary device in Chinese.

Needless to say, Prince Shōtoku did not make this statement, but it sounded good enough, and historicity was not a vital concern of medieval minds. Far more striking to them would have been Kanetomo's bold attempt to turn the tables on Buddhism and Confucianism, and assert the primacy of Shinto after centuries of subservience.

Yoshida revealed his indebtedness to Buddhism, particularly to Esoteric Buddhism, at every point in his exposition of Shinto principles; it often appears as if he has merely substituted a Shinto word in an otherwise Buddhist context:

Kami or Deity is spirit, without form, unknowable, transcending both cosmic principles, the yin and the yang . . . changeless, eternal, existing from the very beginning of Heaven and Earth up to the present, unfathomable, infinite, itself with neither beginning nor end, so that the so-called "Divine Age" is not only in the past but also in the present. It is, indeed, the eternal now.[8]

This is an enunciation of the Shingon doctrine of *aji hompushō* (the eternity of creation) decked in Shinto garments; in the following passage we find Shingon cosmotheism, expressed in the characteristic three aspects:

With reference to the universe we call it *kami,* with reference to the interactions of nature we call it spirit (*rei*), in man we call it soul (*kokoro*). Therefore, God is the source of the universe. He is the spiritual essence of created things. God is soul (*kokoro*) and soul is God. All the infinite variety of change in nature, all the objects and events of the universe are rooted in the activity of God. All the laws of nature are made one in the activity of God.[9]

The significant thing about Yoshida's teachings is that by his time the long period of Shinto apprenticeship to alien ideologies had ended, and Shinto spokesmen not only knew the intricacies of Buddhist and other foreign doctrines, but were adept in rewriting them in Shinto terms with ease and vigor. Yoshida was a member of the Urabe family, one of the oldest and most important Shinto families of diviners. For centuries this family had experienced all the tribulations which had befallen Shinto during its period of subservience to Buddhism; with Yoshida Kanetomo at last Shinto once more came into its own, and the persistent devotion of the Urabe family was justified.

[8] Yoshida, *Shindaishō,* translated in D. C. Holtom, *The National Faith of Japan,* pp. 39–40.
[9] Translated in Holtom, p. 40. The word "God" should not, of course, be interpreted in the Christian sense; it is the Japanese *kami.*

THE EMPRESS SHŌTOKU
Edict on the Great Thanksgiving Festival
[From *Rikkokushi, Shoku Nihongi*, II, 126]

Today is the day of plenteous feasting attendant on the Great Thanksgiving Festival.[1] This occasion differs from the usual celebrations in that we, as a disciple of Buddha, have received the ordination of a bodhisattva. Therefore, deeming that we should serve the Three Treasures with our highest devotion, should next reverence the gods of the shrines of heaven and earth, and should next cherish and love the princes, the ministers, the officials of the hundred departments, and all the people of this land who serve us, we have returned [to the throne] and again rule over the nation. . . .[2]

Some people believe that the gods shun and will not touch the Three Treasures. However, it may be seen in the sūtras that it is the gods who protect and exalt the Law of Buddha. For this reason we consider that there can be no objection to both Buddhist priests and ordinary laymen joining together in the service.

Hearken all ye people to the imperial command: we do direct that on the occasion of this Great Thanksgiving Festival that which has hitherto been avoided should not be avoided.[3]

KITABATAKE CHIKAFUSA
The Records of the Legitimate Succession of the Divine Sovereigns

The most important document of medieval Shinto is *The Records of the Legitimate Succession of the Divine Sovereigns* by Kitabatake Chikafusa (1293–1354). Like the *Records of Ancient Matters* (712), but far more conspicuously so, Kitabatake's work is a political tract as well as a theological one. It was written at a time when Japan was split between two contending courts, and

[1] Held on the twenty-third day of the eleventh moon of 765, or January 8, 766. This was a traditional celebration held after the accession to the throne of a new sovereign. Shōtoku had recently reascended the throne.

[2] A few lines dealing with the wines and viands of the ceremony have been omitted at this point.

[3] That is, the participation of Buddhist priests in the ceremony. The word here translated as "avoid" has the implication of "to be tabooed."

Kitabatake, as a loyal supporter of the southern court, sought to prove its legitimacy by tracing the descent of the emperor he served from the Age of the Gods. Later Japanese historians for the most part have agreed with Kitabatake in considering the emperors of the southern court to have been in the true line of succession.

The extracts here given include the opening pages of the work and also one of its most famous sections, the interpretation of the meaning of the three sacred regalia of the imperial family. Most of the rest of the book consists of summaries of the reigns of successive monarchs.

The first extract may be divided into three sections—the names of Japan; Japan's position according to (primarily) Buddhist geographical concepts; and the relation between Buddhist, Chinese, and Japanese accounts of the creation of the world. Kitabatake's preoccupation with names and the etymologies is characteristic of Shinto from earliest times, as is shown for example in the explanation of the name "Yamato." Later Shinto scholars never wearied of tracing the origins of such words as Yamato and *kami*.

The second and third sections of the first extract show Kitabatake's familiarity with Buddhist and Chinese writings. He did not reject the foreign theories, but attempted instead to show that they were imperfect renderings of Shinto truths. Buddhist and Confucian books are useful in that they help to spread Shinto doctrines, but they do not give a full picture of Japan's glory, her uninterrupted line of sovereigns. The avowed purpose of *The Records of the Legitimate Succession of the Divine Sovereigns* was to supplement this deficiency and so reveal to Japanese the uniqueness of their country.

[From the *Jinnō Shōtō-ki*, pp. 1–22]

Japan is the divine country. The heavenly ancestor it was who first laid its foundations, and the Sun Goddess left her descendants to reign over it forever and ever. This is true only of our country, and nothing similar may be found in foreign lands. That is why it is called the divine country.

THE NAMES OF JAPAN

In the Age of the Gods, Japan was known as the "ever-fruitful land of reed-covered plains and luxuriant ricefields." [1] This name has existed since the creation of heaven and earth. It appeared in the command given by the heavenly ancestor Kunitokotachi to the Male Deity and the Female Deity. [2] Again, when the Great Goddess Amaterasu bequeathed the land to her grandchild, that name was used; it may thus be considered

[1] Toyoashihara no Chiihoaki no Mizuho no Kuni. Translations of ancient names of places and deities are only approximate.

[2] The Male Deity (Izanagi) and the Female Deity (Izanami) were ordered to descend to earth and produce the terrestrial world.

[268]

the primal name of Japan. It is also called the country of the great eight islands. This name was given because eight islands were produced when the Male Deity and the Female Deity begot Japan. It is also called Yamato, which is the name of the central part of the eight islands. The eighth offspring of the deities was the god Heavenly-August-Sky-Luxuriant-Dragon-fly-Lord-Youth [and the land he incarnated] was called Ō-yamato, Luxuriant-Dragon-fly-Island. It is now divided into forty-eight provinces. Besides being the central island, Yamato has been the site of the capital through all the ages since Jimmu's conquest of the east. That must be why the other seven islands are called Yamato. The same is true of China, where All-Under-Heaven was at one time called Chou because the dynasty had its origins in the state of Chou, and where All-Within-the-Seas was called Han when the dynasty arose in the territory of Han.

The word Yamato means "footprints on the mountain." Of old, when heaven and earth were divided, the soil was still muddy and not yet dry, and people passing back and forth over the mountains left many footprints; thus it was called Yama-to—"mountain footprint." Some say that in ancient Japanese *to* meant "dwelling" and that because people dwelt in the mountains, the country was known to Yama-to—"mountain dwelling."

In writing the name of the country, the Chinese characters Dai-Nippon and Dai-Wa have both been used. The reason is that, when Chinese writing was introduced to this country, the characters for Dai-Nippon were chosen to represent the name of the country, but they were pronounced as "Yamato." This choice may have been guided by the fact that Japan is the Land of the Sun Goddess, or it may have thus been called because it is near the place where the sun rises. . . .

According to the Buddhist classics, there is a mountain called Sumeru which is surrounded by seven gold mountains. In between them is the Sea of Fragrant Waters, and beyond the gold mountains stretch four oceans which contain the four continents. Each continent is in turn composed of two smaller sections. The southern continent is called Jambu (it is also known as Jambudvīpa, another form of the same name) from the name of the jambu-tree. In the center of the southern continent is a mountain called Anavatapta, at the summit of which is a lake. A jambu-tree grows beside this lake, seven yojanas in circumference and one hundred yojanas in height. (One yojana equals forty *li;* one *li* equals 2,160 feet.) The tallest of these trees grows in the center of the continent, and gives it its name. To the south of Anavatapta are the Himālayas and to the north are the Pamirs. North of the Pamirs is Tartary; south of the Himālayas is India. To the northeast is China, and to the northwest, Persia. The continent of Jambu is seven thousand yojanas long and broad; that is, 280,000 *li*. From the eastern sea to the western sea is 90,000 *li;* from the southern sea to the northern sea is also 90,000 *li*. India is in the very center, and is thus the central land of Jambu; its circumference is likewise 90,000 *li*. However big China may seem, when compared with India it is only a remote, minor country. Japan is in the ocean, removed from China. Gomyō Sōjō of Nara and Saichō of Hiei designated it as the Middle Country, but should not that name refer to the island of Chāmara, which lies between the northern and southern continents? When, in the *Kegon Sūtra,* it states that there is a mountain called Kongō [Diamond], it refers to the Kongō Mountain in modern Japan, or so it is believed. Thus, since Japan is a separate continent, distinct from both India and China and lying in a great ocean, it is the country where the divine illustrious imperial line has been transmitted.

JAPAN'S POSITION CHRONOLOGICALLY

The creation of heaven and earth must everywhere have been the same, for it occurred within the same universe, but the Indian, Chinese, and Japanese traditions are each different. According to the Indian version, the beginning of the world is called the "inception of the kalpas." (A kalpa has four stages—growth, settlement, decline, and extinction—each with twenty rises and falls. One rise and fall is called a minor kalpa; twenty minor kalpas constitute a middle kalpa, and four middle kalpas constitute a major kalpa.) A heavenly host called "Light-Sound" [3] spread golden clouds in the sky which filled the entire Brahmāloka. Then they caused great rains to fall, which accumulated on the circle of wind to form the circle of water. It expanded and rose to the sky, where a great wind blew from it foam which it cast into the void; this crystallized into the palace of Brahmā. The water gradually receding formed the palaces

[3] These divine beings "spoke" with light instead of sound—hence the name.

of the realm of desire, Mount Sumeru, the four continents, and the Iron Enclosing Mountain. Thus the countless millions of worlds came into existence at the same time. This was the kalpa of creation. (These countless millions of worlds are called the three-thousand-great-thousand worlds.)

The heavenly host of Light-Sound came down, were born, and lived. This was the kalpa of settlement. During the kalpa of settlement there were twenty rises and falls. In the initial stage, people's bodies shone with a far-reaching effulgence, and they could fly about at will. Joy was their nourishment. No distinction existed between the sexes. Later, sweet water, tasting like cream and honey, sprang from the earth. (It was also called earth-savor.) One sip of it engendered a craving for its taste. Thus were lost the godlike ways, and thus also was the light extinguished, leaving the wide world to darkness. In retribution for the actions of living creatures, black winds blew over the oceans, bearing before them on the waves the sun and the moon, to come to rest half-way up Mount Sumeru, there to shine forth on the four continents under the heavens. From that time on there were the day and the night, the months, and the seasons. Indulgence in the sweet waters caused men's faces to grow pale and thin. Then the sweet waters vanished, and vegetable food (also called earth-rind) appeared, which all creatures ate. Then the vegetable food also vanished, and wild rice of multiple tastes was provided them. Cut in the morning, it ripened by evening. The eating of the rice left dregs in the body, and thus the two orifices were created. Male and female came to differ, and this led to sexual desire. They called each other husband and wife, built houses, and lived together. Beings from the Light-Sound Heaven who were later to be born entered women's wombs, and once born became living creatures.

Later, the wild rice ceased to grow, to the dismay of all creatures. They divided the land and planted cereals, which they made their food. Then there were those who stole other people's crops, and fighting ensued. As there was no one to decide such cases, men got together and established a Judge-King whom they called kshatriya (which means landowner). The first king bore the title of People's Lord [*Minshu*].[4] He enjoyed the love and respect of the people because he ruled the country with laws which

---

[4] Kitabatake's source for this statement, the *Busso-tōki*, indicates that the first king was chosen by the people to administer equal justice.

embodied the ten virtues. The realm of Jambu was prosperous and peaceful with no sickness or extremes of cold or heat. Men lived so long that their years were almost without number. Successive descendants of People's Lord ruled the land for many years, but as the good laws gradually fell into abeyance, the life-span decreased until it was only 84,000 years. People were eighty feet tall. During this period there was a king, the wheels of whose chariot rolled everywhere without hindrance. First the precious Golden Wheel came down from heaven and appeared before the king. Whenever the king went abroad, the wheel rolled ahead of him, and the lesser rulers evinced their welcome and homage. No one dared do otherwise. He reigned over the four continents and enjoyed all treasures—elephants, horses, pearls, women, lay-Buddhists, and military heroes. He who is possessed of these Seven Treasures is called a Sovereign of the Golden Wheel. There followed in succession [sovereigns of] Silver, Copper, and Iron Wheels. Because of the inequality of their merits, the rewards also gradually diminished. The life-span also decreased by one year each century, and human stature was similarly reduced by one foot a century. It was when the life-span had dropped to 120 years that Shākya Buddha appeared. (Some authorities say that it was when the life-span was 100 years. Before him three Buddhas had appeared.)

When the life-span has been reduced to a bare ten years, the so-called Three Disasters will ensue, and the human species will disappear almost entirely, leaving a mere 10,000 people. These people will practice good deeds, and the life-span will then increase and the rewards improve. By the time that a life-span of 20,000 years is reached, a King of the Iron Wheel will appear and rule over the southern continent. When the life-span reaches 40,000 years, a King of the Copper Wheel will appear and rule over the eastern and southern continents. When the life-span reaches 60,000 years, a King of the Silver Wheel will appear and rule over three continents, the eastern, western, and southern. When the life-span reaches 84,000 years, a King of the Golden Wheel will appear and rule over all four continents. The rewards in his reign will be those mentioned above. In his time a decline will again set in, followed by the appearance of Maitreya Buddha. There are then to follow eighteen other rises and falls. . . .

In China, nothing positive is stated concerning the creation of the world even though China is a country which accords special importance to the keeping of records. In the Confucian books nothing antedates King Fu-hsi.[5] In other works they speak of heaven, earth, and man as having begun in an unformed, undivided state, much as in the accounts of our Age of the Gods. There is also the legend of King P'an-ku,[6] whose eyes were said to have turned into the sun and the moon, and whose hair turned into grasses and trees. There were afterwards sovereigns of Heaven, sovereigns of Earth, and sovereigns of Man, and the Five Dragons, followed by many kings over a period of 10,000 years.

The beginnings of Japan in some ways resemble the Indian descriptions, telling as it does of the world's creation from the seed of the heavenly gods. However, whereas in our country the succession to the throne has followed a single undeviating line since the first divine ancestor, nothing of the kind has existed in India. After their first ruler, King People's Lord, had been chosen and raised to power by the populace, his dynasty succeeded, but in later times most of his descendants perished, and men of inferior genealogy who had powerful forces became the rulers, some of them even controlling the whole of India. China is also a country of notorious disorders. Even in ancient times, when life was simple and conduct was proper, the throne was offered to wise men,[7] and no single lineage was established. Later, in times of disorder, men fought for control of the country. Thus some of the rulers rose from the ranks of the plebeians, and there were even some of barbarian origin who usurped power. Or, some families after generations of service as ministers surpassed their princes and eventually supplanted them. There have already been thirty-six changes of dynasty since Fu-hsi, and unspeakable disorders have occurred.

Only in our country has the succession remained inviolate, from the beginning of heaven and earth to the present. It has been maintained within a single lineage, and even when, as inevitably has happened, the succession has been transmitted collaterally, it has returned to the true line. This is due to the ever-renewed Divine Oath, and makes Japan unlike all other countries.

[5] Fu-hsi was the legendary founder of Chinese culture, being credited, among other things, with the establishment of the laws of marriage, the invention of writing, and the first instruction in hunting and fishing.
[6] The legend of P'an-ku was apparently of Central Asiatic origin and not "naturalized" by the Chinese until post-Han times.
[7] This refers to the decisions of the legendary emperors Yao and Shun to hand over the throne to wise men rather than to their own sons.

It is true that the Way of the Gods should not be revealed without circumspection, but it may happen that ignorance of the origins of things may result in disorder. In order to prevent that disaster, I have recorded something of the facts, confining myself to a description of how the succession has legitimately been transmitted from the Age of the Gods. I have not included information known to everyone. I have given the book the title of *The Records of the Legitimate Succession of the Divine Sovereigns*. [pp. 1–9]

Then the Great Sun Goddess conferred with Takami-musubi and sent her grandchild to the world below. Eighty million deities obeyed the divine decree to accompany and serve him. Among them were thirty-two principal deities, including the gods of the Five Guilds—Ameno Koyane (the first ancestor of the Nakatomi family), Ameno Futodama (the first ancestor of the Imbe family), Ameno Uzume (the first ancestor of the Sarume family), Ishikoridome (the first ancestor of the mirror-makers), and Tamaya (the first ancestor of the jewel-makers). Two of these deities, those of the Nakatomi and the Imbe, received a divine decree specially instructing them to aid and protect the divine grandchild. The Sun Goddess, on bestowing the three divine treasures on her grandchild, uttered these words of command, "The reed-plain-of-one-thousand-five-hundred-autumns-fair-rice-ear land is where my descendants shall reign. Thou, my illustrious grandchild, proceed thither and govern the land. Go, and may prosperity attend thy dynasty, and may it, like Heaven and Earth, endure forever."

Then the Great Goddess, taking in her own hand the precious mirror, gave it to her grandchild, saying, "When thou, my grandchild, lookst on this mirror, it will be as though thou lookst at myself. Keep it with thee, in the same bed, under the same roof, as thy holy mirror." She then added the curved jewel of increasing prosperity and the sword of gathered clouds, thus completing the three regalia. She again spoke, "Illumine all the world with brightness like this mirror. Reign over the world with the wonderful sway of this jewel. Subdue those who will not obey thee by brandishing this divine sword." It may indeed be understood from these commands why Japan is a divine country and has been ruled by a single imperial line following in legitimate succession. The Imperial Regalia have been transmitted [within Japan] just as the sun, moon, and stars remain in the heavens. The mirror has the form of the sun; the jewel contains the essence of the moon; and the sword has the substance of the stars. There must be a profound significance attached to them.

The precious mirror is the mirror made by Ishikoridome, as is above recorded. The jewel is the curved bead of increasing prosperity made by Tamanoya, and the sword is the sword of gathered clouds, obtained by the god Susa-no-o and offered by him to the Great Goddess. The goddess's commands on the Three Regalia must indicate the proper methods of governing the country. The mirror does not possess anything of its own, but without selfish desires reflects all things, showing their true qualities. Its virtue lies in its response to these qualities, and as such represents the source of all honesty. The virtue of the jewel lies in its gentleness and submissiveness; it is the source of compassion. The virtue of the sword lies in its strength and resolution; it is the source of wisdom. Unless these three virtues [8] are joined in a ruler, he will find it difficult indeed to govern the country. The divine commands are clear; their words are concise, but their import is far-reaching. Is it not an awe-inspiring thing that they are embodied in the imperial regalia?

The mirror stands first in importance among the regalia, and is revered as the true substance of ancestor-worship. The mirror has brightness as its form: the enlightened mind possesses both compassion and decision. As it also gives a true reflection of the Great Goddess, she must have given her profound care to the mirror. There is nothing brighter in heaven than the sun and the moon. That is why, when the Chinese characters were devised, the symbols for sun and for moon were joined to express the idea of brightness. Because our Great Goddess is the spirit of the sun, she illuminates with a bright virtue which is incomprehensible in all its aspects, but dependable alike in the realm of the visible and invisible. All sovereigns and ministers have inherited the bright seeds of the divine light, or they are the descendants of the deities who received personal instruction from the Great Goddess. Who would not stand in reverence before this fact? The highest object of all teachings, Buddhist and Confucian included, consists in realizing this fact and obeying in perfect consonance its principles. It has been the power of the dissemina-

[8] Cf. *Book of History* (Hung-fan); Legge, *The Chinese Classics, Shoo-King*, p. 333: "The three virtues: The first is correctness and straightforwardness; the second, strong rule; and the third, mild rule."

tion of the Buddhist and Confucian texts which has spread these principles.[9] It is just the same as the fact that a single mesh of a net suffices to catch a fish, but you cannot catch one unless the net has many meshes. Since the reign of the Emperor Ōjin, the Confucian writings have been disseminated, and since Prince Shōtoku's time Buddhism has flourished in Japan. Both these men were sages incarnate, and it must have been their intention to spread a knowledge of the way of our country, in accordance with the wishes of the Great Sun Goddess. [pp. 20–22]

[9] That is, Buddhist and Confucian texts have helped to spread a knowledge of Shinto because they contain the same essential principles.

CHAPTER XIV

THE VOCABULARY OF
JAPANESE AESTHETICS II

The collapse of the Heian society is all too apparent in the terrible wars that mark the close of the period, in the growth of new religious sects (some of which preached that the world had entered its last, degenerate days), and in the successive disasters which befell the once lovely capital. During much of the period from 1100 to 1600 there was bitter warfare, marked usually by the triumphs of the lower rank of warlord over the higher, a tendency which culminated in the victory of Hideyoshi, a man of extremely humble birth. The wars brought so much destruction and death that it must have seemed at times the whole country would become one huge graveyard. It is small wonder that ghosts so frequently figure in the literature, and that the prevailing tone is one of intense tragedy. *The Tale of the Heike,* written at the beginning of this long period of warfare, opens with the words: "In the sound of the bell of the Gion Temple echoes the impermanence of all things. The pale hue of the flowers of the teak-tree show the truth that they who prosper must fall. The proud ones do not last long, but vanish like a spring night's dream. And the mighty ones too will perish in the end, like dust before the wind."

It might be expected that parallel changes in aesthetic principles would at once have developed, and that the new masters of Japan would have imposed new standards of taste. We find, however, that although changes did occur, they were soon softened by the influence of *miyabi* and the son of an upstart warlord was likely to compose verses on the sadness of the falling cherry blossoms. The third of the Kamakura shoguns prided himself on being an accomplished poet of the traditional school, and exchanged *aware*-laden verses with members of the court.

The new aesthetic standards in literature and art which eventually emerged did not represent any sharp break with the past, but were instead an intensifying and a darkening of the Heian ideals. Fujiwara no

Shunzei (1114–1204) declared, "We should seek to express emotions which our predecessors have not already described, but in so doing retain the language which they used." In other words, he did not advocate a rejection of the means of earlier poets, but rather the use of the old means in the search for new ends. It was the ends involved which characterize the period from the end of the twelfth century to the seventeenth century.

The aesthetic ideals which pervaded the poetry, drama, painting, gardens, tea ceremony, and most other artistic activities during this period were summarized largely in the concept of *yūgen*. *Yūgen* was a word used to describe the profound, remote, and mysterious, those things which cannot easily be grasped or expressed in words. Its closest equivalent in Western terms is probably "symbolism," not the obvious symbolism of a flag standing for a country or a bird in a cage for a captive spirit, but what Poe called "a suggestive indefiniteness of vague and therefore of spiritual effect." To intimate things rather than state them plainly was what Japanese of the medieval period no less than nineteenth-century Europeans were trying to do.

The connection between the ideal of *yūgen* and that of *aware* is obvious, but there was a difference. The Heian poet felt *aware* when he saw wrinkles reflected in the mirror and realized that time was passing by and the years of his youth vanished. But this realization was in a sense the end of the emotion: it did not extend to the dark and mysterious regions of *yūgen*. On the other hand, when a Nō actor slowly raises his hand in a play, it corresponds not only to the text which he is performing, but must also suggest something behind the mere representation, something eternal—in T. S. Eliot's words, a "moment in and out of time." The gesture of the actor is beautiful in itself, as a piece of music is beautiful, but at the same time it is the gateway to something else, the hand that points to a region as profound and remote as the viewer's powers of reception will permit. It is a symbol, not of any one thing, but of an eternal region, of an eternal silence. Again, in T. S. Eliot's words,

> . . . Words, after speech, reach
> Into the silence. Only by the form, the pattern,
> Can words or music reach
> The stillness, as a Chinese jar still
> Moves perpetually in its stillness.[1]

---

[1] Burnt Norton, in *Four Quartets*, p. 7.

To suggest the stillness there must be form or pattern. If that form or pattern is beautiful, it is enough for many people, and they do not feel a need for any deeper meaning. Others might even doubt whether such a thing as silence beyond the form really exists, and whether one can seriously consider anything like *yūgen* which defies definition or description.

Such doubts are not peculiar to our time. A work written in the year 1430 contains these words: "*Yūgen* may be comprehended by the mind, but it cannot be expressed in words. Its quality may be suggested by the sight of a thin cloud veiling the moon or by autumn mist swathing the scarlet leaves on a mountainside. If one is asked where in these sights lies the *yūgen,* one cannot say, and it is not surprising that a man who does not understand this truth is likely to prefer the sight of a perfectly clear, cloudless sky. It is quite impossible to explain wherein lies the interest or the remarkable nature of *yūgen.*" [2]

It may be impossible to explain *yūgen,* but we can intuitively sense it. "It is just as when we look at the sky of an autumn dusk. It has no sound or color, and yet, though we do not understand why, we somehow find ourselves moved to tears." [3] *Yūgen* is the quality of the highest realm of art, an absolute domain to which all forms point. It tends to be expressed in bare and simple terms, as if to keep the mind from dwelling too long on the beauty of the form presented, and thereby to allow it to leap to that realm. There is *yūgen* in the simple perfection of the Chinese jar which "moves perpetually in its stillness," but not in the Dresden figurine. There is *yūgen* in the sound of the Nō flute, which stirs us imprecisely but with an almost painful urgency to an awareness of the existence of something beyond the form, but not in the ravishing melodies of the sextet from *Lucia*. There is *yūgen* in the sight of a tea-master dipping water into a kettle with simple movements that have about them the lines of eternity.

Although *yūgen* may be discovered in many forms of Japanese medieval art, the Nō theatre was the medium which carried it to the highest degree. It was in fact the effect at which the masters of the Nō, and particularly the great Seami (1363–1443), consciously aimed. From what little we know of the Nō before Seami's day it seems clear that it was essentially a representational theatre, with the attempt being made in a

[2] *Shōtetsu Monogatari* in *Zoku gunsho ruijū,* Book 16, p. 929.
[3] *Mumyō Hisho* in *Gunsho ruijū,* Book 13, p. 366.

manner not very different from that employed in the West to portray on the stage the actions of dramatic personages. Seami, however, chose to make of the Nō a symbolic theatre, in which the most important actions were not represented but suggested. The central character in many of his plays is a ghost, someone from a world beyond our own which can only be symbolized. Often this ghost returns in his former appearance in the second part of the play, and during the interval between the first and second parts harsh music and inarticulate cries from the musicians suggest the distance of the world of the dead and the pain of being born. The climax of the play is the final dance which symbolizes and resolves the character's anguish.

Seami wrote that spectators of the Nō sometimes found the moments of "no-action" the most enjoyable, when it was not any gesture of the actor which suggested the eternity beyond gestures, but only the unconsciously revealed spiritual strength of the actor. However, *yūgen* was more normally achieved through the means of beautiful forms, and in deciding what was beautiful Seami was guided by the Heian principle of *miyabi*. He says, for instance, that "the *yūgen* of discourse lies in a grace of language and a complete mastery of the speech of the nobility and the gentry so that even the most casual utterance will be graceful." This is another instance of how it was attempted to achieve *yūgen* by using Heian aesthetic means and not by denying them. But what had stopped at the level of being "charming" or "touching" in the Heian Period became in the medieval period the profoundly moving *yūgen*. It is tempting to speculate that in an age of painful changes and destruction like the Japanese medieval period, the need for eternal incorruptible values might well give rise to such an aesthetic ideal as *yūgen*.

Towards the end of the medieval period another aesthetic ideal, that of *sabi*, joined *yūgen*. *Sabi* was a very old word, found as far back as the *Manyōshū*, where it has the meaning of "to be desolate." It later acquired the meaning of "to grow old" and it is related to the word "to grow rusty." In *The Tale of the Heike* we find it used in the sentence, "It was a place *old* with moss-covered boulders, and he thought it would be pleasant to live there." It seems likely that already by this time (the thirteenth century) *sabi* suggested not only "old" but the taking of pleasure in that which was old, faded, or lonely. To achieve the end of *yūgen*, art had sometimes been stripped of its color and glitter lest these externals distract; a bowl of highly polished silver reflects more than it suggests, but one of oxidized silver has the mysterious beauty of stillness, as Seami realized when he used for stillness the simile of snow piling in a silver bowl. Or one may prize such a bowl for the tarnished quality itself, for its oldness, for its imperfection, and this is the point where we feel *sabi*.

If the Nō is the highest expression of *yūgen*, *sabi* is most profoundly felt in the tea ceremony, and to attend one even today is to get a glimpse of *sabi* at its purest. The tea hut is extremely bare and almost devoid of color. If a flower is arranged in a vase, it is usually a single, small blossom of some quiet hue or white. The tea utensils are not of exquisite porcelain but of coarse pottery, often a dull brown or black and imperfectly formed. The kettle may be a little rusty. Yet from these objects we receive an impression not of gloominess or shabbiness but one of quiet harmony and peace, and watching the ceremony we may experience an intimation of *yūgen*.

The love of imperfection as a measure of perfection in pottery and other forms of art and nature is very old with the Japanese. We find a beautiful statement of it in the *Essays in Idleness* (*Tsuredzure-gusa*) of Yoshida Kenkō (1283–1350) when he asks:

Are we only to look at flowers in full bloom, at the moon when it is clear? Nay, to look out on the rain and long for the moon, to draw the blinds and not to be aware of the passing of the spring—these arouse even deeper feelings. There is much to be seen in young boughs about to flower, in gardens strewn with withered blossom. . . . They must be perverse indeed who will say, "This branch, that bough is withered, now there is nought to see." [4]

The love for the fallen flower, for the moon obscured by the rain, for the withered bough is part of *sabi*. Unlike *yūgen* (to which, however, it is not opposed) *sabi* does not necessarily find in these things symbols of remoter eternities. They are themselves and capable in themselves of giving deep pleasure. *Sabi* also differs from the gentle melancholy of *aware:* here one does not lament for the fallen flower, one loves it. This quality is superbly captured in the *haiku* of Bashō (1644–1694) who, although he lived after the end of the medieval period, was heir to its aesthetic traditions. Many of his *haiku* give expression to a love for old and faded things.

Kiku no ka ya	Scent of chrysanthemums—
Nara ni wa furuki	And in Nara all the many
Hotoketachi	Ancient Buddhas.

[4] Sansom, "Tsuredzure-gusa," p. 85.

In this *haiku,* which unfortunately depends a great deal for its effect on an exquisite choice of words that cannot be approximated in translation, there is suggested the correspondence between impressions of *sabi* received through different senses. The scent of chrysanthemums, astringent and somewhat musty, blends into the visual impression of the statues in the old capital of Nara—dark, with flaking gold leaf and faded colors. The *sabi* quality found alike in the chrysanthemums and the ancient statues may be contrasted with the Heian love for the fragrance of plum blossoms, recalling the memories of past springs, and for richly colored images, or with the common Western preferences for the heavy perfume of the rose and the polish of white marble statues.

In *sabi* art is valued as a refuge, a haven of tranquility, as is not surprising when we read the early history of the tea ceremony, born amidst the terrible warfare of the medieval period. Even when the warfare ceased in the seventeenth century the need for spiritual peace continued to be met largely by the *sabi* aspects of beauty.

Yūgen can probably only be understood by a person of developed aesthetic perceptions who is spiritually capable of seeing beyond symbols to the eternal things adumbrated, but *sabi* has become very much a part of Japanese life. The Japanese, like every other people, love bright colors, but they are unusual in that they also love the old, the faded, and the underdecorated. This is not always understood by foreigners. During the days of the American occupation, for example, Americans who requisitioned Japanese houses often painted the woodwork to "brighten" the subdued harmonies of the buildings, much to the dismay of the Japanese owners. More recently, when the Golden Pavilion was rebuilt in Kyoto, its dazzlingly gilded walls reflected in the temple pond brought delight to many tourists, but the people of Kyoto said, "Wait ten years, wait till it acquires some *sabi.*" This love for the old and unobtrusive may be the best defense the Japanese have against the harsher aspects of mechanization which are otherwise all too apparent today.

SEAMI

On Attaining the Stage of Yūgen

Yūgen is a term which it is difficult either to define or to translate. It primarily means "mystery," and however loosely used in criticism generally retains some-

[282]

thing of the sense of a mysterious power or ability. The term was employed as a standard of criticism long before Seami, but it was only with him that it attained its full meaning as the unifying aesthetic principle underlying all parts of the Nō. In this section of a longer essay he gives some of the ways of attaining *yūgen*. It should be noted, however, that he concludes by insisting that it is not enough for an actor to learn about *yūgen* from others—he must attain it through his own efforts.

[From Nosé, *Seami Jūrokubushū Hyōshaku,* I, 358–66]

Yūgen is considered to be the mark of supreme attainment in all of the arts and accomplishments. In the art of the Nō in particular the manifestation of *yūgen* is of the first importance. In general, a display of *yūgen* in the Nō is apparent to the eye, and it is the one thing which audiences most admire, but actors who possess *yūgen* are few and far between. This is because they do not in fact know the true meaning of *yūgen*. There are thus none who reach that stage.

In what sort of place, then, is the stage of *yūgen* actually to be found? Let us begin by examining the various classes of people on the basis of the appearance that they make in society. May we not say of the courtiers, whose behavior is distinguished and whose appearance far surpasses that of other men, that theirs is the stage of *yūgen?* From this we may see that the essence of *yūgen* lies in a true state of beauty and gentleness. Tranquility and elegance make for *yūgen* in personal appearance. In the same way, the *yūgen* of discourse lies in a grace of language and a complete mastery of the speech of the nobility and gentry, so that even the most casual utterance will be graceful. With respect to a musical performance, it may be said to possess *yūgen* when the melody flows beautifully and sounds smooth and sensitive. In the dance there will be *yūgen* when the discipline has been thoroughly mastered and the audience is delighted by the beauty of the performer's movements and by his serene appearance. In acting, there will be *yūgen* when the performance of the Three Roles is beautiful. If the characterization calls for a display of anger or for the representation of a devil, the actions may be somewhat forceful, but as long as the actor never loses sight of the beauty of the effect and bears in mind always the correct balance between his mental and physical actions and between the movements of his body and feet,[1] his

---

[1] Seami elsewhere discusses the relation between what the actor expresses with his body and what he knows but does not overtly express. At first an actor who has studied with a master does not know any more than what he has learned and what he expresses, but as he

appearance will be so beautiful that it may be called "the *yūgen* of a devil."

All these aspects of *yūgen* must be kept in mind and made a part of the actor's body, so that whatever part he may be playing *yūgen* will never be absent. Whether the character he portrays be of high or low birth, man or woman, priest, peasant, rustic, beggar, or outcast, he should think of each of them as crowned with a wreath of flowers. Although their positions in society differ, the fact that they can all appreciate the beauty of flowers makes flowers of all of them.[2] Their particular flower is shown by their outward appearance. An actor, by the use of his intelligence, makes his presentation seem beautiful. It is through the use of intelligence that the above principles are thoroughly grasped; that poetry is learned so as to impart *yūgen* to his discourse; that the most elegant costuming is studied so as to impart *yūgen* to his bearing: though the characterization varies according to the different parts, the actor should realize that the ability to appear beautiful is the seed of *yūgen*. It is all too apt to happen that an actor, believing that once he has mastered the characterization of the various parts he has attained the highest stage of excellence, forgets his appearances and therefore is unable to enter the realm of *yūgen*. Unless an actor enters the realm of *yūgen* he will not attain the highest achievements. If he fails to attain the highest achievements, he will not become a celebrated master. That is why there are so few masters. The actor must consider *yūgen* as the most important aspect of his art and study to perfect his understanding of it.

The "highest achievement" of which I have spoken refers to beauty of form and manners. The most careful attention must therefore be given to the appearance presented. Accordingly, when we thoroughly examine the principles of *yūgen* we see that when the form is beautiful, whether in dancing, singing, or in any type of characterization, it may properly be called the "highest achievement." When the form is poor, the performance will be inferior. The actor should realize that *yūgen* is attained when all of the different forms of visual or aural expression

---

himself acquires mastery there are things which he comes to understand beyond what he has been taught and which he suggests rather than expresses.

The relation between the movements of the body and feet refers to a principle of Seami's that if the body and feet move in the same manner the effect will be crude. Thus, in an agitated passage if the feet are stamping wildly, the movements of the body should be gentle. Otherwise a disorderly effect will be produced which will mar the enjoyment of the spectators.

[2] That is, their love of beauty makes them beautiful, however humble their station may be.

are beautiful. It is when the actor himself has worked out these principles and made himself their master that he may be said to have entered the realm of *yūgen*. If he fails to work out these principles for himself, he will not master them, and however much he may aspire to attain *yūgen*, he will never in all his life do so.

On the One Mind Linking All Powers

The influence of Zen Buddhism is particularly apparent in the following section. The "mindlessness" which transcends mind, the moments of "no-action" which excite greater interest than those of action, the mind which controls all the powers—all these are familiar ideas of Zen, and show to how great an extent Seami's aesthetic principles relied on the Zen teachings.

[From Nosé, *Seami Jūrokubushū Hyōshaku*, I, 375-79]

Sometimes spectators of the Nō say, "The moments of 'no-action' are the most enjoyable." This is an art which the actor keeps secret. Dancing and singing, movements and the different types of miming are all acts performed by the body. Moments of "no-action" occur in between. When we examine why such moments without actions are enjoyable, we find that it is due to the underlying spiritual strength of the actor which unremittingly holds the attention. He does not relax the tension when the dancing or singing come to an end or at intervals between the dialogue and the different types of miming, but maintains an unwavering inner strength. This feeling of inner strength will faintly reveal itself and bring enjoyment. However, it is undesirable for the actor to permit this inner strength to become obvious to the audience. If it is obvious, it becomes an act, and is no longer "no-action." The actions before and after an interval of "no-action" must be linked by entering the state of mindlessness in which one conceals even from oneself one's intent. This, then, is the faculty of moving audiences, by linking all the artistic powers with one mind.

> Life and death, past and present—
> Marionettes on a toy stage.
> When the strings are broken,
> Behold the broken pieces.[3]

This is a metaphor describing human life as it transmigrates between life and death. Marionettes on a stage appear to move in various ways,

---

[3] Buddhist verse by an unknown Zen master. The last two lines may mean, "When life comes to an end the illusions of this world also break into pieces."

but in fact it is not they who really move—they are manipulated by strings. When these strings are broken, the marionettes fall and are dashed to pieces. In the art of the Nō too, the different sorts of miming are artificial things. What holds the parts together is the mind. This mind must not be disclosed to the audience. If it is seen, it is just as if a marionette's strings were visible. The mind must be made the strings which hold together all the powers of the arts. If this is done the actor's talent will endure. This resolution must not be confined to the times when the actor is appearing on the stage. Day or night, wherever he may be, whatever he may be doing, he should not forget this resolution, but should make it his constant guide, uniting all his powers. If he unremittingly works at this his talent will steadily grow. This article is the most secret of the secret teachings.[4]

The Nine Stages of the Nō in Order

The *Nine Stages* is a summary and systematization of the aesthetic principles of Seami found in his various other writings. It appears to be a late work, and of all his works of aesthetic criticism is the most difficult to understand, partially because of the unexplained technical terms and partially because of its Zen form of expression. As the leading authority on the work, Nosé Asaji, wrote, "In order to understand this work properly one must have had considerable experience with Zen practices and have discovered how to decipher the Zen riddles (kōan). One must also have studied Seami's aesthetic criticism thoroughly. Unless this work is approached with the wisdom gained from both aspects of it, it will not be possible to give any definitive explanation of the text." Nevertheless, thanks mainly to Nosé's work, we can now understand much of what Seami was seeking to express in his deliberately elusive manner.

The influence of Zen teachings is apparent throughout this work. Most of the sentences or phrases used to characterize the different stages of the Nō are taken from poems written by Japanese Zen monks; the use of such symbols itself is a typical Zen device. But the general structure, synthetic character, and much of the terminology of this essay are reminiscent of Tendai and Shingon doctrine.

[From Nosé, *Seami Jūrokubushū Hyōshaku,* I, 547–83]

THE HIGHER THREE STAGES

1. The flower of the miraculous
   "At midnight in Silla the sun is bright." [5]

[4] The tradition of secret teachings transmitted from teacher to student is here indicated.
[5] From a Chinese Zen work also paraphrased in Japan by Musō Kokushi. The reason for mentioning Silla (Korea) here is uncertain, but since Korea is to the east of China it may

The miraculous transcends the power of speech and is where the workings of the mind are defeated. And does "the sun at midnight" lie within
the realm of speech? Thus, in the art of the Nō, before the *yūgen* of a
master-actor all praise fails, admiration transcends the comprehension
of the mind, and all attempts at classification and grading are made
impossible. The art which excites such a reaction on the part of the
audience may be called the flower of the miraculous.

2. The flower of supreme profundity

"Snow covers the thousand mountains—why does one lonely peak
remain unwhitened?"

A man of old once said, "Mount Fuji is so high that the snow never
melts." A Chinese disagreed, saying, "Mount Fuji is so deep. . . ." [6]
What is extremely high is deep. Height has limits but depth is not to
be measured. Thus the profound mystery of a landscape in which a
solitary peak stands unwhitened amidst a thousand snow-covered mountains may represent the art of supreme profundity.

3. The flower of stillness

"Snow piled in a silver bowl."

When snow is piled in a silver bowl, the purity of its white light appears
lambent indeed. May this not represent the flower of stillness?

THE MIDDLE THREE STAGES

1. The flower of truth

"The sun sinks in the bright mist, the myriad mountains are crimson."

A distant view of hills and mountains bathed in the light of the sun
in a cloudless sky represents the flower of truth. It is superior to the art
of versatility and exactness, and is already a first step towards the acquisition of the flowers of the art.

2. The art of versatility and exactness

"To tell everything—of the nature of clouds on the mountains, of
moonlight on the sea."

To describe completely the nature of clouds on the mountains and of
moonlight on the sea, of the whole expanse of green mountains that fills
the eyes, this is indeed desirable in acquiring the art of versatility and

---

signify that the sun is already rising there while it is still night in China—a typical device
in Taoism and Zen to show that nothing is impossible but only appears so due to the limitations in time and place of the individual.

[6] Both the "man of old" and the Chinese are as yet unidentified. The meaning is apparently
that height can be measured, but depth cannot.

exactness. Here is the dividing point from which one may go upward or downward.

3. The art of untutored beauty

"The Way of ways is not the usual way." [7]

One may learn the Way of ways by traveling along the usual way. This means that the display of beauty should begin at the stage of the beginner. Thus the art of untutored beauty is considered the introduction to the mastery of the nine stages.

THE LOWER THREE STAGES

1. The art of strength and delicacy

"The metal hammer flashes as it moves, the glint of the precious sword is cold."

The movement of the metal hammer represents the art of strong action. The cold glint of the precious sword suggests the unadorned style of singing and dancing. It will stand up to detailed observation.

2. The art of strength and crudity

"Three days after its birth the tiger is disposed to devour an ox."

That the tiger cub only three days after its birth has such audacity shows its strength; but to devour an ox is crude.

3. The art of crudity and inexactness

"The squirrel's five talents."

Confucius said,[8] "The squirrel can do five things. He can climb a tree, swim in the water, dig a hole, jump, and run: all of these are within its capacities but it does none well." When art lacks delicacy it becomes crude and inexact.

In the attainment of art through the nine stages, the actor begins with the middle group, follows with the upper group, and finally learns the lower three. When the beginner first enters the art of the Nō, he practices the various elements of dancing and singing. This represents the stage of untutored beauty. As the result of persistent training, his untutored style will develop into greater artistry, constantly improving until, before he is aware of it, it reaches the stage of versatility and exactness. At this stage if the actor's training is comprehensive and he expands his art in versatility and magnitude until he attains full competence, he will be

[7] Paraphrased from the opening of the *Tao Te Ching*, but the meaning given by Seami to the phrase is not the one currently accepted.

[8] Said by Hsün-tzu and not Confucius.

at the stage of the flower of truth. The above are the stages from the learning of the Two Disciplines to the mastery of the Three Roles.

Next the actor progresses to the stage of calm and the flower that arouses admiration. It is the point where it becomes apparent whether or not he has realized the flower of the art. From this height the actor can examine with insight the preceding stages. He occupies a place of high achievement in the art of calm and the realization of the flower. This stage is thus called the flower of stillness.

Rising still higher, the actor achieves the ultimate degree of *yūgen* in his performance, and reveals a degree of artistry which is of that middle ground where being and nonbeing meet.[9] This is the flower of supreme profundity.

Above this stage, words fail before the revelation of the absolute miracle of the actor's interpretation. This is the flower of the miraculous. It is the end of the road to the higher mysteries of the art.

It should be noted that the origin of all these stages of the art may be found in the art of versatility and exactness. It is the foundation of the art of the Nō, for it is the point where are displayed the breadth and detail of performance which are the seeds of the flowers of the highest forms of the art. The stage of versatility and exactness is also the dividing line where is determined the actor's future. If he succeeds here in obtaining the flower of the art he will rise to the flower of truth; otherwise he will sink to the lower three stages.

The lower three stages are the turbulent waters of the Nō. They are easily understood and it is no special problem to learn them. It may happen, however, that an actor who has gone from the middle three stages to the upper three stages, having mastered the art of calmness and the flower of the miraculous, will purposely descend and indulge in the lower three stages.[10] Then the special qualities of these stages will be blended with his art. However, many of the excellent actors of the past who had mounted to the upper three stages of the art refused to descend to the lower three. They were like the elephant of the story who refused to follow in the tracks of a rabbit. There has been only one instance of an actor who mastered all the stages—the middle, then the upper, and

[9] Expression used in Tendai philosophy of a region "which is not being and not nonbeing, and is being and nonbeing."

[10] Suggested by the Mahāyāna doctrine of the bodhisattva who voluntarily leaves the highest rank to go down to save those at the bottom.

then the lower: this was the art of my late father.[11] Many of the heads of theatres have been trained only up to the art of versatility and exactness and, without having risen to the flower of truth, have descended to the lower three stages, thus failing in the end to achieve success. Nowadays there are even actors who begin their training with the lower three stages and perform with such a background. This is not the proper order. It is therefore no wonder that many actors fail even to enter the nine stages.

There are three ways of entering the lower three stages. In the case of a great master who has entered the art by way of the middle stages, ascended to the upper stages of the art, and then descended to the lower stages, it is quite possible to give a superb performance even within the lower stages. Actors who have dropped to the lower stages from the level of versatility and exactness will be capable only of parts which call for strength with delicacy or crudity. Those actors who have wilfully entered the art from the lower three stages have neither art nor fame and cannot be said even to be within the nine stages. Although they have taken the lower three stages as their goal, they fail even in this, to say nothing of reaching the middle three stages.

THE BOOK OF THE WAY OF THE HIGHEST FLOWER (*SHIKADŌ-SHO*)

In this piece Seami, one of the great masters of the Nō drama, sets forth the criteria for consummate mastery in the performance of this art. "Flower" here signifies "beauty" or "perfection," a meaning which derives from the use of the Lotus as a symbol of supreme truth or perfection in Buddhism, especially as represented in the *Lotus* (*Hokke*) and *Flower Wreath* (*Kegon*) *Sūtras*.

Seami was chiefly instrumental in defining and shaping the Nō drama, and his views reflect the synthetic character of the art form which he and his father, Kan'ami, helped to develop. In it elements from earlier dance-drama forms, especially temple and folk dances, were combined to produce an art of the greatest refinement and sophistication. Much of the subtlety and striking simplicity of the Nō manifest the influence of Zen Buddhism, then dominant at the Ashikaga court in Kyoto. But the extreme stylization, precision, and gorgeous costuming of the Nō also reveal the deep and lasting influence of Esoteric Buddhism on Japanese art, though this is today less generally appreciated. The elaborate symbolism, conventionalized movements, and stylized

[11] Kan'ami (1333–1384), the first great master of the Nō.

gestures of the Nō relate it closely to the maṇḍala, that typical expression of the esoteric teaching in the field of painting, which, like the Nō, is so inaccessible to those who are ignorant of the conventions which have surrounded these arts from the beginning. To them Esoteric Buddhism has contributed, not so much the conventions themselves, as the essential concern for proper form in the representation of sacred mysteries and the performance of symbolic acts. Through the exercise of all men's faculties, not just the intellectual, Esoteric Buddhism made the widest use of all the riches of the natural world to enhance the efficacy of its secret formulas and thus achieve the unity of matter and spirit in the perfection of Buddhahood. To accomplish this was a great art, requiring perfect mastery. Seami's conception of mastery in the Nō, his insistence on prolonged training in orthodox disciplines and in imitation of one's teacher, as well as his neat numerical formulations and philosophical categories, all attest to the formative influence of this earlier tradition. Seami served his apprenticeship in Nara, the stronghold of Buddhist catholicism which left its seal on the fundamentals of his art. Only later in the Ashikaga court at Kyoto did he find in Zen the final quickening insight which brought these dramatic elements into sharp focus and raised his mature art to the threshold of perfect ease and freedom.

[From Nosé, *Seami Jūrokubushū Hyōshaku,* I, 435–80]

1. The Two Mediums and the Three Roles

Although there are many different items of training in the art of the Nō, the initial preparation should be confined to the Two Mediums and the Three Roles. By the Two Mediums is meant dancing and singing; the Three Roles refer to the types of people represented. First of all, singing and dancing must be thoroughly studied and practiced under the guidance of a master. While the actor is still a boy, from his tenth to his fifteenth years, he should not study the Three Roles; he should merely perform the singing and dancing of these roles while remaining in a boy's attire. He should not wear a mask. His miming should be nominal, and his appearance in keeping with his age. It is similar to the way in which the dancing-boys perform the Ryō-ō, the Nassori, and other court dances in outline only, wearing no masks, and retaining their youthful appearance. This training as a boy is the root of the flower which will maintain its beauty in all an actor's later performances.

When an actor has been initiated into manhood [12] and has come of age, he wears a mask and changes his appearance according to the role he

---

[12] The *gembuku* ceremony took place when a boy reached the age of fifteen. His personal name was changed and he wore for the first time the hat and clothes of an adult.

assumes. There are many types of impersonation, but the beginner may attain to the highest flower of true art through the Three Roles only. The old man, the woman, the warrior—these are the three. These roles must be thoroughly studied and practiced, and then combined with the various types of singing and dancing which have already been learned. No other training exists in the art of the Nō.

The other forms of miming all derive from the Two Mediums and the Three Roles, and one should wait for ability in them to develop naturally. The noble perfection of the dances of the gods derives from the mastery of the role of the old man; beauty and elegance in the singing and gestures derive from the role of the woman; and vigor in the movements of the body and the feet derives from the role of the warrior. The actor will naturally express in his performance his own conception of the role. If his talents are inadequate and natural mastery does not develop, he may still be considered an actor of the highest flower if he is thoroughly trained in the Two Mediums and the Three Roles. That is why they are known as the measure, essence, and basis of the art of the Nō.

When we examine contemporary methods of training in the Nō, we find that the initial steps are not made on the main road of the Two Mediums and the Three Roles, but instead all kinds of unorthodox fashions of miming are practiced. This results in a lack of mastery, a feebleness of performance and general inferiority—there are thus no actors today who are worthy of the name of "masters."

Having entered the art in a way other than the Two Mediums and the Three Roles, to indulge in fripperies of style constitutes a denatured and peripheral training.

(Author's note: It should be borne in mind that the beauty of an actor's boyhood appearance is preserved in the Three Roles, and the mastery derived from the three roles can impart vividness to every performance.)

2. The lack of mastery

In the art of the Nō a lack of mastery is to be deplored. This matter deserves careful consideration. It seems likely that natural gifts make one a master. May it not be also that natural gifts are developed through an accumulation of experience in this art? Take the case of singing and dancing. As long as an actor is trying to imitate his teacher, he is still without mastery. Even once he has perfected his imitation, until he makes the performance his own it will be lacking in vigor and inadequate: he will still be an actor without mastery. The master-actor is one who has trained himself thoroughly in imitation of his teacher, and having absorbed his art and made it his own, part of his own body and mind, thus achieves effortless proficiency. His performance is then imbued with life. An actor may be said to be a master when, by means of his artistic powers, he quickly perfects the skills he has won through study and practice, and thus becomes one with the art itself. I must insist on the importance of recognizing the demarcation between mastery and lack of mastery. Mencius said, "To do is not difficult; to do well is difficult." [13]

3. The master-actor

In the art of the Nō it sometimes happens that a master-actor who has scaled the topmost heights of the profession and who is aware of his degree of attainment will perform in an unusual manner, which is then copied by beginners. The perfect freedom exercised by the accomplished veteran should not be imitated thoughtlessly. What, I wonder, do beginners think that they are doing when they copy him?

The art of the accomplished veteran lies in the spiritual strength of his interpretations. It may occasionally lead him to demonstrations of the skill which he has attained after having spent the years from youth to old age in intensive training in all aspects of the Nō, and after having gathered to himself all the good techniques and rejected the bad ones. He may then at his stage of perfection mix a little of the bad techniques, which he has hated and rejected during his years of training, with the good ones. Why, it may be wondered, should a master indulge in faulty techniques? The answer is that it is a method of demonstrating his virtuosity. The master-actor by definition has only good techniques. Thus, if, as it may happen, his excellences lose their unusualness and become somewhat stale to the audience, he may occasionally introduce faulty techniques which will be acclaimed for their novelty in a master's performance. In this way, faulty techniques may actually seem good ones to the audience. This is a case where the talents of the master seem to transform faults into merits. It thereby creates an interesting effect. If beginners in the art, finding such techniques an interesting method

[13] This statement is not by Mencius; it is not even in normal Chinese.

of winning applause, believe that they should copy them, their imitations will represent the admixture of essentially faulty techniques with their own immature style; it will be "adding fuel to the flames" of their mediocrity. Imagining that maturity in art is a matter of techniques, they may not realize that it comes from the attainment of mastery. This fact requires careful attention.

The actions which the master performs with full awareness that they are wrong are imitated by the young actors in the delusion that they are right. They thus differ as much as black and white. How can the beginner hope to attain the level of the master-actor without having accumulated experience? When a beginner imitates the mannerisms of the master actor, he is imitating faults, which make him all the worse an actor, do they not? Mencius said, "To do what you do to seek for what you desire is like climbing a tree to seek for fish." [14] He adds, by way of comment, "If you climb a tree to seek for fish, it is merely stupid, and does you no harm. But to do what you do to seek for what you desire assuredly does you harm." The fact that faults of technique in the hands of the veteran master-actor may actually become merits shows that artistic achievements may be obtained by a master-actor, but this does not lie within the competence of an unskilled performer. Thus, if with the limited powers at his disposal, he seeks to emulate the inimitable feats of the master-actor, there is certain to be harm done. It is like "doing what you do to seek for what you desire." As long as the beginner confines his imitations to consummate performances of the correct techniques, however inadequate he may be there is not likely to be much harm done. It is like "climbing a tree to seek for fish." I repeat: the beginner must not imitate the eccentricities and mannerisms of the master-actor's performance. To do so invites mishaps.

Beginners should remain close to their master, ask his advice on their problems, and find out everything they can about their art. Even when they witness examples of the kind of unusual performance I have described they should direct their efforts towards the mastery of the Two Mediums and the Three Roles. The *Lotus Sūtra* states, "Be wary of those who consider entlightenment yet to come as enlightenment attained, and

[14] Legge, *The Chinese Classics, Mencius* IA:7. The passage concerns the use of improper means to achieve an end, aspiring to greatness without first qualifying for it through personal cultivation.

mystic insight yet to be achieved as mystic insight won." Bear this in mind.

4. The skin, flesh, and bones

The art of the Nō has its skin, flesh, and bones, but the three are never found together. In calligraphy as well they say that the three have never been found together except in Kūkai's writing. The skin, flesh, and bones of the Nō may thus be identified: the display in this art of the special powers which have enabled one to become a master-actor naturally, by virtue of inborn abilities, may be designated the bones; the display of the perfect powers which have come from study and experience of dancing and singing may be called flesh; and an appearance which exhibits these qualities at their highest pitch, with perfect gentleness and beauty, may be termed the skin. If these three aspects are equated with the senses, seeing may be called the skin, hearing the flesh, and feeling the bones. Moreover, the three aspects may be found in singing alone or dancing alone. (In singing the voice is the skin, the style the flesh, and the breathing the bones; in dancing, the appearance is the skin, the movements the flesh, and the expression the bones.) These distinctions should be noted carefully.

When I look over the contemporary Nō performers, not only do I fail to find anyone who possesses these three aspects of the art, but there is not a single person who even realizes that such things exist. I myself learned of them through the secret teachings of my late father. The contemporary performers whom I have seen limit themselves to a feeble representation of just the skin, and even that is not the real skin. Again, the fact that they imitate only the skin proves that they are actors without mastery.

Even if an actor happens to possess all three qualities, there is another point to be borne in mind: he may have natural gifts (the bones), consummate attainments in dancing and singing (the flesh), and personal beauty (the skin), but it may be that he merely *possesses* the three. He still cannot be said to be an actor with full control of them. To say of an actor that he has attained full control of the three qualities means that he has developed to their limits all of his inborn talents, and being already in the highest rank, reaches to effortless and ineffable performance. His performances on the stage will offer pure enjoyment, and the audience will lose itself in the wonder of his art. Only on careful reflection after the performance will the audience appreciate its flawlessness; this is the feeling aroused by accomplishment in the art of the bones. The audience will then also be aware of the actor's inexhaustible wealth of skill: this is the feeling aroused by accomplishment in the art of the flesh. And it will realize that, in whatever way it might be considered, the performance was of perfect beauty: this is the feeling aroused by accomplishment in the art of the skin. In view of the effect that he has produced on the audience, the actor may then be known as a master in full control of the skin, flesh, and bones.

5. Essence and performance [15]

We must distinguish in the art of the Nō between essence and performance. If the essence is a flower, the performance is its fragrance. Or they may be compared to the moon and the light which it sheds. When the essence has been thoroughly understood, the performance develops of itself.

Among those who witness Nō plays, the connoisseurs see with their minds, while the untutored see with their eyes. What the mind sees is the essence; what the eyes see is the performance. That is why beginners, seeing only the performance, imitate it. They imitate without knowing the principles behind the performance. There are, however, reasons why the performance should not be imitated. Those who understand the Nō see it with their mind and therefore imitate its essence. When the essence is well imitated, the performance follows of itself. The untutored, believing that the performance is the thing to follow, imitate it; they show themselves unaware of the fact that the performance when imitated becomes an essence as well.[16] Since, however, it is not the true essence, both the essence and the performance are doomed eventually to perish, and the style which they are imitating will cease to exist. It will then be Nō without direction and without purpose.

When we speak of the essence and the performance, they are two. Without the essence, however, there cannot be any performance. There is no such thing as performance by itself, and it thus does not deserve to

[15] By essence is here meant the inner understanding of the Nō, the true accomplishment of the actor; the performance is the actual manifestation on the stage of his qualities.

[16] That is, sets up within the actor a basic misconception of the art.

be imitated. If, however, it is considered to exist and is copied, does it not become a false essence? The connoisseur realizes that the performance lies in the essence and not apart from it, and that there is no reason to imitate it. Such a person understands the Nō.

Since there is no reason to imitate the performance, it must not be imitated. It should be realized that to imitate the essence is in fact to imitate the performance. I repeat: he who bears in mind the fact that to imitate the performance is to create a false essence may be termed an actor who has distinguished between essence and performance. It has been said, "What one should desire to imitate is skillfulness; what one should not imitate is skillfulness."[17] To imitate is performance, to have achieved resemblance is essence.

These items of training in the Nō, some simple and some profound, were not very much considered in the past. A very few of the actors of the old style were able by their innate talents to attain the heights of the art. In those days, the criticism made by the courtiers consisted entirely of praise for the excellences which they observed; they did not criticize the faults. At present, however, their powers of observation have greatly developed, and they have come to criticize the most trifling faults. Thus, unless performances are as polished jade or chosen flowers, they will not meet with the approval of the patrons on high. That is why there are few masters of this art. The Nō is steadily declining as an art, and if training in it is neglected, it may well perish. With this in mind I have recorded in outline my convictions about the Nō. The rest of the instruction will depend on the degree of talent of the inquirer, and must be privately transmitted in person.

Ōei 27 [1420] Sixth Month   [*signed*] Seami

[17] One should supply the words "of essence" and "of performance" to complete the meaning of each part of this curious statement.

THE TOKUGAWA PEACE

In the Tokugawa Period (1603–1868), which followed the military re-unification of the country in the late sixteenth century, modern Japan began to take definite shape. It is for this reason that many historians have been tempted to identify the beginning of the modern era in Japan with the founding of the Tokugawa regime. True, there is some in-congruity in calling "modern" a period which saw the perpetuation of a feudal system and military government inherited from medieval times; and a question might also be raised, with respect to the drastic changes made after Japan's opening to the West, as to why, by that time, she should still have been so much in need of modernization. Yet we should have even more difficulty explaining Japan's success in undertaking such a vigorous reorganization of her national life and assuming a very active role in the modern world, if during the preceding centuries Japan had not already been traveling, though perhaps somewhat more slowly, in the direction of her subsequent rapid progress. And among the changes in Japanese society which helped to prepare her for this role, we may point to several significant trends in thought which were already well established in the Tokugawa Period.

The first of these is a marked shift in attention from religious ques-tions—from the Buddhist search for release from the bonds of this world —to more mundane problems. This is not to suggest that Buddhism suddenly went into eclipse or that its light ceased to shine among the Japanese people as a whole, but rather that there was an almost im-mediate response in the intellectual world to the need felt by the Toku-gawa shoguns for a secular ideology that would buttress their own rule. What they sought was less peace of mind than the peace of the nation, and it was natural that they should turn to Confucianism for this, since it was par excellence the philosophy which devoted itself to the problem of achieving social peace and order. Consequently the new "this-worldliness" of the Tokugawa era did not directly concern the

[298]

material or physical world so much as the world of social ethics, and it was in this domain that the Neo-Confucianism adopted from China had its greatest impact. At the same time, however, from the Neo-Confucianism which the Tokugawa officially endorsed flowed other streams that nourished and invigorated Japanese thought in the seventeenth and eighteenth centuries.

As compared to Buddhism's emphasis on the evanescence of this world, Neo-Confucianism stressed its substantiality, orderliness, and intelligibility. In the minds of a significant few among Tokugawa thinkers this attitude helped eventually to foster a new interest in the study of nature. More directly, however, it expressed itself in the typical Confucian concern for the study of human history as revealing the constant laws of human behavior and political morality. As applied to Japan this study took forms for which there was no precedent in China's experience: first, it focused attention on the question of legitimate imperial rule and the unbroken succession of the reigning house, which ultimately enkindled a new loyalty to the Throne and prepared the way for an imperial restoration; second, it inspired a new study of native religious traditions which contributed to the revival of Shinto. In time both of these trends fused in an intense nationalism, which consciously rejected Chinese influence while yet incorporating essential elements from the great residue of Confucian moral indoctrination. Perhaps the most striking example of this is the development of *Bushidō,* the "way of the warrior," which joined Japanese feudal traditions with Confucian ethics and placed them at the service of the emperor.

If Confucian historicism thus inadvertently reinforced a growing sense of nationalism, Confucian rationalism, along with some exposure to Western science through the Dutch at Nagasaki and no doubt a certain measure of native realism, helped to keep that nationalism from developing a total blindness to Japan's own weaknesses. We are speaking here of a much less pervasive force in the nation's life—indeed, one which affected only a few exceptional individuals in the educated class. Nonetheless it was from this same limited class that the leadership came for Japan's eventual modernization, and we cannot help but be struck by the fact that the samurai, whose qualifications to rule had once been strictly martial, by the end of the Tokugawa Period had developed in some of its members a competence in other fields of leadership, intellectual

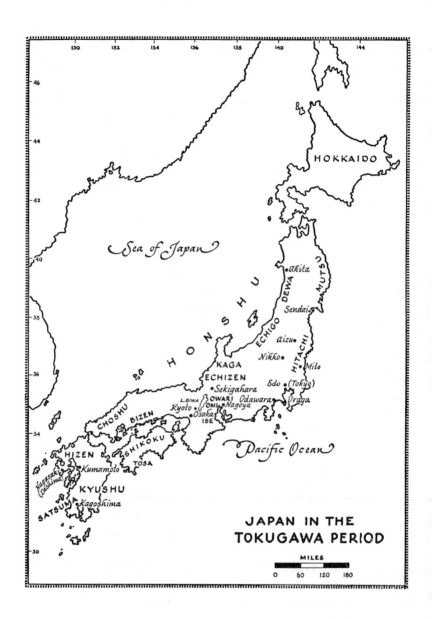

Sea of Japan

HOKKAIDO

HONSHU

Akita

DEWA

MUTSU

Sendai

ECHIGO

Aizu

KAGA

Nikko

HITACHI

Mito

ECHIZEN

Sekigahara

Edo (Tokyo)

OWARI

Odawara

L.BIWA

OMI

Nagoya

Uraga

Kyoto

Osaka

CHOSHU

BIZEN

ISE

Pacific Ocean

SHIKOKU

HIZEN

TOSA

Nagasaki

Kumamoto

(Deshima)

KYUSHU

SATSUMA

Kagoshima

JAPAN IN THE
TOKUGAWA PERIOD

MILES

0   60   120   180

as well as political. The example of Yoshida Shōin, a great hero of the Restoration movement who combined fanatic nationalism, Confucian moral discipline, and an intense awareness of the need to learn from the West, is exceptional. Still, there were other educated Japanese before Yoshida, and these for the most part samurai, who were already grappling with some of the most challenging problems of their own society, economic ones especially, and some questions which only became acute when Japan's doors were forcibly opened. Even when these individual thinkers had no direct influence on their own age, they gave evidence that despite the backwardness of the shogunate itself and the Tokugawa attempt to exact a rigid conformity of thought in the interests of their own security, other forces were at work which would better prepare Japan to take her place in the new world.

CHAPTER XV

HEROES AND HERO WORSHIP

The medieval period in Japan, from the twelfth to the sixteenth centuries, was one of incessant change which nevertheless served to quicken the economic, social, and religious life of the people. It was only in the political sphere that the powerful centrifugal tendencies of feudal society seemed for long to permit no regrouping of forces which might conform to a more orderly pattern of development. Yet it was precisely during the worst period of disorder, in the first half of the sixteenth century that the centrifuge of war separated out, from over sixty more or less independent domains, a few powerful feudal houses which were to provide the leadership for a new era in Japanese history. Out of the elimination contest among them issued forth three great generals, Nobunaga, Hideyoshi, and Ieyasu, and through their efforts Japan emerged suddenly united. While they left till a much later time the destruction of feudalism itself and the establishment of a modern state, nevertheless these titanic figures did succeed in bringing Japan to the threshhold of a new era, as remarkable for its stability as the old one had been for its turbulence. And in this process the intellectual life of the country underwent an equally striking transformation, step by step with political changes, from the dominance of Buddhist institutions and ideals to that of a new Confucian rationalism concerned with the problems of this changed society.

ODA NOBUNAGA

Significantly, one big step in this process of political unification was the destruction of the power of the chief strongholds of Buddhism. This was the work of Oda Nobunaga (1534–1582), who did not live to receive the submission of his secular rivals, but did succeed in eliminating from contention the religious communities which had for centuries played a questionable and sometimes crucial role in the unending struggle for power over the Kyoto court. Nobunaga, who thus humbled such a mighty —and seemingly indestructible—bastion of Buddhist tradition as Mt. Hiei, was himself of a rather obscure family, a typical product of the upheavals which Japanese historians described, in language taken from the Book of Changes, as *ge-koku-jō,* "the overturning of those on top by those below." His ambition, which he narrowly failed to achieve, was "to bring the whole country under one sword" (*tenka-fubu*), a motto inscribed on his personal seal. His qualifications for this stupendous task were somewhat paradoxical: a singleminded, ruthless determination to attain his ends, coupled with an amazing flexibility and open-mindedness as to means. His rise to power, though swift, was by no means direct, and a man less stubborn and resourceful than he could not have recovered from the many setbacks he experienced, nor would he have persisted so tenaciously in prosecuting long, grueling campaigns which almost exhausted human endurance and ingenuity. Nobunaga had schooled himself in self-reliance, alertness, and adaptability, and he looked for these qualities in his men, prizing those who could act without orders and granting them the utmost freedom of action. In this respect it may be noteworthy that the only Buddhist teaching for which he seems to have had any use was that of Zen, which likewise emphasizes these qualities. But beyond this Nobunaga was also a master of the art of treachery, and did not hesitate to use the most deceitful stratagems when fair means failed. Moreover, he had a long memory for old injuries and his vindictiveness led him to exact the most cruel punishments from those with whom he had a score to settle—as for instance a man who had once taken a pot-shot at him and who, when caught many years later in religious seclusion, had had his head sawed off at the neck while his body was planted in the ground; or for another instance, the monastic inmates of Mt. Hiei, every one of whom he took elaborate steps to capture and slaughter, irrespective of age or guilt, just to show the world how awful his vengeance could be.

The fact is, however, that Nobunaga was almost as hard on his friends as his enemies. His preoccupation with his own plans, his impatience with whatever did not seem to contribute to their advancement, and sometimes also the depth of his inmost feelings, made him appear wayward and heedless of ordinary conventions. He appeared at his father's funeral in a dishevelled condition and was criticized for the disrespectful manner in which he tossed at his parent's corpse the incense which he should have burned in homage. Eventually his eccentric behavior, upon which the remonstrances of his aged tutor failed to have any effect, forced this faithful retainer to commit suicide as the only means of bringing Nobunaga to his senses.

Yet his hostility to established tradition and convention left Nobunaga receptive to much that was strange and new, as well as quick to turn recent developments to his own advantage, so that his name became associated with several innovations of lasting significance in Japanese history. Thus his cordiality toward the Christian missionaries newly arrived in Japan seems to have been inspired fundamentally by a desire to learn, but perversely also by his antipathy for traditional Buddhism. In any case his obvious admiration for the high intelligence and nobility of these intrepid Jesuits, as well as his generous treatment of them, won for Nobunaga the distinction of being the first great Japanese leader for whom Western accounts of Japan were to become important biographical sources. He became identified, moreover, with the development of another importation from the Portuguese in the sixteenth century—firearms. Not only was he quick to train himself in the offensive uses of those weapons, but he also took the lead in working out a solution to the defensive problems they presented: the massive castle of the type he built at Azuchi, with its extensive moats and high stone ramparts, which served as a model for the monumental fortifications erected by Hideyoshi at Osaka and Ieyasu at Edo (Tokyo). The protection afforded by this type of virtually impregnable fortress also served to attract those interested in trade, an increasingly important element in the economy of the country and of great potential benefit to the financing of Nobunaga's ambitious schemes. In his indecisive siege of Osaka we find the same historical forces juxtaposed: his recognition of the vital importance of seaports and control of the Inland Sea route; his bull-headed attempt to crush the religious communities controlling these commercial centers, such as the Ikkō followers of the Pure Land Sect in Osaka; and his use of iron-clad ships, for the first time in Japanese history, to blockade the port and cut its lines of communication and supply with its allies in Western Japan.

There is reason to think that he had a keen awareness of the vistas opened up by Japanese overseas trade, and that he hoped, once national unity had been achieved, to exploit Japan's growing maritime power for the launching of military expeditions on the Asiatic mainland. It remained, however, for his successor, Hideyoshi, to act on this ambitious plan. Before final unity had been won, Nobunaga died in the prime of life at the hands of one of his own generals—a fitting recompense, as the Buddhists pointed out, for one who had risen to power through violence and treachery.

The Burning of Enryaku Temple and the Slaughter of Monks and Inmates

Perhaps no other incident in the life of Nobunaga reveals more vividly than does the burning of the Tendai monastery on Mt. Hiei his ruthless determination to crush any power in his way, secular or religious. In this account by an early biographer, condensing a longer contemporaneous account, Nobunaga justifies his destruction of this venerable center of Japanese Buddhism, with its 3,000 buildings and 20,000 inmates, as necessary to the maintenance of law and order in the country. It is not a vindictive desire to avenge himself on the monks, but—he protests—a selfless devotion to the cause of unification which motivates him.

[From *Hoan Nobunaga-ki,* Ch. 4 in *Dai-Nihon Shiryō,* Part 10, Vol. 6, pp. 871–74]

On September 11, the second year of *Genki* [1571], Nobunaga encamped at Gyokurin-sai's place in Seta, and . . . he ordered his principal retainers to set fire to and to destroy all temples, halls, and quarters on Mount Hiei and to annihilate all monks and inmates. Devoid of compassion, he relentlessly commanded his men to hasten with the destruction. Although vassals close to him, alarmed and confounded, remonstrated with him not to go ahead with the order, Nobunaga's indignation increased and he could not be restrained. Thus, all helplessly acceded to his order. Then one [Sakuma] Nobumori and a lay-bonze Takei [Sekian] of Higo came forward with an offer to remonstrate with Nobunaga. They told him that this mountain center, since its founding during the *Enryaku* Era [782–805] by the joint efforts of the fiftieth Emperor Kammu and Dengyō Daishi,[1] had been the guardian of the imperial palace for 800 years, and that its complaints to the Throne—even the most audacious—had not

[1] Saichō, founder of the Tendai Sect.

gone unheeded. "Although it is said that ours is a degenerate age," they continued, "such an act as the destruction of the center is an unprecedented, unheard-of act." In the face of this strong remonstrance Nobunaga explained that he was not entirely insensitive to the warning, but he requested that they listen calmly to what he had to say. He said, "I am not the destroyer of this monastery. The destroyer of the monastery is the monastery itself. As you know I am one who has not known a moment of peace. I have risked my life. I have devoted myself to hard work and to a life of denial of my personal desires. I have given myself to the hardships of warrior life in order that I might restrain the turbulence within the land, check the decline of imperial prestige and restore it, improve the prevailing manners and customs, and perpetuate the benefits of government and religion. But last year, when Noda and Fukushima of Settsu Province were about to be subdued and their strongholds about to fall, Asakura and Asai seized the opportunity of my absence to invade Shiga in this province at the head of several tens of thousands of mounted troops. Thus, I was compelled to return here and to expel them from Sakamoto. The following day I drove the rebels to the hilltop of Tsubogusa. The deep snows retarded their flight and they were about to be slain by our men when the monastic inmates of Mt. Hiei came to their assistance. You were sent to dissuade and to reason with the monks, but they would not listen. Whereupon, I sent another envoy —Inaba—to inform them that if they persisted in their decision, all buildings without exception, including the central cathedral and the Shrine of the Mountain King,[2] would be burned and destroyed, and all inmates—clergy and otherwise—would be decapitated. Still they would not yield. I do not speak falsehoods. It is they who obstruct the maintenance of law and order in the country. Those who would help rebels are themselves traitors to the country. If, moreover, they are not destroyed now, they will again become a peril to the nation. Therefore not a single life should be spared." So convincing was his reasoning that even Sekian, the lay-bonze, succumbed to his arguments without a word of protest.

Thereupon, one Ikeda Katsusaburō offered a suggestion, saying, "The day is drawing to a close and the rebels will withdraw and disperse, and their numbers will diminish. Thus, if we encircle them under cover of

---

[2] Mountain King, a Shintō deity, whom Dengyō Daishi found enshrined on Mt. Hiei. He chose the Mountain King as the guardian deity of his Tendai headquarters.

darkness and launch the attack at the crowing of the cock tomorrow, not a single soul will escape." Nobunaga agreed. Thus, the attack was not carried out during the day; but in the dead of night his men completely encircled the broad expanse of Mt. Hiei, leaving no room for escape. Then when horns were sounded as a signal for the attack, the men launched the assault from all sides with a fierce battle cry. Although the troops of the monastery contested every inch of the hill, they were not equal to the occasion. Everything, everywhere, from the central cathedral to the twenty-one shrines of the Mountain King, the bell tower and the library, were burned to the ground. Moreover, the holy scriptures—both esoteric and exoteric—and the records of the imperial capital under generations of emperors were destroyed at once. Great scholars, men of rare talents, aged priests and young boys—still with their innocent, delicate features—were either beheaded or taken captive. Some pleaded innocence, claiming that they held no enmity; but they were told merely to cease their pretense and their connivance. Some begged to be spared while others remained steadfast in their faith, saying, "As the world, after the lapse of 500 years, has entered upon the period of the Latter Degenerate Days of the Law,[3] there can be no hope for the future. If we burn together with the icons and the images of the Mountain King, the Great Founder [Dengyō Daishi], and the Buddhas and Bodhisattvas, it may create for us the merit of attaining Buddhahood. Let us concentrate our attention on the Moon of Perfect Enlightenment, and chastise our hearts in the water that flows from the hillside of Shimei.[4] Scalding water and charcoal fire are no worse than the cooling breeze." So saying they threw themselves into the raging flames, and not a few were thus consumed by the flames. The roar of the huge burning monastery, magnified by the cries of countless numbers of the old and the young, sounded and resounded to the ends of heaven and earth. The noise was at once deafening and pathetic. A historian has said: "The fall of the Six Kingdoms was the work of the Six Kingdoms and not the work of the Ch'in. The destruction of the Ch'in was the work of the Ch'in and not the work of the nation." Thus, it may be said that the destruction of the mountain center was its own doing and not that of Nobunaga.

[3] A period foretold by Buddha in which his teaching would decline and perish.
[4] Shimei—symbolic name of Mt. Hiei deriving from the Ssu-ming mountains of China where the original headquarters of the Tendai Sect was located.

The Reverend Sakugen of West Kyoto wrote in sorrow over the development:

> In all buildings, great and small, on Mount Hiei
> The Law has been in decline;
> What a pity that the Three Calamities of fire, sword, and death
> Have sent their fumes to heaven.
> Even the waters of the lake [5] that wash the twenty-four provinces
> Have grown hot,
> And the ashes and the embers of three thousand sanctuaries
> Are turning cold.
> Though the imperial solicitude, like the sun and the moon,
> Stood high in a pagoda,
> And the Shrine of the Mountain King
> Has stood long in history,
> The gray-haired deity [6] has resided there
> Who has been witness of the sea
> Which seven times has turned to land.

The Introduction of Firearms
(As described by Nampo Bunshi in the *Teppō-ki* for Lord Tanegashima Hisatoki)

Sixty years after the introduction of the Portuguese arquebus to Japan, this account was written for a descendant of the local lord of Tanegashima, an island off the southern tip of Japan which was the site of this historic incident. In the intervening years the use of firearms spread so rapidly that it became a large factor in the campaign of unification prosecuted by Nobunaga and Hideyoshi, threatening to revolutionize battle tactics and the construction of defense works (including castles). A delightful feature of this account is the purported attempt of the Japanese involved to interpret the nature and uses of firearms in terms of traditional Oriental philosophy.
[Okamoto, *Jūroku seiki Nichi-Ō kōtsū-shi no kenkyū*, pp. 187–89]

To the south of Ōsumi [Province] 18 *ri* off the shore, there is an island called Tanegashima. My forbears had lived there for generations. Ac-

---

[5] Biwa, largest lake in Japan, located at the foot of Mt. Hiei.

[6] Reference is to Shiragi Myōjin, the deity enshrined at Onjō-ji on the shores of Lake Biwa. Onjō-ji, a rival of Enryaku-ji, had been attacked and burned several times by the monks of Enryaku-ji; thus the allusion to the "sea which seven times has turned to land," i.e., the sea, in reflecting the burning of Onjō-ji, looked like land.

cording to an ancient legend, the name Tane is derived from the fact that despite the smallness of the island, the number of inhabitants has continued to grow and to prosper, like a seed planted in season. During the Temmon Era [1532–1554], on the 25th of the eighth month of the year of the Water and the Hare [1543], there appeared off our western shore a big ship. No one knew whence it had come. It carried a crew of over a hundred whose physical features differed from ours, and whose language was unintelligible, causing all who saw them to regard them suspiciously. Among them was a Chinese scholar of whose family or given name no one was certain, but whose pen name was Goho. There was at the time a man called Oribe, the chieftain of a village on the west coast, who was quite well-versed in Chinese. Thus, upon meeting Goho he conversed with him by writing Chinese words on the sand with his cane. He wrote: "Those passengers on the ship—of what country are they? Why do they appear so different?" Goho wrote in answer: "They are traders from among the south-western barbarians. They know something of the etiquette of monarchs and ministers, but they do not know that polite attitudes are part of etiquette. Thus, when they drink, they do not exchange cups. When they eat they use their hands, not chopsticks. They know how to gratify their appetites but they cannot state their reasons in writing. These traders visit the same places in the hope of exchanging what they have for what they do not have. There is nothing suspicious about them."

Then Oribe wrote: "About 13 *ri* from here there is a seaport called Akaogi where the family to whom I owe allegiance has lived for generations. The population of the seaport is several tens of thousands of households. The people are rich and prosperous, and merchants from the south and traders from the north come and go continuously. Now this ship is anchored here, but it is far better there as the port is deep and calm." When the report of the foreign ship was made to my grandfather and to my aged father, the latter sent several tens of junks to fetch the ship at Akaogi, where it arrived on the 27th.

At that time there lived at the port a certain Zen student of senior grade who had once been a disciple of Ryōgen of Hyūga. Desirous of attending the lectures on the Lotus Gospel of Universal Enlightenment, he remained in the port, and, in the end, he became a convert to the

[309]

Lotus Sect at a monastery called Jūjō-in. Well-versed in the scriptures and the classics, he was capable of writing fast and intelligently. He met Goho with whom he carried on conversation through the written word. Goho regarded him as a true friend in an alien land—a case of like attracting like. [He reported:]

"There are two leaders among the traders, the one called Murashusa, and the other Christian Mota. In their hands they carried something two or three feet long, straight on the outside with a passage inside, and made of a heavy substance. The inner passage runs through it although it is closed at the end. At its side there is an aperture which is the passageway for fire. Its shape defies comparison with anything I know. To use it, fill it with powder and small lead pellets. Set up a small white target on a bank. Grip the object in your hand, compose your body, and closing one eye, apply fire to the aperture. Then the pellet hits the target squarely. The explosion is like lightning and the report like thunder. Bystanders must cover their ears. . . . This thing with one blow can smash a mountain of silver and a wall of iron. If one sought to do mischief in another man's domain and he was touched by it, he would lose his life instantly. Needless to say this is also true for the deer and stag that ravage the plants in the fields."

Lord Tokitaka saw it and thought it was the wonder of wonders. He did not know its name at first nor the details of its use. Then someone called it "iron-arms," although it was not known whether the Chinese called it so, or whether it was so called only on our island. Thus, one day, Tokitaka spoke to the two alien leaders through an interpreter: "Incapable though I am, I should like to learn about it." Whereupon, the chiefs answered, also through an interpreter: "If you wish to learn about it, we shall teach you its mysteries." Tokitaka then asked, "What is its secret?" The chief replied: "The secret is to put your mind aright and close one eye." Tokitaka said: "The ancient sages have often taught how to set one's mind aright, and I have learned something of it. If the mind is not set aright, there will be no logic for what we say or do. Thus, I understand what you say about setting our minds aright. However, will it not impair our vision for objects at a distance if we close an eye? Why should we close an eye?" To which the chiefs replied: "That is because concentration is important in everything. When one concentrates, a broad vision is not necessary. To close an eye is not to dim one's eyesight but rather to project one's concentration farther. You should know this." Delighted, Tokitaka said: "That corresponds to what Lao Tzu has said, 'Good sight means seeing what is very small.' "[1]

That year the festival day of the Ninth Month fell on the day of the Metal and the Boar. Thus, one fine morning the weapon was filled with powder and lead pellets, a target was set up more than a hundred paces away, and fire was applied to the weapon. At first the people were astonished; then they became frightened. But in the end they all said in unison: "We should like to learn!" Disregarding the high price of the arms, Tokitaka purchased from the aliens two pieces of the firearms for his family treasure. As for the art of grinding, sifting, and mixing of the powder, Tokitaka let his retainer, Shinokawa Shōshirō, learn it. Tokitaka occupied himself, morning and night, and without rest in handling the arms. As a result, he was able to convert the misses of his early experiments into hits—a hundred hits in a hundred attempts. . . .

So interested was Tokitaka in the weapon that he had a number of iron-workers examine and study it for months and from season to season in order to manufacture some. His product resembled the foreign weapon in outward appearance, but he did not know how to close the end of the barrel. The following year foreign traders came again to a bay in Kumano, one of our islands. . . . Fortunately, there was among the traders an iron-worker whom Tokitaka regarded as a godsend. He ordered the Commandant Kimbei Kiyosada to learn from the iron-worker how to close the end of the barrel. He learned that there was a spring within the barrel, which discovery led to the production of several tens of firearms in a period of a little more than a year. Then the wooden stock and the ornament resembling a key were manufactured. Tokitaka's interest lay not in the stock or the ornament but in their use in warfare. Thus, his retainers, far and near, all practiced the use of the new arms with the result that soon there were many who could score a hundred hits in a hundred attempts. Later, a man named Tachibana-ya Matasaburō, a merchant, who stayed on our island for one or two years, learned the art of the firearm. He became quite skilled in it, and upon his return home everyone called him, not by his name, but as Teppō-mata.[2] Following this the provinces in the Inner Circuit learned the art, and in time

[1] Lao Tzu (Tao te ching), LII.   [2] Teppō means "firearm."

not only the Inner Circuit but also the provinces in the West as well as those in the East learned the art. . . .

It is more than sixty years since the introduction of this weapon into our country. There are some gray-haired men who still remember the event clearly. The fact is that Tokitaka procured two pieces of the weapon and studied them, and with one volley of the weapon startled sixty provinces of our country. Moreover, it was he who made the iron-workers learn the method of their manufacture and made it possible for that knowledge to spread over the entire length and breadth of the country.

The ancients have said that if the achievements of our forbears are obscure, the fault lies with posterity; so, here is the record.

TOYOTOMI HIDEYOSHI

The greatest success story in Japanese history is probably that of Hideyoshi (1536–1598), a peasant boy who first came into Nobunaga's service as a menial, and who, eight years after the latter's death in 1582, became the undisputed master of all Japan. This burly, big-hearted son of the soil had started life without even a family name, and the names he subsequently adopted indicate the successive steps in his rise from obscurity to unprecedented power. Under Nobunaga he was known first as Kinoshita, "under-the-shade-of-a-tree," suggesting his original homeless condition. Next he put together the names of two of Nobunaga's lieutenants whom he desired to emulate and got Hashiba. After Nobunaga's death his ambition to become shogun found expression in the choice of Taira, a family name appropriate to one who hoped to succeed the Ashikaga shoguns of Minamoto descent. Failing in this, he aspired to and won the premiership, adopting the name of the Fujiwara family which had monopolized this post for centuries. Finally, at the peak of his power he took for himself the title, Taikō (His Highness, lit. "Great Palace"), and a new family name, Toyotomi, "abundant provider." This latter desire to be identified with wealth and largesse, rather than with military might, was confirmed by the posthumous title with which he was enshrined, Hōkoku, "Wealth of the Nation," and also by the song sung at his shrine in Kyōto:

Shihyaku yoshū o	Who's that
Ryōte ni nigiri	Holding over four hundred provinces
Cha-no-yu asobasu hito wa	In the palm of his hand
Tare?	And entertaining at a tea-party?
Taikō san	It's His Highness
Do erai go-itoku	So mighty, so impressive!

Hideyoshi had all the ambition of Nobunaga, but with it a reputation for magnanimity which contributed as much to the achievement of his aims as sheer power. He could use the arts of persuasion and compromise —as when he achieved a settlement with religious communities which had been at odds with and were left unsubdued by Nobunaga—or he could apply overwhelming force with unremitting pressure, as when he besieged his last remaining enemy in the north, the Hōjō at Odawara, for four months with a force of 200,000 men. Yet unlike Nobunaga he dealt generously even with those he had defeated in battle and did not seek their utter extermination.

This characteristic of Hideyoshi's is in keeping with the kind of unity he sought to achieve for Japan: cooperative endeavor by all the feudal houses of the land under his personal leadership. At this crucial juncture in the nation's history Hideyoshi did not contemplate the employment of his unprecedented military power for the achievement of a more thoroughgoing national unification, involving drastic political reforms. Economic forces, such as the growth of commerce and manufacturing, the spread of a money economy, and the extension of overseas enterprises were impelling sixteenth-century Japan along the same path as the rising nation-states of Western Europe, and this impulse toward unity might have been further strengthened by the threatening appearance of these Western powers in Japanese waters. Yet Hideyoshi did not respond with a plan of integration which would have placed Japan on the threshold of progress as a modern state and world power. His own hegemony over the daimyō and their domains was expressed in feudal ties and personal relationships; his ascendancy was that of the overlord, not that of the systematic nation-builder who establishes a new pattern of power on the ruins of the old. Thus he created a new alignment without disturbing the traditional organization of Japanese society. Within it, however, there was a place both for representatives of the old military aristocracy and for new leaders of humbler origin, such as Katō Kiyomasa, a peasant from Hideyoshi's own village, and Konishi Yukinaga, a drug-merchant and Christian convert, who became an expert in naval matters and an outstanding general in the Korean campaign.

Just as this alignment centered upon the commanding figure of Hideyoshi, so also the objectives it served were bound up with the personal ambitions of Hideyoshi, who looked upon himself as embodying the destiny of the Japanese nation to rule all of East Asia. This grandiose scheme was by no means an outpouring of sudden enthusiasm or a momentary diversion, hastily conceived. The dream of conquering China was part of Nobunaga's legacy to Hideyoshi, and much methodical planning was devoted to achieving the maximum employment of Japan's naval power and logistic capabilities in the Korean expeditions of 1592 and 1597. Nevertheless, it took only the sudden death of one man, Hideyoshi, to bring about the total collapse of this vaunted enterprise and to show how prematurely Japan had been cast in the role of empire. It revealed, too, how much the new regime had been held together by a single figure. With Hideyoshi's passing his power was rapidly dispersed among contending generals and his own son lost out in the ensuing struggle.

Hideyoshi had not been so preoccupied with dreams of empire that he overlooked entirely the business of strengthening the internal administration of the country, and yet the character of those reforms he did undertake indicates how far short they fell of creating a regime which could survive his own demise. Some of his measures to stabilize the existing feudal order, such as prohibitions on change of residence and employment and on the carrying of arms by others than samurai, had the effect of creating a rigid class system which did indeed endure into the nineteenth century under Tokugawa auspices. But these ordinances, issued individually to the feudal lords in various domains on the personal authority of the Taikō, tended more to confirm local autonomy and the status-quo than to assert the direct control of a centralized state over all Japan. Further evidence of this tendency is found in the extensive land survey conducted over the years from 1582 to 1595. The first such survey had been made in the seventh century, following the example of T'ang China, with a view to establishing a tax system which would secure for the state assured revenue from the land, revenue to sustain the large Chinese-type bureaucracy then envisaged. For Hideyoshi, on the contrary, the purpose of this survey was not to bring all land under the taxing power of the state, but to serve as the basis for awarding such land to faithful retainers and for fixing the income which *they* might derive from it.

If Hideyoshi thus failed to devise a political mechanism which could operate independently of himself, he was nonetheless successful in achieving unprecedented personal power and wealth. He could assign or reassign the feudal lords to such domains as he chose, and he could exact from them substantial contributions to projects which showed forth his own magnificence, such as the construction of a Great Buddha image in Kyoto and a massive castle in Osaka. His great wealth enabled him to become a virtual patron of the impoverished imperial court, upon which he lavished his generosity as no shogun had done for centuries, and to entertain notables from all segments of Japanese society—political, religious, intellectual, and artistic—at his elaborate performances of the tea ceremony. At his death he was already an almost legendary figure, and the imperial court took the lead in expressing the people's reverence for him by granting Hideyoshi the posthumous Shinto title, Hōkoku, or "Wealth of the Nation," and by raising a shrine to his memory on the southeastern heights of Kyoto, above the Great Buddha image he had erected. Almost immediately this shrine, known as Toyokuni (also meaning "wealth of the nation"), became the cynosure of the capital and the nation, the center of a new form of national hero-worship in honor of the godlike leader who had unified Japan and inspired in her people the dream of overseas empire.

Had Hideyoshi's family been able to maintain its position, this shrine would no doubt have been accorded a place among the so-called "Big Five" national shrines. Ironically, however, it was the inscription on the bell Hideyoshi's son gave in honor of the Great Buddha that served as a pretext for Ieyasu's campaign against him.[1] After a long siege the seemingly impregnable walls of Osaka castle fell to Ieyasu's assault in 1615, and under Tokugawa rule Toyokuni Shrine became an object of deliberate neglect rather than of national reverence. This fate had almost been foretold in the poem said to have been composed by Hideyoshi just before his death.

[1] Part of the inscription expressing a desire for the nation to be at peace (*kokka ankō*) contained the two characters of Ieyasu's name, and since they happened to lie just at the point where the bell was usually struck, this was interpreted as putting a curse on Ieyasu.

Tsuyu to oki	Like dew I came,
Tsuyu to kienan	Like dew I go.
Waga mi kana	My life
Naniwa no koto wa	And all I have done at Osaka
Yume no mata yume	Is just a dream in a dream.

Even centuries of Tokugawa rule, however, could not wholly obscure Hideyoshi's vision of a larger world in which Japan was to play a part, of a horizon that stretched beyond Asia to Africa and Europe. Two maps he had had made kept this vista constantly before him, one mounted on a folding screen in his palace and the other on a fan with which, while cooling himself, he had fanned the flames of his ambition. During the years that followed the memory of Hideyoshi's exploits lingered on in the consciousness of an isolated, insular Japan, as a reminder of the world beyond her shores and of a destiny which some day would carry her warriors again to the banks of the Yalu.

TOYOTOMI HIDEYOSHI

Letter to the Viceroy of the Indies

Three years before the date of this letter, Hideyoshi had received a letter from the Viceroy of the Indies (Portuguese Goa) through a Jesuit missionary. This letter, which Hideyoshi wrote in reply, and a similar letter he was to send in 1597 to the Governor-General of the Philippines, reveal his attitude toward Christianity and religion generally, and incidentally his ambition to rule all of East Asia.

[From Akiyama, Nisshi kōshō-shi kenkyū, pp. 65–66]

Reading your message from afar, I can appreciate the immense expanse of water which separates us. As you have noted in your letter, my country, which is comprised of sixty-odd provinces, has known for many years more days of disorder than days of peace; rowdies have been given to fomenting intrigue, and bands of warriors have formed cliques to defy the court's orders. Ever since my youth, I have been constantly concerned over this deplorable situation. I studied the art of self-cultivation and the secret of governing the country. Through profound planning and forethought, and according to the three principles of benevolence, wisdom, and courage, I cared for the warriors on the one hand and looked after the common people on the other; while administering justice, I was able to establish security. Thus, before many years had passed, the unity of the nation was set on a firm foundation, and now foreign nations, far and near, without exception, bring tribute to us. Everyone, everywhere, seeks to obey my orders. . . . Though our own country is now safe and secure, I nevertheless entertain hopes of ruling the great Ming nation. I can reach the Middle Kingdom aboard my palace-ship within a short time. It will be as easy as pointing to the palm of my hand. I shall then use the occasion to visit your country regardless of the distance or the differences between us.

Ours is the land of the Gods, and God is mind. Everything in nature comes into existence because of mind. Without God there can be no spirituality. Without God there can be no way. God rules in times of prosperity as in times of decline. God is positive and negative and unfathomable. Thus, God is the root and source of all existence. This God is spoken of by Buddhism in India, Confucianism in China, and Shinto in Japan. To know Shinto is to know Buddhism as well as Confucianism.

As long as man lives in this world, Humanity will be a basic principle. Were it not for Humanity and Righteousness, the sovereign would not be a sovereign, nor a minister of state a minister. It is through the practice of Humanity and Righteousness that the foundations of our relationships between sovereign and minister, parent and child, and husband and wife are established. If you are interested in the profound philosophy of God and Buddha, request an explanation and it will be given to you. In your land one doctrine is taught to the exclusion of others, and you are not yet informed of the [Confucian] philosophy of Humanity and Righteousness. Thus there is no respect for God and Buddha and no distinction between sovereign and ministers. Through heresies you intend to destroy the righteous law. Hereafter, do not expound, in ignorance of right and wrong, unreasonable and wanton doctrines. A few years ago the so-called Fathers came to my country seeking to bewitch our men and women, both of the laity and clergy. At that time punishment was administered to them, and it will be repeated if they should return to our domain to propagate their faith. It will not matter what sect or denomination they represent—they shall be destroyed. It will then be too late to repent. If you entertain any desire of establishing amity with this land, the seas have been rid of the pirate menace, and merchants are permitted to come and go. Remember this.

As for the products of the south-land, acknowledgment of their receipt is here made, as itemized. The catalogue of gifts which we tender is presented on a separate paper. The rest will be explained orally by my envoy.

Tenshō 19 [1591]: Seventh Month, 25th Day [signed] The Civil Dictator

Memorandum on the Korean Expedition

The Korean expedition, which was only the initial step in Hideyoshi's grand scheme to bring China—and eventually all of Asia—under his control, had been launched only a few weeks before the date of this memorandum. This communication from Hideyoshi to his nephew reflects Hideyoshi's supreme confidence of victory and his expectation that China could be governed by the kind of feudal regime he was accustomed to in Japan. Hideyoshi had assembled at Nagoya (now Karatsu) in northern Kyushu a force variously estimated at from 300,000 to 480,000 men, and the division of about 130,000 men which he reports in this memorandum as having reached the Korean capital (Seoul) had achieved its objective within twenty days of its landing near Pusan.

[From Akiyama, *Nisshi kōshō-shi kenkyū*, pp. 55-57]

[1] Your Lordship [Hidetsugu] must not relax preparations for the campaign. The departure must be made by the First or Second Month of the coming year.

[2] The Capital of Korea fell on the second day of this month. Thus, the time has come to make the sea crossing and to bring the length and breadth of the Great Ming under our control. My desire is that Your Lordship make the crossing to become the Civil Dictator of Great China.

[3] Thirty thousand men should accompany you. The departure should be by boat from Hyōgo. Horses should be sent by land.

[4] Although no hostility is expected in the Three Kingdoms [Korea], armed preparedness is of the utmost importance, not only for the maintenance of our reputation but also in the event of an emergency. All subordinates shall be so instructed. . . .

[The next thirteen items deal with supplying, equipping and staffing the expeditionary force.]

[18] Since His Majesty is to be transferred to the Chinese capital, due preparation is necessary. The imperial visit will take place the year after next. On that occasion, ten provinces adjacent to the Capital shall be

presented to him. In time instructions will be issued for the enfeoffment of all courtiers. Subordinates will receive ten times as much [as their present holdings]. The enfeoffment of those in the upper ranks shall be according to personal qualifications.

[19] The post of Civil Dictator of China shall be assigned, as afore-mentioned, to Hidetsugu who will be given 100 provinces adjacent to the Capital. The post of Civil Dictator of Japan will go to either the Middle Counsellor Yamato,[1] or to the Bizen Minister,[2] upon declaration by either of his readiness.

[20] As for the position of Sovereign of Japan, the young Prince or Prince Hachijō shall be the choice.

[21] As for Korea, the Gifu Minister[3] or Bizen Minister shall be assigned. In that event the Middle Counsellor Tamba shall be assigned to Kyūshū.

[22] As for His Majesty's visit to China, arrangements shall be made according to established practices for Imperial tours of inspection. His Majesty's itinerary shall follow the route of the present campaign. Men and horses necessary for the occasion shall be requisitioned from each country involved.

[23] Korea and China are within easy reach, and no inconvenience is anticipated for any concerned, high or low. It is not expected that anyone in those countries will attempt to flee. Therefore, recall all commissioners in the provinces to assist in preparation for the expedition. . . .

Hideyoshi [*Seal*]

Tenshō 20 [1592]: Fifth Month, 18th Day
To: His Lordship the Civil Dictator [of China]

The Sword Collection Edict

Of more enduring significance than Hideyoshi's dreams of conquest were the measures he adopted to solidify his power and stabilize the existing order. Since the twelfth century Japan had been dominated by warriors, but the very warfare which had put an increasing premium on military prowess in medieval times showed little regard for hereditary rights or class distinctions. In the hurly-burly struggles of the sixteenth century peasants and seafaring people fought alongside aristocrats, and through such an exacting test of individual

---

[1] Hideyoshi's half-brother, Hidenaga.   [2] His adopted son (*yushi*) Ukita Hideie.
[3] Hashiba Hideyasu, a relative by marriage.

merit men of humble origins like Hideyoshi could rise to great power. But Hideyoshi's avowed purpose was to put an end to this disordered state of affairs, and thus to deny others the opportunities which had been afforded to him. One of the many means he had used to accomplish this was his famous Sword Hunt, which deprived the peasantry of their weapons and made fighting the exclusive prerogative of an hereditary class. In justification of this he offered a pious motive as well: the confiscated metal could be used for the casting of a great Buddha image.

[From Kuroita, *Kokushi gaikan*, p. 236]

[1] The people of the various provinces are strictly forbidden to have in their possession any swords, short swords, bows, spears, firearms, or other types of arms. The possession of unnecessary implements [of war] makes difficult the collection of taxes and dues and tends to foment uprisings. Needless to say, the perpetrators of improper acts against official agents shall be summarily punished, but in that event the paddy fields and farms of the violators will remain unattended and there will be no yield of crops. Therefore the heads of provinces, official agents, and deputies are ordered to collect all the weapons mentioned above and turn them over to the government.

[2] Swords and short swords thus collected will not be wasted. They shall be used as nails and bolts in the construction of the Great Image of Buddha. This will benefit the people not only in this life but also in the life hereafter.

[3] If the people are in possession of agricultural implements only and devote themselves exclusively to agriculture, they and their descendants will prosper. Sincere concern for the well-being of the people is the motive for the issuance of this order, which is fundamental for the peace and security of the country and the happiness of the people. In other lands, such as China, the ruler Yao converted rare swords and sharp weapons into agricultural implements after he had established peace. In our country such an experiment has never been made. Thus, all the people should abide by and understand the aims of this act and give their undivided attention to agriculture and sericulture.

All implements mentioned above shall be collected and submitted forthwith.

Hideyoshi [*Seal*]

Tenshō 16 [1588]: Seventh Month, 8th Day

Restrictions on Change of Status and Residence

The beginnings of the rigid class system of the Tokugawa Period are found in ordinances such as this issued by Hideyoshi. In the absence of more direct control by a centralized administration, it was essential that the activities and movements of the people be regulated by the feudal lords in each locality and that the responsibility for this be clearly defined. The principle of collective responsibility, so much in evidence here, was also embodied in Hideyoshi's revival of the Five and Ten-man Group Responsibility System, which likewise became an important feature of Tokugawa rule.

[From *Kokushi shiryō shū*, III, 280–81]

[1] If there should be living among you any men formerly in military service who have taken up the life of a peasant since the seventh month of last year, with the end of the campaign in the Mutsu region, you are hereby authorized to take them under surveillance and expel them. If persons of this type are kept concealed in any place, the entire town or village shall be brought to justice for this evasion of the law.

[2] If any peasant abandons his fields, either to pursue trade or to become a tradesman or laborer for hire, not only should he be punished but the entire village should be brought to justice with him. Anyone who is not employed either in military service or in cultivating land shall likewise be investigated by the local authorities and expelled. If local officials fail to take action in such cases, they shall be stripped of their posts for negligence. In cases involving concealment of peasants who have turned to trade, the entire village or town shall be held responsible for the offense.

[3] No military retainer who has left his master without permission shall be given employment by another. A thorough investigation should be made of the man's previous status and he should be required to provide a guarantor.

Those who fail to report that they already have a master are to be arrested for violating the law and returned to their former master. Whenever this regulation is violated and the offender allowed to go free, the heads of three men shall be offered in compensation to the original master. If restitution is not made in this manner, there will be no alternative except to hold the new master responsible and bring him to justice.

Such are the provisions of this ordinance.

Hideyoshi [*Seal*]

Tenshō 19 [1591]: Eighth Month, 21st Day

TOKUGAWA IEYASU

Tokugawa Ieyasu (1542–1616), from the lower ranks of the feudal gentry, rose to prominence in the armies of Nobunaga and won undisputed mastery over Japan after Hideyoshi's death, first by defeating a powerful coalition of rivals at Sekigahara in 1600 and finally by reducing the Osaka fortress of Hideyori in 1615. Short, stout, and somewhat ugly to look at, he was powerfully built and famous as a commander for his thunderous battle-cry. Less impetuous than Nobunaga, less colorful and dramatic than Hideyoshi, Ieyasu surpassed both in foresight and political acumen, which enabled him to climax his military triumphs by the achievement of a lasting peace. It was to be the longest period of peace—and for the most part, prosperity—which Japan has ever known, one which saw his own family retain unbroken control of the shogunate down to 1868.

For this achievement Ieyasu was revered—almost to the point of idolatry—as a national hero by many generations of Japanese, his cult quickly displacing that which had so lately grown up around the magnificent Hideyoshi. Neither a thinker nor a writer, Ieyasu nevertheless figured prominently in the history of Japanese thought for over two centuries, and in the popular mind became the focus of some of the most diverse and persistent tendencies in the religious life of the time. We have tangible evidence of this in the famous shrine at Nikkō, dedicated to him. There is a common saying,

Nikkō minai de   Speak not of beauty
Kekkō to yū na   Until you have seen Nikkō.

Some discriminating judges may dispute whether the pretentious architecture and ornate design of the Nikkō shrine justify such high praise as is proverbially accorded to it, but none can deny it a place as one of the great monuments of Japanese architecture, heightened by a natural setting of picturesque mountains and giant evergreens which overlook vast stretches of the eastern plains. Officially it is classed as one of the five lead-ing Shinto shrines of Japan (designated as *miya* or *gū*) among which is the famous shrine to the Sun Goddess at Ise.[1] Built at a great cost, in gold, silver, and rice, to the shogunate treasury, supplemented by size-able contributions from the Tokugawa feudatories, this lavish creation was obviously meant to associate the cult of Ieyasu with the Sun Goddess, if not to rival Ise itself. Nikkō means "Sunshine" and the title granted the new shrine was Tōshō-gū, "Shrine of the Sun God of the East." Even the Emperor in Kyoto, who claimed to be a living descendant of the Sun Goddess, gave his imprimatur to the title by autographing a scroll painted by the foremost artist of the time, Kanō Tanyū, called "An Illustrated Account of the Sunshine Shrine."

One of the most distinctive features of the Nikkō cult, however, is the fact that it is not merely Shintoist. An attempt was initially made by the exclusive "One and Only" Shinto sect to have Ieyasu enshrined like Hideyoshi as a Shinto deity alone, but the venerable Abbot Tenkai, who had been Ieyasu's closest religious and political adviser, prevailed in the choice of the posthumous title, Tōshō Gongen, "Buddha Incarnate as the Sun God of the East." Ieyasu had indeed been a devout Buddhist all his life. Amidism was especially strong in the region he came from, and his most intimate spiritual confidant was the Amidist, Zon'ō. Ieyasu's humility, his forbearance, his sense of equity, his love of peace, and his abiding concern for the life hereafter, all suggest the deep and persistent influence of the Pure Land teaching. But his creed, which verged on monotheism in its exclusive devotion to Amida, was an embarrassment politically. It had no place for the Shinto deities or even for the other Buddhas, and yet Ieyasu, the overlord of Japanese of many faiths, some-how had to reconcile their claims. In the catholic syncretism of the Tendai school, as represented by Abbot Tenkai, he found a doctrine which em-braced Shinto particularism in Buddhist universalism—native deities are so many manifestations of the cosmic Buddha. It is appropriate, then, that Tenkai should have succeeded in identifying Ieyasu with the Cosmic Buddha, known in Japanese as Dainichi or "Great Sun." He thus became both the Sun God and the Sun Buddha of the East.

Of all the schools of thought in Japan, however, the one which owed

---

[1] The other three are the shrine to Hachiman in Kamakura; Temmangū, dedicated to Sugawara Michizane at Kitano in Kyoto; and the Kasuga Shrine in Nara.

most to Ieyasu and had the most reason to venerate him was the Confucian school, which was to dominate the intellectual life of the Tokugawa Period. After the nation had been united in submission to the new shogun, his great task was to restore social order, stability, and peace. Confucianism he found well suited to assist him in this task, especially the Neo-Confucian philosophy of Chu Hsi which had already gained wide acceptance and official sanction in China, though centuries of turmoil and disunity had hindered its spread in Japan. Buddhism, which had long since declined on the Continent but was still a living force in Ieyasu's homeland, generally took a pessimistic view of life in this changing uncertain world. It had little hope in human society or the moral order; all laws but the one Law of Buddha's Liberating Truth were delusive and burdensome. The Buddhist solution was to "leave the world," to seek total emancipation by Enlightenment or through the saving power of Amida. But Ieyasu and his successors sought peace and order here and now, and the rational humanism of Chu Hsi gave some promise of this in its stress on the rule of law and order throughout the universe, its optimistic view of man's political and social intelligence, and its insistence upon individual morality as the foundation of the state.

A soldier with little time for formal education, Ieyasu nevertheless was as noted for his interest in the "arts of peace" as for his accomplishments in war. He surrounded himself with learned men, and greatly encouraged the printing of books. Still, his intellectual concerns were intensely practical; not the metaphysical theories of the Sung philosophers, but the political history of China and Japan was what attracted him most. One of his idols was the founder of the T'ang dynasty, T'ai-tsung, the greatest organizer and administrator of empire which the Far East had so far seen. It is significant, however, that Ieyasu was far more inclined to emulate the personal virtues of a T'ang T'ai-tsung than to imitate the imperial institutions of China. He was no more tempted, indeed, than Hideyoshi to undertake the wholesale revamping of Japanese institutions which such an ambition would have required.

As it was, the stable political system which Ieyasu handed on to his long line of Tokugawa successors contained little that was new and much that derived from the rule of Hideyoshi. Unlike the civil bureaucracy of China, it was an avowed military government predicated upon a feudal organization of society and a hereditary aristocracy. The shogunate's principal concern was with the disposition of the feudal houses, which it placed in such a manner that its closest adherents could afford maximum support and protection to the new regime and its potential enemies the least possible resistance. Following this policy earlier, Hideyoshi had been responsible for moving the Tokugawa to new headquarters in the strategic fishing village of Edo, which has since become Tokyo. From its massive fortress there the shogunate saw to it that their feudatories did not build castles of comparable size, and that they took up periodic residence or left hostages in Edo as insurance against hostile activities. Such general measures as the Bakufu, or military government, enforced were meant to regulate the relations of the feudal lords among one another, so as to prevent any horizontal combination from forming which might cut through or disrupt the vertical control of the Tokugawa overlords. The effect of this policy was to seal off the feudatories and set them apart, to encourage dispersion of power, decentralization, and particularism. Within these bounds the various domains enjoyed their traditional autonomy, and the Bakufu refrained from interfering in their internal administration except insofar as necessary to preserve the status quo in all things. Frankly and unqualifiedly conservative, and opposed in principle to any "innovation," the Tokugawa confirmed the class restrictions of Hideyoshi as a bar to social mobility, and also Hideyoshi's stern system of collective responsibility in five-man groups (gonin-gumi) for individual crimes.

Though not uniformly successful in preventing change or innovation, the shogunate did at least maintain its rule unbroken for two and a half centuries, due partly to superior management of the Tokugawa household by a Council of Elders ensuring continuity of administration regardless of the capabilities of the incumbent shogun. In addition, among the other considerations which may explain the durability of so reactionary a government is the basic fact that it did not attempt to do too much, but concentrated its efforts on the maintenance of peace and security, which in turn fostered prosperity and general well-being. Another factor is certainly the effectiveness of that ethical code, feudal and Confucian, which it promoted so assiduously among all segments of the population. Much of the legal code of the Tokugawa consists of ethical maxims or injunctions, which today may appear naive and quaint or else unduly to infringe upon the domain of private morality. Yet in a feudal society, where the governmental structure was built upon personal relationships and so much depended upon the loyalty, fitness, and discretion of the individual members of the ruling class, such a code served a vital need and its universal acceptance took the place to a large extent of centralized control backed by force. The Tokugawa appreciated that the voluntary, internalized restraints of Confucian morality, reinforcing the rigid self-discipline of feudal tradition, could be a potent force in itself for the maintenance of order. The effectiveness of this policy is indicated by the infrequent application of armed force in the seventeenth and eighteenth centuries, so much so that the samurai, or warrior, class was deprived of any real opportunity to discharge its military function. Whatever else may have contributed to this remarkable development, there can be no doubt that the Tokugawa succeeded admirably in inculcating among all ranks of Japanese a system of ethics which served well its own security requirements, and which became so deeply ingrained in the life of the people that it long outlived the shogunate itself.

Laws Governing the Military Households

The character of Tokugawa rule is nowhere better shown than in the laws governing the military aristocracy promulgated in 1615, a year before Ieyasu's death, by his successor as shogun, Hidetada. The object of these laws was to insure peace and order among the feudal domains, not to interfere unduly in local matters. Extremely precise in regard to certain security requirements affecting the interests of the Tokugawa as military overlords, this code gave only the most generalized sort of moral guidance to the feudal nobility in other areas of administration. It thus reflects the continuing force of feudal traditions, stressing individual rule, personal loyalties, and martial virtues, and also Confucian emphasis upon personal morality as the foundation of the social order.

Similar regulations were later issued for the imperial household, the court families and the Buddhist communities, setting forth the conditions and procedures according to which these largely self-governing bodies were to conduct their own affairs.

The commentary on the various provisions below contains numerous maxims and quotations from earlier authorities, legal and canonical, often loosely applied to the case in hand and without attribution as to source. To avoid excessive annotation, only a few sample quotations are identified.

[From Ono Kiyoshi, *Tokugawa seido shiryō,* pp. 2-4]

[1] The arts of peace and war, including archery and horsemanship, should be pursued single-mindedly.

From of old the rule has been to practice "the arts of peace on the left hand, and the arts of war on the right"; both must be mastered. Archery and horsemanship are indispensable to military men. Though arms are called instruments of evil, there are times when they must be resorted to. In peacetime we should not be oblivious to the danger of war. Should we not, then, prepare ourselves for it?

[2] Drinking parties and wanton revelry should be avoided.

In the codes that have come down to us this kind of dissipation has been severely proscribed. Sexual indulgence and habitual gambling lead to the downfall of a state.

[3] Offenders against the law should not be harbored or hidden in any domain.

Law is the basis of social order. Reason may be violated in the name of the law, but law may not be violated in the name of reason. Those who break the law deserve heavy punishment.

[4] Great lords (daimyō), the lesser lords, and officials should immediately expel from their domains any among their retainers or henchmen who have been charged with treason or murder.

Wild and wicked men may become weapons for overturning the state and destroying the people. How can they be allowed to go free?

[5] Henceforth no outsider, none but the inhabitants of a particular domain, shall be permitted to reside in that domain.

Each domain has its own ways. If a man discloses the secrets of one's own country to another domain or if the secrets of the other domain are disclosed to one's own, that will sow the seeds of deceit and sycophancy.

[6] Whenever it is intended to make repairs on a castle of one of the feudal domains, the [shogunate] authorities should be notified. The construction of any new castles is to be halted and stringently prohibited.

"Big castles are a danger to the state." [1] Walls and moats are the cause of great disorders.

[7] Immediate report should be made of innovations which are being planned or of factional conspiracies being formed in neighboring domains.

"Men all incline toward partisanship; few are wise and impartial. There are some who refuse to obey their masters, and others who feud

---

[1] Legge, *The Chinese Classics, Tso Chuen*, pp. 2, 5. "Any metropolitan city, whose walls are more than 3,000 cubits round, is dangerous to the state. According to the regulations of the former kings, such a city . . . can have walls only a third as long as the capital."

with their neighbors."[2] Why, instead of abiding by the established order, do they wantonly embark upon new schemes?

[8] Do not enter into marriage privately [i.e., without notifying the shogunate authorities].

Marriage follows the principle of harmony between yin and yang, and must not be entered into lightly. In the *Book of Changes,* under the thirty-eighth hexagram (*k'uei*), it says, "Marriage should not be contracted out of enmity [against another]. Marriages intended to effect an alliance with enemies [of the state] will turn out badly."[3] The Peach Blossom ode in *The Book of Poetry* also says that "When men and women are proper in their relationships and marriage is arranged at the correct time; then throughout the land there will be no loose women."[4] To form an alliance by marriage is the root of treason.

[9] Visits of the *daimyō* to the capital are to be in accordance with regulations.

The *Chronicles of Japan, Continued,* contains a regulation that "Clansmen should not gather together whenever they please, but only when they have to conduct some public business; and also that the number of horsemen serving as an escort in the capital should be limited to twenty. . . ." Daimyō should not be accompanied by a large number of soldiers. Twenty horsemen shall be the maximum escort for daimyō with an income of from one million to two hundred thousand *koku* of rice.[5] For those with an income of one hundred thousand *koku* or less, the escort should be proportionate to their income. On official missions, however, they may be accompanied by an escort proportionate to their rank.

[10] Restrictions on the type and quality of dress to be worn should not be transgressed.

Lord and vassal, superior and inferior, should observe what is proper to their station in life. [Then follows an injunction against the wearing of fine white damask or purple silk by retainers without authorization.]

[11] Persons without rank shall not ride in palanquins.

[2] From the Constitution of Prince Shotoku. See Chapter III.

[3] These passages have been pieced together from the sub-commentary on the 38th hexagram, in which context they have quite a different significance from that indicated here.

[4] Legge, *The Chinese Classics, She King,* Prolegomena, p. 38, Preface to the 6th ode, T'ao yao. The original text reads "throughout the land there will be no *widowers.*" A character has been substituted here which means "unattached female" and also has the misleading connotation of "seductive and frivolous." There is only the remotest connection between the original context and the purpose which the quotation is made to serve here.

[5] Rank was indicated by the estimated revenue from lands held in fief.

From of old there have been certain families entitled to ride in palanquins without special permission, and others who have received such
permission. Recently, however, even the ordinary retainers and henchmen of some families have taken to riding about in palanquins, which is
truly the worst sort of presumption. Henceforth permission shall be
granted only to the lords of the various domains, their close relatives and
ranking officials, medical men and astrologers, those over sixty years of
age, and those ill or infirm. In the cases of ordinary household retainers
or henchmen who willfully ride in palanquins, their masters shall be held
accountable.

Exceptions to this law are the court families, Buddhist prelates, and the
clergy in general.

[12] The samurai of the various domains shall lead a frugal and simple life.

When the rich make a display of their wealth, the poor are humiliated
and envious. Nothing engenders corruption so much as this, and therefore it must be strictly curbed.

[13] The lords of the domains should select officials with a capacity for
public administration.

Good government depends on getting the right men. Due attention
should be given to their merits and faults; rewards and punishments
must be properly meted out. If a domain has able men, it flourishes; if
it lacks able men it is doomed to perish. This is the clear admonition of
the wise men of old.

The purport of the foregoing should be conscientiously observed.

Military Government and the Social Order

This anecdote told by a contemporary of Ieyasu gives the latter's views on the
functions of the emperor, the shogun, and the four classes of society. They
reflect both the warlike virtues of the feudal society through which he struggled
to power and the Confucian social theories by which he hoped to preserve that
power in peace. Note that the Emperor's duties are largely ceremonial, while
the shogun serves as actual ruler.

[From Korō shodan, in Dai-Nihon shiryō, Part 12, Vol. 24, pp. 546–49]

Once, Lord Tōshō [Ieyasu] conversed with Honda, Governor Sado, on
the subject of the emperor, the shogun, and the farmer. "Whether there
is order or chaos in the nation depends on the virtues and vices of these
three. The emperor, with compassion in his heart for the needs of the

people, must not be remiss in the performance of his duties—from the early morning worship of the New Year to the monthly functions of the court. Secondly, the shogun must not forget the possibility of war in peacetime, and must maintain his discipline. He should be able to maintain order in the country; he should bear in mind the security of the sovereign; and he must strive to dispel the anxieties of the people. One who cultivates the way of the warrior only in times of crisis is like a rat who bites his captor in the throes of being captured. The man may die from the effects of the poisonous bite, but to generate courage on the spur of the moment is not the way of a warrior. To assume the way of the warrior upon the outbreak of war is like a rat biting his captor. Although this is better than fleeing from the scene, the true master of the way of the warrior is one who maintains his martial discipline even in time of peace. Thirdly, the farmer's toil is proverbial—from the first grain to a hundred acts of labor. He selects the seed from last fall's crop, and undergoes various hardships and anxieties through the heat of the summer until the seed grows finally to a rice plant. It is harvested and husked and then offered to the land steward. The rice then becomes sustenance for the multitudes. Truly, the hundred acts of toil from last fall to this fall are like so many tears of blood. Thus, it is a wise man who, while partaking of his meal, appreciates the hundred acts of toil of the people. Fourthly, the artisan's occupation is to make and prepare wares and utensils for the use of others. Fifthly, the merchant facilitates the exchange of goods so that the people can cover their nakedness and keep their bodies warm. As the people produce clothing, food and housing, which are called the 'three treasures,' they deserve our every sympathy."

Ieyasu's Secret

From the reminiscences of an elderly man who had followed Ieyasu's activities at his military headquarters, we learn of this occasion on which the Tokugawa leader summed up his philosophy of life in just four words. Here the influence of "tender-minded" Amidism and Taoism is quite strong on this "tough-minded" general.

[From Daidō-ji Yūzan, *Iwabuchi Yawa-besshū* in *Dai-Nihon shiryō*, Part 12, Vol. 24, pp. 438–39]

At Suruga Castle one evening after the Osaka campaign, Ieyasu summoned his attendants before him and spoke thus: "As you know, I was born in the very midst of the period of turbulent warfare. Every day, from dawn to dusk and since my boyhood, my body and soul have been given to the councils of war. I have had little time to pursue learning. However, there is a line from a text I have studied which I have always retained in my mind. Since my days at the castle in Okazaki, Mikawa to the present time of the unification of the country, I have always acted according to the principle expressed in that one line in attempting to establish by deeds the fortunes of my family. What do you think that line is, and where does it come from: the Confucian canon or the biographies of the sages, or the words of Buddha? I should like you to think about it," he ordered.

Among those in attendance on that occasion were some who possessed great learning. They ventured one answer after another, only to be told they were incorrect. Soon all admitted that they did not know the answer. Then Ieyasu spoke thus: "From the statements you have just made suggesting the presence of the line in the Four Books and the Five Classics, or in the sayings of the sages and the scholars, this line must indeed be an important text in literary studies. However, as you know, I am unlettered, and therefore I am not certain of its source. At any rate, the line which I learned in my boyhood and which I have always retained in my mind runs, 'Requite malice with kindness.' [1] It has been useful to me on many occasions, great and small. That is the secret formula I wish to confide to you today" said Ieyasu smiling.

Ieyasu and the Arts of Peace

Although Ieyasu had had little formal education and left no writings of significance, anecdotes told by his contemporaries reveal him as a man with a deep respect for learning, and especially for that which bore on the conduct of life, government or war. The following excerpt from an official chronicle indicates his breadth of mind, his particular interest in Chinese political history and thought, and his encouragement of learning through the promotion of printing. Movable type had been introduced to Japan from Korea and the West at the turn of the century.

[From *Tōshō-gū go-jikki*, by Narushima Motonao, in Kuroita, *Kokushi gaikan*, p. 282]

Having lived from boyhood to manhood in military encampments, and having suffered hardship after hardship in countless battles, large and

From Lao Tzu, LXIII.

small, His Lordship had little time to read or study. Although he had conquered the country on horseback, being a man of innate intelligence and wisdom, he fully appreciated the impossibility of governing the country on horseback. According to his judgment there could be no other way to govern the country than by a constant and deep faith in the sages and the scholars, and as a human being interested in the welfare of his fellow human beings, he patronized scholarship from the very beginning of his rule. Thus, he soon gained a reputation as a great devotee of letters and as one with a taste for elegant prose and poetry. On one occasion, Shimazu Yoshihisa, whose Buddhist name was Ryūhaku, took the trouble to arrange a poetry composition party in Ieyasu's honor, only to learn that His Lordship did not care at all for such a vain pastime. He listened again and again to discourses on the *Four Books*, the *Records of the Historian* by Ssu-ma Ch'ien, the *History of the Former Han Dynasty,* and the *Precepts and Policies of T'ang T'ai-tsung (Chen-kuan cheng-yao)* as well as the *Six Tactics* and *Three Strategies.*[1] Among Japanese works he gave special attention to the *Institutes of Engi,* the *Mirror of the East,* and the *Kemmu Regulations.*[2]

He kept the company of Fujiwara Seika and Hayashi Dōshun as well as the Three Elders of Nanzen-ji, the Elder Tetsu of Tōfuku-ji, the Courtier Kiyohara Hidekata, Lieutenant General Minase Chikatomo, Sanyō of the Ashikaga School, the Elder [Shōda] of Rokuon-in, and the Abbot Tenkai in whose discourses about [The Confucian sage-kings] Wen and Wu, the First Han Emperor's magnanimity and tolerance, and T'ang T'ai Tsung's openmindedness and amenability to suggestion he found constant delight. He also extolled the spirit of personal sacrifice and the utterances and deeds of loyalty to the state of such [great Chinese statesmen] as T'ai Kung-wang, Chang Liang, Han Hsin, Wei Cheng, and Fang Hsuan-ling. And among the warriors of our country he constantly asked for discourses on the General of the Right of Kamakura (Minamoto Yoritomo). Whatever the subject, he was interested, not in the turn of a phrase or in literary embellishments, but only in discovering the key to government—how to govern oneself, the people, and the country.

[1] The *Liu t'ao* and *San-lüeh,* works on the art of war falsely attributed to Lu Wang of the early Chou and Huang Shih-kung of the third century B.C., respectively.

[2] The *Engi shiki,* a compilation of governmental regulations in A.D. 927; the *Azuma kagami,* a chronicle of the Kamakura Shogunate from 1180 to 1266; and the *Kemmu shikimoku,* a compilation of governmental by-laws during the reign of the Emperor Go-daigo, 1334–35.

Ieyasu declared, "If we cannot clarify the principles of human relations, society and government will of itself become unstable and disorders will never cease. Books are the only means whereby these principles can be set forth and understood. Thus, the printing of books and their transmission to the public is the first concern of a benevolent government." For this reason steps were taken for the printing of various books.

The Sun God of the East

More than a century after Ieyasu's rule this appreciation of him was written by the noted scholar Ogyū Sorai. Believing in the importance of governing according to fixed laws and institutions, in contrast to the usual Confucian reliance on the efficacy of personal virtue, Sorai especially admired Ieyasu's attention to the establishment of lasting institutions of government. At the same time Ogyū's deification of Ieyasu reflects not only his personal predilections, but the general awe in which the founder of the Tokugawa shogunate was held by posterity. The title "Sun God of the East" (Tōshō) was originally accorded to Ieyasu by the Tendai abbot Tenkai, one of his personal advisers.

[From *Ken'en dan'yo*, Ogyū Sorai in *Dai-Nihon shiryō*, Part 12, Vol. 24, pp. 441–42]

The Great Sun God of the East seemed to have been blessed with the wisdom of a sage. The great achievement of his lifetime—that of restoring order throughout the country—cannot be appreciated by the ordinary mind. I, as a scholar, would regard his age as essentially one of strife and warfare. True, the *Nō* play, tea ceremony, and other pastimes were in vogue, but serious attention to literature and Confucianism did not exist. . . . It was at such a time that [Hāyashi] Razan was invited to become Ieyasu's tutor while [the scholarly Sūden], the Elder of Konji-in, was also invited to serve as his companion during his military campaigns. He always put great store in books. He collected the ancient texts of China and Japan, the classics and their commentaries, philosophical works and historical accounts—all of which he sent to his library in Edo. Such works which have come down to our time as the *Administrative Code*,[1] the *Institutes of Engi, Selected Writings in Chinese*,[2] and the *Mirror of the East*, all appeared in print in his time and were made widely available. He also invited, year after year, eminent Buddhist priests from

---

[1] That is, the Yōrō Code of 718 together with its commentaries.
[2] The *Honchō monzui*, a collection of prose and poetry in Chinese written by Japanese, compiled in A.D. 999.

Kyōto, Nara, and other Buddhist centers in the provinces to lecture on and discuss their doctrines before him at his headquarters in Suruga. And he made gifts of gold and silver to them upon their departure for home. We appreciate now his noble intentions to change the rough and violent customs of a warring age into cultured, genteel ways as the basis for eternal peace. In this connection there is a noteworthy anecdote about something he did during the Osaka campaign. He went to Kyoto, which was still in the midst of war and confusion, to borrow the records of the imperial court and also to gather books and manuscripts from courtiers and long-established families so that he might examine precedents and procedures for the drafting of laws and regulations. This is the mark of a monarch capable of ruling the country. Thus, his plans for laws to administer the country have been effective, and today, more than a hundred years later, the government maintains its equilibrium and remains firmly established on a solid foundation. Education is spreading from day to day, and in the observance of the principle of the five human relationships between the ruler and the ruled, parent and child, etc., we excel the past. Even China and Korea cannot attain our position in this regard. This is a matter which only the well-informed can appreciate.

CHAPTER XVI

NEO-CONFUCIAN
ORTHODOXY

Confucianism, though a product of China, has not, historically speaking, been confined to a role as the national creed or cult of the Chinese, but has entered deeply into the lives of other East Asian peoples as well. Its transmission to these other countries is all the more remarkable, however, since Confucianism has had no missionaries of its own to win converts abroad. The scholar and the official, rather than the monk or pilgrim, is the usual symbol of Confucianism in action; its natural orbit is the family and the state, not the "uncivilized" world. Consequently when Confucianism was first introduced into Japan in the sixth and seventh centuries, Buddhist monks had to serve as the intermediaries, bringing Chinese culture with them as naturally as Christian missionaries of the twentieth century brought Western medicine, for example, to strange lands. Similarly, when the second great wave of Confucian influence reached Japan, Buddhist monks again served as intermediaries—this time the Zen monks who played such a prominent part in trade and intercourse with China, and who made their monasteries centers of Chinese studies in the Ashikaga period. We have already seen how great an impression had been made on the Japanese by the artistic achievements of the Sung dynasty. Another outstanding product of Sung times was Neo-Confucian philosophy, which likewise attracted the attention of learned monks in fifteenth- and sixteenth-century Japan.

It is nevertheless to other factors than its reception by Zen monks that Neo-Confucianism owes the ascendancy which it achieved in the early years of the Tokugawa Period. Neo-Confucian orthodoxy in Japan was a creation of both scholarship and state sponsorship. The achievement of peace and unity, under a new and stronger military government, provided an opportunity to Neo-Confucianism which it had lacked in more disordered times. Circumstances had enhanced its importance to men confronted by precisely those problems which Confucianism took most seriously, and whose outlook and interests differed greatly from its original clerical sponsors. It was not long, therefore, before those who espoused the cause of Neo-Confucianism at court, like Fujiwara Seika and Hayashi Razan, attempted to liberate themselves from clerical dominance and establish Neo-Confucianism, not only as an independent teaching, but also as a creed and code having undisputed state sanction.

FUJIWARA SEIKA AND THE RISE OF NEO-CONFUCIANISM

The first interview between Tokugawa Ieyasu and Fujiwara Seika (1561–1619) took place as early as 1593 when Toyotomi Hideyoshi was still the Tycoon of Japan and Ieyasu one of his lieutenants. The meeting was a momentous one, for it led eventually to wholesale renovation of the cultural and educational policy of the new shogunate. History remains silent as to who it was that took the initiative for that interview, from which both had much to gain. Ieyasu had been inspired by the example of China's great empire builder, T'ang T'ai-tsung (r. 627–649) whose reconstruction policies were outlined in a Japanese movable-type edition of the *Chen-kuan cheng-yao* appearing at that time, and he was eager to learn how peace and stability could be restored to his own war-ravaged land. Seika, at the same time, was anxious to promote a new center of study outside the Five Zen Monasteries. There is strong evidence that a third party interested in overseas trade might have been instrumental in bringing the two together. We may well believe that enterprising traders of the time wanted a man like Ieyasu, of firm character and steady temper, to take the lead in establishing a regime devoted to peace and prosperity, and that they looked upon Seika as one well-suited to serve such a regime as commissioner of foreign trade and ambassador extraordinary, since he was a learned student of things Chinese, able to write Chinese as well as the Zen monks, and acquainted with adjacent countries as well.

Two such traders were Yoshida Sōan and his father Ryōi, well-established Kyoto capitalists engaged exclusively in overseas trade. Ryōi and Sōan were Seika's ardent admirers and disciples, on whose behalf Seika

[336]

later wrote his *Bunshō Tattoku Kōryō,* and also a letter addressed to the merchant prince of Annam.

A scion of the Fujiwara aristocracy, Seika was a twelfth-generation descendant of Fujiwara no Teika, the foremost poet and arbiter elegantium of the thirteenth century, and Seika himself was a poet of great skill. Much reduced by circumstances, he made his way to Kyoto to study Chinese poetry and prose at one of the Five Zen Monasteries, hoping to prepare himself for the post of emissary to China. Seika's deep interest in Chinese studies can be seen in his *Bunshō Tattoku Kōryō,* the most extensive and systematic study of Chinese poetry and prose until then attempted from the creative point of view. He also took every opportunity to acquaint himself personally with Korean captives and Chinese envoys arriving in Japan at irregular intervals. He even attempted to visit China in 1596, but a shipwreck upset his plans.

One thing he became aware of in the course of his preparatory studies was the complete change that had taken place in China and adjacent countries, through the establishment of Neo-Confucianism or Chu Hsi philosophy as the official basis of all instruction. The decline of Buddhism was already well-advanced in China. Zen teaching, especially, was held to be purely negative in regard to secular affairs; more particularly, as far as Seika was concerned, it failed to offer an ethical code such as was needed to govern the peaceful pursuit of international trade. Chu Hsi philosophy, however, being thoroughly secular and rational in character, and also by now officially accepted in all the countries of East Asia, could serve as a moral basis for international dealings.

It may be noted in this connection that Seika's adherence to Chu Hsi philosophy was qualified, being less exclusive than was later the case with his follower Hayashi Razan. For the latter, it was Chu Hsi alone that mattered; but for Seika, any system of philosophy (including the unorthodox Wang Yang-ming school) would suffice providing that it offered a secular and rational standard of conduct for the peaceful transaction of business, and was acceptable to all countries.

Seika's awareness of the need for such a code or standard in international dealings must have impressed Ieyasu; for the latter was much interested in overseas commercial ventures, as he later proved when shogun. Indeed, he wished to enlist Seika's services for this purpose, but the latter declined, and recommended in his stead one of his young and rising disciples, Hayashi Razan. It was through the efforts of Razan and his descendants that Neo-Confucianism became the official philosophy and code of the shogunate, in both external and internal affairs.

FUJIWARA SEIKA

Letter to the Prince of Annam

The following letter was written in behalf of the Kyoto merchant, Yoshida Ryōi, who was sending a trading expedition to Annam. Like Korea and Japan, Annam was in the Chinese cultural sphere, within which diplomatic and commercial intercourse were usually conducted on the basis of the Chinese language and customs.

[From *Fujiwara Seika shū*, I, 125–26]

To Lord Huang, Chief of Annam:

The going and coming of ships to your country in recent years bears certain witness to the amicable friendship between our two countries and is a source of deep satisfaction.

Last year during the sixth month our crew arrived home safely bearing your reply to our letter and also some exquisite gifts. Words cannot express our appreciation for your generous good-will.

Your letter says that the only thing important is the word "good faith"; it is the essence of morality in the nation and the home. We too hold to the belief that good faith is inherent in our nature, that it moves heaven and earth, penetrates metals and rocks, and pervades everything without exception; its influence is not just limited to contact and communication between neighboring countries. The winds may blow in different directions in countries a thousand miles apart, but as to good faith every quarter of the world must be the same, for this is the very nature of things.

It will be seen therefore that men differ only in secondary details, such as clothing and speech. Countries may be a thousand or even ten thousand miles apart and differences may be found in clothing and speech, but there is one thing in all countries which is not far apart, not a bit different: that is good faith.

Our former representatives were not virtuous; on their way back and forth, they went astray in both conduct and speech and were guilty of many irregularities. So they were punished according to the law of our country. We imagine that this is what your country would do under the same circumstances.

The crews of our ships are drawn from among street boys and shop clerks, who are apt to lose their sense of honor when they see a chance to get something for themselves. They say whatever suits their fancy at the moment, so their word cannot be fully trusted. From now on therefore let the good faith of our two countries be embodied in written form, and let the written forms be stamped with a seal to certify their genuineness.

We are taking the liberty of sending, in the care of our crew, an answer to your letter of last summer which we want you to examine carefully. We are sending along with it several samples of our native products as tokens of good-will. Your letter also says that your "country is a land of poetry, history, good manners, and justice, not a land crowded with traders and merchandise. When merchants and traders crowd around, they are only bent on profit, which is really deplorable."

Generally speaking, however, the four classes of people [1] are all people, the eight departments of government are all parts of the government; and aside from people and government, poetry, history, good manners, and justice do not mean anything. This is likewise a fixed truth in all lands, and the basis of good faith everywhere. What your country is really concerned about is that a lack of good faith may produce all kinds of undesirable results. But as long as our two countries are not lacking in good faith, even if there be a few contemptible men among the crews, there need be no fear of such undesirable incidents arising. Of course one cannot afford to be careless or lax, and if such incidents occur, each of our two countries has its own code of punishment, has it not?

Ship's Oath

This oath was drawn up by Fujiwara Seika in connection with the same trading mission referred to above. It represented a policy declaration on the part of the owners and captain of the ship, whose crew members were to conform to

---

[1] Scholar-officials, farmers, artisans, and merchants. Defending the merchant class from the aspersions of the Confucian-minded Annamese, Seika shows that merchants have a legitimate place even in the Confucian scheme of things.

its provisions. Note the characteristic Confucian subordination of the profit motive to equity and mutual benefit.

[From *Fujiwara Seika shū*, I, 126–27]

1. Commerce is the business of selling and buying in order to bring profit to both parties. It is not to gain profit at the expense of others. When profit is shared the gain may be large but the benefits are small. "Profit is the happy outcome of righteousness." So while the greedy merchant bids for five, the decent one bids for three. Keep that in mind.

2. Foreign lands may differ from our own in manners and speech, but as to the nature bestowed upon men by heaven there cannot be any difference. Do not forget the common identity and exploit differences. Beware even of minor lies and cheating, of arrogance and cursing. The foreigner may not be aware of them but you certainly will be. "Good faith reaches to the pig and fish, and trickery is seen by the seagulls." Heaven does not tolerate deception. Be mindful, therefore, not to bring disgrace upon our country's tradition. In case you meet men of benevolence and education, respect them as you would your own father or teacher. Inquire into the restrictions and taboos of the country, and act in accordance with its customs and religion.

3. Between heaven above and earth beneath all peoples are brothers and things are the common property of all, everyone being equal in the light of Humanity. It must be the more so with one's fellow countrymen and still more so with men on the same ship. In trouble and tribulation, in sickness and hunger, relief should go to everyone equally. Never should anyone think only of his own escape.

4. Raging waters and angry waves, dangerous as they are, are not so dangerous as human passions. Human passions are numerous, but none are so dangerous as the passion for liquor and women that drowns men. Those who go around together, wherever it may be, should act as a team for restraining and correcting each other. The old adage says that the dangerous road lies in a soft bed, in eating and in drinking. Be on guard.

The Common Basis of Confucian Teaching

In contrast to the spirit of strict Neo-Confucian orthodoxy later fostered by the Tokugawa, Fujiwara Seika inclined toward an easy eclecticism, avoiding controversy on metaphysical questions and pointing instead to the common ethical principles of the Neo-Confucian philosophers. This excerpt is from a letter to his disciple Hayashi Razan, who became the champion of orthodox Chu Hsi philosophy.

[From Inoue, *Shushi gakuha*, pp. 26–27]

Chu Hsi was by nature conscientious and consistent; he had a taste for the profound and the precise. Those who followed him were therefore liable to suffer from the defect of hair-splitting. Lu Hsiang-shan was by nature superbly brilliant and craved unfettered simplicity. Those who followed him, therefore, were inclined to suffer from a lack of restraint. That is where they differed, and people took note of their differences without taking note of their agreement on fundamentals.

Where did they agree? They agreed on the approval of [the sage-kings] Yao and Shun, and on the disapproval of [the tyrants] Chieh and Chou. Both also agreed on reverence for Confucius and Mencius, and on the rejection of Shākyamuni Buddha and Lao Tzu. They also considered an action in accord with heaven's law as public-spirited and an action that follows human desire as selfish-minded.

What all students should do therefore is keep a right mind, be prompt in action, and practice patience and perseverance. Then one day in the course of time, a sort of self-revelation independent of everyday knowledge will overtake them all of a sudden, and the question of agreements and disagreements will solve itself.

THE OFFICIAL SCHOOL: THREE GENERATIONS OF THE HAYASHI FAMILY

It took father, son, and grandson—three generations of the Hayashi family—to initiate, establish, and entrench Sung Neo-Confucianism as the creed and code of the ruling class under the Tokugawa Shogunate. The father was Hayashi Razan (1583–1657), also known as Dōshun. A precocious youth, he began his Chinese studies in his early teens at Kyoto under the guidance of Zen monks, but being dissatisfied both with the Zen method of study and with the traditional way of the court scholars, he went to Fujiwara Seika, unofficial Confucian adviser to Tokugawa Ieyasu, to study further under his guidance. This was a case in which the younger scholar proved abler than the older, both in philosophical studies and literary ability. Recommended by his master to serve as Confucian tutor to the shogun in 1608, he rose steadily in influence and importance. His biographers maintain that after his appointment, "there was not a single line in the laws or edicts of the first Tokugawa Shoguns that was not drafted by him." The most important of these laws served as a virtual constitution for Tokugawa Japan: the Laws Governing the Military Households, the Imperial Court and the Buddhist religious communities.

To set forth the vast system of Neo-Confucian philosophy which Hayashi Razan embraced is not our purpose here, but it is worth noting some features of Chu Hsi's thought which were to have a profound influence upon Japanese intellectual and political life for the next three centuries. One of these is its fundamental rationalism. The Ch'eng-Chu school was known as the "philosophy of reason (or principle, *li*)," since it stressed the objective reason or principle in all things as the basis of learning and conduct. Intellectually this required exhaustive study of things and human affairs in order to determine their underlying principles, pursuing what the *Great Learning,* a favorite text of this school, called "the investigation of things." This positivistic and quasi-scientific approach was a notable characteristic of Japanese thought and scholarship in the Tokugawa period, which showed a new interest in observing the constant laws of nature and human society, as contrasted to the medieval, Buddhistic view of the world as subject only to ceaseless change, the Law of Impermanence.

Another important feature of Chu Hsi's philosophy is its essential humanism, which, like his rationalism, derives from the earlier Confucian tradition. The moral doctrines of this school focus directly upon man and his closest human relationships, not upon any supernatural order or divine law. These are expressed most concretely in the Five Human Relationships and their attendant obligations (between father and son, ruler and subject, husband and wife, older and younger brother, and between friends). Such an emphasis upon human loyalties and personal relationships was obviously congenial to the feudal society of Japan in this period, and provided a uniform, secular code by which the Tokugawa could maintain social order in all their domains, no matter how divided they might be by local loyalties or religious allegiances. It is a noteworthy fact that public morality until recent times, as well as the peculiar code of the warrior-aristocrat known as *bushido,* drew more upon the ethical teachings and terminology of Confucianism than upon any other doctrine.

A third characteristic of Chu Hsi's thought is what might be called its historicism. For Chu Hsi, good government depended not only on the personal moral cultivation of the ruler and his subjects, but also upon the study of history. In the record of the past could be found the principles of human affairs, which a ruler must understand in order to discharge his function properly. Chu Hsi took it upon himself to compile a general history of China, the *Outline and Digest of the General Mirror,*[1] pointing up the moral implications of past events. His followers in Japan devoted much of their study to history, and were responsible for reviving interest in Japan's own past, which had been largely neglected in medieval times. On the whole Neo-Confucianists in Japan distinguished themselves, not in the realm of speculative philosophy, but in historical studies, and exerted the greatest influence on their own and later times by their interpretations of Japanese history and traditions.

This brings us to a fourth feature of Neo-Confucianism, ethnocentrism, which tended strongly to reinforce an already well-developed sense of nationalism. The Neo-Confucian revival in the Sung Dynasty had brought a reassertion of Chinese cultural traditions and values against a foreign faith, Buddhism, and in the face of imminent conquest by Turkic and Mongol barbarians. Chu Hsi's history had put special stress, in its moralistic judgments, upon the distinction between legitimate and illegitimate rulers, and upon Chinese civilization as opposed to foreign barbarism. In the Japanese mind this same attitude inspired loyalty to the Throne and intense xenophobia, both of which became increasingly significant toward the end of the shogunate.

Furthermore, Confucian economic thinking was traditionally agrarian and hostile to the development of commerce. This was due partly to an ethical viewpoint in which the sense of equity dominated over the sense of utility or profit, and also to two basic facts of Chinese political economy: that the fortunes of government (and revenues of the state) rose or fell with the condition of agriculture, and that the monopolistic Chinese state resented large-scale private enterprise which might challenge its own interests. Notwithstanding the great social and economic disparities

[1] The *T'ung-chien kang-mu,* a condensation of Ssu-ma Kuang's *Tzu-chih t'ung-chien.*

between China and Japan, and disregarding especially the tremendous expansion of Japanese commerce in recent years, the Tokugawa and their Neo-Confucian advisers adopted the traditional Chinese attitude of opposing commerce and imposing social disabilities upon the merchant class.

Finally, related to nationalism and agrarianism is the traditional isolationism of the Chinese Confucianist, his conviction of Chinese self-sufficiency and cultural superiority, his disbelief in the advantages of cultural relations or trade with the world beyond the pale of China, and his usual preoccupation with security problems at home rather than expansion abroad. There can be no doubt that this kind of thinking carried over into the minds of Neo-Confucian officials in Japan and disposed them to adopt a seclusionist policy similar to that of the Ming dynasty.

Tokugawa Ieyasu was a cautious administrator who, as we have seen, kept in his service two older and very astute advisers, Abbot Tenkai (1536–1643) of the Tendai sect and the Elder Sūden (1569–1633) of the Zen sect. The former was director of the Nikkō shrines, with all Esoteric Buddhist temples and syncretic Shinto shrines under his jurisdiction; while the latter was superintendent-general of all Zen denominations, with the traditional privilege of supervising government correspondence with foreign countries. Razan raised objections to the meddling of Buddhists in the secular affairs of the government, but was soundly beaten by Tenkai, it is said, in a debate held in the presence of Ieyasu. While thus carrying on the old struggle of the Neo-Confucianists against the Buddhists—a rivalry already centuries old in China—Razan found a natural ally in native Shinto. With a view to strengthening this alliance by showing the essential unity of the Shinto religion and Confucian ethics, and perhaps also to establish himself at court as an authority on Japanese history and Shinto, he undertook extensive research into Shinto which resulted in his *Study of Our Shinto Shrines* (*Honchō jinja-kō*). He also studied the history of Japan and wrote a *General History of Our State* (*Honchō tsugan*) with Chu Hsi's *T'ung-chien kang-mu* as his model. In philosophy, history, prose, and poetry, Chinese as well as Japanese, Razan worked with amazing speed and industry to provide authoritative compilations which would stand as guides to the three shoguns he served. His collected works ran to 150 titles, and his residence at Ueno grew into a true college of liberal arts with the largest private library in Japan attached to it.

Still the elder Hayashi was unable by himself to overcome Buddhist influence in the government; in fact, to maintain his own position at court he was forced to comply with an old custom requiring the Buddhist tonsure of all those entrusted with educational duties. It is fortunate, therefore, that he had worthy successors in his own son, known as Shunsai and also as Gahō (1618–1680), and in his grandson Hōkō (1644–1732). It was the former who compiled the 300-volume *Family Genealogies* in 1643, and who completed the aforementioned *General History of Our State* in 310 volumes, by 1670. There is also a collection of his complete works, including commentaries on all the Confucian Classics, in 120 volumes. As a consequence of this great scholarly achievement the college came to gain official recognition as the shogunate university with the title of *Kōbunin,* and Gahō was named the first doctor of literature (*Kōbunin gakushi*). The award of the official title, Head of the State University (*Daigaku-no-kami*), had to wait for another generation.

In 1691, the fifth shogun, Tsunayoshi, himself an ardent Confucianist, conferred on Hōkō that eminent title, which became hereditary in the Hayashi family. At the same time the university was renamed The School of Prosperous Peace (*Shōhei-kō*) and located at a new site in Yushima, where it stood throughout the long Tokugawa rule as the center of official instruction. It was indeed not only an educational center, but a Confucian religious center as well, for images of Confucius and his disciples were installed in the building, and the shoguns came to pay homage there every year, with the head of the Hayashi family always acting as master of ceremonies.

Following are the Hayashi family leaders, all of whom except Razan and Gahō were Heads of the State University (*Daigaku-no-kami*) under the Tokugawa Shogunate.

1. Razan	1583–1657		7. Kimpō	1767–1793
2. Gahō	1618–1680		8. Jussai [2]	1768–1841
3. Hōkō	1644–1732		9. Teiu	1791–1844
4. Ryūkō	1681–1758		10. Sōkan	1828–1853
5. Hōkoku	1721–1773		11. Fukusai	1800–1859
6. Hōtan	1761–1787		12. Gakusai	1833–1906

[2] Adopted heir from the Ogyū family.

HAYASHI RAZAN

On Mastery of the Arts of Peace and War

As Confucian adviser to Tokugawa Ieyasu, Hayashi Razan represented the Chinese tradition of civil government and polite learning at the center of Japanese military government. His function was to assist Ieyasu, the man of war, to become a man of peace as well, to crown his military success with the achievement of an enduring social order based on Confucian ethical ideals. In this excerpt Razan explains why the members of the military aristocracy, the samurai, should cultivate the arts of peace and devote themselves to Confucian learning. It was the pursuit of this aim which led, in the course of the long Tokugawa period, to the "civilizing" of the warrior class, to the Confucianizing of feudal ethics, and to increasing acceptance of the idea that the samurai's role as a member of the ruling class partook of political and intellectual functions akin to those of the Chinese scholar-bureaucrat. In making his point Razan identifies the samurai with the knight or gentleman (*shih;* Jap. *shi*) of whom Confucius spoke, and who, in the evolution of Chinese social thought, came to represent the ideal scholar-bureaucrat. Razan thus attempts the conversion of the samurai to a new concept of moral and intellectual leadership (in somewhat the same way that Confucius had the "knight").

[From *Hayashi Razan bunshū*, pp. 309–10]

Someone asked for an explanation of the samurai's mastering both the arts of peace and the arts of war. The reply was: "Armies achieve victory by the arts of war. That by which they achieve victory is strategy. Strategy is derived from the arts of peace. This is why the precepts of T'ai Kung included a chapter on civil arts as well as a chapter on military arts.[1] These two together make up the art of the general. When one is unable to combine one with the other, as in the cases of Chuang Hou and Kuan Ying, who lacked the arts of peace, and Sui Ho and Lu Chia, who lacked the arts of war, there will be cause for regret. Warfare involves knowledge of one's opportunity. Stratagems involve secrecy. Opportunities are not easy to see, but one can learn them through stratagems so long as the stratagems are not divulged. Therefore, those who are adept at the handling of troops regard the arts of peace and the arts of war as their left and right hands.

"Let us consider [the teaching of] the Sage that 'to·lead an untaught

[1] Referring to the *Liu t'ao,* falsely attributed to Lü Wang, a minister to King Wen of Chou according to traditional Chinese accounts.

people into war is to throw them away.'[2] Teaching the people is a civil art, but warfare is a military art. Without both of them, the people would be thrown away. Therefore it is said that the man of civil affairs must also have military preparedness. There may be no lack of daring in hunting a tiger unarmed or in crossing a river without a boat, but this is not the same thing as prowess in the arts of war. There may be no lack of magnanimity in refraining from making old people prisoners of war, but this is not the same thing as mastery of the arts of peace. To have the arts of peace, but not the arts of war, is to lack courage. To have the arts of war, but not the arts of peace, is to lack wisdom. Keeping both in mind, generals employ or disperse their troops and advance or retreat according to the proper time. This is the Way of the general. A general is no other than a true man. A man who is dedicated and has a mission to perform is called a samurai (or *shi*). A man who is of inner worth and upright conduct, who has moral principles and mastery of the arts is also called a samurai. A man who pursues learning, too, is called a samurai. A man who serves [at court] without neglecting the mountains and forests is also called a samurai. The term samurai (or *shi*) is indeed broad. Thus of ranks [in the Chou dynasty] it was said that they ascended from officer [*shi*] to high official; from high official to chief minister; and from chief minister to prince. Nevertheless, when a man became a chief minister and entered the service of the king to administer the government, he was also called a 'minister-officer' (*kyō-shi*).[3] At court he was a statesman; in the field he was a general. The Book of Odes says: 'Mighty in peace and war is Chi-fu / A pattern to all the peoples.'[4] How can a man discharge the duties of his rank and position without combining the peaceful and military arts?"

The Confucian Way

The early leaders of the Neo-Confucian revival in China had been strongly opposed to Taoism and Buddhism as being essentially amoral and antisocial. In Japan Hayashi Razan, as founder of the official Neo-Confucian school, took issue with these philosophies on the same grounds. Against their view of the way as transcending human reason and ethical relations, he reaffirms the fun-

[2] *Analects*, XIII, 30.
[3] That is, the term *shi* (Ch., *shih*) was used for the lowest rank of the feudal aristocracy, but also in the titles of the highest officials.
[4] Waley (trans.), *The Book of Songs*, No. 133, p. 127.

damental rationalism of the Confucian Way and the universal moral constants upon which human society rests. In this excerpt the immediate antagonist is Lao Tzu, but the language Razan uses makes it clear that he has Zen Buddhism in mind as well.

[From *Hayashi Razan bunshū*, p. 852]

Lao Tzu said: "The Way that can be told of is not an Unvarying Way."[5] What he considered the Way was quiescence and nonstriving, and what he spoke of was the original undifferentiated state of nature. But man is born into the world of today and cannot even achieve the untroubled state of high antiquity; how much less can he put himself in the original undifferentiated state of nature? If it is true in the case of nature that in the original state of unresolved chaos there was no thought [mental discrimination], still while men live and breathe how can they avoid thinking? Man is essentially an active living thing. How can he be compared to desiccated bones? That old fool [Chuang Tzu]'s arguments based on withered trees, dead ashes, and old faggots[6] are of the same sort—all weird, perverted talk.

The Way of the Sages is altogether different from this. Their Way consists in nothing else than the moral obligations between sovereign and subject, father and child, husband and wife, elder and younger brother, and friend and friend. One practices it with the five virtues. The five virtues are rooted in the mind, and the principle which inheres in the mind is the nature [of man]. What all men partake of together is the Way, and attainment of the Way in one's mind is called virtue. Therefore, the Way, virtue, humanity, righteousness, decorum, and wisdom are different in name but the same in essence. It is not what Lao Tzu called the Way. If one casts aside the moral obligations of man and calls something else the Way, then it is not the Confucian Way, it is not the Way of the Sages, and it is not the Way of Yao and Shun.

Essay on the Emperor Jimmu (*Jimmu Tennō Ron*)

Hayashi Razan, though not a philosopher of much originality, was deeply enough influenced by Chu Hsi's rationalism that he re-examined some of the legends concerning Japan's imperial house, such as the divinity of the first

---

[5] Opening lines of the *Tao Te Ching*.

[6] Symbols used by Chuang Tzu for the state of seeming unconsciousness or superconsciousness.

emperor, Jimmu. He was also enough of a sinologue and sinophile to convince himself that Japan's first civilized rulers were Chinese immigrants and that the so-called Three Imperial Regalia were of continental rather than divine origin. While Razan's views did not gain general acceptance, they are typical of his attempt to reconcile Chinese and Japanese traditions, by giving the latter a naturalistic and moralistic interpretation in line with Confucian teaching.

[From *Hayashi Razan bunshū*, pp. 280–81]

The Zen monk, Engetsu, of the East Hill Monastery undertook to compile a history of the nation. Because the court disapproved of it, his work was cast into the fire before it was finished. Engetsu's idea, as far as I can gather, was to cite certain historical records indicating that the Japanese were descended from Wu T'ai-po of China.[7] T'ai-po found his refuge among barbarians, cut his hair, tattooed his body and lived with dragons. His descendant made his way to Tsukushi [in Kyushu], where the people considered him a deity; that may correspond to the imperial grandson's descent to the summit of Takachiho in Hyūga. [Then follow other alleged correspondences between Japanese imperial traditions and the legend of Wu T'ai-po]. . . . Although this is just a patchwork of conjecture, there seems to me to be an element of truth in it. If the imperial grandson was the son of Heavenly Gods, as the *Chronicles* say, how can you explain his descent on a remote hill of the western countryside, instead of on the central province? How can you explain that for three generations from Ninigi and Hikohoho to Ugaya, they made a protracted sojourn in Hyūga and passed away there without establishing their capital in central Japan? Jimmu, on his expedition to the East at the age of forty-five, first went to Aki and then made his way to Kibi a year later. He spent three years, therefore, readying his forces and gathering provisions; only then did he proceed to Kawachi, to win his great victory over Nagasune-hiko in the battle of Kushae Hill. Killing Nagasune, he made a triumphal entry into great Yamato, there to establish his court at Kashiwabara. Why did he have to overcome such difficulties, if he possessed divine powers in war? Just as the imperial grandson met resistance from Ōnamochi, so Jimmu was opposed in battle by Nagasune. Does it not give rise to suspicion? Is it not reasonable to assume that Ōnamochi and Nagasune were ancient tribal chieftains whom

---

[7] According to tradition, noble scion of the house of Chou, who left the Chou state so that a younger brother could succeed to the throne, c. thirteenth century B.C.

Jimmu supplanted when he established his rule? Thus, the Wu prince and his descendants, having already held sway for a hundred generations in succession, will continue their reign for ten thousand generations to come. Is it not glorious? The once-powerful Wu may have been overcome [in China] by the Yüeh state, but their reign in our country is coeval with heaven and earth. I am therefore more and more inclined to believe in the sovereign virtue of T'ai-po. If Engetsu could come back to life, I would like to ask him what he thought of this.

Some may say: Our country regards the Yata mirror, the Kusanagi sword, and the Yasaka jewel as the Three Imperial Regalia. These Three Regalia have been handed down since the divine deities came to rule the land succeeding Heaven. Since the mirror, the sword and the jewel are heaven-made, succeeding reigns have treasured them. If we accept your interpretation, however, they are no more than man-made treasures from a foreign land, are they not?

In answer, I would state that when T'ai-po left his country, he most certainly brought with him articles and implements which would be bequeathed to his heirs. . . . [Razan goes on to show that objects similar to the Three Regalia were available to Wu T'ai-po in his native land.]

As to the distinction between Heaven-made and man-made, "We call what is metaphysical 'principle' and what is physical 'object'" but Heaven and man are one and principle and object are inseparable. Where there is reason there is matter, where there is matter there is form, and where there is form, there is object. The evolution of matter has its root in nature. Take the case of an ox's nose or a horse's neck; one is strung by a rope, the other yoked with a rod. We all know that the rope and the yoke are man-made, but we are not aware of the fact that the rope and yoke are made because of the ox and the horse. So it is with the Three Imperial Regalia. And likewise it is true, not of these divine objects alone, but of all the institutions created by the ancient sages. Where is there anything strange in this?

I have been trying to fathom the significance of the sacred scriptures on this subject. The Three Regalia are three virtues. The human mind is empty, alert, and transparent; it reflects and it apprehends. Is it not truly a mirror? The human mind is round and perfect in its virtue, as stainless as jade, the symbol of humanity (*jin*). It is a jewel, is it not? The human mind is brave and resolute, and makes decisions in accord-

[350]

ance with its sense of duty (*gi*). This signifies courage, which is represented by the sword, is it not? The Three Regalia are divine, and the
three virtues are those of the human mind, which is the abode of the
divine. So they are one in three and three in one, essentially inseparable.
The divine is not finite; only in the object does it become manifest. The
mind leaves no trace of itself; only through the medium of matter do
we observe its reactions. The interrelation of Heaven and man is truly
wondrous. How can we set them apart from each other?

If one who becomes the leader of men rules the land with these three
virtues, long may he keep as his own the great treasure of the Three
Regalia. But if the Regalia be taken while the virtues are abandoned,
that will be the end. The ancients who read sacred scriptures were aware
of this truth but did not talk about it; men today who read sacred scripture talk as if they understood but actually do not. So I have taken
the liberty of discussing the matter.

Conversation with Three Korean Envoys

In Japan (as in other Far Eastern countries influenced by Confucian traditions
of diplomatic intercourse) foreign relations were entrusted to men of superior
intellectual attainments, capable of matching wits on all levels of discourse and
thus upholding the moral and cultural prestige of their country. Here we
find Hayashi Razan acting as a sort of foreign secretary for the shogunate and
feeling out some Korean envoys on their position with respect to Chu Hsi's
metaphysics. Since they could not speak each other's tongue, the "conversation" was conducted *by writing* in Chinese, the diplomatic language.

[From *Hayashi Razan bunshū*, p. 840]

The Bakufu [shogun] asked me, "What did you discuss in writing with
the three Korean envoys?" I told him that I asked whether principle (*ri*)
and material force (*ki*) are to be regarded as one or two. Their answer
was, "Principle is just one; as to material force there is the pure and the
impure. The four impulses," they said, "come from principle, but the
seven emotions arise from material force." I asked what that meant.
Their answer was, "When pleasure, anger, sorrow, and happiness are
normal, they are called pure; when they are abnormal, they are called
impure. However, material force itself also comes from principle." [8]
I then asked which is greater, Chu Hsi or Lu Hsiang-shan. Their

[8] Whereas Chu Hsi's philosophy had emphasized a dualism of principle and material force,
Razan himself tended to reduce everything to principle or reason (Jap., *ri;* Ch., *li*).

answer was, "Chu Hsi achieved the supreme synthesis of the various philosophies. Hsiang-shan cannot be compared to him." I had special reason to ask the above question. I wanted to test their position. As to the foregoing opinions, they are set forth in many books already known to me and there was nothing to be learned by asking them. Their responses were what one would expect from Confucian scholars, and have no special significance.

On Wang Yang-ming

Wang Yang-ming, the Chinese Neo-Confucian thinker who departed from Chu Hsi's philosophy, was equally well known as a statesman and general. Razan, a strong partisan of Chu Hsi, suggests that Wang had one serious defect as a scholar: he was addicted to the study of military strategy and tactics.
 [From *Hayashi Razan bunshū*, p. 878]

Wang Yang-ming was the most gifted scholar of the Ming dynasty. Proclaiming his doctrine of "good knowledge," he attracted many followers, and his schoolmen are seen everywhere today. When, in obedience to the imperial decree, he subdued the rebel Ch'en Hao, he often gave instruction to his officers and men by quoting from [the Military Classics] of Sun and Wu, but [instead of identifying them] he would say, "According to the Classics. . . ." Wang Yang-ming was a man of profound intelligence and excellent memory, but even so in military matters he turned to the stratagems of Sun and Wu. . . . Examine the *Collected Works of Yang-ming* and see for yourself. They are full of strategies and intrigue which do violence to our best instincts, as the reader cannot fail to observe. That is one thing which readers must keep in mind. Is it not said that "those who like to fight are doomed to the heaviest punishment"? [9] True gentlemen do not devote themselves to this kind of study.

THE SPREAD OF NEO-CONFUCIANISM IN JAPAN

The Hayashis' success in establishing Neo-Confucianism as the official system of instruction was due in large part to the wholehearted support given them by leading members of the Tokugawa family. Among the

[9] An adage very similar to: "He who lives by the sword shall perish by the sword."

many sons of Ieyasu who contributed to the promotion of Neo-Confucianism, Yoshinao (1600–1650) may be noted especially. Representing one of the three Tokugawa branch families chosen to guard the interests of the shogunate in the provinces, with strategic Owari as his domain, Yoshinao was an early convert to Confucianism and a steadfast advocate of Chu Hsi philosophy. It was this scion of the Tokugawa who erected the Sage's Hall, in which Confucius' image was installed at Ueno and where Razan had his official residence. It was he, too, who induced the third shogun, Iemitsu, to pay personal homage to the image, thus helping to make it a center of religious veneration. Another Tokugawa prince who became especially interested in Confucianism was Tsunayoshi (r. 1680–1709), the fifth shogun. Given as he was to extremes of enthusiasm, Tsunayoshi outdid himself in promoting Confucianism. Through his lavish patronage, a new Paragon Hall was built near the center of Edo, with all the splendor of a national shrine. At the annual commemoration ceremony held there, one of the Hayashis acted as master of ceremonies, and the shogun took great pride in giving a personal lecture on one of the Confucian Classics, which was an outstanding feature of the program. From this time until the end of the shogunate, the School of Prosperous Peace (Shōheikō) was the cultural and educational center of the nation. At this center the Hayashis officiated as Commissioners of State Education and spread Neo-Confucian teachings throughout the metropolitan era of Edo.

But in the provinces it was a different matter. Topographically Japan was divided by steep hills and fast-running rivers into many comparatively isolated regions that could only be penetrated slowly and with difficulty. It was fortunate for the new movement that it found champions in a pair of Tokugawa princes, one Hoshina Masayuki (1611–1672), third son of the second shogun, Hidetada, and newly created lord of ancient Ainu-land in the remote northeast of Japan; and the other Tokugawa Mitsukuni (1628–1701), a grandson of the first shogun, who had the strategic Tone River basin of Hitachi as his feudal domain. The former was assisted by a hot-tempered Chu Hsi scholar of the Southern school, Yamazaki Ansai; the latter was under the tutelage of a high-minded Chinese political refugee, Chu Shun-shui.

YAMAZAKI ANSAI

The importance of Yamazaki Ansai (1618–1682) lies in his wide influence as a teacher of Chu Hsi's philosophy and in his role as the chief formulator of a new system of Shinto doctrine. Yamazaki was much impressed by the structure and clarity of Neo-Confucian metaphysics, but his natural inclinations led him away from this type of speculation toward a much simpler ethical teaching. In his hands the encyclopedic system of Chu Hsi was thus reduced to the much less complex formula "Devotion within, righteousness without." "Devotion" for Yamazaki was the traditional Confucian virtue of reverence or seriousness given a plainly religious significance. In his later years Yamazaki was increasingly drawn to the study of Shinto, and therefore interpreted this formula in terms strongly suggestive of worship and service of the gods. From one of his Shinto teachers he borrowed the expression *Suika*, which in turn derived from a Shinto text wherein men were enjoined to pray for the blessings of the gods and to rely on divine grace in all their actions. This expression eventually served as the distinctive mark of Yamazaki's brand of Confucian-Shinto, or *Suika Shinto*, combining the ethical maxims of the former teaching with the religious doctrines of the latter.

Actually Yamazaki went to much greater lengths than this to establish the unity of the two teachings. Not only did he equate Shinto creation legends with Chinese cosmology, and the Shinto pantheon with the metaphysical principles of the Neo-Confucianists, but he further identified the supreme moral virtue, devotion, with the primal stuff of the universe. In spite of his attempt, however, to embrace these disparate elements in what seemed to him a rationally coherent system, in the end he had to insist that human reason was inadequate to deal with such truths and much had to be taken simply on faith. Later Shintoists were glad enough to dispense with Yamazaki's tortuous rationalizations, while retaining his emphasis on faith, on the moral virtues, and particularly on devotion to the gods as expressed through devotion to their living embodiment, the emperor. In these respects Yamazaki serves as a striking example in the seventeenth century of three tendencies which became increasingly significant in modern times: the popularization of Confucian ethics in Japan; the revival of Shinto and its development as an articulate creed;

[354]

and finally the intense nationalism which combined Confucian reverence with Shinto tradition to produce emperor worship.

Principles of Education
(From the Preface to the Collected Commentaries on Chu Hsi's Regulations for the School of the White Deer Cave)

Yamazaki Anasi was a forceful teacher who impressed others with his earnestness and air of moral authority. As an exponent of Chu Hsi's teaching in Japan, he paid special attention to a somewhat neglected aspect of Chu's writing: the ethical maxims of the school in which the latter had taught. In his preface, Yamazaki is at pains to establish the authoritative character of this particular formulation by showing that it embraces all the teachings of the sacrosanct *Great Learning*. As such it provides a convenient résumé of the type of Confucian indoctrination to which many Japanese were exposed in this period.
[From *Zoku Yamazaki Ansai zenshū*, III, 1–5. Text abridged and commentary deleted]

The philosopher Chu, styled Hui-an, was conspicuously endowed with intellectual leadership. Following in the line of [the Sung philosophers] Chou Tun-i and the Ch'eng brothers, he advanced the cause of Confucianism in both elementary education and higher education. For the guidance of his students he established these regulations, but they failed to gain wide acceptance in his own time because of opposition from vile quarters. . . .

It would seem to me that the aim of education, elementary and advanced, is to clarify human relationships. In the elementary program of education the various human relationships are made clear, the essence of this education in human relationships being devotion to [or respect for] persons. The "investigation of things" in advanced studies [as set forth in the *Great Learning*] simply carries to its ultimate conclusion what has already been learned from elementary instruction. . . .

Chu Hsi's school regulations list the Five Human Relationships as the curriculum, following an order of presentation which complements the curriculum of advanced education [as found in the *Great Learning*]. Studying, questioning, deliberating and analyzing—these four correspond to the "investigation of things" and "extension of knowledge" in advanced education. The article dealing with conscientious action goes with the "cultivation of one's person." From the emperor to the common people, the cultivation of one's person is essential, including both "making the thoughts sincere" and "rectifying the mind." The "managing of affairs" and "social intercourse" [in Chu's Regulations] refer to "regulating the family," "governing the state" and "establishing peace" [in the *Great Learning*]. These Regulations thus contain everything, and they should be used for instruction together with the *Book of Elementary Instruction* and the *Book of Advanced Education* [*Great Learning*]. But so far they have gone almost unnoticed among the items in Chu's collected works, scarcely attracting any attention from scholars. I have taken the liberty, however, of bringing them out into the light of day by mounting and hanging them in my studio for constant reference and reflection. More recently I have found a detailed discussion of these regulations in *Some Reflections of Mine* by the Korean scholar Yi T'oege. It convinced me more than anything else that these Regulations are the true guide to education. . . .

[*Signed*] Yamazaki Ansai
Keian 3 [1650]: Twelfth Month, 9th Day

REGULATIONS FOR THE SCHOOL OF THE WHITE DEER CAVE

[*The Five Regulations*]

Between parent and child there is intimacy.

Between lord and minister there is duty.

Between husband and wife there is differentiation.

Between elder and junior there is precedence.

Between friend and friend there is fidelity.

These five articles of teaching are what [the sage-kings] Yao and Shun commanded Ch'i, the Minister of Education, solemnly to promulgate as the five subjects of teaching. All that the student should study is contained in these five regulations, but in studying them he should follow five steps, as given below:

Study widely.

Question thoroughly.

Deliberate carefully.

Analyze clearly.

Act conscientiously. . . .

In speech be loyal and true; in action be conscientious and reverent. Subdue ire and stifle passion. Change yourself for the better; do not hesitate to correct your errors. These things are essential to personal culture.

Do not do to others what you do not care for yourself. When action fails to get results, seek the reason for failure in yourself. These are important in social intercourse.

The aim of teaching and guidance given by ancient sages and scholars, it seems to me, is nothing more than to set forth moral principles, in order, first, to cultivate them in one's own person, and then to extend them to others. Simply to accumulate knowledge and learn to write well in order to gain fame and a well-paid position, is far from being the true function of education. Nevertheless that is what most men pursue learning for today. . . .

Devotion and Righteousness

Pedagogically it was the practice of Confucian scholars to sum up their teachings with a key word or phrase, which could be fixed easily in people's minds. Yamazaki Ansai's key virtues of Devotion and Righteousness were taken from a slogan of the Neo-Confucian philosopher Ch'eng Yi. The original Chinese term *ching*, rendered here as Devotion, covers a wide range of meaning, including "reverence," "seriousness," "conscientiousness," etc. As Yamazaki's Shintoist leanings became more pronounced, he stressed that aspect of the term having to do with worship of the gods and the emperor. Eventually he equated these two virtues with terms found in native texts concerning primitive Shinto mythology; namely: prayer (*negigoto* or *kitō*) and honesty or forthrightness (*massugu* or *shōjiki*).

What follows is a typical attempt to demonstrate that one's own favorite slogan contains the essence of the Confucian classics.

[From *Yamazaki Ansai zenshū*, I, 90, Suika-sō 11]

" 'By Devotion we straighten ourselves within; by Righteousness we square away the world without.' The significance of these eight characters cannot be exhausted by even a lifetime of application." [1] Indeed, the Master Chu was not exaggerating at all in saying this.

In the *Analects* of Confucius when it says "the superior man cultivates himself with reverent care [Chinese *ching*, Japanese *kei*]," [2] it simply means "By Devotion [*kei*] we straighten ourselves within." What is said further in the *Analects*, "To put others at ease by cultivating oneself, and

---

[1] Chu Hsi's comment on a saying by Ch'eng Yi.　　[2] *Analects*, XIV, 45.

thus to put all men at ease" is the same as "By Righteousness we square away the world without."

. . . "The virtue of Sincerity [as taught in the *Mean*] is not merely for perfecting oneself alone; it is also for perfecting things [around us]. Perfection of self is Humanity; perfection of things is Knowledge. These are virtues which manifest our nature; this is the Way which joins the inner and the outer [worlds]." [3] Ch'eng I also said: "Devotion and Righteousness hold each other together and ascend straightway to attain the Virtue of Heaven." Thus when Chu Hsi said that these eight characters of Ch'eng I are inexhaustible in their application, he was not exaggerating at all.

Lecture Concerning the Chapters on the Divine Age

(in the *Kojiki* and *Nihongi*)

When Yamazaki Ansai took up Shinto studies late in life, he developed a cosmology based on early Japanese texts, which in spite of his own denials, obviously betrays the influence of Chinese models, especially the yin-yang and Five Elements theories incorporated into Neo-Confucian metaphysics. Fundamentally a monist who asserted the identity of the human and divine, Yamazaki saw all phenomena as produced by Fire and regulated by the interaction of two powers, Soil and Metal. With these powers he identified the supreme virtues of Devotion and Righteousness.

The following passage reveals the devious rationalizations by which Yamazaki tried to establish the relationship between Devotion and Soil and Metal. Some of the complicated philological arguments have been eliminated to smooth the way for the reader, but enough remain to illustrate Yamazaki's method.

[From *Zoku Yamazaki Ansai zenshū*, III, 207-12]

There is one important matter to be learned by those beginning the study of Shinto. If a student takes up the chapters on the Divine Age without first learning it, he will not readily understand the chapters' true significance; whereas, having the proper instruction, everything in these chapters can be understood without further inquiry. This is the key to Shinto which explains it from beginning to end. This you certainly must know.

[3] *The Mean*, XXV, 3.

I am not sure whether you have heard about it yet or not, but this is the teaching on soil and metal [*tsuchi-kane*]. . . . Do you recall that in the Divine Age text soil [*tsuchi*] is represented as five [*itsutsu*]? Izanagi cut the fire-god Kagu-tsuchi into five, its says.[1] You may not see what that really means, but it indicates the conversion of soil into five. . . .

Soil comes into being only from fire. Fire is mind and in mind dwells the god. This is not discussed in ordinary instruction, and it is only because of my desire to make you understand it thoroughly that I am revealing this to you. Now here is the secret explanation of something very important: why a [Shinto] shrine is called *hokora*. *Hokora* is where the god resides, and is equivalent to *hi-kura* [storehouse of fire]. *Ho* is an alternate form of *hi* [fire], as seen in the words of *ho-no-o* [fire tail, i.e., flame] and *ho-no-ko* [fire-child, i.e., spark]. It is interesting to note that Steadfast-Devotion [*tsutsushimi*] comes only from the mind, which is fire, the abode of the god. Now when the fire-god Kagu-tsuchi was cut into five pieces, it led to the existence of soil [*tsuchi*]. That can be understood from the theory that fire produces soil.

As to soil, it does not produce anything if it is scattered and dissipated. Only where soil is compacted together are things produced. So you can see what is meant by *tsutsushimi* [steadfast devotion]: it is the tightening up of the soil [*tsuchi wo shimuru*]. Soil is a solid thing, which holds together firmly (here the Master held out his two fists by way of demonstration). Water always is running downward; but soil does not run downward, it holds fast. Because it holds fast, things are produced. The mountain that produces metal is particularly hard, as we all know. Metal is formed when the essence of soil is drawn together and concentrated. Metal [*kane*] is joined together [*kane*] with soil. Because of metal the soil is held firmly together, and because the soil holds together firmly, the metal power is produced. This is going on now right before your eyes.

If there were no soil, nothing would be produced; but even if there were soil, without steadfastness [*tsutsushimi*], the metal power would not be produced. That steadfastness is something in man's mind. Just as nothing is produced when the soil is scattered and dissipated, so if man becomes dissipated and loose, the metal power cannot be produced. The

[1] Aston, *Nihongi*, I, 29.

metal power is actually nothing other than our attitude in the presence of the God. There is something stern and forbidding about the metal power. When this power reaches the limit of its endurance, we must expect that even men may be killed. So unyielding is it that it allows of no compromise or forgiveness.

As we see every day, only soil can produce metal. That is the principle of soil begetting metal. But do not confuse it with the Chinese theory that fire produces earth and earth produces metal. Whatever the Confucian texts may say does not matter. What I tell you is the Way of the Divine Age, and it is also something which goes on right before your eyes. The Sun Goddess, you see, was female, but when the Storm God got out of hand, she put on warlike attire and took up a sword. Even Izanagi and Izanami ruled the land by use of the spade and sword. From very earliest times Japan has been under the rule of the metal power. And that is why I have been telling you that Japan is the land of the metal power. Remember that without steadfastness the metal power would not come into being, and steadfastness is a thing of the mind.

There are still more important things to be explained in connection with soil and metal, but these are beyond your capacity now. Without the moral discipline which would prepare you for them, you are not allowed to hear such things.

Anecdotes Concerning Yamazaki Ansai

A QUESTION OF LOYALTIES

A recurring question among Tokugawa scholars was the dual allegiance seemingly implied by adherence to Chinese ethics on the part of patriotic Japanese. Yamazaki Ansai's handling of the question suggests the possibility of being faithful to Confucius and yet anti-Chinese. Neo-Shintoists carried this a step further by rejecting Confucius himself out of national loyalty.

[From *Sentetsu sōdan*, pp. 124–25]

Once Yamazaki Ansai asked his students a question: "In case China came to attack our country, with Confucius as general and Mencius as lieutenant-general at the head of hundreds of thousands of horses, what do you think we students of Confucius and Mencius ought to do?" The students were unable to offer an answer. "We don't know what we should do," they said, "so please let us know what you think about it."

"Should that eventuality arise," he replied, "I would put on armor and take up a spear to fight and capture them alive in the service of my country. That is what Confucius and Mencius teach us to do."

Later his disciple met [the Sinophile] Itō Tōgai and told him about it, adding that his teacher's understanding of Confucius and Mencius was hard to surpass. Tōgai, however, told him smilingly not to worry about the invasion of our country by Confucius and Mencius. "I guarantee that it will never happen."

YAMAZAKI ANSAI AND HIS THREE PLEASURES

Though Yamazaki in general typifies the fusion of Confucian ethics with the feudal virtues of medieval Japan, this anecdote shows how Confucian insistence upon the moral worth of the individual militated against the principle of hereditary aristocracy basic to feudalism.
[From *Sentetsu sōdan*, pp. 122–23]

The Duke of Aizu asked Yamazaki Ansai if he enjoyed any pleasures of his own. In answer Yamazaki said:

"Your vassal enjoys three pleasures. In between heaven and earth there are innumerable creatures, but I [as a man] am the highest of all creatures. That is one source of pleasure. In between heaven and earth, peace and war come in defiance of all calculation. Fortunately, however, I was born in a time when peaceful arts flourish. Thus I am able to enjoy reading books, studying the truth, and keeping the company of the ancient sages and philosophers as if they were in the same room with me. That is another pleasure."

The Lord then said, "Two pleasures you have already told me about; I would like to hear about the third one." Yamazaki replied, "That is the greatest one though difficult to express, since your Highness may not take it as intended, but instead consider it an affront." The Duke said, "Ignorant though I am, I am still the devoted disciple of my teacher. I am always thirsty for his loyal advice and hungry for his undisguised opinions. I cannot see any reason why this time you should stop halfway."

Yamazaki then declared, "Since you go to such lengths, I cannot hold back even though it may bring death and disgrace. My third and greatest pleasure is that I was lowborn, not born into the family of an aristocrat."

"May I ask you the reason why?" the Duke insisted. "If I am not mistaken, aristocrats of the present day, born as they are deep inside a palace and brought up in the hands of women, are lacking in scholarship and wanting in skill, given over to a life of pleasure and indulgence, sexual or otherwise. Their vassals cater to their whims, applaud whatever they applaud, and decry whatever they decry. Thus is spoiled and dissipated the true nature they are born with. Compare them with those who are low-born and poor, who are brought up from childhood in the school of hardship. They learn to handle practical affairs as they grow up, and with the guidance of teachers or the assistance of friends their intellect and judgment steadily improve. That is the reason why I consider my low and poor birth the greatest of all my pleasures." The Duke was astounded and said with a sigh, "What you say is quite right."

THE MITO SCHOOL

The interest of Tokugawa Mitsukuni in Chinese studies was aroused by the great histories Chinese writers had produced, rather than by their religion or philosophy. This may well be considered one of the distinctive influences of Chinese culture on Japan, in contrast to Indian influence, which was confined to religion, philosophy, and the arts. As early as 1657, Mitsukuni set out to organize his own committee for the rewriting of Japanese history, a task which was to take nearly two hundred fifty years for completion. Apparently he was not satisfied with the new history of Japan started by Hayashi Razan in 1644, and in the initial stage of his project he had stiff competition from Hayashi Shunsai who was carrying on his father's work. As mentioned elsewhere, the Hayashis' work was completed in 1670 and accepted by the shogunate as the official history of Japan, having been accorded the title *General History of Our State (Honchō tsugan)*. Fortunately Mitsukuni was able to persuade a Chinese political refugee of wide experience and considerable scholarship to participate in his new undertaking as general adviser. Chu Shunshui (1600–1682), a steadfast adherent of the Ming dynasty who had crossed the Eastern seas many times in hopes of raising outside help for the Ming cause, was finally forced by the dynasty's collapse to seek refuge in Nagasaki in 1659. In 1665, after repeated invitations from Mitsukuni to serve on his historical commission, Chu accepted and came to settle

in Mito. To Japanese Confucianists Chu symbolized above all else unswerving loyalty to his dynasty. This was what Chu Hsi had called
"the highest duty of all (*taigi meibun*)," and what had served as a
guiding principle in the great Sung scholar's rewriting of the *General
Mirror,* as the *Outline and Digest of the General Mirror* (*T'ung-chien
kang-mu*). There is no doubt that the presence of this staunch loyalist
on the commission made itself felt, for patriotism and loyalty to the
throne became the paramount themes of Mitsukuni's history, as well as
the cardinal doctrines of those who later carried on the tradition of the
Mito school. Through them these ideas were to exert a profound influence on the course of Japanese history during the Restoration period.
Still later Chu Shun-shui's unceasing resistance to the Manchus was to
serve as an inspiration to Chinese students in Japan, who returned home
to lead in the struggle that brought the Manchu dynasty to an end.

TOKUGAWA TSUNAEDA
Preface to *The History of Great Japan* (*Dai-Nihon-shi*)

This preface was written in 1715 by Tsunaeda, then head of the Mito branch
of the Tokugawa family, who records the aims of his predecessor Mitsukuni
in launching this monumental history project. Two points are emphasized:
loyalty to the legitimate imperial house (though not at this time suggesting
active rule by the Emperor), and the contribution of objective historiography
to the social order. Both are characteristic of Neo-Confucian thought.
[From *Dai-Nihon-shi*, I, i–ix]

My Sire [Mitsukuni] at the age of eighteen once read the biography of
Po-i[1] and became a staunch admirer of his high character from that
time on. Patting the volume containing it, he remarked with emotion,
"Only by the existence of this book is the culture of ancient China made
available to us; but for the writing of history how could posterity visualize
the past?"

Thereupon he resolved to compile a history of Japan. Official chronicles
were sought out as sources, and private records were hunted for far and

---

[1] Po-i, legendary figure of classical China whose biography is contained in the *Records
of the Historian* by Ssu-ma Ch'ien. He and his brother were said to have starved themselves
in the wilderness rather than live on the bounty of King Wu of Chou, whom they considered
a usurper of the Shang throne. Since King Wu was a great hero to Confucianists, many of
them have condemned this account as fraudulent.

wide. Famous religious centers were visited for rare documents, and eminent personages were approached for their personal memoirs. Thus scores of years have been spent in the work of compilation and editing in order to complete this history.

It was the Sun in person who laid the foundation of this nation over two thousand years ago. Since then, divine descendants have occupied the throne in legitimate succession; never did an impostor or traitor dare to usurp it. The Sun and Moon shone bright where the Imperial Regalia found their abode, splendid and wondrous. The ultimate reason for this can only be traced, I respectfully surmise, to the benevolence and charity of our imperial forbears, which served to keep the people's hearts united in solid support of the country. As to the doings and sayings of the wise ministers and able officials of early times, they may in general be ascertained from ancient records. In the Middle Ages, able sovereigns appeared who preserved the dynasty and maintained its prestige, pursuing policies as beneficial as those of early times. But because there is a dearth of sources for this period the contributions of individual ministers and advisers are gradually fading into oblivion, to my profound regret. That is the reason why this history was planned.

Having lived close to my Sire, [I], Tsunaeda, enjoyed the privilege of listening to his pregnant remarks concerning history as a record of the facts. "Write it faithfully on the basis of the facts, and the moral implications will then make themselves manifest. From antiquity to the present time, the customs and manners of the people, whether refined or vulgar, as also the government and administration of successive eras, whether conducive to prosperity or ruin, should be put down in black and white as clearly as if they were things held in our own hands. Good deeds will serve to inspire men and bad deeds to restrain them, so that rebels and traitors may tremble in fear of history's judgment. The cause of education and the maintenance of social order will thus greatly benefit. In writing one must be true to fact, and the facts must be presented as exhaustively as possible. Arbitrary selection or willful alteration has no place in authentic history. So in this history, all pains have been taken to make it true to fact, even at the expense of literary excellence. An excess of detail is preferable to excessive brevity. As to its final form and arrangement, I shall leave that to some great writer to come." Before the history was completed, however, my Sire passed away.

[364]

Among Japanese Neo-Confucianists there is perhaps none who combines more strikingly than Kaibara Ekken (1630–1714) both the moralistic and rationalistic tendencies of this movement. More than anyone else he brought Confucian ethics into the homes of ordinary Japanese in language they could understand. Other Neo-Confucianists might have taken great pride in demonstrating their command of Chinese style writing. Kaibara was content to set forth in comparatively simple Japanese the basic moral doctrines which should govern the everyday conduct of the people, their relations with others, their duties within the family and to their feudal lords, their duties in war and peace, etc. Though Kaibara addressed himself particularly to the samurai, his writings had a very general appeal to all classes and ages, and he gained a reputation for having made Confucian moral teachings "household talk" among the people. To do this he had especially to reach the women and children. In this way he (along with the playwright Chikamatsu) performed for Confucian ethics the service which the great apostles of the Pure Land Sect had performed for Buddhism in the medieval period—bringing it down from the realm of philosophical discussion and into the households of all who could read.

As a fact of incidental importance we should note that Kaibara, though childless, enjoyed a married life of rare happiness and genuine mutuality. His wife, trained in philosophy and history, skilled in calligraphy and poetry, provided him with intellectual companionship and accompanied him on his travels throughout Japan to historic sites. For forty-five years they lived happily together and then died within a year of each other.

Kaibara was from the feudal domain of the Kuroda clan in the southern island of Kyushu, where Christianity had so recently flourished and where the local lord had become so taken with things Western that he adopted Roman initials for his seal. We cannot help wondering whether these circumstances had something to do with the almost religious quality of Kaibara's approach to Neo-Confucianism, in particular his interpretation of the virtue of humanity (*jin*) as love for all things. In an orthodox follower of Chu Hsi like Kaibara, however, this is not too surprising a development of the Sung philosopher's own view of *jin* as representing a cosmic love identified with the creativity of nature. And it was rather in his special emphasis on creativity and the life-force that Kaibara eventually qualified his acceptance of Chu Hsi by taking issue, in a book entitled *Grave Doubts* (*Taigi-roku*), with the latter's dualism of principle (*ri*) and material force (*ki*) in favor of a monism of *ki* understood as the life-force.

Kaibara's methodical study of natural life is also not without its antecedents in the more naturalistic and rationalistic tendencies of Neo-Confucianism, and yet he pursued this interest in nature much further than most other men in his school. In his youth he was trained as a physician, and from this profession he may have acquired the sort of objective approach which distinguishes him from most Confucianists of the day. Moreover, since he enjoyed the security of a feudal stipend and was not, like Confucianists at the shogunate capital, encumbered by political ambitions or official duties, Kaibara was free to put into practice and carry to its logical conclusion the dictum of the Great Learning: "Investigate things and make your knowledge perfect!" Virtually all Chinese and Japanese Confucianists had been content to confine their "investigation of things" to the classics, but Kaibara carried his inquiry further into the field of nature. His *Catalogue of Vegetables, Catalogue of Flora*, and *Medicinal Herbs of Japan*, together with his last work, *How To Live Well*, are samples of his extensive studies in the biological realm. But his interests in this sphere were not pursued to the exclusion of humanistic studies. To Kaibara, man and nature are allied and inseparable; an understanding of nature is indispensable to the understanding of man. In this respect it may be said that Kaibara still reflects the essential humanistic and ethical concerns of Confucianism, which distinguish him from the more independent "scientific" thinkers and "Dutch" schoolmen of the eighteenth century in Japan. Kaibara's contributions to the study of nature were nonetheless significant enough to attract the attention of Westerners, among them Dutch visitors, and also the American, Swingle, with the U. S. Agricultural Experimental Station after the Restoration, whose enthusiasm for Kaibara's works led him to collect a complete set of them in first editions.

KAIBARA EKKEN
Precepts for Children

This opening passage to his *Precepts for Children* (*Shogaku-kun*) sets forth with great simplicity Kaibara's view of the interrelation of man and nature through the supreme Confucian virtue of humanity or benevolence (Ch. *jen,* Jap. *jin*). To make clear that this virtue is understood by him as not only involving but transcending "humanity," we render the term here as "benevolence." The reader should not fail to observe, however, that it is precisely that which makes man truly man which unites him with nature.

In the first paragraph the compound standing for "nature" is rendered literally as "heaven and earth" so that the correspondence to "father and mother" may be brought out.

[From *Ekken zenshū*, III, 2–3]

All men may be said to owe their birth to their parents, but a further inquiry into their origins reveals that men come into being because of nature's law of life. Thus all men in the world are children born of heaven and earth, and heaven and earth are the great parents of us all. The *Book of History* says, "Heaven and earth are the father and mother of all things" (T'ai-shih 1). Our own parents are truly our parents; but heaven and earth are the parents of everyone in the world. Moreover, though we are brought up after birth through the care of our own parents and are sustained on the gracious bounty of the ruler, still if we go to the root of the matter, we find that we sustain ourselves using the things produced by nature for food, dress, housing, and implements. Thus, not only do all men at the outset come into being because of nature's law of life, but from birth till the end of life they are kept in existence by the support of heaven and earth. Man surpasses all other created things in his indebtedness to the limitless bounty of nature. It will be seen therefore that man's duty is not only to do his best to serve his parents, which is a matter of course, but also to serve nature throughout his life in order to repay his immense debt. That is one thing all men should keep in mind constantly.

As men mindful of their obligation constantly to serve nature in repayment of this great debt, they should not forget that, just as they manifest filial piety in the service of their own parents, so they should manifest to the full their benevolence toward nature. Benevolence means having a sense of sympathy within, and bringing blessings to man and things. For those who have been brought up on the blessings of nature, it is the way to serve nature. It is the basic aim of human life, which should be observed as long as one lives. There should be no letting up on it, no forgetting of it. Benevolence in the service of nature and filial piety are one in principle: it is a principle which must be known and observed by anyone insofar as he is a man. There is none greater than this, none more important. All men living in their parents' home should expend themselves in filial service to their father and mother; and serving their lord should manifest single-minded loyalty to him. Just so, living as we do in the wrap of nature, we must serve nature and manifest to the full our benevolence. For a man to be unaware of this important duty, to let the days and years pass idly by and let one's life go for naught, is to make oneself unworthy of being a man. Indeed, how can anyone who would be a man ignore this fact? It is in this that the way of man lies. Any way apart from this cannot be the true way.

To persist in the service of heaven means that everyone who is a man should be mindful of the fact that morning and evening he is in the presence of heaven, and not far removed from it; that he should fear and reverence the way of heaven and not be unmindful of it. He should not, even in ignorance, oppose the way of heaven or commit any outrage against it. Rather, following the way of heaven, he should be humble and not arrogant toward others, control his desires and not be indulgent of his passions, cherish a profound love for all mankind born of nature's great love, and not abuse or mistreat them. Nor should he waste, just to gratify his personal desires, the five grains and other bounties which nature has provided for the sake of the people. Secondly, no living creatures such as birds, beasts, insects, and fish should be killed wantonly. Not even grass and trees should be cut down out of season. All of these are objects of nature's love, having been brought forth by her and nurtured by her. To cherish them and keep them is therefore the way to serve nature in accordance with the great heart of nature. Among human obligations there is first the duty to love our relatives, then to show sympathy for all other human beings, and then not to mistreat birds and beasts or any other living things. That is the proper order for the practice of benevolence in accordance with the great heart of nature. Loving other people to the neglect of parents, or loving birds and beasts to the neglect of human beings, is not benevolence.

[368]

陽明

CHAPTER XVII

THE ŌYŌMEI (WANG YANG-MING) SCHOOL IN JAPAN

Deep and lasting as was the influence of Chu Hsi's philosophy in Tokugawa Japan, its dominance, even with the backing of the shogunate, was far from complete. Indeed, from the vantage point of history one of the most striking features of Japanese thought in this period is seen to be its diversity and vitality. Not only during the waning years of the Bakufu when its control was loosened, but even during the heyday of its power there were men of independent mind who offered alternatives to the established Neo-Confucian orthodoxy, even if they did not directly attack it. Among them an important strain of independent thought is represented by Nakae Tōju (1608–1648), considered the founder of the Wang Yang-ming school in Japan, and Kumazawa Banzan (1619–1691), an outstanding example of those personal and political virtues which had already made this school a center of reformist activity in China.

NAKAE TŌJU

Ōyōmei is the Japanese rendering of the name Wang Yang-ming, the sixteenth-century Chinese Neo-Confucianist who became the outstanding spokesman of the School of Intuition (or Mind, *shin*), as opposed to Chu Hsi's School of Reason (or Principle, *ri*). Two features of Wang's teaching appealed especially to Nakae Tōju, who was introduced to it after he had spent many years in the study of Chu Hsi. One was his stress upon man's intuition or moral sense, rather than upon the intellect as with Chu Hsi. Everyone does not have to be a scholar but everyone ought to be a good man. For Nakae the moral sense innate in every man, the inner light which he later called the "Divine Light of Heaven," is man's only sure guide in life. Nakae was also attracted to Wang's teaching because of its emphasis on deeds rather than words. The dictates of one's conscience should be carried out directly in action. Wang had explained the unity of knowledge and action by showing that no matter how much a man read or talked about filial piety, he could not be said truly to have learned or understood it until he had put it into practice. Nakae himself gave an excellent example of this. Because his conscience told him that the well-being of his parents should be the first concern of every pious son, Nakae resigned a post he held in the service of a feudal lord in Shikoku and returned to his native village near Lake Biwa in order to care for his aging mother. This meant virtually retiring from the world to take up the life of a farmer in a rather remote and rugged region of hills and streams. Nevertheless his fame was spread abroad as a teacher whose precepts were taken to heart by country folk as well as educated men. That he attracted such able men as Kumazawa Banzan to his school, and influenced such great scholars as Arai Hakuseki and Dazai Shundai, was due less to his intellectual brilliance than to his gentle-hearted and single-minded pursuit of this way of life, guided only by the Heavenly voice within him. It is this same single-minded and selfless determination which we find among his followers in the late Tokugawa, the reformer Ōshio Chūsai, and those zealous patriots, Sakuma Shōzan and Yoshida Shōin, whose example made such an impression upon the leaders of the Meiji Restoration. Even in the twentieth century the philosophy which Nakae Tōju espoused has had a considerable vogue (one periodical is devoted solely to studies and writings of this school), and the famous Western-trained preceptor to the Emperor Taishō (1912–1926), Sugiura Jūgō, paid this tribute to Nakae: "He was the Sage of Ōmi Province; but is he not also the sage of Japan, the sage of the East, and indeed, the sage of the entire world? For a sage is a sage in the same way in the present as in the past, in the East and in the West. That he was already the sage of Ōmi province is reason enough for calling him the sage of the entire world."[1]

NAKAE TŌJU

Control of the Mind Is True Learning

According to Nakae Tōju the fundamental truths of life were the same for all men, regardless of their station in life. Where other Confucianists addressed

[1] Inoue, Yōmei gakuha, p. 18.

themselves generally to scholars and officials, Nakae offered guidance to the humblest of men and even to women, whom Confucianists and Buddhists often neglected.

[From *Tōju sensei zenshū*, II, 569–73]

There are many degrees of learning, but the learning that teaches control of the mind is the true learning. This true learning is of the utmost importance in this world and the chief concern of all mankind. The reason is that it aims at "exemplifying illustrious virtue,"[1] which is the greatest treasure of mankind. Gold, silver, and jewels are treasures, of course, but they are incapable of severing the root of all human suffering and of providing lasting happiness. So they are not man's greatest treasure.

When illustrious virtue shines forth, human suffering of all kinds will cease and our hearts will be filled with lasting happiness. Everything will be as we want it. Wealth and rank, poverty and lowliness, prosperity and adversity, will have little effect upon our enjoyment of life. Moreover everyone will love and respect us, Heaven itself will help us, and the gods will protect us, so that natural calamities and disasters will not harm us, thunder and earthquake will not injure us. Storms may destroy buildings but will leave us untouched. Fire will not burn us nor floods drown us. The devil will be afraid of us and the demon plague will not pester us. The spirits of evil and resentment will not come nigh. The fox and badger will be powerless with their magic. The tiger, wolf, and adder will not hurt us. Thieves and robbers will also be helpless to do us ill. Even swords and arms will be of no use against us. The seven sufferings will vanish and the seven happinesses will appear. In this world the enjoyment of life will be indescribable, and in the life hereafter we will be born in Heaven. Because of its boundless merits and blessings, this is called "the greatest treasure in the world." It is found in every human being, high or low, old or young, male or female, in the inexhaustible treasure-house of the Mind, but not knowing how to seek it, people in their pitiful ignorance go on searching for treasure in external things, only to sink into a sea of suffering. . . .

Some say that learning seems not to be the business of women. I say that there are many women busy composing poetry in both Chinese and Japanese, and though poetry would seem not to be the business of women,

[1] From the opening lines of the *Great Learning*.

they are not criticized for it. Control of the mind is of the utmost importance to women, and it would be a great mistake to say that it is not their business. The outward manner and temper of women is rooted in the negative (yin) power, and so temperamentally women are apt to be sensitive, petty, narrow, and jaundiced. As they live confined to their homes day in and day out, theirs is a very private life and their vision is quite limited. Consequently, among women compassion and honesty are rare indeed. That is why Buddhism says that women are particularly sinful and have the greatest difficulty in attaining Buddhahood. Thus women are in special need of mental discipline. If a wife's disposition is healthy and pious, obedient, sympathetic, and honest, then her parents and children, brothers and sisters, and, in fact, every member of her family, will be at peace and the entire household in perfect order, so that even lowly servants benefit from her gracious kindness. That kind of family is certain to enjoy lasting happiness and succeeding generations will continue to prosper as a result. . . .

It may be added that in ancient times when a girl reached ten years of age, she was turned over to a woman-teacher in order to learn the virtues and duties of womanhood. Now that practice has been discontinued, and "study" for women means only a little reading. Completely forgotten is the fact that cultivation of the mind is the essence of all learning. It is because of this that the question now has arisen as to whether or not learning is the business of women. It is imperative that this truth be fully understood, and that great care be given to the proper education of women, lest they should turn out to be the cause of domestic discord and family disaster.

The Divine Light in the Mind

Nakae Tōju's doctrine of innate or intuitive knowledge is directly derived from Wang Yang-ming, according to whom this sense constituted the goodness of human nature and rendered man one with Heaven. For Nakae, however, this doctrine has strong theistic overtones which reflect his tendency to reinterpret both Confucianism and Shinto in order to show their essential unity.

[From Inoue, *Yomei gakuha*, pp. 81–85]

The superior man will be watchful over those inmost thoughts known to himself alone. In his everyday thinking, he will not think anything for which he would have to fear if brought into the presence of the

Divine. In his everyday actions he will not perform an act of which he might be ashamed if it were known to others. By mistake an evil idea may arise, a wrong deed may present itself; but since there is within the mind a divine awareness illuminating it, what we call "enlightenment" will come. Once this realization occurs, rectification will follow, the evil idea and wrong deed will disappear, and the mind will revert to its normal state of purity and divine enlightenment. The ordinary man, unfortunately, continues to think such evil thoughts and goes on doing what he knows is wrong. Nevertheless, since the divine light in the mind makes the man aware [that he is doing wrong], he tries to hide it. In everybody's mind there is this divine light, which is one with the Divinity of Heaven, and before which one stands as if in a mirror, with nothing hidden either good or bad. [p. 81]

. . . .

There is no distinction among men, be they sages or ordinary persons, so far as their Heaven-bestowed nature is concerned. They are all gifted with the divine light that tells good from bad. All men hate injustice and are ashamed of evil because they are born with this intuitive knowledge.[1] It is only from the self-watchfulness of the one and the self-deceit of the other that the vast distinction arises between the superior man and the inferior man. If, however, the inferior man realizes where he has erred and becomes watchful over himself, correcting his mistakes and turning to the good, he may then become a superior man. [pp. 84–85]

The Supreme Lord and God of Life

While Nakae Tōju accepted in general the pantheistic view of Heaven or the Supreme Ultimate prevailing among the Neo-Confucian scholars, he frequently confuses this impersonal concept with the idea of a personal or even anthropomorphic God, which harmonized readily with Shinto belief. Both of these tendencies are present, but unreconciled, in the following passages.
[From *Tōju sensei zenshū*, I, 128–38]

The Supreme Lord Above is infinite and yet He is the final end of all. He is absolute truth and absolute spirit. All forms of ether are His form; infinite principle is His mind. He is greater than all else and yet there is nothing smaller. That principle and that ether are self-sustaining and unceasing. Through their union He produces lives throughout all time, without beginning or end. He is the father and mother of all

[1] *ryōchi*, the "good-knowledge" of Wang Yang-ming.

[373]

things. Through division of His form He gives form to all things; through division of His mind He gives all things their nature. When form is divided, differences result; when mind is divided, the minds remain the same. [p. 128]

. . . .

The Great God of Life [1] is called in the *Book of History* the Supreme Lord Above. The Supreme Lord Above is the spirit of the God of Life. He is the ruler and parent of all things in the universe; not a single particle of the six directions of the universe, nor a single second of all time, is hidden from the light of His omniscience. But all particular things in the universe partake of just one virtue, and do not combine all of the virtues of the Supreme Being. The sun and the moon shine only at certain periods, and cannot match the everlasting splendor of the Supreme Lord. The sun and moon are dimmed at times, yet He shines on; heaven and earth may come to an end, yet His life is infinite. Trace back, and you cannot tell where He has arisen; stretch forward, and you cannot tell where He reaches to. Stop Him, and His organs will continue to operate. Start Him, and He will leave no trace of His activity. There is nothing He does not know, nothing He cannot do. His body fills all space. Without noise, without scent, His mysterious activity pervades all space. Most miraculous, most spiritual, reaching to where there is no circumference, penetrating to where there is no center, He alone is worthy of devotion and without peer. His virtues are exquisite and unfathomable. Nameless Himself, He has been called by the sages "The Supreme Heavenly God of Life," in order to let men know that He is the source of all creation so that they may pay homage to Him. [pp. 137-38]

Filial Piety

As pointed out in the case of Yamazaki Ansai, it was the practice among Confucian philosophers to single out some particular virtue or expression from the Classics as the focal point of their teaching. For Nakae Tōju this was "filial piety," which he regarded as the underlying moral power in the universe.

[From *Tōju sensei zenshū*, I, 215-17]

Filial piety is the root of man. When it is lost from one's heart, then one's life becomes like a rootless plant, and if one does not expire instantly, it is nothing but sheer luck. . . .

[1] A Chinese Deity, *Daiotsu-Sonshin*, incorporated into medieval Shinto as *Ō-kinoto no Ō-mikoto*.

Filial piety is what distinguishes men from birds and beasts. When men are not filial, Heaven will visit upon them the six major punishments. It was said in ancient times that a man without filial piety turned into a man with a dog's head, clearly indicating that he was a beast. Reflect upon this and take heed!

An orphan would seem to have no obligations to look after parents. Yet I say that one's own moral endowment is the true inheritance from one's parents, and to care for one's own moral endowment is to care for one's parents, to respect one's own moral nature is to respect one's parents. That is the essence of filial piety in a larger sense. To be with them in person does not matter much. . . .

Filial piety is the summit of virtue and the essence of the Way in the three realms of heaven, earth, and man. What brings life to heaven, life to earth, life to man, and life to all things, is filial piety. Therefore those who pursue learning need study only this. Where is filial piety to be found? In one's own person! Apart from one's own person, there is no filial piety to be found; and without filial piety, there is no person who can practice the Way that illumines the four seas and communes with the Divine Light.

KUMAZAWA BANZAN, A SAMURAI REFORMER

A characteristic of Wang Yang-ming's teaching concerning "the unity of knowledge and action," as exemplified by the master himself, had been its dual emphasis on self-understanding and self-discipline in action. Wang, the philosopher and moralist, had been at the same time a soldier and statesman. In Japan the character of Nakae Tōju and his personal circumstances lent themselves better to carrying out this same teaching in the more limited sphere of personal conduct and private instruction. It was left to his ablest pupil, Kumazawa Banzan (1619–1691), to apply Wang's principles in the wider field of political action.

Like many other intellectual figures of his time, Kumazawa was a low-ranking samurai with the status of *rōnin,* that is, having no allegiance to a specific feudal lord nor any support from one. During his youth Kumazawa's family lived in difficult circumstances, and he was fortunate at the age of fifteen to gain employment with Ikeda Mitsumasa, lord of Okayama (Bizen). During five years of such service, including visits with his master to the Tokugawa capital at Edo, Kumazawa pursued an intensive program of training in the military arts to achieve his ideal of the model samurai. He was already twenty-one when, for the first time, he read the famous Four Books of the Confucian school and resolved to make up for his deficiencies in the liberal arts. A free agent again, he determined to pursue his education under the guidance of Nakae Tōju, to whose personal character and teachings he is said to have been attracted by chance contact with a student of Nakae remarkable for his integrity. It is typical of the antischolastic bent of the Wang Yang-ming school, however, and its distaste for much book learning, that Nakae confined his instruction to just three short texts: the *Book of Filial Piety,* the *Great Learning,* and the *Mean.* Apart from this, Kumazawa was largely self-taught and became known more for his personal knowledge of practical matters than for wide learning.

In 1647 Kumazawa re-entered the service of Lord Ikeda, and soon rose to become chief minister of Okayama. The reform program which he then launched upon was such a signal success that his fame spread across the land. When he visited Edo in 1651 and 1653 high dignitaries and officials of the shogunate came to pay their respects to him; indeed the third shogun is said to have arranged an audience with him, though the shogun fell sick and died before the appointed day. But in feudal times fame was as often the cause of personal downfall as of advancement. Kumazawa became the target of a concerted attack by a conservative group in the Ikeda fief, which led to his resignation in 1656. His remaining years were spent largely in study and writing, but he still found himself harassed for his unorthodox and independent views. Though his counsel was sometimes still sought by persons in positions of power, a program of reform which he submitted to the shogun in 1687 caused such a furor that he was kept in custody or under surveillance the rest of his life. A year before his own death in 1691, he was preceded by his devoted wife. Their marriage had been a union of free lovers, rather unusual in feudal Japan, and so romantic that it was dramatized in a play entitled *Diary of a Morning Glory (Asagao-nikki).*

Kumazawa's views on political and economic questions are known chiefly through his dialogue on the *Great Learning,* which is less a discussion of the text itself than a dissertation that takes as its point of departure the political principles of the Confucian school as set forth in this canonical work. This being so, Kumazawa's outlook often strikes the reader today as quite in keeping with earlier Confucian tradition, and it is indicative more of the shogunate's deep conservatism than of any extreme radicalism or heterodoxy on Kumazawa's part that his ideas should have given so much offense. Thus his reassertion even of the traditional Confucian view supporting individual merit as against hereditary privilege in politics could not help but alarm a regime based so completely on hereditary position, though Kumazawa stopped well short of advocating the abolition of feudalism. At the same time Kumazawa's Confucianism was far from doctrinaire. He put great stress upon the adaptation of general principles to the particular time, place, and circumstances confronting the statesman, and many of the suggestions which Kumazawa made on the basis of his own experience and observations definitely ran counter to policies with which the shogunate had been identified from its inception. For instance, Kumazawa believed that no general economic improvement could be expected unless the shogunate relaxed the restrictions and lightened the financial burdens which it had imposed on the feudal lords. Specifically he opposed the system which required the lords to maintain residences in Edo and make regular visits there to pay their respects to the shogun. Yet the Tokugawa had good reason to fear for the maintenance of their own supremacy if greater freedom of action were granted the daimyō. On the other hand even when Kumazawa suggested that the shogunate itself take a stronger hand in directing the economic life of the country, he could not overcome the almost instinctive resistance of the Tokugawa to any change in their way of doing things. It is doubtful that the measures proposed by Kumazawa—such as the use of rice as a medium of exchange (returning to a "natural" or barter economy), the discouragement of cotton, tobacco, and tea raising in favor of rice production, greatly increased rice storage to provide against famine and national emergency, and similar measures —would have sufficed to cope with the grave problems posed by Japan's expanding population and money economy. Yet at least Kumazawa pointed to the urgent need for facing these problems and taking action to meet them. In doing so he set an example for later reformers whom the Tokugawa could not shrug off or silence.

[377]

KUMAZAWA BANZAN

The Model Samurai

Kumazawa was concerned that years of peace and indolence might have a debilitating effect on the samurai class. Believing that the Manchus, who had just completed the conquest of China, might repeat the Mongols' attempted invasion of Japan in the thirteenth century, he warned his countrymen of the danger of foreign invasion and of the need for maintaining a constant state of physical readiness. In this passage from his memoirs, Kumazawa tells how as a young man he disciplined himself to that end. His ideas and example were an inspiration to leaders of the Restoration of 1868, who likewise feared a foreign invasion and were disturbed over the ineffectuality of the Tokugawa aristocracy.

[From Fisher, "Kumazawa Banzan," pp. 230–31]

When I was about sixteen I had a tendency toward corpulence. I had noticed a lack of agility in other fleshy persons and thought a heavy man would not make a first class samurai. So I tried every means to keep myself agile and lean. I slept with my girdle drawn tight and stopped eating rice. I took no wine and abstained from sexual intercourse for the next ten years. While on duty at Edo, there were no hills or fields at hand where I could hunt and climb, so I exercised with spear and sword. When I was on the night watch at my master's residence in Edo, I kept a wooden sword and a pair of straw sandals in my bamboo hamper, and with these I used to put myself through military drill in the darkened court after every one was asleep. I also practiced running about over the roofs of the out-buildings far removed from the sleeping rooms. This I did so as to be able to handle myself nimbly if a fire should break out. There were a few who noticed me at these exercises and they were reported to have said that I was probably possessed by a hobgoblin. This was before I was twenty years old. After that I hardened myself by going into the fields on hot summer days and shooting skylarks with a gun, since I did not own a falcon for hawking. In the winter months I often spent several days in the mountains taking no night clothes or bed quilt with me, and wearing only a lined jacket of cotton over a thin cotton shirt. My little hamper was almost filled by my inkstand, paper, and books, and two wadded silk kimonos. I stayed overnight in any house

I came across in my rambles. In such a way I disciplined myself until I was thirty-seven or -eight years old and avoided becoming fleshy. I was fully aware of my want of talent and believed I could never hope to be of any great service to my country, so I was all the more resolved to do my best as a common *samurai*.

The Development and Distribution of Wealth

[From *Kumazawa Banzan shū*, pp. 13–16, 17, 44. Revised from Fisher, "Daigaku Wakumon," pp. 277–80, 282, 317]

Question: Should something be done to develop our "material wealth"? [1]

Answer: Benevolent rule cannot be extended throughout the land without first developing our material wealth. In recent times there have been a great many people with no one to turn to: that is, with no one to depend upon, no place to go for help, and no work by which to support their parents, wives, and children. The benevolent rulers of the past attended first to the needs of such persons with no one to turn to. Today the worst off of these people are the *rōnin*. There are innumerable cases of their starving to death during the frequent famines. Even rich harvests and the consequent lowering of the price of rice would not give much relief to those who are already hard up. Every year there are many cases of starvation which are unknown to the general public. This is due to the impoverished condition of the feudal lords who are thus forced to stop giving allowances to some of their retainers. The retainers in turn cut off their dependents.

The other causes which produce so many *rōnin* are evident to all. When daimyō and their retainers suffer from debts which are out of proportion to their incomes, they tax the people more and more heavily, even though they know the taxes are excessive. This leads the common people to increase their indebtedness far beyond their resources. Thus all classes of society come to be saddled with crushing debts. When samurai and farmers are hard up, merchants and artisans are soon reduced to poverty, and society at large is reduced to indigence. The public treasure of the shogunate would not suffice to pay so much as one percent of the people's

[1] As spoken of in the *Book of Changes* (*Chi tzu*, 5) where material wellbeing is linked to social and moral order. [Ed.]

debts, even if all the stored up money and grain were devoted to the purpose. For the aggregate debt of the people would be more than one hundred times as much as all the money now in circulation. Nevertheless it would be quite easy to relieve the situation if benevolent rule were adopted, for there is a Great Principle[2] which can be applied in the present better than ever in the remote or recent past.

Question: What is that kind of government?

Answer: It has to do with wealth. To the ordinary mind, wealth is one man's gain and another man's loss, gratifying to the possessor, but displeasing to others. If the feudal lords are rich the people resent it, and if the shogun is rich the people are envious—for this is wealth in a small sense. However, if the lord of a province had wealth according to the Great Principle, the entire province would be happy, and if the shogun had such wealth, the whole country would be happy—for this is wealth in peace and good fortune. Their descendants would enjoy every felicity, and their good reputation would be passed on to their posterity. During the more than five hundred years since the establishment of the military regency at Kamakura there have been many shoguns naturally fitted for the task, but I deeply regret that they seem never to have heard of the principle. And just as a good carpenter cannot build a house without following proper rules, so even an eminent ruler cannot govern a whole country in lasting peace, unless he follows the example of the ancient sage-kings.

Question: The laws of the sage-kings are recorded in the Chinese Classics. Why cannot rulers naturally fitted for the task avail themselves of such examples?

Answer: The ideal examples involved a combination of the most favorable circumstances, including the right time, place and political position. It is hard to reduce them to writing. There may be exceptional rulers who succeed on account of inborn wisdom, but as a rule, it is well-nigh impossible for men of such high rank as the shoguns or the feudal lords to attain the ideal combination by their own efforts alone. The ideal can only be comprehended by those who, while of lowly extraction, still have deep insight into events and into the workings of the human heart, and who at the same time have learning, administrative talent, and true

[2] As set forth in the *Record of Rites* (*Li-yün*, 1), this principle or Way involves the exercise of power and the use of the world's goods for the benefit of all. [Ed.]

loyalty. Only men of such character are qualified to be the teachers of kings.

Question: Never before has there been such a high rate of tax remissions, or have the people been in such dire straits as they are now. How can wealth be developed under such conditions?

Answer: There is a mode of government by which the remission can be allowed as it is now and yet the samurai in the various provinces may become well-to-do; and by which the rice granaries of both the shogun and the daimyō may be filled to overflowing with the harvest. At present there is an immense quantity of rice wasted to no one's profit. But in the present social situation, people manage to support themselves not in spite of but simply because of such waste. After the farmers have paid their annual taxes and the samurai have taken in their regular share, the greater the waste of the rice crop, the easier do all classes of people find it to get on. If the present social situation should continue, but all waste were prevented, it would be harder for the people to get along. If there were no waste of rice, the price would fall lower and lower. Witness the rich harvests of recent years, because of which both the samurai and the common people have been made poorer and poorer. When these two classes are hard up, business transactions in general become sluggish in consequence. And this in turn causes trade to languish and the artisans to suffer more than ever. Cheap rice may appear to be an advantage to *rōnin,* but the contrary is the case. As the whole class of samurai is hard up, there is almost no one to give assistance to *rōnin,* and they stand less chance of being engaged by the provincial lords. Cheap rice would seem to be beneficial to day laborers, but the contrary is the case. When samurai, farmers, artisans, and merchants are all hard up, there is no one to hire the laborers. This general distress among the people is caused by there being a little too much rice.

Question: Do the people, then, find rich harvests undesirable?

Answer: The people too have heavier debts and are all the worse off because of the rich harvests of recent years. The money they borrowed when a *koku* of rice was worth seventy or eighty *me* they must pay back when the price has fallen to thirty or forty *me,* so that the principle alone will double, and adding the interest in too, will more than double. And since a bumper crop never amounts to twice an average harvest, the poor farmer is the loser. . . . The common people will suffer from the high price of rice in a year of bad harvest, for they will have no rice to sell; and when there is a bumper crop they will find it very hard to get on, for rice will be too cheap. Hence it is not advisable, so long as the present mode of government lasts, either to prevent the crop from being wasted or to cultivate new fields for rice. . . .

Question: What kind of government will make both the upper and lower classes happy, without wasting rice or reducing its value?

Answer: Since only gold and silver are legal tender, neither imposts nor tribute can be paid without selling one's rice [to obtain money]. But while there is an abundance of rice waiting to be sold in the harbors of Osaka and Edo, there are few merchants to buy it. This causes the price to go lower and lower, to the distress of the people at large. In fact, the amount of rice stored in the provinces is even smaller than one would expect. If the price of rice were fixed in relation to currency, all sorts of rice could be used in buying and selling cloth and other articles at Kyoto, Osaka, and Edo, as well as in the provinces; and wages to working men could also be paid with rice. Men in the eastern provinces could give bills of rice exchange to those of the western provinces for goods from the capital. Some inconvenience might occur in the practical execution of the system, but in time it could easily be overcome. We must first make it unnecessary for the people to sell all their rice in exchange for money just to support themselves. Then the great quantity of rice, which is now so largely wasted, could be stored unhulled in the different provinces, to be given out to famine sufferers and to be eaten by the soldiers in time of invasion by the northern barbarians [Manchus]. . . .

Question: Since I understand that there is no place to store the material wealth thus obtained, are there not still likely to be shortages?

Answer: Wealth here means wealth for the whole country. If grain for which there is no storage space is used for the civil government and military preparedness, there will be no shortage, and poverty will be reduced everywhere. When all things are set in order, wealth will not be wasted. When the old system of farmer-soldiers [3] is restored and a tribute of only one tenth is paid, wealth will be widely distributed and the people's hearts will be won. When it has become the custom generously to share wealth with those in need, then the people will know no lack. When the samurai become farmer-soldiers, the martial spirit of the nation will be greatly

---

[3] Believed to have prevailed in ancient China and adopted in seventh-century Japan. [Ed.]

strengthened and it will deserve to be called a martial country. Ever since the samurai and farmers became separate classes, the samurai have become sickly and their hands and feet have grown weak. It avails nothing to boast of a brave spirit if the warrior plays out when he confronts an enemy or if he dies of disease. His young retainers of lower rank will lose all respect for such a samurai and want to quit the service in a year. This will surely weaken the military forces. On the whole, a noble and lasting social order can only be built on a farmer-samurai basis. Now is the time to restore the farmer-soldier of olden times.

CHAPTER XVIII

THE REDISCOVERY OF CONFUCIANISM

Neo-Confucianism in seventeenth- and eighteenth-century Japan, as represented by Chu Hsi's synthesis of speculative thought in the Sung school, was only the culmination of a movement begun much earlier in the Sung period to revive the original Confucian tradition and reassert its validity for later times. One feature of this movement had been a strong reaction against Buddhism as being antithetical to the Confucian belief in an enduring moral order and the value of social action. Another feature had been a reaction against the kind of Confucian scholarship which during the intervening centuries had become increasingly antiquarian or else a mere accessory to bureaucratic rule. Tokugawa scholars, for their part, fully appreciated the role which Sung thinkers had played in reasserting and revitalizing the basic teachings of the Confucian school. More belatedly they came to appreciate the extent to which these teachings, admittedly much amplified by the Neo-Confucianists, had also been subject to considerable reinterpretation by them.

As we have seen, even among those who upheld the orthodoxy of Chu Hsi's philosophy in Japan, there was a tendency to disregard certain aspects of this vast system of thought while emphasizing others that seemed more especially to meet Japanese needs at that time. Neo-Confucian metaphysics, for example, though much admired for its systematic and all-embracing character, seems to have been less congenial a subject for discussion among orthodox Japanese scholars than ethics and history. In pursuing the latter, moreover, there was a natural tendency to apply or adapt them to specifically Japanese problems or traditions. In this way Hayashi Razan and the Mito school were drawn to the study and reinterpretation of Japanese history, Yamazaki Ansai and Kaibara Ekken to the codification of Japanese feudal ethics, and virtually all of them—but Hayashi and Yamazaki in particular—to the re-examination of Shinto.

Thus even within the limits of orthodoxy as upheld by the shogunate, Japanese scholars from the outset had imitated their Chinese masters most closely in adapting the Confucian tradition to their own requirements. Pursuing this same line of development, only one further step had to be taken to dispense with Sung philosophy itself. It was a big step indeed—involving as it did a break with the official orthodoxy and an implied repudiation of Tokugawa authority in intellectual matters—yet it was one for which the Sung Neo-Confucianists themselves had set a precedent by insisting upon a return to the classical sources of their own tradition.

YAMAGA SOKŌ AND THE ORIGINS OF BUSHIDŌ

The first important thinker to take this bold step was Yamaga Sokō (1622–1685), a figure celebrated in Japanese history for his intellectual powers and fierce independence of mind. Among other things he became known as one of the "three great *rōnin*" of the Tokugawa period, the other two being Yui Shōsetsu, who had to commit suicide in 1651 after the exposure of his part in a plot against the shogunate, and Kumazawa Banzan, who died in exile after his reform program had incurred the shogunate's ire. Though the influence of these two in their own time was comparatively limited, Yamaga acquired an enormous following, and this, as much as his refusal to conform in intellectual matters, proved a cause of his misfortunes. A brilliant student of Hayashi Razan, while still a young man he had established a wide reputation for his mastery of Shinto, Buddhism, and Taoism as well as Neo-Confucianism. It was especially as a student of military science, however, and one with very decided convictions about the role of the warrior class in peacetime, that Yamaga attracted attention from numerous samurai eager to employ their leisure time in self-improvement. Among those he taught, while serving as military instructor under the lord of Akō, was the future leader of the famous "Forty-seven *Rōnin*," who later won fame for themselves and their teacher by the spectacular manner in which they avenged the death of their lord.

Like Kumazawa Banzan, Yamaga was concerned over the prolonged inactivity of the warrior class under peaceful Tokugawa rule. Even in these circumstances he believed that the samurai had an important function to perform which justified his special status—something more than simply keeping himself fit for possible military service, important as that was. If the samurai was provided with a stipend by his lord, it was not so that he could enjoy a parasitic existence at the expense of the other social classes, eating the food of the peasant and using the goods of the artisan or merchant, but so that he would be free to cultivate those arts and virtues which would enable him to serve as a model and leader for all others. Above all he should set a high example of devotion to duty (*gi*, or righteousness). If this sense of duty required the other classes to perform their respective functions conscientiously, it required the samurai specifically to serve his lord with the utmost loyalty and in general to put devotion to moral principle (righteousness) ahead of personal gain. The achievement of this high ideal involved a life of austerity, temperance, constant self-discipline, and a readiness to meet death at any time—qualities long honored in the Japanese feudal tradition but now given a systematic form by Yamaga in terms of Confucian ethical philosophy. To set forth the lofty mission of the warrior class and its attendant obligations he wrote a series of works dealing with "the warrior's creed" (*bukyō*) and "the way of the samurai" (*shidō*) in extremely detailed fashion. This series, it is generally conceded today, represents the first systematic exposition of what later came to be known as the Way of the Warrior (*bushidō*).

It is well to remember, however, that for Yamaga the way of the warrior was not all moral indoctrination and martial discipline, and his contribution to it lay in more than simply codifying and providing a philosophical basis for Japanese feudal traditions. Yamaga stressed also the so-called peaceful arts, letters and history, as essential to the intellectual discipline of the samurai. In this he reflects one of the most characteristic features of the age: the union of military power, as represented by the shogunate, with the civil arts, as the Tokugawa encouraged them through humanistic studies of the Confucian type. At the same time Yamaga symbolizes a historical trend of momentous significance: the conversion of the samurai class during the long Tokugawa peace from a purely military aristocracy to one of increasing political and intellectual leadership. This development helps to explain why the samurai, instead of becoming a wholly idle and effete class relying on its hereditary privileges, could serve as the brains of the Restoration movement, take the initiative in dismantling feudalism itself, and play an important role in Japan's subsequent modernization.

Significantly, however, Yamaga's intellectual interests did not conform exactly to the Confucian pattern of civil arts and peaceful pursuits. He had an intense concern for military science, devoting himself to the study of strategy and tactics, weapons, and the obtaining of military intelligence —subjects for which the average Chinese Confucianist would have expressed a lofty disdain. On the other hand, considering the great stress which he and other Japanese Confucianists placed upon moral indoctrination as the essence of *bushidō*, Yamaga's affirmation that intelligence too was one of the martial virtues had important implications. He himself drew attention to the need for studying and adopting Western weapons and tactics as introduced by the Dutch, and it is a striking fact that his heirs in the nineteenth century, antiforeign though they were, quickly realized the necessity for "knowing the enemy" and thus for learning more about the West. Yoshida Shōin, the fiery hero of the Restoration era who was arrested for stowing away on one of Perry's ships in order to visit the West, was from a family that conducted a military school based on the teachings of Yamaga Sokō.

Considering the purpose to which he wished to put his Confucianism in a feudal age, it is not surprising that Yamaga should have chosen as his teacher Confucius himself, who had lived in a period of feudal transition, rather than the Neo-Confucianists, whose social concerns were those of a highly developed civil bureaucracy in a centralized state and whose philosophical outlook reflected the greater urbanity, sophistication, and cultural maturity of the Sung. In 1665, however, no such allowances could be made in mitigation of Yamaga's offense when he publicly avowed his antipathy for Neo-Confucianism in the *Essence of Confucianism* and was arrested the following year at the instigation of Hoshina Masayuki, Lord of Aizu. In this work Yamaga proclaimed his belief that the unadulterated truth could only be found in the ethical teachings of Confucius, and that subsequent developments within the Confucian tradition—especially the metaphysical theories of the Sung Neo-Confucianists —represented perversions of the original doctrine. Confucius, the common-sense sage who taught men about their everyday duties in life, was a far better guide for the samurai than all the abstract thinkers of later times. Actually, Yamaga was much less severe in his strictures on

Chu Hsi than on the Sung school in general, but this did not serve to lessen the author's crime in the eyes of Hoshina, a staunch upholder of the Neo-Confucian synthesis who saw in this attack upon it a potential challenge to Tokugawa authority itself.

After Yamaga went into exile, in the custody of the lord of Akō, his studies and writing turned more toward the Japanese tradition than to the Chinese. He became convinced that Japanese civilization was even more glorious than that of its neighbor, and wrote *The True Facts Concerning the Central Kingdom* (*Chūchō jijitsu*) to show that his own country, not China, was the center and zenith of all culture. This claim he based on the fact that Japan was divinely created and ruled over by an imperial line coeval with heaven and earth. The truths which Confucius taught had already been revealed by the divine ancestors of the imperial house and of course were no less true on that account. But the Japanese alone had been true to the highest concept of duty as set forth by Emperor Jimmu and Confucius; they alone had set an example of unswerving loyalty to the dynasty. In China, on the other hand, dynasties had come and gone and Confucian teaching itself had been corrupted almost beyond recognition.

In thus pointing to the emperor as the focus of all loyalties, Yamaga had no intention of undermining the authority of the shogunate. He contended, indeed, that the recognition by Japan's successive military rulers of the imperial sovereignty was proof both of the continuity of imperial rule and the legitimate exercise of power by the shoguns as deputies of the emperors. Loyal service to the shogunate was therefore one more manifestation of that hierarchy of loyalties so uniquely upheld by the Japanese. Also, since Yamaga's teaching had so greatly emphasized the samurai's duty to his own lord, his conception of *bushidō* had direct application for everyone in the existing feudal structure without calling for a change in the status of the emperor himself. Nevertheless much later, as hostility to the shogunate grew, Yamaga's devotion to the imperial house became of increasing significance and enhanced his stature greatly among those who sought to put *bushidō* to the service of the emperor as opposed to the shogun.

YAMAGA SOKŌ
The Way of the Samurai

The opening passage to *The Way of the Samurai* (*Shidō*), which follows, lays the groundwork for Yamaga's exhaustive discussion of this subject as recorded by his disciples. Reflecting the general Neo-Confucian approach to ethics (compare, for example, Yamazaki Ansai's discussion of the guiding principles of Chu Hsi's own school), it is entitled "Establishing One's Fundamental Aim: Knowledge of One's Own Function." Here Yamaga stresses a correct understanding of one's place and function in a feudal society, and the application to it of Confucian ethics based on personal relationships.

[From *Yamaga Sokō bunshū*, pp. 45–48]

The master once said: The generation of all men and of all things in the universe is accomplished by means of the marvelous interaction of the two forces [yin and yang]. Man is the most highly endowed of all creatures, and all things culminate in man. Generation after generation men have taken their livelihood from tilling the soil, or devised and manufactured tools, or produced profit from mutual trade, so that peoples' needs were satisfied. Thus the occupations of farmer, artisan, and merchant necessarily grew up as complementary to one another. However, the samurai eats food without growing it, uses utensils without manufacturing them, and profits without buying or selling. What is the justification for this? When I reflect today on my pursuit in life [I realize that] I was born into a family whose ancestors for generations have been warriors, and whose pursuit is service at court. The samurai is one who does not cultivate, does not manufacture, and does not engage in trade, but it cannot be that he has no function at all as a samurai. He who satisfied his needs without performing any function at all would more properly be called an idler. Therefore one must devote all one's mind to the detailed examination of one's calling.

Human beings aside, does any creature in the land—bird or animal, lowly fish or insect, or insentient plant or tree—fulfill its nature by being idle? Birds and beasts fly and run to find their own food; fish and insects seek their food as they go about with one another; plants and trees put their roots ever deeper into the earth. None of them has any respite from seeking food, and none neglects for a day or an instant in a year its flying, running, or going about [for food]. All things are thus. Among men, the farmers, artisans, and merchants also do the same. One who lives his whole life without working should be called a rebel against heaven. Hence we ask ourselves how it can be that the samurai should have no occupation; and it is only then as we inquire into the function of the samurai, that [the nature of] his calling becomes apparent. If one does not apprehend this by himself, one will depend on what others say or [understand] only what is shown in books. Since one will not then truly comprehend it with one's heart, one's purpose will not be firmly grounded. When one's purpose is not firmly grounded, owing to the long engrained bad habits of lethargy and vacillation hidden within, one will be inconstant and shallow. [In this condition] can the purpose of the samurai by any means mature? For this reason one must first establish the basic principle of the samurai. If one follows the suggestion of some-one else or leaves matters to the shifting dictates of one's own heart, though one may, for example, achieve what one is about in a given in-stance, it is difficult for one to accomplish his purpose in any true sense.

If one deeply fixes his attention on what I have said and examines closely one's own function, it will become clear what the business of the samurai is. The business of the samurai consists in reflecting on his own station in life, in discharging loyal service to his master if he has one, in deepening his fidelity in associations with friends, and, with due con-sideration of his own position, in devoting himself to duty above all. However, in one's own life, one becomes unavoidably involved in obliga-tions between father and child, older and younger brother, and husband and wife. Though these are also the fundamental moral obligations of everyone in the land, the farmers, artisans, and merchants have no lei-sure from their occupations, and so they cannot constantly act in accord-ance with them and fully exemplify the Way. The samurai dispenses with the business of the farmer, artisan, and merchant and confines himself to practicing this Way; should there be someone in the three classes of the common people who transgresses against these moral principles, the samurai summarily punishes him and thus upholds proper moral prin-ciples in the land. It would not do for the samurai to know the martial and civil virtues without manifesting them. Since this is the case, out-wardly he stands in physical readiness for any call to service and in-wardly he strives to fulfill the Way of the lord and subject, friend and friend, father and son, older and younger brother, and husband and wife.

Within his heart he keeps to the ways of peace, but without he keeps his weapons ready for use. The three classes of the common people make him their teacher and respect him. By following his teachings, they are enabled to understand what is fundamental and what is secondary.

Herein lies the Way of the samurai, the means by which he earns his clothing, food, and shelter; and by which his heart is put at ease, and he is enabled to pay back at length his obligation to his lord and the kindness of his parents. Were there no such duty, it would be as though one were to steal the kindness of one's parents, greedily devour the income of one's master, and make one's whole life a career of robbery and brigandage. This would be very grievous. Thus I say that one must first study in detail the duties of one's own station in life. Those who have no such understanding should immediately join one of the three classes of the common people; some should make their living by cultivating the fields, some should pass their lives as artisans, and some should devote themselves to buying and selling. Then the retribution of heaven will be light. But if perchance one should wish public service and desire to remain a samurai, he should sustain his life by performing menial functions, he should accept a small income, he should limit his obligation to his master, and he should do easy tasks [such as] gate-keeping and night-watch duty. This then is [the samurai's] calling. The man who takes or seeks the pay of a samurai and is covetous of salary without in the slightest degree comprehending his function must feel shame in his heart. Therefore I say that that which the samurai should take as his fundamental aim is to know his own function.

Short Preface to *The Essence of Confucianism*

In this preface to the *Seikyō yōroku* [lit. "The Essential Teachings of the Sages"] Yamaga's pupils explain the risks involved in publishing his work and the reasons why Yamaga nevertheless insisted on going ahead with it.
 [From *Yamaga Sokō shū*, VI, 167–68]

The Sages lived far in the past and their precise teachings have gradually sunk into oblivion. The scholars of the Han, T'ang, Sung, and Ming dynasties have misled the world, piling confusion upon confusion. And if this has been true in China, how much the more has it been true in Japan.
Our teacher has made his appearance in this country when it is already

2,000 years since the time of the Sages. He has held high the way of the Duke of Chou and Confucius, and been the first to set forth their essential teachings. Whatever the problem—of the individual, of the family, the state, or the world—and whether it has concerned the arts of peace or the arts of war, his teaching has never failed to solve it and deal with it effectively. Truly the presence of such a teacher among us is a sign of the beneficial influences which emanate from our good government.

In order to keep his teaching in book form for posterity, but not knowing whether the general public would be allowed to share in its benefits, we, his disciples, made a collection of his sayings and then made this request of our master: "These writings should be kept secret and sacred to us; they should not be spread abroad among men. Your criticisms of Confucian scholarship in the Han, T'ang, Sung, and Ming dynasties run contrary to the prevailing view among scholars. Some readers might complain to the authorities about it."

The master answered, "Ah, you young men should know better. The Way is the Way of all the world; it cannot be kept to oneself. Instead, it should be made to permeate the whole world and to be practiced in all ages. If this book can help even a single man to stand on his own convictions, that will be a contribution to the moral uplift of our times. The noble man must sometimes give his life in the fulfillment of Humanity. Why should my writings be kept secret?

"Moreover, to talk about the Way and mislead people concerning it is the greatest crime in the world. The textual commentators of the Han and T'ang, the metaphysicians of the Sung and Ming, who were so clever of speech and full of talk, wanted to clear up the confusion but only ended by making it worse. The Sages were left sitting in filth and mud— a dreadful spectacle!

"The Sages' scriptures are self-evident to all the world; there is no need for lengthy comment. And I, deficient in scholarship and no master of letters—how could I aspire to write a new commentary on these sacred texts, or engage in controversy with other scholars over them? And yet unless this is done, the filth and defilement of these other scholars cannot be cleansed away and the texts restored to their original purity.

"I am mindful of future generations and aware of my own shortcomings. Once my sayings are out in public, all the world will publicize them, condemn them, and criticize them. Should these reports, accusations, and criticisms contribute to the correction of my mistakes, it will be a great blessing to the Way. They say, 'A pig of a barbarian invites ridicule, the boastful ass is apt to fall on his own knee.' The weakness of us all lies in seeing only our own side and not seeing that of others—in the lack of openmindedness.

"Let me state again that I look up to the Duke of Chou and Confucius for guidance, but not to the Confucianists of the Han, T'ang, Sung, or Ming. What I aim to master is the teaching of the Sages, not the aberrant views of deviationists; in my work I occupy myself with everyday affairs, not with things fanciful and transcendental. In the pursuit of knowledge I want to be thoroughgoing; in action I want to leave no stone unturned. Even so, I am afraid that I am quick in speech but slow in action. The Way of the Sages is not one person's private possession. That which can be practiced by one individual, but not by all the world, is not the Way. My sole aim is to reveal it to the world and await the judgment of true gentlemen in the future."

We, his disciples, respectfully carrying out his wishes, have taken steps to print and publish this work. As for his basic discourses on the relationships between the lord and retainer, parent and child, husband and wife, older and younger brothers, and between friends, as well as concerning personal moral cultivation and the teachings of the Sages, readers are referred to the Master's *Classified Discourses (Gorui)*.

The Sage as the Moral Man

In this passage from Yamaga's *Takkyo dōmon* his view of Confucianism as essentially an ethical teaching is revealed in his conception of the sage, who possesses no supernatural powers or transcendent wisdom but simply fulfills the moral nature common to all men.

[From *Yamaga Sokō shū*, VI, 240–42]

In order to know what the real master of the Way is like, you should first have a very clear understanding of what the sage is like. The sage, according to the prevailing notion among conventional scholars, is one who has a mien of moral superiority—a distinctive personality, remarkably conspicuous in a crowd of men. His inner excellence being so eloquent of itself, the fact that he is no ordinary man is sensed immediately. Endowed as he is with supernatural and superhuman qualities, his speech and conduct are anything but human. Amidst whatever sensations of sound or sight, his emotions remain unmoved just as if he were a dead tree or burnt ashes. To him personal gain and a fat salary are more fleeting attractions than a snowflake on a red-hot stove. And in scholarship, he is versed in almost everything. Therefore, when entrusted with the government of the land, he will sweep away in an instant evils that have festered and bred for years; sweet dewdrops will gather on earth, while [such lucky omens as] giraffes and phoenixes will be constant visitors; all the people will follow the Way, practicing humanity and righteousness. Just one interview with the sage, and a man of plain mediocrity will shine with intelligence; overnight he will become unselfish and pure in body and mind—or so it is thought.

Now this indicates a lack of real knowledge concerning the sages. Upon studying the utterances, the actions, and the political ordinances of the Duke of Chou and Confucius we find that they were not at all like this. The sage represents only the best of humankind and is not a bit different from other men. He is fully accomplished in those things which make a man a Man, is well-informed of things and affairs, and is not perplexed by them at all. As to his personality and character, he is warm, amicable, humble, frugal, and self-sacrificing. Toward the ruler he is a model of decorum; to parents he is filially pious in a wholesome measure. In liberal arts he can express himself well when writing; in military affairs he is preparedness itself, being warm-hearted but not hot-headed, commanding respect without being violent, working hard when at work but relaxing fully when at rest. He takes what is due to him, gives to others what is due them, is generous when liberality is called for, and sparing when to be sparing is in order. His sayings and actions are hard to characterize in simple terms. Those who do not know him well call him unselfish at the sight of his charity; but take him for a miser when he is sparing. They think him flattering when he is merely being polite, and consider him arrogant when he is not flattering. Their judgments fail because they are ignorant of what the sage is really like.

The sage is fully aware of Heaven's will, so he seeks that which ought to be sought, he plans for that which ought to be planned for, saves when it is proper to save, and is not concerned over personal success or failure. Contented with his own lot, he never deviates from the course of duty. Managing things well in the sphere which it is his responsibility to administer, he never lets his plans or proposals overreach his own position. If questioned concerning the formalities to be observed in a given matter, he explains them in terms of basic principles. If questioned concerning the highest principles of duty to the state, he does not neglect their detailed application.

As to his everyday living, in clothing, in housing, utensils, and implements, he will spend when the expense is justified; he will be simple when simplicity is in order. Sometimes he will strive for the utmost in beauty, going to the limit of his resources, and at other times he will not so strain his resources. Thus, in all that he does, there is nothing strikingly different from what others do. If you get close to him, and try to live up to his teachings, you will undergo a change for the better day-by-day. If you do not live up to his teachings, he will not constrain you to adopt his ways. Only when an opportunity is presented for him to serve mankind and the world will he exert himself to the utmost.

From *An Autiobiography in Exile*

In *An Autobiography in Exile* (*Haisho zampitsu*), the last of Yamaga's important works, he traces his own intellectual development from Neo-Confucianism through Taoism and Buddhism to his "rediscovery" of the authentic traditions of Confucianism and Shinto.

[From *Yamaga Sokō bunshū*, pp. 481–88]

I am taking this occasion to write down some of my views about learning. For a long time I have been fond of the study of foreign books. Though I am not acquainted with those writings which have reached this country only in recent years, still I have gone through all the books received from China a decade or more ago. I feel, therefore, that with things Chinese at least I am quite well acquainted.

I once thought that Japan was small and thus inferior in every way to China—that "only in China could a sage arise." This was not my idea alone; scholars of every age have thought so and devoted themselves to the study of Chinese. Only recently have I become aware of the serious errors in this view. We have "believed too much in what we heard and not enough in what our own eyes could see; we have ignored what is near at hand in our search for the distant." Truly this is without doubt the chronic weakness of our scholars. This point I tried to make clear in my *True Facts Concerning the Central Kingdom* (*Chūchō Jijitsu*). The following is a short summary of what I said there:

In Japan the one true imperial line, legitimate descendants of the Sun Goddess, has ruled from the divine ages down to the present time without the interruption of a single generation. The Fujiwara too, loyal vassals and supporters of the Throne, have survived, with men of every generation serving as premier or minister. Such unbroken succession has no doubt been due to the inability of rebels and traitors to succeed in treachery and intrigue; but has not this in turn been due to the wide prevalence in Japan of the cardinal virtues of humanity and righteousness?

From the divine ages on for seventeen generations there have been on the throne sovereigns of supreme virtue, supported by wise and eminent ministers, who have upheld the way of heaven-and-earth, who have set up the court administration and control over the provinces, who have laid down formal regulations for the four classes of people regarding the necessaries of life—clothing, food, and dwelling, as well as the proper procedures for initiations, marriages, funerals, and festivals—so that in all these things the mean was achieved; and who have pointed out the respective paths of ruler and ruled, setting an example for all ages so that the people were at ease and the country at peace. Is not all this a manifestation of their heavenly virtues of supreme intelligence and holy wisdom?

No less deserving of mention is Japan's pursuit of the way of martial valor. The three kingdoms of Han[1] were conquered and made to bring tribute to the court. Korea was subjugated and its royal castle made to surrender.[2] Japanese military headquarters was established on foreign soil and Japanese military prestige was supreme over the four seas from the earliest times down to the present day. Our valor in war inspired fear in foreigners. As for invasion from abroad, foreigners never conquered us or even occupied or forced cession of our land. In fact, in the making of armor for man and horse, in the making and use of sword and spear, and again in military science, strategy and tactics, no other

[1] Three kingdoms of Han: means Korea. The name derives from three early kingdoms in South Korea known to Japanese as Ma-han, Mu-han, and Shin-han. The conquest of Korea referred to here is that of the Empress Jingō (r. c. 362–380). At the time of this invasion the three Kingdoms of Korea were Silla, Koguryo, and Paekche.
[2] Refers to the invasion of Korea by Hideyoshi in 1592.

country can equal us. Within the four seas, then, are we not supreme in military valor?

Wisdom, humanity, and valor are the three cardinal virtues of a sage. When even one of these three is lacking, a man falls short of being a sage. When we compare China and Japan with these virtues as criteria, we see that Japan greatly excels China in each of them and undoubtedly merits the name of Middle Kingdom far more than does China. This is no mere fancy of mine but a just estimate made by the world.

Prince Shōtoku was the only one throughout our history who did not esteem China too highly. He was aware of the fact that it was enough for Japan to be Japan. But the records were destroyed by fire at the time of the Iruka incident [3] and all of his writings have been lost to later times.

Many paths to learning have existed in the past and present. Confucianism, Buddhism, and Taoism each has its own basic principle. In my own case from boyhood to manhood I devoted myself to study of the Ch'eng-Chu system, and consequently my writings in those days were generally in accord with the Ch'eng-Chu system. Then in middle age I became interested in Lao Tzu and Chuang Tzu and accepted as basic such mystical concepts as emptiness and nothingness. At the same time I developed a particular esteem also for Buddhism and visited the eminent masters of the five Zen monasteries, including even the Abbot Ingen, because of my eagerness to pursue the path to enlightenment.

While I was engaged in the study of the Ch'eng-Chu system, perhaps owing to my own ineptitude, I was too much given to the practice of sustained reverence and silent sitting and found myself becoming too taciturn and grave. In comparison with the Ch'eng-Chu system, however, the approach of Lao Tzu, Chuang Tzu, and Zen proved far more full of life and freedom. The identification of human mental activity with the mystic activity of nature produced deep insight. From that point on I followed the impulse of my own nature; all was spontaneous. Heaven and earth might fail but as to the eternal and unchanging principle remaining in itself active and untrammeled, there would be no doubt.

[3] Iruka incident: in 645 Nakatomi Kamatari and Prince Naka-No-Ōe (later Tenchi Tennō) brought about the death of Soga no Iruka and his father, Soga no Emishi, in a struggle over the imperial succession. Before his death Emishi is said to have burned most of the historical records compiled by his father Soga no Umako and Shōtoku Taishi in A.D. 620—probably the first histories written in Japan.

Nevertheless, when it came to everyday matters, there was still much that I did not comprehend. Thinking that this might again be due to my own ineptitude, I pursued this method all the more assiduously in the hope that I might improve. It might be, I thought, that daily affairs are of such slight importance that it is as well to let them take their own course. Still we find ourselves bound by the five obligations of human relationship and are so much involved in everyday affairs that we cannot go on thus—we are held in their grip. If we should make our abode under the trees or upon some rock in lonely solitude, scorning worldly honor and fame, we might be able to attain to an inexpressible state of unselfish purity and mystical freedom. But when it comes to the affairs of the world, of the state, and of the four classes of the people, needless to say we should be able to accomplish nothing in that manner. Even in minor matters, we should have less comprehension of things than the uneducated man in the street.

Some say that if the perfection of virtue (*jin*) could be fully realized in one's mind, all the things of this world and all the affairs of men would be taken care of; others say that if the compassion of Buddha were made the basic principle, all would work out for good in the three existences—past, present and future. All these ideas, however, serve only to keep learning apart from the real world. Whatever others may think, I myself cannot believe otherwise or accept that kind of learning as satisfactory. I have consulted both Confucianists and Buddhists on this question, made inquiry of persons reputed to be of eminent virtue, and carefully observed their methods and actions, only to find that they are not in accord with the real world. Their teaching goes one way and life another.

Shinto is the way of our own country but the early records of it are lost: what we know is fragmentary and incomplete. From it we might have obtained the guiding truths concerning the affairs of men and of the state, but after the Iruka incident the old records ceased to exist. I began to wonder about those studies and proceeded to read more widely and to ponder on what earlier scholars had left behind them; but on many points my doubts were not clarified. I thought that this might be due to misunderstanding on my part but for many years those doubts still remained unresolved. Then, early in the Kambun era [1661–1672], it occurred to me that my failure to comprehend might be due to the fact that I had been reading the scholars of the Han, T'ang, Sung, and

Ming. By going directly to the writings of the Duke of Chou and Confucius, and taking them as my model, the guiding lines of thought and study could be correctly ascertained. After that I ceased to make use of later writings, but day and night applied myself to the works of the sages. Then for the first time I understood clearly the guiding teachings of the sages and their underlying principle became firmly fixed in my mind.

When you try to cut paper straight without a ruler to guide your hand, try as you will, you cannot get it accurate. Even if you should manage to do it well yourself, you could not expect others to do so. But with the use of a ruler even a child can cut along the guiding line. Even though one person may be considerably less skilled than another, he can almost always follow the guiding line. In the system of the sages, likewise, if one acquires by careful reading a sort of guiding rule, one can understand the way of the sages in all things according to the degree of one's individual scholarship.

Now to learn the guiding principles of the sages neither language nor scholarship is needed, because [the thing is so simple that] if I am told about it today, I can understand what I am to do today. Neither the "moral training" nor the "sustained reverence" nor the "silent sitting" [of the Neo-Confucianists] is required. Even if one goes through strict discipline of both speech and act and carries in memory almost all the sayings of the sages, it is clear that these are merely digressive pursuits and do not follow the guiding principle of the sages. I can tell at once, when someone even so much as utters a word or a phrase, whether he understands the guiding principle of the sages, simply because I measure him by the use of my guiding rule. Even when it comes to things out of reach of sight and hearing, with this approach one can understand in at least five or seven cases out of ten; whereas those who pursue conventional or digressive studies may be unable to understand in even three cases out of ten. Of this I am certain. This is the reason why men of wide scholarship often become the laughingstock of the less educated. One cannot shape a bullet without a cast; one cannot cut paper without a ruler. Those who try labor in vain and struggle long and painfully to no avail. The more they pursue their studies, the more they become involved in ignorance.

Among the paths to learning there is one which exalts personal virtue and cultivates benevolence through the intensive practice of moral training and silent sitting. There is another which involves personal cultivation, the guidance of others, and maintaining of peace and order in the world, and the winning of honor and fame. There is also that which arises from a love of books and stresses the writing of poetry or prose. Into these three classes scholars may be divided, each having his own attitude or approach.

As far as I can observe, however, it is difficult in our times for men to attain the degree of righteousness which prevailed in the days of the Yellow Emperor and the sage-kings Yao and Shun, such that rule by virtue alone was sufficient through its beneficent influence to keep the country under control without a word of command being given, or to make peace reign supreme within the four seas without any action from above, or to enable cultivation of the arts of peace so as to win without coercion the willing submission of any enemy. Even though we should take them as our model, no good result would come of it. Scholars who advocate such a course are lofty in their aims, but in the end they turn their backs upon the world and retire in solitude to commune only with the birds and the beasts. On the other hand, the love of books and the pursuit of writing are merely scholarly diversions; they are not matters of everyday concern. Writing is a corollary of learning and I do not cast any aspersions upon it. The writing of poetry and prose is something that should not be neglected "if one has spare time for them." [4]

To me, therefore, the guiding path to the teaching of the Sages is that which involves personal cultivation, the guidance of others, the maintaining of peace and order in the world, and the winning of honor and fame. I come from a samurai family and have the five obligations of human relationship which attach to my person and station. My own thought and conduct, as well as my five obligations in relations with others, are what I as a samurai must give first attention to. In addition, however, there are both major and minor matters to which the samurai must give his attention. In minor matters, such as dress, food, dwelling, and all implements and their uses, he must live up to the best samurai traditions of good form. This is particularly true in connection with training in the arts of war and with the manufacture and use of armor and horse trappings. Among major matters there are the maintenance of

[4] Paraphrasing *Analects*, I, 6.

peace and order in the world; rites and festivals; the control of feudal states and districts; mountains and forests, seas and rivers, farms and rice fields, temples and shrines; and the disposition of suits and appeals among the four classes of people. In addition, there is military command and organization, strategy in war and tactics in battle, the quartering and provisioning of troops, and the building of fortifications—all those preparations for war which are the daily concern of generals and officers.

No matter how much training he undergoes, if the studies pursued by a samurai do not enable him to get results in all these fields, then they serve no useful purpose and fail to follow the guiding principle of the sages' teaching. For this reason thought and study will have to be given to these matters, and some research done into the records of history and of court procedure. Thus there will be less time for meditation, silent contemplation and quiet sitting. I do not mean, however, that we must have an exhaustive knowledge of all these numberless things. As I have pointed out elsewhere, we need only have a good understanding of the guide-rule provided by the sages' teaching and use it as a measure and standard. Then, whatever we see or hear can be comprehended in its true light. No matter what task presents itself, it may be clearly understood in terms of these aforementioned categories, and therefore no matter what befalls, we need not falter—we are on safe ground. Truly we find ourselves "with mind open and body free." [5]

If one follows this approach to learning, intelligence will renew itself, and virtue will of itself be heightened; humanity will be deepened and courage strengthened. Finally, one will attain to a state of mind in which success and fame are of no account, in which unselfishness and self-forgetfulness will be the rule. Thus one starts out with the idea of success and honor, but comes to the stage in which success and honor have no meaning and one simply goes on fulfilling the way by which man becomes truly man. The Book of Filial Piety says: "Cultivate yourself and follow the way; fame will be the natural outcome of filial piety."

ITŌ JINSAI'S DEVOTION TO CONFUCIUS

The tendency to break with Neo-Confucianism and return to the classical sources of Confucian teaching was given added impetus by a

[5] *Great Learning*, VI, 4.

very different type of Japanese from Yamaga Sokō, the gentle but per-suasive Itō Jinsai (1627–1705). Where Yamaga stands for the basic Con-fucian virtues as exemplified in the true samurai, Itō, the son of a Kyoto merchant, represents the best in Confucian scholarship and dedication to humanistic ideals. What they had in common was a staunch independ-ence of mind, which Itō demonstrated not only in his thinking but also by making study and teaching a profession in itself and refusing all offers of lucrative employment from powerful feudal lords. In this respect he followed the example of Confucius himself, who was probably the first to establish teaching as an independent profession in ancient China rather than as an official function. Itō himself enjoyed great success as a teacher, attracting students in even larger numbers than Yamaga. The private school which he set up with the able assistance of his son, Tōgai, was devoted to the study of the original classics, known as the "Kogi-dō," or roughly, "School for Study of the Ancient Meaning." Here the *Analects* of Confucius and the book of Mencius were the basic texts. In subjecting them to the most careful and critical scrutiny, however, Itō was less concerned with the niceties of conventional scholarship than with dis-cerning the underlying truths of Confucius' teaching. The measure of his exclusive devotion to the latter is reflected not only in the superlative terms in which he described Confucius as the "supreme sage of the uni-verse," but also in the fact that he did not hesitate to attack even the Great Learning as spurious, though the Neo-Confucianists had elevated it to a position of the first importance as a Confucian classic.

Itō also took issue with the Neo-Confucianists on metaphysical grounds, rejecting Chu Hsi's dualism of principle (*ri*) and material force (*ki*) in favor of a monism which denied any standing to *ri* as a first principle. It was *ki,* conceived as the vital force, which underlay all three realms of existence—heaven, earth, and mankind. It contrast to Chu Hsi's more static view of the universe in terms of ultimate and immutable law, Itō saw it as dynamic in character. The universe is the progression of the life force, and the only reality in life, death being nothing but the absence of life and purely negative. By conserving and developing the life force within him, man achieves the fullness of manhood in the virtue of hu-manity (*jin*), which for Itō means "love"—love as expressed in the four great virtues of loyalty, good faith, reverence and forgiveness.

In contrast to Yamaga Sokō, whose studies and thinking turned in the direction of Shinto later in life, Itō consistently devoted himself to the rediscovery of Confucianism in its original Chinese sources, and there is in him little of the nationalistic type of thinking which increasingly characterized Japanese Confucianism in the later Tokugawa Period. Like Arai Hakuseki he represents the concern for universal human values which remained a significant, though less widely appreciated, aspect of Confucian thought into modern times. At the same time, Itō's rediscovery and systematic exposition of the classics partake of much the same character as earlier Neo-Confucian writing: that is, they present the "original" teaching of Confucius in new terms which reflect to some extent the metaphysical temper of the Sung School, as well as the reaffirmation of life and love found in so much of Japanese thought in this period, be it Confucian (as in Kaibara and Itō) or Neo-Shintoist.

ITŌ TŌGAI
The Devolution of Confucianism

Itō Jinsai was not a prolific writer; indeed, his teachings were not committed to writing until late in life and only published after his death. In this respect Itō's son, Tōgai (1670–1736), rendered his school a great service by editing his father's works and adding many more of his own to amplify their point of view. In this preface to *Changes in Confucian Teaching, Past and Present* (*Kokon gakuhen*), Tōgai explains how Confucianism was radically altered by the metaphysical interpretations of Han and Sung scholars, and why it is necessary to return to the original teachings of Confucius.
[From Inoue, *Rinri ihen*, V, 216–17]

The change from the Way of the Sages in the Three Dynasties to the Confucian teaching of today has been a gradual one and not something that happened overnight. There was one great change during the Han dynasty and a second during the Sung dynasty. Quietly and surreptitiously the teaching has been altered or done away with throughout ten centuries or more, with the result that present-day teaching is no longer identical with early Confucianism.

The rise and decline of good government from the age of the sage-kings T'ang and Yü to the Chou dynasty can be understood through the examination of history. Prior to the Duke of Chou, those who occupied the throne introduced rites and festivals, arms and punishments; they also established fiefs and farms, shrines and schools, so that all the people would be brought under beneficent moral and cultural influences. Government was in accord with the Way, and political rule was exercised through moral virtue; the self-cultivation of the ruler was the means by which the country was governed. After the Duke of Chou, sages were unable to occupy the throne. Privately, therefore, they gathered together with men of accomplished virtue and sterling character for study in their own homes. They said that the Way of the early kings was perfect in every respect, either for general practice or for individual application. Therefore they formulated it in writing according to various topics and subtopics, which would help them to cultivate themselves and also to teach all the people. They did not accomplish what [the able ministers] I, Fu, Chou, and Chao had done [in earlier times], it is true, but inasmuch as they deemed everyday human relations to be their proper concern, considered the achievement of social order and the security of the people to be their supreme task, and wanted all the people of the world to follow the same way, there was no deviation whatever [from the ancient Way]. The four virtues of humanity, righteousness, decorum, and wisdom they held to be the greatest and most important in life. More than this they did not say.

The decline of the Chou was followed by the Warring States period. Rites and music were allowed to deteriorate and were then abandoned. Warfare raged day after day. Steady decline led to the rise of the ruthless Ch'in, who burned the classics and had Confucian scholars killed. The Way of the early kings vanished from the earth completely.

With the rise of the Han dynasty the Books of Odes and History came into a certain vogue, and Confucian scholarship was favorably regarded. Still at that time the government adopted its own political system and its own regulations, while the surviving documents of the early kings were relegated to learned men dealing with the past. Thereupon the Confucianists of that day made the transmission of this heritage the private and exclusive business of their own schools. Thus the conduct of government and the teaching of the Way took separate paths.

In addition, the interpretation of portents in terms of the five elements theory became fashionable. Everything in heaven and earth was reckoned in fives. In this way the virtue of faith was joined to the four virtues of humanity, righteousness, decorum, and wisdom, to make up the five norms corresponding to the five elements. Some looked upon them as part

[404]

of man's inherent nature which is not subject to increase and decrease, like the five organs hanging inside the body or the four limbs growing outside. Earlier it had been on the basis of actualities that the teaching concerning the four virtues had been formulated; now these virtues were taken as fixed and unchanging things within us. Thus the first great change took place in the ancient teaching. Thereafter Confucian scholarship was turned into the study of textual commentaries, the mastery of literary style, and the art of making rhetorical allusions. Thus the Way of the Sages was left in darkness and obscurity for more than a thousand years.

Nevertheless, even though their theories were superficial, still because of the [Han Confucianists'] proximity in time to the ancients, the essential truth concerning the Way and virtue, as well as of human nature and the Mandate of Heaven, survived from the ancient tradition. In no time, however, the teachings of Gautama Buddha and Lao Tzu threw the world into a commotion. Not only were their rituals enthralling, but also their doctrines concerning "consciousness of the mind" and "seeing one's own nature" were so lofty and dazzling that scholars and officials, upon hearing of them, eagerly followed after such teachings. So enthusiastic and enslaved were some that they considered Gautama Buddha and Lao Tzu to have surpassed Yao and Shun and advanced beyond Confucius. This was worse still than merely separating the conduct of government from the teaching of the Way!

In the Sung dynasty true Confucianists appeared to champion the Way of the Sages and denounce heretics. The profundity of their scholarship and the thoroughness of their research went far beyond that of the Han and T'ang Confucianists. Nevertheless, they considered man's true nature to be principle in its disembodied and unmanifested state, and believed that the eradication of physical desires was the method for attaining sagehood. As for the various works and undertakings of life, the Sung Neo-Confucianists did not go so far as to declare them nonessential or diversionary, but did in effect regard them as less than ideal pursuits. They insisted that man's true nature must be sought in an original unformed and undetermined state. So humanity, righteousness, decorum, and wisdom could not be seen or heard any more than sound within a bell or fire within a stone [before they are struck]. Names they were, but not real things. Thus Confucianism underwent a second change.

Since then, because [Neo-Confucianism] has been accepted in the schools for so long and become so completely systematized, entwining and entangling everything, patching here and thatching there, its bonds could not be broken. While there has been some leeway in interpretation within the system, yet in the final analysis no one has been able to break outside its confines. Restricting themselves to the commentaries and interpretations of the Sung and Ming dynasties, scholars have tried to evaluate and criticize them without ever attempting to trace out the history of the past two thousand years or more in order to find out for themselves the source of these ideas. Unhesitatingly they accept present-day teaching as the teaching of the Three Dynasties of old. They do not realize that it has endured so many vicissitudes and changes that they could hardly be dealt with in a few words.

My father's belief in returning to the ancient source [of Confucianism] was not the blithe expression of a momentary personal fancy. He had been under the spell of the [Neo-Confucian] philosophy of "human nature and principle" for years. At first he was a reverent and wholehearted follower of this teaching, but then as he got further into it found himself involved in controversial questions requiring further research. A few doubtful points he studied from all angles, analyzing and classifying, comparing and contrasting them until at long last he became aware of the fact that present-day Confucianism was no longer the Way of the Three Dynasties.

The Neo-Confucianist's Erroneous View of Human Nature

These extracts from Itō Tōgai's *Critique of the Doctrine of Returning to One's Original Nature (Fukusei-ben)* argue that the Neo-Confucian philosophy of human nature is essentially Buddhist or Taoist in character and antithetical to the original ethical doctrines of Confucius.

[From Inoue, *Rinri ihen*, V, 210–11]

The teaching of the sages was not limited to a single method, but all of the methods used were intended without a single exception to achieve full development through cumulative achievement. . . . The teachings of Buddha and Lao Tzu have been expressed in different ways but all have been based without exception on the theory of returning to the original state of nature. Lao Tzu, for instance, wants to dispense with humanity and righteousness, and put an end to rites and music, in order to return to so-called "vacuity." As for the Buddhists, they also want to extinguish human desires, dispel illusions, transcend transmigration, and through realization of what they call Enlightenment (Bodhi) or Suchness (Tathatā) attain to the Buddhaland. Here the return to Nirvāna and return to Suchness are being emphasized.

The Way as understood among Confucianists of later times has emphasized living according to moral standards and social norms; rites and music, justice and administration are taken seriously, and, of course, Buddhism and Taoism are considered by them inadequate to serve as the Way. In practice, however, these later Confucianists have also tried to eradicate physical desire and modify man's physical nature in order to return to the original state. As to what they consider the Way, they differ; but as to their methods, there is no difference at all.

Nevertheless, all living things have some root or basis for their existence, from which by tiny increments they attain full size or by imperceptible degrees manifest their full brilliance. There is not a single instance in which mere return to the original state has led to fulfillment or completion. Only such fixed things as a clean mirror or still water may return to their original state by getting rid of dirt and dust. But active, living things develop gradually; not only is this true of running water and sprouting plants, but of all human undertakings as well; and not merely of all human undertakings, but also of human progress in the Way and even the sage's achievement of virtue.

Confucius at fifteen had dedicated himself to study, but only at seventy was he able to say, "I follow my heart's desire without trespassing the rules of conduct." The Sage's gifts were of course extraordinary, but only with advancing age did his virtues shine more and more resplendently and his knowledge reach such a state that he knew what no other man did. If he had only had to return to the original state of nature, the excellence of non-trespassing the rules of conduct, which he achieved at seventy, should have been attained in his boyhood or infancy. With his proverbial genius both in knowledge and in conduct, what could possibly have prevented him from achieving that state of nontrespassing the rules of conduct until the age of seventy?

Consequently one can see that even the Sage's virtue attained its fullness only by dint of steady cultivation. All of the great men and heroes in history, who have set an example for all time either by the attainment of virtue or through personal accomplishment, have done so by a steady husbanding of effort to bring their powers to maturity. Look at what they started with; and you will find that they did not have much in reserve then to fall back upon. See how the same principle applies to all the affairs of the world: all those whose artistry and craftsmanship have been acclaimed as "divine" or "wondrous," all those who have reached the very zenith of creative excellence, have been able to achieve their end only through sustained effort. When they started out in life they did not have much knowledge. Therefore men always say that "study progresses," but no one ever says that "study returns." This is what you call "checking a theory against the facts" and finding that it is not so. And it is for this reason that, even after the Sung school had completed its work, some questions still had to be reopened for discussion.

In this preface to *Boys' Questions* (*Dōji-mon*), containing Jinsai's instructions to his students, Togai attempts to show how the Neo-Confucian view of human nature is in conflict with the correct view of Mencius.

[From Inoue, *Rinri ihen*, V, 74]

There is no part of the world in which the Way does not apply, and no time in which it ceases to be true. It does not owe its existence to the Sage, nor can petty men cause it to disappear. Immutable throughout the ages, normative all over the world, the Way operates every day in human relations—it is no abstract principle intangible to the senses. It has four aspects: humanity, righteousness, decorum, and wisdom. Therefore Confucius said, "The Way prevails under Heaven, and I do not seek to alter it." [1]

Now if we go to the root of things, it may be seen that any individual, insofar as he is a man, possesses four impulses,[2] just as he possesses four limbs. The sense of sympathy is the impulse from which humanity develops; the sense of shame and aversion is the impulse from which righteousness develops; the sense of humility and reverence is the impulse from which decorum develops; the sense of right and wrong is the impulse from which wisdom develops. These impulses are what con-

---

[1] *Analects*, XVIII, 6. The passage is usually understood: "If the Way prevailed under Heaven, I should not seek to alter things"; which is just the opposite of what Itō seems to intend here.

[2] The doctrine of Mencius that human nature tends to the good, because it is characterized by four impulses which, if properly developed, become four cardinal virtues: humanity, righteousness, decorum, and wisdom.

stitute the goodness of human nature and what distinguish man from all other things. If brought to fulfillment, they become the virtues of humanity, righteousness, decorum, and wisdom. If, however, nothing is done to cultivate the impulses with which we are born, then they will remain weak rather than develop their full power, and when put to a test may be lost together with that into which they were born. The Sage was concerned about this, so he established moral training in order to let people expand and fulfill that which they were born with. Men cannot endure the suffering of others, so he brings them to where they can endure them; they do not dare to act, so he brings them to where they dare to act. Thus gradually but steadily they move towards good and reject evil, so as to attain the fulfillment of virtue. . . .

In later times, however, [Neo-Confucian] teaching has not been in accord with the original aim of the Sages. Humanity, righteousness, decorum, and wisdom are considered to be complete in man's original nature. Only the waywardness of the life force and the beclouding effect of matter, they say, cause this natural brilliance to be obscured; so we must try to get rid of the beclouding screen and sweep away the dust in order to restore the original, as a mirror cleansed of dust regains its brightness, or as water when kept still becomes clear again. Therefore the virtues of humanity and righteousness do not need to be acquired through cultivation; they are there already. Thus the method of expansion and fulfillment has been turned into a discipline for extinguishing desires. Still, who can fail to realize that in the teaching of the Sages there was a method of fulfillment and cultivation, but no such thing as "returning to the original state of nature"? How could sagehood be attained by nothing more than a return to one's original nature? Therefore, while it is correct to say that the way of humanity, righteousness, decorum, and wisdom is based on the goodness of nature, it is wrong to assert that these virtues are complete in nature from the start.

ITŌ JINSAI
The Primacy of Confucius and the Analects

The following extracts from Jinsai's two basic works *The Meaning of Terms in the Analects and Mencius* (*Gomō-jigi*) and *Boys' Questions* represent the main features of his own teaching.

[From Inoue, *Kogakuha no tetsugaku*, pp. 187–89]

Before Confucius' time, education was provided in a general sort of way; but true learning had not yet been established and the Way and virtue had not yet clearly been set forth. Only with the appearance of Confucius was true learning based on the Way and virtue fully brought into the light of day, so that scholars generation after generation could learn to walk on the single path of humanity and righteousness. Only then were the many kinds of superstitious and supernatural beliefs dealt with in the light of reason in order to avoid confusion with the Way and virtue. Thus true learning was inaugurated by Confucius on an entirely original and constructive basis. Mencius, citing statements by Ts'ai Yü, Tzu Kao, and Yo Jo, called Confucius wiser than Yao and Shun by far. He also said that "since man first appeared on earth no other man has ever achieved the greatness of Confucius." [1] Those gentlemen were fortunate enough to enjoy the personal guidance of Confucius; they became aware of Confucius' superiority to all other sages and gave testimony to it. That is the reason why I consider the *Analects* to be the highest, supreme, and foremost book of the universe.

Since the Han and T'ang dynasties, however, scholars have looked up to the Six Classics as the highest authority, without knowing that the *Analects* was the foremost book of all, rising high above the Six Classics. Some had an idea that the *Book of Changes* or the *Book of History* was to be revered above all others; some thought the *Great Learning* and the *Mean* stood ahead of all the rest. Never did they realize that it was the *Analects* alone which set forth the teaching that made the Way clear to all, penetrating everything from first to last as no other classic has done. That the Way of Confucius has come to be known throughout the world is mainly due to this book. [pp. 188–89]

. . . .

The *Analects* alone is a book which can serve as the standard and guide for the teaching of the Way in all times. What it says is supremely right and supremely true, penetrating everything from first to last. Add one word to it and it is one word too long; take one word away and it is one word too short. In this book the Way finds its ultimate expression and learning discovers its highest realization. The *Analects* is like the boundless universe which men live in without comprehending its full magnitude. Enduring and immutable throughout the ages; in every part of the world it serves as an infallible guide. Is it not, indeed, great! [p. 187]

---

[1] A paraphrase of *Mencius*, II A, 2.

Mencius as a Guide to the Analects
[From Inoue, *Kogakuha no tetsugaku*, pp. 189–90]

The *Book of Mencius* is the key that opens the gate of Confucianism at all times. Confucius' sayings are plain and direct. Seemingly simple and clear, they are really profound; seemingly easy to understand, they are actually difficult to grasp. They reach high into the sky and deep to the bottom of the earth, so unfathomable and immeasurable are they. Yet having Mencius to point out the meaning in so felicitous a manner, scholars can find their way through to the origin and trace the descent of Confucian teaching. So all discussion of human nature, the Mandate of Heaven, the Way and virtue, humanity and righteousness, decorum and wisdom, can be understood with Mencius' words as a commentary instead of trying to exhaust the significance of every character in the text of the *Analects* [as the later commentators have done]. For in Confucius' time the sun was still at its zenith and everyone with a pair of eyes was able to see where he was going; so in teaching it was enough to tell men what to do and there was no need to explain why in great detail. But Mencius' time was like a dark night when a lighted lantern is needed very badly; therefore reasons had to be clearly explained and directions had to be explicitly indicated. To try to understand the way of Confucius without the help of Mencius is like trying to go by water in a rudderless boat; the crossing will be thwarted. The *Book of Mencius* is for all of us of later times a magnet, a lantern in the dark.

Love as the Supreme Virtue
[From Inoue, *Rinri ihen*, V, 95–97; Spae, *Itō Jinsai*, pp. 150–52]

Humanity is the virtue! It is great! But to extol it in one word, it is called love. For what is called righteousness [or duty] between sovereign and subject, paternal affection between father and son, distinction between husband and wife, precedence between elder and younger brothers, faith between friends, this all comes from love!

Because love originates from a genuine heart, these five feelings, when they come forth from love, are true; when not from love, they are feigned. Therefore, in the eyes of the gentleman, there is no virtue above compassionate love, and nothing more pitiable than a vicious, hardened, and shallow heart. In Confucianism, humanity is considered the fountain-head of the virtues. That is the reason for it. [Inoue, p. 95; Spae, pp. 150–51]

. . . .

A disciple asked: "About humanity being the perfect Virtue, may I beg to hear something?" Jinsai answered: "Yes! A compassionate and loving heart reaching everywhere, that is precisely called humanity. To keep it in this action and not to practice it in that one, this is not humanity; to bestow one's love on an individual and not on ten men, this is not humanity. That which exists in every moment of life, extend-ing into one's sleep and dreams; a heart that does not relinquish love; love completely in that heart; both then forged into one whole: that is humanity. Therefore, among virtues, there is none greater than the love of man; and nothing is worse than the hatred of beings. This is the reason why in Confucianism humanity is believed to be the ultimate aim of learning." [Inoue, p. 97; Spae, p. 152]

The Life Force as the Ultimate Reality
[From Inoue, *Rinri ihen*, V, 12, 21]

The Buddhist takes emptiness (*śūnyatā*) as the Way, while Lao Tzu considers vacuity (*hsü*) the Way. The Buddhist thinks that mountains, rivers, and the great earth are all illusions, and Lao Tzu says all things are produced out of nothing. Still heaven overspreads us and earth up-holds us throughout eternity; the sun and moon shine and shed their light on us throughout eternity.[1] The four seasons come and go in order, while mountains stand and rivers flow for eternity. Feathered creatures, furry creatures, scaly creatures, and naked creatures, as well as plants and vines, continue as they are for eternity. Those who propagate in definite form have always done so in definite form; that which exists in formless ether will always exist in formless ether. And thus they go on, life follow-ing life endlessly. Where do you find this so-called emptiness and vacuity? [p. 21]

. . . .

The *Book of Changes* says, "The great virtue of Heaven and Earth is life." This means that life following life unendingly is the Way of

[1] That is, in contradiction to the Buddhist law of impermanence and insubstantiality, the natural world is real and enduring.

Heaven and Earth; or put another way, in the Way of Heaven and Earth there is life but not death; there is accumulation but not dissolution. Death is nothing but an end of life, and dissolution is just a conclusion of accumulation. This is because Heaven and Earth are just one life. Parents and grandparents may pass away, but their spirits are carried on by their sons and grandchildren, who will transmit them to their own sons and grandchildren. Thus life following life for eternity is in truth deathlessness. That is the case with everything. So in the Way of Heaven and Earth there is life but not death. Therefore it is all right to say that all living things die and all accumulations dissolve, but it is wrong to say that where there is life there must be death, and where there is accumulation there must be dissolution, because that makes life and death interdependent. [p. 12]

OGYŪ SORAI AND THE STUDY OF THE PAST

Umegaka ya	The scent of plum blossoms!
Tonari wa	And close to it—
Ogyū Soemon.	Ogyū Soemon.

Thus wrote the poet Bashō, who was at one time Ogyū's neighbor, associating this great Confucianist of the Tokugawa Period with the plum flower that thrives amidst the rigors of winter and early spring. Having spent fourteen years in the land of his father's exile, during which he kept working away at his studies, Ogyū Sorai (1666–1728) returned at the age of twenty-five to the metropolis of Edo, where he started a free, open-air lecture course beside the front entrance of the famous temple, Zōjō-ji. There he eventually attracted the attention not only of the prelate of that Buddhist center, but also of the shogun himself. Through the latter's special permission, equivalent to a recommendation, Ogyū was made private secretary to Premier Yanagisawa and thereafter rose rapidly to acquire an unusually large stipend.

At his school, which he later set up in the very stronghold of orthodox Chu Hsi teaching, Ogyū Sorai offered a radically new approach to Confucian studies. He had followed for a time both the orthodox school and Itō Jinsai, but concluded that they had equally failed to fulfill the basic aim of scholarship—to provide for the needs of the people and the general social welfare. The Neo-Confucianists were too much given to meta-physics, philosophical idealism and personal cultivation. Itō, while correct in trying to rediscover the original basis of Confucian teaching, had likewise concerned himself with personal ethics to the neglect of social questions. In addition, Itō, by insisting upon the authority of the *Analects* alone, had failed to recognize that this work could be properly under-stood only in relation to its historical context. Taking a broader view of things, one could see that the Six Classics (including the Books of History, Odes, Rites, etc.) were the basic deposit of China's classical heritage, while the Four Books (including Confucius and Mencius) merely represented personal interpretations of these primary sources. In fact, from Ogyū's point of view, the classical philosopher Hsün Tzu was a much better guide in such matters. Hsün Tzu's realism in regard to the evil nature of man and the necessity for correcting it through social institutions was upheld by Ogyū against the more subjective, idealistic, and optimistic view of Mencius that social betterment could only be achieved in the last analysis through moral cultivation to fulfill the original goodness of human nature. Ogyū therefore stressed the im-portance of rites (understood broadly to include virtually all social in-stitutions) and political administration, as against the virtues of humanity and righteousness narrowly conceived in terms of personal ethics. Indeed Ogyū is frankly utilitarian in asserting that morality, as embodied in the traditional Confucian "Way," has no other basis than the social function which the ancient sage-kings meant it to serve. In this respect he did not hesitate to take a stand very close to that of the foremost "realists" and utilitarians of ancient China, the Legalists, in giving primacy to law, its strict enforcement through a system of punishments and rewards, and the need to reform institutions as well as men.

One can hardly imagine a teaching more calculated to arouse the antagonism of orthodox Confucianists than this, and the fact that Ogyū was permitted to propagate it in open competition with the Hayashi family school suggests that the enforcement of Chu Hsi orthodoxy was much less strict than is commonly supposed. From the political point of view, however, Ogyū's nonconformism involved no great risks for the shogunate. His respect for the rule of law backed by superior force accorded well with the realities of the Tokugawa situation, seeming to justify the maintenance of a military government rather than reliance on the virtue of the imperial house and its subjects to maintain order. Beyond this, too, a positive interest was taken in Ogyū's ideas by the eighth shogun, Yoshimune, who was greatly impressed by his breadth of scholarship and practical approach to political problems. Ogyū's *Discourses on Government* (*Seidan*), written expressly for Yoshimune, offered detailed suggestions on a wide variety of such problems, pointing to the need for stricter controls and more uniform policies to achieve a stable social order. Yoshimune, it is said, was about to give the author a high post in the government when Ogyū suddenly died at the age of sixty-three.

We might expect that the natural outcome of Ogyū's teaching, as well as of his associations with the Edo court, would have been to direct the attentions of his school to political and social institutions in contemporary Japan. It was, on the contrary, with the study of ancient China that his school continued to be identified. Ogyū's forte was scholarship, and from the start he had put a premium on a thorough knowledge of the Chinese language. Thus, as the Sinologist par excellence of his time, he communicated a love of all things Chinese to his disciples and perhaps also a touch of intellectual snobbery, which made the most of his own acknowledged mastery in the Sinological sphere, while deprecating the importance of things Japanese. It was this attitude which carried over to his leading disciple, Dazai Shundai (1680–1747), a thorough-going Sinophile, who represents probably the highwater mark of Chinese influence in Tokugawa thought. Thereafter the tide ran strongly in a nationalistic direction, as if in reaction to the excessive adulation of Sino-Confucian culture. But it is significant that here, too, Ogyū's teaching had its effect. One of his own students was the first to show that the study of antiquity and classical learning could be applied to Japan as well as to China. This led to the School of National Learning and the Shinto revival.

OGYŪ SORAI
The Confucian Way As a Way of Government

In this passage from Ogyū's *Distinguishing the Way* (*Bendō*), which is aimed at both Itō Jinsai and the Neo-Confucianists, he tells how the Way arose from human efforts to meet social needs, and not from Confucius' unique discovery of a constant moral order or natural process.

[From Inoue, *Rinri ihen*, VI, 12–14]

The Way of Confucius is the Way of the early kings. The Way of the early kings was the way by which all under Heaven were brought peace and contentment. Confucius always wished to serve the Eastern Chou dynasty by training his disciples and perfecting their talents so that they could be employed in the government. In the end, however, failing to achieve a position of authority, he devoted himself to editing the Six Classics so that they might be handed down to posterity. Thus the Six Classics[1] embodied the way of the early kings, and they are quite wrong who say today that the way of Confucius is not the same as the way of the early kings.

The basis for bringing peace and contentment to all under Heaven was personal cultivation—but always with a mind to achieving peace in the world. This was what one called humanity. After the appearance of Tzu Ssu and Mencius, when the Confucianists became a separate school, they devoted themselves to the reverent following of their master's way and foolishly thought that through study alone they could achieve sagehood. Having once achieved sagehood, they could then set an example for all under Heaven and the world would govern itself. This was like the theory of Lao Tzu and Chuang Tzu concerning "sageliness within and kingliness without." But to deprecate the importance of what lies without [politics] and to attach all importance to what lies within [personal virtue] is quite contrary to the old way of Confucius and the early kings. Therefore in their schools the Confucianists have been unable to train students so as to develop their capacities, and outside of their schools they have been unable to mold the characters of the nation by perfecting its customs. This is why the Confucianists could not escape the charge that their learning was useless.

The Way is an all-embracing term. It takes rites, music, law enforcement, and political administration—everything the early kings established—and brings them together under one designation. There is no such thing as the Way apart from rites, music, law enforcement, and political

[1] The *Books of History*, of *Odes*, of *Changes*, of *Rites*, of *Music* (later lost) and the *Spring and Autumn Annals*.

[416]

administration. . . . The Way of the early kings was something the early kings themselves created; it was not the natural way of Heaven and Earth. The early kings, by virtue of their high intelligence and perspicacity, received the mandate of Heaven and ruled over the world. They were of one mind in making it their duty to bring peace and contentment to the world. Thus by expending all of their spiritual resources and exerting to the utmost their mental capacities, they produced this Way so that all men in later generations might act in accordance with it. How could Heaven-and-earth of themselves have produced it? Fu Hsi [who first domesticated animals], Shen Nung [who started agriculture], and the Yellow Emperor [who invented writing, etc.] were also sages, though what they produced only contributed to the Way in a utilitarian and material sense. After the intervening reigns of Chuan Hsü and Ti K'u, there came Yao and Shun who first inaugurated rites and music, and only after the Hsia, Shang, and Chou dynasties did rites and music become fully established. Thus it took several thousands of years, as well as the combined spiritual resources and mental capacities of several sages before the Way was fully developed. It was not something which could be put forth by the efforts of just one man in one lifetime.

Distortion of the Way through Ignorance of the Past

Ogyū's critique of the later Confucian tradition, which appears as a kind of prolegomenon to his *Distinguishing the Way,* points to the need for broader and more intensive study of the classical age and ancient Chinese writing in order to rescue Confucianism from the effects of historical change and excessive partisanship.

[From Inoue, *Rinri ihen,* VI, 11–12]

The Way is difficult to know and difficult to express because of its magnitude. What the Confucianists of later times saw of the Way was only one aspect of it. The true Way is the Way of the early kings of China, but after the appearance of Tzu Ssu and Mencius it degenerated into the Confucianist school which began to contend for supremacy among the "hundred philosophers" of the late Chou, and by so doing, itself demeaned the Way. Take the case of Tzu Ssu who wrote the *Mean* in opposition to Lao Tzu. Lao Tzu had called the Way of the Sages artificial. Tzu Ssu therefore said the Way was in conformity with nature, in order to show that the Confucian Way was not artificial. This brought him in the end to his theory of absolute sincerity. . . . In ancient times an originator was considered a sage, but as Confucius was no originator, absolute sincerity was spoken of in the *Mean* as the virtue of the Sage, and the three-fold explanation [of the virtue of the Sage] was put forward in order to rescue Confucius from embarrassing criticism.[2] Sincerity, however, is only one virtue of the Sage. How could it be thought of as all-sufficing and all-inclusive?

Mencius' conception of human nature as good is an example of the same sort as Tzu Ssu. By likening human nature to the willow [which can be bent into any form], Kao Tzu had said all that could be said about it. Mencius' attempt at refutation went too far. Now what Tzu Ssu had really meant to say was that when the Sages established the Way, they did so in conformity with nature; he did not mean to say that every human being is in conformity with nature and that therefore all men are naturally in conformity with the Way. It is true that while other trees cannot be bent or twisted, the willow is by nature bendable and twistable; but this does not mean that to be bent and twisted is the natural state of the willow. The sense of sympathy and shame point to the fact that humanity and righteousness have their origin in nature, but the sense of sympathy is not all there is to humanity, and the sense of shame and aversion may not necessarily constitute righteousness. It is a case of a slight misstatement that leads to a tremendous error. The latter-day School of the Mind had its inception in this. Hsün Tzu's criticism of it was correct. So I say that Tzu Ssu and Mencius were defenders of the Confucian school while Hsün Tzu was a loyal minister to Tzu Ssu and Mencius.[3]

Nevertheless, this was not long after Mencius' time and things had not changed greatly, so that their world of discourse was essentially the same. By the time Han Yü made his appearance in the T'ang, however,

[2] That is, since Confucius had not been an "originator" (like the early kings Ogyū speaks of in the preceding selection), the Confucianist author of the *Mean* offered a new conception of the Sage which would fit Confucius even though he had failed to establish anything new. This three-fold conception is referred to in the *Mean,* ch. 29, and has been variously interpreted. Ogyū seems to have in mind a three-fold conception of sincerity such as is found in ch. 26, where the attributes of Heaven, Earth, and Infinity are ascribed to absolute sincerity.

[3] In Confucian parlance "loyal minister" is often used to signify a forthright critic devoted to his Master's best interests.

writing had undergone a great change. Thereafter came the two Ch'engs and Chu Hsi, admittedly scholars of great stature, yet nonetheless unacquainted with the ancient language. Unable to read and understand the Six Classics properly, they showed a preference for the *Mean* and *Mencius* because these texts were easy to read. Thus, the writings of philosophers contending with other philosophers came to be taken as the true expression of the Way of the Sages in its original form. In addition to that, they read the ancient style of writing as if it were the modern style and, since they were ignorant of what was actually referred to, a discrepancy arose between reality and discourse, whereupon sense and reasoning took separate paths. Thus the teaching of the early kings and Confucius was seen no more.

In recent years Mr. Itō Jinsai, also a scholar of great stature, has become aware of this general state of things. Nevertheless, in the interpretation of the *Analects* he has depended on *Mencius* and has read the ancient style of writing as if it were the modern, just as the Ch'eng and Chu schoolmen did. Moreover, he has openly divided the Way of the early kings and Confucius into two ways, and put the Six Classics aside in favor of the *Analects* alone. Also he has not succeeded in avoiding the errors of those who read Chinese in Japanese fashion. So when I read what he has put forth as the ancient meaning, I wonder indeed how it could ever be called "ancient"!

Alas, the Way of the early kings degenerated into the "Confucianist" school and there appeared Hsün Tzu and Mencius; then it degenerated again with the appearance of Chu Hsi and Lu Hsiang-shan. As if it were not enough to have them in opposition to one another, each spawned his own partisan following. The more the division, the greater grew the contention; and the greater the flow of words, the less the importance of what was said. Who could not but be saddened by all this?

Thanks to Heaven's special favor, this writer obtained access to the works of two eminent scholars, Wang and Li,[4] and for the first time became acquainted with the ancient style of Chinese writing. Thus equipped, I painstakingly went through the Six Classics for a great many years. Gradually I arrived at an understanding of the terms and their corresponding realities, and thereupon the interpretation of the texts became

[4] Wang Shih-cheng and Li P'an-lung, sixteenth-century Chinese scholars who advocated a return to the language and prose style of ancient times.

clear. Only then I felt I was able to discuss the Six Classics properly. The Six Classics contain facts while the *Book of Rites*[5] and *Analects* offer interpretations. Interpretations must be supported by facts, however, before they can be accepted as definitive explanations of the Way. If facts are disregarded and interpretations are accepted of themselves, it will scarcely be possible to avoid generalization, exaggeration, and arbitrary judgment. These are the faults found among scholars following Han Yü and Liu Tsung-yüan, the Ch'engs and Chu Hsi.

I am already past fifty. If I do not exert myself before I die, what will be the judgment of Heaven? Mindful of this, whenever I have had time to spare, I have applied myself to writing in appreciation of Heaven's favor. The contents of this work include many tens of items, all intended for students who may come under my guidance.

Conclusion to *Discourses on Government*

Ogyū's *Discourses* take up a wide variety of problems affecting Japanese society at great length and in great detail. In this conclusion he sums up his general approach and principal recommendations. Note the great emphasis on strong legal controls and the comparative depreciation of the ruler's personal example (such as leading a life of austerity) as an influence on the people.

[From *Ogyū Sorai shū*, 214–15]

In my lengthy remarks contained in the foregoing four volumes, I have often gone into minor details in order to bring prevailing conditions to your attention.

Since the laws of today are not based on mature consideration, important matters are left entirely uncontrolled by law, while a tremendous amount of legislation is devoted to minor matters. Everyone lacks discipline, and customs are shifting constantly. Today laws are handed down as law, but people feel that it has no connection with them. Therefore I wanted to call to Your Highness' attention the fact that laws are becoming wholly ineffectual.

Current affairs have been discussed above, some out of my personal experience, some on the basis of information from other sources. There may be certain misunderstandings on my part; there may also be mistakes in judgment. The way of government, however, is not a series of

[5] The compilation containing the *Great Learning* and the *Mean*.

disconnected affairs; a knowledge of the whole world and what goes on in it is essential for the ruler. The important thing to understand today is that present conditions all go back to two facts: first, that people all over are living like transients in a hotel, and second, that everything is out of legal control. Therefore, family registration should be instituted so that people would settle down in a fixed place of residence. Controls should be adopted to maintain the distinction between military households, merchants, and farmers. Controls should also be set up over the daimyō. Finally, it is necessary for the government to stop buying in the rice market.[1]

For the most part these measures will help the nation to recover and become prosperous. Other measures will follow in natural sequence as things improve. The ruler himself may adopt economy and austerity measures to put his household on a sound basis, but it will do no good if the people continue to suffer from dire poverty. My fervent desire is to see that both ruler and ruled grow rich and prosperous together, so that Your Highness' reign will last forever.

In the third volume, I discussed the functions of office and the way to pick men for official employment. That is also a secret of the Sage. Laws may be as good as one could wish, but if the right man to administer them is lacking, the laws will prove of no use.

These are the main points of what I have written. It is said that "unless plans be kept secret, harm will follow." And since matters relating to your administration of the government may not be divulged to others, I have written out these discourses myself without asking the help of my students, though my eyes are weak and my handwriting poor. I trust therefore that when Your Highness has finished perusing it, my work will be thrown into the fire.

For a Merit System in Government

As we have seen, Ogyū not only favored the hereditary class system but advocated strict controls to preserve it. In the government, however, he believes that hereditary succession to high office inevitably results in power falling into the hands of incompetents. Though he advocates no general replacement of

---

[1] An attempt to control the price of rice by buying when the price was low and selling when the price was high. It also aimed at storing surpluses which could be used for relief in times of famine.

the hereditary system by a civil service, like many a Confucianist before him Ogyū must plead the case of the man of ability if he is to have any opportunity to put his own ideas into effect. No doubt Ogyū's criticisms are directed in part at the Hayashi family, whose hereditary monopoly over state education he attacks elsewhere in the *Discourses*.

[From *Ogyū Sorai shū*, pp. 124–28]

It is a general law of nature that old things gradually disappear and new things come into being. All things in heaven and earth are like this. We might like to keep old things forever, but that is beyond our power. Timber rots, grain varies in yield from year to year. So too with men: the old pass away and the young come in. In this they follow the law of nature, by which things from below rise gradually to the top and on reaching the top decline and disappear. This is an invariable rule, with which even the law of [the *Book of*] *Changes* accords. It is in keeping with the principles of good government that a family which has rendered distinguished service should be well treated so as to preserve it as long as possible. In a family with old people, prayers are said for great grandparents, grandparents, and parents in hopes of their living till the end of time. It is only human not to entertain the thought of their early death, but the law of the universe is one thing and human sentiment is another; the things of old, which you want to preserve so much, are destined to disappear. To say that things of the past might just as well disappear immediately is to go too far in the other direction and is not in accord with the Way of the Sages. Nonetheless, to attempt to preserve the things of the past forever is sheer stupidity and also not in accord with the Way of the Sages. The Way of the Sages gives due place to human sentiments so that human feelings will not be outraged, but at the same time the everlasting law is transparently clear and there is no way of ignoring it. Consequently not to keep dwelling foolishly on human sentiment is the key to fair treatment of all mankind.

Because of the law mentioned above, the descendants of Kings Yao and Shun, Yü and T'ang, Wen and Wu, have vanished without a trace in China. In Japan there is no longer any trace of the once great shoguns Yoritomo and Takauji. It is the same with all famous families. On the other hand, the powerful families we call daimyō today were in former days of little account. Because of their achievements in war they have risen to the top. Even so today there are few powerful families which have maintained direct, legitimate succession. To try foolishly to preserve hereditary status by forever keeping those on top at the top and those below at the bottom is in violation of the law of the universe, for it helps to preserve from oblivion those at the top who have reached the point where they should give way. When men of talent and wisdom are no longer at the top, it signifies the end of a regime; confusion and disorder will open the way for men of talent and wisdom to rise up and overthrow the dynasty. Being profoundly aware of this truth and solicitous of preserving the dynasty, the sages instituted the system of punishments and rewards in order to raise up men of talent from below and at the same time leave to Heaven's will the elimination of those who have no legitimate heir to succeed them or whose wickedness has foredoomed them to destruction.

If this were adhered to, the wise would always be on top and the stupid would always stay at the bottom, in perfect accord with the universal law; and thus the reign would go on forever. To be unaware of this natural balance means ignorance of the law that prevails over heaven, earth and mankind. This means in turn lack of accord with Heaven's will; which again is not the true way of government. . . .

Why is it that during a period of prolonged peace men of ability are only found among the lower classes, while men of the upper class grow increasingly stupid? As far as I can see, men's abilities are developed only through hardship and tribulation. In the case of our bodies, use makes the members strong. Use the hands and the arms grow strong, use the legs and the feet become hardened. If one practices aiming as in archery or gunnery, one's eyesight will improve. Likewise, when the mind is used, intelligence develops. If hardship and tribulation are encountered in different forms, these experiences will bring out one's abilities; that is the natural law. So in Mencius it is noted that when Heaven has a great mission for a man to perform, it will first put him to an acid test. When he develops his ability through such an acid test, he is especially fit for the task of government because he is familiar with conditions among the people. Therefore, in the Way of the Sages too it is recommended that able men be advanced by bringing them up from below. Through the study of history also we may see, as clearly as in a mirror, that men of intelligence and talent have all come from below; rarely have they come from hereditarily privileged families. Even those men of the hereditary nobility have come to that high estate because their forebears risked their lives during the Warring States period, developed their abilities the hard way through bitter experience, and rendered distinguished service in order to attain high office and large feudal grants. Their descendants, however, having held high office and large feudal grants for generations, find themselves on top from birth and suffer no hardship at all. How then can they develop their abilities? Set apart from those below by their high rank, they are uninformed of conditions among the people. Brought up amidst the constant flattery of those around them, they pride themselves on their wisdom without in truth having any. As they are recipients of respect by birthright, they take it so for granted that they accept even favors from the shogun without heartfelt appreciation, as if these were to be expected. Full of self-will, they look upon the people as so many insects; this feeling is natural to man in such circumstances and such conduct only follows the natural law. Even when gifted with talent, the highborn are likely to have such a weakness. Though they may be intelligent and clever enough, they live so far apart from the people that they are simply unaware of how the people feel. As they are inured to the formalities of polite society, their talents are well-developed in this direction. But common people are not inured to such formalities, so they often appear uncouth to the high-born, whose egotism is thereby further inflated. Such is human nature, the same in the present as in the past. For this reason, in the Way of the Sages, prime importance was placed on raising up wise and talented men of low station, while hereditary succession in high office from generation to generation was strongly disapproved.

MURO KYŪSŌ'S DEFENSE OF NEO-CONFUCIANISM

Muro Kyūsō (1658–1734), the son of a physician (like many other thinkers of his time), came to the defense of Chu Hsi's philosophy at a time when it was under heavy attack from such able men as Yamaga, Itō, and Ogyū. Having acquired his belief in the rightness of Chu Hsi only after a long intellectual struggle, it was a matter of intense personal conviction with him and not just a passive acceptance of the established teaching. Therefore, although he did not seek to formulate any new philosophy of his own, he was far more effective in revitalizing the teaching of the old doctrine than its official defenders in the Hayashi school. In this role he strongly reinforced the ethical attitudes by which the Tokugawa had originally hoped, through their sponsorship of Neo-Confucianism, to secure the bases of their own rule. Among these was the sense of duty (or "righteousness," *gi*) as manifested in personal relationships, especially in loyalty to one's lord or ruler which was regarded as the highest duty. Related to this was a deep sense of one's indebtedness or obligation (*on*) to one's parents for the original gift of life and to one's ruler for sustaining and protecting it.

In contrast to Yamaga, however, whose sense of loyalty was increasingly directed to the imperial house, Muro became a staunch supporter of the shogunate, for which he found a justification in Mencius' theory of the Mandate of Heaven being conferred on those who best serve the interests of the people. On this basis, for instance, he regarded Ieyasu as virtually heaven-sent to bring order out of chaos and establish a benevolent regime after centuries of bloodshed and disorganization. Indeed, he contributed in no small measure to the hero-worshipping cult of Ieyasu, which persisted to the end of the Tokugawa Period, and to the general buttressing of the shogunate's position and authority. By thus identifying himself so wholeheartedly with the existing regime and Chu Hsi orthodoxy, however, Muro stood squarely in the face of two powerful currents of thought which eventually swept all before them: nationalism (particularly as embodied in the revival of Shinto, which he considered unworthy of association with Neo-Confucianism) and the growing sense of loyalty to the imperial house.

MURO KYŪSO
In Defense of Neo-Confucian Orthodoxy

In his prefatory remarks to the *Conversations at Suruga-dai* (*Shundai zatsuwa*) Muro, identified as the "Old Man," describes how he became a convinced Neo-Confucianist only after many years of study. Now, with the Ch'eng-Chu school

[425]

under attack from many quarters, he feels that he has a mission to defend it similar to that of the great Han Yü in T'ang dynasty China, who turned the tide against Buddhism and Taoism and led the way to the later revival of Confucianism.

[From Inoue, *Rinri ihen,* VII, 82–84; cf. Knox, "A Japanese Philosopher," in *TASJ,* XX, 28–31]

One day as the Old Man was talking with his students, the discussion turned to developments in Confucian thought since the Sung school, and one of those present expressed doubts as to the Ch'eng-Chu philosophy. The Old Man said to him:

"When I was young I pursued conventional Chinese studies, memorizing and reciting the classics and studying composition. I had devoted many years and months to this when suddenly I realized the folly of it and thought of devoting myself to that teaching of the ancients which was concerned with one's true self. Unhappily, however, I had neither able teachers nor worthy friends to guide me, and was simply bewildered by the many theories of the different philosophers. I half believed in the Ch'eng-Chu system, and half doubted it. Unable to arrive at any settled view of things, I saw the years and months pass by without anything having been gained. Then at about the age of forty I came to the deep realization that nothing could take the place of the Ch'eng-Chu teaching. Now for thirty years I have studied the writings of the Ch'eng-Chu school, considering them deep in my heart and reflecting upon them in my mind. I find that the higher one gazes the loftier they seem; the more carefully one analyzes them the more impervious they are to criticism. Neither too abstruse nor too superficial, these teachings would undoubtedly obtain the full assent of even a sage, if one arose again. For the Way of Heaven-and-earth is the Way of Yao and Shun; the Way of Yao and Shun is the Way of Confucius and Mencius; the Way of Confucius and Mencius is the Way of Ch'eng and Chu. If we refuse to follow the Way of Ch'eng and Chu, we cannot attain the Way of Confucius and Mencius; if we refuse to follow the Way of Confucius and Mencius, we cannot attain the Way of Yao and Shun; and if we refuse to follow the Way of Yao and Shun, we cannot attain the Way of Heaven-and-earth. I do not expect that my teaching should be accepted implicitly, but this much I know to be true from my own knowledge, and

I should take upon myself the punishment of Heaven-and-earth if I spoke not from my own knowledge and uttered what was perhaps not true—such is my solemn oath!"

At this everyone seemed to listen all the more intently, and the Old Man went on:

"What I say has already been confirmed by five centuries of scholarly opinion and consequently stands in no need of an oath from me to affirm it today. After the time of Chu Hsi, beginning with such eminent scholars as Chen Hsi-shan and Wei Hao-shan in the Sung dynasty, Hsü Lu-chai and Wu Ts'ao-lu in the Yüan dynasty, and Hsüeh Ching-hsüan and Hu Ching-chai in the Ming dynasty, there were many others devoted to the study of the True Way and all of them believed in Ch'eng and Chu. . . . Thus until the middle of the Ming period, scholarship was conducted on the correct lines and the true teaching suffered no decline. But when Wang Yang-ming appeared he proclaimed the doctrine of innate knowledge ["good knowledge"] and attacked Chu Hsi. Thus the temper of thought in the Ming underwent a change, and after Yang-ming's death such followers of his as Wang Lung-ch'i turned in the direction of Zen Buddhism. Thereafter scholars became intoxicated with intuitive knowledge and grew tired of pursuing first principles. By the end of the Ming the deleterious effects of this were such that scholars throughout the land became Confucianists by day and Buddhists by night. . . . Men with only a particle of the learning of Ch'eng and Chu criticized them in the most flippant manner, like the wren who mocked at the [wider knowledge of the far-flying] roc and the caterpillar who presumed to measure the expanse of the sea. As Han Yü said, 'They sit in a well and, looking up at the sky, pronounce it small.' Nevertheless there are countless numbers of men, shallow and deficient in knowledge, who eagerly take to new and strange teachings and love to echo the opinions of others.

"In our state peace has endured for a hundred years and learning has flourished, so that scholars have appeared in great numbers. Their scholarship may not always have been of the best, but at least they held firmly to the Ch'eng-Chu philosophy and preserved what was worthy of imitation from the past—which must be counted a blessing. More recently, however, there have been some who misled men into new and dangerous paths, trying to set up their own schools of thought and gathering followers about them, so that they might enjoy some kind of ascendancy in the company of scholars long used to prostituting themselves, and make much of their own wild ideas—without the least sense of shame. All the dogs join in when one starts barking, and that is the reason why vile teachings and outrageous doctrines abound in the world today. Truly the Way is in a critical phase. Therefore, just as Han Yü rose up when Buddhism and Taoism were flourishing and attacked them single-handedly, likening himself to Mencius and swearing an oath by the gods of Heaven-and-earth, so this old man swears too, that though his merits may not equal those of Mencius, still he dares not fail to answer the call of Han Yü. And you, too, see that my words are not listened to in vain!"

Economics and the Traditional Virtues

The next two selections from Muro's *Conversations* are typical of the official attitude toward the rising merchant class and the spreading influence of bourgeois life and values. It springs from concern over the deterioration of samurai standards and from a feeling that the prosperity of the merchant was gained at the expense of the peasant and tended to discourage agriculture. Muro is obviously guided by the traditional Chinese policy, which became established as early as the Han dynasty (second century b.c.), of discrimination against the merchant class and at least nominal support for agriculture. His reflections on the contemporary scene are a striking commentary on the rapid social and economic changes Japan was undergoing despite the shogunate's attempt to preserve the status quo.

[From Inoue, *Rinri ihen*, VII, 294–97; cf. Knox, "A Japanese Philosopher," *TASJ*, XX, 129–30]

Nothing is more important to the samurai than duty. Second in importance comes life, and then money. Since both life and money are also of value, a man is likely when confronted by a life-or-death situation or when faced with money matters to depreciate the precious thing called duty. Hence, only if the samurai is careful not to think nor speak of greed for life or greed for money can he remove himself entirely from avaricious desires. What I call avaricious desires is not limited to love of money, for concern with one's own life is also avarice. Is one's life not more precious than money? When faced with however unpleasant a duty, the way of the samurai consists in regarding his own wishes—even his life itself—as of less value than rubbish. How much less should he value money? Since [life and money] are of intrinsic value, it is good to take care of one's health and avoid spending money wantonly. Even so, to cherish in one's heart or even to speak of overfondness for one's life or the worship of money may be suitable for the merchants, but it is hardly so for the samurai. I have seen in a book of old tales that in the T'ang dynasty there was a servant woman who had been employed for a long time in the household of Liu Kung-ch'üan.[1] Leaving the Liu household, she went to work for Yang Chü-yüan.[2] There she saw the mistress of the house selling silk and haggling with wholesalers over prices. Suddenly dismayed, she made her apologies and left the Yang household. . . . As one might expect from a family of hereditary office-holders of the T'ang, the Liu family retained unsullied customs and were distinguished from families which had arisen recently. This story is preserved simply because [such customs] were exceptional in the middle of the T'ang dynasty.

In ancient Japan, in keeping with its name of "the country of the sages," manners were pure and simple, and not perverted by [consideration for] prices and profits. Even where duty was not rigorously defended, there was an inbred sense of honor which had not entirely disappeared. Though manners changed greatly with the coming of military government, the samurai still knew nothing at all of money matters, and they were frugal and direct, and not the slightest bit given to extravagance. This was true until recent times. . . .

As I remember my youth, young men of that time never mentioned prices, and there were some who blushed when they heard erotic stories. Most of them delighted in listening to stories about old battles and loved to discuss duty to one's lord or father and the samurai's resolute will. I hear that when young men nowadays get together, they often amuse each other by telling stories of profit and loss or talking about sexual pleasures. Thus have social standards changed since fifty or sixty years ago. At about that time there was a samurai in Kaga named Aochi Uneme. His son, named Kurando,[3] was a friend of mine. Uneme said to his sons and disciples: "Though the attainment of prosperity by exchanging goods with others is practiced freely in the world, you should have nothing to

---

[1] T'ang official, poet, and calligrapher (778–865). [2] Poet (eighth-ninth century).
[3] Aochi Saiken, praised by Muro as a model samurai.

do with it. In buying at a loss, it is all right for the gain to be on the other side. However, winning in trade differs from winning at chess, for when one buys at a profit and the gain is to oneself, there is no satisfaction, but on the contrary the heart becomes spiteful. To rejoice when one makes a profitable transaction or buys valuable merchandise cheaply is part of the merchant's trade, but it is unpardonable in a samurai."

Some years ago, when Arai Chikugo-*no-kami* [i.e., Arai Hakuseki] was attendant lecturer in the Confucian temple, I heard him say: "Never say, in reporting of another man, that he is greedy, for if he is greedy of money, then you can be sure that he will ultimately be greedy of life. In that case, you should use the blunter word, and say that he is cowardly." This is quite true.

The People Should Be As Heaven to the King

[From Inoue, *Rinri ihen*, VII, 155–59; cf. Knox, "A Japanese Philosopher," in *TASJ*, XX, 81–84]

Once, at the end of his exposition of the tenth book of the *Analects*, concerning the passage, "He bowed to those who bore the tables of the census" (X, 16), the Old Man asked his guests: "What is the meaning of the phrase, 'The king takes the people to be Heaven, while the people take food to be Heaven'?"

"The people," replied one, "are the foundation of the state; when they are obedient the state remains, but when they rebel it is destroyed. As its preservation or destruction is up to the people, the king must always honor them as Heaven. Food is the people's life. With it they live, but without it they die. . . . Therefore, the people honor food as Heaven."

"You have explained both of them correctly," continued the Old Man. "Both phrases refer to the idea that agriculture should be highly valued. When Heaven begets man it brings forth grain for his food. If there are men there is grain and if there is grain there are men; if there is no grain there are no men. Nothing on earth is more important than food. The farmers produce it and are entrusted by Heaven to the king, who must honor them as he honors Heaven itself. He should not despise even one of them. This is why the census in ancient times was received with honor by the king, and Confucius bowed when he met those who bore it. The

[430]

people too should remember that they are entrusted with the production of the most essential thing in the land, given by Heaven for the continuance of human life, and should honor it as Heaven itself. They must not be idle, for their industry is the basis of social standards and customs, and has a bearing on the tranquility of the state. . . .

"Under the Three Dynasties the rulers regarded the people as Heaven. Therefore they lightened taxes and aided the people in times of distress, so that the people were not reduced to fleeing elsewhere and wandering about the country. They lived at home without anxiety and gave their produce to the king and no one failed to 'take food to be Heaven.' Their spirit carried over to the capital, from the officials down to the tradesmen, and all were frugal and none lazy or extravagant. But later, in the time of the Ch'in dynasty, there no longer existed the feeling that the people were as Heaven, and cruel taxes were imposed until provinces broke away or rebelled. The country crumbled like earth, and bands of ruffians appeared everywhere. Again from the time of the Han dynasty, though there was peace and safety, yet many were intent on gain and the great merchants lived like princes . . . and in imitation the country folk too fell into extravagance and competed in costly amusements. Chia I complained to the government, and as something of the spirit that takes the people to be Heaven remained, the emperor repeatedly proclaimed that agriculture is the foundation of the empire, remitted the taxes and warned the local officials against greed. He exhorted to filial obedience, brotherly respect, and industry. . . . So in the time of [the emperors] Wen and Ching, lord and servant were frugal and the land grew rich. At no time since the Three Dynasties had there been such good government. The study of the past and the present shows that ancient times were unique. In later ages, when the social standards of the countryside extended to the capital, times were good; but when the social standards of the capital extended to the countryside, times were bad. This is because the custom of the capital was to value luxury, while the provinces had not lost their simplicity.

"From what I have heard about the recent state of the capital, the provinces are full of avaricious officials, and the towns are full of money-grubbers. Many of them, while they seem outwardly to obey the law and be above bribery, work privately for profit and love luxury. Furthermore, they flaunt their cunning and hide their faults; they deceive the government, slander others, and plot shrewdly. From what I hear of their intercourse with one another, they strive for sumptuousness in their banquets, they vie with one another in the elegance of songs and dances, and spend immense sums in a day. They take all this to be in refined taste. It staggers the imagination. When they see a man who is frugal and honest they ridicule him as rustic and unaccustomed to the ways of the world. Since an individual can do nothing against the multitude, these fashions become universal, and even the remote regions are extravagant and false. Alas! All the world praises extravagance and all the world desires money without which these lusts cannot be gratified. So those who are strong seize the wealth of the empire, and its circulation is stopped. Gold and silver are scarce. But food is produced every year, so money grows dear, while grain grows cheap. The samurai who are paid in rice must exchange cheap grain for dear cash and have not enough, while the money-grubbers buy cheap grain with dear coin and increase their goods. But with limited coin their extravagance is unlimited and useful money goes for useless things. . . .

"This has not come about in a day. Until sixty or seventy years ago there was greater prosperity than there is today. Some vulgar people liked luxury, but the majority were frugal, for many old men of the former age still remained, men who . . . had endured hardship as soldiers and had known no luxury even in their dreams. They trained their sons and grandsons too in the family traditions. Though we would speak of them today as having rustic ways, they were naturally without ostentation, and were rich in character. They were lacking in falseness and full of genuineness. They were earnest, dependable, hardworking, and kind. Later, such men disappeared. Samurai and officials now wallow in their hereditary pensions. In times of peace, they know nothing of hardships. All they want is comfort. They are unaware of its poisons. Extravagant and vain and profligate—no wonder we are in such a condition! Still worse are the money-grubbers and the providers of great entertainments. And the evil spreads to the provinces. In the country there is still some of the old spirit which has already disappeared from the capital. Of course country folk are often foolish and profligate, and some commit great crimes; moreover, having for the most part little discretion, they become angry when faced with hard times, and sometimes rise against the government. Still they are not cunning like the towns-

[432]

people. They are naturally honest, simple, easily moved by blessings, quick to follow reason and satisfied with their daily food. When the officials of a province remember the spirit that takes the people to be as Heaven, modify the taxes according to circumstances and so treat the people that they may nourish parents and children without fear of death from cold and hunger, then the people will be contented and will not abandon their land to escape suffering. When the laws are made known, showing the punishments that will be meted out to criminals, forbidding extravagance, and reproving the idle and dissolute, then the people of that province will respectfully obey, and thus their customs will be improved. As customs improve in one province after another their influence will naturally be felt in the capital. The townspeople are not one tenth so numerous as the country folk; yet whatever is in fashion at the capital soon spreads to the provinces. Were the farmers content and prosperous, still more readily then would their fashions go throughout the empire conquering extravagance and evil. Without doubt extravagance would give way gradually to frugality."

CHAPTER XIX

THE VOCABULARY OF
JAPANESE AESTHETICS III

The student of Tokugawa Japan is everywhere faced with seeming contradictions. He finds first of all a military dictatorship which ruled the country for more than two hundred and fifty years virtually without warfare, and which sacrificed the chance of an overseas empire in favor of peace. He finds also a society which subscribed to strict Confucian principles but which distinguished itself especially by its devotion to sensual pleasures. And when he considers the aesthetic vocabulary of the period he discovers no less curious contradictions.

Part of the difficulty in attempting to establish the typical words used by Tokugawa writers in making aesthetic judgments stems from the fact that there was no uniformity. That is, we have no reason to suppose that the touchstone of taste in 1650 remained such in 1850, or that the ideals which guided a chronicler of the glories of the gay quarters were the same as for a poet living in a tranquil hermitage. Nevertheless, certain words and ideas can be mentioned as having possessed especial significance during much of the period.

The most brilliant part of the Tokugawa Period was undoubtedly the Genroku era (1688-1703), which lent its name to much of the culture of the late seventeenth and early eighteenth centuries. One term which first came into prominence about this time was *ukiyo,* a word which in another meaning was much older. In Heian literature the word was used to mean "sorrowful world," and was a typical Buddhist description of the world of dust and grief. However, about 1680 the same sounds acquired a new meaning, by making a pun between *uki* meaning "sorrowful" and *uki* meaning "floating." The new term, the "floating world," was quickly taken up, probably because it gave so vivid a picture of the unstable volatile society which had succeeded the medieval world of sorrow and gloom. One typical expression of the "floating world" may be found in the numerous Genroku paintings of waves—the most changeable and exciting of natural forms. The word *ukiyo* itself came to be applied to many products of Genroku culture, including the *ukiyo-e,* the woodblock prints which were the most famous if not the best works of Tokugawa art. *Ukiyo* was used especially of the licensed quarters—the brothels and other places of amusement which were the center of urban society at the time. The Genroku literary figure par excellence, the hero of the novel *The Man Who Spent His Life at Love-making* (1683), was named Ukiyonosuke, and his complete familiarity with the denizens and arts of the "floating world" made him the envy and the object of emulation of many lesser men. This book (an outstanding example of *ukiyo-zōshi,* or demi-monde fiction) was written by Ihara Saikaku (1642-1693), the leading Genroku novelist, who portrayed in a fascinating manner the two great interests of the "floating world"—sex and money. He who gained a full mastery of these two disciplines was entitled to be known as a *tsūjin,* or expert. Saikaku himself was a great *tsūjin* and could boast of many and varied experiences in the *ukiyo*. His description of the ideal woman of Genroku times proves, among other things, how careful a study he made of his chosen field:

When I asked what type of woman he was hoping to get, the old man took from a scroll-case of paulownia wood a picture of a beautiful woman, saying that he would like to hold in his arms a living replica made from this model. When I examined it I saw that the woman in the picture was from fifteen to eighteen years of age. Her face, which had an up-to-date look, was roundish and of the color of pale cherry blossoms. Her features were flawless: the eyes, by his wish, were not narrow; the thick brows did not grow too close together; the nose was straight; the mouth was small with regular, white teeth; and the long ears, which had delicate rims, stood away from the head so that one could see through to the roots. Her hair at the forehead grew naturally and with no trace of artificiality. The back hair fell over her downless slender neck. Her fingers were pliant and long with thin nails. Her feet could not have had the breadth of eight copper coins; the big toes curled upwards and the soles were translucently delicate. Her body was above average in size. The hips were firm and not fleshy, the buttocks full. Elegant in movement and in dress, her bearing possessed both dignity and gentleness. She excelled in the arts required of women, and was ignorant of nothing. There was not a single mole on her entire body.[1]

[1] *Kōshoku ichidai onna* 1, in *Saikaku zenshū,* I, 320.

Saikaku's ideal woman differed greatly from the one described in *The Tale of Genji*. The Heian beauty was distinguished primarily by her accomplishments and her tastes, and her genealogy was never over-looked. She was, of course, ravishingly beautiful too, but no Heian writer would have entered into the precision of details to which Saikaku treats us. It was obviously more important for him that his ideal woman's toes curl up than that she write with exquisite brush strokes. And, since Saikaku does not even mention what moral qualities she should possess to complement her physical charms, there is no reason to suppose that he sought any in this paragon of women.

In the plays of Chikamatsu (1653–1725), however, we find depicted quite a different type of woman—which serves to show how far from uniform the aesthetic ideals of the Tokugawa Period were. Chikamatsu's heroines were usually either figures from Japanese history or else women from the same *ukiyo* milieu that Saikaku so lovingly treated. But unlike Saikaku's heroines, who surrendered themselves entirely to their passions, Chikamatsu's were also influenced by *giri,* a concept of great importance in Tokugawa Japan. *Giri* had both Buddhist and Confucian antecedents, developing equally from the awareness of the law of causality and the concern for moral justice. The word may be translated as "duty" or "moral obligation," but its implications extended far beyond the usual sphere of the English words. To control the passions (*ninjō*) one had to exercise *giri;* when the passions were too strong to be controlled there was likely to be tragedy, as Chikamatsu demonstrated.

The *ukiyo* world of the passions and the stern dictates of *giri* remained dominant themes in Tokugawa literature. Well into the nineteenth century we find books with such titles as *The Ukiyo Bath-house* or *The Ukiyo Barbershop,* as well as numerous works with the avowed intention of "encouraging virtue and chastising vice" (*kanzen chōaku*). The *ukiyo* books usually consisted of gay (and even pornographic) material; the other type of literature which enjoyed great popularity was the didactic romance, in which the author attempted painlessly to inculcate moral teachings. The outstanding work in the latter category was Bakin's monumental *Hakken-den* ("Biographies of Eight Heroes"), written between 1814 and 1841. Each of Bakin's eight heroes represents one of the Confucian cardinal virtues, a device similar to that employed by Spenser in *The Faerie Queene.* In the course of the thousands of pages of the *Hakken-den,* the various heroes are often sorely tempted and tried, but their Buddhist conviction that good brings only good while evil leads only to evil enables them to surmount all difficulties. In its time the *Hakken-den* enjoyed immense popularity because of its combination of exciting incidents with sage admonitions. And, even though most modern readers prefer Saikaku's *ukiyo* to Bakin's *giri,* the *Hakken-den,* both by its magnitude and its summary of ways of thought developed during the preceding two hundred years, may be considered to represent the grand culmination of the Tokugawa culture and aesthetic ideals.

CHIKAMATSU MONZAEMON

On Realism in Art
  (From the preface to *Naniwa Miyage* by Hozumi Ikan)
  [From Keene, *The Battles of Coxinga,* pp. 93–96]

This is what Chikamatsu told me when I visited him many years ago. "*Jōruri* differs from other forms of fiction in that, since it is primarily concerned with puppets, the words should all be living things in which action is the most important feature. Because *jōruri* is performed in theatres that operate in close competition with those of the *kabuki,* which is the art of living actors, the author must impart to lifeless wooden puppets a variety of emotions, and attempt in this way to capture the interest of the audience. It is thus generally very difficult to write a work of great distinction.

"Once, when I was young and reading a story about the court, I came across a passage which told how, on the occasion of a festival, the snow had fallen heavily and piled up. An order was then given to a guard to clear away the snow from an orange tree. When this happened, the pine tree next to it, apparently resentful that its boughs were bent with snow, recoiled its branches. This was a stroke of the pen which gave life to the inanimate tree. It did so because the spectacle of the pine tree, resentful that the snow has been cleared from the orange tree, recoiling its branches itself and shaking off the snow which bends it down, is one which creates the feeling of a living, moving thing. Is that not so?

"From this model I learned how to put life into my *jōruri.* Thus, even

[437]

descriptive passages like the *michiyuki,* to say nothing of the narrative phrases and dialogue, must be charged with feeling or they will be greeted with scant applause. This is the same thing as is called evocative power in poets. For example, if a poet should fail to bring emotion to his praise of even the superb scenery of Matsushima or Miyajima in his poem, it would be like looking at the carelessly drawn picture of a beautiful woman. For this reason, it should be borne in mind that feeling is the basis of writing. . . .

"The old *jōruri* was just like our modern street story-telling and was without either flower or fruit. From the time that I began to write *jōruri* . . . I have used care in my writing, which was not true of the old *jōruri.* As a result, the medium was raised one level. For example, inasmuch as the nobility, the samurai, and the lower classes all have different social stations, it is essential that they be distinguished in their representation from their appearance down to their speech. Similarly, even within the same samurai class, there are both daimyō and retainers, as well as others of lower rank, each rank possessed of distinct qualities; such differences must be established. This is because it is essential that they be well pictured in the emotions of the reader.

"In writing *jōruri,* one attempts first to describe facts as they really are, but in so doing one writes things which are not true, in the interest of art. To be precise, many things are said by the female characters which real women could not utter. Such things fall under the heading of art; it is because they say what could not come from a real woman's lips that their true emotions are disclosed. If in such cases the author were to model his character on the ways of a real woman and conceal her feelings, such realism, far from being admired, would permit no pleasure in the work. Thus, if one examines a play without paying attention to the question of art, one will probably criticize it on the grounds that it contains many unpleasant words which are not suitable for women. But such things should be considered as art. In addition, there are numerous instances in the portrayal of a villain as excessively cowardly, or of a clown as being funny, which are outside the truth and which must be regarded as art. The spectator must bear this consideration in mind.

"There are some who, thinking that pathos is essential to a *jōruri,* make frequent use of such expressions as 'it was touching' in their writing, or who when chanting do so in voices thick with tears, in the manner of the *Bunyabushi*.[1] This is foreign to my style. I take pathos to be entirely a matter of restraint.[2] Since it is moving when all parts of the art are controlled by restraint, the stronger and firmer the melody and words are, the sadder will be the impression created. For this reason, when one says of something which is sad that it is sad, one loses the implications, and in the end, even the impression of sadness is slight. It is essential that one not say of a thing that 'it is sad,' but that it be sad of itself. For example, when one praises a place renowned for its scenery such as Matsushima by saying, 'Ah, what a fine view!' one has said in one phrase all that one can about the sight, but without effect. If one wishes to praise the view, and one says numerous things indirectly about its appearance, the quality of the view may be known of itself, without one's having to say, 'It is a fine view.' This is true of everything of its kind."

Someone said, "People nowadays will not accept plays unless they are realistic and well reasoned out. There are many things in the old stories which people will not now tolerate. It is thus that such people as *kabuki* actors are considered skillful to the degree that their acting resembles reality. The first consideration is to have the chief retainer in the play resemble a real chief retainer, and to have the daimyō look like a real daimyō. People will not stand for the childish nonsense they did in the past."

Chikamatsu answered, "Your view seems like a plausible one, but it is a theory which does not take into account the real methods of art. Art is something which lies in the slender margin between the real and the unreal. Of course it seems desirable, in view of the current taste for realism, to have the chief retainer in the play copy the gestures and speech of a real retainer, but in that case should a real chief retainer of a daimyō put rouge and powder on his face like an actor? Or, would it prove entertaining if an actor, on the grounds that real chief retainers do not make up their faces, were to appear on the stage and perform, with his beard growing wild and his head shaven? This is what I mean by the slender margin between the real and the unreal. It is unreal, and yet it is not unreal; it is real, and yet it is not real. Entertainment lies between the two.

[1] The style of Okamoto Bunya, noted for its sentimentality.
[2] The word here translated as "restraint" is *giri*, which normally means "propriety" or "duty." If one acts in accordance with propriety one will not gush over into uncontrolled emotion but will be restrained.

"In this connection, there is the story of a certain court lady who had a lover. The two loved each other very passionately, but the lady lived far deep in the women's palace, and the man could not visit her quarters. She could see him therefore only very rarely, from between the cracks of her screen of state at the court. She longed for him so desperately that she had a wooden image carved of the man. Its appearance was not like that of any ordinary doll, but did not differ in any particle from the man. It goes without saying that the color of his complexion was perfectly rendered; even the pores of his skin were delineated. The openings in his ears and nostrils were fashioned, and there was no discrepancy even in the number of teeth in the mouth. Since it was made with the man posing beside it, the only difference between the man and this doll was the presence in one, and the absence in the other, of a soul. However, when the lady drew the doll close to her and looked at it, the exactness of the reproduction of the living man chilled her, and she felt unpleasant and rather frightened. Court lady that she was, her love was also chilled, and as she found it distressing to have the doll by her side, she soon threw it away.

"In view of this we can see that if one makes an exact copy of a living being, even if it happened to be Yang Kuei-fei,[3] one will become disgusted with it. Thus, if when one paints an image or carves it of wood there are, in the name of artistic license, some stylized parts in a work otherwise resembling the real form; this is, after all, what people love in art. The same is true of literary composition. While bearing resemblance to the original, it should have stylization; this makes it art, and is what delights men's minds. Theatrical dialogue written with this in mind is apt to be worthwhile."

[3] The most celebrated of Chinese beauties, concubine of the Emperor Hsüan-tsung (r. 712–755).

CHAPTER XX

THE HAIKU *AND THE* DEMOCRACY OF POETRY IN JAPAN

The *haiku,* quite possibly the shortest of all verse-forms, represents a distinct Japanese contribution to the poetic literature of the world, if only because it proves how great an effect can be obtained with the barest minimum of words. In spite of its extreme brevity—a *haiku* consists of only 17 syllables—the Japanese have often considered *haiku* poetry the greatest produced in their country, and it has attracted wide attention and even imitation in the West. Like the Japanese wood-block prints, it possesses universal appeal, largely perhaps because of its unpretentiousness.

The *haiku* has another importance in the history of Japanese literature and society: it is a verse-form evolved for the ordinary man, in contrast to most other Japanese poetry, which is aristocratic in form and tradition.

There must, of course, always have been poetry composed by unlettered people in Japan. We may find examples of such crude, almost meaningless verse in the earliest surviving book, the *Records of Ancient Matters* (*Kojiki,* A.D. 712). Some of it may have been composed in connection with ritual observances like the following one (which, however, is apparently of a later date):

Ajime o o o o	Ajime! O! O! O! O!
Oke ajime o o o o	Go to it! Ajime! O! O! O! O!

The anthropologist would find more of interest in such verses than the student of poetry, but even among the songs of the *Records of Ancient Matters* we can find some here and there of literary quality, and by the end of the eighth century the first and possibly the greatest anthology of Japanese poetry was compiled—the *Manyōshū.* There is an amazing diffence in quality between the poetry of the *Manyōshū* and the songs preserved in the *Records.* Even the poems attributed to antiquity have an elegance usually lacking in those songs, and the poetry composed in the eighth century itself has a power and a nobility seldom again to be equaled in Japan. It is not very difficult to see how this came about. With the establishment of a permanent capital in Nara (in 710) court life of complexity and refinement became possible in Japan as never before. Among the necessary accomplishments of the courtiers, perhaps in imitation of Chinese usage, was the ability to write verse. The preponderant part of the poetry in the *Manyōshū* was in fact composed by sovereigns and members of their courts, although poems by unknown authors, some of them apparently peasants, were also included.

It was not long, however, before the composition of poetry fitted for the court-sponsored anthologies became far too difficult for casual amateurs. This was not because the rules of prosody were too demanding: the standard verse-form, the *waka*, consists of only 31 syllables, arranged in five lines of 5, 7, 5, 7, and 7 syllables, without rhyme or quantity. Anyone could compose a *waka*, but it was deemed unworthy of attention unless it showed a mastery of the poetic traditions of the past. A technique was evolved which may be characterized as "virtuoso." Only a restricted number of themes was recognized as being suited to poetry, and this meant that there were innumerable poems composed on such popular subjects as the cherry blossoms or the autumnal moon, often with only a slight change in wording or imagery between one poem and its much appreciated imitation of a century later. The poetry in the *Manyōshū* covered a wide variety of subjects, including some obviously of the common people:

My hands so chapped from rice-pounding—
To-night again, he will hold them, sighing,
My young lord of the mansion! [1]

In later times such subjects as "chapped hands" were considered indecorous and rather vulgar by the poets, who far preferred to write their love-poetry about tear-drenched sleeves. Although lip service continued to be paid to originality of sentiment, this in general meant little more than a new twist to some familiar poetic formula. According to Fujiwara no Teika (1162–1241), the celebrated arbiter of poetic excellence, poets must imitate the masterpieces of their predecessors and restrict themselves to the same vocabulary. He enjoined a constant study of the

[1] *Manyōshū*, No. 850, Nippon Gakujutsu Shinkōkai edition.

old poetry, and the members of the court actually appear to have spent much of their time in this pursuit. It was not only for use in composing new poetry worthy of the anthologies that a knowledge of old poetry was indispensable: the courtier who missed an allusion or who failed to respond with an impromptu verse in an appropriate mood was likely to be disgraced.

It may be seen that this type of poetry could thrive best in a society preoccupied with few other tasks. Little time for the arduous study Teika recommended could be spared by soldiers, farmers and villagers, and from the twelfth or thirteenth centuries onwards, poets from these classes began to express themselves not in the classical *waka,* but in linked-verse *(renga).* As far back as the *Records of Ancient Matters* occurs an elementary form of linked-verse, one *waka* composed by two people. That is, one man gave the first three lines (or 5, 7, and 5 syllables) and the other man "linked" on the two remaining lines (of 7 and 7 syllables) to make up a normal *waka.* In time this type of poetry became quite popular at the court, where it gradually developed into long poems in many "links" composed by three or more poets at a special meeting.

When samurai returned to their provinces after service in the capital they must have aroused widespread interest with their accounts of linked-verse gatherings. The special appeal of linked-verse to such people was probably its communal quality—it could furnish an evening's entertainment to small groups of samurai, merchants, or farmers living a lonely country life. The rules of linked-verse drawn up at the court and transmitted to the provinces were extremely complicated, but they were essentially the rules of a game and not abstract poetic dicta based on purely aesthetic considerations. Thus, one can imagine a group of people shouting down a man who attempted to mention cherry blossoms before the proper "link" for them, as stated in the book of rules. This was quite a different matter from knowing by heart a dozen anthologies of poetry so as to be able to spot an allusion, and it is easy to see why linked-verse gained such popularity with people in the provinces.

Between the thirteenth and sixteenth centuries two main varieties of linked-verse flourished. The first was the linked-verse of the court— refined, melodious, and melancholy, in the aristocratic tradition; the second was the linked-verse of the provinces—gay, simple, and often so crude that only their obedience to the codes of linked-verse preserved a semblance of poetic form about them. Linked-verse of the first type became a great art, and at times possessed a unique beauty that resulted from the fusion of the imagery of several poets' minds. Although the form was different, the substance of the linked-verse became essentially one with that of the *waka* especially after the victory of the "serious" over the "humorous" faction.

The countrified linked-verse, however, had a special importance in the medieval period with its decentralized culture. An account written in 1470, for example, relates that even in the most wretched village the sound of people making verse of 1,000 or even 10,000 "links" filled the ears of passing travelers, indicating how popular a pastime it was. At many temples and shrines, which were the centers of local culture, linked-verse meetings were regularly held in which samurai, farmers, and villagers alike participated. Sometimes such meetings served other purposes than the mere composition of verse; that at least was the view of the Muromachi Shogunate which occasionally attempted to prohibit linked-verse meetings because it was feared they might actually be gatherings of dissident factions.

The greatest master of linked-verse, Sōgi (1421–1502), came from the lowest class of society. Though he ultimately rose to be an arbiter of poetic taste almost comparable to Teika before him, and he enjoyed the patronage of the aristocracy, there always remained a strong contact between Sōgi's art and the linked-verse of the common people. Sōgi's chief works were not composed at the court, but in different parts of the country, where he was welcomed by all ranks of people.

The popular linked-verse did not represent a conscious revolt against the aristocratic traditions of poetry. Rather, it was a form which ordinary, untutored people enjoyed because it gave them the chance to compose verse together as a kind of game governed by clearly stated rules. The level of poetic quality tended to remain very low, but this did not dampen the enthusiasm of the participants, and the popular linked-verse, largely through its use of a modern, colloquial vocabulary, retained a vitality that the court linked-verse lost. It was almost in spite of its elegance and purity of diction that Sōgi's linked-verse achieved greatness; most poets could say very little of permanent value within the stereotyped framework of the court linked-verse. With the shift in cultural supremacy from the aristocrats and the great samurai (who absorbed the aristocratic culture through widely circulated textbooks) to the merchant class in the seventeenth century, a real revolt occurred in linked-verse stemming from the active desire of the newly risen class to have its own forms of all types of literary activity.

The kind of poetry which best suited the exuberant, volatile, rather vulgar society dominated by the merchant class was called *haikai*. This word may be translated "comic," "light-hearted," or "free," and was used in opposition to the serious, formal *waka* and linked-verse. Already in the sixteenth century Yamazaki Sōkan (1465?–1553?) had pioneered in the use of the familiar language and ideas of the popular linked-verse in compositions of a more artistic nature. Sōkan compiled an anthology called the *Collection of Canine Linked-Verse,* "canine" to indicate the lowly and sometimes crude nature of the verse. A famous pair of "links" from this collection, one which was denounced by later advocates of refined *haikai* as the negation of filial piety, ran:

| Niganigashiku mo | Bitter, bitter it was |
| Okashikarikeri. | And yet somehow funny. |

To which was added:

Ware oya no	Even when
Shinuru toki ni mo	My father lay dying
He wo kokite.	I went on farting.

This "link" is certainly in very poor taste, but it cleverly captures the mixed emotions of the previous link, and in some ways embodies the genius of *haikai* poetry by showing the contrast between the most solemn moment of a man's life and the coarse actions which may involuntarily accompany it.

The new *haikai* linked-verse was immediately popular with poets tired of the stale vocabulary and images of the court linked-verse, but it did not take long for a reaction to set in against the excessive liberty of expression found in Sōkan's collection. Matsunaga Teitoku (1571–1653) led a new movement in *haikai* poetry which attempted to lift its artistic level while retaining its freedom of language. Teitoku compiled a *haikai* code which differed very little from the old linked-verse codes. What marked his linked-verse as being *haikai* was his use of words drawn from common speech or from Chinese, unlike the court linked-verse which restricted itself to old and pure Japanese words. Thus, according to Teitoku, if a verse contained such words as "slap" or "existence" instead of "strike" or "life" (to use approximate English parallels) it was *haikai* even though the subject was as hackneyed as the moonlight and cherry blossoms of the court linked-verse.

It looked very much as if the fate of the new *haikai* poetry was to be that of the earlier linked-verse, with a great cleavage developing between the work of professional poets and that of ordinary people. *Haikai* was saved by the vigorous reaction of the Danrin school, and was made the glory of the Japanese people by the greatest of its poets, Bashō (1644–1694). The Danrin school insisted that it did not suffice for the language of *haikai* poetry to be modern; the ideas must also be new. The great attention paid by Danrin *haikai* to the humor of the details of daily living won its popularity with people of every class. The masters of Teitoku's school, finding their pupils deserting them for the new school, declared that Danrin *haikai* went against the sacred Way of Poetry, which enjoyed the blessings of the gods and Buddha, and even that Danrin's irreverence constituted a menace to the well-being of the nation. They could point, for example, to a Danrin verse in which Buddha was depicted in a privy, the victim of diarrhea. The Danrin poets, in demonstrating their emancipation from traditional ideas about linked-verse, often went to excess as in such an example. Danrin linked-verse could be composed very rapidly by several poets or even one talented man because it did not insist on any fixed number of syllables for a given link, thus removing virtually the last formal restriction. It may be imagined that the quality of much of the verse was very poor. The Danrin insistence on up-to-dateness also meant that their verse quickly became dated, if not quite unintelligible, in a few years' time. The allusions to contemporary life and literature which in its day won Danrin verse such popularity thus ultimately spelled its oblivion.

It was Bashō who saw the problem of rules versus freedom most clearly and solved it by his insistence that the poetry of his school embody both change and permanence. Change, or novelty, he felt to be the essence of *haikai* poetry, and the one thing which could keep it from becoming in time as stale as the conventional *waka* or linked-verse. For centuries the Japanese poets had been taught to imitate the writings of their predecessors; Bashō declared that in *haikai* there were no predecessors. His philosophy of poetry is perhaps best summarized in his advice to a pupil, "Do not seek to follow in the footsteps of the men of old; seek what they

[446]

sought!"[2] Here we have the most vivid example of the two principles of change and permanence. Bashō urged his pupil not to imitate, but at the same time to retain in mind the permanent objectives of poetry instead of frittering away his talents on the ephemeral subjects so dear to Danrin versifiers.

Bashō began life as a samurai, but renounced all privileges when he took up the career of a *haikai* master. He lived as a commoner and had nothing to do either with the emperor's court in Kyoto or the shogun's court in Edo (Tokyo). Nor did Bashō, like Sōgi and many other famous poets, become a Buddhist priest, although he dressed and in some ways acted like one. He likened himself to a bat, being "neither priest nor layman, bird nor rat, but something in between."[3] His pupils included men of every walk of life from rich samurai and merchants down to poor farmers; the two for whom he showed the most affection were a criminal and a beggar. The democratic quality of his school was typical of the entire *haikai* movement, and explains in part why *haikai* poetry found adherents everywhere. Bashō's journeys around Japan, although usually made under difficult and even disagreeable circumstances, had something of the triumphal progress about them. Wherever he went Bashō found amateur poets who begged him to join in making a chain of *haikai* linked-verse. Even the man who led Bashō's horse across the fields surprised him by asking for a poem.

Bashō was famous both for his *haikai* linked-verse and for his *hokku*. The latter originally meant specifically the opening verse of a linked-verse series, and although it retained its potentiality of serving as the first link in a chain, it also developed into a complete and independent form, now usually called the *haiku*. Bashō's *haiku* covered a wide range of subjects. Nothing was too commonplace for him to treat, and nothing too sublime. Early in his career Bashō had mastered the Danrin techniques, and he remained capable of turning out a gay verse when he chose, but he is most renowned for the verses which show his warm sympathy and identification with the sights of nature and human life. The splash of a frog jumping into a pond, the sight of a monkey shivering in the wintry

[2] Bashō attributes this statement to Kūkai, who actually said, "In writing poetry, a study of the old forms is an excellent thing, but it is no mark of ability to copy old poems. In calligraphy too, it is good to imitate the old conceptions, but it is not a mark of skill to make one's writing resemble the old examples." *Shōryōshū* in *Kōbō Daishi zenshū*, III, 427.

[3] *Kashima Kikō* in *Bashō Zenshū*, I.

rain, or of a grasshopper under the brazen helmet of some long dead warrior, or of a boatman smoking his pipe in the spring breeze—each became in his poetry a microcosm which suggested the macrocosm, a perception of universal truth from one essential detail. The connection between the art of Bashō's *haiku* and Zen Buddhism is particularly noteworthy.

Many of Bashō's best poems were composed while on a journey, the most important of which was the one to the northern part of Japan described in *The Narrow Road of Oku*. Many poets before Bashō had traveled to see the cherry blossoms at Mt. Yoshino and other famous spots in the general area of Kyoto, but it remained for Bashō to celebrate the neglected northern half of the country. The lonely beauty of half-forgotten places attracted him far more than the gaiety of the cities, and he was constantly stirred by wanderlust. Bashō died on a journey, as he once had predicted. His last poem was:

Tabi ni yamite	Stricken on a journey
Yume wa kareno wo	My dreams through withered fields
Kakemawaru.	Go wandering still.

Among the many great successors of Bashō, Issa (1763–1828) was one of the most original and well-beloved. Unlike Sōgi, who rose from the lowest class to official recognition as the leading poet of the nation, or Bashō, who left the ranks of the samurai to lead the life he chose, Issa remained throughout his life a farmer. With Issa the many generations of anonymous peasant-poets at last found their authentic voice. Like them, but with genius, Issa wrote of sparrows, frogs, mosquitoes, fleas, spiders, and farmers, with extreme simplicity and great feeling. Everyone can understand Issa, and since his poetry comes from the two true sources, the heart and nature, it is no wonder that it is so loved by the Japanese people. With him the democracy of poetry attained universality.

Yasegaeru	Skinny frog,
Makeru na Issa	Don't give up!
Koko ni ari.	Issa is here.

Japanese peasants have not always been poets, by any means. There is a common saying among them: "It is better to work in the fields than to write poetry (*Shi o tsukuru yori, ta o tsukure*)." But this homespun reminder that the bodily need for food comes ahead of aesthetic satisfactions would have little point among people with less of a flair for versification than the Japanese. Today at New Years thousands of humble folk still respond to the emperor's invitation to submit a poem (*waka*) on a theme he has selected for that year. During the Tanabata festival young girls still write poems on a thin streamer and attach them to a stalk of green bamboo, telling of their yearning for a lover. And virtually all daily newspapers have a section devoted to *haiku*. Japan is perhaps the only country in the world where poetry can be called a national pastime.

MATSUO BASHŌ
The Rustic Gate

Farewell words to Kyoroku, who was returning to his province [1]
[From Ebara, *Bashō bunshū*, pp. 175–76]

It was just in the autumn of last year that, quite by chance, I met him, and already I am lamenting deeply our separation. One day, when the time of parting approached, he knocked at the door of my thatched hut, and we spent the whole day in quiet conversation.

Talented as he is, he loves both painting and *haikai* poetry. I asked him once as a test why he liked painting, and he said it was because of poetry. "And why do you love poetry?" "Because of painting." Two things he studied for one purpose. Indeed, since it is said that it is shameful for a gentleman to have many accomplishments,[2] it is admirable that he makes one use of the two arts.

In painting he was my teacher; in poetry I taught him and he was my disciple. My teacher's paintings are imbued with such profundity of spirit and executed with such marvelous dexterity that I could never approach their mysterious depths.

I said to him as we parted, "My poetry is like a stove in the summer or a fan in winter. It runs against the popular tastes and has no practical use. But there is much that is affecting even in the poems of Toshinari and Saigyō[3] that were lightly tossed off. Did not the retired Emperor Go-

---

[1] Morikawa Kyoroku (1656–1715), a samurai from Hikone, was one of Bashō's favorite pupils.
[2] See *Analects*, IX, 6. "Does it befit a gentleman to have many accomplishments? No, he is in no need of them at all." (Tr. by Waley.)
[3] Fujiwara no Toshinari (or Shunzei) (1114–1204) and the priest Saigyō (1118–90). The latter poet, together with Sōgi, were the earlier poets whom Bashō most admired.

Toba [4] say of their poetry that it contained truth tinged with sorrow? Take strength from his words and follow unswervingly the narrow thread of the Way of Poetry. Do not seek to follow in the footsteps of the men of old; seek what they sought. That is what Kūkai wrote, [5] and it is true of *haikai* poetry as well." Saying these words I lifted my lantern and showed him outside the rustic gate, where we parted.

Summer [1693]

KYORAI

Conversations with Bashō

The brevity and apparent simplicity of the 17-syllabled *haiku* led to its wide popularity in Japan, where only a very inarticulate person remained incapable of an extemporary verse. However, in the hands of its masters, the *haiku*, far from representing an impromptu reaction to the sights of nature, was usually a highly conscious form of verse, demanding compliance with exacting aesthetic principles. Bashō was famous not only as the supreme *haiku* poet, but as the foremost interpreter of its theories. His conversations with his pupil Kyorai (1651–1704) contain a fair sample of his critical views. Some of them are translated below.

The method employed by Kyorai in demonstrating various facets of the "Master's" opinions was to give a verse, either a *haiku* or a 14-syllabled "second-verse" (*waki*), and then report what the "Master" said about it. The editorial comments are intended to help elucidate special points.

[From Iwata, *Kyoraishō hyōkai*, pp. 14–67]

One of the ideals of the *haiku* was to have each word indispensable and inalterable. This was no doubt a product of the brevity of the form. In the following a critic suggests that the wording of a poem by Bashō might have been changed.

Yuku haru wo	The departing spring
Ōmi no hito to	With the men of Ōmi
Oshimikeru	Have I lamented.
	Bashō

The Master said, "Shōhaku criticized this poem on the grounds that I might just as well have said 'Tamba' instead of 'Ōmi' or 'departing year'

---

[4] The Emperor Go-Toba (1180–1239) was one of the best poets among the sovereigns of Japan.

[5] See note 2, page 447.

instead of 'departing spring.' How does this criticism strike you?" Kyorai replied, "Shōhaku's criticism misses the mark completely. What could be more natural than to regret the passing of the spring, when the waters of the Lake of Ōmi are veiled so enchantingly in mist? Besides, it is especially fitting a poem for one who lives by the lake to have written." The Master said, "Yes, the poets of old loved spring in this province almost as much as in the capital." Kyorai, deeply struck by these words, continued, "If you were in Ōmi at the close of the year, why should you regret its passing? Or, if you were in Tamba at the end of spring, you would not be likely to have such a feeling. What truth there is in the poetry of a man who has genuinely been stirred by some sight of Nature!" The Master said, "Kyorai, you are a person with whom I can talk about poetry." He was very pleased. [p. 14]

· · · ·

Haiku poets, particularly of the schools before Bashō, often erred in the direction of excessive ingenuity in their choice of words. Kakei's verse, though here criticized by Bashō, may appeal to modern readers more than Kyorai's.

Kogarashi ni	Will the two-day moon
Futsuka no tsuki no	Be blown from the sky
Fukichiru ka	By the winter wind?

Kakei

Kogarashi no	Kept by the winter wind
Chi ni mo otosanu	From falling to earth—
Shigure ka na	The drizzling rain.

Kyorai

Kyorai said, "I feel that Kakei's verse is far superior to mine. By asking if it will be 'blown from the sky' he makes his mention of the two-day moon all the more clever." Bashō answered, "Kakei's verse is built around the words 'two-day moon.' Take away the 'two-day moon' and there is nothing left to the poem. It is not apparent on what you based your poem. It is good all around." [p. 19]

· · · ·

Kiyotaki ya	Clear cascades!
Nami ni chiri naki	In the waves immaculate,
Natsu no tsuki	The summer moon.

Bashō

One day when the Master was lying on his sickbed in Osaka, he called me to him and said, "This verse resembles one I composed not long ago at Sonome's house:

Shiragiku no	The white chrysanthemum
Me ni tatete miru	Even when lifted to the eye
Chiri mo nashi	Remains immaculate.

Bashō

I have therefore changed the 'Clear cascades' verse to:

Kiyotaki ya	Clear cascades!
Nami ni chirikomu	Into the waves scatter
Aomatsuba	Blue pine-needles.

Bashō

The rough draft of the original version must be in Yamei's house. Please destroy it." But it was too late—the poem had already appeared in several collections.

This example demonstrates what pains Bashō took with every verse, master though he was. [p. 22]

. . . .

The Monkey's Cloak (*Sarumino*) was a collection of verse by Bashō and members of his school, published in 1691. In the following excerpt Bashō is struck by the words 'skylark of Akashi' because of the graceful allusion to another poem.

Omokaji ya	Port the helm!
Akashi no tomari	There, by Akashi harbor,
Hototogisu	A skylark!

Kakei

This poem was being considered for inclusion in *The Monkey's Cloak*. Kyorai said, "It is just like the Master's

No wo yoko ni	Across the fields
Uma hikimuke yo	Turn the horse's head—
Hototogisu	A skylark!

Bashō

It should not be included." The Master said, "The 'skylark of Akashi' is not a bad image." Kyorai replied, "I don't know about the 'skylark of Akashi,' but the poem merely substitutes a boat for a horse. It shows no originality." The Master commented, "He hasn't made any advance in the conception of the verse, but you may include it or not as you please on the basis of the Akashi skylark." We finally did not include it. [p. 25]

. . . .

Kyorai's poem has been interpreted as referring to himself, older but less talented than most of Bashō's pupils—"a back number." The question here treated is how openly emotional a poem may be.

Furumai ya	The attitudes they strike!
Shimoza ni naoru	I straighten on the lower shelf
Kozo no hina	Last year's dolls.

Kyorai

I wrote this verse because of the special meaning it had for me. For the first line I had at first tried "the old court cap" or else "the paper cloak," but they left nothing to the imagination, and mentioning the doll's costume obscured my underlying thought. On the other hand, an expression like "how pitiable!" or "how unfortunate!" was too feeble. When, having finally hit on the present opening line, I asked the Master about it, he replied, "If you really insist on putting your heart into the first line, you ought to say something like Shintoku's 'Ah, the world of men!' Your 'attitudes they strike' is not quite right, but it will do." [p. 28]

. . . .

Iga was Bashō's native place and he took a special interest in its poets.

Ta no heri no	Along the borders of the fields
Mame tsutai yuku	Following the bean plants
Hotaru ka na	Go the fireflies.

Banko

This verse was originally one by Bonchō which the Master had corrected. When we were compiling *The Monkey's Cloak*, Bonchō remarked, "This verse has nothing special to recommend it. Let's leave it out." Kyorai answered, "The lights of the fireflies following the bean plants at the edge of a field splendidly evoke a dark night." But Bonchō was not convinced by my words. The Master said, "If Bonchō throws it away, I'll pick it up! It fortunately happens that one of the Iga poets has a similar verse which I can modify into this one." Thus it finally appeared as Banko's poem. [p. 29]

The art of making a *haiku* from a trifling incident.

Kiraretaru	Stabbed to death!
Yume wa makoto ka	Was my dream true?
Nomi no ato	The marks of a flea.

Kikaku

Kyorai said, "Kikaku is really a clever writer. Who else would ever have thought of writing a poem merely about being bitten by a flea?" The Master said, "You're quite right. He's the Prince Teika of the *haiku*. He deals with trifling matters in a most grandiloquent way." This criticism seemed to me to describe Kikaku's art completely. [p. 35]

* * * *

Ototoi wa	The day before yesterday
Ano yama koetsu	I crossed the mountain over there—
Hanazakari	With the full bloom of the cherry.

Kyorai

I wrote this verse two or three years before *The Monkey's Cloak* was compiled. At the time the Master told me, "I doubt whether anyone will appreciate this verse now. You'll have to wait a year or two." Later he wrote me on his journey with Tokoku to Yoshino, "My mind has been so dominated now by one poem about the cherry blossoms of Yoshino and now by another, each of which so completely describes the scene, that I myself have not written a single verse at Yoshino. All I do every day as I go along is to recite your 'The day before yesterday I crossed the mountain over there.'" The poem was acclaimed when I later read it to other people. How did the Master know that it would be popular in a year or two? I for one never dreamt it. [p. 36]

* * * *

Bashō likens himself to a wild duck stricken while in flight; a fisherman's hearth has not only crickets but shrimps.

Yamu kari no	A sick wild duck
Yosamu ni ochite	Falling in the evening cold—
Tabine ka na	These traveler's lodgings!

Bashō

Ama no ya wa	The fisherman's hut—
Koebi ni majiru	Mixed with little shrimps
Itodo ka na	Some crickets!

Bashō

When we were compiling *The Monkey's Cloak* we were asked to choose one of these two poems for inclusion. Bonchō said, "The verse about the sick wild duck is good, but the other about the crickets mixing with the little shrimps has a freshness which makes it truly outstanding." Kyorai answered, "The verse about the shrimps is unusual, but had I thought of the scene in the fisherman's hut I could have written it myself. The one about the wild duck, on the other hand, is so noble in tone, so subtly perceptive, that I wonder how anyone could have conceived it." After some discussion we finally asked permission to include both verses. The Master later said laughing, "You seem to have argued yourselves into thinking that a sick duck and a little shrimp have about equal value." [pp. 37–38]

. . . .

In the attempt to make the *haiku* as suggestive as possible, deliberately ambiguous language was often used. Here, however, Bashō discovers a meaning in Kyorai's poem which the author did not think of.

Iwahana ya	The tips of the crags—
Koko ni mo hitori	Here too is someone,
Tsuki no kyaku	Guest of the moon.

Kyorai

Kyorai said, "Shadō thinks that the last line should be 'monkey of the moon,' but I think that 'guest' is better." The Master asked, "How can he suggest such a word as 'monkey'? What had you in mind when you wrote the poem?" Kyorai answered, "One night, when I was walking in the mountains by the light of the harvest moon, composing poetry as I went along, I noticed another poet standing by the crags." The Master said, "How much more interesting a poem it would be if by the lines 'Here too is someone, guest of the moon' you meant yourself. You must be the subject of the verse." [pp. 39–40]

. . . .

Shimokyō was a very quiet district of Kyoto.

Shimokyō ya	Shimokyō!
Yuki tsumu ue no	On the piled-up snow
Yo no ame	The night rain.

Bonchō

This verse at first lacked an opening line, and everyone from the Master downwards tried to think of one. At length the Master settled on the above line. Bonchō said "yes" to it, but still didn't seem satisfied. The Master said, "Bonchō, why don't you think of a better opening line? If you do, I'll never write another *haiku!*" Kyorai said, "Anyone can see how good a line it is, but it's not so easy to appreciate that no other line would do. If members of some other school of poetry heard what you said, they would think that you were ridiculously self-assured, and they would make up any number of opening lines. But the ones which they considered to be good would seem laughably bad to us." [p. 43]

. . . .

The difference in subjects suited to the classical *waka* and the *haiku*.

Inoshishi no	Is that the path
Ne ni yuku kata ya	The wild boar travels to his lair?
Ake no tsuki	The moon at dawning.

Kyorai

When I asked the Master what he thought of this verse he pondered for a long time without saying whether it was good or bad. I mistakenly thought that, master though he was, he didn't know how hunters wait at night for a boar to return to his lair at dawn, and I explained it all to him in great detail. Then he remarked, "The interest of that sight was familiar even to the poets of former times. That is why we have the *waka:*

Akenu to te	Now that it has dawned
Nobe yori yama ni	A wind from the clover
Iru shika no	Wafts away the spoor
Ato fukiokuru	Of the deer returning
Ogi no uwakaze	From the fields to their mountains.

When a subject can be treated even within the elegant framework of the *waka,* there does not seem to be much point in giving within the freer compass of the *haiku* so prosy a description. The reason why I stopped to think for a while was that the verse seemed somehow interesting and I was wondering if something couldn't be done with it. But I fear it's hopeless." [pp. 44–45]

. . . .

Kyorai takes Bashō too literally.

Yūsuzumi	The evening cool—
Senki okoshite	I got lumbago
Kaerikeri	And went back home.

Kyorai

When I was first studying the *haiku* I asked the Master how to write an opening verse. He replied, "It must be written firmly and clearly." As a test of my abilities I composed the above verse. When I asked his opinion of it, he gave a great laugh and said, "You still haven't got the idea!" [p. 54]

. . . .

The importance of using words exactly appropriate to the season of *haiku*.

| Ume ni suzume no | In the plum tree the swallows |
| Eda no hyaku nari | Form countless clusters on the branches. |

Kyorai

This was a "second-verse" composed at the New Year. The Master heard it while he was at his retreat in Fukagawa. He commented, "Plum blossoms are a sight of the second month. Kyorai, how ever did you make the mistake of using that image in a New Year's poem?" [p. 62]

. . . .

| Detchi ga ninau | The water the apprentice |
| Mizu koboshikeri | Was carrying spilled over. |

Bonchō

At first he used the word "nightsoil." Bonchō asked, "Is it permissible to mention urine and nightsoil in a poem?" The Master replied, "You need not avoid mentioning them. You should not do so more than twice in a hundred verses, and it is quite all right if they aren't mentioned at all." Bonchō changed it to "water." [p. 64]

. . . .

On the need for sharpness in the imagery of a *haiku*.

| Tsuma yobu kiji no | The pheasant calling his mate |
| Mi wo hosō suru | Draws in his body. |

Kyorai

At first it was "The pheasant calling his mate confusedly cries." The Master said, "Kyorai, don't you know even that much about poetry? A

[457]

poem should have shape. If you say the same thing in the way I suggest your poem will have shape." [p. 65]

. . . .

Bashō's techniques in linked-verse demonstrated: by evoking the excitement caused by the blossoming of the cherry tree he gives a most dramatic picture of the arrival of spring in a dark wood.

| Kuromite takaki | Somber and tall |
| Kashi no ki no mori | The forest of oaks |

Saku hana ni	In and out
Chiisaki mon wo	Through the little gate
Detsu iritsu	To the cherry blossoms.

Bashō

When the former verse was given, I thought how difficult it would be to add a verse about cherry blossoms without losing the image of the forest of oaks. When I asked the Master to add a verse, this was how he did it. [p. 67]

CHAPTER XXI

EIGHTEENTH-CENTURY RATIONALISM

As Japan moved into the eighteenth century the Tokugawa Shogunate was already a century old, with its power and prestige firmly established and its policy of peace enforcement a proven success. The country was entering a stage of economic and cultural prosperity which brought an outburst of intellectual activity and originality unprecedented in Japan's long history. Despite the shogunate's adherence to a seclusion policy, the events of the late sixteenth century leading up to its adoption had also left indelibly printed on many Japanese minds the vision of a new and larger world in which the West played so dynamic a part. At the same time the official program of instruction based upon Chu Hsi's philosophy, which for almost a century had been spreading its influence throughout the land, greatly stimulated scholarly study in general, sometimes along lines not anticipated by its Tokugawa sponsors. Furthermore in the port cities and towns around the feudal castles the growing merchant class, restricted by the lack of opportunities for overseas trade, tended to develop new outlets for their energies and talents at home. There, as patrons of men like the novelist Saikaku, the poet Bashō, and the playwright Chikamatsu, they assisted in giving birth to a variety of popular arts which richly displayed the increasing wealth and culture of the people. In some instances these merchants and their fast-growing towns also contributed materially to the development of independent thinkers and scholars.

One epoch-making development in peaceful eighteenth-century Japan was the successful construction of a new calendar by an official commission of scholars, working with new methods similar to those then in use in the West. It had been the fond dream of Yoshimune (1684–1751) to issue a calendar using the services of his newly built observatory, and great satisfaction was expressed in the proclamation of a new era name, Precious Calendar (*Hōreki*) in 1751. The satisfaction was doubly felt because it meant that the Japanese no longer had to rely on the Chinese for what was considered to be the almost sacred duty of calendar making.

The newly awakened sense of cultural independence was far reaching in its effect. As the eighteenth century brought to full flower the needs of independent, and particularly scientific, thought sown in the preceding period, along with this there was a steady rise in both rationalistic and nationalistic thinking. The latter trend is dealt with in other sections. Here we can offer only a few examples of the growing rationalism in this period. One is Tominaga Nakamoto (1715–1746), the son of an Osaka merchant, whose name is associated with an original method of historical criticism. Another is Miura Baien (1723–1789), a rural physician in Kyushu, under no feudal bond, who carried on in the tradition of Kaibara Ekken. Ekken, another Kyushu man, had brought Chu Hsi's spirit of objective investigation into the open field of nature, regarding the study of man and nature as one. Baien went further to insist that man cannot be understood except in terms of nature, and that nature can only be understood if man divests himself of his anthropocentric point of view. The third representative is Kaiho Seiryō (1755–1817), who was born by the shores of the Japan Sea, and came from a warrior family of good standing but renounced his hereditary status to become a teacher among merchants and farmers. He argued in favor of the realistic study of the laws governing social and economic behavior as against the narrowly ethical approach of the traditional Confucianist.

None of these three figures had a wide influence in his own time and none can be considered representative of the eighteenth century as a whole. They are, rather, symptomatic of an intellectual ferment that threatened eventually to break down the narrow limits within which the Tokugawa and their Neo-Confucian advisers had sought to confine Japanese thinking. It is true that this trend toward greater independence in thought, which had risen steadily throughout the eighteenth century, was partly checked by a shogunal decree of 1790 known as the Prohibition of Heterodox Studies. Nevertheless the fact that such a prohibition was felt to be a matter of urgent necessity indicates in itself the extent to which independent minds were active and articulate by the end of the century.

Before turning to these more striking cases of independent thought, however, we shall do well to observe how, in the person of a far more widely recognized scholar and statesman, Arai Hakuseki, the rationalistic tendency received great impetus from within the ranks of orthodox Confucianism. This will serve as a reminder of the fact, sometimes lost sight of in connection with the growing revolt against Chu Hsi orthodoxy, that this rationalistic temper of mind owes more to the Neo-Confucianism it sought to displace than to any other single influence in Japanese thought. Neo-Confucianism itself provided the instruments with which its disciples gained their intellectual freedom.

THE ENLIGHTENED CONFUCIANISM OF ARAI HAKUSEKI

A samurai whose family was greatly reduced in circumstances, Arai Hakuseki (1657–1725) was independent enough twice to decline offers of marriage into wealthy families and high-minded enough to decline a lucrative post in favor of a former classmate who needed it more. Endowed with a brilliant mind and striking appearance (he is described as having eyes that flashed like lightning and a mustache stiff as spears), Arai eventually rose high in the service of the shogunate court. First as mentor to the sixth shogun, Ienobu, and then as adviser to his successor, Ietsugu, Arai became the chief architect of government policy and temporarily deprived the Hayashi family of their function as top consultants to the Tokugawa in educational and cultural matters. Ietsugu, however, died prematurely in 1715 (at the age of eight). When Yoshimune came in as the eighth shogun, Arai was summarily dismissed in favor of the conservative Muro Kyūsō.

During his six years in power, from 1709 to 1715, Arai distinguished himself as a statesman who attempted to bring some kind of order and sense into the Tokugawa administration. One of his chief accomplishments was the systematic revision of the basic law of the shogunate, the Laws Governing the Military Households (*Buke Hatto*), to make them less rhetorical and more practical (see Chapter XV). Another was reform of the currency, which had been seriously debased in the previous administration of Tsunayoshi. Along with this he instituted for the first time a system of budgeting and accounting to bring order out of the chaos of Tokugawa finances. Finally, to stabilize the currency he tried to stop the drain on gold and silver caused by what he considered the one-sided trade at Nagasaki. Arai's solution, however, was not to free Japan from the self-imposed limitations of the seclusion policy, so as to develop an export trade which would balance imports from the Chinese and Dutch. Rather he favored even more stringent controls over the Nagasaki trade to limit its volume and prevent bootlegging, adhering strictly to the traditional Sino-Confucian policy of discouraging, regulating, and monopolizing foreign trade.

Nevertheless among the growing number of Confucian scholars in a secluded Japan, Hakuseki was almost the only one who sensed that his country was now called upon to play a part in a larger world. Ahead of all other shogunal officials he realized that in its dealings with foreign countries, Japan must be represented as a sovereign state and that the unresolved conflict in authority between the shogunate at Edo and the imperial court at Kyoto must somehow be settled. At the same time, as a thoroughgoing Confucianist, he believed that social order and political authority rested upon a clearly defined hierarchy and a unified system of social and ceremonial observances reflecting that hierarchical order. To achieve such unity in Japan he proposed that the heir to the shogunate be married to an imperial princess, and that all ceremonial practices at Edo conform to the Kyoto model. Also, he settled for a time at least the delicate question: how are foreign embassies to address the shogun, in such a way as to indicate that he is the *de facto* ruler of Japan without challenging the nominal rule of the emperor? Hakuseki instructed them to use the term "king" (*ō*), which in Chinese usage signified an autonomous ruler who acknowledges the suzerainty of the emperor (and which often can best be translated "prince"), while it also connoted all of the moral authority associated with the ancient sage-kings.

It is one of the paradoxes of Neo-Confucianism in Japan that, much as it encouraged nationalism by its stress on loyalty to the ruler and hostility to barbarians, among its abler adherents this tendency was offset by the very fact of their appreciation of things Chinese (indeed this was held against them as proof of disloyalty by the more narrow-minded Shintoists). This circumstance set a limit to xenophobia among Japanese Confucianists and distinguished them from their Chinese confreres whose ethnocentrism was not similarly modified by an appreciation of another culture such as the Japanese. Here the case of Arai Hakuseki is highly illustrative, for as a scholar he typifies this cosmopolitan spirit and breadth of mind. With the installation of Yoshimune, a staunch reactionary who had faith only in the traditional Tokugawa policy of a divided court and narrow isolationism, Arai was forced to retire and spend the rest of his life in political oblivion. For a man of his tremendous energy and industry such enforced idleness could have been a calamity, but for Arai it provided an opportunity for study and writing which established him as a scholar of the first rank. As his collected works indicate, he wrote voluminously on a wide range of subjects, such as language (treating Korean, Chinese, and even Dutch, as well as his own), historical archeology, geography (including the Ryukyus, the land of the Ainus, and also Europe), and sociological case studies on artisans, artists, stage actors, etc., as well as on political, legal, economic, and religious institutions. In the field of history, his major interest, he produced the first complete historical gazetteer of the feudal domains, the *Hankampu: Essays on Political History* (*Dokushi-yoron*), famous for its evolutionistic viewpoint; *The Understanding of Ancient History* (*Koshi-tsū*), a study of the so-called Divine Age of Japanese history in terms of rationalistic humanism; and his own incomparable autobiography *Oritaku shibanoki*.

As a letter to one of his disciples indicates, Arai's consuming interest in his old age was to write a new Japanese history, different from either Hayashi's *General History of Our State* (*Honchō-tsugan*) or Mitsukuni's history later known as the *History of Great Japan* (*Dai-Nihon-shi*). For Arai, Hayashi's work is no more than a chronological compilation of administrative records, akin to the Six National Chronicles of early Japan. It is conspicuously lacking in coordination of the social, economic, and cultural factors in history. Mitsukuni's history, not yet completed but widely heralded, conceived of Japanese history as autonomous, with the seclusion or isolation idea quite pronounced both in arrangement and content. To set forth his own conception of Japanese history Arai started a series of historical essays entitled *Problems of History* (*Shigi*) emphasizing the coordination of many different factors in the making of history, and also viewing Japan in the general frame of East Asia and to some extent of the world at large. Unfortunately these essays have been lost, except for a few that found shelter in his posthumously collected miscellaneous essays.

ARAI HAKUSEKI
A Critical Approach to Japanese History

In this letter to Sakuma Dōgan, Arai Hakuseki discusses his aims as a historian, his dissatisfaction with the Mito historians' uncritical acceptance of traditional accounts, and the need for objective research. He also reflects upon his public career and its aftermath.

[From *Arai Hakuseki zenshū*, V, 517–20]

You are very kind to inquire about my writings. . . . As to *The Understanding of Ancient History* (*Koshi-tsū*), it has little appeal for ordinary men; but it is likely to startle people and arouse suspicion. It is a modern interpretation of the Divine Age. Only one copy of it was made, and that was taken to Kaga. *The Manual of Government Precedents* (*Keiseitenrei*) is a compilation which can be kept anywhere without any trouble arising over it. I will have the pages counted very soon; if I remember correctly, it consists of twelve volumes. The collected *Policies and Acts of Government* (*Hōsaku*) was written partly for my own amusement; its loss would not be serious. As I had finished most of what concerned my own self, I started last year to deal with debatable points in our national history under the title *Problems of History* (*Shigi*), putting it in the form of questions and answers. Early last winter I was able in three chapters to discuss the accounts in the *Nihongi*'s two chapters on the Age of the Gods, as well as the *Kujihongi* and *Kojiki,* insofar as they corroborated or conflicted with one another. Minor problems are left out and only major issues discussed. Of the three volumes, one is a general review of *Kujihongi, Kojiki,* and *Nihongi,* together with the six national chronicles; and in the other two volumes problems of the Divine Age are treated. My hope is that they will clarify the position I took when I wrote *The Understanding of Ancient History* (*Koshi-tsū*). . . . After the Age of the Gods was finished, I moved on to the reign of the emperors. Because of illness, however, I will need more time to finish it. If I survive the illness and become strong enough to resume work, I am hoping to finish the parts covered in the *Nihongi,* though the present state of my health does not warrant such optimism.

I have been expecting that the history of our country being undertaken at Mito would correct errors in the national chronicles, but through contact with the staff of the Mito Historical Commission, I have found that all ancient events are to be left as described in the *Nihongi, Shoku Nihongi,* and other chronicles. If that is the case, the true history of Japan, as far as I can see and prejudiced as I may be in that, will be left unwritten.

Japanese sources on this period are scarce, it is true, but in the Chinese histories, starting with the *History of the Latter Han Dynasty,* there are accounts dealing with our country and much accurate information is given. This is regarded, however, as so much hearsay and prevarication coming from foreign sources, and is passed over without any scrutiny or study. Then again, the three Han States of Korea were overseas domains of our country for four hundred years, and their records often confirm or supplement our information, but they are similarly disregarded. Thus the Mito historians rely on the *Chronicles,* nothing but the *Chronicles;* and so the history of our country is turning into an account of dreams told in a dream. This old man's *Problems of History,* even if he only succeeds in completing the discussion to the end of the *Nihongi,* will serve as a reliable record of the facts. Its completion, however, is simply up to the will of Heaven. When young, I may have conceived a plan, but lacked the ability to execute it; in middle age, official responsibilities left me no time; and in old age, when I have had the leisure for it, my mind has lost its vigor and everything is running against my expectations.

Concerning Chinese history and Confucianism there are almost too many books to be studied. In Japan, however, there are no books that give a critical examination of historical facts and serve a practical purpose in government. So wretched has been the state of historical writing that I was roused to do something about it, but the circumstances are such as to preclude any hope of success. Something might be accomplished if other scholars were invited to join hands in the project, but in my old age I am not inclined to do this. Last year it so happened that Mito sent me a message encouraging me to launch this undertaking, but in my reply I discouraged them, adding that it would do no good to them and no good to myself. . . .

Men customarily wish to be known for their scholarship and good reputation, but since my reputation for scholarship reached China, Korea, the Ryukyus, and even Holland, visitors from those countries occasionally asked how I was faring, and their interest in me was one cause of my misfortunes. In view of my advanced age, I have had to consider how my children and grandchildren might suffer from this. Now for seven or eight years I have tried to stay out of the limelight, and I am told that my critics are decreasing in number. For these reasons I am extremely reluctant to let my writings appear in public. Frankly, I am entrusting myself to the judgment of men a century or two after my death.

A Superstition Concerning Era Names

In East Asian countries great significance was attached to the choice of the names by which periods of imperial rule were identified, since these era names were regarded as "signs of the times." Hayashi Hōkō, minister of education by hereditary succession, cited Chinese authorities of the Ming dynasty in his successful attempt to have the Chinese character meaning "correct" or "true" declared taboo in era names, on the ground that it had brought bad luck to previous rulers who used it. This passage from Arai Hakuseki's autobiography argues in the name of Confucian rationalism against such a superstitious interpretation.

[From *Arai Hakuseki zenshū*, III, 127–30]

It is true that Chinese of the Ming dynasty have asserted, in connection with the choice of era names, that inasmuch as misfortune has been the lot of those eras which have had the ideograph *shō* [meaning "correct," "true"] in their designations, this ideograph should be debarred from use. Indeed, the same argument appears in works other than those cited by Nobuatsu (Hōkō). Nevertheless this does not represent the thinking of a true gentleman.[1] Whether a state rises or falls, whether a ruler enjoys long life or suffers untimely death, depends either upon the will of Heaven or on the actions of men. Fortune or misfortune does not come from the use of particular words in an era name. . . .

An era name does not differ from the designation for a month. . . . If the use of the ideograph *shō* in an era name augurs ill, its use in a month name must likewise augur ill. But from the days of the ancient sages to our own time, the first month of the year has always been known as the *shō* month. Confucius, speaking of the "four beginnings" in his *Spring and Autumn Annals,* refers to the *shō* month as the beginning of the year. If the ideograph *shō* is indeed an unlucky word, there has

[1] That is, a man with a sense of moral responsibility, who does not resort to superstition in explaining his failures and misfortunes.

never been an auspicious year, for every year of every dynasty since Confucius' time has started with a *shō* month. This should be obvious enough to all, but if anyone considers my argument to be trifling I should still like to be told why the ideograph *shō* is unlucky in era names and not so in month names. . . .

Ever since the adoption of era names in our country the events of era after era, if examined closely, may be seen to include both lucky and unlucky events, and no matter what the character used in era names, each has endured misfortunes. The reason is that for both China and Japan era names have been changed with the appearance of heavenly signs or earthly calamities, such as floods, droughts, and epidemics. Thus, none of the ideographs which have been adopted in era names has been entirely free of unfortunate associations. If names brought misfortune, it would be best to return to the ancient custom of using none. But even in remote antiquity when era names were not used either in China or Japan, states rose and fell and rulers enjoyed long life or suffered untimely death era after era. Further, I have met with men from Italy, Holland, and other lands who say that only two or three countries use era names, and that the rest do not, speaking rather in terms of so many thousands and hundreds of years since the creation of the world. Yet, few countries in Europe in the past twenty years have escaped upheavals caused by the death of rulers and struggles for succession. Last winter and this spring, they said, many have been killed in war. How do you account for such disasters? Even if era names are not used, decline and destruction are inevitable when heaven so decrees or men fail to conduct themselves properly.

On the Regulation of Shipping and Trade at Nagasaki

In his autobiography *Oritaku shibanoki* Arai gives the following account of the measures which he recommended for the strict control of shipping and cargoes at Nagasaki, in order to eliminate bootlegging and the steady drain of gold and silver from Japan. Here his restrictive policy is typical of the traditional Sino-Confucian concern for economic control at the expense of economic expansion.

[From *Arai Hakuseki zenshū*, III, 166–68]

During the spring of this year, in the second month, the opinions of the Port Commissioner and other local officials of Nagasaki were sought regarding the shortage of copper coins for foreign trade. As there was nothing worthy of official adoption in the written reports submitted by them I was assigned to write out and submit a set of revised regulations along the lines suggested during the rule of the former shogun [Ienobu, d. 1712]. These regulations which I drafted contained 211 articles in approximately eight rolls. . . .

I am not going to say anything about the events which occurred before the present dynasty of shoguns. In 1601 there was no regulation on foreign ships coming here to trade. This was at a time when Ming China maintained strict prohibitions against overseas trade, especially during the Wan-li era (1573-1620). Thus, Chinese ships were not seen here as they are now.[1] Only Western ships cast their anchor at Nagasaki. At the beginning of the Kan'ei era (1624-1644) when the order was issued that foreign ships should come to Nagasaki to trade, Dutch ships continued to anchor at Hirado in the province of Hizen. Toward the end of the Kan'ei era the Dutch ships began to anchor at Nagasaki.[2] There were also some local lords and merchants who requested crimson seals[3] and dispatched trading vessels abroad, but these ventures were stopped in 1634. During these days there was no regulation as to the number of foreign ships coming here or the volume of trade permitted. In 1685 the regulation was first made that trade with the Chinese should be limited to 6,000 kan[4] in silver and with the Dutch to 50,000 ryō[5] in gold. Then in 1688 the number of Chinese ships permitted to trade was set at 70. This was due to the fact that the number of Chinese ships arriving in Japan had reached 200, following the lifting of trade restrictions in China during the reign of the K'ang-hsi emperor. Since it was possible after 1695 to use copper as a medium of exchange in addition to silver, ten more Chinese ships were allowed to come to Japan after 1698, thus increasing the number of Chinese ships to 80 and the volume of Chinese trade by 2,000 kan in copper in addition to the amount per-

---

[1] The ban was not, in fact, wholly effective and some Chinese ships did come to Japanese ports. Arai is not too well informed concerning the situation in the early seventeenth century, and his statements are sometimes erroneous or misleading.

[2] Actually the Dutch had put in at Nagasaki before, but at this time were confined to the use of this port exclusively.

[3] Those authorized to trade with foreign countries received a patent bearing the crimson seal of the Shogun.

[4] One kan of silver was about 8¼ lbs.

[5] At this time the ryō was roughly equal to a half ounce.

mitted in silver. As the number of Chinese ships permitted to trade was fixed, all ships in excess of the fixed number were called "cargoes to be sent home" and were not allowed to trade. Moreover, as ships even within the specified number were permitted to trade only to the extent of 160 *kan* per ship, in accordance with the regulations limiting trade, there have been ships which returned emptyhanded and without profit, notwithstanding the great bulk of cargo they had brought, the great distance they had traveled or the great dangers they had faced. Thus, they tried to dispose of their merchandise in any manner they could, even at the risk of violating the law. As for our merchants, they too sought to purchase in any manner possible the "cargoes to be sent home," for buying legal cargo entailed payment of high commissions and the incurring of heavy expenses with resulting low profits. Thus, the volume of illicit trade increased from year to year. (This trade and illegal cargo were known variously as "outside trade," "trading through brokers," "chance goods," and "chance trading.")

During the reign of the last shogun the Port Commissioner's Office in Nagasaki was ordered to find out the volume of gold, silver, and copper spent in Nagasaki for foreign trade. The records for the 46-year period from 1601 to 1647 are lacking. In the sixty years that followed—from 1648 to 1708—2,397,600 *ryō* of gold and 374,229 *kan* of silver flowed out of the country. As for copper there are no data for the 61-year period prior to 1662, but in the 44-year period from 1663 to 1707, the total reached 1,114,498,700 catties (*kin*). These figures, which come from the records of the Nagasaki Port Commissioner, represent only the trade of Nagasaki. But trade was not limited to Nagasaki. As stated elsewhere foreign ships stopped at various places to trade just as our ships go to various ports in foreign countries to trade. Thus, we cannot estimate the volume of export trade, as for example to Korea via Tsushima, or to the Ryukyu Islands via Satsuma.

If an estimate is made on the basis of reports submitted by the Nagasaki Commissioner as to the volume of gold and silver lost to foreign countries for the 107-year period since the *Keichō* era (1596–1615), and if that figure is compared with the amount of gold and silver coined in our country for the same period, it would indicate that one-fourth of the gold and three-fourths of the silver had been lost.[6] At this rate half the

[6] Arai's estimates have been strongly questioned by Yosaburo Takekoshi in his *Economic Aspects of the History of the Civilization of Japan*, Vol. II, ch. LIV.

gold will be lost in another hundred years while the silver supply for use in our country will be completely lost before another century. As for copper, there is a shortage not only in meeting the present needs of foreign trade but also to meet our country's annual expenditures. Thus, treasures of permanent value which our country produces are being diverted in exchange for curios of momentary value which come from afar. It must be realized that such commercial dealings are against our national interest and prestige. If payment abroad is necessary for the purchase of medicines and books, an estimate should be made of the current need for them in our country and the annual production of them in other countries, and a limit fixed on the annual payment to be made for such products at Nagasaki, Tsushima and Satsuma. I cannot understand the purpose of only limiting the annual volume of gold, silver, and copper to be used for foreign trade at Nagasaki. Even if such a limit is set, private, illicit trade will continue unchecked unless the number of ships and the cargo of each ship are also regulated. Therefore, I suggest that an estimate be made of the annual production of gold, silver, and copper in our country as well as of their volume of flow into foreign countries; then fix an annual limit on their use for foreign trade. A record should also be kept of the number of foreign ships arriving here and of the volume of cargo which they carry, and a limit fixed as to their numbers and volume of cargo. If such cargoes are purchased in their entirety we shall neither lose our national treasures in illicit trade as in the past, nor will foreigners continue to defy our country's laws. Our national prestige will prevail far and wide and our national wealth will prove adequate for all time.

THE HISTORICAL RELATIVISM OF TOMINAGA NAKAMOTO

Osaka, where Tominaga Nakamoto (1715-1746) was born, had something of a reputation for independence and individual initiative. It was there, at the end of the Middle Ages, that a militant Buddhist organization had asserted its independence by resisting the attacks of Nobunaga for nearly a decade. Subsequently Osaka had been proud to serve as headquarters for the ambitious Hideyoshi in his heyday of power; and even after the triumph of Ieyasu, it was the first city to recoup its economic fortunes, win a measure of self-rule from its Tokugawa masters, and lead in the development of a new bourgeois culture. Here Saikaku's novels were written, with sex and money as their leading themes, and here Chikamatsu's dramas, with their love triangles and suicides, filled theatres to capacity. At Osaka too, in 1726, the Shogun Yoshimune saw an opportunity to start a Confucian educational center, with financial support from the merchants of the town. And it was from this new center that the son of one such enterprising merchant struck out on his own, against formidable opposition from many quarters, to explore the past.

Tominaga, who passed away at the age of thirty-one after a protracted illness aggravated by persecution and penury, did not live to write the complete history of Japan that he had in mind. Apparently much of his writing was lost as a result of the Prohibition Act of 1790, according to which it would have been classed as non-conforming and dangerous. But fortunately two of his important works, the *Historical Survey of Buddhism* (*Shutsujō kōgo*) and the *Testament of an Old Man* (*Okina no fumi*) preserve for us something of his original historical method. Another work, now lost, *Failings of the Classical Philosophers* (*Seppei*), seems to have been a critical examination of Chinese thought in the pre-Ch'in period. That it was an outspoken and provocative piece is certain, for it started the stone of persecution rolling over him before he was twenty. Not only did it lead to his expulsion from the Confucian school his father had helped to establish, but it also forced the young man out of his father's home. Thereafter he managed to earn a meager living at the Zen Monastery of Uji, working as a proofreader of the newly edited *Tripiṭaka*. This afforded him an opportunity for testing his historical method and textual criticism in the field of Buddhism. The *Historical Survey* was a result. At that time there were thirteen Buddhist sects with sixty-three subdivisions established throughout the nation, and as Tominaga's historical analysis left none of them unscathed, a great furor arose over it. "The rise of the sects and denominations is due to everybody's striving for 'advancement,'" he writes in the second chapter of his *Historical Survey*. "It is an effort to promote a certain teaching by making an additional contribution of one's own, without which religion would never spread. In the past as in the present, it is the nature of religion to develop in this way. Students of later times, however, consider that all religions were the same originally as they are found to be in later transmission, unaware that a great many innovations and reforms have taken place." Elsewhere (in paragraph 9 of the *Testament*) he says that in all historical religions the authority of the founders is appealed to by followers seeking to rise above or push beyond those who preceded them. That is the rule and not the exception, and it is the reason why, in the study of religion, historical criticism is indispensable. It is not difficult to see in this the logical extension to other schools of thought of the critical method Ogyū Sorai advocated for the study of Confucianism.

As criteria for textual criticism, Tominaga gives three "things" and five "categories." "My method of study emphasizes three things by which all human discourse can be properly understood," he writes. "As long as one's approach is made through these three things, there is no discourse which defies clear understanding." In the first place, discourse has man behind it, and as one man or one group of men differs from another, so does discourse. Tominaga illustrates this by showing how the terminology employed in the various Buddhist scriptures reflects the difference in language and outlook of various authors, and shows that they do not derive from one original source. Secondly, discourse is related to time, and as each age has its own characteristics so human discourse too partakes of them. Thirdly, discourse falls into different "categories." These types or categories are not fully explained by Tominaga, but they seem to have had particular reference to the ways in which different teachings or truths were further developed or modified in the hands of others. First there was assertion or expansion; second, generalization; third, collision or contradiction; fourth, reversion or inversion; and fifth, transformation or modification.

The terms Tominaga used to represent these categories are metaphorical and suggest the movement of water at the seashore as a wave swells up and lunges forward, spreads out, breaks against the shore, washes back and then turns away. The examples he gives, however, are drawn from Buddhist teaching and their exact significance is not always clear. First, when a Buddhist says that the historical personage Shākyamuni attained Buddhahood, it is a case of assertion or expansion. Second, to say that all creatures are potential Buddhas is a case of generalization. (The original meaning of Tathāgata as applied to the Buddha was "He who comes thus." As the storehouse of the Mind, however, it was described in the

Laṅkāvatāra Sūtra as the source of good and evil, and in the *Prajñā Pāramitā Sūtra* all creatures from Heaven to Hell are seen as embraced in the storehouse of the Tathāgata.) Third, to say that the Buddha's Truth-body (Dharmakāya) does not exist apart from the world of passion, or, in other words, that in the storehouse of the Tathāgata, the Tathāgata is found amidst all the passions of the sentient world, is a case of collision or in this instance, perhaps, paradox. (That is, as absolute Truth the Tathāgata transcends good and evil, but as the perfection of virtue Tathāgatahood proceeds from the stilling of the passions.) Fourth, the use of the expression "to follow one's own bent" as a translation for the Sanskrit *pravāraṇa* is a case of inversion ("to follow one's own bent" originally had the bad connotation of lacking restraint; here it takes on the good one of acting spontaneously in accord with one's true nature). Fifth, that a member of the shūdra caste, originally considered to be lacking a Buddha-nature, should as a sentient creature capable of spiritual conversion possess the seeds of Buddhahood, is an example of modification or transformation (i.e., a modification or transformation of the idea of potentiality for Buddhahood as deriving from the possession of spiritual selfhood rather than from one's status among men).[1] Thus Tominaga goes on to show in detail how Buddhism evolved in the course of time into so many different schools, sects and denominations through individual contributions following the different possible lines of development.

In his *Testament,* Tominaga tried to synthesize his historical interpretations of the three existing religions—Shinto, Buddhism, and Confucianism—into a kind of ethical culture which he called *Makoto no oshie* or "the religion of true fact." It was long preserved in a manuscript from which only a few copies were made, and did not attract the attention it deserved until 1923 when Professor Naitō Konan of Kyoto Imperial University had reproductions made of it for distribution among his friends. To Dr. Anesaki Masaharu, an outstanding modern authority on the history of Japanese religion and the author of *Historical Criticism of the Buddhist Scriptures (Bukkyō seiten shiron),* Tominaga Nakamoto seemed like a lotus in the quagmire because of the critical

---

[1] As reconstructed from *Shutsujō Kōgo,* sec. 11, by Ishihama Juntarō in *Tominaga Nakamoto,* pp. 96–107.

powers and broad knowledge of cultural history which he displayed at a time when the historical sense was almost wholly lacking in the study of religion.

TOMINAGA NAKAMOTO
Testament of an Old Man

Having provoked great hostility from the established religions because of his unorthodox views, Tominaga found it prudent to represent this brief work as expressing the opinions of an anonymous old man rather than himself. It nevertheless provides a convenient summary of his own philosophy and his critique of established teachings.

[From *Nihon jurin sōsho*, VI, *Okina no fumi*, pp. 1–14]

This writing is the work of a certain Old Man, and was lent to me by a friend. In spite of the fact that this is a degenerate age, the author appears to be a wise old man. Departing from the three teachings of Buddhism, Confucianism, and Shinto, he advocates what he calls the Way of Truth. Truly, it seemed to me that if one conducted oneself in accordance with what the Old Man said, one would make no mistakes in life. And having thus subscribed to his teaching, I asked my friend what the Old Man's name was, only to be told that he did not know and there was no way of finding out. The Old Man must have been like those personages in ancient times who chose to live in obscurity that they might be free to say what they thought. Wishing to preserve this as my own family teaching and also to pass it on to others, I have copied it all down from beginning to end.

Gemmon 3 [1738]: 11th Month, Ban no Nakamoto.

I. In the world today there are three religions: Buddhism, Confucianism, and Shinto. Some think they represent the three different countries, India, China and Japan; while others consider them essentially one, or else dispute with one another over the truth or falsity of each. However, the way which may be called the Way of all ways is different from these, and what each of these three teachings calls the Way is not in accord with the Way of Truth. The reason is that Buddhism is the Way of India, and Confucianism is the Way of China. Because they are

[474]

peculiar to these countries, they are not the Way of Japan. Shinto is the Way of Japan, but because of the difference in time, it is not the Way for the present generation. Some may think that the Way is always the Way despite differences in nationality and differences in time; but the Way is called the Way because of its practicality, and a Way which is not practical is not the true Way. Thus, the Way as taught by the three teachings mentioned above is not a Way practicable in present-day Japan.

. . . . .

VI. What is the Way of Truth, then, that will be practicable in present-day Japan? It is simply this: Be normal in everything you do. Consider today's work of primary importance. Keep your mind upright. Comport yourself properly. Be careful in speech. Be respectful in manner and bearing. Care for and honor your parents.

(The Old Man's footnote refers to the [Buddhist Sūtra] *Rokkōhai-kyō,* where the five human relationships are specially dealt with. Confucianists also consider these relationships important and the Shinto decrees likewise mention these five things. Therefore just as these three things are indispensable to the Three Teachings, so are they to the Way of Truth.)

If you have a master, serve him well. If you have children, educate them well. If you have retainers, manage them well. If you have an elder brother, show him every respect; if you have a younger brother, show him every sympathy. Toward old people, be thoughtful; toward young people, be loving. Do not forget your ancestors. Be mindful of preserving harmony in your household. When associating with men, be completely sincere. Do not indulge in evil pleasures. Revere those who are superior, while not despising the ignorant. What you would not have done to yourself, do not do to others. Be not harsh; be not rash. Be not obstinate or stubborn. Be not demanding or impatient. Even when you are angry, do not go too far. When you are happy, be so within bounds. You may take pleasure in life, but do not indulge in sensuality. Be not lost in sorrow; whether you have enough or not, accept your lot as good fortune and be content with it. Things which you ought not to take, even if they seem insignificant, do not take; when you ought to give, do not hesitate to do so even if it means giving up all, even your country. As to the quality of your food and clothing, let it conform to your station in life and avoid extravagance. Do not be stingy, do not steal, do not lie. Do not lose yourself in lust, be temperate in drinking. Do not kill anything that does no harm to mankind. Be careful in the nourishment of your body; do not eat bad things; do not eat too much.

(The Old Man has a footnote saying: In the [Buddhist] Yoga Shāstra cases of untimely death are listed under nine types such as: 1) too much eating; 2) untimely eating; 3) eating again before food has digested; and so forth. The *Analects* too say that one should not eat in the wrong proportions or at the wrong time, or in excessive amounts. They all have insight into the Way of Truth.)

In your free time study the arts of self-improvement; try to be better informed.

(The Old Man's footnote says: The *Analects* has it that when one has energy to spare, one should study the polite arts. The [Buddhist] *Vinaya* also says that to understand order and gradation, history should be studied. Also the young bhikshus are permitted to study arithmetic. These too are in accord with the Way of Truth.)

To write with present-day script, to use present-day vernacular, to eat present-day food, to dress in present-day clothes, to use present-day utensils, to live in present-day houses, to follow present-day regulations, to mix with present-day people, to do nothing bad, to do all good things—that is the Way of Truth. That is the Way which is practicable in present-day Japan.

(All of these things are already mentioned in Confucian and Buddhist writings, and do not need to be made a special point of. But the Old Man is presenting these ideas as if they were something new of his own, so as to induce people to discard all that is useless and go straight to the Way of Truth. His aim is truly praiseworthy.)

．．．．

VIII. That it is difficult to invent any system of teaching which can do without the Way of Truth can be surmised from the fact that Buddha preached the Five Commandments and Ten Virtues; called greed, anger, and folly the Three Poisons; and declared filial piety to parents and loyal service to teachers to be one of the Three Blessings. "Not to do anything bad, but to do everything good and keep one's motive pure, is the essence of all the Buddha's teaching," it is said.

Confucius also talked about filial piety, brotherliness, loyalty, and tolerance. He taught fidelity and reverent devotion; Wisdom, Humanity, and Valor he called the Three Cardinal Virtues. Restraint of anger, stifling of passion, correction of mistakes and conversion to goodness were also emphasized. "The superior man is always poised in action, while the inferior man is ill at ease," he said.

Shinto people also taught cleanliness, simplicity and honesty.

These are all in accord with the Way of Truth, well expressed and to the point, each resembling the other. As long as the followers of the Three Teachings abide by their respective beliefs, without bias or prejudice, not giving themselves over to the strange and exotic, but living in the society of men to the end of their lives—then they are also following the Way of Truth.

(In the foregoing the Old Man has expressed his main ideas. He does not mean to discard the Three Teachings in their entirety. He simply wants every one to act upon the Way of Truth.)

At this point, however, the Old Man has his own theory. Generally speaking it has been the rule that all those who have started teaching what they call the Way as handed down from ancient times, have inevitably appealed to the authority of a Founder, while at the same time trying to go further than any predecessor has gone. Posterity, however, has been ignorant of this fact and it has resulted in great confusion.

. . . .

Tominaga proceeds to explain how the teaching of the Buddha and the various schools of Buddhism successively appealed to some earlier authority, while at the same time either reacting against or attempting to surpass their immediate predecessors. These teachings, instead of representing a pure and untouched revelation from the past, were actually the product of a considerable development in human hands. The same pattern of evolution is indicated for the Confucian tradition. Finally he takes up Shinto.

XII. As to Shinto, it is what certain medieval Japanese dressed up as ancient traditions of the Divine Ages and called the Way of Japan in an attempt to outdo Confucianism and Buddhism. In the time of Ābhāsvara in India, for instance, or of P'an Ku in China,[1] there were no such definite teachings as Buddhism and Confucianism. What later came to be known as Buddhism and Confucianism were wholly purposeful and conscious creations of men in later times. In exactly the same way there could be no such thing as Shinto in the Divine Ages. The first Shinto taught was the syncretism known as Dual Shinto, which was a combina-

[1] The first beings to appear in these countries.

tion of Confucianism and Buddhism arbitrarily put together to suit the occasion. Then followed the Shinto called *Honjaku Engi* which regarded Shinto deities as Japanese manifestations of Indian Gods and Buddhas. This was an attempt on the part of Buddhists envious over the rise in popularity of Shinto, who taught Shinto outwardly but inwardly wanted to capture it for Buddhism. Then came another form of Shinto known as *Yui-itsu Sōgen* [the One and Only Original Source]. It was an attempt to transcend Confucianism and Buddhism, and to proclaim Shinto as pure and unique. All three of these made their appearance in medieval times.[2] A new type of Shinto that has recently appeared is known as *Ōdō Shintō,* the Shinto of the Sovereign Way. It teaches that Shinto has no particular way of its own, and that the Way of the Sovereign is the Way of the Gods. There is also a form of Shinto which professes Shinto outwardly but inwardly identifies it with Confucianism.[3] None of these things existed in Divine Antiquity; they have simply arisen from the struggle of each one to get ahead of the other. But ignorant people of the world, not realizing this, believe one of these to be the True Way, identify themselves as partisans of this teaching or that, and start violent controversies. It is at once pitiful and ridiculous, to this Old Man's way of thinking.

. . . .

XV. The vice of Confucianism is rhetoric. Rhetoric is what we call oratory. China is a country which greatly delights in this. In the teaching of the Way and in the education of men, if one lacks proficiency in speech, he will find no one to believe in or follow him. For example, take the word Rites (*ri*). It originally signified simply the ceremonies on the four great occasions in life: coming of age, marriage, mourning, and religious festivals. But as you know they talk now of what is the Rite of a man as the son of his father, what is the Rite of a man as the subject of his sovereign; they speak of it in connection with human relationships, they speak of it in regard to seeing, hearing, speaking, and acting. They also assert that Rites owes its inception to the division of heaven and earth, and embraces the whole universe. Take another example, that of music (*gaku*). The character *gaku* originally meant to be entertained by the music of bell and drum. But then they began to

---

[2] Concerning the foregoing types of Shinto, see Chapter XIII.
[3] The *Suika Shintō* of Yamazaki Ansai.

say that music was not necessarily confined to bell and drum. Music, they said, was the harmony of heaven and earth. You can see the way they talk. Take again the character for "sage" which originally signified a man of intelligence. They have gradually stretched it to the point where a sage is the highest type of humanity, even capable of working miracles. Thus we know that when Confucius talked of humanity, Tseng Tzu of humanity and righteousness, Tzu Ssu of sincerity, Mencius of the Four Beginnings and the goodness of human nature, Hsün Tzu of the badness of human nature, the *Book of Filial Piety* of filial piety, and the Great Learning about [what the superior man] loves and hates, the *Book of Changes* about heaven and earth—all of these are just ways of presenting the plainest and simplest things in life with an oratorical flourish in order to arouse interest and make people follow them. Chinese rhetoric is like Indian magic, and neither of them is particularly needed in Japan.

(The Old Man speaks here of the "plainest and simplest things in life," but he also knew full well that the Way transcends all else, and that some things are extremely difficult to explain and transmit. So you must not be misled by what he says or fail to grasp his true meaning.)

XVI. The vice of Shinto is secrecy, divine secrets, secret and private transmission, such that everything is kept under the veil of secrecy. Hiding things leads to lying and theft. Magic and oratory are interesting to see or to listen to—they thus have some merit. But this vice of Shinto is of the lowest sort. In olden times people were simple, and so secrecy may have served certain educational purposes, but the world today is a corrupt world in which many people are addicted to lying and stealing, and it is a deplorable thing for Shinto teachers to act in such a way as to protect and preserve these evils. Even in such lowly things as the Nō drama and the Tea Ceremony, we find them all imitating Shinto, devising methods of secret transmission and authentication and attaching a fixed price to the transmission of these "secrets" for selfish gain and benefit. It is truly lamentable. If you ask the reason why they devise such practices, their answer is that their students are immature and untried, and must not be granted too ready an access to their teachings. It sounds plausible, but any teaching which is kept secret and difficult of access, and then is imparted for a price, cannot be considered in accord with the Way of Truth.

MIURA BAIEN'S SEARCH FOR OBJECTIVITY

Miura Baien (1723–1789) was the son of a village physician in the southern island province of Kyushu. He carried on in his father's profession and declined all invitations to take office in the service of a feudal lord. He nevertheless achieved wide recognition outside his own locality, first of all as a true gentleman and worthy successor of his father, then as a master of Chinese language and poetry, and finally as the bold advocate of a new rationalism. This new philosophy he set forth in three outstanding essays: *Discourse on Metaphysics* (*Gengo*, lit. "Abstruse Talk"); *Discourse on Corollaries* (*Zeigo*, lit. "Talking On and On"); and *Discourse on Morality* (*Kango*, lit. "Presumptuous Talk"). Miura also wrote a political guide known as *Heigo Hōji*, which is said to have been highly prized by its recipient, a feudal lord in Kyushu. Lastly he produced an essay on economics known as *The Origin of Price* (*Kagen*), which later attracted attention in Europe because of the similarity of Miura's views on currency with those of his contemporary, Adam Smith (born the same year), and also because of his analysis of the circulation of bad money, identical with Gresham's Law. Among Miura's other accomplishments was the creation of a cooperative plan for saving against emergencies in his village. It is related that when he finished his thirtieth revision of the *Discourse on Metaphysics* and was in a quandary because commercial publishers did not consider it a marketable book, his neighbors—mostly hard-working thrifty peasants—got together and collected money for its publication.

There is some reason to believe that before Miura died in 1789, the shogunal premier (Matsudaira Sadanobu [1758–1829]) entertained the idea of bringing Miura into the government service. A little later, however, in 1790, Sadanobu was a signer of the notorious Act of Prohibition, the adoption of which had been urged by staunch traditionalists, at court, who were determined to uphold Chu Hsi orthodoxy. Miura was not a direct object of persecution, since his death preceded the Act by a year. His new philosophy suffered, nonetheless, because the Act deprived students of opportunities to study this new system, which required long and careful examination owing to the utter originality of

Miura's ideas and his use of entirely new terminology. Also few students had a knowledge of mathematics and astronomy sufficient to follow Miura's thought.

A distinctive feature of Miura's philosophy is his radical departure from all traditional systems of thought. Even the long-accepted Confucian view of yin and yang he subjected to searching analysis:

"People say fire belongs to yang, and therefore it is hot; water belongs to yin, so it is cold. I ask myself, however, why that which belongs to yang is hot and why that which belongs to yin is cold. Again people say that which belongs to yang is light and goes upward, while that which belongs to yin is heavy and goes down. Most men's thinking stops right there, but my own doubts rise higher at that point. Why do a pair of dark things on the forehead see; why do a pair of holes in the head hear? Why don't eyes hear, why don't ears see? When most people come to these points they just leave them alone, but I simply can't leave them alone. . . . They refer the question to past authority, and when they find a book that deals with it, they accept whatever answer it gives. I can't convince myself entirely in that way. When they discuss the natural world, they do so in a wild, hit-or-miss manner; when they talk of life and death, they do so in an absurd or obscure manner. Though their evidence may be flimsy and their arguments preposterous, this does not disturb people at all. Yet I cannot content myself with this. I keep reconsidering such matters and probing further into them." [1]

For Miura the final source of knowledge is neither tradition nor the writings of men, but nature and man himself. If one wants a true view of the universe, one must test in heaven what one believes true of heaven, and test in man what one believes true of man. Readers of books must therefore check what they read by looking into the book of nature; if nature confirms it, they may accept it, but otherwise they must set it aside.

As we have already seen, Kaibara Ekken, in his *Grave Doubts,* questioned Chu Hsi's basic dualism of principle and material force. Miura went on to question Chu Hsi's entire system. In the preface to his *Discourse on Metaphysics* he says, "From boyhood I have asked questions about whatever I laid my hands on. All around me there have been people noisily explaining things, but what they said was too absurd and

[1] *Baien Zenshū,* I, 2.

defied any test. . . . They were usually ready to condemn those who did not possess what they themselves possessed and to discriminate against those who did not act according to their own standards. Thus they easily arrived at some conclusion, while I still remained in doubt." [2]

Though a stout skeptic toward tradition, convention, book learning, and even scholarly authority, Miura was no nihilist. He was, instead, a thoroughgoing positivist, who rejected the traditional Buddhist view of the emptiness of things. He believed that the universe, including space, is one endless reality. For him there is no such thing as complete extinction; even death is nothing but an organic change. On this point Miura comes quite near to Itō Jinsai's position: for both of them the universe is dynamic energy or vitality, which has neither beginning nor end.

Being a native of Kyushu, Miura had come under the influence of Western science at the port of Nagasaki and devised an astronomical spheroid for his own use at the age of eighteen. He was also a steadfast friend and admirer of Asada Gōryū (1734-1799), much younger, but the foremost mathematician and astronomer of his time. There is reason to believe that his insistence on the priority of nature over man had its inception in the deep impression made upon him by Western astronomy. But his questioning mind carried him beyond the study of geography and astronomy to work out a system of metaphysics which he called the study of *jōri*, which can be understood as a system of natural order, or the "logic of things."

"The comprehensive way of understanding Heaven-and-earth [nature] is the study of the logic of things, and the essence of this logic is the dialectics of antithesis and synthesis, setting aside all bias or prejudice, and verifying everything by empirical evidence. Setting aside all bias or prejudice means freeing ourselves from preconceptions. In regard to empirical verification, however, we must recognize that empirical evidence is sometimes misleading. The sun and the moon look as if they are traveling westward, but in reality they travel east. Water appears as the foe of fire, but fire comes from water. The way of Heaven-and-earth is yin and yang; and yin and yang are antithetical. Because they are contradictory, together they constitute a unity or synthesis, and thus become Heaven-and-earth [nature]. Because they represent unity through

[2] *Baien Zenshū*, I, 2.

mutual contradiction, we must view them as deriving their identity from contradiction if we are to understand their true nature. Thus [in mathematical terms], the logical principle [jōri] may be stated: one has two in it, and two lead to one. As two, a difference exists which serves as the basis for a logical relationship [jōri]; as one, a combination exists which transcends difference. Antithesis and synthesis are the dialectical principles for our study of this logic of things [jōri] without which there would be no means of understanding yin and yang. With no means of understanding yin and yang, even though we possessed the broadest knowledge, the widest experience, the keenest intelligence and the deepest insight we should still be incapable of seeing inside the structure of the universe. So this logic [jōri] is the key for opening the gates of Heaven." [3]

As may be seen here, jōri is used by Miura in a number of related senses, but it is primarily botanical in conception, jō meaning "branch" and ri (principle) originally meaning "the grain of wood." According to Miura everything embodies reason and order, just as the external structure of the tree is manifested in its branches and the internal structure in the grain of the wood. Also, just as many branches grow from one trunk but the grain of each branch shows its unity with the whole, so the universe goes on dividing or multiplying, but even the manifold forms produced are identical in nature. For Miura philosophy is the study of the dialectics of the one becoming two (many) and the two becoming one in all realms of existence. Thus Miura's dialectic is not merely logical but also existential, as is Hegel's. It is the essential character of reality that everything has its antithesis. One does not remain one, and yet when there is two, the identity of the two is apparent. This logic of things is to be reasoned toward, on the one hand, and to be tested, on the other. That is why Miura felt he had to rewrite his *Discourse on Metaphysics* more than thirty times, checking and revising it throughout his life.

MIURA BAIEN

Man's Preconceptions
[From a letter to Taga Boku, *Zenshu*, II, 83–85]

I have your letter of inquiry on the dialectics of nature. As Heaven-and-earth [nature] are the permanent residence of humanity, they come

[3] *Baien Zenshū*, II, 89.

first among the things to be studied by scholars. Astronomy, geography, and solar mathematics are steadily gaining in accuracy, thanks to the introduction of Western science; but that is about all. As to the logic (*jōri*) of Heaven-and-earth I have yet to see any scholar who could be considered an expert in it.

The world is wide enough, and time has been going on for eternity. Countless men have pondered and worked on this problem, yet even though Heaven-and-earth are in plain sight day and night, nobody has succeeded in viewing them aright. Why?

I think it is because our curiosity and wonder have ceased to be stirred. From the day of our birth, when we know nothing, we become so accustomed to seeing, hearing, and touching in such and such a way that in the course of time we have unconsciously developed habits which have become prejudices with us and have deadened our sense of curiosity about things. These prejudices represent a persistent attachment of the mind which the Buddhist calls *vijñāna*. As long as this acquired habit is unbroken, the mind cannot be expected to function as it should.

That Ānanda was a monkey in his former existence and was unable to get rid of his apish habits,[1] is, I think, an interesting fable. As man thinks and judges with a human mind, he cannot help doing so with human predilections. Intelligent thinkers, ancient and modern, have been victims of this habit of mind (*vijñāna*) and have painted everything in heaven and earth with the colors of humanity, thus failing to obtain a true picture of things.

Men walk with feet and work with hands; for them walking and working have the *vijñāna* of being associated with feet and hands. When they see snakes without feet or fish without hands they are likely to think them somewhat ineffective beings. But there is Heaven, which has no feet, yet goes round and round on its way day and night; and there is the creativity of nature, which has no hands, yet makes flowers bloom, brings children into the world, and creates fish and birds. From an anthropomorphic point of view, the revolution of the sun and creativity of nature should be objects of curiosity, but no one watches them with wonder. Being accustomed to these sights every morning and evening, people simply pass them by with utter indifference.

From the objective point of view, nature is an object, as water and

[1] Ānanda was Buddha's nephew and disciple, who is said to have recited from memory what Buddha taught during his lifetime. All sūtras start with the expression "Thus I have heard." From this habit of verbatim recitation Ānanda became known as apish.

fire are. Grass and trees, birds and animals, are also each of them objects. Even we ourselves, all human beings, are just so many objects. Despite this fact, because of his anthropomorphic habits, man views other objects in terms of himself—that is an almost inescapable fixation with him.

Thus a human peculiarity is to view everything as human. Take, for example, children's picture books, *The Betrothal of Rats* or *Monsters and Goblins*. Rats are never kept as rats in their true shape; instead all of them are turned into human forms. The bridegroom appears in the book in ceremonial robes with a pair of swords, while the bride is shown with a flowing gown on and snowy cap of cotton, and is carried in a palanquin with an escort of footmen and young guards. In the book of *Monsters and Goblins,* no cases are found of an umbrella turning into a tea-mortar, or of a broom changing into a bucket. But all monsters and goblins are given eyes and noses and hands and feet, so as to look like members of the human family. A well-known picture of the *Parinirvāna*[2] represents the Dragon-King in a human form with regular royal garments on; the only suggestion of his being a dragon is a fireman-style hat he wears. It is such an imagination as this that populates heaven with a supreme God, and earth with gods of wind and thunder. Monstrous in form, they all move by foot, and do their work by hand. Wind is put in bags, thunder is beaten out on drums. If they are real bags, how were they made? And there must be skin to make a drum. If such imaginings are carried further, the sun will be unable to go on revolving unless it gets feet, and nature will be helpless in her work unless she has hands.

Let us take a more familiar example: Animals have sex, male and female; but plants do not. Without sex, animals as a rule will not procreate, while without sex, plants, as a rule, have no difficulty propagating. So the rule in one case will not apply to the other.

Take another example: if fire, imbued with a will, starts to think about water, asking how water will burn or dry, arguing mainly from what the former has to what the latter has not; or the other way round, if water, also imbued with a will, demands of fire what water itself has, it is obvious that nothing useful will result, even if a lifetime is spent working on the problem.

[2] Scene depicting the creatures of the world which assembled to witness the Buddha's final translation into Nirvāna.

[485]

The Disinterested Study of Nature
[From a letter to Asada Gōryū, *Zenshu*, II, 752–54]

From the pavilion the evening haze could be seen floating between the azure sky and blue water. The sun was gradually setting, its golden hue changing into crimson, while its evanescent glory was cast upon the clouds and reflected in the waves. Suddenly a breeze blew up out of the duckweed and vanished into the pine grove yonder; it sounded like a passing shower or like a phoenix calling to its mate.

At home, my head against a pillow, I thought of the scene that had stirred me with joy and wonder. It was made up of real things, true enough, but it was at the same time far from being real. And I thought of the sayings of those philosophers and scholars whose writings are so bulky that oxen perspire pulling them and libraries are full to overflowing with them. Are they not inspired by so many evening scenes from pavilions which aroused and delighted the senses of these philosophers? We know that *sake, su, moro,* and *amasake* are all made of rice. They are not brewed by the rice itself, but in each case the nature of rice is adapted to suit the taste and flavor [the brewer has] in mind.

The Chinese sages were sovereigns in antiquity who ruled the people well. The Buddha was a recluse who was adept at mind-control. So the Classics of the sages contained the principles for ruling men and the Buddhist scriptures revealed the secret of controlling the mind. One derived from a concern for the world of men, which was going from bad to worse, and the other from compassion for the masses who were drowning themselves in passion. Out of a feeling of paternal solicitude they sought to save the people of their time from plunging to self-destruction. The ancient Chinese did use crystal orbs and jade measures for astronomical observation, it is true, but the purpose was only to give a calendar to the people. The Bhājana-loka [3] was referred to by the Buddhists, but it was no more than their own mental creation. There were other schoolmen who also touched upon the problem [of the natural world] incidentally, but put it aside as a vague and remote problem, not an important one. Though occasionally skeptics have appeared, they have eventually become entangled in traditional notions; captives in

[3] Buddhist term for the physical environment or inanimate world.

the human prison, they have not penetrated into the heart of things.

Now the universe shelters all things in it, and man is just one of those things. As all things come into existence, they are provided with innumerable distinct natures. Though afforded the same means, children cannot be just like their parents; fire cannot be like water. The landlord (nature) provides what the tenant (man) occupies, but the landlord is not the tenant, and the tenant is not the landlord, each being different in character and capacity. . . . To know the world of Heaven (nature), therefore, man must put his own interests aside in order to enter into the world of Heaven. In order to know objects, man must again put his own interests aside and enter into the world of objects; only in that way can his intellect hope to comprehend Heaven-and-earth and understand all things. All beings exist together with us, and we are just one of them. Realization that Heaven is universal, while man is individual, must be the starting point for all discussion of humanity. This is what I call opening the windows of the human sphere. The reason men have remained in the dark about the universe is that, remaining fixed in the human sphere, they have considered their own position to be of the highest dignity and their own intellect to be the most exalted. To view Heaven-and-earth in this way, or to study creation and its manifold objects with this attitude, is exactly the same as the brewers of *sake, su, moro,* and *amasake* who consider rice only in terms of taste and flavor.

In the comprehension of the universe, knowledge is most important. But as long as students approach creation without opening the windows of the human sphere, and persist in keeping a smug sense of their own importance and intelligence, their approach is certain to give rise to delusions, as a mote in the eye casts a shadow on what one sees. Concern for the world and compassion for the masses is benevolent in motive, but the study of creation in human terms is not conducive to true knowledge. Those whom the world acclaims as leaders in thought and action take humanity and human motives as the basis of their thinking and speculation in order to set up standards for what is to be believed and done. But human minds are like human faces; their preferences differ one from another. Each considers what he has arrived at to be right, a revelation from Heaven or a deposit of truth from antiquity, and thinks those who do not accept his standards should be exterminated. It is my conviction, therefore, that there is no systematic truth or logic [*jōri*] except that which enables man to comprehend the universe without setting up standards conceived in terms of humanity or human motives. . . .

In a letter you wrote me last year, you said something to the effect that in the observation of an object, one's mind must be unfettered. If the mind is in bondage, it will drag the object into the confines of its own prejudices. Your friendly solicitude was so sincere that I was most profoundly moved. But I have an explanation for this in terms of my own method for understanding the logic of things [*jōri*]. Suppose that a thesis is available, but not its antithesis. At least for a while something will have to be hypothesized for it. If that is found unsatisfactory, then something else will have to be hypothesized; if it fails again, still another thing must be hypothesized. Thus one hypothesis after another will be tried till at long last true accord is reached. It is just as in the case of a circle; if its true antithesis, a straight line, is not hit upon, a square will be used until the time comes when a straight line is finally hit upon. Or as in the case of the sun: if its true antithesis, shadow, is not hit upon, the moon will be tried as a hypothesis, until at last shadow is hit upon. The logic of things [*jōri*] has never been studied before, and my lone efforts for fifty years have not sufficed to arrive at finding the true antithesis in every case. So in my *Discourse on Metaphysics* the true and the hypothetical will be found side by side. You will do me a great favor indeed by bringing the critical powers of your brilliant mind to bear on this book.

KAIHO SEIRYŌ AND THE LAWS OF ECONOMICS

Kaiho Seiryō (1755–1817) was born into a warrior-class family of some standing, an eldest son who waived his inheritance in favor of his younger brother. When called to serve as secretary and lecturer to one of the three Tokugawa families, he resigned this too on the ground of poor health. He was thus free of any allegiance or responsibilities and spent most of his life as a wayfarer, covering the length and breadth of the country. That he never married was due, not to any ascetic convictions on his part, but simply to his love of independence. In an autobiographical sketch at the end of his *Lessons of the Past* (*Keikodan*), he writes:

"After I resigned from service, I visited Echigo for a year. The following year I made my way to Kaga, spending more than a year there and climbing Mt. Tate for the sake of my health. After that I visited Kyoto twice and traveled to the Eastern circuit (from Edo to Kyoto) back and forth, ten times. Twice I journeyed to remote Kiso; the northwestern coast, by the Sea of Japan, was also visited. Altogether the places I visited for longer or shorter stays numbered nearly forty and the mountains I climbed numbered a few hundred. I never had a wife, never spent money on concubines, and have no children. . . . Being fifty-nine years old, I have so far been fortunate enough not to have starved and free enough to keep on writing whatever I wanted to write. Without a guilty conscience, without obligation to any offspring, I have felt that my way of life was quite enjoyable." [1]

As he traveled through Japan, Kaiho Seiryō went about talking with farmers, shopkeepers, and tradesmen, emphasizing that human society rests on two pillars: labor and the exchange of merchandise. Society is basically economic in character. And the first principle of government is the law of economic balance: unless both ends meet, distress and disaster are inevitable. In order to achieve this balance of goods and needs, unproductive classes such as Buddhist priests, Confucian scholars, and hereditary warriors should be strictly regulated as to size. The first two should never be allowed to increase in numbers; in fact, total elimination of them is desirable. As to the warrior class, handcrafts and home industries should be encouraged among them, for it is the law of Heaven that everybody should work. It is preposterous to assume that the ruling warrior class is exempt from this fundamental law of economics; for according to this economic rationalist, warriors themselves are only so much human merchandise sold into the hands of a feudal lord. Feudal service is basically a business transaction. The exchange of commodities is the primary mechanism for sustaining society. But unfortunately the ruling class is unwilling to recognize this basic mechanism of society, and its members are inevitably condemned to a life of poverty or utter destitution.

This rationalist and mercantilist also believed in the rule of law instead of the arbitrary rule of man. "To act in strict accordance with Heaven's law, completely restricting one's own arbitrary desires is the secret for

---

[1] *Kaiho Seiryō Shū, Keikodan,* pp. 191–92.

bringing happiness and forestalling evil," he writes.[2] In respect to legal codes, however, Kaiho strongly advocated a minimum of laws with a maximum of enforcement. An extensive and detailed code with vague means of enforcement oftener than not defeats its own purpose. In this way Kaiho mediates between the traditionally opposed Confucian and Legalist positions: he agrees with the former that too much legal regulation is self-defeating, and with the latter that ultimate authority must rest in the law rather than in the individual ruler. His view of law as universal and transcending all personal considerations thus reflects this general belief in a system of natural law which prevails throughout the universe—in the political and economic sphere as well as in the physical or moral.

The fact that Kaiho conceives of this natural order in characteristically Neo-Confucian terms as the "principles [reason or law] of heaven-and-earth" suggests again how much even the most independent of Japanese rationalists owed to the conception of a rationally ordered universe which was part of their Neo-Confucian heritage. In Kaiho's case, however, as in that of Miura Baien, the moral aspect of things (or the moral order as understood in human terms) assumes much less importance than their intelligibility in scientific terms. For Kaiho "a sage is one who understands the law of nature, who keeps the ways of heaven and earth and all creatures in mind. Since he knows the quality of the soil and the nature of the tree, the trees planted by him have a better chance of taking root." [3] Thus it is his intelligence, not his virtue, that really makes a man a sage or saint. For Kaiho, the great founders of Buddhist sects in Japan, such as Kūkai, Shinran, and Nichiren, were appreciated simply because their intelligence was far above that of contemporary Confucianists.

KAIHO SEIRYO

THE LAW OF THE UNIVERSE: COMMODITIES TRANSACTIONS

The following selections are from *Lessons of the Past* (*Keikodan*), a summation of Kaiho's economic thought written in 1813. The title, as he explains it in the opening lines of the work, means "comparing the past with the present, considering the outstanding excellences of the past, and making use of them."

[2] *Kaiho Seiryō shū, Yorozu-ya dan*, p. 294. [3] *Kaiho Seiryō shū, Yorozu-ya dan*, p. 299.

"Study should not be for the acquisition of detailed information concerning the past," he writes elsewhere. "It should seek detailed accounts of affairs today." Kaiho's use of his own classical learning is well illustrated in the references to Mencius in the following passage. Even the style demonstrates his freedom from conventional practices and independence of mind. Not content to quote verbatim from the words of the sage, he paraphrases them expansively, almost in the language of the market place.

[From *Kaiho Seiyō Shū, Keikodan,* pp. 11–37]

It is a ridiculous thing that the aristocracy and military class in Japan should disdain profit, or that they should say that they disdain profit. When a man does not disdain profit, he is called a bad person. Such is the perverse practice of the times. In China it is the same. A man who is clever at making profits is called a sharp enterpriser or some such bad name. But if collecting taxes from those beneath you is to be a sharp enterpriser, then the *Rites of Chou* is a book for sharp enterprisers; and if lending rice and money to the people and exacting interest from them is to be a sharp enterpriser, then the Duke of Chou himself was a sharp enterpriser. Let us first make a general case of this, go to the root of it, and examine it close at hand.

What sort of thing was it when rice fields were originally handed over to the people and rice collected from them in return? By what logic was rice taken from the people? If we only recognize the natural principle by which this was done, we shall understand it completely. Rice fields, mountains, the sea, gold, rice, and everything between heaven and earth, are commodities. The natural principle is commodities and the realization of commodities. The realization of rice from rice fields is no different from the realization of profit from gold. The realization of timber from mountain land, the realization of fish and salt from the sea, and the realization of profit from gold and rice are the natural principle of heaven and earth. If one lets a field go uncultivated, nothing is grown on it; if one lets gold lie unused, nothing is produced from it. But if one lends a rice field to the people and exacts an annual tribute [tax] of one-tenth on it, then one makes a profit of 10 percent. . . . Of course, the realization of profit is fast or slow depending on the case, so the rate of interest should vary accordingly. Taxes on rice fields and taxes on mountain land are both alike forms of interest, levied on commodities that have been lent. Such commodities are things on which interest must be levied. This is not sharp enterprise or anything of the sort; it is the natural principle of heaven and earth.

Po Kuei was an economist of ancient times. He said to Mencius: "I think I shall take a twentieth of the produce as a land tax." He boasted that since the state had become wealthy, even a tax of that little would be enough for its needs. Then Mencius said: "You had better exact a tax of one-tenth. A tax of one-twentieth would be the way of the barbarians, but the barbarians have no fortifications, no palaces, and no rites or music, so even that little is sufficient for the needs of the state. However, China has a splendid way of life, so a tax of one-tenth must be levied." [1] . . . From ancient times it has been said that the relations between lord and subject are according to the way of the market place.[2] A stipend is offered for the service of a retainer, and the retainer obtains rice by trading his ability to his lord. The lord is a buyer and the retainer is a seller. It is simply a business transaction, but business transactions are good, not bad. When it is said that business transactions are not things for a superior man to concern himself with, this is a misunderstanding which comes from everyone's having swallowed whole the idea that Confucius despised profit. Much parasitism and wasted labor have resulted from the notion that the relation between lord and subject is not a trade relationship. . . .

The universe is made up of Law [principle, *ri*]; buying, selling and paying interest are all parts of the Law of the universe. In order to make the nation wealthy, the ruling class should return to Law. . . . The ruling house is a great family which owns the commodity known as the country. The feudal houses are also rich families, owning the commodities called feudal states. They lend these commodities to the people and live on the interest therefrom. Ministers are those who sell their talents to the ruler and live on the wages he pays. Foot carriers are those who obtain wages for their labor on the roads, in order to get something to drink or a bite to eat. They all live in the same way. . . .

The unity of law and punishment is also a law of the universe. . . . In Chinese antiquity when a death sentence was passed, the sentence was

---

[1] *Mencius*, VI, B, 10.

[2] A reference to *Shih Chi*, Ch. 81: "Relationships in the nation are according to the way of the market place. If the lord is powerful, I shall follow him. If he is without power, I shall leave him."

reported to the sovereign; then the sovereign would request a reprieve three times, but the penal officer would not listen to the request and proceeded to execute the death sentence. To repay a capital crime offender with capital punishment is a matter of simple business arithmetic. That the death sentence had to be executed, even in spite of the sovereign's request for a reprieve, is proof that the law is higher than the will of the ruler and that business arithmetic is more important than the will of the sovereign. [pp. 11-14]

. . . .

The warrior laughs when told that the King of Holland engages in commerce. But he himself buys and sells commodities; it is a law of the universe that one must sell in order to buy, and hardly a thing to be laughed at. [p. 37]

THE PROHIBITION OF HETERODOX STUDIES

The Kansei Edict

This edict, issued in 1790 during the administration of Matsudaira Sadanobu, strongly reaffirmed support by the shogunate for the traditional Chu Hsi teaching. In form, however, it was merely a directive to the head of the Hayashi school, hereditarily entrusted with the supervision of education, to stamp out unorthodox teachings in his own and other official schools. Five years later another directive called for the enforcement of this ban in the official schools maintained by the other feudal lords. The main effect of these decrees was to discourage the open propagation of heterodox views, without actually suppressing the schools in which they were privately taught. To us these measures serve as a reminder of the restrictions which curbed the activity and influence of independent thinkers, as well as an indication of the alarm felt by shogunal leaders over the spread of nonconformist thought.

[From Inoue, *Shushi gakuha*, pp. 522-23]

The teaching of Chu Hsi has had the full confidence of successive shoguns since the Keichō era [1596-1615, i.e., since the founding of the shogunate] and your family, generation after generation, has been entrusted with the duty of upholding and expounding this teaching. It has been expected, therefore, that orthodox studies would be pursued without remiss and your students trained in accordance with it. Lately, however, various new theories have been put forward, heterodox teachings have become popular, and social standards have been broken down. Indeed, since it points to a complete decline in orthodox studies, this is a matter for the most profound regret and concern. Even among your own students, we have heard from time to time of those whose thinking is not pure and correct. Consequently in order to tighten discipline at the Confucian college, we are assigning Shibano Hikosuke and Okada Seisuke responsibility in these matters, and you are requested to consult with them upon this question, so as strictly to bar your students from heterodox teachings. Not only in your own school, but in all others as well, you are advised to see to it that the orthodox doctrine alone is taught as the basis for the training of men for public service.

The Justification for the Kansei Edict
(Letter of Nishiyama Sessai to Akamatsu Sōshū)

As the text of the edict indicates, two men were specially appointed to insure that the new ban would be complied with in the official school, probably because the eclectic views of Hayashi Kimpō, then head of the school, did not inspire confidence in his readiness to enforce the new policy wholeheartedly and vigorously. One of these men, Shibano Hikosuke, who was instrumental in having the edict promulgated, had himself been influenced by the views of Nishiyama Seṣsai, a convert from the school of Ogyū Sorai. When a friend of Shibano's sent him a letter protesting against this narrow view of Confucian orthodoxy, Nishiyama was eventually entrusted with formulating a reply. In this it becomes clear that the primary targets of the ban are followers of the Ancient Learning propounded by Ogyū and Itō Jinsai, as well as those identified with the Wang Ying-ming school. Quite evidently the popularity of these teachings had grown to the point where they threatened completely to overshadow the orthodox doctrine.

[From Nihon Jurın sōsho, III, Kansei igaku-kin kankei monjo, p. 6]

Since the fall of the Chou dynasty, the conduct of education has declined and heresies have sprung up. Yang Chu upheld self-interest and cast doubt on righteousness; Mo Ti upheld all-embracing love and cast doubt on humanity. Both of them talked about humanity and righteousness, but were mistaken in what they said. Mencius exposed them as perverters who, failing to acknowledge [the claims of the] sovereign and

[494]

[the peculiar affection due to a] father, thwarted humanity and righteousness. Han Yü paid tribute to Mencius, saying that his merit [in exposing these heretics] was no less than that of the [sage-king] Yü.

Lu Hsiang-shan with his "sudden enlightenment" and Wang Yang-ming with his "good knowledge" both talked about sage wisdom, but were mistaken about it. Wise men of the Sung and Ming dynasties exposed them as openly Confucianist and inwardly Buddhist, and as destroyers of the moral law. . . .

How much the more in recent times with Itō and Ogyū, who opposed the tradition of the *Great Learning* and the *Mean* as being contrary to the original [doctrine] of Confucius, and slandered Tzu Ssu, Mencius, Ch'eng, and Chu, saying that they contradicted the Way of the Sages! With sophistry and eloquence they seduced their followers; while pretending to speak for the "ancient learning" they simply peddled their own pernicious doctrines. What small men they were! . . . Since their time second-rate Confucian scholars have imitated them. Arrogant and conceited, each has insisted upon his own mistaken interpretation of the classics and slandered the Ch'eng-Chu school. Hundreds of them now vie with one another in setting up their own schools, in which they propound new teachings under the strange name of "ancient learning."

You have said: "There have been many different methods of reading the texts and studying the Way, but what all alike revere and believe in are the teachings of Confucius. These consist of nothing more than filial piety, duty toward elder brothers, loyalty, fidelity, [the study of] the *Odes* and the *Book of History,* rites and music, governing the country, and pacifying the people. If this be so, then why must one take as one's foundation the Sung Confucianists alone? Those who use the Han and T'ang commentaries, or follow Wang Yang-ming, or adopt the teachings of [Itō's] Horikawa school or of Ogyū Sorai, or choose at will from among the interpretations of many different schools do no injury to the Way as a consequence." If it were as you say, however, those who study the Way of the Sages would have no need of true guidance and the art of teaching would have nothing to do with the conduct of ordinary life. Your students, I believe, are well aware that Buddhism and Taoism are heretical and false doctrines, for the followers of Buddhism and Taoism state explicitly what each regards as the Way and the heretical nature of their doctrines is immediately apparent. But these stupid Confucianists appeal to the authority of the classics and commentaries to advance their own false beliefs, so that what is false, yet appears true, utterly contaminates the eyes and ears of men and greatly confounds the world.

INDEX

Actor, *see* Nō theatre

Aesthetics, 115; of Heian period, 137-38, 172-80; in medieval Japan, 181-82, 277-97; in Tokugawa period, 434-40

Agrarianism, 343, 344, 428-33; *see also* Farmer

Ainu, xx, 11, 188

Aji hompushō, 266

Amaterasu (Sun Goddess), xix, 14-15, 22, 24, 27-29, 32-33, 274

America, *see* United States

Amida (Amitābha), 152-53, 185-212

Amidism, xxi, 182; *see also* Pure Land Buddhism

Amoghavajra, 143

Analects, 409-11, 414, 419

Ancestry and ancestor worship, 12, 15-17, 22, 25, 275

Anesaki Masaharu, cited, 473-74

Animism, 22, 25

Annam, 338

Anthology of poetry, 441-42

Arai Hakuseki, xxii, 370, 403, 461-70

Aristocracy, 52-53, 184-85, 324-25; *see also* Court; Samurai

Art of "avoiding calamities," 56-58

Artisan: function of, 329-30; one of four classes of people, 339*n*

Arts, the, 138; in Pure Land Buddhism, 189-90; Zen Buddhism and, 255-60; in Heian period, 277-97

Asada Gōryū, 482

Ashikaga Shogunate, xxi, 256-57

Ashikaga Takauji, xxi, 235, 250

Ashikaga Yoshimitsu, xxi, 256-57

Ashiku (Akshobhya), 152-53

Astrology, 55-58

Astronomy, 84, 93

Aware, 172-73, 174, 277, 278, 281

Bakin, 436-37

Bakufu, *see* Military government

Bashō, *see* Matsuo Bashō

Ben Kemmitsu Nikyō-ron (Kūkai), 144-46

Bendō: Distinguishing the Way (Ogyū), 415-17

Bin, priest, 77

Bodhidharma, 227-28

Bodhisattvas, meaning of, 127-28

Body and mind, 248-49; *see also* Three Mysteries

Book of Advanced Education, see *Great Learning*

Book of Changes, quoted, 328, 412-13

Book of Elementary Instruction, 356

Book of Filial Piety, 376

Book of History, 1, 374

Book of Poetry, quoted, 328

Brāhmanism, 146, 148

Bu (Emperor Yūryaku), 8, 9

Buddha, 92; biography of, 95-97; quoted, 98-99; three bodies of, 144, 213; *see also* Three Treasures

Buddhism: introduction of, to Japan, xix, 10, 11, 34; and Seventeen-Article Constitution, 36, 47; in Nara period, 91-108; fusion with other religions, 262-66; destruction of power by Nobunaga, 302-8; *see also* specific types of, e.g., Mahāyāna Buddhism

Buddhist Law (Dharma), *see* Law; Three Treasures

Buddhist monastic orders, *see* Monastic orders; Three Treasures

Buddhist sūtras, 93; *see also* under specific name, e.g., *Golden Light Sūtra*

Bukkyō seiten shiron: Historical Criticism of the Buddhist Scriptures (Anesaki), 473

Bunshō Tattoku Kōryō (Fujiwara Seika), 337

Temple of the Original Vow: in Osaka, 205; in Kyoto, 206
Tempyō Hōji era, 87
Tempyō Shōro era, 87
Ten States of Religious Consciousness (Kūkai), 135-37, 146, 150-51, 184-85
Tenchi, emperor, 11, 68-69, 87
Tendai (T'ien-t'ai) Buddhism, xx, 110, 113-32; Kūkai on, 137; spread of, 152-71, 184-85; and Shinto, 264; syncretism of, 323
Tenkai, abbot, 323, 344
Tennōism, 59-88 *passim*
Tenryū monastery, 235, 250, 252
Theatre, see Nō theatre
Three Deities, 57, 60-61
Three Divisions of the Eight-fold Path, 149
Three Human Relationships, 147
Three Imperial Regalia, 17-18, 27, 30, 274-76, 349
Three Mysteries, 135, 138, 145, 156, 185
Three Pleasures, 361-62
Three Realms, 55-58
Three Treasures, 48, 92, 97, 205
Three Vehicles, 125*n*, 126*n*, 145
Three virtues, 275
Tokugawa Mitsukuni, 353, 362-63
Tokugawa period, xxi-xxiii, 181, 257, 298-496 ,
Tokugawa Shoguns: Ieyasu, xxi, 302, 304, 315, 322-34, 344, 425; Yoshimune, xxii, 459, 461, 463, 471; Tsunayoshi, 345, 353; Iemitsu, 353
Tokugawa Tsunaeda, 363-64
Tokugawa Yoshinao, 353
Tokyo (formerly called Edo), 325
Tominaga Nakamoto, xxii, 460, 470-79
Toyokuni shrine, 315
Toyotomi Hideyoshi, see Hideyoshi
Tripiṭaka, 92, 157-62, 471
True Pure Land Sect, xxi, 203-12
Tsūjin, 435
Tsunayoshi, see Tokugawa Shoguns
Tsurezure gusa: Essays in Idleness (Yoshida Kenkō), 281
Tung Chung-shu, 54
Twelve Links of Causation, 148
Two Essences, see Yin-yang
Tzu-chih t'ung-chien: Outline and Digest of the General Mirror (Chu Hsi), 343

Uda, emperor, 157
Ueno, 353

Ukiyo, xxi, 434-37 *passim*
Ukiyo-zōshi, 435
Universality, in Tendai Buddhism, 113-14, 117-24, 126
University, State (Daigaku), xxii, 345

Vairochana (Cosmic Buddha), 135, 137, 138, 143, 144, 152-53, 163, 323; discipline, 128; *sūtra*, 262-63
Vajra Mandala, 156
Vajrabodhi, 143
Vijñāna, 484
Vimalakīrti Sūtra (*Yuima-Kyo*), 99-104
Vinaya school, 213, 227
Vocabulary: of Japanese aesthetics I, 172-80; of Japanese aesthetics II, 277-97; of Japanese aesthetics III, 434-40

Wa, 3, 11, 269; *see also* Japan, names of
Waka, 442-45
Wang Yang-ming, 352
Wang Yang-ming school (Ōyōmei), 369-83
War, 3, 346-47
Warrior class, *see* Samurai
Warrior-monks, 155-56
Way of the Sages, 348
Way of the Warrior, see *Bushidō*
Wealth, development and distribution of, 379-83
Wei, kingdom of, 3, 4-7
White pheasant, discovery of, 76-78
Womb (*Garbha*) Mandala, 138
Women, 5, 74; in Amidism, 186-87; and tea ceremony, 257-60; and learning, 371-72; in Tokugawa literature, 435-37

Yakushi (the Healing Bodhisattva), 96
Yamaga Sokō, xxii, 385-401
Yamato, 4, 25-27, 31, 34, 268, 269
Yamazaki Ansai, xxii, 353-62, 384
Yamazaki Sōkan, 445
Yasumaro, 12
Yin-yang, 57-60, 62, 84, 358, 481-83
Yoritomo, xx
Yorozu, 37-41
Yoshida Kanetomo, xx, 265-66
Yoshida Kenkō, 281
Yoshida Ryōi, 336
Yoshida Sōan, 336
Yoshida Torajiro (Shōin), influence of, 301, 370, 387
Yoshimitsu, *see* Ashikaga Yoshimitsu
Yoshimune, *see* Tokugawa Shoguns